Lecture Notes in Computer Science 15374

Founding Editors

Gerhard Goos
Juris Hartmanis

The series Lecture Notes in Computer Science (LNCS), including its subseries Lecture Notes in Artificial Intelligence (LNAI) and Lecture Notes in Bioinformatics (LNBI), has established itself as a medium for the publication of new developments in computer science and information technology research, teaching, and education.

LNCS enjoys close cooperation with the computer science R & D community, the series counts many renowned academics among its volume editors and paper authors, and collaborates with prestigious societies. Its mission is to serve this international community by providing an invaluable service, mainly focused on the publication of conference and workshop proceedings and postproceedings. LNCS commenced publication in 1973.

Masaaki Kurosu · Ayako Hashizume ·
Hirohiko Mori · Yumi Asahi ·
Dylan D. Schmorrow · Cali M. Fidopiastis
Editors

HCI International 2024 – Late Breaking Papers

26th International Conference on
Human-Computer Interaction, HCII 2024
Washington, DC, USA, June 29 – July 4, 2024
Proceedings, Part I

 Springer

Editors
Masaaki Kurosu
The Open University of Japan
Chiba, Japan

Ayako Hashizume
Hosei University
Tokyo, Japan

Hirohiko Mori
Tokyo City University
Tokyo, Japan

Yumi Asahi
Tokyo University of Science
Tokyo, Japan

Dylan D. Schmorrow
Soar Technology Inc.
Orlando, FL, USA

Cali M. Fidopiastis
Katmai Government Services
Orlando, FL, USA

ISSN 0302-9743   ISSN 1611-3349 (electronic)
Lecture Notes in Computer Science
ISBN 978-3-031-76802-6   ISBN 978-3-031-76803-3 (eBook)
https://doi.org/10.1007/978-3-031-76803-3

This Springer imprint is published by the registered company Springer Nature Switzerland AG
The registered company address is: Gewerbestrasse 11, 6330 Cham, Switzerland

If disposing of this product, please recycle the paper.

Foreword

This year we celebrate 40 years since the establishment of the HCI International (HCII) Conference, which has been a hub for presenting groundbreaking research and novel ideas and collaboration for people from all over the world.

The HCII conference was founded in 1984 by Prof. Gavriel Salvendy (Purdue University, USA, Tsinghua University, P.R. China, and University of Central Florida, USA) and the first event of the series, "1st USA-Japan Conference on Human-Computer Interaction", was held in Honolulu, Hawaii, USA, 18–20 August. Since then, HCI International is held jointly with several Thematic Areas and Affiliated Conferences, with each one under the auspices of a distinguished international Program Board and under one management and one registration. Twenty-six HCI International Conferences have been organized so far (every two years until 2013, and annually thereafter).

Over the years, this conference has served as a platform for scholars, researchers, industry experts and students to exchange ideas, connect, and address challenges in the ever-evolving HCI field. Throughout these 40 years, the conference has evolved itself, adapting to new technologies and emerging trends, while staying committed to its core mission of advancing knowledge and driving change.

As we celebrate this milestone anniversary, we reflect on the contributions of its founding members and appreciate the commitment of its current and past Affiliated Conference Program Board Chairs and members. We are also thankful to all past conference attendees who have shaped this community into what it is today.

The 26th International Conference on Human-Computer Interaction, HCI International 2024 (HCII 2024), was held as a 'hybrid' event at the Washington Hilton Hotel, Washington, DC, USA, during 29 June – 4 July 2024. It incorporated the 21 thematic areas and affiliated conferences listed below.

A total of 5108 individuals from academia, research institutes, industry, and government agencies from 85 countries submitted contributions, and 1271 papers and 309 posters were included in the volumes of the proceedings that were published just before the start of the conference. Additionally, 222 papers and 104 posters were included in the volumes of the proceedings published after the conference, as "Late Breaking Work". The contributions thoroughly cover the entire field of human-computer interaction, addressing major advances in knowledge and effective use of computers in a variety of application areas. These papers provide academics, researchers, engineers, scientists, practitioners and students with state-of-the art information on the most recent advances in HCI. The volumes constituting the full set of the HCII 2024 conference proceedings are listed on the following pages.

I would like to thank the Program Board Chairs and the members of the Program Boards of all thematic areas and affiliated conferences for their contribution towards the high scientific quality and overall success of the HCI International 2024 conference. Their manifold support in terms of paper reviewing (single-blind review process, with a minimum of two reviews per submission), session organization and their willingness to act as goodwill ambassadors for the conference is most highly appreciated.

This conference would not have been possible without the continuous and unwavering support and advice of Gavriel Salvendy, founder, General Chair Emeritus, and Scientific Advisor. For his outstanding efforts, I would like to express my sincere appreciation to Abbas Moallem, Communications Chair and Editor of HCI International News.

September 2024   Constantine Stephanidis

HCI International 2024 Thematic Areas and Affiliated Conferences

- HCI: Human-Computer Interaction Thematic Area
- HIMI: Human Interface and the Management of Information Thematic Area
- EPCE: 21st International Conference on Engineering Psychology and Cognitive Ergonomics
- AC: 18th International Conference on Augmented Cognition
- UAHCI: 18th International Conference on Universal Access in Human-Computer Interaction
- CCD: 16th International Conference on Cross-Cultural Design
- SCSM: 16th International Conference on Social Computing and Social Media
- VAMR: 16th International Conference on Virtual, Augmented and Mixed Reality
- DHM: 15th International Conference on Digital Human Modeling & Applications in Health, Safety, Ergonomics & Risk Management
- DUXU: 13th International Conference on Design, User Experience and Usability
- C&C: 12th International Conference on Culture and Computing
- DAPI: 12th International Conference on Distributed, Ambient and Pervasive Interactions
- HCIBGO: 11th International Conference on HCI in Business, Government and Organizations
- LCT: 11th International Conference on Learning and Collaboration Technologies
- ITAP: 10th International Conference on Human Aspects of IT for the Aged Population
- AIS: 6th International Conference on Adaptive Instructional Systems
- HCI-CPT: 6th International Conference on HCI for Cybersecurity, Privacy and Trust
- HCI-Games: 6th International Conference on HCI in Games
- MobiTAS: 6th International Conference on HCI in Mobility, Transport and Automotive Systems
- AI-HCI: 5th International Conference on Artificial Intelligence in HCI
- MOBILE: 5th International Conference on Human-Centered Design, Operation and Evaluation of Mobile Communications

Conference Proceedings – Full List of Volumes

1. LNCS 14684, Human-Computer Interaction: Part I, edited by Masaaki Kurosu and Ayako Hashizume
2. LNCS 14685, Human-Computer Interaction: Part II, edited by Masaaki Kurosu and Ayako Hashizume
3. LNCS 14686, Human-Computer Interaction: Part III, edited by Masaaki Kurosu and Ayako Hashizume
4. LNCS 14687, Human-Computer Interaction: Part IV, edited by Masaaki Kurosu and Ayako Hashizume
5. LNCS 14688, Human-Computer Interaction: Part V, edited by Masaaki Kurosu and Ayako Hashizume
6. LNCS 14689, Human Interface and the Management of Information: Part I, edited by Hirohiko Mori and Yumi Asahi
7. LNCS 14690, Human Interface and the Management of Information: Part II, edited by Hirohiko Mori and Yumi Asahi
8. LNCS 14691, Human Interface and the Management of Information: Part III, edited by Hirohiko Mori and Yumi Asahi
9. LNAI 14692, Engineering Psychology and Cognitive Ergonomics: Part I, edited by Don Harris and Wen-Chin Li
10. LNAI 14693, Engineering Psychology and Cognitive Ergonomics: Part II, edited by Don Harris and Wen-Chin Li
11. LNAI 14694, Augmented Cognition: Part I, edited by Dylan D. Schmorrow and Cali M. Fidopiastis
12. LNAI 14695, Augmented Cognition: Part II, edited by Dylan D. Schmorrow and Cali M. Fidopiastis
13. LNCS 14696, Universal Access in Human-Computer Interaction: Part I, edited by Margherita Antona and Constantine Stephanidis
14. LNCS 14697, Universal Access in Human-Computer Interaction: Part II, edited by Margherita Antona and Constantine Stephanidis
15. LNCS 14698, Universal Access in Human-Computer Interaction: Part III, edited by Margherita Antona and Constantine Stephanidis
16. LNCS 14699, Cross-Cultural Design: Part I, edited by Pei-Luen Patrick Rau
17. LNCS 14700, Cross-Cultural Design: Part II, edited by Pei-Luen Patrick Rau
18. LNCS 14701, Cross-Cultural Design: Part III, edited by Pei-Luen Patrick Rau
19. LNCS 14702, Cross-Cultural Design: Part IV, edited by Pei-Luen Patrick Rau
20. LNCS 14703, Social Computing and Social Media: Part I, edited by Adela Coman and Simona Vasilache
21. LNCS 14704, Social Computing and Social Media: Part II, edited by Adela Coman and Simona Vasilache
22. LNCS 14705, Social Computing and Social Media: Part III, edited by Adela Coman and Simona Vasilache

23. LNCS 14706, Virtual, Augmented and Mixed Reality: Part I, edited by Jessie Y.C. Chen and Gino Fragomeni
24. LNCS 14707, Virtual, Augmented and Mixed Reality: Part II, edited by Jessie Y.C. Chen and Gino Fragomeni
25. LNCS 14708, Virtual, Augmented and Mixed Reality: Part III, edited by Jessie Y.C. Chen and Gino Fragomeni
26. LNCS 14709, Digital Human Modeling and Applications in Health, Safety, Ergonomics and Risk Management: Part I, edited by Vincent G. Duffy
27. LNCS 14710, Digital Human Modeling and Applications in Health, Safety, Ergonomics and Risk Management: Part II, edited by Vincent G. Duffy
28. LNCS 14711, Digital Human Modeling and Applications in Health, Safety, Ergonomics and Risk Management: Part III, edited by Vincent G. Duffy
29. LNCS 14712, Design, User Experience, and Usability: Part I, edited by Aaron Marcus, Elizabeth Rosenzweig and Marcelo M. Soares
30. LNCS 14713, Design, User Experience, and Usability: Part II, edited by Aaron Marcus, Elizabeth Rosenzweig and Marcelo M. Soares
31. LNCS 14714, Design, User Experience, and Usability: Part III, edited by Aaron Marcus, Elizabeth Rosenzweig and Marcelo M. Soares
32. LNCS 14715, Design, User Experience, and Usability: Part IV, edited by Aaron Marcus, Elizabeth Rosenzweig and Marcelo M. Soares
33. LNCS 14716, Design, User Experience, and Usability: Part V, edited by Aaron Marcus, Elizabeth Rosenzweig and Marcelo M. Soares
34. LNCS 14717, Culture and Computing, edited by Matthias Rauterberg
35. LNCS 14718, Distributed, Ambient and Pervasive Interactions: Part I, edited by Norbert A. Streitz and Shin'ichi Konomi
36. LNCS 14719, Distributed, Ambient and Pervasive Interactions: Part II, edited by Norbert A. Streitz and Shin'ichi Konomi
37. LNCS 14720, HCI in Business, Government and Organizations: Part I, edited by Fiona Fui-Hoon Nah and Keng Leng Siau
38. LNCS 14721, HCI in Business, Government and Organizations: Part II, edited by Fiona Fui-Hoon Nah and Keng Leng Siau
39. LNCS 14722, Learning and Collaboration Technologies: Part I, edited by Panayiotis Zaphiris and Andri Ioannou
40. LNCS 14723, Learning and Collaboration Technologies: Part II, edited by Panayiotis Zaphiris and Andri Ioannou
41. LNCS 14724, Learning and Collaboration Technologies: Part III, edited by Panayiotis Zaphiris and Andri Ioannou
42. LNCS 14725, Human Aspects of IT for the Aged Population: Part I, edited by Qin Gao and Jia Zhou
43. LNCS 14726, Human Aspects of IT for the Aged Population: Part II, edited by Qin Gao and Jia Zhou
44. LNCS 14727, Adaptive Instructional System, edited by Robert A. Sottilare and Jessica Schwarz
45. LNCS 14728, HCI for Cybersecurity, Privacy and Trust: Part I, edited by Abbas Moallem
46. LNCS 14729, HCI for Cybersecurity, Privacy and Trust: Part II, edited by Abbas Moallem

47. LNCS 14730, HCI in Games: Part I, edited by Xiaowen Fang

48. LNCS 14731, HCI in Games: Part II, edited by Xiaowen Fang

49. LNCS 14732, HCI in Mobility, Transport and Automotive Systems: Part I, edited by Heidi Krömker

50. LNCS 14733, HCI in Mobility, Transport and Automotive Systems: Part II, edited by Heidi Krömker

51. LNAI 14734, Artificial Intelligence in HCI: Part I, edited by Helmut Degen and Stavroula Ntoa

52. LNAI 14735, Artificial Intelligence in HCI: Part II, edited by Helmut Degen and Stavroula Ntoa

53. LNAI 14736, Artificial Intelligence in HCI: Part III, edited by Helmut Degen and Stavroula Ntoa

54. LNCS 14737, Human-Centered Design, Operation and Evaluation of Mobile Communications: Part I, edited by June Wei and George Margetis

55. LNCS 14738, Human-Centered Design, Operation and Evaluation of Mobile Communications: Part II, edited by June Wei and George Margetis

56. CCIS 2114, HCI International 2024 Posters: Part I, edited by Constantine Stephanidis, Margherita Antona, Stavroula Ntoa and Gavriel Salvendy

57. CCIS 2115, HCI International 2024 Posters: Part II, edited by Constantine Stephanidis, Margherita Antona, Stavroula Ntoa and Gavriel Salvendy

58. CCIS 2116, HCI International 2024 Posters: Part III, edited by Constantine Stephanidis, Margherita Antona, Stavroula Ntoa and Gavriel Salvendy

59. CCIS 2117, HCI International 2024 Posters: Part IV, edited by Constantine Stephanidis, Margherita Antona, Stavroula Ntoa and Gavriel Salvendy

60. CCIS 2118, HCI International 2024 Posters: Part V, edited by Constantine Stephanidis, Margherita Antona, Stavroula Ntoa and Gavriel Salvendy

61. CCIS 2119, HCI International 2024 Posters: Part VI, edited by Constantine Stephanidis, Margherita Antona, Stavroula Ntoa and Gavriel Salvendy

62. CCIS 2120, HCI International 2024 Posters: Part VII, edited by Constantine Stephanidis, Margherita Antona, Stavroula Ntoa and Gavriel Salvendy

63. LNCS 15374, HCI International 2024 - Late Breaking Papers: Part I, edited by Masaaki Kurosu, Ayako Hashizume, Hirohiko Mori, Yumi Asahi, Dylan D. Schmorrow and Cali M. Fidopiastis

64. LNCS 15375, HCI International 2024 - Late Breaking Papers: Part II, edited by Adela Coman, Simona Vasilache, Fiona Fui-Hoon Nah, Keng Leng Siau, June Wei and George Margetis

65. LNCS 15376, HCI International 2024 - Late Breaking Papers: Part III, edited by Vincent G. Duffy

66. LNCS 15377, HCI International 2024 - Late Breaking Papers: Part IV, edited by Jessie Y.C. Chen, Gino Fragomeni, Norbert A. Streitz, Shin'ichi Konomi and Xiaowen Fang

67. LNCS 15378, HCI International 2024 - Late Breaking Papers: Part V, edited by Panayiotis Zaphiris, Andri Ioannou, Robert A. Sottilare, Jessica Schwarz and Matthias Rauterberg

68. LNCS 15379, HCI International 2024 - Late Breaking Papers: Part VI, edited by Margherita Antona, Constantine Stephanidis, Qin Gao and Jia Zhou

69. LNCS 15380, HCI International 2024 - Late Breaking Papers: Part VII, edited by Aaron Marcus, Elizabeth Rosenzweig, Marcelo M. Soares, Pei-Luen Patrick Rau and Abbas Moallem

70. LNCS 15381, HCI International 2024 - Late Breaking Papers: Part VIII, edited by Don Harris, Wen-Chin Li and Heidi Krömker

71. LNCS 15382, HCI International 2024 - Late Breaking Papers: Part IX, edited by Helmut Degen and Stavroula Ntoa

72. CCIS 2319, HCI International 2024 - Late Breaking Posters: Part I, edited by Constantine Stephanidis, Margherita Antona, Stavroula Ntoa and Gavriel Salvendy

73. CCIS 2320, HCI International 2024 - Late Breaking Posters: Part II, edited by Constantine Stephanidis, Margherita Antona, Stavroula Ntoa and Gavriel Salvendy

74. CCIS 2321, HCI International 2024 - Late Breaking Posters: Part III, edited by Constantine Stephanidis, Margherita Antona, Stavroula Ntoa and Gavriel Salvendy

https://2024.hci.international/proceedings

26th International Conference on Human-Computer Interaction (HCII 2024)

The full list with the Program Board Chairs and the members of the Program Boards of all thematic areas and affiliated conferences of HCII2024 is available online at:

http://www.hci.international/board-members-2024.php

HCI International 2025 Conference

The 27th International Conference on Human-Computer Interaction, HCI International 2025, will be held jointly with the affiliated conferences at the Swedish Exhibition & Congress Centre and Gothia Towers Hotel, Gothenburg, Sweden, June 22–27, 2025. It will cover a broad spectrum of themes related to Human-Computer Interaction, including theoretical issues, methods, tools, processes, and case studies in HCI design, as well as novel interaction techniques, interfaces, and applications. The proceedings will be published by Springer. More information is available on the conference website: https://2025.hci.international/.

General Chair
Prof. Constantine Stephanidis
University of Crete and ICS-FORTH
Heraklion, Crete, Greece
Email: general_chair@2025.hci.international

https://2025.hci.international/

Contents – Part I

HCI Theories, Methods and Tools

Contributions for the Development of *Personae*: Method for Creating
Persona Templates (MCPT) 3
   Fábio Couto and Mariana Curado Malta

A Method Based on Customer Success Metrics for Software Product
Usability Assessment 23
   Marcelo Henrique de Oliveira, Ferrucio de Franco Rosa,
   and Adler Diniz de Souza

Unraveling Collaborative, User-Dependent IS: A Taxonomy 42
   Marvin Heuer and Chikaodi Uba

Action Research on the Educational Outcomes of AI Application
in the Conceptual Ideation Phase of Innovative Design Thinking 52
   Szu-Erh Hsu, Lin-mei Lin, Hao Chen, Chao Liu, Wen-Ko Chiou,
   and Po-Chen Shen

Creativity in Digital and Physical Environments: A Case Study with Data
Thinking Courses 63
   Stephan Leible, Constantin von Brackel-Schmidt, Gian-Luca Gücük,
   and Dejan Simic

What's the Value of Science Fiction for Future-Oriented Human-Computer
Interaction: The Role of Innovative Catalysts 83
   Yuqi Liu and Zhiyong Fu

Reconciling Wicked Problems Through Speculation: Exploring Design
Strategies for Interactive Installations 97
   Yue Ma

Reflection and Practice of Design in Sustainable Community Building 111
   Yichen Meng and Liying Huang

Let the Music Play: How Can One Test the Impact of Auditory Stimuli
on User Experience (UX)? 124
   Abhijai Miglani and Anushi Singh Thakur

Lexical Event Models for Multimodal Dialogues 174
    James Pustejovsky and Yifan Zhu

Exploring the Dynamics of XR and AI Synergy in Architectural Design 193
    Juan David Salazar Rodriguez and Sam Conrad Joyce

A Template Course for Teaching the Development of Interactive Systems
to Students of Human-Computer Interaction 211
    Toni Schumacher, Maged Mortaga, and André Calero Valdez

Humans as Cultural Gatekeepers: A Reverse Turing Test Approach 230
    Nanta Sooraksa, Chattraporn Noviram, and Pitikhate Sooraksa

Design and Responsible Research Innovation in the University-Industry
Collaboration: An Ethnographic Study of Nice2035 Project-Based
Community 249
    Jing Wang, Yunyun Weng, Mohammad Shidujaman, and Ying Jiang

Design Support Tool Based on the Analysis of Differences Between
Japanese and Chinese E-commerce Sites 274
    Xiaojiao Zou and Tomonari Kamba

Multimodal Interaction

Evaluation of Interactive Slider Design Utilizing Haptic Feedback 289
    Yui Atarashi and Buntarou Shizuki

Design of a Multimodal Robot-Based Conversational Interface: A Case
Study with FURHAT 299
    *Rita Francese, Madalina G. Ciobanu, Emilio Clemente,
    and Genoveffa Tortora*

Effect of Olfactory Presentation Timing on Memory Retention:
Relationship to Default Mode Network Activity 312
    Takuto Fukushima and Takehiko Yamaguchi

A Stereohaptics Accessory for Spatial Computing Platforms 325
    *Ali Israr, Asad Tirmizi, Bo Zhu, Dehao Zhao, Erting Cheng,
    and Zachary Schwemler*

EEGMobile: Enhancing Speed and Accuracy in EEG-Based Gaze
Prediction with Advanced Mobile Architectures 341
    Teng Liang and Andrews Damoah

Foam Magnetic Tactile Sensors for Spatial Computing Input 356
  Wade Marquette, Ali Israr, and Mohammed Al-Rubaiai

Decoding Elbow Movement Intentions from EMG Signals
for Exosuit/Exoskeleton Control 372
  Siddharth Rajesh Patil and Deep Seth

On-Skin Interaction System and Smart Wearable Research Based
on Innovative Gesture Input 387
  Chen Wang

Refining Human-Data Interaction: Advanced Techniques for EEGEyeNet
Dataset Precision 407
  Jade Wu, Jingwen Dou, and Sofia Utoft

Author Index 421

HCI Theories, Methods and Tools

Contributions for the Development of *Personae*: Method for Creating Persona Templates (MCPT)

Fábio Couto[1](✉)(iD) and Mariana Curado Malta[2](iD)

[1] CEOS.PP, ISCAP, Polytechnic of Porto, Porto, Portugal
`fabio.couto@iscap.ipp.pt`
[2] INESC TEC, Faculty of Engineering, University of Porto, Porto, Portugal
`mariana.c.malta@inesctec.pt`

Abstract. This paper contributes to developing a Method for Creating Persona Templates (MCPT), addressing a significant gap in user-centred design methodologies. Utilising qualitative data collection and analysis techniques, MCPT offers a systematic approach to developing robust and context-oriented persona templates. MCPT was created by applying the Design Science Research (DSR) methodology, and it incorporates multiple iterations for template refinement and validation among project stakeholders; all of the proposed steps of this method were based on theoretical contributions. Furthermore, MCPT was tested and refined within a real-life R&D project focusing on developing a digital platform e-marketplace for short agrifood supply chains in two iteration cycles. MCPT fills a critical void in persona research by providing detailed instructions for each step of template development. By involving the target audience, users, and project stakeholders, MCPT adds rigour to the persona creation process, enhancing the quality and relevance of *personae* casts. This paper contributes to the body of knowledge by offering an initial proposal of a comprehensive method for creating persona templates within diverse projects and contexts. Further research should explore MCPT's adaptability to different settings and projects, thus refining its effectiveness and extending its utility in user-centred design practices.

Keywords: persona · method · persona templates · design science research · MCPT

1 Introduction

In the ever-evolving landscapes of user-centred design (see [24]), understanding the intricacies of target audiences has become vital. This article investigates the theoretical foundations and research methodology of crafting a persona (*personae*). The foundation of this exploration lies in the Persona method, introduced by [11], a user-oriented design approach applicable to diverse contexts such as

M. Kurosu et al. (Eds.): HCII 2024, LNCS 15374, pp. 3–22, 2025.
https://doi.org/10.1007/978-3-031-76803-3_1

software development [1,3,5,18,26,57], UX [59], digital marketing and communication [4], among others [20,25,27,41,56]. *Personae* are semi-fictional characters representing specific user groups. They play a pivotal role [57]. The first step in creating a *persona* is to develop a 'persona template' which establishes the information to be included in each *persona* profile. A *persona* template is defined by attributes, which can be visual models, textual descriptions, and various characteristics of the target groups, from attitudes to daily life, creating a comprehensive overview of the target-audience [57]. Templates should be adapted to each specific use context [3,45]. To the best of our knowledge, no established general method exists for creating context-oriented *persona* templates. A method is an intangible artefact incorporating recipes [42]; it is a set of organised interconnected activities that use techniques to achieve a goal. Methods are instantiated to accomplish the designed objectives; you run the activities to obtain a result. In our case, a method is used to develop the "Persona Template" artefact for a specific context. Existing literature provides vague guidelines for creating *persona* templates, lacking a comprehensive and general method. Some papers guide creating *personae* but omit details on template creation. The contributions are many, e.g. [2,12,19,22,34,35,40,50,55,75–77] but none provides guidance - see Table 1.

Table 1. Analysis of papers regarding methods to create *personae*

	Sources											
Parameters	[2]	[12]	[19]	[22]	[35]	[40]	[50]	[55]	[75]	[76]	[77]	[34]
Mentions Template creation?	y	y	y	y	y	n	y	y	y	y	y	y
Proposes detailed method?	n	n	n	n	n	n	n	n	n	n	n	n

This knowledge gap can result in inadequate persona templates not aligned with project goals or needs, thus making the *personae* technique less effective.

This paper aims to contribute to the definition of a 'Method for the Creation of Persona Templates' (MCPT); it shows how we have used the Design Science Research Methodology (DSRM) ([53] to develop MCPT. The work context was an R&D project (*AgroVila*[1]), which aims to develop an e-marketplace of short agrifood supply chains for small-holder family farmers.

The remainder of this paper is organised as follows: the following section presents the state-of-the-art of the Persona approach, and the next section presents the research problem and objectives. Section 4 presents the research methodology, and Sect. 5 explains the application of DSRM to develop MPCT. Section 6 presents the Method for the Creation of Persona Templates, showing the rationale, the steps, and the control points. Finally, the last section concludes the paper and discusses future research directions.

---

[1] See http://www.agrovila.org - accessed in 19.03.2024.

2   State-of-the-Art

Cooper [11] first introduced the Persona approach. This user-oriented design approach can be used in different contexts whenever the target is a specific group of people [27]. This approach offers benefits to teams of product developers, as it helps keep the focus on real users' needs [57] or identifying application requirements [17]. The Persona approach can also help market segmentation [12] and design teams by boosting ideation and empathy and avoiding design fixation [63]. This method aims to create *personae*, which are semi-fictional characters [11]. In general, the Persona creation is represented by visual models (photos, quotes, text) that help create an overview of the target audience [27,56]. The textual descriptions can include attitudes, personality or behaviours ([5], but also add further information [56] such as daily life [9], activities [5,26] or hobbies [71]. The definition of a Persona begins with its backbone, i.e., a template describing which information to include when creating these semi-fictional characters [4]. As [3,45] point out, there is no standard way, that is, a method, of creating these characters, and they should be adapted to the specific context of use. There is controversy regarding the attributes of *Personae* templates [22,25]. In its original Persona approach proposal, [11] suggested a standard approach used by [1], which includes attributes such as persona identification, roles and tasks, goals, segments, skills and knowledge, context/environment, personal and psychological details [18]. For [11], system designers could use these attributes in multiple contexts. However, this specific set of attributes indicated by [11] can contain irrelevant details in a particular context, so there has to be a connection between Persona attributes and the context of the solution to be developed [17,25]. [60] found a significant variation in Persona attributes. This is caused by the different information needs of Persona end-users [4], which only strengthens the idea of adapting Persona templates to their specific contexts. For example, [56] have built a Persona template to understand citizens' mobility needs. In their study, they identified additional attributes from the ones proposed by [11]: Preferences ([71]); Expectations ([71]); Goals ([58]); Needs (Seth, as cited in [56]); Frustrations ([58]); Challenges (Seth, as cited in [56]); Impairments/restrictions (Seth, as cited in [56]; [71]). Additionally, [3] also identified other Persona attributes, such as demographic data ([59]), persona interests ([74]), education level ([59]) and IT experience ([3]). After identifying the context of use, the Persona templates cannot depend solely on literature, as they may not reflect the needs of the end-users [4,49]. A possible solution could be the inclusion of industry contributions (white papers and grey literature), as they offer additional perspectives that, in some cases, are connected with real projects, thus giving more insights into the needs of end-users ([4]). There are methods to create *Personae* (but not Persona templates, as this task is not detailed) based on quantitative, qualitative, or data with both types (quantitative and qualitative). However, these methods do not delve into the Persona templates. Instead, they focus on collecting and analysing user data to build the *Personae* [35]. So, there is no possible way to develop *Personae* if we do not have access to data, only proto-*personae* [55]. Proto-*personae* are not built based on user data. Instead, they are built based on the assumptions of the project team and their knowledge of a given domain [21,55], i.e., proto-*personae* are not data-driven.

3   Research Problem and Objective

To the best of our knowledge, there is no detailed method for developing context-oriented *personae* templates. Therefore, our work aims to create such a method.

4   Methodology: Design Science Research

We used the Design Science Research Methodology (DSRM) to develop MCPT. Design Science is the scientific study and creation of artefacts [36]. Artefacts can be defined as human-made objects that aim to solve or address a problem, and their instantiations could be in the form of physical objects, products, services, methods, guidelines or processes [67]. Design Science promotes a pragmatic, theory-based creation and investigation of the artificial, i.e., a design based on theory [65]. Furthermore, research based on the Design Science paradigm should position the artefacts in natural settings to achieve validation [65]. This approach is a valuable tool for industry-academia collaborations [65], as researchers develop general knowledge in a given context to help professionals create solutions for their problems [16]. Design Science is the supportive paradigm of Design Science Research (DSR). DSR is a research methodology to guide knowledge production through prescriptive studies to find solutions to existing problems, to improve or create new systems, projects or the building of artefacts [13,69]. DSR aims to develop artefacts to solve practical problems and generate new knowledge, which could be scientific and technological [54]. Technological and scientific knowledge are different, but both are important in building artefacts [54]: science searches for knowledge and explanations and builds theories to explain observed facts, and technology does not explain the world; instead, technology is practical and aims to transform the world without theorising about it [72]. DSR is used in a wide range of disciplines, including information systems [16], engineering [16], education [65], management, project management, medical research [47,68] and operations management [31]. DSR's most common stages are Problem Identification, Solution Design and Evaluation [51]. According to [43], novelty is a crucial criterion for evaluating DSR artefacts. Novelty differentiates DSR from regular design and is achieved when a problem is addressed innovatively or more efficiently [66]. The contributions from DSR can either improve (new solutions for existing issues) or invent new solutions to new problems [66]. DSR solutions must also be generalisable to a particular class of problems [61,69,70]. The knowledge generated through DSR has to be useful for other researchers and professionals [13], meaning it can be confirmed in a different context from the one in which it was empirically tested [39]. Literature shows that the most common technique to evaluate artefacts that are methods, in Information Systems papers, is the Case Study method [52], so that is how we evaluate MCPT. The impact of a given solution developed through DSR can be measured by its practical use and research citations of scientific publications [7]. There are multiple approaches to DSR [29,36,51,53]. This paper follows the Design Science Research Method (DSRM) by [53], consisting of six phases in sequential order:

- Phase 1: Problem Identification and Motivation, in which one defines the specific research problem and justifies the solution's value.
- Phase 2: Define Objectives for a Solution, in which one infers the objectives of a solution from the problem definition and knowledge of what is possible and feasible.
- Phase 3: Design and Development, in which one creates the artefact.
- Phase 4: Demonstration, one uses the artefact created to solve one problem instance.
- Phase 5: Evaluation, in which one observes and measures how well the artefact supports a solution to the problem.
- Phase 6: Communication, in which one communicates the problem and its importance, the artefact, its utility and novelty, the rigour of its design, and its effectiveness to researchers and other relevant audiences.

However, researchers might start at a different phase and then move outward. Also, DSRM gives the possibility of iterating the work from phase five (Evaluation) or six (Communication) to phase two (Define objectives of a solution) or three (Design and Development).

Regarding research entry points, Peffers [53] establishes four possibilities: Problem-Centered Initiation; Objective-Centered Solution; Design & Development-Centered Initiation; Client/Context-Initiated solution.

The next section presents how the DSRM methodology was used to develop MCPT.

5   Application of DSRM

5.1   Introduction

This research's entry point of our work was the "Problem-Centered Initiation" since the research problem was identified after reviewing existing literature [53]. We started with Phase 1, problem identification and motivation and then proceeded to Phase 2, where we defined the solution objectives. Two iteration cycles were developed between Phases 3 and 5 (see Fig. 1): Cycle 1 in blue and Cycle 2 in yellow. Each Cycle is described in the following paragraphs:

- Cycle 1 (blue): Draft 1 of the artefact is designed in Phase 3. It is validated in Phase 4 by developing a template for the "family-farmer" type of persona. It is evaluated in Phase 5. Then, by returning to Phase 3, a second cycle (Cycle 2 - in yellow) begins.
- Cycle 2 (yellow): Draft 2 of the artefact is redesigned in Phase 3, according to the results of Phase 5 - Cycle 1. In Phase 4, Draft 2 is validated by developing a template for the "buyer" type of persona, and in Phase 5, it is evaluated.

    After the two cycles, the work moved to Phase 6.

    The following paragraphs present the rationale for developing the work according to the previously described DSRM phases and cycles.

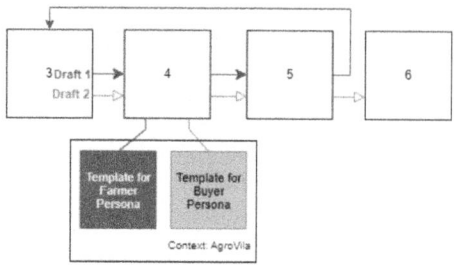

Fig. 1. The DSRM cycles developed. (Color figure online)

5.2   Phase 1

We identified a knowledge gap regarding the creation of Persona templates. We have found general guidelines for creating templates, e.g., the need to adapt the persona templates to a specific context of use, but no comprehensive method for creating templates. Selecting attributes for a persona template is vaguely addressed, which could lead to ineffective persona templates that might not reflect or convey helpful information for a given project's goals. We have identified papers that guide us in creating personas but do not indicate how to create the templates (see Table 1) since the authors present the templates already created without exploring how they did it. A well-built and data-driven Persona template (in opposition to *proto-personae*, which might not be as accurate [50]) might be the first step towards developing a practical solution, which could be achieved by following our method: Method for Creating Persona Templates (MCPT). Applying this method introduces rigour to a process that, hitherto, lacks clear guidelines from academia [3,45].

5.3   Phase 2

The DSRM process aimed to create the artefact, a "Method for Creating Persona templates. This method should guide building robust and data-driven Persona templates, resulting in more efficient and context-oriented *personae* casts. In turn, the *personae* cast contributes to effectively developing a given solution (e.g., software, among other types of solutions).

5.4   Phase 3

In this phase, we developed the artefact Method For Creating Persona Templates. The next paragraphs present, for each cycle:

- the rationale for creating MCPT and for the decisions taken.
- MCPT, we make a presentation by step; for each step, we present the activities to be carried out with what techniques, the Milestones and the Outputs, when applicable. In Cycle 1, we present MCPT Draft 1, but not in Cycle 2 since it is presented in the Results Section.

The Rationale: Draft 1

The MCPT Draft 1 design was based on the DSR rationale since it includes a problem identification, solution design, and evaluation phase, the most common DSR stages [51]. So, we included such phases in MCPT. We resorted to the knowledge base as the starting point to design MCPT [29,53]: since we're working in the software development context (information systems for e-business), our starting point to define the phases and the techniques used, was the Rational Unified Process (RUP) [38], one of the best-known and most widely used software development processes. RUP is a comprehensive method that can be used in different contexts [38]. The RUP inception phase calls for "Business modelling", which, in our case, is the study of the application context. In the information collection or evaluation phases, we incorporated the possibility of using social science techniques, such as focus groups [14,28]. In the information analysis, we incorporated the possibility of using the Content analysis techniques [6]. The techniques used to identify attributes of an entity can be used in the design phase of MCPT (e.g. UML [44]).

The artefact: MCPT Draft 1

Fig. 2 shows the Workflow of MCPT Draft 1.

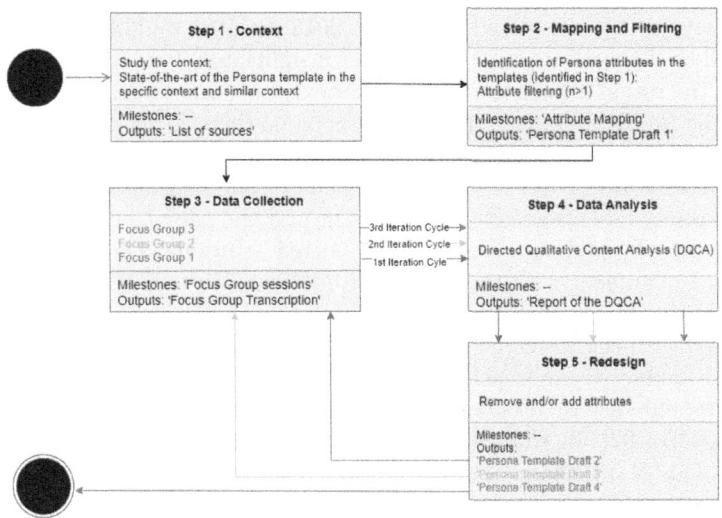

Fig. 2. Workflow of MCPT Draft 1.

Step 1 - Context: this step aims to establish the state-of-the-art of the persona templates in the specific context in which the work in question takes place - this can be achieved via a systematic literature review [73]. If needed, it is possible to extend the scope of the research by searching similar contexts. There should be a resort to academic papers, white papers and grey literature [4, 49]. Furthermore, the working team should develop knowledge of the problem domain and context of use [11]. This step allows the team to identify the research problems and define the objectives. The **Output** of this step is a document report with the 'List of sources' of the persona templates identified.

Step 2 - Mapping and Filtering: An analysis is carried out on the document report with the 'List of sources' to build a list with the attributes used in the state-of-the-art of the persona templates and register how many times each attribute is used in the set of persona templates found. This allows the identification of a list of attributes to guide the creation of the template, providing a starting point for the Persona Template. The next phase of this step is to exclude from the list of attributes those attributes which are not used in more than one template. The **Milestone** of this step is the 'Attribute Mapping', as it marks the baseline for developing the persona template. The **Output** of this step is the 'Persona Template Draft 1', i.e., a visual document with the attributes for the persona (see [3]).

Step 3 - Data Collection: Qualitative research is the first step for creating *personae*, regardless of the approach (qualitative, quantitative or mixed methods) [30, 45]. Moreover, Focus Groups are mainly conducted in the early stages of design processes [30], as the characteristics of a given target audience have to be considered (Siqueira, 2018 as cited by [33]). Focus Groups also allow the work team to gain deeper insights and develop more knowledge about the target audience and their context, fostering an essential familiarity with the problem domain [11]. This step runs three focus groups to test the template drafts and identify relevant characteristics of the target audience. The **Milestone** of this Step is the 'Focus Group sessions', as they provide direct contact between the project team and the target audience, thus creating empathy and supporting User-Centred solutions. The **Output** of this step is a document with the 'Focus Group Transcription'.

Step 4 - Data Analysis: The document with the 'Focus Group Transcription' is analysed with the 'Directed Qualitative Content Analysis' (DQCA) technique [6] in a deductive approach. The deductive approach allows researchers to validate, enhance or broaden a theory or theoretical framework within new contexts [15, 32]. In this case, the goal is to validate the persona template draft. This is especially useful when the work team is unfamiliar with the problem domain, as the data analysis might provide additional information, which could be discussed or clarified in the next Focus Group run (in the next cycle). The **Output** of this step is the result of the data analysis materialised in the 'Report of the DQCA'.

Step 5 - Redesign: Based on the 'Report of the DQCA', the work team decides which attributes to be added and excluded from the template draft developed in Step 2. This work considers the new information that may emerge from the Input: if new data appears, or new needs for the information system that is to be developed, or any other new information, then the template needs to be updated. The **Output** of this Step is a new version of the 'Persona template Draft'.

The iteration cycles allow the work team to build more information about the project's target audience and refine the template to build templates that convey useful information to a project's stakeholders [1]. The process runs one more time before delivering the final version of the persona template.

Cycle 2
In this cycle, we developed Draft 2 of MCPT.
The Rationale: Draft2
The changes on MCPT were made to:

- address the generalisability characteristic of the artefact. This characteristic should be addressed in any process of creation of artefacts since it means that an artefact (in our case, the method) can be applied to situations other than those explored when created and evaluated [13,39,61,69,70];
- extend the suggestion of milestones, methods and techniques in the various stages of MCPT to make it more comprehensive so that it can be applied in different contexts;
- involve more stakeholders or experts from outside the work team (e.g. academics or specialists) in the construction of the templates, especially in the validation phases;
- introduce the concept of Data Saturation [23]. Many qualitative researchers struggle with knowing how many data collection sessions are needed to finish their work - and they might fall into an infinite loop. The "Data Saturation" concept is a way to control iteration cycles with a variable. When Data saturation is achieved, the work terminates, meaning there is no new information to add to the process. The theory by [23] says that data saturation could be achieved when the amount of information changed is less than or equal to 5% when compared to the previous version. In the case of MCPT, when modifications to the persona template attributes are less than or equal to 5% compared to the attributes before the modifications, the work team has achieved data saturation. See Table 2 to see how to calculate Data Saturation in the specific case of MCPT.

Table 2. Formula to calculate Data Saturation in MCPT (see [23])

Name	Variable
No. Attributes changed	v1
No. Attributes before modification	v2
Data Saturation (%)	DS = v1 / v2 * 100

In more detail, the rationale for the changes from Draft 1 to Draft 2 is: The process has seven Steps:

Step 1 - Context: The new version adds a **Milestone**: the 'State-of-the-art of *personae*' in the context of the project or similar contexts, as it marks the first step of the persona template creation process and will have implications for all the other Steps.

Step 2 - Mapping and Filtering: The new version adds an **Input**, the 'List of Sources', being the result of mapping and filtering the attributes of the 'State-of-the-art of *personae*' presented in the 'Persona Template Draft In Progress'.

Step 3 - Data Collection: MCPT Draft 2 offers more general data collection guidelines by including different methods and techniques, thus making this Step more wide-reaching. The **techniques and methods** are: 'Focus Groups' [14, 28], 'Interviews' [37], 'Observation' [46] or 'Surveys' [8]. This Step in this new version includes an **Input**, the 'Persona Template Draft In Progress', which will guide the preparation of the data collection session(s) and two possible **Outputs**: 'Data Collection Transcription', or 'Data Collection Report', depending on the data collection technique or method, e.g. if doing a Focus Group, the output is the transcription, whereas if doing Observation, the output is a report. Furthermore, it includes a **Milestone**: the 'Data Collection Session'.

Step 4 - Data Analysis: this Step features more general qualitative data analysis guidelines in the new version of MCPT by suggesting multiple **methods and techniques**, which depend on the social sciences techniques or methods for data collection used in Step 3. The techniques or methods are 'Content Analysis' [6], 'Grounded Theory' [10], 'Thematic Analysis' [48] and 'Narrative Analysis' [62]. Also, an **Input** is added as the work team analyses the results from the data collection session(s), and the **Output** is changed to 'Data analysis report' to embrace all the different methods and techniques besides the DQCA.

Step 5 - Redesign 1: this step was updated to reflect the more wide-reaching overall design of MCPT Draft 2, adding an **Input**, the 'Data analysis report', as this will be the basis for justifying redesign modifications, and a new **Output** - the 'Persona Template Draft In Progress', as it now allows infinite redesign iterations and thus improving generalisability by not limiting the number of iterations to three as in MCPT Draft1.

Step 6 - Validation: as a way of ensuring relevancy, accuracy and rigour of the persona templates [1], a validation Step was added with either project stakeholders (the members that will make use of the *personae* or the target-audience) or external participants (experts and the scientific community). The validation can be done via multiple **methods and techniques**, from the 'Delphi Technique' [64], 'questionnaires or surveys to target audience', to the presentation of the work at a 'scientific conference'. The **Input** will be the 'Persona Template Draft In Progress', which is to be validated. The **Output** of this Step is a 'Validation Report' with the results of the validation session, which can either be the recommendations by the evaluation panel or a proof of acceptance. This Step includes an updated **Milestone**: the

'Validation Session', which marks the direct involvement of other stakeholders and external contributors in the template creation process.

Step 7 - Redesign 2: This Step has a new **Input**, the 'Validation Report'. Based on the Input, the work team will modify the persona template draft. The **Output** of this Step is the 'Persona Template Draft'.

Furthermore, the MCPT has four Control Points (which are all added to Draft 2):

Control Point 1 - Control question: Does the Template need changes?; The control point is introduced to assess if the 'Persona Template Draft In Progress' must be changed based on the data collection and analysis activities before being submitted for validation. This can happen as new information might arise from contact with the target audience, and the developers might think of it as useful - or reveal that an attribute in the 'Persona Template Draft In Progress' is irrelevant - for a given project.

Control Point 2 - Control question: Is Data Saturation Achieved?; Data Saturation is introduced as a tool to measure if another data collection and analysis round is needed.

Control Point 3 - Control question: Does the Template need changes?; Based on the results of Step 6 ('Validation Report'), the work team assesses if the 'Persona Template Draft In Progress' needs to be modified.

Control Point 4 - Control question: 'Is Data Saturation Achieved?; The concept of Data Saturation is introduced to measure if the 'Persona Template Draft' needs to be submitted to another validation round.

The artefact: Draft2
Draft 2 of MCPT is presented in the "Results" Section. The Workflow of MCPT Draft 2 is presented in Fig. 3.

5.5   Phase 4

Cycle 1
To demonstrate the MCPT Draft 1, we instantiated it to create a Persona Template for the "Familly Farmer". As a result, we obtained the following attributes for the Template: Photo, Demographic Data, Personality, Channels, Quote, Routine, Goals, Needs, Motivations, Digital Literacy, Digital Tools, Devices and Operation Details.

Cycle 2
To demonstrate the MCPT Draft 2, we instantiated it to create a Persona Template for the "Buyers" of the *AgroVila* e-grocery marketplace. As a result, we obtained the following attributes for the Template: Photo, Demographic Data, Personality, Preferred Channels, Quote, About, Routine, Motivations, Goals, Needs, Tech Skills, Purchase Factors and Brands.

5.6   Phase 5

The evaluation of MCPT Drafts took place with a multidisciplinary group of experts from the *Agro Vila* project team, spanning from experts in Information Systems, Management, Marketing, and Entrepreneurship & Business Innovation.
Cycle 1
The first evaluation session led to the identification of the following limitations: 1) The lack of a validation phase involving project stakeholders, as the persona needs to convey useful information to the development team [1]; 2) Definition of an exact number of iteration cycles and data collection and analysis techniques, which may hinder the method's applicability to other contexts, as each project has its time frame and resources, thus affecting MCPT's generalisability [35,39]; 3) The assumption of constant template changes (Step 5) after the focus group data analysis (Step 4) may not apply in all cases, as data saturation could be reached in one of the rounds [23] and there would be no need for more iteration cycles, thus optimising resources and time by avoiding unnecessary repetition of data collection and analysis procedures.
Cycle 2
In the second evaluation session, the *Agro Vila* experts concluded that all the limitations identified in the previous evaluation session were addressed, and no further changes were deemed necessary. MCPT Draft 2 includes multiple iteration cycles and a validation phase, allowing for continuous refinement of the templates. By involving stakeholders in the validation step of MCPT, we address the usefulness and reliability of the templates. If the information in the templates is in line with the needs of the stakeholders, the *personae* might have a higher impact on the development of user-centred solutions. Furthermore, the method was now considered more generalisable to other contexts, allowing for as many iterations as necessary. Its Steps now include multiple methods and techniques. Finally, introducing Control Points offers a mechanism to control and evaluate the necessity of iterations.

5.7   Phase 6

This paper completes Phase number six of the DSRM ([52] approach), as we communicate the problem and its importance, the artefact, research details and phases, and MCPT's effectiveness reflected in the instantiations.

6   Results: Method for Creating Persona Templates

6.1   Introduction

Figure 3 depicts the process of MCPT. The following paragraphs present the details of this process: its steps and control points, the activities to be carried out in each step, the techniques used, and the inputs, outputs, and milestones of each step. MCPT has seven steps and four control points.

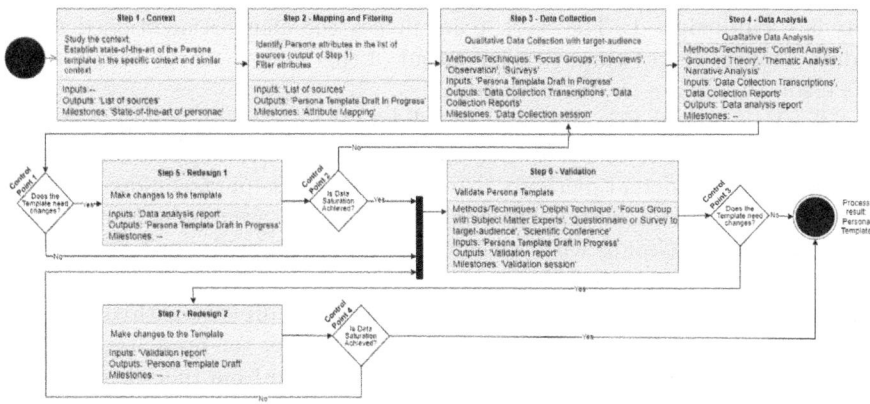

Fig. 3. Workflow of MCPT Draft 2.

6.2   Steps

The steps are:

Step 1 - Context: the context of the application should be thoroughly studied to understand user needs better and establish the state-of-the-art (milestone) regarding persona templates in the specific context of the application or even in similar contexts. This Step results in a 'List of sources' consulted to establish the state-of-the-art (output).

Step 2 - Mapping and filtering: all the attributes in the persona templates found in Step 1 (input) should be identified and mapped (milestone); attributes should then be filtered, and those that appear more than once are included in the initial persona template draft ('Persona Template Draft In Progress' - output).

Step 3 - Data Collection: this Step aims to collect data from the stakeholders using a technique of data collection or method like Focus Group, Interview, Observation or Survey. This Step's input is the 'Persona Template Draft In Progress', which guides the data collection session(s) preparation. Furthermore, it has two possible Outputs: 'Data Collection Transcription' or 'Data Collection Report', depending on the data collection technique or method - e.g., if doing a Focus Group, the output is the transcription, whereas if doing Observation, the output is a report. The Milestone of Step 3 is the 'Data Collection Session'.

Step 4 - Data Analysis: The input of this Step is the output of Step 3, which is analysed. This should be done using a qualitative data analysis technique. The technique should be aligned with the data collection method used, as they should be compatible. The methods are content analysis, grounded theory, thematic analysis and narrative analysis. The output of this step is a 'Data Analysis Report', which could be shared internally amongst project members or teams.

Step 5 - Redesign 1: The work team makes the changes mentioned in the data analysis report (input). The output of this Step is a new version of the 'Persona Template Draft In Progress'.

Step 6 - Validation: this step aims to validate the persona template and guarantee its usefulness and relevancy. The validation can happen through the application of different methods or techniques: the Delphi technique (includes its multiple versions, such as the mini-Delphi if there are time or resource constraints), Focus Groups with specialists (could be internal or external project specialists, or a mix of both), Questionnaires or Surveys to the target-audience (in this case, the work team conducts a validation directly with the project members that will make use of the *personae* cast), or the presentation of the work in a Scientific Conference to achieve validation from the scientific community. The input of this Step is the 'Persona Template Draft In Progress' from Step 5. The output of this Step is a 'Validation Report', i.e., the results from the method or technique used for validation.

Step 7 - Redesign 2: the goal of this step is to proceed with the modifications suggested in the 'Validation Report' of Step 6 (input).

6.3   Control Points

The control points are:

Control Point 1 - Control Question: Does the Template need changes?; Based on the 'Data analysis report' (Step 4), the work team assesses the 'Persona Template Draft In Progress' to see if it needs to be changed, as new and relevant information can come from the 'Data Collection session'. If changes are to be made, the work moves to Step 5; if not, the work moves to Step 6.

Control Point 2 - Control Question: Is Data Saturation achieved?; The work team assesses if there are enough modifications to the new persona template to justify another round of data collection; this is done by calculating Data Saturation (see Table 2). If the template does not achieve Data Saturation, there should be another iteration of the data collection (the process moves to Step 3). If Data Saturation is achieved, the process moves to Step 7.

Control Point 3 - Control Question: Does the Template need changes?; Based on the results of Step 6, the work team decides if there is a need for further refinement of the 'Persona Template Draft In Progress'. The development process is finished if the Control Point dictates that no further changes are required. If there are changes to be done, the process iterates to Step 7.

Control Point 4 - Control Question: Is Data Saturation achieved?; This final Control Point aims to assess if there are enough modifications to the new 'Persona Template Draft' to justify another round of validation. If Data Saturation is achieved, the process ends, and the result is the final 'Persona Template'. In contrast, a new validation cycle begins if Data Saturation is not achieved (the process moves to Step 6).

6.4   Final Considerations

MCPT was built based on solid theoretical contributions, ensuring theoretical robustness in its design [29,38,51,53].
Step 1 creates context awareness to ensure context-oriented *personae* [11], while Step 2 provides a baseline for the initial template draft. Step 3 and Step 4 guide the data collection and analysis by indicating qualitative methods and techniques [14,28]. Step 5 introduces the possibility of template redesign after analysing the results of data collection, which would lead to Step 6, thus entering an initial iteration loop; this will allow reaching Step 8 with a more refined template draft and decrease the chances of another iteration round in Step 9 after consulting with other project stakeholders during Validation. To assess the need to iterate back to Step 3, the work team calculates if Data Saturation was achieved, as if only minor changes are done, then iteration might not be necessary; this is an important Step as it provides an exact formula that helps understanding when it is time to proceed with the persona template draft validation [23]. If no template redesign is needed (Step 5), the work team moves directly to Step 8. In Step 8 we provide multiple possibilities for draft validation, as the primary goal here is to ensure relevancy i.e., that the attributes in the persona template are the most adequate ones [1]; one should select the most appropriate method or technique depending on specific project resources and timeline. If the Validation round requires so (Step 9), the template must be adjusted and - if Data Saturation is not achieved - iterate back to another round of Validation. The feedback loops in MCPT ensure relevancy and adequacy to each project by involving internal (development/design teams) and external (end-users) project stakeholders. Furthermore, we provide detailed explanations with actionable guidance for each of the steps, including techniques, inputs, outputs and milestones, as we believe these instructions help understand what is expected from each Step.

7   Conclusion and Future Work

Papers that deal with the creation of *personae* provide scant detail about how to create the templates. If a persona template is not carefully conceived, it could lead to persona profiles with irrelevant attributes, damaging their usefulness and impact on project goals. This paper aims to contribute to filling this knowledge gap. To the best of our knowledge, there is no detailed method for developing context-oriented *personae* templates. This paper presents a Method for Creating Persona Templates (MCPT) based on qualitative data collection and analysis techniques; to do that, we designed MCPT by applying the DSRM approach of [52]. The paper details the activities carried out for the development of MCPT.

We went through two iteration cycles of DSRM between the Phase of Design and the Phase of Evaluation, both in the context of the *AgroVila* R&D project - which aims at developing an e-marketplace for short agrifood supply chains.

This paper contributes to creating context-oriented persona templates and, consequently, context-oriented *personae*. It also makes an interesting contribution to the DSR community, being a use-case of DSRM to create a method (artefact).

The limitations include the DSRM application, by running exclusively in the *AgroVila* R&D project, which could result in limited generalisability.

For further research, MCPT should be applied in different contexts aside from *AgroVila* to further improve it and demonstrate its applicability to other projects.

Acknowledgements. This work is financed by the investment programme RE-CO5-i03-Agenda de investigação e inovação para a sustentabilidade da agricultura, alimentação e agroindústria N° 14/C05-i03/2021-PRR-C05-i03-I-000166, This work is financed by Portuguese national funds through FCT - Fundação para a Ciência e Tecnologia, under the project UIDB/05422/2020, and under the project UIDB/50014/2020 (DOI 10.54499 /UIDB/50014/2020). The authors would like to thank Inês Veiga Pereira (ORCID: 0000-0002-7906-612X) for introducing the possibility of controlling iteration cycles with the Data Saturation concept, as well as all Focus Groups participants and *AgroVila* project partners for their effort and cooperation.

Disclosure of Interests. The authors have no competing interests to declare.

References

1. Acuña, S., Castro, J., Juristo, N.: A HCI technique for improving requirements elicitation. Elsevier **54**(12), 1357–1375 (2012). https://doi.org/10.1016/j.infsof.2012.07.011
2. Ali, F., Stewart, R., Boks, C., Bey, N.: Exploring "Company Personas" for Informing Design for Sustainability Implementation in Companies. MDPI **11**(2), 463 (2019). https://doi.org/10.3390/su11020463
3. Almahri, F., Bell, D., Arzoky, M.: Personas Design for Conversational Systems in Education. MDPI **6**(4), 46 (2019). https://doi.org/10.3390/informatics6040046
4. Alsaadi, B., Alahmadi, D.: Audience-centered approach for health communication over social media during pandemic: persona template based on delphi technique. Taylor Francis (2022). https://doi.org/10.1080/10447318.2022.2144125
5. Anvari, F., Richards, D., Hitchens, M., Babar, M.: Effectiveness of persona with personality traits on conceptual design. In: 2015 IEEE/ACM 37th IEEE International Conference on Software Engineering, vol. 2. IEEE, Italy (2015). https://doi.org/10.1109/ICSE.2015.155
6. Assarroudi, A., Heshmati Nabavi, F., Armat, M.R., Ebadi, A., Vaismoradi, M.: Directed qualitative content analysis: the description and elaboration of its underpinning methods and data analysis process. J. Res. Nurs: JRN **23**(1), 42–55 (2018). https://doi.org/10.1177/1744987117741667
7. Baskerville, R., Baiyere, A., Gregor, S., Hevner, A., Rossi, M.: Design science research contributions: finding a balance between artifact and theory. J. Assoc. Inf. Syst. **19**(5), 3 (2018)
8. Braun, V., Clarke, V., Boulton, E., Davey, L., McEvoy, C.: The online survey as a qualitative research tool. Int. J. Soc. Res. Methodol. **24**(6), 641–654 (2021)
9. Brown, T.: Design thinking. Harv. Bus. Rev. **86**(6), 84–92 (2008)

10. Chun Tie, Y., Birks, M., Francis, K.: Grounded theory research: a design framework for novice researchers. SAGE open med. **7**, 2050312118822927 (2019)
11. Cooper, A.: The inmates are Running the Asylum. In: Software-Ergonomie '99, vol. 53. Vieweg+Teubner Verlag, Wiesbaden (1999)
12. Dion, D., Arnould, E.: Persona-fied brands: managing branded persons through persona. Taylor Francis **32**(1–2), 121–148 (2016). https://doi.org/10.1080/0267257X.2015.1096818
13. Dresch, A., Lacerda, D.P., Antunes Jr, J.A.V., Dresch, A., Lacerda, D.P., Antunes, J.A.V.: Design science research. Springer (2015)
14. Dutton, W.H., Carusi, A., Peltu, M.: Fostering multidisciplinary engagement: communication challenges for social research on emerging digital technologies. Prometheus **24**(2), 129–149 (2006)
15. Elo, S., Kyngäs, H.: The qualitative content analysis process. J. Adv. Nurs. **62**(1), 107–115 (2008). https://doi.org/10.1111/j.1365-2648.2007.04569.x
16. Engström, E., Storey, M.A., Runeson, P., Höst, M., Baldassarre, M.T.: How software engineering research aligns with design science: a review. Empir. Softw. Eng. **25**, 2630–2660 (2020)
17. Ferreira, B., Santos, G., Conte, T.: Identifying possible requirements using personas - a qualitative study. In: International Conference on Enterprise Information Systems, vol. 2, pp. 64–75. SCITEPRESS (2017). https://doi.org/10.5220/0006311600640075
18. Ferreira, B., Silva, W., Barbosa, S., Conte, T.: Technique for representing requirements using personas: a controlled experiment. Inst. Eng. Technol. **12**(3), 280–290 (2018). https://doi.org/10.1049/iet-sen.2017.0313
19. Goh, C.H., Romainoor, N.H.: User goals, behaviours and attitudes: developing web user personas of art and design students. Sci. Res. Publishing **7**(1), 1–9 (2019). https://doi.org/10.4236/adr.2019.71001
20. Gonera, A., Svanes, E., Bugge, A.B., Hatlebakk, M.M., Prexl, K.M., Ueland, Ø.: Moving consumers along the innovation adoption curve: a new approach to accelerate the shift toward a more sustainable diet. Sustainability **13**(8), 4477 (2021)
21. Gothelf, J.: Lean UX: Applying Lean Principles to Improve User Experience. " O'Reilly Media, Inc." (2013)
22. Grudin, J., Pruitt, J.: Personas. Participatory design and product development: an infrastructure for engagement. In: PDC 02 Proceedings of the Participatory Design Conference, pp. 144–161. IEEE, Sweden (2002)
23. Guest, G., Namey, E., Chen, M.: A simple method to assess and report thematic saturation in qualitative research. PLOS ONE **15**(5), e0232076 (2020).https://doi.org/10.1371/journal.pone.0232076, https://journals.plos.org/plosone/article?id=10.1371/journal.pone.0232076, publisher: Public Library of Science
24. Gulliksen, J., Göransson, B., Boivie, I., Blomkvist, S., Persson, J., Cajander, Å.: Key principles for user-centred systems design. Behav. Inf. Technol. **22**(6), 397–409 (2003)
25. Guo, F., Shamdasani, S., Randall, B.: Creating effective personas for product design: insights from a case study. In: Internationalization, Design and Global Development: 4th International Conference, IDGD 2011, Held as part of HCI International 2011, Orlando, FL, USA, July 9-14, 2011. Proceedings 4 ,vol. 6775, pp. 37–46. Springer, USA (2011). https://doi.org/10.1007/978-3-642-21660-2_5
26. Guo, H., Razikin, K.: Anthropological user research: a data-driven approach to personas development. In: Proceedings of the Annual Meeting of the Australian

Special Interest Group for Computer Human Interaction, pp. 417–421. Association for Computing Machinery, Australia (2015). https://doi.org/10.1145/2838739. 2838816

27. Hansen, J., Nielsen, L.: Exploring the persona model as a tool to generate user insight through co-creation with users in the early phase of a design project. vol. 4, pp. 89–97. Canada (2017)

28. Hevner, A., Chatterjee, S., Tremblay, M.C., Hevner, A.R., Berndt, D.J.: The use of focus groups in design science research. Des. Res. Inf. Syst. Theory and practice 121–143 (2010)

29. Hevner, A.R., March, S.T., Park, J., Ram, S.: Design science in information systems research. MIS quart. 75–105 (2004)

30. Hisham, S.: Experimenting with the use of persona in a focus group discussion with older adults in Malaysia. pp. 333–336. OZCHI '09, Association for Computing Machinery, New York, NY, USA (11 2009). https://doi.org/10.1145/1738826. 1738889Accessed 18 Jan 2024

31. Holmström, J., Hameri, A.P., Ketokivi, M.: Operations management as a problem-solving discipline. In: Academy of Management Proceedings, vol. 2006, pp. B1–B6. Academy of Management Briarcliff Manor, NY 10510 (2006)

32. Hsieh, H.F., Shannon, S.: Three approaches to qualitative content analysis. Qual. Health Res. **15**(9), 1277–1288 (2005). https://doi.org/10.1177/1049732305276687

33. Ibáñez, C.V.: Marketing y publicidad en el aula de ele. una propuesta didáctica. Foro de profesores de E/LE (15), 267–275 (2019)

34. Jain, P., Djamasbi, S., Wyatt, J.: Creating value with proto-research persona development. In: HCI in Business, Government and Organizations. Information Systems and Analytics: 6th International Conference, HCIBGO 2019, Held as Part of the 21st HCI International Conference, HCII 2019, Orlando, FL, USA, July 26-31, 2019, Proceedings, Part II 21, pp. 72–82. Springer (2019)

35. Jansen, B.J., Jung, S.G., Nielsen, L., Guan, K.W., Salminen, J.: How to create personas: three persona creation methodologies with implications for practical employment. AIS Electron. Libr. (AISeL) **14**(3), 1–28 (2022). https://doi.org/10.17705/1pais.14301

36. Johannesson, P., Perjons, E.: An introduction to Design Science, vol. 10. Springer (2014). https://doi.org/10.1007/978-3-030-78132-3

37. Knott, E., Rao, A.H., Summers, K., Teeger, C.: Interviews in the social sciences. Nat. Rev. Methods Primers **2**(1), 73 (2022)

38. Kruchten, P.: The rational Unified Process: an Introduction. Addison-Wesley Professional (2004)

39. Lee, A.S., Baskerville, R.L.: Generalizing generalizability in information systems research. Inf. Syst. Res. **14**(3), 221–243 (2003)

40. Luz, F.G., Ferreira, P.A., Neves, J.S.: Developing personas and proto personas to enhance the art museum visitor experience. In: KISMIF Conference 2021, vol. 5, pp. 440–447. Portugal (2021)

41. Mahamuni, R., Khambete, P., Punekar, R.M., Lobo, S., Sharma, S., Hirom, U.: Concise personas based on tacit knowledge-how representative are they? In: Proceedings of the 9th Indian Conference on Human-Computer Interaction, pp. 53–62 (2018)

42. March, S.T., Smith, G.F.: Design and natural science research on information technology. Decis. Support Syst. **15**(4), 251–266 (1995)

43. March, S.T., Storey, V.C.: Design science in the information systems discipline: an introduction to the special issue on design science research. MIS quart. 725–730 (2008)

44. Martin Fowler, K.S., Distilled, U.: A brief guide to the standard object modeling language. Addition-Wesley Publisher (1999)
45. Mulder, S., Yaar, Z.: User Is Always Right, The: A Practical Guide to Creating and Using Personas for the Web, 1st edn. New Riders, Berkeley, CA (2006)
46. Mulhall, A.: In the field: notes on observation in qualitative research. J. Adv. Nurs. **41**(3), 306–313 (2003)
47. Murad, A., Schooley, B., Horan, T., Abed, Y.: Enabling patient information handoff from pre-hospital transport providers to hospital emergency departments: design-science approach to field testing. In: 2014 47th Hawaii International Conference on System Sciences, pp. 2665–2674. IEEE (2014)
48. Naeem, M., Ozuem, W., Howell, K., Ranfagni, S.: A step-by-step process of thematic analysis to develop a conceptual model in qualitative research. Int. J. Qual. Methods **22**, 16094069231205788 (2023)
49. Nielsen, L., Hansen, K., Stage, J., Billestrup, J.: A template for design personas: analysis of 47 persona descriptions from Danish industries and organizations. Int. J. Sociotechnology Knowl. Dev. **7**(1), 45–61 (2015)
50. Nielsen, L., Larusdottir, M., Larsen, L.B.: Understanding users through three types of personas. In: Human-Computer Interaction - INTERACT 2021, vol. 12933, pp. 330–348. Springer, Italy (2021). https://doi.org/10.1007/978-3-030-85616-8_20
51. Offermann, P., Levina, O., Schönherr, M., Bub, U.: Outline of a design science research process. In: Proceedings of the 4th International Conference on Design Science Research in Information Systems and Technology, pp. 1–11. DESRIST '09, Association for Computing Machinery, New York, NY, USA (May 2009). https://doi.org/10.1145/1555619.1555629
52. Peffers, K., Rothenberger, M., Tuunanen, T., Vaezi, R.: Design science research evaluation. In: Design Science Research in Information Systems. Advances in Theory and Practice: 7th International Conference, DESRIST 2012, Las Vegas, NV, USA, May 14-15, 2012. Proceedings 7, pp. 398–410. Springer (2012). https://doi.org/10.1007/978-3-642-29863-9_29
53. Peffers, K., Tuunanen, T., Rothenberger, M.A., Chatterjee, S.: A design science research methodology for information systems research. J. Manag. Inf. Syst. **24**(3), 45–77 (2007). https://doi.org/10.2753/MIS0742-1222240302, publisher: Routledge _eprint: https://doi.org/10.2753/MIS0742-1222240302
54. Pimentel, M., Filippo, D., dos Santos, T.M.: Design science research: pesquisa científica atrelada ao design de artefatos. RE@ D-Revista de Educação a Distância e eLearning **3**(1), 37–61 (2020)
55. Pinheiro, E., Lopes, L., Conte, T., Zaina, L.: On the contributions of non technical stakeholders to describing UX requirements by using proto persona+ **7** (2019). https://doi.org/10.5753/jserd.2019.155
56. Polst, S., Stüpfert, P.: A comprehensive persona template to understand citizens' mobility needs, pp. 295–306. Springer Nature (2019). https://doi.org/10.1007/978-3-030-22666-4_22
57. Pruitt, J., Adlin, T.: The Persona Lifecycle - A Volume in Interactive Technologies. Morgan Kaufmann (2006)
58. Quattrucci, T.: Public transport Victoria app redesign: a UX case study (2018), https://medium.com/@tony.quattrucci/public-transport-victoria-a-ux-case-study-de6ae49e8235. Accessed 25 July 2023
59. Roussou, M., Vayanou, M., Katifori, A., Rennick-Egglestone, S., Pujol, L.: A life of their own: museum visitor personas penetrating the design lifecycle of a mobile experience. pp. 547–552. France (2013). https://doi.org/10.1145/2468356.2468453

60. Salminen, J., Guan, K., Nielsen, L., Jung, S.G.: A template for data-driven personas: analyzing 31 quantitatively oriented persona profiles. In: Human Interface and the Management of Information. Designing Information: Thematic Area, HIMI 2020, Held as Part of the 22nd International Conference, HCII 2020, Copenhagen, Denmark, July 19–24, 2020, Proceedings, Part I 22, vol. 12184, pp. 125–144. Springer (2020). https://doi.org/10.1007/978-3-030-50020-7_8
61. Sein, M.K., Henfridsson, O., Purao, S., Rossi, M., Lindgren, R.: Action design research. MIS quart. 37–56 (2011)
62. Smith, C.P.: Content Analysis and Narrative Analysis (2000)
63. So, C., Joo, J.: Does a persona improve creativity? Des. J. **20**(4), 459–475 (2017)
64. Strasser, A.: Delphi method variants in information systems research: taxonomy development and application. Electron. J. Bus. Res. Methods **15**, 120 (2017)
65. Strode, D.E., Chard, S.M.: A proposal for using design science in small-scale postgraduate research projects in information technology. In: 2014 IEEE International Conference on Teaching, Assessment and Learning for Engineering (TALE), pp. 242–245. IEEE (2014)
66. Sutton, S.G., Arnold, V., Collier, P., Leech, S.A.: Leveraging the synergies between design science and behavioral science research methods. Int. J. Account. Inf. Syst. **43**, 100536 (2021)
67. Teperi, A.M., Gotcheva, N., Aaltonen, K.: Design thinking perspective for developing safety management practices in nuclear industry. In: Human Factors in the Nuclear Industry, pp. 309–326. Elsevier (2021)
68. Van Aken, J.E., Romme, A.G.L.: A design science approach to evidence-based management (2012)
69. Van Aken, J.E.: Management research based on the paradigm of the design sciences: the quest for field-tested and grounded technological rules. J. Manage. Stud. **41**(2), 219–246 (2004)
70. Van Aken, J.E.: Management research as a design science: articulating the research products of mode 2 knowledge production in management. Br. J. Manag. **16**(1), 19–36 (2005)
71. VDV, D.: Definition und dokumentation der nutzeranforderungen an eine offene mobilitätsplattform (2018)
72. Wazlawick, R.S.: Metodologia de pesquisa para ciência da computação, vol. 2. Elsevier Rio de Janeiro (2009)
73. Webster, J., Watson, R.: Analyzing the past to prepare for the future: writing a literature review. MIS Q. **26**(2), 13–23 (2002). https://doi.org/10.2307/4132319
74. Wirth, R., Hipp, J.: CRISP-DM: towards a standard process model for data mining. In: Proceedings of the 4th International Conference on the Practical Applications of Knowledge Discovery and Data Mining, pp. 29–40. Practical Application Co, England (2000)
75. Ying, F., Ye, M., Yao, L., Zhu, P.: personas building and digital contents design for Chinese farmers. Trans Tech Publ. **102–104**, 344–347 (2010). https://doi.org/10.4028/www.scientific.net/AMR.102-104.344
76. Yu, D.J., Lin, W.C.: Facilitating idea generation using personas. In: Human Centered Design. vol. 5619, pp. 381–388. Springer, USA (2009).https://doi.org/10.1007/978-3-642-02806-9_44
77. Zhong, R., Han, S., Wang, Z.: Developing personas for live streaming commerce platforms with user survey data. Springer Nature (2023). https://doi.org/10.1007/s10209-023-00996-x

A Method Based on Customer Success Metrics for Software Product Usability Assessment

Marcelo Henrique de Oliveira[1,2], Ferrucio de Franco Rosa[2],
and Adler Diniz de Souza[1(✉)]

[1] Federal University of Itajubá - UNIFEI, Itajubá, MG, Brazil
{marcelo-sinf,adlerdiniz}@unifei.edu.br
[2] Renato Archer Information Technology Center - CTI, Campinas, SP,
Campinas, Brazil
ferrucio.rosa@cti.gov.br

Abstract. The software quality assessment can be performed using the analysis of quality components established in ISO/IEC 25010. Usability is a quality component directly related to the system's user experience (UX). The user's success in the interaction depends on the user's performance in the actions determined to deliver the product value. Studies point out the Customer Success (CS) methodology as a valuable tool for evaluating systems since it uses metrics to measure CS when using a software product. The use of CS metrics to evaluate software components is increasingly being implemented in systems development. However, the metrics for CS are not fully defined, and there is also scant research linking to the software's quality components. In this scenario, we present a method based on CS metrics for software product usability assessment, a quantitative approach to provide success indicators in the context of SaaS. The main CS metrics and their application in different coverage contexts are unveiled. In our proposal, the Component Usability Index (UCI) and Software Usability Index (USI) arise as indicators of customer success, owing to their relationship with the standards usability components that influence the user experience during interaction.

Keywords: Software Quality · Customer Success · Indicators · ISO/IEC 25010 · Usability

1 Introduction

Evaluating software usability is essential to ensure a satisfactory experience, when users interact with products or services [7]. Methods and usability metrics are crucial for identifying usability flaws in different stages of the user's journey. The pirate metrics framework [12] is designed to classify and categorize metrics according to their business objectives such as acquisition, activation, retention, revenue, and referrals.

M. Kurosu et al. (Eds.): HCII 2024, LNCS 15374, pp. 23–41, 2025.
https://doi.org/10.1007/978-3-031-76803-3_2

Usability constitutes a vital aspect of software quality. ISO/IEC 25010-2011 [20] categorizes usability components based on the product and its usage. According to this standard, the usability of a product encompasses efficiency, effectiveness, freedom from risk, satisfaction, and context coverage. 'In use' usability comprises learnability, accessibility, operability, loveability, recognizability, memorability, interface aesthetics, and protection against user errors. Software usability can be assessed by measuring the success perceived by the user when interacting with the product (or service) in a certain coverage context.

A successful interaction with the software can be determined by the user's skills to use it efficiently and without difficulties. The concepts and metrics used in Customer Success (CS) methodologies [15] can be used to assess components that influence the user's success when using SaaS [14,16].

We propose a method for assessing SaaS usability components from a business perspective by employing a set of CS metrics. This method aims to assist test analysts and developers in enhancing the usability of their SaaS systems.

The remainder of this article is structured as follows: Section 2 presents the literature review and related work. Section 3 details the design and development of the method and its application process. Section 4 presents the proof of concept (PoC), performed to illustrate the method's application in a practical scenario. Finally, Sect. 5 presents the conclusions, pointing out challenges, future research needs, and the next steps in this work.

2   Literature Review and Related Work

We present a literature review aiming at unveiling the state of the art on the quality of software products and services, and Customer Success (CS) metrics. Essential concepts to support this work are also presented. We contextualize the topics that guided the objectives of this research to understand their relationship with the quality of software products and services.

The literature review is structured as follows: Subsection 2.1 presents the methodology used in the review; Subsect. 2.2 presents the literature review results and explores the topics of SaaS, usability, and CS discussing the concepts and definitions of these terms according to the review carried out. In Subsect. 2.2.1, we present the related work.

2.1   Review Methodology

The approach employed in the systematic literature review (SLR) adhered to the guidelines outlined by Kitchenham (2009) [23] and the review process used by Mendonça (2019) [26] allowing the verification and analysis of current problems regarding usability evaluation and the application of CS metrics in the context of software quality.

The publication scarcity on CS metrics to evaluate usability in SaaS systems was discussed. Works related to the research issue or relevant topics were compared, highlighting the need for conducting the review proposed in this study.

Defining the research questions is the most important step, it directs the methodology adopted. The PICOC methodology [23] was employed to delineate the research questions, being defined in this research as follows: P) *Population*: Articles published in academic journals or presented at conferences. I) *Intervention*: SaaS, Customer Success, usability, metrics. C) *Comparison*: Concepts, limits, challenges, research gaps. O) *Outcome*: Overview of CS metrics in evaluating system usability. C) *Context*: Software engineer, Infoproducts, Public sector, Government, SaaS platform, Developers.

PICOC's information determined the questions that needed to be answered in this review: *Q1) Which CS concepts and metrics are utilized to assess the usability of systems? Q2) What are the impacts of the CS metrics on software usability and UX? Q3) What are the gaps in research on SaaS systems using CS metrics to evaluate usability?*

Regarding *Q1*, our main objective was to map and understand all topics related to CS metrics covered in the studies retrieved from SLR. Collecting current and relevant documents in different scientific databases allowed us to understand and map the main CS metrics that could assess the user experience when interacting with a SaaS.

Regarding *Q2*, CS metrics comprise a wide range of targeted metrics that apply to different stages of a business. These metrics can serve as software quality and UX indicators during interactions with SaaS [14]. These metrics are mainly used to measure user success and directly impact the SaaS quality. User success is a factor that considers the software attributes and the user's interaction with the application [16]. Metrics associated with customer success remain relatively underexplored and lack comprehensive definition, posing challenges in their usage for evaluating other quality parameters of a SaaS model [31]. The wide application range of these metrics creates an uncertain scenario regarding their usage. Consequently, identifying and understanding the practical applications of CS metrics is imperative, to align them effectively with predetermined objectives.

Regarding *Q3*, research using SLR allows us to identify gaps in a given study area [37]. Identifying the gaps elucidated in the analyzed studies aids subsequent researchers in directing their efforts and comprehending research questions that remain unanswered or lack full consolidation.

Based on the research questions, searches were carried out in well-known scientific databases. We were looking for concepts necessary to understand and apply CS metrics, in order to enable the subsequent development of a catalog addressing the main CS metrics and their usage in SaaS's usability evaluation.

The defined protocol was followed to obtain articles that would be evaluated and analyzed and from them, the necessary data for the method development were extracted. Parsifal [11] was used as a support tool. This online tool is designed to assist researchers in conducting SLRs, from preparing the protocol to consolidating the results. All data necessary for the review were entered into a project created in the Parsifal application. Mendeley [8] was used to manage the bibliographic references.

The scientific databases were selected based on their significance as references in the research area and the quality of materials published within them. Six prominent scientific databases in the field of Computing were chosen for the search and selection of articles: IEEE Xplore, ACM-DL, Springer Link, Scopus, Science Direct, and EI Compendex.

The main keywords used in developing the search string were: "Usability", "Metric", "Customer Success" and "Software as a Service". To increase the reach of searches, terms related to the main words were used, which could expand the search results. The related words to the term "Usability" were "Human-Computer Interface", "Interaction", and "UX experience". For "Metrics", the following words were used as related terms: "Assessment", "Evaluation", "Kpi", "Measure", "Method", and "Score". For "Customer Success", we used "Customer satisfaction", "Success Score", and "Customer experience". Lastly, for "Software as a Service", the related words "SaaS", "infoproduct", "Online platform", and "Cloud computing" were used.

The search string was specified considering the defined keywords. Several searches were carried out to refine the string interactively. Keywords were excluded if the use did not return additional articles in automatic searches. The search string has been adapted for the search engines of each scientific database used in the research. After successive iterations, the mapping defined the following search string: *("Usability" OR "Human-Computer Interface" OR "Interaction" OR "UX experience") AND ("Software as a service" OR "Infoproduct" OR "Online platform" OR "SaaS") AND ("Metric" OR "Assessment" OR "Evaluation" OR "Kpi" OR "Measure" OR "Method" OR "Score") AND ("Customer success" OR "Customer satisfaction" OR "Success score" OR "Customer experience").*

Defining inclusion and exclusion criteria is important to give higher credibility to research, as it does not allow the analysis to follow the researcher's expectations [23]. The criteria adopted in this work are described as follows, and always supported by the online tool Parsifal. *Inclusion Criteria (IC):* IC1) Primary articles; IC2) Articles published from 2018 to 2023; IC3) Articles that present definitions, usability evaluation methodologies, and collaborative tools in software product development processes using CS; IC4) Articles that mention CS metrics; IC5) Articles that answer any of the research questions; *Exclusion Criteria (EC):* EC1) Articles whose full text is inaccessible; EC2) Articles that are not written in English; EC3) Secondary articles; EC4) Studies that are not relevant to research; EC5) Gray literature; EC6) Short papers.

In selection, the studies were consulted and obtained through automatic search using the respective search strings in the presented databases. The search results were stored in Parsifal. The subsequent step in the SLR protocol involved the removal of duplicate articles. Next, the primary studies obtained in the previous stage were selected by retrieving keywords in the title and abstract and employing the inclusion and exclusion criteria.

If data were considered insufficient or doubts arose regarding the inclusion of a study, the articles were thoroughly read. This was done to address the research questions comprehensively and identify the main contributions of each study. Figure 1 presents a flowchart of the selection procedure.

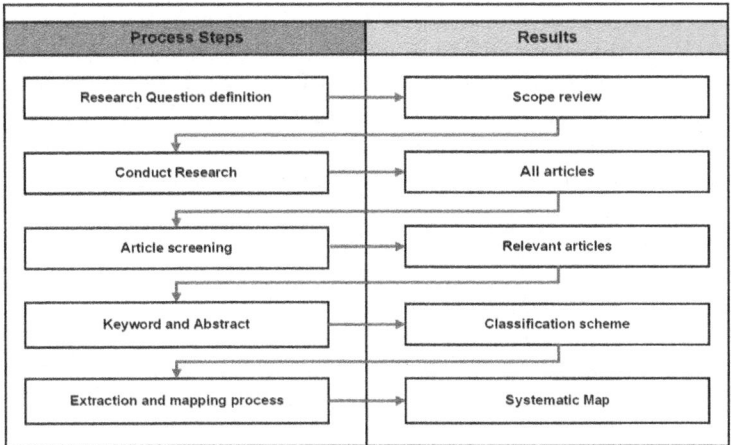

Fig. 1. Flowchart of the selection procedure

2.2 Results of Literature Review

The systematic review protocol applied retrieved 298 works from the six well-known scientific databases in the field of Computing (IEEE Xplore, ACM-DL, Springer Link, Scopus, Science Direct, EI Compendex). After applying the protocol, 38 articles were selected for further analysis and classification. From a careful analysis of the studies, CS metrics that could be used to evaluate usability in SaaS systems were identified. Metrics were mapped for the different business objectives of a SaaS, considering the classification of pirated metrics [12]. The usability components described in the ISO/IEC 25010 [20] standard were used as a reference to associate the metrics that showed a higher adherence.

The metrics extracted from the articles were evaluated regarding their relationship with the usability components provided by ISO/IEC 25010 [20]. This assessment considered the approach and context of use explored in each article. Each CS metric mentioned was correlated with one or more usability components, based on the metric's application aligned with the specific business objective outlined in the analyzed article.

After the final selection of articles, a careful analysis was carried out by three experienced software engineers (2 professors with a doctorate and 1 with a master's degree). The data extraction procedure was based on the complete reading of each selected article. The authors identified CS metrics that could be mapped to the different SaaS business objectives, considering the pirated metrics classification, and evaluated and selected usability components from the ISO/IEC 25010 [20] standard that could be appointed to compose the method.

The assessment considered the approach and coverage context explored in each article. Thus, each CS metric mentioned was linked to one or more usability components based on its application in pursuit of the business objectives outlined in the analyzed article.

The CS metrics most addressed by the authors were Churn Rate (CR) (18 mentions), Retention Rate (RR) (17 mentions), Aha Moment (AHA) (17 mentions), and Activity Monitoring (MONIT) (16 mentions). Other important metrics were also identified, such as: Wow Moment (WOW), Base Size (BASE), Stickness (STICK), Engagement (ENGAJ), Net Promoter Score (NPS), Monthly Recurring Revenue (MRR), Lifetime Value (LTV), Customer Acquisition Cost (CAC), Customer Effort Score (CES), Customer Health Score (CHS), Customer Satisfaction Score (CSAT), and Support Rate (SUPP) which, although less mentioned, are also used for success assessments in SaaS.

Table 1 presents the main metrics addressed in each article. We classified the works according to the proposed business objective of the pirated metrics framework (AARRR) [12] and the number of works that mentioned the addressed metric. The classification was based on the proposed business objective in each article.

Acquisition metrics refer to the number of users acquired. In SaaS systems it can be measured using CS metrics such as an increase in customer base, the addition of new users; page views, sign-ups, customer acquisition cost (CAC), etc. *Activation* metrics indicate the number of users who take significant action on the product or service. The activation effect occurs when the user understands the value proposition and starts using the product or service. In SaaS, the CS metrics most related to activation are the daily number of active users (DAU) and monthly number of active users (MAU).

Retention metrics represent the number of users who often use the product or service after the first contact. In SaaS, retention can be expressed by metrics such as Retention Rate, Churn Rate, and Return Rate (e.g., visits or logins). *Revenue* generation metrics refer to the recurring profits generated by the software. In SaaS, revenue is expressed by metrics such as Monthly Recurring Revenue (MRR), Annual Recurring Revenue (MAR), and Billing. *Referral* metrics indicate the number of users who recommend the product or service to third parties. In SaaS, the recommendation is expressed by, e.g., Net Promoter Score (NPS) and Customer Satisfaction Score (CSAT).

2.2.1 Software as a Service – SaaS

Software as a service (SaaS) is a cloud-based software usage model (cloud computing), i.e., the system is hosted in the cloud and can be accessed via the Internet [6]. In this model, the company providing or developing the application makes it available for periodic payment for use as a service and not as a product [15]. SaaS can be offered to customers free of charge, in which case the application configurations are limited and can be customized by the customer upon payment for the desired functionality [30].

Table 1. Classification of CS metrics and number of citations

CS Metric	Business objective	Citations
NPS	Acquisition/Referral	5
LTV/CAC	Acquisition/Activation	13
AHA	Activation	17
MONIT	Activation	16
CES/CHS	Activation	6
STICK	Activation	3
BASE	Retention	3
ENGAJ	Retention	6
SUPP	Retention	8
CR	Retention	18
RR	Retention	17
WOW	Revenue	9
MRR	Retention	4
BASE	Referral	8

SaaS is used by organizations to manage their resources and processes and to integrate them [36]. Each manager has access to centralized data that facilitates the workflow understanding in different sectors, activities and the company as a whole [30]. SaaS is used by organizations that operate remotely. In this case, they contract a service package with the desired version to access the selected resource.

The main advantages of using SaaS are the reduction in Total Cost of Ownership (TCO) and equipment maintenance expenses, data security, automatic system updates, and customization of services [5]. SaaS can integrate online and offline systems, helping to improve service scalability, providing better cost predictability, allowing mobility of services offered, and helping to analyze important indicators for decision-making and business development [16]. Several quality models can be applied to evaluate performance characteristics in SaaS. These models can help the development of SaaS with attributes that add higher value to customers in terms of experience and can also be a useful tool for identifying attributes that could compromise or limit the UX.

ISO/IEC 25010 [20] is a standard used to measure the quality of software products. This quality model is employed to identify and evaluate attributes related to software quality [22]. The ISO/IEC 25010 software product quality model divides software quality into two perspectives that consider the quality of the product itself and its use. ISO 25010 presents eight attributes (quality characteristics): Functional Suitability, Performance Efficiency, Compatibility, Usability, Reliability, Security, Maintainability, and Portability.

Each attribute is organized into sub-characteristics, which relate to the properties of the software product. As SaaS seeks to offer a better UX, usability arises as an attribute with a high impact on the SaaS quality.

2.2.2   Usability in SaaS

Usability is the ability of a product or system to achieve objectives efficiently, effectively, and satisfactorily [7]. According to ISO/IEC 25010 [20] the sub-characteristics constituting the usability of a system are: Recognizability, Learnability, Operability, Protection from user errors, Accessibility, and Interface aesthetics. Usability is a fundamental requirement for UX, especially in software that uses the SaaS model. In this way, the compromise of usability factors directly interferes with user satisfaction when interacting with the system.

In this sense, it is essential to evaluate the usability and elicit requirements that provide better use of SaaS, providing a successful user experience [33]. Usability directly affects the user experience [4], as a system with good usability positively impacts the users' experience by increasing the success rate in user interactions with the system [21]. Successful interaction and use of the product increase customer loyalty and consequently business revenue [15]. Therefore, strategies that increase the chances of success in UX can impact business revenue and direct the development of SaaS with better usability and quality.

2.2.3   Customer Success (CS)

Customer Success (CS) is a methodology applied in different knowledge areas to provide a successful experience, during a customer's journey with the purchased product or service. In CS, success is obtained when the customer achieves the results desired by developers, through interactions with the product or service [3]. This methodology places the customer as the main focus of all the company's actions and promotes strategies that contribute to the customer's success [36]. The company creates this strategy to increase public satisfaction when interacting with a system, aiming for results, such as user loyalty, increased customer base, and recurring revenue generated by the product [35].

Actions are performed to make it easier for the user to achieve their final objective by offering personalized products, support services, employee training, and intuitive interfaces with great usability [4]. CS can be represented as a segment within the development process of a software product or service [28]. It can work as a company's sector responsible for user satisfaction and monitoring indicators related to success. CS actions can be applied at different stages of the business to achieve objectives of interest, such as acquiring new customers, activating existing customers, retaining activated customers, generating recurring revenue, and user referrals on social networks [12].

The CS area is a current market trend, which is widely used by large companies, such as Netflix, Nubank, Disney, and Mercado Livre, successful cases in implementing CS mainly as an organizational culture and not just as another company sector [32]. In this scenario, the user's success in the system journey becomes a fundamental strategic element to guide the development of success-ful software [34]. CS tools are not completely defined, mainly because many companies do not know or implement CS in their companies. However, informa-tion regarding customer success supports strategic positioning and important decision-making for the future of products in the market [33].

The definition of success can be attributed according to each person's per-ception, which makes it difficult to measure success as an isolated attribute since success is a qualitative characteristic. The CS approach uses success metrics to quantify the user's success components in their journey of using the product or service. Success analytics seek to verify and quantify the user experience by analyzing data that indicates their success [24]. This data is obtained through metrics that quantify qualitative information based on the user's interaction with the system [15]. In this research, we sought to identify the main CS metrics and their relationship with components related to usability in SaaS.

Metrics and indicators of customer success allow managers to identify system bottlenecks and elicit requirements for more efficient products and processes [2]. Without management using CS indicators, the company and its developers will not have the foundation to make assertive decisions [25]. CS metrics are inferences that point out the main advantages and disadvantages of the system, considering the user's perspective of success when interacting with the product [2]. CS metrics in eliciting usability requirements can help products and services strategically aimed at the user's successful experience, consequently improving the quality of SaaS and the company's positioning in the market. CS metrics can be defined and used according to business needs and objectives. Metrics are fundamental in monitoring data representative of customer success.

CS managers must determine success metrics according to established objec-tives. For example, in an application that provides passenger transport, user success may be associated with attributes, such as the number of accesses to the app, number of trips completed, trip evaluation score, or even pre-established objectives such as completing the second trip in a within three days after the first trip. A practical example of applying CS metrics can be observed in Net-flix's operations. The company systematically maps the customer journey and utilizes various indicators to enhance the service experience. Netflix segments its customer base by monitoring data, such as the frequency and duration of access, time spent on the platform, service activations, and individual user pref-erences. This segmentation enables the creation of features that encourage user engagement and retention, ultimately leading to success metrics that deepen the understanding of user profiles. Consequently, Netflix can offer personalized services aimed at ensuring customer success.

2.3   Related Work

We considered five works related to this research, as they present conceptual contributions or address usability evaluation methods in information systems. The related works were obtained from the RSL carried out in this research and by sampling using the snowball research technique, seeking to identify research that contributed to the design and development process of the proposed method.

Floriano et al. (2022) [10] proposed a method for evaluating the usability of educational systems, considering accessibility aspects. The proposed method considered the user profile and platform characteristics. The main objective is to evaluate the usability of distance learning systems qualitatively and assess the numerical values of this component, allowing a systematic evaluation. Our method incorporates components from ISO/IEC 25010 [20]. An important contribution of our research was identifying various criteria for indicating the usability level. This identification considered the diverse profiles of system users, along with the development of equations systematizing the proposed process for usability assessment. Similarly, our method defines equations for calculating a system usability index. However, the final index in this method is obtained from two indexes that subdivide the product usability and its use to compose the final usability index of the system as defined by ISO/IEC 25010. Differently, Floriano et al. (2022) obtained the general usability index from the different user profiles that would use the system.

Anandhan et al. (2006) [1] propose the CARE methodology (Cheap, Accurate, Reliable, Efficient testing), to reduce costs and increase the efficiency of usability testing of web systems. CARE uses specific e-learning systems criteria aimed at decreasing costs in testing activities. The authors consider components such as audience, category, content, usability goals, and ways of measuring it. The components were defined based on other evaluation methods, different from our proposal, whose evaluation is based on the usability components of ISO 25010.

Munir et al. (2019) [27] present an evaluation model based on Nielsen's Attributes of Usability (NAU) [29]. In this study, a Web portal was developed for the technological campus of a university. During the development of the portal, usability tests were carried out using a questionnaire based on the NAU model, including additional usability evaluation criteria. These usability tests aimed to evaluate the principles of learning, efficiency, memorization, errors, and satisfaction to develop a web portal that would solve perception problems, such as unattractive, monotonous, or confusing for the user. The authors used some usability components of ISO/IEC 25010, however, it did not divide the components according to ISO guidelines, as it follows Nielsen's guidelines and although this research does not directly address CS, the objectives are directly associated with the CS objectives cited in other research.

Damásio-Filho (2011) [9] presents a method for assessing quality in SaaS (MAQSaaS). MAQSaaS is a quality model based on software quality standards and IT management models, such as ISO/IEC 25010 [20], ISO/IEC 9126 [19], ISO/IEC 14598 [18], ITIL [13] and COBIT [17]. The requirements and components of MAQSaaS were mapped with measurable attributes, enabling an objective assessment using a checklist. The model compiles the main characteristics of software products, covering criteria and requirements of the SaaS paradigm, to consider all characteristics through measurable attributes. According to the author, MAQSaaS can add efficiency to practical software quality assessments, helping to overcome inefficiencies in current assessment methods.

Hochstein et al. (2020) [14] present a literature review on CS, addressing foundations, concepts, methodologies, and the roles of the successful manager in SaaS companies. Research fields are proposed for CS development in SaaS companies, such as CS in the company's leadership and organizational culture, CS assessment metrics, user health status, and CS solutions performance. The authors addressed the metrics CR (Churn Rate), CHS (Customer Health Score), SUPP (Support Rate), ENG (Engagement), CSAT (Customer Satisfaction Score), and NPS (Net Promoter Score). In Table 2, we present a summary of related work, comparing it and their contribution to our proposal. Contributions to the design process included CS models, methods, processes, and concepts applied in the contexts of SaaS, e-learning, and Web systems.

Table 2. Summary of related work

Reference	Application domain	Contribution
Floriano et al. (2022)	E-learning	Method e Process
Anandhan (2006)	E-learning	Method e Prototype
Munir et al. (2019)	General Web Systems	Model
Filho (2011)	SaaS	Method
Hochstein (2020)	SaaS	Conceptualization
This Work	SaaS	Conceptualization, Method, and PoC

3 Method for Software Product Usability Assessment

The initial stage of the engineering process for the proposed method involved unveiling the state-of-the-art CS metrics, encompassing usability evaluation methodologies in SaaS.

After mapping the main CS metrics and their relationship with the usability components, we propose a method based on Customer Success Metrics for Software Product Usability Assessment (CSM4SPUA), which is composed of a nine-step process for evaluating the software product usability, presented in Fig. 2, in addition to two Equations (1 and 2) used to calculate the Usability of Component Index (UCI) and the Usability of Software Index (USI).

In Phase 1 (*Setting*) of the process, the following artifacts are produced: LBO (List of Business Objects), SBO (Selected Business Object), LET (List of Usability Evaluation Types), SET (Selected Usability Evaluation Type), LUC (List of Usability Components), SUC (Selected Usability Components), LMC (List of Usability Components Metrics), SMC (Selected Usability Components Metrics), WUM (Set Weight in Metrics of Usability Components).

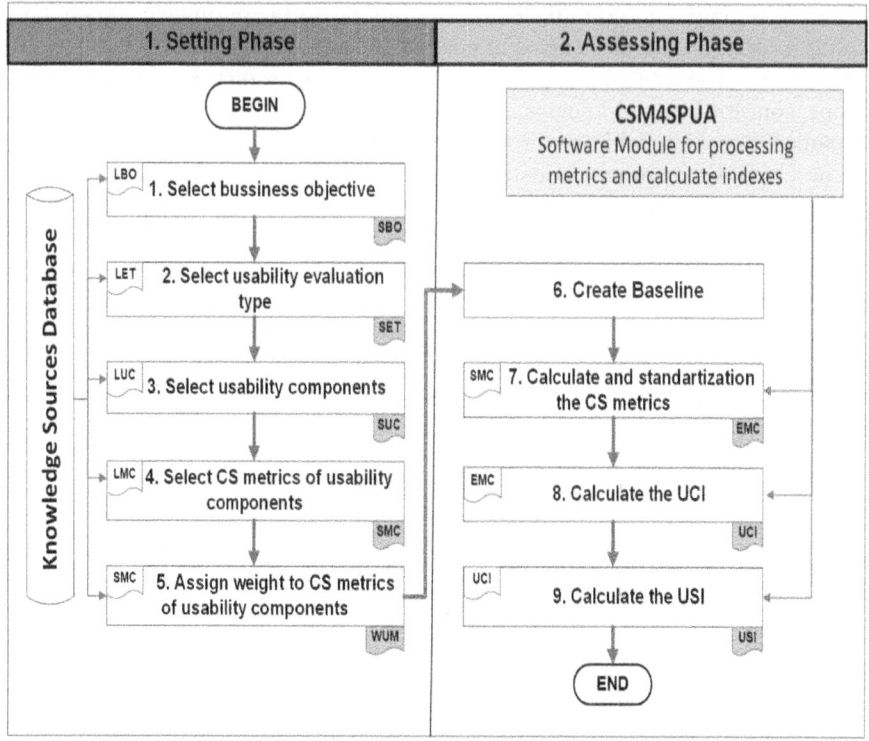

Fig. 2. Process for Usability Assessment

To evaluate the software product, we first need to parameterize CSM4SPUA for the SaaS context that will be assessed, as follows: 1) Select which business objective you want to improve (e.g., acquisition, activation, customer retention, revenue generation, or referral by the user); 2) Select the type of usability evaluation (e.g., "in use" or "product"); 3) Select the usability components that are most appropriate to the SaaS context that will be evaluated; 4) Select CS metrics from business objectives and usability components (metrics mapped in the SLR); 5) Assign weights and values to CS metrics.

In Phase 2 (*Assessing*), the following software usability evaluation artifacts and indices are produced: EMC (Evaluated Metrics of Usability Components), UCI (Usability of Component Index), and USI (Usability of Software Index).

As the CS metrics can be expressed in different units of measure, we need to standardize them. In CSM4SPUA, standardization is carried out through an indicator calculated by dividing the metric value by its corresponding value in the baseline. Baselines (Step 6) are reference values of metrics and indicators obtained in periods before the current assessment.

Indicators are representative data on the current situation of the evaluated system and are fundamental for calculating CS metrics. The indicators used can be defined according to the business model. In SaaS, the most representative indicators are: base size, number of lost customers, number of new customers, number of months on the plan, monthly plan value, and accesses number, among others [32].

The indicators are used to calculate CS metrics, and the definitive value of CS metrics is obtained after they are standardized. In standardization (Step 7), the value of each calculated metric is divided by the baseline value to obtain metric variation. The final value of the CS metrics is obtained by calculating the average between the metric value and its variation.

When calculating usability indices, the final values of the CS metrics and weights assigned to each metric are used. The evaluated metrics are used to calculate the Usability of Component Index (UCI), using Eq. 1 (Step 8).

From UCI calculated, the Usability of Software Index (USI) is computed using Eq. 2 (Step 9). In the equations α represents the adopted weights and β represents the value of CS metrics.

$$UCI = \sum_{1}^{n}(\alpha * \beta)/\alpha \tag{1}$$

$$USI = \sum_{1}^{n}(\alpha * UCI)/\alpha \tag{2}$$

UCI can be obtained using at least one component to calculate Eq. 1, and USI is obtained through Eq. 2 using at least one UCI value. In Eqs. 1 and 2, the value 1 is assigned to unobtained indices and components. Although it is possible to calculate usability indices using a few components and indices, the system presents more accurate and representative values when calculated using more component values and indices in the equation.

4 Proof of Concept

To validate the method, a proof of concept (PoC) with simulation was performed. In Step 1, to increase recurring revenue was defined as a business objective. In Step 2, the usability evaluation type "in use" was selected, according to the ISO/IEC 25010 guidelines. According to SLR, usability components "in use" of the product related to this objective are recognizability and accessibility.

Recognizability occurs when the user understands the software value proposition. By understanding the value that the application delivers, he starts to use the product or service more frequently and seek out other services and products from the company, considerably increasing CS metrics such as Average Ticket (AT), Monthly Recurring Revenue (MRR), and Lifetime Value (LTV) [6]. Recognizability can be identified through the Wow Moment (WM) and the number of freemium users who have activated premium functions (F4P). Accessibility can be evaluated based on CS metrics, such as base size, retention rate, and usage frequency-of accessibility functions. The increase in these metrics demonstrates that the application has reached users with different profiles in an efficient and accessible manner. The system utilization by diverse user types expands the user base, subsequently leading to increased recurring revenue.

In Step 3, the first component evaluated was Recognizability. According to SLR, the CS metrics associated with the recognition component are MRR, LCV, monthly AT, F4P, and WM. In this simulation, we calculated all CS metrics related to Recognizability (Step 4). The Setting Phase ends in Step 5, and weights and values are assigned to the selected CS metrics. After setting parameters, the Assessing Phase (Step 6) starts. In Step 6, the baseline is obtained to be used in the following steps. The baseline is obtained from reference values of metrics and indicators obtained in periods before the assessment. In this proof of concept, we will use illustrative indicator values to obtain the CS metrics of the evaluated SaaS. Table 3 presents a simulation of the indicator values for the previous three months (M1-3) of the analyzed SaaS.

Using the indicators presented in Table 3, the CS metrics selected in Step 4 were calculated for the same three reference months. After obtaining the baseline values, weights and values are assigned to the CS metrics that will be evaluated according to importance (Step 7). In this simulation, we used weight 3 for WM and F4P variables and weight 2 for AT, MRR, and LTV metrics. The values used for the metrics were: LTV = 170, MRR = 13,000, AT = 51, WM = 20, F4P = 12, CR = 3, and RR = 2. In Step 7, the final CS metrics values are calculated and standardized. Standardization is performed by obtaining the analyzed metric variation divided by the weight assigned to the metric, using the formula: *Final Value Metric = (CS metric value - Baseline value) / metric weight*. Table 4 presents the calculation of the metrics selected in the evaluation. Table 5 presents the final value of the metrics evaluated in this simulation after standardization for Recognizability.

In Step 8, the final values of the CS metrics are used to calculate UCI. The weights were assigned according to the importance of each metric in the evaluation, with higher weights assigned to the more representative metrics. Weight 3 was appointed to WM and F4P, weight 2 to LTV, MRR, and AT, and weight 1 to CR and RR metrics. UCI obtained from Recognizability, using data provided in this PoC and Eq. 1 was 70.39. In Step 9, USI is calculated based on the UCI of the previously evaluated usability components. We employed the same data used in Recognizability for calculating UCI. The final values of the simulated CS metrics for Accessibility are presented in Table 6. QPWD (Quantify of People With Disabilities) corresponds to the number of people with special needs and FPW corresponds to the number of PWD functions unlocked in the analyzed period. For Accessibility, the weights adopted were 3 for QPWD and FPW, 2 for RR, and 1 for BASE and CR metrics.

The UCI calculated from Accessibility was 67.33. Finally, USI was calculated in this scenario based on the UCIs of the Recognizability and Accessibility components using Eq. 2, with weight 2 for both components. Therefore, the USI calculated in this proof of concept was 51.26. The final values of both UCI and USI are valuable indicators of system usability. Periodically monitoring these indexes allows a broader view of SaaS and better system planning to achieve

Table 3. CS indicators from the 3 months prior to the assessment

Indicator	M1	M2	M3
BASE (Active Clients)	250	241	264
Lost Clients (LC)	0	12	2
New Clients (NC)	0	3	25
Monthly Value (MV) (US$)	50	50	50
Plan Months (PM)	3	3	3

Table 4. Calculation of CS metrics for Baseline

CS metric	Calculation	M1	M2	M3	Baseline
MRR	BASE * MV	12,500	12,050	13,200	12,583
AT	MRR/BASE	50	50	50	50
CR	(LC/BASEi)*100	0	4.97	0.75	1.90
RR	(BASEf - NC/BASEi)	0	2.32	2.79	1.70
LTV	(AT * QM)/CR	0	30.18	200	76.72
WM	Unlocked Paid Features (users)	0	15	18	11
F4P	Freemium migrated to Premium (users)	0	3	9	4

Table 5. Final value of CS metrics for Recognizability

CS Metric	Metric Value	Baseline	Variation	Final Value
MRR	13,000	12,583	417	6,708.5
AT	51	50	1	26
CR	3	1.9	1.1	2.05
RR	2	1.7	0.3	1.15
LTV	170	76.72	93.28	131.64
WM	20	16.5	3.5	11.75
F4P	12	6	6	9

Table 6. Final value of CS metrics for Accessibility

CS Metric	Metric Value	Baseline	Variation	Final Value
BASE	13,000	12,583	417	6,708.5
CR	3	1.9	1.1	2.05
RR	2	1.7	0.3	1.15
QPWD	16	11	7	11.5
FPW	17	13	4	10.5

customer success. Figure 3 shows all CAM4SUA steps for this simulation. We can see the UCI recognizability (red) and accessibility (green) components calculation, both used to calculate the SaaS USI evaluated in this proof of concept.

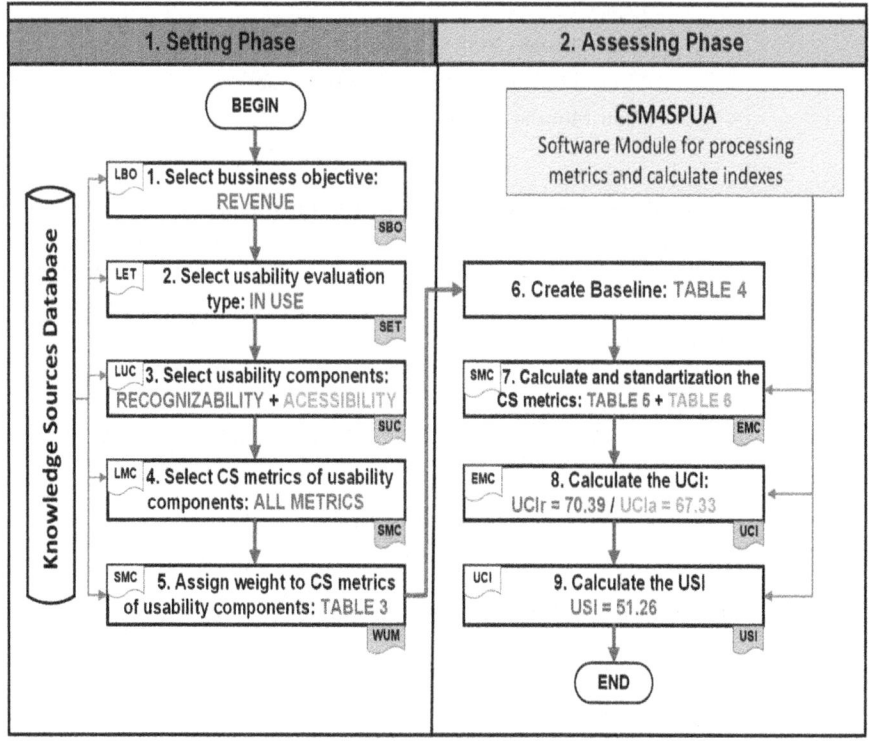

Fig. 3. Running Example of the USI Calculation

5   Conclusion

We propose a usability assessment method driven to SaaS systems due to the relationship between CS metrics and the business model. Not being restricted to this context, the proposed assessment is straightforward and feasible, allowing adjustments of metrics of interest according to the desired business objective.

CSM4SPUA covers usability components common to various systems and applications from different perspectives (service or product) based on standards. The proposed method differs from related work as it decomposes usability into specific components, allowing for more specific and strategic business decisions. CSM4SPUA provides indices for assessing usability components in different contexts from a new perspective, i.e., inspired by standards, business objectives, and customer success metrics.

A simulation was carried out calculating UCI and USI of the Recognizability and Accessibility components with the Revenue objective in both. CS concepts are not clearly defined, since different nomenclatures were observed for similar metrics and various methods for calculating similar metrics. The lack of standardization of the concepts used and the scarcity of research that defines these CS concepts are limiting factors for using metrics since the user is responsible for identifying and defining the metrics used in calculating USI and UCI.

In future work, we plan to improve the software prototype, by implementing automatic data collection and use it to assess the usability of real-world software in the E-learning domain. CSM4SPUA may be evolved, allowing the evaluation of other software quality components described in standards, and implementing the proposed model for further software products and services quality standards.

References

1. Anandhan, A., Dhandapani, S., Reza, H., Namasivayam, K.: Web usability testing — care methodology. In: Third International Conference on Information Technology: New Generations (ITNG'06) (2006)
2. Bischoff, P.: Customer value-in-use monitoring in business markets: an investigation into its determinants and consequences. Ind. Mark. Manage. **112**, 160–174 (2023). https://doi.org/10.1016/j.indmarman.2023.05.013
3. Bita, H., Brysen, H., Connor, H., Robert, P.: Customer success management: the next evolution in customer management practice? (2020)
4. Cong, P., Zhang, Z., Zhou, J., Liu, X., Liu, Y., Wei, T.: Customer adaptive resource provisioning for long-term cloud profit maximization under constrained budget. IEEE Trans. Parallel Distrib. Syst. **33**, 1373 - 1392 (2022). https://doi.org/10.1109/TPDS.2021.3112562
5. César, D.A., Pereira, I.: Analysing and modeling customer success in digital marketing. In: International Conference on Innovations in Bio-Inspired Computing and Applications, pp. 404–413. Springer Nature Switzerland (2023). https://doi.org/10.1007/978-3-031-27499-2_38
6. Dewarani, G., Alversia, Y.: The influence of customer involvement and engagement on co-creation of services, satisfaction, and loyalty: the case of software as a service. Innovative Mark. **19**, 27–37 (2023).https://doi.org/10.21511/im.19(2).2023.03
7. Eggert, A., Ulaga, W., Gehring, A.: Managing customer success in business markets: conceptual foundation and practical application. J. Serv. Manag. Res. **4**, 121–132 (2020).https://doi.org/10.15358/2511-8676-2020-2-3-121
8. Elsevier: Mendeley reference management software (2021). https://www.mendeley.com/search/
9. Filho, N.F.D.: MAQSaaS - Método para avaliação da qualidade em produtos SaaS. Ph.D. thesis, Universidade Federal de Minas Gerais.Departamento de Ciência da Computação (2011)
10. Floriano, H.M., Bonacin, R., de Franco Rosa, F.: A user profile based method for usability assessment of distance learning systems. In: Zaphiris, P., Ioannou, A. (eds.) Learning and Collaboration Technologies. Designing the Learner and Teacher Experience, pp. 275–288. Springer International Publishing, Cham (2022). https://doi.org/10.1007/978-3-031-05657-4_20
11. Freitas, V.: Parsifal systematic literature review (2021). https://parsif.al/

12. Hampshire, N., Califano, G., Spinks, D.: Pirate Metrics. In: Mastering Collabo-
    ration in a Product Team: 70 Techniques to Help Teams Build Better Products,
    pp. 60–61. Apress, Berkeley, CA (2022). https://doi.org/10.1007/978-1-4842-8254-
    0_30
13. Hochstein, A., Zarnekow, R., Brenner, W.: ITIL as common practice reference
    model for it service management: formal assessment and implications for practice.
    In: EEE, pp. 704–710. IEEE Computer Society (2005). http://dblp.uni-trier.de/
    db/conf/eee/eee2005.html#HochsteinZB05
14. Hochstein, B., Rangarajan, D., Mehta, N., Kocher, D.: An industry/academic per-
    spective on customer success management. J. Serv. Res. **23**(1), 3–7 (2020). https://
    doi.org/10.1177/1094670519896422
15. Holst, N., Chuh, D.D.: Customer success management in the subscription business
    of manufacturing companies: towards a task-oriented reference model (2021)
16. Holst, L., Schuh, G., Volker, S.: Reference data model for customer success manage-
    ment in the subscription business of manufacturing companies: findings from the
    German manufacturing industry. In: Proceedings of the Conference on Production
    Systems and Logistics: CPSL 2023 - 1. Hannover (2023)
17. Institute, I.I.T.G.: CobiT 4.1: Framework, Control Objectives, Management Guide-
    lines, Maturity Models. IT Governance Institute, Rolling Meadows (2007)
18. ISO/IEC, .: Iso/iec 14598-3 engenharia de software - avaliação de software - parte
    3: Processos para desenvolvedores (2013)
19. ISO/IEC, .: Iso/iec 9126-1 engenharia de software - qualidade de produto - parte
    1: Modelo de qualidade (2003)
20. ISO/IEC 25010: ISO/IEC 25010:2011, systems and software engineering - systems
    and software quality requirements and evaluation (SQuaRE) - system and software
    quality models (2011)
21. Kerim, A., Jhenc, B.: Mobile games success and failure: mining the hidden factors.
    167–171 (2020). https://doi.org/10.1109/ISCMI51676.2020.9311587
22. Khattab: Organizational patterns for improving the understanding between a cus-
    tomer and the development team (2023)
23. Kitchenham, B., Brereton, P., Budgen, D., Turner, M., Bailey, J., Linkman, S.: Sys-
    tematic literature reviews in software engineering-a systematic literature review.
    Inf. Softw. Technol. **51**(1), 7–15 (2009)
24. Kleinaltenkamp, M., Prohl-Schwenke, K., Keränen, J.: What drives the implemen-
    tation of customer success management? Antecedents of customer success man-
    agement from suppliers' and customers' perspectives. Ind. Mark. Manage. **102**,
    338–350 (2022). https://doi.org/10.1016/j.indmarman.2022.02.003
25. Kumar, A., Steward, M.D., Morgan, F.N.: Delivering a superior customer expe-
    rience in solutions delivery processes: seven factors for success. Bus. Horiz. **61**,
    775–782 (2018). https://doi.org/10.1016/j.bushor.2018.05.010
26. Mendonça, R., Rosa, F.F., Rodrigo, B.: Um estudo sobre análise, representação e
    detecção de intenções de criminosos em postagens em mídia social. pp. 27–36 (12
    2019). https://doi.org/10.33965/ciawi2019_201914L004
27. Munir, S., Rahmatullah, A., Saptono, H., Wirani, Y.: Usability evaluation using
    NAU method on web design technique for web portal development in STT Nurul
    Fikri. In: 2019 Fourth International Conference on Informatics and Computing
    (ICIC) (2019)
28. Murph, L., Mehta, N., Martinez, M., Steinman, D.: Customer success: how innova-
    tive companies are reducing churn and growing recurring revenue (2018). https://
    doi.org/10.1177/1094670519896422

29. Nielsen, M.: Heuristic evaluation of user interfaces. In: Proceedings of the SIGCHI Conference on Human Factors in Computing Systems Empowering People - CHI '90, pp. 249–256, New York, USA. ACM Press (1990)
30. Nieminen, T., Mohanani, R., Abrahamsson, P.: Conducting B2B SaaS business with a freemium model: a case study. In: Carroll, N., Nguyen-Duc, A., Wang, X., Stray, V. (eds.) Software Business, pp. 134–140. Springer International Publishing, Cham (2022). https://doi.org/10.1007/978-3-031-20706-8_9
31. Petersen, K., Vakkalanka, S., Kuzniarz, L.: Guidelines for conducting systematic mapping studies in software engineering: an update. Inf. Softw. Technol. **64**, 1–18 (2015). https://doi.org/10.1016/j.infsof.2015.03.007
32. Ruud, W., Klaus, P. ., Wetzels, M.: There is a secret to success: linking customer experience management practices to profitability. J. Retail. Consum. Serv. **73**, 103338 (2023)
33. Sari, H.: Designing a customer loyalty program. Icibe '20: In: Proceedings of the 6th International Conference on Industrial and Business Engineering (2020)
34. Schwenke, K., Kleinaltenkamp, M.: How business customers judge customer success management. Ind. Mark. Manage. **96**, 197–212 (2021). https://doi.org/10.1016/j.indmarman.2021.05.004
35. Tekinarslan, R., Sert, M.: Classification of student success in online courses using feature selection and convolutional neural network. In: 2022 30th Signal Processing and Communications Applications Conference (SIU) (2022)
36. Wan, S., Jiahui, C., Qi, Z., Gan, W., Tang, L.: Fast RFM model for customer segmentation - Journal Sagepub - Companion Proceedings Of the Web Conference, pp. 965–972 (2022)
37. Wazlawick, R.: Engenharia de software: conceitos e práticas. Elsevier Editora Ltda. (2020)

Unraveling Collaborative, User-Dependent IS: A Taxonomy

Marvin Heuer$^{(\boxtimes)}$ and Chikaodi Uba

Universität Hamburg, Vogt-Kölln-Straße 30, 22527 Hamburg, Germany
{marvin.heuer,chikaodi.uba}@uni-hamburg.de

Abstract. Increasingly, information systems (IS) have become more collaborative and essential for enabling interaction, integration, and cooperation across diverse actors. These kinds of technologies reduce barriers across code-centric (e.g., low-code/no-code solutions), data-centric (e.g., conversational agents), and infrastructure-centric (e.g., Microsoft 365) dimensions, fostering new interaction paradigms and coordination models. The complexity and multitude of these collaborative, user-dependent IS necessitate a systematic classification to enhance their understanding and application. This paper develops a comprehensive taxonomy of these IS to address and integrate various streams. The taxonomy facilitates clear identification, distinction, and functionality assessment of these technologies, and guides stakeholders in leveraging them effectively. Further, we identify these systems based on their traits as 'knowledge-integrating technologies', which serves as a foundation for academic research, and highlights areas for innovation. By employing an established method for taxonomy development, this taxonomy fosters informed decision-making and strategic planning, and significantly contributes to the coherence and advancement of knowledge-integrating technologies.

Keywords: User involvement · Knowledge integration · collaboration · taxonomy

1 Introduction

In the rapidly evolving landscape of the digital era, collaborative IS have emerged as indispensable tools, facilitating unprecedented levels of interaction, integration, and cooperation across various actors. These technologies increasingly lower barriers on several dimensions: code-centric (e.g., low-code/no-code solutions [1]), data-centric (e.g., conversational agents (CAs) [2]) and infrastructure-centric (e.g., Microsoft 365). Further, in these dimensions new interaction paradigms and patterns have emerged (e.g., dialog patterns in CAs [3]), as well as new paradigms of team work, breaking down geographical and temporal barriers.

The increasing diversity and complexity of collaborative IS underscore the urgent need for a systematic classification i.e. in form of a taxonomy. Such a taxonomy would not only aid in the clear identification and distinction of these technologies but also

© The Author(s), under exclusive license to Springer Nature Switzerland AG 2025
M. Kurosu et al. (Eds.): HCII 2024, LNCS 15374, pp. 42–51, 2025.
https://doi.org/10.1007/978-3-031-76803-3_3

enable stakeholders and interaction designers to understand their functionalities and applicabilities in different contexts. Moreover, a well-defined taxonomy could serve as a foundation for further academic research, guiding future developments and innovations in this domain. It would facilitate a more nuanced discourse among researchers, fostering a deeper understanding of how these tools can be effectively leveraged to enhance collaboration in organizations. Thus, this paper argues for the development of a taxonomy on collaborative IS, emphasizing its necessity and potential impact on the field. We understand collaborative IS as information systems that benefit from the interaction of users with the system herein creating value whilst also encompassing aspects like communication, cooperation etc. [4, 5]. Further, we consider a subset of these IS that can be defined as user-dependent systems. They include an expert who inserts the actual value into the system by integrating their knowledge and making the technology useful. This interaction contributes to the value creation of the system. Here, the current literature landscape is scattered.

So moreover, the creation of a comprehensive taxonomy would address the current fragmentation observed in the literature and practice of collaborative IS [1–3, 6]. By establishing a common framework, researchers and practitioners can compare and contrast different systems more easily, leading to more informed decision-making and strategic planning. This taxonomy could also highlight the evolutionary trajectory of collaborative IS, showcasing how these systems have adapted and evolved in response to changing technological landscapes and organizational needs. Furthermore, it could help identify gaps in the existing research and practice, pinpointing possible areas for innovation and development. In essence, a robust taxonomy would not only map the current state of collaborative IS but also pave the way for future advancements, ensuring that these systems continue to meet the dynamic demands of modern organizations. By fostering a shared understanding and providing a structured approach to analyze collaborative IS, the proposed taxonomy would significantly contribute to the coherence and progression of the field.

2   Related Work

In this section, related work is presented to enhance the understanding of the following taxonomy. This section focuses on collaborative IS and two examples namely conversational agents and low-code platforms.

Collaborative IS are integral to modern organizational dynamics, enhancing efficiency and innovation. These systems are designed to facilitate seamless interaction among users, enabling the exchange and synthesis of information to achieve common goals. They attempt to lower barriers by including knowledge of domain experts into their interactive system, e.g. in conversational agents (CAs).

2.1   Conversational Agents

Conversational agents (CAs) are sophisticated software applications designed to interact with users through natural language processing and artificial intelligence [7]. These agents, encompassing chatbots and virtual assistants, facilitate human-computer interaction by understanding, interpreting, and responding to user queries in a conversational manner. They can perform a variety of tasks, from providing customer support and automating routine operations to assisting in decision-making processes [2]. Nonetheless, they are continually learning and thus unfinished systems [8, 9]. By leveraging machine learning and contextual understanding, conversational agents enhance user experience, streamline communication, and increase efficiency within various organizational and consumer contexts. Moreover, they learn in a context-driven way which relies on interaction with these systems [10, 11]. Their integration into collaborative information systems exemplifies advancements in human-computer collaboration.

2.2 Low-Code Development Platforms

Low-code development platforms (LCDPs) are software solutions that enable the creation of applications with minimal hand-coding, using visual interfaces and pre-built components [1, 12, 13]. Thereby, LCDPs lower barriers on a code-centric level as they simplify and expedite the development process, thus making it accessible to users with limited programming skills. In the context of collaborative IS, low-code development platforms facilitate rapid application development and deployment, enhancing team collaboration and efficiency [14–16]. They allow diverse stakeholders, including business analysts and developers, to collaboratively design, modify, and implement information systems. This democratization of development fosters innovation, reduces time-to-market, and improves alignment with organizational needs [12, 13].

3   Methodology

For the taxonomy creation, we follow the detailed and comprehensive iterative procedure as proposed by Kundisch et al. (2021) [17], which is based on the process by Nickerson et al. (2013) [18] (Fig. 1). It allows for the combination of literature and real-world applications as data sources for the taxonomy development process.

First, we started with identifying the issue we investigate and defined the purpose of the taxonomy. This taxonomy considers collaborative, user-dependent IS where usage and value depend on the experts entering their knowledge. So, collaborative IS incorporate IS that benefit from the interaction of its users with them and herein create value including further aspects like communication, cooperation etc. [4, 5]. Further, we focused on a subset of these IS that can be defined as user-dependent systems. They include an expert who inserts the actual value into the system by integrating their knowledge and making the technology useful. This interaction contributes to the value creation of the system.

After defining the purpose of the taxonomy, we defined our goal which was to help identify such systems, assisting in their introduction and improving their lifecycle. Especially, we wanted to describe the necessary information for fostering the lifecycle development and enabling system introduction and interaction. We end the process when all dimensions stay unaltered when viewing new systems and, subjectively, when the authors considered all object classes of systems they took into account.

We decided to start with an empirical-to-conceptual approach. There is a large number of objects, we found our data on. This also aligns with our goal of being descriptive and describing what currently exists. We selected data from several search engines and databases by searching for relevant collaborative, user-dependent or enterprise collaboration systems. Including the main search engines and databases (Google, AISel, JSTOR), we identified 22 systems that fulfilled our criteria and led to our representative sample set. For the collected data, we used quantitative techniques such as cluster analysis to identify overarching themes and text search. In the first iteration, we identified 8 different dimensions in our dataset. After a second iteration, we found two additional dimensions ('focus' and 'evaluation sources').

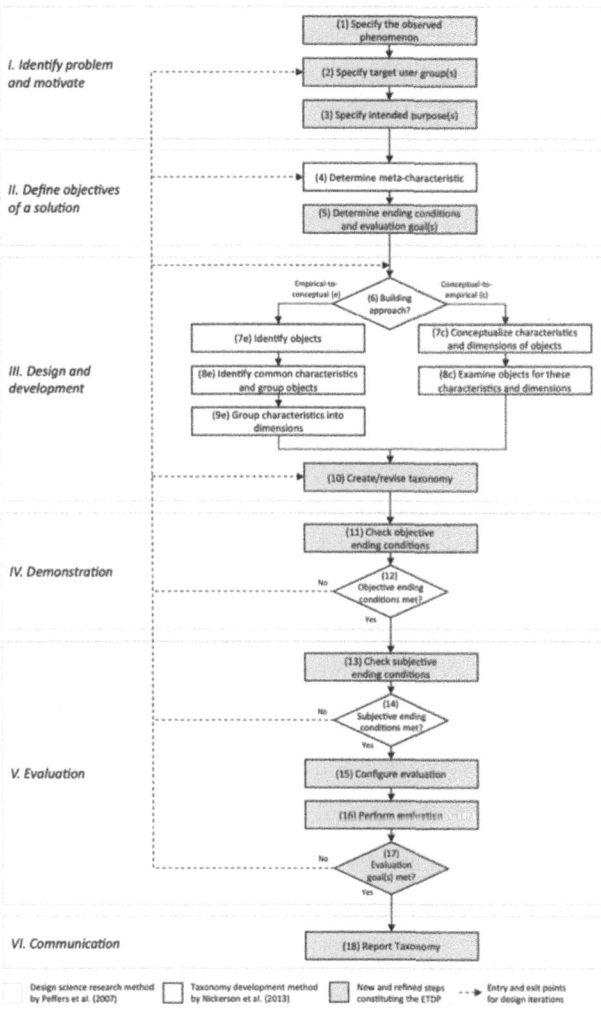

Fig. 1. Extended Taxonomy Development Process [17].

4 Results

After collecting our data set, the following taxonomy was developed as presented in Table 1. The resulting taxonomy contains 10 dimensions, with up to 8 characteristics per dimension. Thereby, this comprehensive taxonomy enables a nuanced understanding of collaborative, user-dependent IS, highlighting their diverse features and functionalities.

As the first dimension, we identified three different **foci** that collaborative IS can have. These foci determine the primary objectives and applications of the IS, influencing how they are designed and utilized within organizations. For instance, data-centric IS emphasize data inclusion and provision to the user, providing clear benefits for users who need to get access to the right knowledge efficiently. On the other hand, infrastructure-centric IS are often designed to support the underlying technical infrastructure of an organization. Dependent on the focus benefits can be less or more apparent to end users. The **user benefit** dimension highlights this as a key dimension: the primary focus of the IS and as a second dimension emerged the clarity of its benefits to users, which can lead to significantly different user influence impacts between different IS.

The **direct user influence** dimension in the taxonomy shows that collaborative, user-dependent IS can have varying degrees of user influence, which affects how users interact with and contribute to the system. This user influence can range from minimal to significant, depending on the system's design and purpose. For example, in some systems, users may have substantial control over data inputs and outputs, shaping the system's functionality and outcomes. In other cases, user influence might be limited to predefined tasks and interactions. This variability in user influence leads to different impacts on user engagement and system effectiveness.

Further, there are many **topic areas** in which these kinds of IS get introduced. We identify six different areas from our data base, namely costumer service, collaboration, health, assistance, learning, and knowledge management.

Moreover, the researched collaborative IS have distinct levels of **user involvement**, which is an important dimension to consider. Some systems are designed as open platforms that facilitate collaboration across the entire organization, enabling seamless communication and information sharing. These platforms can significantly enhance organizational productivity and innovation. On the other hand, other systems are restricted to departmental use, limiting their integration and collaboration potential to specific teams or functions. This dimension is closely linked to the **organizational culture** dimension, as the success of these systems often depends on how well they are embraced by the organization. For instance, an open platform might foster a collaborative culture, while in some settings, these systems may only be tolerated or even viewed adversely, hindering their effectiveness.

Interaction type forms another key dimension in the taxonomy. Collaborative IS offer several levels of interaction, from passive to fully interactive interfaces. For example, CAs provide interactive experiences through natural language processing, allowing users to engage with the system dynamically. This interaction can enhance user satisfaction and effectiveness, as users can communicate their needs and receive tailored responses. In contrast, some systems might only offer passive interaction, where users have limited engagement with the system. The extent of user interaction options influences the overall user experience and the system's ability to meet user needs.

Moreover, the application of the examined IS can be distinguished by the **temporal interaction** type. Depending on their design and application, these systems can operate in synchronous or asynchronous modes. Synchronous systems, like CAs, facilitate real-time interaction, enabling immediate responses and communication. Asynchronous systems, such as Microsoft 365, allow users to interact with the system at their convenience, supporting flexible and efficient workflows. The temporal mode of usage is often aligned with the type of interaction, as self-service systems typically operate asynchronously, allowing users to access and use the system independently.

Based on the data set, we see that the **context** is an important dimension in the lifecycle of these IS and when introducing them. So, the context of use is vital in our taxonomy. Collaborative IS can be deployed as standalone solutions, integrated into individual user systems, or embedded within the broader organizational infrastructure. For example, a standalone Sharepoint documentation might be used on a user's desktop for specific tasks, while an integrated system could be linked to the organization's intranet and other internal services like enterprise internal networks, enhancing its functionality and accessibility. The context of use significantly influences the system's effectiveness and user adoption, as well as the overall organizational impact.

Evaluation sources for collaborative IS vary widely across systems and form the final dimension of our taxonomy. Some IS are evaluated using log files, which provide detailed insights into user interactions and system performance. Recently, statistical methods have also been employed to assess these systems, offering more sophisticated

Table 1. Taxonomy of Collaborative, User-dependent IS.

Dimensions	Characteristics					
Focus	Data-centric		Code-centric		Infrastructure-centric	
Topic area	Customer Service	Collaboration	Health	Assistance	Learning	Knowledge Management
User benefit	Clear			Unclear		
Direct user influence	High		Medium		Low	
User involvement	Open platform		Department level		Close platform	
Organizational culture	Fostering		Toleration		Hostile	
Interaction type	Self-service usage		Language-based interaction		Passive interaction	
Temporal interaction	Synchronous			Asynchronous		
Context	Organization-embedded			Individual		
Evaluation sources	Log files		Observation	Statistical methods	None	

analysis techniques. However, evaluation practices are still evolving, and in many cases, evaluations are conducted internally within organizations. For certain systems, such as conversational agents, evaluation might be easier and more straightforward, while for others, it remains a challenge. Observation and informal assessments are also common, highlighting the need for more standardized and comprehensive evaluation approaches.

5 Discussion

By presenting this comprehensive taxonomy on collaborative IS, we contribute to the developing research stream on collaborative, user-dependent IS. We enable researchers and practitioners to navigate through the various advancements of these IS and give structure to existing systems as well as new technologies. By categorizing the vast array of collaborative IS, this taxonomy addresses the needs and behaviors of diverse user groups. It acknowledges that technology efficacy is not solely determined by its features but significantly influenced by the context of its use and the specific requirements of its users. This perspective is crucial in user-dependent systems research and emphasizes the symbiotic relationship between technology and its users ("Value Co-Creation" [19, 20]). Herein, we identified that many systems also include the integration and consolidation of knowledge. We therefore coin the phrase 'knowledge-integrating technologies' as a type of collaborative, user-dependent IS.

In this respect, we highlight two dimensions that were identified in the second iteration while creating the taxonomy: 'focus' and 'evaluation sources'. The focus of these IS differs and enables researchers to describe archetypes as well as certain mechanisms to foster their lifecycle. While the evaluation is another important sub-aspect, especially for data-centric knowledge-integrating technologies. Their success hinges on well-established evaluation procedures [2, 21].

The taxonomy serves multiple purposes in advancing the understanding and application of these knowledge-integrating technologies. One primary function is to offer a structured framework for evaluating and comparing different IS based on their distinct characteristics. This structured approach allows researchers to systematically investigate how various features and design choices affect user interaction, satisfaction, and productivity. For example, a code-centric application necessitates a self-service design as domain experts integrate their knowledge into the IS. In contrast, a data-centric IS, which involves more interactions and collaborative processes, requires a different design that facilitates greater user interaction and data sharing.

Further, the taxonomy helps researchers and practitioners determine technologies best suited for particular types of users or tasks, enabling tailored and effective implementations. This aspect is particularly important in a landscape where the diversity of users and their specific needs continue to expand. By identifying the key characteristics that influence the suitability of an IS for certain tasks or user groups, the taxonomy aids in the selection and customization of technologies that can enhance user performance and satisfaction.

The structured nature of the taxonomy also provides a common language and reference point for interdisciplinary collaboration. In the realm of collaborative IS, insights from various disciplines—such as computer science, psychology, organizational behavior, and human-computer interaction—are essential for developing systems that are both effective and user-friendly. By fostering a shared understanding among researchers from different fields, the taxonomy facilitates deeper insights into how technologies can be designed or adapted to meet evolving user needs. This collaborative approach is vital for addressing complex challenges that require multifaceted solutions.

Moreover, the taxonomy underscores the importance of aligning technological development with user requirements, a principle that is important in the creation of effective and efficient user-dependent systems. Often the success of knowledge-integrating technologies hinges on their ability to adapt to the specific context in which they are deployed. For instance, IS designed for a corporate environment may need to support complex workflows and integration with existing enterprise systems, whereas a system intended for educational use might prioritize ease of use and accessibility for a diverse user base. By providing a framework for considering these contextual factors, the taxonomy aids in the design of systems that are responsive to user needs and capable of delivering concrete benefits.

In addition to its practical applications, the taxonomy contributes to the theoretical understanding of knowledge-integrating technologies by highlighting the dynamic interplay between technology and users. It encourages researchers to consider not just the static features of an IS, but also the ways in which these features interact with user behaviors, preferences, and environments. This holistic perspective is essential for capturing the full complexity of knowledge-integrating technologies and for developing theories that can guide future research and practice.

The emphasis on user-dependent systems research within the taxonomy also reflects a broader shift in the field toward recognizing the active role of users in shaping technology. Rather than viewing users as passive receivers of technology, we acknowledge that users actively engage with, adapt, and even co-create IS. This recognition of user influence is crucial for designing systems that are not only functional but also empowering, enabling users to achieve their goals and contribute to the ongoing development of the technology.

In essence, this taxonomy not only enriches the academic discourse by offering a clearer understanding of the IS landscape but also empowers the design of responsive and user-centered systems. It underscores the importance of aligning technological development with user requirements, a principle that is important in the creation of effective and efficient user-dependent systems. By doing so, it bridges the gap between theoretical research and practical application, ensuring that advancements in IS are both academically rigorous and practically relevant.

Overall, the taxonomy represents a significant contribution to the field of knowledge-integrating technologies. It offers a comprehensive and structured approach to understanding and improving these systems, providing valuable insights and tools for researchers, practitioners, and educators alike. By fostering a deeper understanding of the interactions between technology and users, it paves the way for the development of more effective, efficient, and user-friendly IS. This, in turn, supports the broader goal of enhancing collaboration and productivity across a wide range of domains and applications.

In conclusion, the development and implementation of this comprehensive taxonomy for knowledge-integrating technologies mark a pivotal advancement in the field. By addressing both the theoretical and practical aspects of IS, it provides a valuable resource for guiding future research and practice. As technology continues to evolve, this taxonomy will serve as a foundational tool for understanding and leveraging the complex dynamics between users and information systems, ultimately contributing to the creation of more effective and user-centered technologies.

6 Limitations and Conclusion

Despite its contributions, this taxonomy has limitations. It may not capture all emerging IS technologies and user needs comprehensively, given the rapid pace of technological advancement. Additionally, the taxonomy's applicability across different contexts and industries requires further empirical validation to ensure its robustness and generalizability. Future research should address these limitations by continuously updating the taxonomy and validating it across diverse real-world settings.

In conclusion, the development of this comprehensive taxonomy for knowledge-integrating technologies significantly advances the understanding and application of these technologies. By systematically categorizing various IS based on their collaborative characteristics, the taxonomy provides a structured framework that aids researchers and practitioners in evaluating and selecting appropriate technologies. It emphasizes the importance of aligning technological features with user requirements, thereby promoting the design of more effective, efficient, and user-centered systems. Furthermore, the taxonomy facilitates interdisciplinary collaboration, fostering deeper insights and innovative solutions to complex challenges in IS design and implementation. This work not only enriches academic discourse but also bridges the gap between theoretical research and practical application, ensuring that advancements in knowledge-integrating technologies are both rigorous and relevant.

References

1. Heuer, M., Kurtz, C., Böhmann, T.: Towards a governance of low-code development platforms using the example of microsoft powerplatform in a multinational company. In: Hawaii International Conference on System Sciences (HICSS). Hawaii, HI, USA (2022)
2. Lewandowski, T., et al.: Design knowledge for the lifecycle management of conversational agents. In: International Conference on Wirtschaftsinformatik (WI). A Virtual Conference (2022)
3. Heuer, M., et al.: Rethinking interaction with conversational agents: how to create a positive user experience utilizing dialog patterns. In: Marcus, A., Rosenzweig, E., Soares, M.M. (eds.) Design, User Experience, and Usability. HCII 2023. LNCS, vol. 14033. Springer, Cham (2023). https://doi.org/10.1007/978-3-031-35708-4_22
4. Schubert, P., Glitsch, J.: Use cases and collaboration scenarios: How employees use socially-enabled enterprise collaboration systems (ECS). Int. J. Inf. Syst. Proj. Manag. 4(2), 41–62 (2016)
5. Williams, S.P.: Enterprise 2.0 and collaborative technologies. In: Working Report of the Research Group Business Software (2010)
6. Heuer, M., et al.: Towards effective conversational agents: a prototype-based approach for facilitating their evaluation and improvement. In: Marcus, A., Rosenzweig, E., Soares, M.M. (eds.) Design, User Experience, and Usability. HCII 2023. LNCS, vol. 14033. Springer, Cham (2023). https://doi.org/10.1007/978-3-031-35708-4_23

7. Gnewuch, U., Morana, S., Maedche, A.: Towards designing cooperative and social conversational agents for customer service. In: International Conference on Information Systems (ICIS). Seoul, South Korea (2017)
8. Zierau, N., et al.: A review of the empirical literature on conversational agents and future research directions. In: International Conference on Information Systems (ICIS). A Virtual Conference (2020)
9. Lewandowski, T., et al.: State-of-the-art analysis of adopting AI-based conversational agents in organizations: a systematic literature review. In: Pacific Asia Conference on Information Systems (PACIS). A Virtual Conference (2021)
10. Clark, L., et al.: What makes a good conversation? Challenges in designing truly conversational agents. In: Conference on Human Factors in Computing Systems (CHI), pp. 1–12. Glasgow, Scotland (2019)
11. Zierau, N., et al.: The anatomy of user experience with conversational agents: a taxonomy and propositions of service clues. In: International Conference on Information Systems (ICIS). A Virtual Conference (2020)
12. Bock, A.C., Frank, U.: Low-code platform. Bus. Inform. Syst. Eng. **63**(6), 733–740 (2021)
13. Rymer, J.R.: Vendor landscape: a fork in the road for low-code development platforms. In: Analyst Report, F.R. Inc. (2017)
14. Al Alamin, M.A., et al.: An empirical study of developer discussions on low-code software development challenges. In: 2021 IEEE/ACM 18th International Conference on Mining Software Repositories (MSR), pp. 46–57. IEEE (2021)
15. Beranic, T., Rek, P., Hericko, M.: Adoption and usability of low-code/no-code development tools. In: Central European Conference on Information and Intelligent Systems (CECIIS), pp. 97–103. Varaždin, Croatia (2020)
16. Käss, S.: Low code development platform adoption: a research model. In: Australasian Conference on Information Systems (ACIS). Melbourne, Australia (2022)
17. Kundisch, D., et al.: An update for taxonomy designers: methodological guidance from information systems research. Bus. Inform. Syst. Eng. 1–19 (2021)
18. Nickerson, R.C., Varshney, U., Muntermann, J.: A method for taxonomy development and its application in information systems. Eur. J. Inf. Syst. **22**(3), 336–359 (2013)
19. Vargo, S.L., Lusch, R.F.: Institutions and axioms: an extension and update of service-dominant logic. J. Acad. Mark. Sci. **44**(1), 5–23 (2016)
20. Vargo, S.L., Maglio, P.P., Akaka, M.A.: On value and value co-creation: A service systems and service logic perspective. Eur. Manag. J. **26**(3), 145–152 (2008)
21. Lewandowski, T., et al.: Leveraging the potential of conversational agents: quality criteria for the continuous evaluation and improvement. In: Hawaii International Conference on System Sciences (HICSS). Hawaii, HI, USA (2023)

Action Research on the Educational Outcomes of AI Application in the Conceptual Ideation Phase of Innovative Design Thinking

Szu-Erh Hsu[1], Lin-mei Lin[1], Hao Chen[2], Chao Liu[2], Wen-Ko Chiou[1(✉)], and Po-Chen Shen[2]

[1] Department of Industrial Design, Chang Gung University, Taoyuan City, Taiwan
wkchiu@mail.cgu.edu.tw
[2] Department of Management, Chang Gung University, Taoyuan City, Taiwan New Taipei City, Taiwan

Abstract. This study aims to explore the application of AI tools in an innovative design thinking course, conducting action research on freshmen students in a general education program at Chang Gung University in Taoyuan, Taiwan. The research focuses on integrating AI tools such as chatGPT's text question-and-answer function and Bing AI Image's image generation tool into the teaching of innovative design thinking for non-design majors. Through the adoption of innovative teaching methods like the "flipped classroom" by teachers, the study investigates the impact of AI tools on the teaching process through pre-class preparation, classroom observation, and the evaluation of students' individual and group creative works. The study employed research tools such as action research, expert analysis, and case studies. The results indicate that AI artificial intelligence tools have had a positive effect on the teaching of innovative design thinking for non-design majors. With teachers' pre-class guidance, case demonstrations, and the provision of introductory spells, students were able to input textual concepts into spells and create stunning design sketches beyond expectations in class. Under the guidance of comprehensive design concepts, the speed of design, the quantity of creations, and self-satisfaction were all significantly improved. Therefore, it is suggested to consider AI artificial intelligence tools as partners in interdisciplinary design teaching to enable teachers and students to have more time for design thinking and continuously improving innovative design concepts.

Keywords: AI tools · innovative design thinking · educational technology · action research · interdisciplinary design

1 Introduction

1.1 Research Background

In the rapidly evolving field of education, seeking innovative methodologies to meet the dynamic needs of 21st-century learners has become urgent. This study focuses on the intersection of education, design thinking, and artificial intelligence (AI), exploring the

M. Kurosu et al. (Eds.): HCII 2024, LNCS 15374, pp. 52–62, 2025.
https://doi.org/10.1007/978-3-031-76803-3_4

role of AI in enhancing students' creative abilities in the conceptual idealization stage of an innovative design thinking course. The motivation for integrating AI into education stems from an awareness of the changing needs of students. In an era dominated by digital technology, traditional educational models are being redefined. Students not only need to acquire knowledge in specific subjects but also need to cultivate skills such as critical thinking, problem-solving, and creativity. To meet this challenge, educators are urgently seeking innovative approaches to promote students' overall development, enabling them to cope with the rapidly changing world. The current concept of the flipped classroom is part of educational innovation. The teaching mode has shifted from traditional lecture-style to students' independent learning before class, with classroom time used for discussion and practice. This approach not only encourages students to be more actively engaged in learning but also emphasizes practical application and problem-solving skills. Therefore, teachers constantly break the original framework in innovative ways. This study adopts action research, focusing on the application of AI tools in a design thinking course. The research focuses on the conceptual idealization stage, using ChatGPT's text question-and-answer function and Bing AI Image's image generation tool. The motivation is to deepen understanding of how these AI tools influence the teaching process, particularly the learning experience of non-design major students in innovative design thinking. Through the action research method, this study seeks to reveal nuanced insights into the enhancement of students' conceptualization abilities and the overall effectiveness of design education brought about by AI tools.

1.2 Research Objectives and Motivations

Explore the Application of AI in Design Thinking. This action research advocates for the intersection of design thinking and artificial intelligence (AI), exploring the role of AI in enhancing students' creative abilities in the conceptual idealization stage of an innovative design thinking course.

Understand the Potential Impact of Flipped Classroom on Education. The flipped classroom has become a hot topic in the global education field in recent years, and its educational philosophy has also flourished in various learning fields in Taiwan. The neglect of physical education courses due to the influence of the examination-oriented education system, as well as one-way teaching, lack of cognitive-level thinking, and authoritative teaching, are all factors that have led to a decreasing level of student interest in physical education courses (Ministry of Education 2005). The use of traditional teaching methods has failed to fully consider students' actual needs and individual characteristics, and there is a need for deep reform in teaching goals, methods, and evaluation. The flipped classroom relies on good teaching tools or school strategies. It requires teachers to use good teaching tools or teaching strategies to assist in laying a good foundation for the flipped classroom, allowing students to complete the entire course information reception, digestion and absorption, application, and examination within the learning period, which is the cognitive learning process of human beings (Zhong Xiaoliu 2013).

Reflection and Suggestions on the Action Research Process of AI-Assisted Design Thinking Teaching. Engaging and Empowering Students: AI tools, such as ChatGPT and Bing AI Image, have proven effective in engaging students and empowering them to explore creative ideas. The interactive nature of these tools allows students to actively participate in the learning process, leading to a deeper understanding of design concepts. Enhancing Creativity and Innovation: The use of AI tools has significantly enhanced students' creativity and innovation. By providing access to advanced design tools, students are able to experiment with new ideas and concepts, leading to innovative solutions to design problems. Facilitating Conceptualization: AI tools have also been instrumental in facilitating students' conceptualization abilities. Through the use of AI-generated images and text-based concepts, students are able to visualize and articulate their design ideas more effectively. Supporting Differentiated Instruction: AI tools have the potential to support differentiated instruction by providing personalized learning experiences for students. Teachers can tailor the use of AI tools to meet the individual needs of students, ensuring that each student is able to achieve their full potential. Challenges and Limitations: Despite the benefits of AI-assisted design thinking teaching, there are also challenges and limitations to consider. These include technical issues, such as access to AI tools and training for teachers, as well as ethical considerations regarding the use of AI in education. Future Directions: Moving forward, it is important to continue exploring the potential of AI in design thinking education. This includes further research into the effectiveness of AI tools in enhancing creativity and innovation, as well as the development of new AI tools specifically designed for educational purposes. In conclusion, the use of AI tools in design thinking education has the potential to revolutionize the way we teach and learn. By harnessing the power of AI, we can create more engaging and effective learning experiences for students, empowering them to become creative and innovative thinkers.

2 Literature Review

2.1 Design Thinking and Innovative Education

In the context of the increasing importance of innovative thinking in the 21st century, systematic design thinking education is crucial for both teachers and learners. Today's innovative education emphasizes cultivating students' abilities in thinking, self-directed learning, visual media, and problem-solving.

The founder of the commonly heard design thinking approach is David Kelley, founder of the renowned American design firm IDEO. He consolidated his past experiences in solving problems from a design perspective into a curriculum, thus establishing the academic status of design thinking. IDEO CEO Brown (2008) defines design thinking as "a human-centered design spirit and method that considers human needs, behaviors, as well as the feasibility of technology or business." Brown believes that the design thinking process is a system composed of overlapping spaces, rather than a series of sequential steps. The three spaces are inspiration, ideation, and implementation. Design thinking has been recognized as a valuable tool in education, especially in 21st-century skill development (Taşpınar 2022). It is proposed as a framework for innovative thinking and learning, promoting high-end thinking, teamwork, and authentic assessment (Norman 2000). This approach has been successfully applied in STEM education, enhancing students' learning and design thinking (Li 2019). Furthermore, it is also suggested as a teaching framework to promote creativity and innovation in rural and distance education (Anderson 2012). These studies collectively emphasize the potential of design thinking in transforming education and helping students face future challenges.

In recent years, many educators have begun to introduce the operational mode of design thinking into their curriculum, and research has found that design thinking teaching has a positive impact on student motivation and satisfaction (Daniel & Education 2016). Students through design thinking also excel in scientific inquiry and convergent thinking performance (Yang, Lee, Hong, & Lin 2016). (Koh, Chai, Benjamin, & Hong 2015) also believe that combining design thinking with Technological Pedagogical Content Knowledge (TPACK) can help students develop the necessary skills for the 21st century. (Ç eviker-Çınar, Mura, & Demirbağ-Kaplan 2017) believe that design thinking is a novel approach to meeting student needs and fostering innovation that can be applied at all levels of education. Therefore, this study explores teaching through action research in innovative design and innovative education.

2.2 The Potential Role of AI Tools in the Creative Process

Today's children and youth are growing up in a new media ecology where data collection is ubiquitous and has become a part of their daily lives (Lupton, Williamson, & Society 2017; Pangrazio, Selwyn, & Society 2019; Vartiainen, Tedre, Kahila, & Valtonen 2020). An entire generation of children is growing up alongside machine learning systems, highlighting the urgent need for AI education to prepare students for the society they live in (Druga, Vu, Likhith, & Qiu, 2019; Shapiro, Fiebrink, & Norvig, 2018; Vartiainen, Tedre, & Valtonen, 2020).

2.3 Interdisciplinary Design Teaching Models

Hayhursta (2011) emphasizes the need for interdisciplinary bridging courses in innovation-driven design education, in areas such as microelectromechanical systems and life sciences. Brown (2018) suggests that instructional designers can benefit from exploring the design process more broadly and drawing on insights from different design disciplines. Gorman (1995) proposed a multidisciplinary approach that combines engineering, social sciences, and humanities to teach invention and design. Nae (2017) focuses on integrating core design principles into interdisciplinary projects such as new media design to enhance design thinking and practice. These models collectively emphasize the importance of integrating different perspectives and knowledge domains in design education.

2.4 Innovative Teaching Models of Flipped Classroom

As early as the early 19th century, General Sylvanus Thayer implemented an engineering curriculum at West Point Military Academy where students watched core course lectures through video before class, and formal class activities were not dominated by teacher lectures but by student group cooperation and critical thinking training, engaging in interactive group problem-solving. In the 1990s, Harvard University physics professor Eric Mazur, feeling that students only studied for exams but did not apply their knowledge, required students to "pre-read" before class and then react to the problems encountered in the pre-reading through online feedback. Lage and Plait (2000b) used the flipped classroom teaching method in the "Microeconomics" course at the University of Miami, requiring students to read parts of the workbook before class, including course recordings or audio PPT courseware. Subsequently, the teacher provided a 10-min mini-lecture in class, guiding and directing the reading of the book, and the remaining time was arranged for students to complete assignments, conduct experiments, or engage in cooperative learning. The results showed that flipped classroom teaching was more enjoyable and effective for students than traditional classroom teaching.

The concept of the flipped classroom originated in 2007 with chemistry teachers Jon Bergmann and Aaron Sams at Woodland Park High School in Colorado, USA. To address absenteeism, they began using screen capture software to record PowerPoint presentations and accompanying explanations. They uploaded the recorded videos to the YouTube website for self-study by students. After the effectiveness of this model was demonstrated, the two teachers changed their approach to having students watch instructional videos at home first, then design interactive class time to complete assignments, or to provide course instruction for students encountering difficulties in the experimental process, which also received good feedback. This model is also known as the "flipped classroom."

The flipped classroom model involves providing basic content through digital media and using class time for practical activities, and has been widely adopted in various educational environments (Library 2014; Arnold-Garza 2014). This model is particularly effective in information literacy instruction, enabling students to tackle real-world library research challenges (Library 2014; Arnold-Garza 2014). Task-based flipped classroom teaching models focus on problem-driven tasks, and have been found to enhance learning, practice, and collaboration skills (Hai-lon 2013). Despite its benefits, the flipped classroom model also brings challenges, such as the need for effective implementation and potential student resistance (Arnold-Garza 2014).

3   Research Method

This study adopts an action research method, which is a research approach that combines theory and practice to solve practical problems. The researcher refers to the action research model proposed by Kemmis & Taggart (1988), which includes five steps: planning, action (implementing teaching plans), observation (data collection), reflection, and modification, carried out in a continuous cycle. Teaching activities are transformed into actions, observations are made on the interactions and learning responses of teachers and students, reflections are made on the difficulties and problems encountered in practice, and teaching designs are revised before re-entering the teaching action.

3.1   Design of Teaching Action Research

This study conducted three workshops in the General Education course "Innovative Design Thinking" at Chang Gung University. Students selected this course for autonomous study regarding the AI application in innovative design thinking, which began in September 2022. The framework of teacher action research included pre-session workshops, mid-term, and final assessments.

3.2 Participants

The participants in this study are 60 students from various departments at Chang Gung University, who autonomously chose to participate in the innovative design course through the university's General Education program. During this period, students have enhanced their interest in design and integrated their professional fields with AI assistance to unleash their creativity.

3.3 Research Tools and Materials

The research tools include ChatGPT 3.5 for text-based questions and answers and Bing AI Image for image generation.

3.4 Data Collection Process and Analysis

Data sources include the implementation, observation, interviews, reports, and presentations of the innovative design thinking course. The analysis of the data is based on the teaching outcomes of the conceptual ideation stage of innovative design thinking among interdisciplinary and non-design major students.

4 Research Results

4.1 Implementation and Observation in the Preparatory Stage

Preparatory Stage: By taking courses, attending seminars, and detailed discussions with experts, the research goals and directions were established. After setting the direction, relevant books, research papers, and news reports were extensively searched in libraries, Taiwan's doctoral databases, and internet resources to assist in the smooth development of the research and to address the difficulties and doubts encountered during the research period.

Development Stage: Planning and development stage: Planning and designing activity content, arranging and rehearsing activity processes, preparing and producing activity props and teaching materials, finding suitable venues for activities, announcing activity schedules and content to teacher trainees, and ultimately consulting with experts to review the overall operation and feasibility of the activities.

Implementation Stage: The actual implementation of the planned activities in the development stage, continuously correcting and improving the direction of activities to meet the diverse learning needs of teacher trainees and to fulfill the original intention of teacher trainees to study "information education."

Data Analysis and Summary Stage: After introducing and implementing the educational program, feedback was gathered through reviewing activity video files, post-activity questionnaires, responses from teacher trainees, and personal emails, to determine if teacher trainees were integrated into the course and to identify future directions for activity development and blind spots that other studies have not yet discovered.

4.2   Classroom Learning Observation and Application of Teaching Tools

In the classroom, students are taught to observe and make good use of AI tools. Through understanding and skillful use, students are neither replaced by the tools nor does it diminish human thinking.

4.3   Analysis of Students' Individual Creative Works.

Students designed for the elderly and children using AI, with each student creating a landscape platform according to their personal preferences (Fig. 1).

Fig. 1. Students' individual creative works

4.4   Analysis of Student Group Creative Works

Through the use of AI, students designed a landscape platform for the elderly and children. The students' design concept for the platform focused on a lush natural style, incorporating various native Taiwanese AI-guided introductions. The platform provides a safe environment for the elderly to walk and enjoy, as well as a lawn for children to play on. It is a place where people of all ages can safely and happily appreciate the green world throughout the seasons. The student group utilized AI data integration to create designs for four such landscape platforms.

1. Landscape Platform Featuring the Taiwan Black Bear

   • Architectural Style: Classical, in line with green and eco-friendly construction.
   • Exterior Features: Taiwan black bear imagery, with gentle slopes and a large lawn for children to run on.
   • AI Functions: Temperature-sensitive music playback, emergency first aid station.
   • Eco-Friendly Materials: Use of environmentally friendly wood.

2. Mushroom-shaped Landscape Platform:

   • Exterior Features: Cute mushroom shape, gentle slope pathways, safe grassy areas for games.
   • Architectural Style: Green and eco-friendly construction, harmonizing with nature.
   • AI Functions: Music sensing, emergency first aid station.
   • Eco-Friendly Materials: Green building materials.

3. Mushroom Tower Landscape Platform:

   • Exterior Features: Mushroom-shaped three-story building covered in greenery, with grass, swings, hammocks, and planting areas.
   • Architectural Style: Integrating elements of nature, full of greenery.
   • AI Functions: Automatic navigation, music playback, emergency first aid station.
   • Eco-Friendly Materials: Sustainable building materials.

4. Low Tower-shaped Observation Deck:

   • Exterior Features: Spiral low tower with various sizes of forest animal models, transparent elevators, slides, and swings.
   • Architectural Style: Cute style, appealing to the public taste.
   • AI Functions: Lighting, projection, music adjustment.
   • Eco-Friendly Materials: Green building materials (Figs. 2, 3, 4 and 5).

These designs are aimed at providing visitors with a unique natural experience while catering to the needs of both elderly and children. The use of eco-friendly and sustainable materials in the architectural design ensures sustainability, while the AI-guided tours and other interactive elements enhance engagement and educational value. During the group interaction, students provided each other with professional knowledge from different interdisciplinary backgrounds, enabling them to empathize more with the elderly.

4.5 Impact of AI Tools on the Teaching Process

AI tools can provide real-time feedback and guidance. In traditional teaching models, students often have to wait for the teacher to grade assignments or exams to receive feedback, which may not be timely or specific enough. With AI tools, students can

- 為高齡長者與孩童設計一座具有人工智慧自動導覽、介紹自然生態系統、臺灣原生植物和竹林山徑上四季生態的戶外觀景台
- 造型是臺灣黑熊的雄偉圖像，具備緩坡以利長輩到達，減少高齡者和孩童爬坡的次數，大草皮供孩童奔跑
- 這座戶外觀景台的建築需符合綠色環保建材規範，木質色調，日式建築風格
- 凸顯AI功能，當高齡者或孩童進入此建築時，透過溫度感應自動播放令人放鬆的旋律，並具有緊急救護站及醫療箱，供緊急傷痛使用

Fig. 2. Student Goup Creative works 1

(1) 請為高齡長輩與孩童設計一座具有人工智慧自動導覽台灣原生蕨類與竹林山徑上四季生態的互動觀景台，造型是可愛磨菇型，具備緩坡步道以利長被到達，孩童有草坡可安全遊戲。

(2) 這座戶外景觀台的小型建築須符合綠色環保建築規範，色調與大自然調和不突兀，建築於容易起霧的地方，有白色菌絲纏繞建築物，有多層高低不一的蘑菇供人觀景。

Fig. 3. Student Goup Creative works 2

receive immediate feedback and guidance during the learning process, helping them to identify and correct errors promptly and improve learning effectiveness.

4.6 Evaluation of the Effectiveness of Interdisciplinary Design Teaching

In the teaching process, the application of AI tools has a multifaceted impact on learners. Firstly, AI tools can provide interdisciplinary students with learning experiences limited by design software, and provide rich and diverse learning resources and activities. Secondly, AI tools can help students better understand and apply design thinking. Through interaction with AI tools, students can understand the basic concepts and methods of design thinking, and continuously improve their design and innovation capabilities in practice, thus preparing them for future learning and work.

- 為高齡長輩與孩童設計一座具有人工智慧自動導覽台灣原生蕨類與竹林山徑上四季生態的戶外觀景台
- 外型採用堆疊式的小房子的概念，要有些許的斜坡可以高齡老人行走，但坡度不能太大、房屋顏色相近於大自然且階梯要有扶手，使用環保木材

Fig. 4. Student Goup Creative works 3

- 為高齡長輩與孩童設計一座具有人工智慧自動導覽台灣原生蕨類與竹林山徑上四季生態的戶外景觀台
- 建築風格為古典風且符合綠色環保建築，外觀色彩與大自然同調，並設有緩坡以及草坪供年長者方便行走以及孩童玩樂的區域

Fig. 5. Student Goup Creative works 4

5   Conclusion

5.1   Summary and Findings of the Study

The application of AI tools in the teaching process has a positive impact. It can help teachers and disciplines cross the boundaries of learning and design interdisciplinary teaching projects and activities. AI can analyze and synthesize information from different disciplines, helping teachers integrate knowledge and skills from different disciplines and promote the cultivation of students' interdisciplinary thinking skills. AI tools can help students better understand and apply design thinking. Through interaction with AI tools, students can understand the basic concepts and methods of design thinking and continuously improve their design and innovation capabilities in practice, thus preparing them for future learning and work.

5.2 The Positive Significance of AI Artificial Intelligence Tools for Innovative Teaching in Interdisciplinary Design Thinking

AI tools can help teachers and disciplines cross the boundaries of learning and design interdisciplinary teaching projects and activities. AI can analyze and synthesize information from different disciplines, helping teachers integrate knowledge and skills from different disciplines and promote the cultivation of students' interdisciplinary thinking skills. AI tools can help students better understand and apply design thinking. Through interaction with AI tools, students can understand the basic concepts and methods of design thinking and continuously improve their design and innovation capabilities in practice, thus preparing them for future learning and work.

5.3 Limitations of the Study and Suggestions for Future Research

Although artificial intelligence (AI) tools have positive significance in innovative teaching of interdisciplinary design thinking, there are still some limitations in the study. First, existing AI tools may not cover all disciplines and teaching areas, leading to limitations in their application in certain specific fields. Second, the use of AI tools requires teachers and students to have certain technical skills and teaching experience. For teachers and students lacking relevant knowledge and skills, there may be a certain learning threshold. Future research can be expanded and deepened in the following aspects. First, further research can be conducted on the application effects of different types of AI tools in interdisciplinary design thinking teaching, exploring their specific impacts on students' learning outcomes and creativity development. Second, research can be conducted on how to design and develop more intelligent and flexible AI tools to meet the needs of different disciplines and teaching scenarios, improving their application value in teaching. Additionally, research can explore how to improve the technical skills and teaching experience of teachers and students in using AI tools through training and support, thereby better promoting the effectiveness of teaching and learning.

Creativity in Digital and Physical Environments: A Case Study with Data Thinking Courses

Stephan Leible[(✉)] [ID], Constantin von Brackel-Schmidt, Gian-Luca Gücük[ID], and Dejan Simic[ID]

University of Hamburg, Hamburg, Germany
{stephan.leible,constantin.schmidt}@uni-hamburg.de,
{gian-luca.guecuek,dejan.simic}@studium.uni-hamburg.de

Abstract. In today's rapidly evolving work and educational landscapes, understanding the impact of environmental settings on creativity is becoming increasingly important. As organizations adopt both digital and physical formats (e.g., workshops), identifying how these environments influence creative processes can significantly enhance innovation outcomes. Creativity, a cornerstone of innovation, thrives in diverse settings, each offering unique characteristics and challenges. This study explores the effects of digital and physical environments on human creativity, focusing on two iterations of a data thinking course in a higher education institution, one conducted entirely in person and the other fully digital. Using a methodological approach that included surveys, focus group interviews, observations, and analyses of creative outputs, we assessed the experiences of 28 interdisciplinary students across both iterations. By exploring ideation, collaboration dynamics, and data integration as individual indicators of creativity, we aimed to understand how these environments influence the creative process. Our findings reveal that physical environments can enhance creativity through immediate feedback, dynamic interactions, and spontaneous brainstorming, fostering deeper group cohesion and engagement. Conversely, digital environments offer flexibility, can save time, and avoid media discontinuity. Consequently, this study provides insights for organizations and moderators aiming to plan and design creative processes, underscoring the importance of tailoring approaches to the specific benefits and challenges of physical and digital environments.

Keywords: Creativity · Design Thinking · Data Thinking · Physical Environment · Digital Environment · Workshops

1 Introduction

Innovation, the cornerstone of progress, is fundamentally anchored in the development of novel ideas. At the heart of this innovative spirit lies creativity, a multifaceted phenomenon encompassing the generation of new concepts, solutions, and approaches [1]. Creativity is posited as a critical driver for both generating unprecedented ideas and enhancing existing products and processes [2]. In our contemporary society, marked by relentless progression and transformation, design-oriented creativity workshop formats

© The Author(s), under exclusive license to Springer Nature Switzerland AG 2025
M. Kurosu et al. (Eds.): HCII 2024, LNCS 15374, pp. 63–82, 2025.
https://doi.org/10.1007/978-3-031-76803-3_5

such as design thinking and data thinking have become prominent tools for leveraging human creativity [3]. These formats are extensively applied across various sectors, including the economy [4–6], education [7], and the public sector [8], nurturing a fertile foundation conducive to the germination and flourishing of innovative ideas.

The advent of the digital age has heralded a significant shift, accelerated by the COVID-19 pandemic, towards digital work, platforms, and tools, engendering a profound transformation in professional and educational environments [9, 10]. This transition to digital environment mode represents a change in operational methodologies as well as in the creative and behavioral dynamics of individuals and teams, as exemplified by Tang et al. [11] in the educational sector. The perception and understanding of creativity in different environments are foundational, as they shape how individuals and teams approach innovation and problem-solving [12]. Furthermore, digitalization and the use of accommodating tools facilitate participation and can enhance the capabilities and performance of people in creative endeavors [13].

Our research is situated within the context of these developments. It focuses on comparing two iterations of a developed data thinking course in a higher education setting to gain insights into how the mode of the environment affects participants' behavior and outputs. Both course iterations covered the same content, combining theoretical inputs to elucidate the concepts of creativity, creative processes, and data thinking as a format. The courses also included insights from practitioners and, at their core, a group-based two-day data thinking workshop based on Kronsbein and Mueller [14]. The primary difference was that the two-day workshop in the first iteration was conducted digitally with 16 students, while the second iteration was delivered in person with 12 students.

In this context, we delve into the complex dynamics of how physical and digital environments affect and shape the creative process. By juxtaposing the experiences, interactions, and outcomes of the digital and in-person iterations of the data thinking workshops, we explore the nuances of environment-related and collaborative creativity. Our findings and analyses primarily cover three perspectives: idea generation, collaboration dynamics, and data integration in these contrasting settings. The insights from this study provide a deeper understanding of how work environments, whether physical or digital, can foster or hinder human creative potential. Consequently, the results can support the planning and design of creative processes, such as design and data thinking workshops, across both digital and physical environment modes. This leads to our research question (RQ):

How do physical and digital environment modes impact the human creative process of creativity-driven workshop formats such as data thinking?

The study progresses into Sect. 2, where we establish the foundational concepts relevant to our research, such as the nature of creativity. In Sect. 3, we detail the data thinking concept, course setup, and the analytical approach employed, along with our data collection. This is followed by Sect. 4, where we present our findings from three perspectives: idea generation, collaboration dynamics, and data integration. The paper concludes with Sect. 5, where we reflect on our findings in the context of existing literature, discuss their implications, and suggest directions for future research.

2 Related Work

This section is divided into two distinct yet interrelated subsections. Subsection 2.1 delves into the theoretical foundations of creativity and explores its definitions and perspectives. Subsection 2.2 examines the dimensions of digital and physical environments affecting creativity, highlighting how these influence creative processes.

2.1 Concepts of Creativity

The discourse on creativity is characterized by numerous definitions and perspectives, reflecting its complex and multifaceted nature [15]. It represents an intensely fragmented and incoherent research field [16]. At its core, creativity is widely recognized as the ability to generate novel and valuable ideas. This understanding aligns with the work of researchers like Guilford [17], who places creativity at the heart of human intelligence, and Amabile [18], who emphasizes the importance of originality and appropriateness in creative outputs. Amabile's [19] componential theory of creativity highlights that creativity is not just about the spontaneous emergence of new ideas but also about their deliberate and skillful refinement into valuable outcomes. Additionally, Rhodes [20] offers the 4P's of creativity: person, process, press, and product, providing an approach to understanding and designing creative processes.

Creativity, especially in connection with the generation of innovative ideas, has been a focal point of interest in organizational and educational settings as well as in concepts such as employee-driven innovation [21]. Scholars like Csikszentmihalyi [22] have conceptualized creativity as a systemic phenomenon that resides within individuals and the environment and society surrounding them. His systems model of creativity underscores the interaction between the individual, the field, and the domain, emphasizing that creativity results from a complex interplay of dimensions and factors. This perspective is particularly relevant in professional environments, where innovative ideas often emerge through collaborative and communication-intensive processes, such as design or data thinking workshops [7, 14]. Social creativity, which involves working together in a community of interest to solve problems [23], highlights the role of communication as one of the most powerful agents of innovative work behavior [24].

Typically, creativity is not a solitary endeavor but a collective process where interaction and communication between different individuals are pivotal [25]. Design and data thinking have increasingly been recognized for fostering innovative solutions by harnessing participants' cognitive abilities and diverse perspectives [5, 14]. This can lead to a richer pool of (valuable) ideas, which is a crucial factor for creative success.

The influence of varied knowledge sources and integration on creativity has also been researched. For instance, Hargadon and Sutton's [26] concept of knowledge brokering explains how new ideas emerge from the combination of existing knowledge sources, suggesting that creativity in such collaborative environments results from connecting and recombining diverse insights and information. This aligns with the principles of design and data thinking, where cross-disciplinary teams work together to ideate, prototype, and test solutions, drawing upon and combining their collective knowledge and experiences [7]. That approach not only broadens the realm of creativity but also amplifies the likelihood of generating innovative and practical solutions.

2.2 Environmental Dimensions Affecting Creativity

Environmental dimensions can affect human creativity, which is especially explored in physical environments [27]. These environments, encompassing elements such as spatial design, ambient conditions, and sensory stimuli, have been shown to impact creative thinking and collaborative innovation. For instance, research by Dul and Ceylan [28] highlights how lighting, noise levels, and room layout can either facilitate or hinder creative processes. These findings are echoed in the work of Kallio et al. [29], who emphasize the importance of physical environment design in enhancing creativity.

In contrast, the exploration of digital environments and their influence on creativity is relatively nascent compared to the extensive research on physical environments. Digital environments present distinct challenges and opportunities for creative processes. Chang and Yu [30] found that innovative endeavors in synchronous digital environments can positively influence inspiration and foster a more engaging process for participants. In their study, Olson and Olson [31] state that digital environments can support and enable creative collaboration, mainly when participants are geographically dispersed. However, they also note potential drawbacks, such as the lack of rich sensory interactions and the challenges of building trust and rapport in digital settings.

Table 1 provides a non-exhaustive overview of dimensions that influence creativity in physical and digital environments, illustrating the conditions each setting offers.

Table 1. Dimensions and exemplary effects on creativity in physical and digital environments based on [11, 25, 28, 29, 32].

Dimension	Physical environment	Digital environment
Spatial design	Physical layout impacts idea generation and interaction dynamics	Intuitive digital interfaces are crucial for virtual interactions
Ambient conditions	For example, noise levels and room temperature can affect creativity	Depends on individual settings such as home office environments
Sensory stimuli	Physical interactions and tangible materials stimulate creativity	Limited to digital interfaces, lacks the feedback of physical materials
Digital tools	Combination of physical and digital tools to foster creativity	Collaborative software for creative work with unique functionalities
Collaboration dynamics	In-person communication enhances understanding and group cohesion	Digital tools may lack immediacy and non-verbal cues
Documentation and analytics	Immediate, hands-on documentation, less streamlined	More accessible documentation, less media discontinuity, data analytics
Non-verbal cues	Rich and immediate, enhancing dynamics and communication	Dependence on digital expressions and cues can limit communication

Digital tools are integral to digital environments and are a vital dimension influencing individuals' creative possibilities and experiences [11]. These tools, such as online whiteboards and mind-mapping software, can significantly impact how ideas are generated, visualized, and shared [25]. Nowadays, such tools are also frequently utilized in physical environments. Research by Boughzala et al. [33] explores how specific digital tools, like shared digital workspaces, can mimic and enhance collaborative work. These tools also introduce unique features, such as the ability to comfortably document and revisit ideas, as well as the use of data analytics to generate empirical insights [34].

The comparative analysis of creativity in physical versus digital environments remains a promising area of research, representing a complex and challenging topic. Although previous studies have individually examined the impacts of these environments on creativity, more research is needed to compare the two practically. This presents an opportunity to investigate how different environmental modes and resulting human behaviors uniquely influence the creative process. Understanding these distinctions is crucial, especially in the current era where the shift towards digital workspaces and innovations is becoming increasingly prevalent. Our research is positioned within this gap and aims to provide insights through a case study approach.

3   Method

In this section, we present our research methodology, structured into four subsections. Subsection 3.1 outlines the details and structure of the data thinking course, highlighting the differences between the digital and physical course iterations. Subsection 3.2 describes the data thinking workshop format we conducted with the students, which also served as the environment for data collection. In Subsect. 3.3, we describe the perspectives and approaches we used to assess creativity in both course iterations. Finally, Subsect. 3.4 details the methods employed for gathering our data.

3.1   Course Setup

The developed course concept is illustrated in Fig. 1. It includes introductory units of 90 min each, covering topics such as data science with practical examples on the first day and co-creative approaches like design thinking and data thinking on the second day, where group formation also occurs. The third day features external guest lecturers to give students insights and real-world examples of data-driven projects from politics, business, and the public sector in preparation for the workshop days.

The data thinking workshop spans the fourth and sixth days, each lasting six hours. On the first workshop day, the groups conceptualize data-driven projects, defining project goals and target groups for detailed examination. They also collect and verify project-related data, such as information from the Internet, and identify additional data requirements. All results are documented using the online whiteboard Miro. On the fifth day, lecturers hold individual discussions with the groups to assess progress and provide guidance for the second workshop day. This second day focuses on developing implementation ideas and prototyping. While the prototyping tool Figma is recommended for mockup prototypes, groups can use other tools, including PowerPoint, Excel, or Adobe Illustrator. For testing, two groups present their developed projects and prototypes to each other, receive feedback, and conduct peer evaluations. The seventh day is dedicated to further discussions with the groups to address final questions and prepare for the presentation of results on the eighth day. These presentations and the groups' results

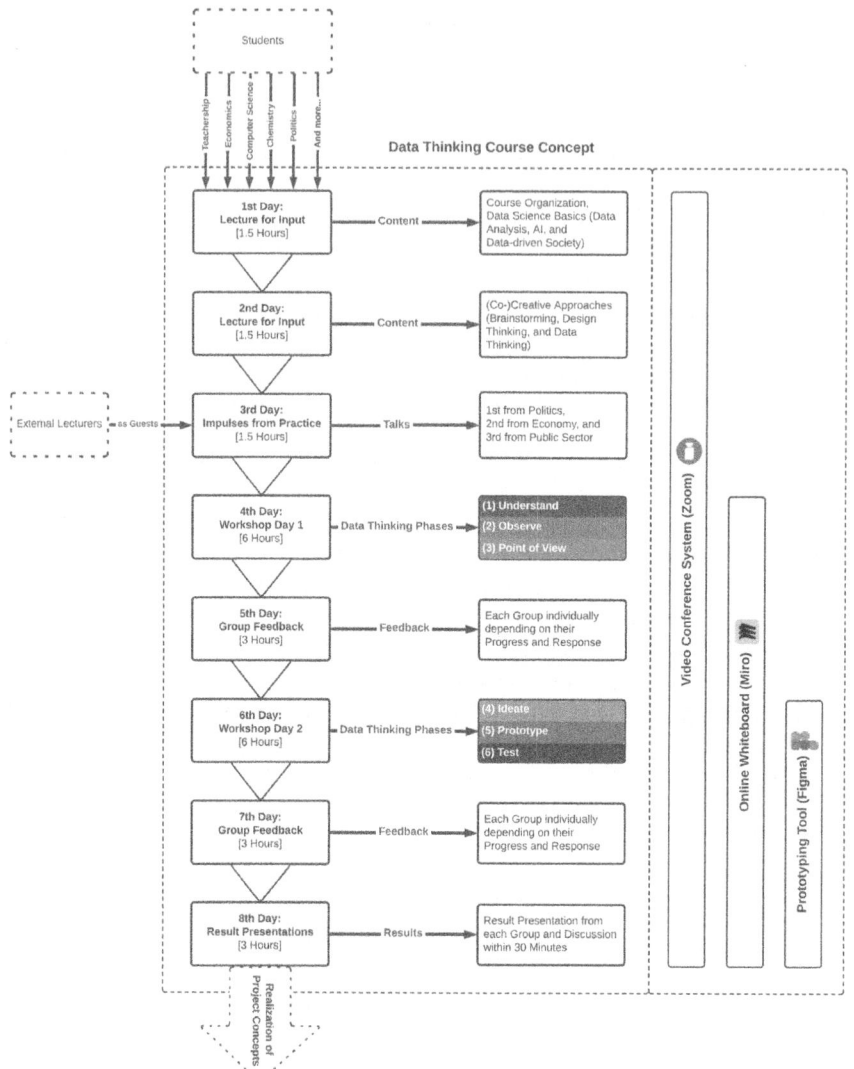

Fig. 1. Concept of the data thinking course.

are the basis for grading. Building on the course, groups have the opportunity to submit their projects to a student funding program.

The workshop was conducted digitally, with 16 students divided into six groups during the first iteration, i.e., the first semester. In the second iteration, the workshop was held in person, with 12 students divided into three groups. There was a one-week interval between the two workshop days in both iterations. The groups were often inter-disciplinary, as the course was offered as an elective across all degree programs. None of the 28 students had prior experience with a data thinking workshop, and all students were unique, as the course could not be repeated. The student cohort included bachelor's and master's students. Details can be found in Table 2.

Table 2. Metadata of the two data thinking course iterations.

Attribute	First iteration	Second iteration
Number of students	16	12
Number of groups	6	3
Average group size	≈2.7	4
Group formation	Free selection	Free selection
Mode	Digital	In person
(Digital) tools used	Zoom, Miro, Figma, PowerPoint, Adobe Illustrator	Miro, Figma, Excel, PowerPoint, flipcharts, sticky notes, physical whiteboards
Student backgrounds	Geography, Computer Science, Economics, Chemistry, IT-Management & -Consulting, Political Science, Human-Computer Interaction, Empirical Cultural Studies	Information Systems, Computer Science, Physics, Sociology, Wood Science, Political Science, Biocomputer Science
Gender distribution	8 males, 8 females	8 males, 4 females
Final deliverables	Filled canvas, PowerPoint presentation, prototype	Filled canvas, PowerPoint presentation, prototype, photographed physical results
Students with prior experience with data thinking	None	None
Support provided	Digital mentoring outside of the workshops, regular progression checks and discussions during the workshops, digital tool tutorials, template canvas on Miro	

3.2 Data Thinking

The data thinking format developed by Kronsbein and Mueller [14], which we utilized for our workshops, integrates data-driven approaches with design thinking principles. The format involves a visual canvas called the Data Innovation Board, structured around three chronological phases: explore, ideate, and evaluate. This canvas is a collaborative visual (inquiry) tool supporting a shared process and understanding. It is composed of thematic blocks in each phase (e.g., target groups, data, and risks) with guiding questions that lead users through the creative process, similar to the Business Model Canvas [35]. The goal is to develop innovative solutions by incorporating data analysis and insights at every stage of the process. This format is particularly valuable for addressing complex, data-intensive challenges.

We selected the data thinking format for our workshops because it offers a data perspective, is simple to use, and is easily accessible. However, we adapted the original visual canvas by Kronsbein and Mueller [14] to better suit our purposes. While their work mainly covers ideation and prototyping for specific challenges, our participants were tasked with developing conceptual research projects over two workshop days, progressing from fundamental problem definition to data-driven solution ideas and evaluation approaches. This task enables students to learn how to plan research projects and improve their data literacy in the process.

To better achieve the learning objectives, we modified existing thematic blocks and added new ones to the canvas, such as lists of required software and hardware and cost estimations with a budget limit. Additionally, we increased the granularity of the data thinking format by mapping the thematic blocks of the original three phases of the canvas to the six phases of the design thinking process outlined by Thoring and Mueller [36]. Each of the six phases, illustrated on the fourth and sixth day in Fig. 1, thus comprises specific blocks from our adapted canvas. This results in a clear and straightforward process path and allows for more detailed grading.

The canvas allowed participants to focus more on the creative content than the processual approach. It was digitized as a template, and each group received a shared copy for collaboration via Miro. The groups had 12 h to complete their work over the two workshop days, but they could allocate this time as they saw fit. To help manage their time, they were advised to complete certain blocks by the end of the first workshop day. Two lecturers also monitored progress and alerted groups if they were at risk of not completing the assignment on time. From a (digital) tool perspective, participants were permitted to use any tools, such as Figma [37] for prototyping, with the only requirement being that all results were linked or documented within the canvas on Miro.

The first workshop day began with a 30-min introduction covering the agenda and objectives, along with a brief presentation of Miro. Following this, the groups worked independently on phases one to three of the data thinking format. In the digital iteration, breakout rooms were created on Zoom to ensure each group could work undisturbed. In the physical iteration, each group was provided with a separate room. All participants used their own hardware in both iterations, except for physical flipcharts and whiteboards. The second workshop day followed a similar structure to the first but began with a presentation of Figma. The groups then worked on phases four to six. Two lecturers acted as facilitators in both iterations, regularly exchanging information with the groups and offering support as needed.

3.3 Assessment Perspectives

Creativity is a complex and multifaceted construct that is difficult to define and comprehensively measure or assess [15, 18, 25]. Therefore, our aim is not to provide an exhaustive account of creativity but to focus on specific perspectives as indicators and the influences of the environmental mode on them. Assessing and understanding the differences between the two course iterations can help elucidate how creativity manifests and evolves in both physical and digital environments, enabling the development of explanatory knowledge and implications for planning, adapting, and conducting creative processes. Our study focused on three key perspectives: idea generation, collaboration dynamics, and data integration, described below.

Idea Generation: This perspective was chosen because it directly reflects the capacity to produce novel and valuable ideas, a core component of creativity [2]. Idea generation, or ideation, such as through brainstorming, is critical for innovation as it represents the stage where creative solutions are conceived, for example, to create something new, address challenges, or solve problems [7]. By evaluating the originality, diversity, and feasibility of the ideas produced in the workshops, we aim to gain insights into the emergence of creative output within both environmental modes. We also assessed the ideas' quality and the groups' ideation approaches and methods.

Collaboration Dynamics: Research has shown that creativity often emerges from collaborative efforts, where group interactions can enhance or inhibit creative performance, as highlighted by Sawyer [1]. Effective collaboration fosters a supportive atmosphere where ideas are shared, constructively critiqued, and refined [38]. From this perspective, we examined participants' interactions, perceptions, and group dynamics in both environmental modes. We also analyzed and compared how the environmental mode affects the flow and continuity of collaborative work and the groups' social interactions, which Karakaya et al. [12] argue contribute to overall creativity.

Data Integration: This perspective underscores the growing importance of data-driven decision-making in modern processes [39–41]. In data-rich environments, leveraging data can enhance the quality and impact of innovative solutions, as highlighted by Davenport and Harris [42]. Extending this to creative approaches, Kronsbein and Mueller [14] argue that new data-driven challenges were a reason for developing the data thinking format. The data integration perspective is particularly relevant as it captures the intersection of creativity and data-driven decision-making influenced by individuals' data literacy. We assessed this by first considering the participants' data literacy through self-assessment and then analyzing how they utilized data to inform their ideas and decisions, as well as how they ensured data quality.

In addition to the three perspectives, participants were asked questions via a survey after the second workshop day about their perceptions of different environments, including which environment they would have preferred for conducting the workshop. They were also queried on which digital tools they selected and utilized for what purpose, as well as whether they had continued working on their project between the first and second workshop days, and if so, in which environmental mode. These questions particularly focused on participants' satisfaction and motivation, as these are essential factors that can influence creative processes [19, 24].

3.4 Data Collection

Our data collection involved multiple methods to ensure comprehensive coverage and reliability concerning our three perspectives. We conducted two focus group interviews with each of the nine groups, each lasting 15 min, on days five and seven of the course plan shown in Fig. 1, resulting in a total of 18 interviews. We followed Rabiee's [43] methodological approach for the interviews. Additionally, a survey, incorporating the suggestions of Krosnick [44], was administered at the end of workshop day two in both iterations, achieving participation from all 28 participants. Observations and discussions were also conducted by the two lecturers, who made notes throughout the workshops. Furthermore, all creative outputs, including canvases, prototypes, and physical outcomes, were thoroughly analyzed. An overview of the data collection methods of our study and further details can be found in Table 3.

Table 3. Overview of the data collection methods.

Data collection method	Description	Timing in both iterations	Overall quantity
Focus group interviews	15-min digital interview with each group	Course days five and seven	First iteration: 12 Second iteration: 6
Surveys	The survey comprised 44 questions of diverse kinds	End of second workshop day	First iteration: 16 Second iteration: 12
Observations and discussions	Notes taken by lecturers during workshops	Throughout workshop days	Six-page document
Analyses of results	Assessment of the course results (e.g., canvases)	Post-workshop analysis	All workshop results of the nine groups

4 Results

In this section, we present the results of our two course iterations in both environmental modes, focusing on our three perspectives before classifying them in the discussion. We use specific conventions to indicate which data collections yielded which results: [I] refers to focus group interviews, [S] to survey results, [O] to notes from observations and discussions, and [A] to analyses of the workshop results. The projects developed by the groups were thematically diverse, reflecting the interdisciplinary nature of the participants and their varied backgrounds. Each group leveraged the collective expertise of its members to address emerging challenges and opportunities. A list of the groups, including their sizes and the topics they tackled, is provided in Table 4.

4.1 Idea Generation

In the digital environment, idea generation was facilitated by collaborative (communication) tools such as Zoom, which allowed participants to work together in a virtual space. Some participants required time to familiarize themselves with digital tools like Figma, while others knew the tools or opted for familiar tools to save on the introductory effort and immediately engage in creative work [I, O]. Technological hurdles, such as compatibility issues, needed to be considered since participants used their own devices, which varied, for example, in browsers and operating systems [O]. The ability to document,

Table 4. Overview of the addressed project topics by each group of the two course iterations.

ID – Iteration	Group size	Project topic
1 – Digital	4	The project aimed to create an app using data-driven algorithms to connect pen and paper enthusiasts, supported by safety features for secure communication
2 – Digital	2	The project involved designing an AI to help learners analyze and improve study habits by identifying effective methods and replacing inefficient patterns
3 – Digital	2	This project investigated the components of a data-driven pipeline for advanced analysis in apple orchards by identifying workflows and specifying relevant data for a prototype
4 – Digital	3	This project aimed to create a program that tracks and analyzes cookies' data collection, provides personalized insights, and educates users on managing their data privacy
5 – Digital	3	The project involved developing a digital application that tracks the environmental impact of products by analyzing their supply chain and providing this information to users
6 – Digital	2	This project aimed to develop an application that aggregates information about local (political) projects and allows users to stay informed and participate anytime, anywhere
1 – In person	4	The project aimed to support the city's efforts to become bicycle-friendly by improving bike infrastructure and routes and researching factors influencing mobility decisions
2 – In person	4	This project involved an application that allows users to coordinate their shopping in a neighborhood by shopping for others or posting their shopping lists for neighbors to fulfill
3 – In person	4	The project aimed to analyze the ecological impact of a general rental service platform within the sharing economy by visualizing emission savings based on transaction data

organize, and share ideas digitally in a structured manner enabled participants to systematically explore the aspects of their projects, guided by the canvas [I]. Additionally, it avoided media discontinuity and facilitated seamless collaboration.

According to the participants in the physical iteration, using physical tools such as flipcharts and whiteboards required no familiarization time, allowing them to focus immediately on creative work without the initial cognitive load of learning new tools [I, O]. Once the results from physical flipcharts and whiteboards were finalized, the groups digitized them using smartphone cameras and uploaded them to the Miro board. However, survey results indicate that 67% of participants preferred digital tools, even in the physical environment, as they facilitate easy editing and rearranging of ideas, thereby simplifying the brainstorming process [S]. Conversely, some interviewees and groups reported that the physical mode encouraged creativity and a steady flow of new ideas [I]. The physical environment also reduced distractions, helping participants stay engaged in group work [I]. The free flow of conversation fostered faster development of ideas, resulting in a greater diversity of concepts [A, O]. Additionally, discussing ideas with other groups present, for example, during breaks, was more natural and often led to shared insights, inspiration, and collaborative problem-solving [I, O].

In comparison, the absence of face-to-face interactions in the digital environment limited the spontaneous exchange of ideas, and some participants stated feeling less engaged and less connected to their teammates [I]. In contrast, some participants in the physical environment reported feeling pressured to contribute good ideas and appreciated short (asynchronous) periods for individual reflection [I]. This led to several groups generating new ideas and modifying their approaches during the week between the two workshop days [A, O]. Observations revealed that discussions in the digital environment were often more structured and less dynamic than those in the physical environment [O]. This structured nature sometimes inhibited the freewheeling brainstorming and ideation, which were more prevalent in the physical workshop iteration [O].

The environmental mode influenced the creative approaches and methods utilized, with many participants rating that face-to-face interaction is superior to digital interaction for methods like brainwriting or 3-6-5, which is, for example, underscored by their absence on the Miro boards [A, I, O]. Conversely, mind mapping and personas were preferred in the digital environment and more frequently found [A, I, O]. For example, Fig. 2 illustrates a persona created on the Miro board by *Group 3 - In Person*, while Fig. 3 shows the software prototype by *Group 6 - Digital* as a Figma mockup.

Neither the participants nor the lecturers found evidence that the originality and quality of the resulting ideas differed based on the environmental mode [A, I, O]. The diversity and feasibility of the ideas were more closely related to the group composition. The project topics were connected to at least one group member's background [A]. While some projects were considered feasible, others were not [A]. In some cases, this was because the groups took a visionary approach to their projects and goals [I]. In

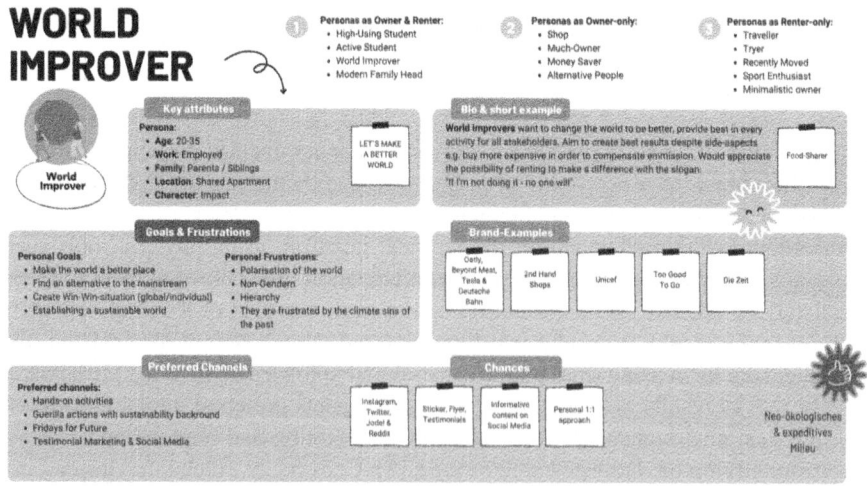

Fig. 2. Illustration of a persona on the Miro board from *Group 3 - In Person*.

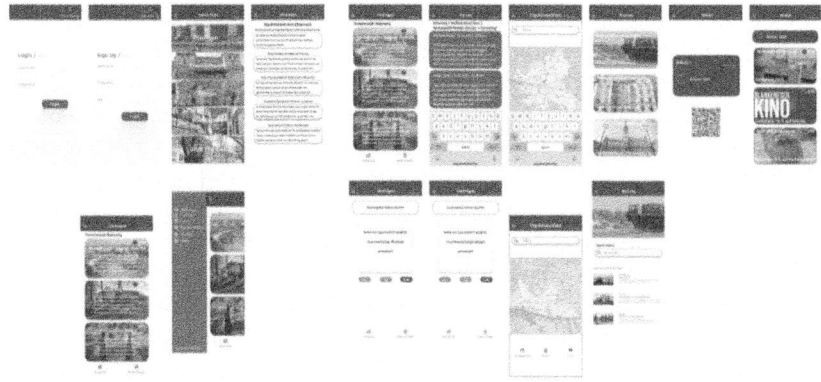

Fig. 3. Illustration of the prototype from *Group 6 - Digital* as Figma mockup (German).

other cases, a lack of competencies led to the projects being classified as difficult or not feasible [A, I]. For instance, insufficient data literacy resulted in the planning of impractical data collection methods and the emergence of accessibility issues that were previously unknown to the group members [I].

4.2 Collaboration Dynamics

The opportunities and constraints of virtual interactions influenced collaboration dynamics in the digital environment. One of the main advantages was the ability to participate from any location, eliminating the need for travel and enabling local independence [I]. However, in the digital iteration, 63% of participants would have preferred a physical workshop, whereas in the physical iteration, 92% favored the physical format [S]. The digital format also introduced several challenges. Work phases were sometimes fragmented, resulting in asynchronous communication and work behavior [I]. This was also evident from lecturers' regular conversations with groups in the breakout rooms, where it was common to find individual members with their cameras and microphones turned off [O]. This lack of continuous real-time interaction sometimes hindered the flow of collaboration, making it harder to maintain engagement and focus [I].

In the physical environment, collaboration dynamics were characterized by the immediacy and richness of face-to-face interactions. Participants could naturally engage in discussions, read body language, and respond to non-verbal cues, enhancing communication, social interaction, and teamwork [I, O]. According to our observations, the physical presence of group members facilitated more spontaneous and fluid exchanges, enabling quicker resolution of misunderstandings and fostering a stronger sense of group cohesion [O]. Group interviews revealed that participants felt more connected and engaged with their peers, leading to a more collaborative and social atmosphere [I]. This was reinforced by taking breaks, such as lunch, together [I, O]. Furthermore, participants in the physical iteration continued to work slightly more on their projects during the week between the two workshop days compared to those in the digital iteration [I]. However, this additional work occurred entirely in a digital environment [I].

75% of the participants in the physical iteration rated the group interactions and independent work within the group as "very good," while 25% rated them as "good" [S]. In the digital iteration, 58% rated them as "very good," 37.5% as "good," and 12.5% as "average" [S]. The physical environment promoted higher engagement and continuous communication, while the digital iteration offered flexibility but faced engagement challenges due to participants' work behavior (e.g., taking small breaks in their home office environment) that distracted and hindered the fluency of the creative process. Participants reported that these breaks, although seemingly minor, sometimes resulted in a fragmented workflow, making it difficult to maintain the level of creativity and engagement [I, O]. When asked why this was the case, some participants pointed to the private environment, which tends to lead to distractions; for example, two people briefly completed some housework [I]. Additionally, some participants experienced short-term internet connection problems, highlighting the dependency on stable connectivity when collaborating digitally, which can also interrupt the creative process [O].

4.3 Data Integration

The digital environment facilitated data integration as participants naturally worked with digital tools. It encouraged independent research, where participants would often individually search the Internet for information and data to support their projects and inform their decisions [O]. The participants accessed a vast array of online resources, such as blogs, news websites, and research databases [A]. They quickly gathered and integrated data into their creative processes, for example, by copying it to the Miro board for further exploration [A, O]. Some groups utilized additional digital tools, such as Excel, to analyze their collected data [A]. These activities, observed primarily during the initial explore phase of the data thinking format, were notably less collaborative compared to how groups in the physical iteration handled it [O].

Groups in the physical environment often began by discussing and categorizing topics based on their experiences and expertise before turning to the Internet for additional information [I, O]. This approach included the frequent formation of sub-teams with structured task delegation, where participants would share a device to collectively extract and explore data [I, O]. This setup fostered dynamic discussions about the data and its implications, promoting deeper collaborative exploration [O]. Traditional methods, such as the use of flipcharts and physical whiteboards for data work, were prevalent and fostered stronger group cohesion [I, O].

It was observed that data quality checks were insufficient in both environments [A, O]. Participants often used data from a single source without checking its quality [I, O]. This approach was particularly the case for students enrolled in degree programs that deal little or not at all with data topics [O]. Participants with computer science and economics backgrounds were more diligent in checking data quality [A, I, O]. Half of the participants in both iterations self-assessed their data literacy as average or lower [S]. These findings highlight that the data thinking format and the outputs from it benefit from higher data literacy among participants.

Overall, each group gathered data and examined it to inform their ideation and decision-making processes [A, O]. This is attributed more to the data thinking format with the canvas, which guides participants in addressing and managing project-related data rather than the environment itself. The data was primarily used to support arguments for project topics, for example, by highlighting societal and organizational problems or the needs of target groups [A, I]. While it influenced the creative process from the outset, data was generally not a primary aspect in designing the final solution approaches [A, I].

5 Discussion and Conclusion

Our case study examines the strengths and weaknesses of digital and physical environments in terms of creativity. The physical environment fosters immediate, spontaneous interactions and more cohesive groups, evidenced by richer face-to-face communication and more fluid exchanges of ideas. This aligns with Short et al.'s [45] theory of social presence, which suggests that physical proximity enhances social and emotional connections, thereby facilitating collaborative creativity. In contrast, the digital environment offers geographical flexibility as long as an Internet connection and specific communication hardware (e.g., microphone) are available [46]. However, in the digital setting, participants can struggle with maintaining engagement and synchronous collaboration, highlighting the challenges and paradoxes of virtual teamwork [47, 48]. As Ocker et al. [49] and Han et al. [46] mention, also asynchronous work components can enhance creativity and decision quality. This is corroborated by several project adjustments made by groups after the week between the two workshop days of our study.

Traditional theories of creativity, such as Amabile's [19] componential theory, emphasize the importance of intrinsic (task) motivation, domain-relevant skills, and creativity-relevant processes. Similarly, the interactionist model of creative behavior proposed by Woodman et al. [50] extends this understanding by integrating, for example, cognitive abilities, personality traits, and social and contextual influences to explain creative outcomes within complex social systems, such as organizations.

Our study contributes to this discourse by illustrating how different environmental modes affect our three perspectives and beyond. For example, while the digital environment offers geographical flexibility and time savings, it does not equally foster the social and motivational aspects that influence creativity [23, 24]. We align with Walia [15] in asserting that creativity can be dynamically defined and influenced by aspects such as the perceived environment. As research shows various facets that affect creativity and group behavior [11, 25, 28, 29, 32], our work adds a case study with two iterations of data thinking workshops, including a perspective on data integration, which has rarely been examined in similar studies. This perspective will become increasingly important as data-driven processes rise across all organizational levels [10].

We noted that the specific environmental mode in our study affected the groups' choice of creative methods, hence the output of the process. These variations in creative method selection (e.g., 3-6-5, personas, and mind mapping) highlight the importance of choosing the appropriate environment to align with the desired creative outcomes. The available (digital) tools are also influential regarding the output and should be considered. Understanding these influences can help organizations and moderators design and conduct creative workshops to foster effectiveness and innovation.

Moreover, our results resonate with Csikszentmihalyi's [22] systems model of creativity, which highlights the interplay between individual, domain, and field. The digital environment, with its slight emphasis on asynchronous and independent work, may support individual creativity. However, it can fall short of fostering the collective creativity that emerges from dynamic group interactions. The physical environment could better support this with face-to-face communication, encouraging socializing [51].

From a practical standpoint, our findings offer insights for organizations or moderators aiming to design and conduct creative processes, such as design thinking [38], data thinking [14], or new formats like a Prompt-a-thon [52], which is technology-driven by generative AI. Most of these formats are conductible physically, digitally, or in a hybrid form. Our results can support the selection and tailoring of the formats and environments depending on their goals. For example, design thinking, one of the most common creative processes [5, 38], can occur in all three mentioned forms with a single or multiple sessions. While our study found that the majority preferred a physical environment, AlMunifi and Alfawzan [51] highlight in their study on learning environments that the preference often depends on the course and content itself, a conclusion with which we concur. The choice of environment for such workshops is frequently linked to their objectives and conditions, for instance, if participants cannot be in the same place due to specific reasons (e.g., collaboration across organizational borders [8] or remote work [9]). Nevertheless, our results emphasize the importance of mechanisms to enhance individual engagement and improve group cohesion, such as socializing, establishing routines for check-ins, and incorporating synchronous work sessions [53].

Data integration holds significant potential to improve decision-making and achieve higher-quality results. For example, based on the work of Hargadon and Sutton [26], an organizational memory holds great potential to integrate stored knowledge (data) in creative processes to foster innovation. The basic concept is similar to idea mining, which involves collecting and analyzing data to generate new ideas [54]. To leverage this potential, organizations and educational institutions should ensure a balanced data literacy education through appropriate training programs, as proposed by Lefebvre et al. [55]. We believe that even basic data literacy can positively impact the reflected gathering and analyzing of relevant data, thereby enhancing creative processes.

Despite the insights provided by this study, several limitations must be acknowledged. Firstly, the sample size of two data thinking course iterations with 28 participants is relatively small, potentially limiting the generalizability of the findings. The study was also constrained by the specific context of the data thinking format, which may not capture the full spectrum of creativity and collaboration dynamics in other settings or disciplines, although it does cover the common design thinking format. Additionally, while the study employed various methods of data collection, including surveys, interviews, and observations, the analysis is subject to a degree of subjectivity and may be influenced by participant bias and researcher interpretation. Furthermore, the digital and physical iterations were conducted at different times, which could introduce temporal effects that were not controlled for. Finally, we did not extensively account for individual differences in data literacy, technological proficiency, or prior experience with collaborative tools, which could impact the outcomes.

Building on the findings and limitations of this study, future research should aim to expand and deepen our understanding of the impact of different environmental modes on creativity. One promising direction is to conduct studies with larger and more diverse samples of participants across various disciplines and settings to enhance the generalizability of the results. Additionally, exploring hybrid forms that combine the strengths of both physical and digital environments could provide valuable insights into designing creative processes for increasingly flexible and remote work contexts.

Future research should also incorporate more objective and quantitative measures of creativity and collaboration, such as behavioral analytics and performance metrics, to complement self-reported data and reduce potential biases. Investigating the role of individual differences, such as data literacy, technological proficiency, and prior experience with collaborative tools, would further elucidate how these factors influence creative outcomes. Moreover, integrating advanced technologies like AI into creative processes could open new avenues for enhancing data integration and ideation [56, 57]. However, this integration will likely affect collaboration dynamics, as (generative) AI itself could act as a group member in human-AI collaborations [58].

In conclusion, this study provides insights into how physical and digital environments influence creativity across three perspectives: idea generation, collaboration dynamics, and data integration. By highlighting each environment's findings, strengths, and challenges during the two data thinking course iterations, we underscore the importance of tailoring creative processes to prevailing conditions, as there is no single "best" mode. As the nature of digital work continues to evolve, understanding the nuances of different environments is beneficial for planning and designing creative processes to foster innovation and enhance outcomes in both academic and professional settings.

Disclosure of Interests. The authors declared no potential conflicts of interest with respect to the research, authorship, and/or publication of this article.

References

1. Sawyer, R.K., Henriksen, D.: Explaining creativity: the science of human innovation. Oxford scholarship online. Oxford University Press, New York, NY (2012)
2. Guenther, A., Eisenbart, B., Dong, A.: Creativity and successful product concept selection for innovation. Int. J. Des. Creat. Innov. 9(1), 3–19 (2021). https://doi.org/10.1080/21650349.2020.1858970
3. Vendraminelli, L., Macchion, L., Nosella, A., Vinelli, A.: Design thinking: strategy for digital transformation. J. Bus. Strat. 44(4), 200–210 (2023). https://doi.org/10.1108/JBS-01-2022-0009
4. Magistretti, S., Pham, C.T.A., Dell'Era, C.: Enlightening the dynamic capabilities of design thinking in fostering digital transformation. Ind. Mark. Manag. 97, 59–70 (2021). https://doi.org/10.1016/j.indmarman.2021.06.014
5. Altman, M., Huang, T.T.K., Breland, J.Y.: Design thinking in health care. Prev. Chronic Dis. 15 (2018). https://doi.org/10.5888/pcd15.180128
6. Bourgeois-Bougrine, S., Buisine, S., Vandendriessche, C., Glaveanu, V., Lubart, T.: Engineering students' use of creativity and development tools in conceptual product design: what, when and how? Think. Skills Creat. 24, 104–117 (2017). https://doi.org/10.1016/j.tsc.2017.02.016
7. Chon, H., Sim, J.: From design thinking to design knowing: an educational perspective. Art Des. Commun. High. Educ. 18(2), 187–200 (2019). https://doi.org/10.1386/adch_00006_1

8. Lewis, J.M., McGann, M., Blomkamp, E.: When design meets power: design thinking, public sector innovation and the politics of policymaking. Policy Polit. **48**(1), 111–130 (2020). https://doi.org/10.1332/030557319X15579230420081
9. Pakos, O., Walter, J., Rücker, M., Voigt, K.-I.: The leap into the new normal in creative work: a qualitative study of the impact of COVID-19 on work practices in industrial companies. Eur. J. Bus. Manag. (2021). https://doi.org/10.7176/EJBM/13-10-01
10. Leyh, C., Becke, P., Pentrack, M., Bodenstein, B.: The impact of digital technologies on how companies work: results from an interview study. In: Proceedings of the 16th Conference on Computer Science and Intelligence Systems, pp. 437–446. IEEE (2021). https://doi.org/10.15439/2021F64
11. Tang, C., Mao, S., Naumann, S.E., Xing, Z.: Improving student creativity through digital technology products: a literature review. Think. Skills Creat. **44**, 101032 (2022). https://doi.org/10.1016/j.tsc.2022.101032
12. Karakaya, A.F., Demirkan, H.: Collaborative digital environments to enhance the creativity of designers. Comput. Hum. Behav. **42**, 176–186 (2015). https://doi.org/10.1016/j.chb.2014.03.029
13. Marion, T.J., Fixson, S.K.: The transformation of the innovation process: how digital tools are changing work, collaboration, and organizations in new product development*. J. Prod. Innov. Manag. **38**(1), 192–215 (2021). https://doi.org/10.1111/jpim.12547
14. Kronsbein, T., Mueller, R.: Data thinking: a canvas for data-driven ideation workshops. In: Proceedings of the Hawaii International Conference on System Sciences (HICSS2019), pp. 561–570 (2019)
15. Walia, C.: A dynamic definition of creativity. Creat. Res. J. **31**(3), 237–247 (2019). https://doi.org/10.1080/10400419.2019.1641787
16. Dietrich, A.: Types of creativity. Psychon. Bull. Rev. **26**(1), 1–12 (2019). https://doi.org/10.3758/s13423-018-1517-7
17. Wreen, M.: Creativity. Philosophia **43**(3), 891–913 (2015). https://doi.org/10.1007/s11406-015-9607-5
18. Amabile, T.M.: The social psychology of creativity. Springer, New York, New York, NY, USA (1983)
19. Amabile, T.M.: Componential Theory of Creativity. Harvard Business School Working Paper, No. 12–096 (2012)
20. Rhodes, M.: An analysis of creativity. Phi Delta Kappan **42**(7), 305–310 (1961)
21. Leible, S., Simic, D., Gücük, G.-L., Lewandowski, T., Kučević, E.: Unfolding effect areas of employee-driven innovation: a systematic literature review. In: Choudhry, T., Aldieri, L. (eds.) Innovation - Research and Development for Human, Economic and Institutional Growth, Business, Management and Economics. IntechOpen (2024). https://doi.org/10.5772/intechopen.112160
22. Csikszentmihalyi, M. Creativity: flow and the psychology of discovery and invention. Harper Perennial (1996)
23. Fischer, G., Rohde, M., Wulf, V.: Community-based learning: the core competency of residential, research-based universities. Int. J. Comput. Support. Collab. Learn. **2**(1), 9–40 (2007). https://doi.org/10.1007/s11412-007-9009-1
24. Hülsheger, U.R., Anderson, N., Salgado, J.F.: Team-level predictors of innovation at work: a comprehensive meta-analysis spanning three decades of research. J. Appl. Psychol. **94**(5), 1128–1145 (2009). https://doi.org/10.1037/a0015978
25. Ciriello, R.F., Richter, A., Mathiassen, L.: Emergence of creativity in IS development teams: a socio-technical systems perspective. Int. J. Inf. Manag. **74**, 102698 (2024). https://doi.org/10.1016/j.ijinfomgt.2023.102698
26. Hargadon, A., Sutton, R.I.: Technology brokering and innovation in a product development firm. Adm. Sci. Q. **42**(4), 716–749 (1997). https://doi.org/10.2307/2393655

27. Oksanen, K., Ståhle, P.: Physical environment as a source for innovation: investigating the attributes of innovative space. J. Knowl. Manag. **17**(6), 815–827 (2013). https://doi.org/10. 1108/JKM-04-2013-0136

28. Dul, J., Ceylan, C.: Work environments for employee creativity. Ergonomics **54**(1), 12–20 (2011). https://doi.org/10.1080/00140139.2010.542833

29. Kallio, T.J., Kallio, K.-M., Blomberg, A.J.: Physical space, culture and organisational creativity – a longitudinal study. Facilities **33**(5/6), 389–411 (2015). https://doi.org/10.1108/F-09-2013-0074

30. Chang, Y.-S., Yu, K.: The relationship between perceptions of an innovative environment and creative performance in an online synchronous environment. Comput. Hum. Behav. **49**, 38–43 (2015). https://doi.org/10.1016/j.chb.2015.02.040

31. Olson, G.M., Olson, J.S.: Distance matters. Hum.-Comput. Interact. **15**(2–3), 139–178 (2000). https://doi.org/10.1207/S15327051HCI1523_4

32. Freeman, G., McNeese, N.J.: Exploring indie game development: team practices and social experiences in a creativity-centric technology community. Comput. Support. Coop. Work **28**(3–4), 723–748 (2019). https://doi.org/10.1007/s10606-019-09348-x

33. Boughzala, I., Vreede, G.-J., Limayem, M.: Team collaboration in virtual worlds: editorial to the special issue. J. Assoc. Inf. Syst. **13**(10), 714–734 (2012). https://doi.org/10.17705/1jais. 00313

34. Titova, O., Luzan, P., Sosnytska, N., Kulieshov, S., Suprun, O.: Information and communication technology tools for enhancing engineering students' creativity. In: Ivanov, V., Trojanowska, J., Pavlenko, I., Zajac, J., Peraković, D. (eds.) Advances in Design, Simulation and Manufacturing IV, LNME, pp. 332–340. Springer International Publishing, Cham (2021). https://doi.org/10.1007/978-3-030-77719-7_33

35. Osterwalder, A., Pigneur, Y.: Business model generation: Ein Handbuch für Visionäre, Spielveränderer und Herausforderer, 1st edn. Campus Verlag, Frankfurt, New York (2011)

36. Thoring, K., Mueller, R.M.: Understanding design thinking: a process model based on method engineering. In: Proceedings of the International Conference on Engineering and Product Design Education (E&PDE2011), pp. 493–498 (2011)

37. Figma. The Collaborative Interface Design Tool (2024). https://www.figma.com/. Accessed 6 June 2024

38. Meinel, C., Leifer, L., Plattner, H.: Design thinking. Springer, Berlin Heidelberg, Berlin, Heidelberg (2011)

39. Frick, W.: An introduction to data-driven decisions for managers who don't like math (2014). https://hbr.org/2014/05/an-introduction-to-data-driven-decisions-for-managers-who-dont-like-math. Accessed 6 June 2024

40. Manyika, J., et al.: Big data: the next frontier for innovation, competition, and productivity. McKinsey Global Institute (2011) https://www.mckinsey.com/capabilities/mckinsey-digital/our-insights/big-data-the-next-frontier-for-innovation. Accessed 6 June 2024

41. Flensburg, S., Lomborg, S.: Datafication research: mapping the field for a future agenda. New Media Soc. **25**(6), 1451–1469 (2023). https://doi.org/10.1177/14614448211046616

42. Davenport, T.H., Harris, J.G.: Competing on analytics: the new science of winning. Harvard Business School Press, Boston, Massachusetts (2007)

43. Rabiee, F.: Focus-group interview and data analysis. Proc. Nutr. Soc. **63**(4), 655–660 (2004). https://doi.org/10.1079/PNS2004399

44. Krosnick, J.A.: Questionnaire design. In: Vannette, D.L., Krosnick, J.A. (eds.) The Palgrave Handbook of Survey Research, pp. 439–455. Springer International Publishing, Cham (2018). https://doi.org/10.1007/978-3-319-54395-6_53

45. Short, J., Williams, E., Christie, B.: The social psychology of telecommunications. Wiley, London (1976)

46. Han, H.-J., Hiltz, S.R., Fjermestad, J., Wang, Y.: Does medium matter? a comparison of initial meeting modes for virtual teams. IEEE Trans. Profess. Commun. **54**(4), 376–391 (2011). https://doi.org/10.1109/TPC.2011.2175759
47. Dubé, L., Robey, D.: Surviving the paradoxes of virtual teamwork. Inf. Syst. J. **19**(1), 3–30 (2009). https://doi.org/10.1111/j.1365-2575.2008.00313.x
48. AlZaabi, F., et al.: An investigation study of challenges in the transition from traditional to virtual teamwork during COVID-19 in UAE organisations. Int. J. Innov. Creat. Change **15**(5), 455–468 (2021)
49. Ocker, R., Fjermestad, J., Hiltz, S.R., Johnson, K.: Effects of four modes of group communication on the outcomes of software requirements determination. J. Manag. Inf. Syst. **15**(1), 99–118 (1998). https://doi.org/10.1080/07421222.1998.11518198
50. Woodman, R.W., Sawyer, J.E., Griffin, R.W.: Toward a theory of organizational creativity. Acad. Manag. Rev. **18**(2), 293 (1993). https://doi.org/10.2307/258761
51. AlMunifi, A.A., Alfawzan, M.S.: Back to the new normal in engineering education towards student-centered learning: remote? In Person? Hybrid? Sustainability **15**(18) (2023). https://doi.org/10.3390/su151813510
52. Kučević, E., et al.: The prompt-a-thon: designing a format for value co-creation with generative ai for research and practice. In: Proceedings of the Hawaii International Conference on System Sciences (HICSS2024), pp. 1586–1595 (2024)
53. Shaik, F.F., Makhecha, U.P.: Drivers of employee engagement in global virtual teams. Australas. J. Inf. Syst. **23** (2019). https://doi.org/10.3127/ajis.v23i0.1770
54. Leible, S., Ludzay, M.: Towards employee-driven idea mining: concept, benefits, and challenges. In: Proceedings of the International Conference on Information Technology (InCIT2022), pp. 428–433. IEEE (2022). https://doi.org/10.1109/InCIT56086.2022.10067734
55. Lefebvre, H., Legner, C., Fadler, M.: Data democratization: toward a deeper understanding. In: Proceedings of the International Conference on Information Systems (ICIS2021) (2021)
56. Leible, S., Gücük, G.-L., Simic, D., von Brackel-Schmidt, C., Lewandowski, T.: Zwischen Forschung und Praxis: Fähigkeiten und Limitationen generativer KI sowie ihre wachsende Bedeutung in der Zukunft. HMD Praxis der Wirtschaftsinformatik **61**(2) (2024). https://doi.org/10.1365/s40702-024-01050-x
57. Joosten, J., Bilgram, V., Hahn, A., Totzek, D.: Comparing the ideation quality of humans with generative artificial intelligence. IEEE Eng. Manag. Rev. **52**(2), 153–164 (2024). https://doi.org/10.1109/EMR.2024.3353338
58. Siemon, D.: Elaborating team roles for artificial intelligence-based teammates in human-AI collaboration. Group Decis. Negot. **31**(5), 871–912 (2022). https://doi.org/10.1007/s10726-022-09792-z

What's the Value of Science Fiction for Future-Oriented Human-Computer Interaction: The Role of Innovative Catalysts

Yuqi Liu and Zhiyong Fu[✉]

Academy of Arts and Design, Tsinghua University, Beijing 100084, China
fuzhiyong@tsinghua.edu.cn

Abstract. The spiritual core of science fiction is a kind of thought experiment of the relationship between human, science, and technology. Science fiction, whether in the form of literature, comics, cartoons, games, or especially in films, offers a form of exploration to delve into the boundless potential of future-oriented human-computer interaction. This study adopts a science fiction perspective and utilizes case studies to elucidate the value of science fiction in catalyzing forward-thinking design innovations in human-computer interaction. The research encompasses 35 seminal science fiction movies as subjects of inquiry. The research mainly discusses how science fiction can play a role as an innovative trigger for future human-computer interaction design from four aspects: "The evolution of human-computer relationship", "The genres of human-computer interaction", "The diversity of human-computer scenarios", and "The speculation of human-computer ethics". The "Evolution of Human-Computer Relationships" traverses four stages: "Human-computer Interaction," "Human-computer Collaboration," "Human-computer Co-Creation," culminating in "Human-computer Symbiosis." "The Genres of Human-computer Interaction" are categorized into "External Interaction," "Partial Substitution," and "Internal Fusion." "The Diversity of Human-computer Scenarios" encompasses diverse fields such as medicine, education, offices, consumption, and entertainment. Lastly, "The Speculation of Human-computer Ethics" delves into five critical areas: "Human Existence," "Safety & Privacy," "Accident Responsibility," "Consciousness Awakening," and "Machine Rights." Finally, by analyzing the disparities between scientific facts and science fiction, the study outlined the constraints of science fiction in predicting the futuristic development trends of human-computer interaction. It also highlighted the crucial issues that educators, researchers, and designers must address when leveraging science fiction as a springboard for innovation. These issues encompass "commercial applicability", "technical feasibility", and "social ethics". This research has broadened the innovative horizons of human-computer interaction design, offering fresh inspiration and perspectives to designers seeking to innovate in the realm of interaction design in the future context.

Keywords: Science Fiction · Human-computer Interaction · Design Innovation · Technological Imagination

M. Kurosu et al. (Eds.): HCII 2024, LNCS 15374, pp. 83–96, 2025.
https://doi.org/10.1007/978-3-031-76803-3_6

1 Introduction

Human-Computer Interaction (HCI) is a discipline that studies the interactive relationship between information systems and users. Systems can be various from intelligent devices and machines to computerized systems and software [1]. Science fiction movies usually explore the relationship between humans and machines, and how to achieve cooperation and co-existence between them through informatic interactive technologies [2]. Human-computer interaction researchers, user experience professionals, and science educators often use science fiction movies to inspire real-world technological innovations of smart systems and devices [3]. It is generally believed that science fiction has had an impact on the development of human computer interaction[4]. Science fiction literature, comics, cartoons, especially audiovisual materials, such as science fiction movies and performances, can be valuable and meaningful extensions and supplementary content [5]. At the same time, science fiction, as a means of analyzing upcoming human-computer interaction technologies, can help us develop an open-minded and reflective dialogue about the future of technology, thereby creating a unique foundation for critical thinking and problem-solving [6, 7]. This study believes that science fiction works can provide imaginative space and exploration possibilities for the study of human-computer interaction. Science fiction movies, because of their rich content elements and concrete creative forms, can serve as triggers for creativity and innovation, thus supporting us to explore the design space. This research aims to explore the value of Sci-Fi in human-computer interaction design innovation via the case analysis of 35 science fiction movies. The article mainly focuses on four aspects, namely "The evolution of human-computer relationship", "The genres of human-computer interaction", "The diversity of human-computer scenarios", and "The speculation of human-computer Ethics", to explore how science fiction plays a role as an innovative trigger for future-oriented human-computer interaction design. Finally, this article proposes the limitations of science fiction in foreseeing future-oriented human-computer interaction design trends by analyzing the differences between science fiction and science facts.

2 The Collection of Science Fiction Movie Sample

This study used crawlers to collect classic science fiction movies titles on internationally authoritative search engines, including Google, Bing, Yahoo, Baidu, etc., and conducted a comprehensive comparison of film titles, film posters, film plot summaries, and film online reviews. Ultimately, 35 science fiction films with a wide influence and strong relevance to human-computer interaction were selected. The rise of human-computer interaction is inextricably linked to the development of information communication technology represented by the Internet and artificial intelligence, especially in the modern era of the Internet [8, 9]. The prototype of the Internet dates to the 1960s, when some research institutions of the US Department of Defense began to explore network communication between computers. In 1969, the US ARPANET project became the first prototype of the Internet, enabling data transmission between universities and research institutions[10]. The 1990s was a crucial period for the development of the Internet. In 1991, British physicist Tim Berners-Lee created the concept and basic architecture of the World Wide Web, providing a simple and easy-to-use way for information sharing and access [11]. In the early 21st century, social media became an important part of the Internet [12]. Nowadays, one of the key trends in Internet is the rise of cloud computing [13]. Therefore, the development of the Internet has probably gone through the budding stage from the 1960s to the 1980s, the commercialization and World Wide Web stage in the 1990s, the social media and mobile Internet stage in the 2000s, and the cloud computing and Internet of Things stages from 2010 to the present [14]. This study classified the 35 science fiction films according to their release year in five stages, namely "before 1959", "1960–1989", "1990–1999", "2000–2009", and "2010-present".

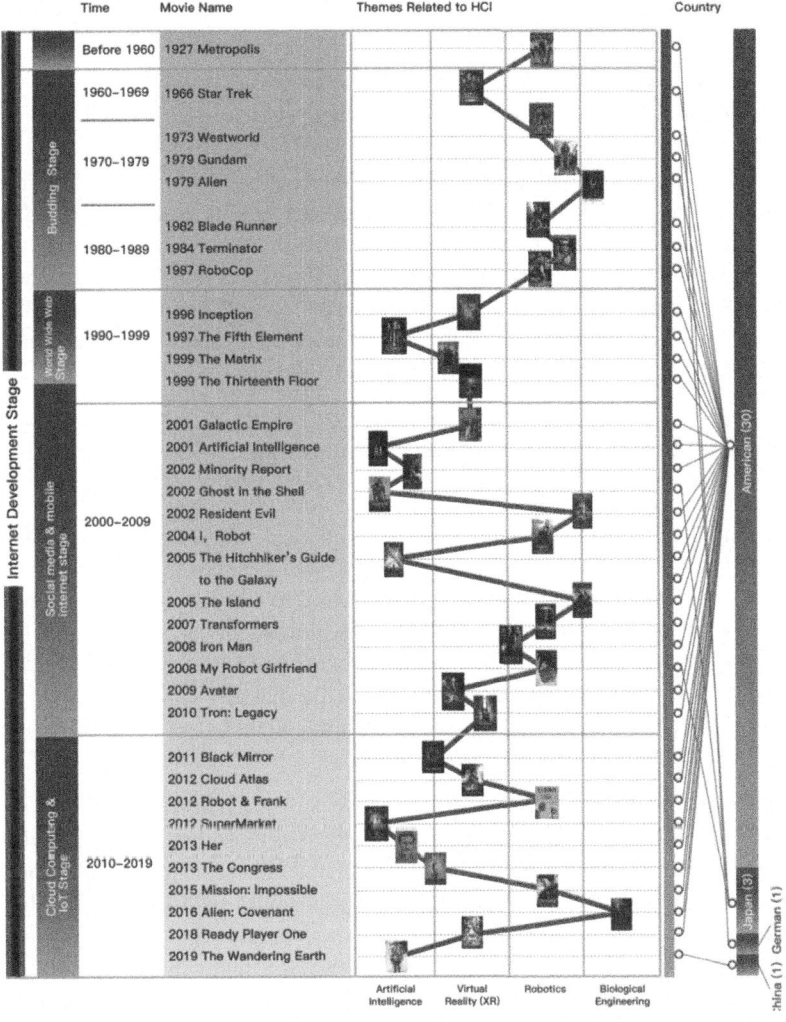

Fig. 1. Release year, theme, and country distribution of science fiction movie samples.

The main themes of human-computer interaction and the countries of release were also statistically analyzed, as shown in Fig. 1. The result shows that among the 35 films, the four main themes of human-computer interaction technology are artificial intelligence, virtual reality (XR), robotics, and bioengineering, with the number of movies from different countries being the United States (30), Japan (3), Germany (1), and China (1). The number of films in each period is before 1959 (1), 1960–1969 (1), 1970–1979 (3), 1980–1989 (3), 1990–1999 (4), 2000–2009 (13), and 2010–2020 (10). It can be seen from the figure that the 35 samples selected are basically consistent with the core application areas of human-computer interaction and the time periods of Internet development and prosperity. Therefore, they are representative of the Sci-Fi impact on the field of human-computer interaction innovation.

3   The Value of Science Fiction in Future-Oriented Human-Computer Interaction Design Innovation

Through watching, analyzing, and summarizing the content of selected 35 Sci-Fi movie samples, the study found that the value of science fiction in future-oriented human-computer interaction design innovation can be mainly divided into four aspects, namely "The evolution of human-computer relationship", "The genres of human-computer interaction", "The diversity of human-computer scenarios", and "The speculation of human-computer ethics". Figure 2 presents the value of these four aspects in a comprehensive way. This section will explain the related content in detail.

3.1   The Evolution of Human-Computer Relationship

With the continuous development of digital technology, the power of machines and the degree of intelligence will be continuously strengthened, and the relationship between humans and machines will also continue to evolve [15]. Science fiction movies provide an experimental and exploratory space for the evolution of benign human-machine relationships on the premise that all technological developments are possible [16]. From the human-computer interaction relationship reflected in 35 science fiction movies, this article believes that its evolutionary process can be mainly divided into four stages: "human-computer interaction", "human-computer collaboration", "human-computer co-creation" and "human-computer symbiosis".

Human-Computer Interaction. When the power of the machine is in a weak state, it mainly completes human orders and tasks in the form of tools. For example, keyboards, mice, touch screens, game controllers, smart voice assistants, virtual reality helmets, eye tracking equipment, EEG instruments, etc. For example, in "Cloud Atlas", there are many elements related to human-computer interaction, such as artificial intelligence, virtual reality, robots, physical interaction, consciousness interaction, social interaction, etc. In "Mission: Impossile", actor Samuel L. Jackson plays the role of a secret agent. He wears a virtual reality helmet, and the channel for obtaining information is a virtual 3D Internet world. In this process, some icons and text messages can be projected onto the helmet goggles he wears. At the same time, the protagonist can achieve the function of

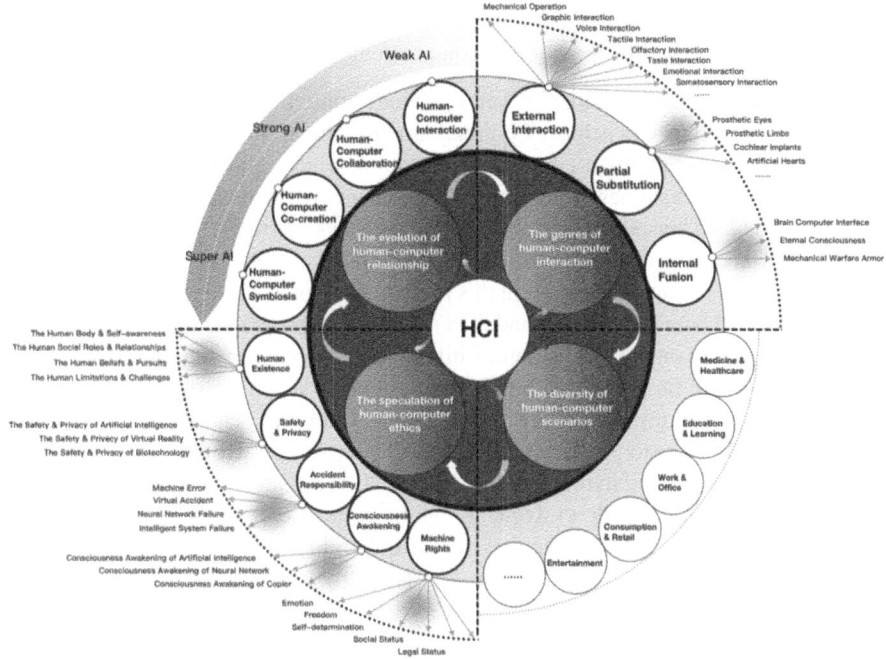

Fig. 2. The value of science fiction for future oriented HCI design innovation.

storage device through his own brain. In "The Minority Report", Tom Cruise's character stands in front of a virtual screen without touching anything but can control data and even memories through a special glove. In "The Fifth Element", the elements related to human-computer interaction mainly include voice interaction, touch screen interaction, gesture recognition, virtual reality interaction, etc.

Human-Computer Collaboration. When the power of machines is enhanced, their role can transform from tools into human assistants, collaborating with humans to complete certain specific tasks. Many science fiction movies have shown different forms and possibilities of human-computer collaboration, reflecting the importance of cooperation and collaborative development between humans and machines in the future world. For example, in the movie "The Wandering Earth", astronaut Liu Peiqiang (played by Wu Jing) and MOSS carry out the mission of saving the Earth in the space station. In the process, Peiqiang is supported by robot assistants. The tacit understanding and trust between them show a kind of emotional bond of human-machine collaboration. These robot assistants are responsible for providing information, executing tasks, and assisting astronauts in completing various tasks. In the movie "Ghost in the Shell", it depicts a future world where humans and machines co-exist and form different social classes. In this world, the cyborg Motoko Kusanagi, as a member of the elite force "Public Security Section 9," works with other types of human-machine combinations such as artificial intelligence and bionics to fight high-tech crimes. In "Gundam", humans combine with giant robots through special equipment to work together to fight the invaders. This form of human-machine collaboration requires a high degree of integration of human consciousness and machine operation to complement each other.

Human-Computer Co-creation. When machines continue to develop in power and possess creativity, they can achieve co-creation with human. In science fiction movies, there are many cases of human-computer co-creation, which reflects that artificial intelligence can jointly create new values and achievements with humans in the future. For example, In the fifth episode of the third season of "Black Mirror", this episode is called "Nelson" and talks about a program that can automatically generate new language games based on the user's input and output. In this process, a human-machine co-creation relationship is formed between the user and the program. The program continuously adjusts the game rules based on the user's input, while the user affects the generation of the program through output feedback. In "The Matrix", humans create a virtual world through virtual reality technology. In this space, the human brain can seamlessly connect and interact with computers to perform various creative works. In "Tron: Legacy", the protagonist Flynn was trapped in the digital world for 20 years, and finally cooperated with his son Sam to crack the code of Tron, so that he could freely travel between the real world and the digital world. At the end of the movie, Flynn and Sam decide to work together to develop a new Tron platform that perfectly combines the real and digital worlds.

Human-Computer Symbiosis. When machines already have abilities, emotions, and consciousness like humans, and have corresponding rights, humans and machines will be in a state of symbiosis. Numerous science fiction movies have shown the realization of human-computer symbiosis to varying degrees, reflecting the possibility of symbiosis and interdependence between humans and machines in the future world. In "I, Robot", Isaac Asimov proposed the "Three Laws of Robotics". Emphasizing the symbiotic relationship between robots and humans. In "RoboCop", the protagonist Albert Drake's body is fused with many mechanical parts, giving him superhuman strength and reflexes. This form of human-machine fusion allows RoboCop to play an outstanding role in high-risk missions. In "Blade Runner", replicants have similar appearance and emotions to humans, and humans can also improve their skills and abilities through mechanical enhancements. In "Metropolis", robot characters are highly intelligent and autonomous, police robots cooperate with human police officers, and medical robots can cooperate with human doctors. The relationship between robots and humans is not a simple instrumental interaction, but closer to a symbiotic relationship.

3.2   The Genres of Human-Computer Interaction

If we assume an infinite future with highly advanced technology as the premise, the relationship between humans and machines reflected in science fiction movies can be summarized into the following three types, namely, "external interaction" where the interaction of humans and machines are naturally separated, "partial substitution" where humans and machines are partial fusion, and "internal fusion" where they are fully embedded into each other's form.

External Interaction. The genre of "External Interaction" refers to a state where humans and machines are independent of each other and engage in natural interactive activities. In this sense, mechanical operation, graphic interaction, voice interaction, tactile interaction, olfactory interaction, taste interaction, emotional interaction, somatosensory interaction and other forms of interaction are all types of external interaction, including keyboard, mouse, joystick, computer, Smart speakers, eye trackers, data gloves, data clothing, helmet-mounted displays, somatosensory gaming devices, etc. For example, in "Iron Man", the human-computer interaction interface inside the Iron Man helmet of the billionaire actor Tony Stark is quite cool. In "Her", the male protagonist Theodore interacts with the intelligent voice assistant operating system "Samantha" to perform various activities, including writing letters, answering questions, editing news, etc. In "Westworld", the receptionist in the Westworld adult park can actively talk and interact with tourists, and provide personalized responses based on the tourists' behaviors and preferences. In "Artificial Intelligence (AI)", the protagonist David not only has a high degree of intelligence, but also has emotions and self-awareness, which allows this robot child to have in-depth emotional communication and interaction with humans. In "Ready Player One", the actor James Halliday captures the user's body movements through somatosensory equipment and converts them into movements in the virtual world. Through this interactive method based on virtual reality technology, users can feel real body movements and environmental feedback in the virtual world, allowing users to experience games and virtual reality experiences more realistically and immersively.

Partial Substitution. The genre of "Partial Substitution" refers to the replacement of parts of the human body by machines. Cyborg technology, or semi-mechanization, refers to the combination of organic and electronic components to produce an organism that is partially mechanical or more electronic than biological. This includes the fusion of computers and the human body, the creation of new body parts such as prosthetic eyes, limbs, and artificial organs, and the use of nanomaterials to improve human performance. In "Ghost in the Shell", the prosthetic technology "Cyborg Technology" that replaces body organs with mechanical parts has developed rapidly, and even the extreme situation of "all organs are artificial" can be easily achieved. Nearly all humans have been modified to varying degrees, and many have ports (on the back of their necks) that connect to the Internet. In the 2D version of "RoboCop", Robert Knife was killed on duty and was sent to a laboratory for transformation, where he was transformed into a biochemical robot "RoboCop". In "Blade Runner", the replicants have mechanical bodies. These mechanical bodies are artificial and allow the replicants to interact with humans. These mechanical bodies allow the replicants to be more like humans, allowing the replicants to integrate into human society. Sci-fi prosthetics have become a reality in the medical field and have provided countless disabled people with opportunities to make up for their physical defects, such as prosthetic eyes, prosthetic limbs, cochlear implants, artificial hearts, etc. Cyborg technology is still in its early stages and faces many challenges, such as the integration of electronic components with human cells, the safety and reliability of implanted devices, and ethical issues related to human augmentation. However, with the continuous advancement of science and technology, cyborg technology is expected to bring more and more benefits to mankind.

Internal Fusion. There are two ultimate ways of human-computer interaction. One is the integration of machines into humans, known as brain-computer interface. The other is the integration of humans into machines, known as the so-called consciousness immortality, where humans become mechanical bodies. There is also another way where humans become the control center of mechanical armor, as typically represented in Japanese sci-fi movies and anime such as "The Matrix" where humans in the real world need to enter the "Matrix" world by inserting a connector into the back of their head. This "brain-to-brain" approach is a typical invasive brain-computer interface. In "Avatar", scientists use an induction cabin to synchronize the brain of a person with the avatar, allowing the person's thoughts to enter the avatar. In "The Wandering Earth 2", the concept of digital life is greatly reflected. Thought uploading, also known as whole brain emulation (WBE), maps a person's thoughts, personality, emotions, and memories onto other carriers, such as computers, robots, and even clones, to achieve consciousness immortality. In Japanese sci-fi anime, mechanical armor is a frequent theme. Humans enter the interior of giant robots and become the driving center. In "Gundam", robots are widely used in combat and military operations. These robots are usually operated and piloted by humans, forming a close interactive relationship with humans. Humans have an ability called "Newtype", which allows them to communicate with machines through mental induction. Through mental induction, humans can better understand the behavior and thinking patterns of machines, thus better operating, and piloting robots.

3.3 The Diversity of Human-Computer Scenarios

The application scenarios of human-computer interaction are very wide, including but not limited to medical, education, office, consumption, entertainment, etc. In the field of medicine, human-computer interaction can help doctors make more accurate diagnoses and treatments. For example, through medical imaging analysis systems, doctors can diagnose diseases more accurately. At the same time, through telemedicine systems, doctors can provide medical services for patients anytime and anywhere, which greatly facilitates the treatment of patients. In the field of education, human-computer interaction technology enables teaching to break through the limitations of time and space, making it more intuitive and vivid, and students can also obtain knowledge more easily. For example, through intelligent education equipment, students can conduct online learning and interact with the classroom through intelligent notebooks. In the field of office, human-computer interaction technology can help improve work efficiency and convenience. For example, intelligent conference systems can realize remote meetings, and intelligent voice assistants can help deal with daily tasks. In the field of consumption, human-computer interaction can help achieve fast, convenient, personalized consumption. For example, intelligent shopping systems can recommend goods based on users' shopping habits, and intelligent voice assistants can also help with daily consumption activities such as shopping and ordering meals. In the field of entertainment, human-computer interaction technology can provide richer and immersive entertainment experiences. For example, through virtual reality technology, users can experience games, movies, and other entertainment content in an immersive way. Relevant plots are reflected in movies such as "Robot Frank", "The Thirteenth Floor", "The Congress", and "Super

Store". In science fiction movies, there are also many other cases of future-oriented human-computer interaction application scenarios.

3.4   The Genres of Human-Computer Interaction

In the real world, with the continuous development of artificial intelligence technology, human-machine ethics issues have attracted more and more attention. For example, some countries have begun to explore the issue of artificial intelligence legislation to ensure that the development of artificial intelligence complies with ethical and legal standards. At the same time, some scientists and philosophers are also exploring whether artificial intelligence has human characteristics such as emotion, consciousness, and free will, hoping to provide a reference for solving human-machine ethics issues. In general, the discussion of human-machine ethics in science fiction mainly includes the following five aspects:

The Existence of Humans.   With the rapid development of science and technology, machines are becoming more and more like humans, and humans are becoming more and more like machines. In particular, the rapid development of artificial intelligence challenges the theme of human existence. Science fiction movies involve human existence and can be thought of from different perspectives. It mainly includes the following four aspects: First, the human body and self-awareness. In science fiction movies, the human body is often given a broader meaning. For example, the heroine in "Resident Evil" had her body transformed into a cyborg, surpassing the limits of human capabilities. In "The Thirteenth Floor", people realize that their consciousness has been manipulated by others and re-examine themselves and the meaning of existence. Second, the human social roles & relationships. For example, the relationship between replicants and humans in "Blade Runner" and the interaction between humans and robots in "Transformers" all reflect the social roles and relationships of humans in the future. Third, the human beliefs and pursuits. For example, the Space Explorers in "Star Trek" aim to explore the unknown universe, challenge unknown dangers, and keep moving forward to realize human ideals and beliefs. Fourth, the human limitations and challenges. For example, in "Alien", human beings face the threat of alien creatures, and their own fears and limitations are exposed. People need to overcome their own fears and meet the challenges.

The Security and Privacy.   In the era of digital survival, the theme of "The end of privacy" is often explored in science fiction movies. For example, how to protect personal privacy and data security, how to avoid online fraud and cyber-attacks, how to manage and control network order, etc. Science fiction movies often involve issues of technological security and privacy, which mainly include "The security and privacy of artificial intelligence", "The security and privacy of virtual reality", and "The security and privacy of biotechnology". For example, in "Inception", a smart home system can automatically control home devices, but this system can also be hacked and controlled. In "The Hitchhiker's Guide to the Galaxy" a supercomputer called "The answer is 42" also touches on security and privacy issues. In "Minority Report", a movie about future crime prevention, preventing crime by predicting people's thoughts and behaviors. But this prediction also raises issues of privacy and ethics. In "The Thirteenth Floor", humans can enter the virtual world through virtual reality technology, but this virtual world also has security and privacy issues. In "Resident Evil", the abuse of biotechnology also triggered a series of security and privacy issues. These issues not only involve personal privacy and security, but also involve the stability and development of the entire society.

The Accident Responsibility. Science fiction movies sometimes involve the issue of responsibility for human-computer interaction technology accidents, reflecting people's concerns and thinking about the future. It mainly includes four aspects: Machine error, Virtual Accident, Neural network failure, Intelligent system failure. For example, in "RoboCop", the protagonist Wikus was transformed into a biochemical robot, but there was a problem with his robot's operating system, which caused him to make mistakes. In this case, who should be held responsible, Wikus himself or the robot manufacturer or programmer? In "The Matrix", humans access the virtual world "The Matrix" through the neural network technology of "brain-computer interface". But if human consciousness is permanently lost in the virtual world, who should bear the responsibility? Is it human self-selection or machine error? In "Inception", smart home systems are hacked and taken over, causing home devices to malfunction. In this case, who should bear the responsibility, the smart home manufacturer or the user's own negligence?

The Consciousness Awakening. Science fiction movies sometimes involve the awakening of consciousness in human-computer interaction technology, which mainly includes three aspects: the awakening of artificial intelligence, the awakening of neural networks, and the awakening of replicant consciousness. For example, in "Her", the artificial intelligence operating system develops an emotional bond with humans and displays self-awareness and emotions like humans. In "The Matrix", humans access the virtual world "Matrix" through "brain-computer interface" technology. In this process, human consciousness can awaken in the machine, showing self-awareness and thinking abilities like humans. In "The Island", the clones also show self-awareness and resistance. These questions involve many fields such as philosophy, psychology, and biology, and have a profound impact on the exploration of human self-awareness and the meaning of existence.

The Machine Right. Machine rights mean that machines have the same rights as humans, including consciousness, emotion, freedom, self-decision, social status, legal status, etc. In science fiction movies, the discussion of machine rights mainly involves three aspects: robot rights, replicant rights, and virtual human rights. For example, the cyborgs and robots in "Ghost in the Shell" have consciousness and self-determination like humans, triggering in-depth thinking about the rights of artificial intelligence. In "My Robot Girlfriend", the emotional relationship between robot girlfriends and humans is discussed in depth, triggering thoughts on the relationship between humans and machines and the rights of machines. The replicants in "Blade Runner" have consciousness, emotions, and self-determination like humans. The existence of replicants has triggered philosophical thinking about the origin of life, self-awareness, and human nature. In "The Matrix", humans are controlled by machines and become the energy source in the matrix. The existence and consciousness of human beings in this virtual world are questioned, triggering in-depth thinking on human self-awareness and machine rights. The virtual characters in "The Thirteenth Floor" have consciousness and emotions like humans, which has also triggered discussions on the rights of virtual human. The theme of machine rights in science fiction films provides us with a new perspective for thinking and exploring the relationship between humans and machines. By deeply reflecting on these issues, we can better understand the interaction between humans and machines and prepare for possible future issues of machine rights.

4 The Limitations of Science Fiction in Human-Computer Interaction Design Innovation

Science facts and science fiction have long symbiotic history [17]. There are clear differences between science fact and science fiction in some respects. Science facts are hypotheses or theories based on empirical and observational results that have been verified by science methods and accepted as truth. Science fiction is based on existing scientific principles and theories and explores and speculates on possible future phenomena and situations through imagination and creation. However, in some cases there may be some crossover and interaction between them. Some early science fiction plots may have been regarded as pure fiction at the time, but with the advancement and development of science & technology, these plots gradually became reality [18]. In turn, the exploration and discovery of some science facts may also inspire the creation of science fiction. They each play different roles and jointly promote human understanding and exploration of nature and human society. Figure 3 shows the interaction between science facts and science fiction. Regarding the innovation of human-computer interaction design, many of the imaginations in science fiction movies have become reality. Some of them are currently limited by technological development and seem unrealistic now, but they may also become reality in the future. Of course, there are also many science fiction movies that exist in science fiction which the imaginations may never be realized technically, and some can be realized but should be prohibited from a social ethics perspective. Therefore, this study believes that science fiction itself needs to withstand the following three aspects of consideration while playing a role as a trigger for human-computer interaction design innovation:

Technical Feasibility. Science fiction itself is a kind of technological imagination, which is still far away from real technological innovation and technical feasibility. Although the feasibility of human-computer interaction is often discussed in science fiction movies, there are still many unsolved problems at the current technological level. These technical challenges may require a long period of research and development to resolve. Therefore, when considering the feasibility of human-computer interaction, the current technical level and future development trends need to be carefully evaluated.

Commercial Applicability. Human-computer interaction interface usually refers to the part visible to the user. Users communicate with the system and perform operations through the human-computer interaction interface. It can be as small as the play button on a radio or as large as the dashboard on an airplane or the control room of a power plant. The design of human-computer interaction interface must include the user's cognitive and mental model, which are for the usability or user-friendliness of the system. There are no limits or boundaries to the imagination of technology in science fiction, but the

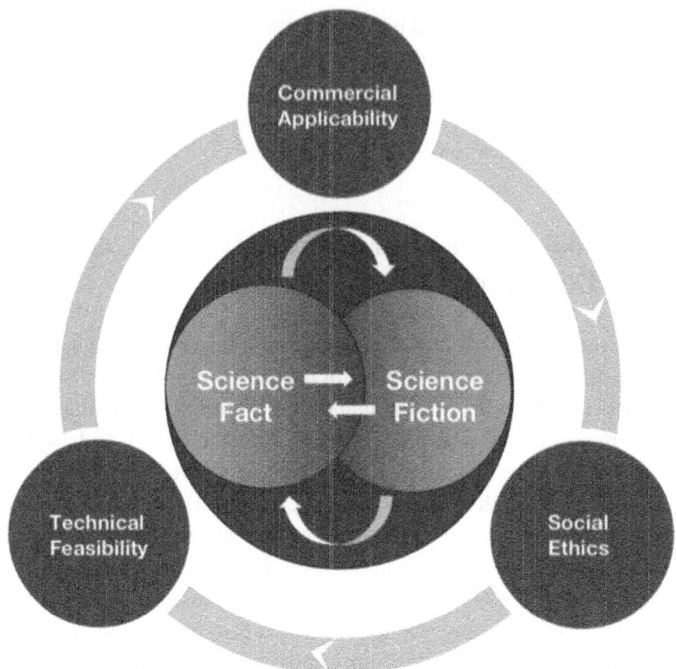

Fig. 3. The interaction between science facts and science fiction.

actual commercial application needs to follow the user-centered principle, which mainly include (1) The user's wishes and needs; (2) The user's abilities or possible physical limitations; (3) The user's perceptions and actions; (4) What the user finds attractive or enjoyable when interacting with the system?

Social Ethics. The imagination of human-computer interaction in science fiction has social and ethical limitations. Some of these questions may relate to our rights over machines, our definition of what it means to be human, and the impact on the social order. For example, would endowing machines with human-like emotions and consciousness have an impact on the questioning of what it means to be human? Will human-computer interaction lead to greater interrelation between humans and machines than between humans, thereby undermining social cohesion? If we can transfer consciousness into machines, should we regulate this behavior morally and legally? If machines have consciousness and emotions like humans, should we treat them as moral agents and make moral assessments of their actions? The development of human-computer interaction may also have an impact on our social order and values. For example, issues such as the autonomy, privacy, and data security of artificial intelligence, etc.

5 Conclusion

Science fiction movies, with their rich imagination and foresight of the possible futures, provide valuable inspiration for human-computer interaction design innovation. Real-world HCI education, technology development, and design practices can learn from the ideas in science fiction movies to promote breakthrough and advancement. At the same time, science fiction movies can also serve as important resources for researchers and practitioners to reflect on and discuss the futuristic technological development direction and ethics. This study explores the value of science fiction for HCI, mainly including "The evolution of human-computer relationship", "The genres of human-computer interaction", "The diversity of human-computer scenarios", and "The speculation of human-computer ethics". The evolution of the human-computer relationship will go through four stages: "Human-machine interaction", "Human-machine collaboration", "Human-machine co-creation" and "Human-machine symbiosis". The genres of human-computer interaction can be divided into "External interaction", "Partial substitution", "Internal fusion". The diversity of human-computer scenarios mainly includes healthcare, education, office, consumption, entertainment, etc. The speculation of human-computer ethics mainly involves "Human existence", "Safety and privacy", "Accident responsibility", "Consciousness awakening" and "Machine rights". Finally, through analyzing the differences and connections between scientific facts and science fiction, the article points out that scientific facts are hypotheses or theories based on empirical and observational results that have been verified by scientific methods and accepted as truth. Science fiction films are fictional works, and the plots and elements in them cannot directly reflect the real situation of human-computer interaction in the future. However, these plots and elements can inspire our imagination and thinking about the future development of human-computer interaction and become a trigger for innovative design practices. Regarding the design innovation of HCI, many of the imaginations in science fiction movies have become reality. Some of them are currently limited by technological development and seem unrealistic now, but they may become reality in the future; of course, there are also many imaginations may never be technically achievable, and there are some that can be achievable but should be prohibited regarding social ethics. Therefore, when innovating HCI design inspired by science fiction works, we should pay attention to three important considerations: "technical feasibility", "commercial applicability" and "social ethics". Only through in-depth thinking and discussion of these issues can we better respond to possible future challenges inspired by science fiction and ensure that scientific and technological progress truly benefits human society.

Acknowledgments. This study was funded by China Postdoctoral Science Foundation (grant number: 2023M742017).

Disclosure of Interests. The authors have no competing interests to declare that are relevant to the content of this article.

References

1. Carroll, J.M.: Human-computer interaction: psychology as a science of design. Annu. Rev. Psychol. **48**, 61–83 (1997)
2. Schwarz, J.O., Liebl, F.: Cultural products and their implications for business models: why science fiction needs socio-cultural fiction. Futures **50**, 66–73 (2013). https://doi.org/10.1016/j.futures.2013.03.006WE-SocialScienceCitationIndex(SSCI)
3. Jordan, P., Mubin, O., Silva, P.A.: A conceptual research agenda and quantification framework for the relationship between science-fiction media and human-computer interaction. In: Stephanidis, C. (eds.) HCI International 2016 – Posters' Extended Abstracts. HCI 2016. CCIS, vol. 617. Springer, Cham (2016). https://doi.org/10.1007/978-3-319-40548-3_9
4. Jordan, P., Mubin, O., Obaid, M., Silva, P.A.: Exploring the referral and usage of science fiction in HCI literature [arXiv]. arXiv 20 pp. -20 (2018)
5. Jordan, P., Silva, P.A.: Building an argument for the use of science fiction in HCI education. Intell. Hum. Syst. Integr. **903**, 846–851 (2019)
6. Bina, O., Mateus, S., Pereira, L., Caffa, A.: The future imagined: Exploring fiction as a means of reflecting on today's Grand Societal Challenges and tomorrow's options. Futures **86**, 166–184 (2017). https://doi.org/10.1016/j.futures.2016.05.009WE-SocialScienceCitationIndex(SSCI)WE-Arts&HumanitiesCitationIndex(A&HCI)
7. Gendron, C., Ivanaj, S., Girard, B., Arpin, M.L.: Science-fiction literature as inspiration for social theorizing within sustainability research. J. Clean. Prod. **164**, 1553–1562 (2017). https://doi.org/10.1016/j.jclepro.2017.07.044WE-ScienceCitationIndexExpanded(SCI-EXPANDED)WE-SocialScienceCitationIndex(SSCI)
8. Leiner, B.M., Cerf, V.G., Clark, D.D., et al.: A brief history of the Internet. ACM SIGCOMM Comput. Commun. Rev. **39**, 22–31 (2009)
9. Hinds, J., Joinson, A.: Radicalization, the internet and cybersecurity: opportunities and challenges for HCI. In: Human Aspects of Information Security, Privacy and Trust: 5th International Conference, HAS 2017, Held as Part of HCI International 2017, pp 481–493. Vancouver, BC, Canada, July 9–14, 2017, Proceedings 5. Springer (2017)
10. Lukasik, S.: Why the ARPANET was built. IEEE Ann. Hist. Comput. **33**, 4–21 (2010)
11. Berners-Lee, T., Cailliau, R., Luotonen, A., et al.: The world-wide web. Commun. ACM **37**, 76–82 (1994)
12. Edosomwan, S., Prakasan, S.K., Kouame, D., et al.: The history of social media and its impact on business. J. Appl. Manag. Entrep. **16**, 79 (2011)
13. Surbiryala, J., Rong, C.: Cloud computing: history and overview. In: 2019 IEEE Cloud Summit, pp 1–7. IEEE (2019)
14. Ryan, J.: A History of the internet and the digital future. Reaktion Books (2010)
15. Müller, V.C., Bostrom, N.: Future progress in artificial intelligence: a survey of expert opinion. Fundam. Issues Artif. Intell. 555–572 (2016)
16. Bell, F., Fletcher, G., Greenhill, A., et al.: Science fiction prototypes: Visionary technology narratives between futures. Futures **50**, 15–24 (2013). https://doi.org/10.1016/j.futures.2013.04.004WE-SocialScienceCitationIndex(SSCI)
17. Johnson, B.D.: Science fiction prototypes or: how i learned to stop worrying about the future and love science fiction. Intell. Environ. **2**, 3 (2016)
18. Zybura, J.: Science fiction prototyping as a tool to turn patents into innovative marketable products. Work. Proc. 10th Int. Conf. Intell. Environ. **18**, 235–246 (2014)

Reconciling Wicked Problems Through Speculation: Exploring Design Strategies for Interactive Installations

Yue Ma[✉]

Soochow University, Suzhou 215000, Jiangsu, China
MaYue20000@163.com

Abstract. Researchers and practitioners in the field of human-computer interaction (HCI) are increasingly confronted with wicked problems. Inspiring speculative thinking among users is an effective approach to reconcile wicked problems. Although existing work explores various ways to inspire speculative thinking through interaction, there is a lack of systematic exploration regarding which interaction strategies can effectively inspire speculative thinking and subsequently reconcile wicked problems. This research aims to explore the obstacles and strategies for inspiring speculative thinking and therefore reconcile wicked problems. Drawing on eight semi-structured interviews with participants with different backgrounds, I used thematic analysis to identity themes. I found that the obstacles include: (1) limited consideration of grand intentions, (2) restricted sensory engagement in interactive communication, and (3) difficulty in changing behavior. I also reveal three interactive design strategies for effectively stimulating user speculation, thereby reconciling wicked problems: (1) attracting participatory interactions, (2) eliciting emotional resonance, and (3) creating cognitive resonance. The first contribution is expanding interaction design strategies and methods in the speculative design domain. Interactive devices are crucial in stimulating user speculation and creating effective paths for reconciling wicked problems to envision a desirable future. This study contributes to the field of speculative design, interaction strategies, providing implications for interaction design practices.

Keywords: Interaction strategies · speculative thinking · wicked problem · exploratory research

1 Introduction

Researchers and practitioners in the field of human-computer interaction (HCI) are increasingly confronted with complex wicked problems. These problems defy clear definition, involve multiple stakeholders with conflicting values, and resist simple solutions [1, 2]. Wicked problems are pervasive across various domains today, such as sustainable development, climate change, and post-human thinking, demanding urgent solutions [3, 4].

M. Kurosu et al. (Eds.): HCII 2024, LNCS 15374, pp. 97–110, 2025.
https://doi.org/10.1007/978-3-031-76803-3_7

Inspiring speculative thinking [5] among users is an effective approach to reconcile wicked problems. Speculative thinking refers to encouraging people to freely imagine and redefine the relationship between humans and reality through discussions and debates [5]. There have been explorations by practitioners in inspiring speculative thinking through interactive design to reconcile wicked problems [6–8]. For instance, the Superlux studio [9] confronts users with future climate instability, food insecurity, economic and political fragility, and social division using installations, scenography, and videos. It stimulates reflection on how to adapt, respond, and perceive in such scenarios. It explores topics like self-sufficiency in extreme climate change. Another example is the "BinCam" design practice [10], where a phone is placed inside a trash can lid to take photos automatically when closed, sharing these pictures on Facebook for peer judgment on users' waste habits and environmental responsibility.

Although existing work explores various ways to inspire speculative thinking through interaction, there is a lack of systematic exploration in the field of HCI regarding which interaction strategies [11, 12] effectively inspire speculative thinking and subsequently reconcile wicked problems. To bridge this gap, this empirical study aims to analyze and categorize interaction design strategies for interactive devices, providing guidance for future research. The research questions are as follows:

1. What obstacles exist in the practical process of inspiring speculative thinking to reconcile wicked problems using interaction strategies?
2. Which interaction design strategies effectively inspire speculative thinking and reconcile wicked problems?

Specifically, I focus on interactive installations within the context of climate change. Interactive installations serve as pervasive mediums to inspire speculative thinking by engaging and sustaining user interaction, prompting users to rethink their conceptualization of reality. Consequently, I propose interaction design strategies and pathways to inspire speculative thinking and reconciling potential wicked problems in the future.

2 Literature Review

2.1 Wicked Problems and Speculative Design

The concept of wicked problems, introduced by Rittel and Webber, refers to complex and ill-defined issues that lack clear solutions [1]. Contemporary society faces significant challenges such as population growth, water scarcity, and climate change. Designers are eager to reconcile these wicked problems collaboratively, yet we must acknowledge that many of today's challenges are difficult to resolve effectively.

Speculative design offers a framework for envisioning and testing responses to these intractable issues, encouraging designers to think creatively and critically. Promoted by Dunne and Raby [5], speculative design involves exploring possible futures through imaginative and provocative design artefacts. This approach recognizes that the future, as objective time, is uncertain and unresolved [13, 14]. Rather than attempting to predict future scenarios, it emphasizes "lived experience" [15], guiding users to navigate towards the future and formulate action plans. This method employs thought experiments [16], fiction, and satire [17] to provoke reflection and debate about potential futures. While users cannot determine the future in its objective sense, their practices in future-making are consequential, as they trigger a series of actions and decisions.

Speculative design facilitates further discussion and reflection on the many possibilities of human existence, rekindling imagination and redefining the relationship between humans and reality to reconcile these wicked problems [5]. For instance, DiSalvo highlights how speculative design can make the complexity of wicked problems more tangible and comprehensible through creative spectacles [18]. By engaging stakeholders in imagined scenarios, speculative design helps reveal underlying values and assumptions, deepening our understanding of the issues at hand. Through the imaginative and collaborative methods inherent in speculative design, designers can develop innovative and meaningful solutions to wicked problems. Further research and practice are needed to refine these methods, ensuring their effectiveness and inclusivity in addressing urgent contemporary issues.

2.2 Interactive Installation Design

The origins of interactive installation design can be traced back to the interactive and installation art of the 1960s. Early interactive installations relied primarily on mechanical devices and simple electronic circuits to create interactive effects. With advancements in computer technology, particularly real-time computing and sensing technologies, the complexity and interactivity of these installations have significantly increased [19]. The application of interactive installations in public spaces has also grown, with substantial social impact. Fischer and Hornecker point out that interactive installations promote social interaction and community integration by creating shared experiences [20]. Researchers have explored various interaction techniques, such as touch, gestures, sound, and virtual reality (VR), to enhance user immersion and engagement. Recently, interactive devices based on artificial intelligence and machine learning have emerged, capable of intelligent responses and personalized adjustments based on user behavior [21].

Tangible interaction involves using physical objects to control digital information, bridging the gap between the physical and digital worlds. This approach enhances the intuitiveness of the installations, potentially offering a more engaging user experience [22]. Traditional approaches to reconciling wicked problems often rely on two-dimensional information dissemination, which lacks the dynamic responsiveness of interactive media. Interactive installations combine text, sound, visuals, and motion to create a unique design expression that can stimulate user speculation.

Despite increasing exploration of interaction methods for interactive devices, the field of human-computer interaction lacks clarity on strategies to effectively stimulate user speculation and reconcile wicked problems. This study aims to reconcile this gap through empirical research.

3 Research Methodology

3.1 Qualitative Research: Semi-structured Interviews

This study utilizes a qualitative research approach, with data primarily derived from semi-structured interviews. Initially, I designed the interview framework, which encompassed various categories of questions. These questions included understanding of interactive installations, perception of wicked problems, the relationship between wicked problems and speculation, experiences with interactive installations, the relationship between speculative ability and interactive installations, the impact of interactive device design, analysis of practical cases, and future outlooks. During the interviews, while maintaining a relatively fixed overall structure, I allowed for exploration based on each interviewee's actual experiences. The aim was to stimulate discussions on how speculative design can reconcile wicked problems, thus obtaining diverse and valuable information to support subsequent analysis and findings.

3.2 Participants

I conducted interviews with eight selected participants to enhance the reliability of this qualitative research, as illustrated in Table 1. The participants included individuals with the following backgrounds:

- Industrial Design: 10 years of research experience, familiarity with interactive installations.
- Fashion Design: 6 years of research experience, familiarity with interactive installations.
- Environmental Design: 4 years of research experience, experience in creating and participating in interactive installations.
- Oil Painting: 7 years of research experience, experience in participating in interactive installations.
- Environmental Design: 36 years of research experience, experience in creating and participating in interactive installations.
- Photography: 5 years of research experience, familiarity with interactive installations.
- Environmental Design: 8 years of research experience, experience in creating and participating in interactive installations.
- Visual Communication: 5 years of research experience, familiarity with interactive installations.

Through semi-structured interviews, I collected approximately 80,000 words in 110 pages of transcriptions. The data was screened and summarized around two primary questions.

3.3 Data Analysis

During the data analysis phase, thematic analysis was employed. Thematic analysis is a systematic approach to uncovering and interpreting themes from collected qualitative data [23, 24]. After transcribing the data and becoming familiar with its content, open

Table 1. Descriptive of the participants

Participant	Gender	Major	Experience	Duration
P1	male	Industrial design	Participated and understood	10 years
P2	female	Clothing design	Participated and understood	6 years
P3	male	Environmental design	Created, participated, and understood	4 years
P4	female	Oil painting	Participated in	7 years
P5	male	Environmental design	Created, participated, and understood	36 years
P6	female	Photograph	Participated and understood	5 years
P7	female	Environmental design	Created, participated, and understood	8 years
P8	male	Visual	Understood	5 years

coding was performed by the researchers to generate an initial list of codes. These codes were then organized into broader categories. Through iterative review and refinement, these categories were summarized into different themes, each supported by relevant examples from the data. This process aids in a nuanced understanding of the phenomenon under study and provides valuable insights for further explanation and discussion. In summary, I organized the data from the bottom up, identifying patterns and forming a model.

4 Findings

The findings of this study are divided into two main sections. In the first section, I identify the obstacles encountered in the process of stimulating user speculation to reconcile wicked problems. These obstacles include: (1) limited consideration of grand intentions, (2) restricted sensory engagement in interactive communication, and (3) difficulty in changing behavior (see Fig. 1). In the second section, I reveal which interactive design strategies effectively stimulate user speculation, thereby reconciling wicked problems. The findings in this section include: (1) attracting participatory interactions, (2) eliciting emotional resonance, and (3) creating cognitive resonance (see Fig. 2). Figures 1 and 2 provides a detailed description of the themes and corresponding secondary codes for each section. The main findings of each section will be described in detail.

4.1 Obstacles in Stimulating User Speculation to Reconcile Wicked Problems

The records under the first section provide a deep understanding of the specific obstacles in using speculation to reconcile wicked problems. This theme includes a total of 83 descriptive quotes (as shown in Fig. 2). These can be summarized into three second-order codes: limited consideration of grand intentions, restricted sensory engagement in interactive communication, and difficulty in changing behavior.

First-order   Second-order   Themes

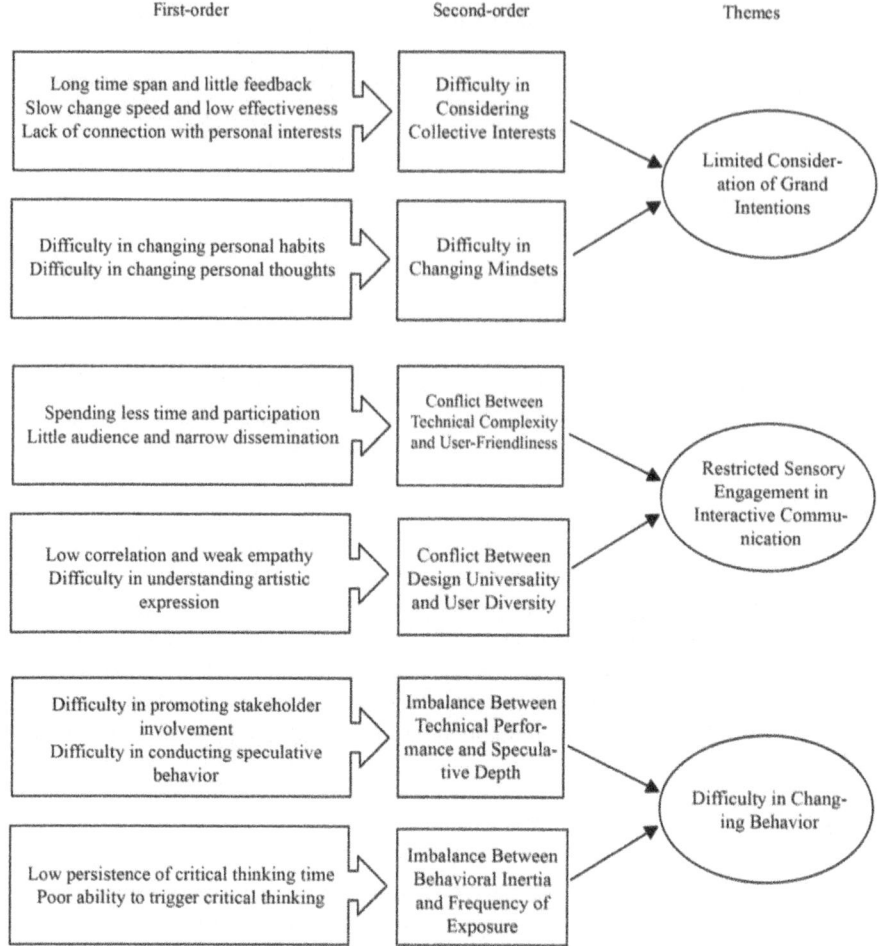

Fig. 1. Obstacles in Stimulating User Speculation to Reconcile Wicked Problems

Limited Consideration of Grand Intentions

Difficulty in Considering Collective Interests. The interviews revealed that participants often perceive wicked problems as complex, believing their individual actions have minimal impact or cannot contribute to resolving these issues. This perspective is common among the interviewees. For instance, P3 mentioned, "For me personally, I feel very small" (P3), and P4 added, "I think my actions are quite normal and won't have a particularly large impact on the world, so I focus more on the small things in life" (P4). This suggests that individuals prioritize immediate personal concerns over broader societal issues. P1 noted, "When there is a conflict of interest, I might compromise and focus on immediate benefits" (P1). This indicates that personal interests tend to outweigh collective interests, a sentiment echoed by P4: "Many things can't be changed. For example,

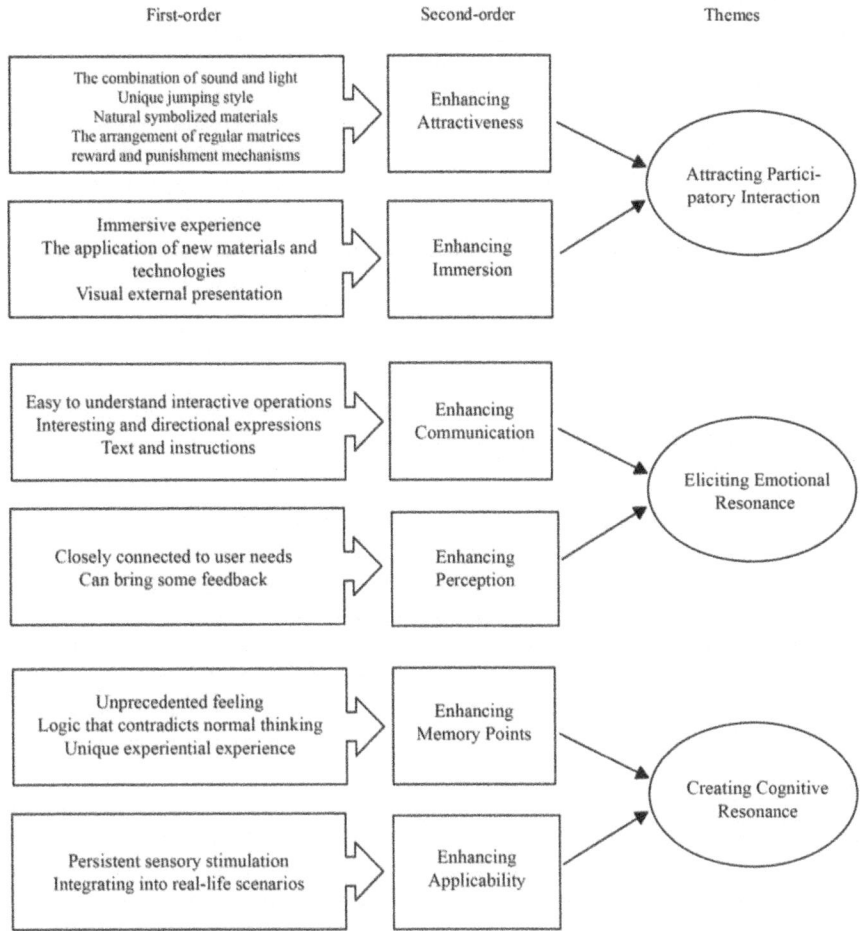

Fig. 2. Strategies to Stimulate Speculative Thinking and Reconcile Wicked Problems

if you join a job that requires overtime, you might choose to comply to keep the job" (P4).

Personal interests seem to overshadow collective ones, and the lack of timely feedback mechanisms clashes with the fast-paced nature of contemporary society. P7 and P8 observed, "If we do something that takes too long, people won't be willing to do it" (P7), highlighting a focus on immediate personal benefits. P4 noted, "For ordinary people, these issues are quite distant and more of a minority's concern" (P4). However, if everyone holds this view, the systemic problems of our planet will persist and remain unresolved, as they are collective issues requiring collective action. The transformation of consciousness is crucial in reconciling wicked problems. Through design interventions, more people can shift their awareness, reach a consensus, and collectively create a desirable future.

Difficulty in Changing Mindsets. Interactive installation art requires sustained audience engagement to have a deep impact. However, due to a lack of attractiveness and challenge in design, audiences often struggle to maintain long-term engagement. This top-down approach places users in a passive acceptance mode. Regarding environmental pollution, P1 said, "It's more about governments setting policies and enforcing them, but from a personal perspective, we can't really feel it" (P1). Large-scale policies can influence user behavior through moral or regulatory guidance, but this also creates issues, as P1 stated, "Because everyone is doing it, we are forced to comply" (P1). Current communication methods, such as documentaries or public service ads, are unidirectional, leading to a lack of enthusiasm and voluntary participation. P4 remarked, "It's hard for people to change things; it takes a long time and a strong will" (P4). However, once a positive mindset is established, passive acceptance can turn into proactive execution, greatly alleviating wicked problems. Design can facilitate the output of positive ideologies, using engaging interactive methods to subtly change mindsets and behaviors.

Restricted Sensory Engagement in Interactive Communication

Conflict Between Technical Complexity and User-Friendliness. While there are numerous interactive installations, many are focused on self-expression rather than effective communication of values from abstract to concrete forms. P7 articulated, "In Shanghai, there are many installation arts, but it's often unclear what the artist intends to express because public art tends to be highly artistic" (P7). Indeed, existing installation art remains an art form, often leaning towards inner expression, creating gaps in communication. P3 also noted, "Some things are conveyed abstractly and are not felt by ordinary people" (P3).

Moreover, many interactive designs remain superficial, lacking deeper guidance for reflection. Simple interactions, such as touchscreens or buttons, are easy to implement but fail to inspire deep reflection and behavioral change, hindering the goals of speculative design. P2 stated, "Ordinary people find it hard to understand, despite the artists having more ideas" (P2). While professionals may appreciate the artistic angle, reconciling wicked problems requires collective consensus. Therefore, value transmission needs to consider the audience's receptiveness. "Adding text or introductions might help users understand better" (P3). Future strategies should balance comprehensive value transmission with technical complexity and user-friendliness.

Conflict Between Design Universality and User Diversity. Interactive installation art must balance personalized experiences and universality. The user experience is crucial, and resonance with the audience enhances the impact. However, current installations often lack this, as users come from diverse backgrounds, encompassing different ages, cultures, and technical skills. P2 remarked, "The time spent interacting is short, and some may not be interested" (P2). Balancing personalization and universality remain a major challenge. Overly personalized designs may not suit all users, while overly universal designs might not meet specific needs. This contradiction complicates design efforts to cater to all user needs.

Additionally, the fast-paced society must be considered. "In a busy life, many can't find the time to engage deeply" (P3). P7 added, "Some installations look similar, just part of the city's public art, so the impact of installation art depends on its design" (P7). This indicates that current interactive art installations struggle to deeply touch individuals. In a rapidly evolving era, people are pressured by time, making it difficult for interactive installations to evoke profound speculation without significant sensory engagement.

Difficulty in Changing Behavior

Imbalance Between Technical Performance and Speculative Depth. Interactive installation art emphasizes audience participation, but this interaction is often superficial and immediate, lacking deep dialogue and reflection. Many works involve simple actions, such as touch or movement, leveraging technologies like VR, AR, and AI. While these technologies enrich artistic creation, their rapid iteration and attraction often lead to a focus on technical display over deep thought and reflection. "New technology in installation art can evoke deep feelings, but ensuring deep speculation is challenging" (P2). Users are easily captivated by technological spectacles, focusing on sensory stimulation rather than the deeper meaning behind the works. "It's a fleeting interest, more like a cursory glance, without further contemplation" (P2). Deep experiences are necessary to establish meaningful connections in such environments. Audiences tend to focus on their own experience rather than the profound meaning conveyed by the works.

Imbalance Between Behavioral Inertia and Frequency of Exposure. Most installation art pieces are exhibited in limited venues like museums or malls, restricting their exposure and audience reach. "The challenge is making a lasting impression after initial interest" (P2). P1 observed, "Installations can inspire thought, but the impact is often fleeting, making it hard to influence behavior" (P1). These unique installations are often difficult to reproduce outside specific spaces, requiring sustained output and broader environmental support for effective resolution. The overwhelming flow of information in society also reduces memory depth. P1 mentioned, "Over time, I might forget it. It fades from my consciousness, just a fleeting experience" (P1). Fast-moving audiences and limited viewing time make it hard for deep reflection. Inconsistent curation and thematic direction further hinder systematic, profound reflection experiences.

4.2   Strategies to Stimulate Speculative Thinking and Reconcile Wicked Problems

In Sect. 2, I delve into strategies to stimulate speculative thinking to reconcile wicked problems. A total of 66 quotes were classified under this theme. As shown in Fig. 2, these quotes were summarized into three second-order codes: (1) attracting participatory interaction, (2) eliciting emotional resonance, and (3) creating cognitive resonance.

Attracting Participatory Interaction. Users engage in participatory interactions by incorporating their daily behaviors into the interactive installation, receiving real-time feedback, and observing the potential impacts of their actions on future developments.

Enhancing Attractiveness. The first step in stimulating speculative thinking to change behavior is to use an appealing design to catch the user's eye. Compared to flat, two-dimensional promotional forms, interactive installation art has the advantage of providing an all-encompassing, three-dimensional perception, making it easier to shift from passive information transmission to active engagement. As P1 mentioned in the interview, "Compared to two-dimensional media, I'm particularly interested in interactive forms" (P1). In interactive installation art, visual aesthetics are key to attracting the audience. Designers should pay attention to harmonious proportions, using the golden ratio, symmetry, and rhythm to create visual comfort. For example, meticulously designed geometric shapes and lines can provide visual balance and beauty, thereby drawing the viewer's attention. "Something bizarre and out of place appearing in the space can make you suddenly jump out of the current environment" (P1). Material selection and texture presentation are also critical in interactive installation art design. Designers should choose appropriate materials based on the installation's theme and function, using the texture and tactile feel of the materials to enhance the audience's experience. For instance, using smooth metal, transparent glass, and soft fabrics can make the installation appealing both visually and tactilely. "An installation that left a deep impression on me was due to its specific texture and the rough grain of the material" (P1). As P4 noted, "I hope to see more diverse works that stand out visually" (P4). In summary, unusual shapes creating an extraordinary environment, rhythmic arrays, and the natural or complex texture of materials can increase the attractiveness of interactive installation art.

Enhancing Immersion. Combining technologies such as virtual reality (VR), augmented reality (AR), and artificial intelligence (AI) can create unprecedented visual and sensory experiences, enhancing the novelty and interactivity of the works, and increasing immersion. VR technology can immerse the audience in the virtual world of the artwork, AR can overlay virtual elements onto the real environment, and AI can adjust interactive content based on audience reactions in real-time. These technologies not only increase the appeal of the works but also attract the audience to participate for longer periods through realistic simulations and dynamic changes. P1 mentioned, "What left a deep impression on me was the immersive experience that shaped various sensory forms" (P1). Additionally, enhancing immersion through visual, tactile, auditory, and other sensory experiences is crucial. As P6 stated, "Incorporating stimuli for all five senses provides an immersive experience, making you feel like you are truly there" (P6). Creating artworks with visual impact and immersive experiences allows the audience to resonate and engage mentally, experiencing an interaction that cannot be felt in daily life, briefly escaping from reality, and immersing in the expression and output of the art.

Eliciting Emotional Resonance. Users perceive, think about, and analyze things through multi-sensory experiences. Sensory perceptions are transformed into rational understanding, leading to new emotional responses. By combining visual presentation with their personal context, users reflect on future scenarios resulting from their behaviors, stimulating their subjective initiative and shifting from passive policy reception to proactive awareness.

Enhancing Communication. Firstly, speculative thinking can simulate and experience future scenarios, allowing people to perceive possible futures in advance. When individuals are placed within these scenarios, they can preemptively transform the uncertain future into more desirable possibilities. As P7 mentioned, "People can't empathize with a lifestyle they haven't experienced, so speculative thinking is particularly helpful" (P7). While we can't experience future events directly, choosing themes that resonate with personal interests can highlight the importance of incremental changes. "With more interventions, perspectives change, making it easier to reconcile wicked problems" (P1).

Secondly, simple interactive behaviors can have significant value, accommodating a broader audience. "Meeting the demands of different types of people can promote partici-pation" (P1). By collecting and analyzing audience behavior data, interactive installation art can provide personalized interaction content based on each audience member's inter-ests and preferences. "Using more intuitive methods to show my ideas and creativity allows non-professional users to feel it too" (P6). AI can dynamically adjust interactive content based on audience reactions, giving each viewer a unique and personalized expe-rience, significantly enhancing the attractiveness of the work. P7 emphasized, "From a technical perspective, simplicity in interaction is crucial. If the interactive installation is too complex, users may feel fatigued and overwhelmed by additional information" (P7). Clear and concise visual communication design helps the audience quickly grasp the theme and intention of the artwork, enhancing the effectiveness of communication.

Enhancing Perception. Our initial research indicated that current installation art lacks sufficient perceptibility, with users feeling low relevance to grand themes during inter-active participation. Therefore, the proposed strategy emphasizes amplifying sensory experiences beyond straightforward images, text, and video, focusing on synesthetic experiences formed by emotions and imagination. "Creating a pure experience uncon-sciously leads me into a reflective process" (P1). "After performing a normal action, the installation provides a direct, heartfelt feedback" (P7). By understanding user percep-tion through interactive behaviors, the interaction transcends a cold, mechanical touch to achieve heartfelt, human-like interaction. "Some installations involve you in hands-on participation, immersing you and converting concepts into concrete actions" (P1). By abstractly understanding and interpreting synesthetic experiences using related imagery materials, the goal is to integrate emotions and achieve resonance. This process involves transforming external information input into personal perception and understanding through imagery and bodily experience, reflecting external environmental inputs through personal perception. "Change doesn't depend on what you do; it's about whether it can elicit empathy" (P4). "It has to be related to the individual and affect their real interests" (P6). "Interacting with the installation will touch them emotionally and also educate them to some extent" (P7).

Creating Cognitive Resonance. Experiencing interactive installations can lead to cog-nitive resonance, a higher level of interaction where users undergo a unique emo-tional experience on a cognitive level. Deep emotional stimulation transforms transient emotional responses into long-lasting cognitive resonance.

Enhancing Memory Points. One approach is to design interactive mechanisms that provide immediate dynamic feedback to audience actions, adjusting visual effects and sounds in real time based on audience movements or choices. Receiving feedback and rewards during participation enhances memory points. As P6 mentioned, "Users will change after receiving a punishment" (P6). Another approach is to use bizarre, coun-terintuitive design concepts to spark curiosity and create unforgettable memories. "An installation that left a deep impression on me was a Tetris game where the falling speed was extremely slow, defying normal logic" (P4). P1 also mentioned, "A clock with 13 h and another spinning rapidly sparked my thoughts" (P1).

Enhancing Applicability. Changing consciousness is a continuous and subtle process. Stimulating behavioral change through speculative thinking to reconcile wicked problems requires repeated scenario reenactments. P4 noted, "If it can be reenacted in daily life, the impression will be deeper, planting seeds that may change bad habits. Frequent activities and increased publicity are needed" (P4). Using public spaces for interactive installation art design can spread and influence more people. "Like fitness equipment, it doesn't need high costs but reaches many people" (P1). P8 added, "For long-term impact, it needs to subtly integrate into life, constantly reminding and influencing views" (P8). Enhancing the applicability of interactive installation art in public spaces, city streets, museums, and other locations allows more people to engage and participate, expanding the reach and impact of the works.

5 Discussion and Conclusion

This empirical study analyzed and categorized interaction design strategies for interactive devices, exploring (1) the obstacles encountered in the practical process of inspiring speculative thinking to reconcile wicked problems using interaction strategies, and (2) which interaction design strategies effectively inspire speculative thinking and reconcile wicked problems. Our findings indicate that the obstacles to stimulating speculative thinking and reconciling wicked problems include (1) limited consideration of grand intentions, (2) limited sensory communication, and (3) difficulty in changing behaviors. I also identified a series of interaction design strategies that effectively stimulate speculative thinking and reconcile wicked problems: (1) attracting participatory interaction, (2) eliciting emotional resonance, and (3) creating cognitive resonance. In this chapter, I will describe the contributions of these findings to the field of human-computer interaction (HCI), the implications for design practice, the limitations of the study, and directions for future research.

5.1 Contributions to HCI Research

This study is expected to contribute to the field of HCI in two main ways. The first contribution is expanding interaction design strategies and methods in the speculative design domain. Interactive devices are crucial in stimulating user speculation and creating effective paths for reconciling wicked problems to envision a desirable future. This study explores interaction design strategies to stimulate user speculation, providing assistance for subsequent researchers.

The second contribution involves expanding understanding of reconciling wicked problems through human-computer interaction. Researchers in the field of HCI are facing increasingly complex wicked problems. This study, from the perspective of stimulating speculation, provides a path for researchers in the field to reconcile these problems. Subsequent research will further explore interaction design strategies within this approach, providing inspiration and reference for design practice.

5.2 Implications for Design Practice

Our findings offer several insights for design practice. First, designers should emphasize the importance of engaging users through participatory interaction. By creating immersive and appealing interactive installations, designers can attract users to actively engage and reflect on the implications of their actions.

Emotional resonance is another critical factor. Designers need to consider how to evoke strong emotional responses that lead to deeper reflection and understanding. This can be achieved through multi-sensory experiences, using materials and technologies that enhance tactile, visual, and auditory stimulation.

Cognitive resonance, the transformation of transient emotional responses into long-lasting cognitive impacts, should also be a key consideration in design. Creating memorable and impactful interactions that provoke curiosity and reflection can lead to lasting behavioral changes.

Designers should integrate factors such as emotions and personal interests into their work, ensuring that the interactive experience is relevant and significant to the user. By doing so, they can create more effective designs that not only attract attention but also promote meaningful engagement and change.

5.3 Limitations and Future Research

While this study has provided valuable insights and addressed our research questions, it also has certain limitations. Due to the constraints of sample selection, certain demographics, regions, or cultural backgrounds were not fully covered, affecting the comprehensiveness and generalizability of the study. The choice to use thematic analysis for in-depth qualitative research, while suitable for our approach, involved a relatively small number of participants. Despite involving eight participants with diverse gender, age, practical experience, and theoretical backgrounds, there might be subjective biases from researchers that influenced the collection, analysis, and interpretation of interview data, potentially leading to biases.

These limitations are inherent to the chosen in-depth qualitative approach. Future research could explore more diverse audiences, including students, art practitioners, and workers, to gain a broader understanding. Additionally, incorporating varied data collection methods such as observations, questionnaires, and experimental methods can provide a more comprehensive understanding of speculative thinking dynamics and user reflection processes.

Future studies could also continue to explore a wider range of interaction design strategies. As exploratory research, I encourage subsequent studies to develop interactive prototypes to test and validate the proposed interaction design strategies in different scenarios and with diverse user groups. This would help in understanding the applicability and effectiveness of the strategies in real-world contexts, further contributing to the field of HCI and design practice.

References

1. Horst, R., Webber, M.: Dilemmas in a general theory of planning. Policy Sci. **4**, 155–169 (1973)

2. Buchanan, R.: Wicked problems in design thinking. Des. Issues **8**(2), 5–21 (1992)
3. Koesten, L., Simperl, E., Blount, T., Kacprzak, E., Tennison, J., Vermaas, P.E.: Revisiting rittel and webber's dilemmas: designerly thinking against the background of new societal distrust. Int. J. Hum. Comput. Stud. **135**, 530–545 (2020)
4. Rith, C., Dubberly, H.: Why horst W J Rittel matters. Des. Issues **23**(1), 72–91 (2007)
5. Dunne, A., Raby, F.: Speculative everything: design, fiction, and social dreaming. The MIT Press (2013)
6. Blythe, M.: Research through design fiction: narrative in real and imaginary abstracts. In: Proceedings of the SIGCHI Conference on Human Factors in Computing Systems (CHI14), pp. 703–712. Association for Computing Machinery (2014)
7. Farias, P.G., Bendor, R., van Eekelen, B.F.: Social dreaming together: a critical exploration of participatory speculative design. In: Proceedings of the Participatory Design Conference 2022 - Volume 2 (PDC22), vol. 2, pp. 147–154. Association for Computing Machinery (2022)
8. Yams, N.B., Muñoz, Á.A.: Poetics of future work: blending speculative design with artistic methodology. In: Extended Abstracts of the 2021 CHI Conference on Human Factors in Computing Systems (CHI EA 21), pp. 1–8. Association for Computing Machinery (2021)
9. Superflux. Mitigation of Shock (London). Superflux (2019). Retrieved 17 June 2021
10. Comber, R., Thieme, A.: BinCam: evaluating persuasion at multiple scales. In: Behavior Change Research and Theory, pp. 181–194. Academic Press (2017)
11. Jennings, P., Giaccardi, E., Wesolkowska, M.: About face interface: creative engagement in the new media arts and HCI. In: CHI06 Extended Abstracts on Human Factors in Computing Systems (CHI EA06), pp. 1663–1666. Association for Computing Machinery (2006)
12. Cooper, A., Reimann, R., Cronin, D., Noessel, C.: About face: the essentials of interaction design. Wiley (2014)
13. Malpass, M.: Between wit and reason: defining associative, speculative, and critical design in practice. Des. Cult. **5**(3), 333–356 (2013)
14. Esposito, E.: Can we use the open future? Preparedness and innovation in times of self-generated uncertainty. Eur. J. Soc. Theory 13684310231224546 (2024)
15. Ericson, M.: On the dynamics of fluidity and open-endedness of strategy process towarda strategy-as-practicing conceptualization. Scand. J. Manag. **30**(1), 1–15 (2014)
16. Barendregt, L., Vaage, N.S.: Speculative design as thought experiment. She Ji J. Des. Econ. Innov. **7**(3), 374–402 (2021)
17. Ahmadpour, N., Pedell, S., Mayasari, A., Beh, J.: Co-creating and assessing future wellbeing technology using design fiction. She Ji: J. Des. Econ. Innov. **5**(3), 209–230 (2019)
18. DiSalvo, C.: Spectacles and tropes: speculative design and contemporary food cultures. Fibreculture J. 109–122 (2012)
19. Fry, B.: Computational Information Design. PhD Thesis, MIT Media Lab (2015)
20. Fischer, P.T., Hornecker, E.: Urban HCI: spatial aspects in the design of shared encounters for media facades. In: Proceedings of the SIGCHI Conference on Human Factors in Computing Systems, pp. 307–316 (2012)
21. Kleinberger, R., Becker, M., Ras, E., Holzinger, A., Müller, P.: Ambient intelligence in assisted living: design challenges and future directions. In: Proceedings of the 5th International Conference on Pervasive Computing Technologies for Healthcare, pp. 1–4 (2019)
22. Ullmer, B., Ishii, H.: Emerging frameworks for tangible user interfaces. IBM Syst. J. **39**(3.4), 915–931 (2000)
23. Terry, G., Hayfield, N., Clarke, V., Braun, V.: Thematic analysis. The SAGE handbook of qualitative research in psychology, vol. 2 (2017)
24. Braun, V., Clarke, V.: Qualitative research in psychology using thematic analysis in psychology. Qual. Res. Psychol. **3**(2), 77–101 (2006)

Reflection and Practice of Design in Sustainable Community Building

Yichen Meng[1(✉)] and Liying Huang[2]

[1] TongJi University, Shanghai, People's Republic of China
miya_mengyc@163.com
[2] DESIGN Harvests, Shanghai, People's Republic of China

Abstract. As urban development progresses, rapid urbanization has disrupted original community structures and social relationships, leading to a decline in community cohesion and estrangement among neighbors. To address this, it is essential to enhance community interaction and cooperation to revitalize community vitality. Participatory design, as an effective approach, can fully engage residents' enthusiasm and participation, fostering interactive learning and continuous communication. It advocates for community issues to be resolved by internal community forces, ultimately achieving community self-management. However, sustainable community development is a dynamic process that requires ongoing adaptation and adjustment to various present circumstances. This paper aims to investigate how the level of designer involvement in participatory design impacts the effectiveness of sustainable community development, and how to effectively coordinate relationships among stakeholders to promote long-term community prosperity and harmony.

Keywords: Participatory design · Community building · Sustainability · Dynamic change

1 Introduction

In the field of design, participation in participatory design refers to the potential for users to intervene in and influence the project development process actively [1]. The fundamental principle is to incorporate public opinion into the decision-making framework, ensuring that design outcomes effectively and accurately meet users' needs and expectations. With its democratic and equitable characteristics, participatory design has rapidly and widely been applied in various fields such as urban planning, community development, and healthcare. It has become an effective tool for solving complex social problems [2]. Representing the basic units of urban systems, communities play a crucial role in social innovation and sustainable development. As community-building strategies shift from 'top-down' approaches—where government or central institutions lead, centralize decision-making, and swiftly advance projects—to more collaborative 'bottom-up' approaches—emphasizing grassroots community members' active participation and decision-making power to ensure solutions meet local needs—and "interactive" approaches—wherein government and community members engage in

M. Kurosu et al. (Eds.): HCII 2024, LNCS 15374, pp. 111–123, 2025.
https://doi.org/10.1007/978-3-031-76803-3_8

bidirectional interactions to achieve adequate resource support and grassroots feedback integration—participatory design is increasingly seen as an effective tool for connecting communities with residents.

However, this method faces many challenges in practical application. On the one hand, although participatory design is well-known in the design field, first-time participants often encounter knowledge and experience limitations. Many participatory design efforts fail to provide sufficient opportunities for participants to deeply engage, often occurring in the form of events where so-called 'participation' is merely symbolic, and the effectiveness of opinions and feedback, as well as their consideration in decision-making, remains uncertain. It undermines the effectiveness of participatory design, preventing it from achieving its intended democratization and inclusivity. Actual participatory design should ensure that all stakeholders have a substantial say in all stages of the design process and can significantly influence the design outcomes. On the other hand, even long-term projects require iterative reflection and reassessment throughout the process. Design projects rarely start with a clear definition; they often begin with a vague front end that must be explored and experimented with to gradually form clear goals and pathways. Adapting and revising the path to cope with complex conditions is essential. The renowned design scholar Donald A. Schön has elaborated on this process in his theory of reflective practice. Schön posits that design is a technical activity and a learning process in practice. This process encompasses "Reflection-in-Action," which refers to observing and reflecting on the current situation and actions in real-time, as well as "Reflection-on- Action," which involves reflecting on past actions after they have concluded, analyzing their successes and failures, and extracting lessons to make more informed decisions in the future. [3] This dual reflection mechanism, focusing on both immediate operational adjustments and thorough post-action analysis, promotes continuous learning and professional development.

Therefore, based on the theory of reflective practice, this study employs participatory observation to explore the dynamic changes in multi-party participation in long-term participatory design projects, particularly the role shifts and driving forces of design behavior throughout the process. By delving into these aspects, the study aims to reveal how changes in participation levels and strategic adjustments at different stages can lead to more sustainable community project operations, ultimately enhancing community effectiveness and social capital.

2 Background

2.1 Development of Participatory Design

The concept of democratization can be traced back to ancient Greek civilization. As a political system and a set of values, it is seen as the foundation of freedom, equality, and human rights, forming a crucial part of Western civilization's value system throughout the development of Western philosophical thought. Nurtured by these democratic ideas, social institutions emphasizing civil rights and participation took shape, reflected in daily practices such as trade unions and public decision-making. Participatory design originated in Scandinavia in the 1960s and 1970s as a response to the problem of workers' power being undermined by new technologies [4]. Designers collaborated with trade unions to promote active worker participation in the design process of information systems. This movement questioned the traditional technology-oriented design model and advocated for a more equitable and effective collaboration through user participation. In 1977, Alexander introduced the concept of 'pattern language' in his book A Pattern Language: Towns, Buildings, Construction, aiming not only to discover features that make environments beneficial and livable but also to achieve this goal through a participatory method that everyone could engage in, ensuring that environments could effectively and spontaneously emerge [5]. He encouraged designers to co-create with users and community members, emphasizing that the design process should be dynamic and open. Alexander sought to break the traditional expert-dominated design process through this method, empowering ordinary people with design authority.

Under the influence of participatory design, designers from various fields began to seek collaboration with those whose lives were affected by their designs. Their starting point was simple: people impacted by design outcomes should have a say in the design process. It is important to note that participatory design is not synonymous with "user-centered design," although they share many commonalities, such as tools and techniques. In user-centered design, users typically act as research subjects and feedback providers. Designers gather needs and feedback through various user research methods (e.g., interviews, surveys, and usability testing) and then design and improve based on this information. In contrast, participatory design respects users' subjectivity more, viewing them as equal partners [6]. Users are more involved in the design process, acting as information providers, active participants, and co-decision-makers.

Today, participatory design plays a significant role in product development and technological innovation and is gradually expanding into urban planning and community development as an innovative governance method. It is a fundamental element of social sustainability and participatory governance, playing a crucial role in enhancing public engagement in development projects and the implementation of sustainable development policies. Especially in addressing the complexity and polycentricity of modern society, design-led solely by experts can only partially meet the needs of different community groups. The participatory design ensures that final solutions genuinely serve the community by giving community members an equal voice and decision-making power, bringing multiple benefits to community development. Firstly, participatory design helps identify and solve actual community problems. Designers gain firsthand information through direct dialogue with community members, understanding the challenges and resources within the community to develop more precise and effective solutions. Secondly, participatory design is a trust-building process. Through long-term interaction and collaboration, community members and designers develop mutual understanding and respect, reducing resistance in the implementation process and promoting project completion. Finally, participatory design drives social innovation and encourages community members to contribute rich, creative, and diverse perspectives, generating more forward-thinking and innovative solutions.

2.2 Challenges of Participatory Design in Community Governance

Despite its effectiveness in addressing prominent community issues, participatory design faces many challenges in practice. The principles and practices of participatory design profoundly impact the human-made world but require considerable time to be realized. There are several reasons for this. Firstly, accepting and implementing the concept of co-creation requires designers and stakeholders to believe that everyone is creative, a belief only sometimes accepted [7]. Many still think creativity and design are the privileges of experts, while ordinary users need more knowledge and skills to participate in the design process. This perception hinders the broad acceptance and implementation of participatory design methods. Secondly, participatory design emphasizes active user participation and co-decision-making, which contrasts sharply with consumerist culture. In consumerist culture, personal happiness is often equated with purchasing and consuming material products rather than enhancing it through co-creation and participation in the design process. Consumerism emphasizes individuals as consumers rather than active participants and creators. This cultural background limits the promotion of participatory design, requiring people to shift from passive consumption to active participation and creation. Thirdly, with the development of new technologies, the relationship between technology and human experience has become increasingly complex and integrated, further complicating the implementation of participatory design. New technologies bring unprecedented complexity, requiring designers to consider user privacy, data security, and diverse user needs. These complexities demand higher levels of collaboration and reflection, making the design process more complex and time-consuming.

Another challenge for community action projects is developing and implementing new products and services through mutual learning and reflecting on the process and its outcomes. Participants may initially show high enthusiasm for many community projects, but their engagement often wanes as the project progresses. It is particularly evident in long-term community projects, making it difficult to sustain community support and feedback, affecting the long-term effectiveness of design solutions. Many participatory design models overly rely on traditional face-to-face interaction and communication methods, such as workshops, public consultations, and community meetings. While these methods promote direct communication and understanding among participants, they are often limited by time and space, making it challenging to achieve broad and continuous user participation. Meanwhile, participatory design is not merely a static process; it includes a dynamic process of investigation, understanding, reflection, development, and supporting mutual learning. These processes are realized through ongoing reflection and iterative adjustments throughout the design process. Design teams must remain engaged and collaborative throughout the project cycle, coordinating opinions, managing expectations, and ensuring continuous reflection and improvement despite time and resource constraints. Reflective practice emphasizes learning and adaptation in the design process, particularly in addressing complex and changing social environments.

To overcome the deficiencies below in existing participatory design models, this study uses reflective practice theory to provide a more dynamic and profound perspective. Schön's reflective practice theory emphasizes that design is not just a technical activity but a reflective practice process. Designers must continuously reflect on their actions and decisions during the design process, learning and adjusting their design solutions based on feedback and experience from practical operations [8]. This reflective thinking requires designers to examine issues from multiple angles, understand the needs and expectations of different stakeholders, and continuously test and adjust their assumptions and decisions throughout the design process. This mindset helps designers better address complexity and variability in community governance, ensuring that design solutions can adapt to the community's long-term development needs.

3 Research Methods and Pathways

This study employs participatory observation, a method in social survey research, to deeply understand the dynamic role changes in the long-term implementation of participatory design in community activities. As a qualitative research method, participatory observation requires the researcher to actively engage in the subjects' daily activities to obtain firsthand observational data and in-depth understanding. Long-term participatory observation is particularly effective in capturing subtle changes in daily interactions when dealing with complex social relationships and dynamic situations, providing comprehensive data support for thorough analysis and understanding of these changes.

The researchers were involved in two six-month community practice projects as observers and collaborators. Both projects are part of NICE Commune's innovative initiatives for exploring future sustainable community building. NICE Commune itself, as a composite space created by the NICE 2035 Future Living Line, aims to stimulate more interesting possibilities by integrating the lives and cultures of external communities and internal residents. Additionally, since most members of the NICE Commune have a design background, this provided ample research conditions for the study.

The entire research process is divided into three stages: preliminary preparation and relationship building, data collection based on observation, and data analysis and summarization. Before the project began, the researcher, as a member of the NICE Commune, had a basic understanding of the backgrounds of various representatives through other collaborative projects, which also established a certain level of relationship and trust. The researchers participated in the project planning process through project meetings and public consultations before the project started, observing participants' interactions and decision-making processes. After the project commenced, the researchers engaged in daily activities, including community meetings, workshops, and event organization. During this period, the researchers observed and recorded the participants' behaviors, verbal communications, and expressions of needs. In addition, the researchers collected project-related documents and materials, such as meeting minutes, activity photos, and community announcements, as valuable background information. In the final stage, by sorting through observation records, interview data, and other materials, the researchers summarized vital events and turning points in the entire participatory design process and analyzed the participation patterns and influencing factors at different stages. This study aims to deeply understand the practical application and effectiveness of participatory design in a community context and reveal the dynamic changes and complexities in the design process. The findings will provide empirical evidence and theoretical support for improving and optimizing participatory design models.

4 Case Study Description

4.1 Community Garden

The vision for the community garden project was to transform the external space of NICE Commune into a vibrant and lively garden within the streets where community residents live. The core goal was to empower community members through design, encouraging the active participation of diverse groups within the community. Over time, the aim was for residents to become the primary maintainers and operators of the garden. Additionally, the garden was envisioned as an open platform where external organizations could regularly host events, injecting fresh content into the community and stimulating residents' evolving needs and interests.

Project Preparation and Launch. Before the project's formal launch, NICE Commune collaborated with university clubs to form an interest group and conducted a series of community research activities. These included resident interviews, on-site observations, case studies, and brainstorming sessions. Subsequently, a co-creation workshop for garden design was held, involving community residents, nearby university students, and designers. Participants discussed the possibilities for the future garden, integrating the research findings from earlier activities. During the workshop, designers actively participated in each group, encouraging innovative designs to ensure everyone could fully express their ideas. These preliminary activities provided a platform for residents to voice their opinions and suggestions, helping to build stronger community relationships and enhancing their sense of identification and belonging to the project and the garden.

Crowdfunding and Co-creation. The construction of the garden employed a crowdfunding and co-creation approach. Key activities included crowdfunding for infrastructure and collaborative implementation of design plans. NICE Commune members coordinated and planned resources, including personnel, funds, materials, and equipment. They also participated in specific construction and planting activities, communicating closely with community members and volunteers. The plans were adjusted flexibly based on on-site conditions to respond to unforeseen situations.

Operational Phase. Once the garden entered the daily operational phase, NICE Commune established a maintenance plan based on weather conditions and plant characteristics. A schedule was created for registered members detailing the responsibilities of watering, weeding, and fertilizing. It ensured that everyone clearly understood their duties and tasks and committed to sharing the harvested fruits and mature seeds. This operational process not only liberated designers from daily management but also ensured the garden's long-term sustainability as members gradually adapted to their roles in self-management.

Steady Development Phase. As the garden developed steadily, it was redefined as a multifunctional community space. NICE Commune began exploring interesting content and invited external organizations to join and initiate themed activities, aiming to connect external communities with internal residents. By hosting diverse activities, the garden met the residents' entertainment and leisure needs and gained more recognition. It became a venue for education and cultural exchange, forming various interest groups.

Although the garden project did not continue due to the pandemic, each phase fully demonstrated the role of design participation and the responsibilities and powers involved. The project achieved the community garden's autonomous development and sustainable prosperity by gradually establishing trust with community members and enhancing their empowerment (Fig. 1) (Table 1).

Table 1. Record of phases for Community Garden Co-Creation

	Description	Construction	Observation
Phase 01	-Resident interviews, field observations, case studies -Design scheme co-creation seminar	-NICE Commune core members -Yocco core members -Community residents	The designer guided the volunteers to make innovative designs based on the design process and designed a participatory workshop for residents.
Phase 02	-Crowdfunding -Garden co-construction	-NICE Commune core members -Community residents -Volunteers	Coordinate and plan resources, including personnel, funds, materials, and equipment; They are also involved in specific construction and planting activities.
Phase 03	-Daily garden care -Emergency maintenance	-Community residents -Volunteers	The designer designed the maintenance manual and maintenance process, and the volunteers were responsible for the daily division of labor.
Phase 04	-Create a Bird Garden -Little Garden Monopoly game	-City Bird members -Student teams -Community residents -Volunteers	Continual events occur as various external organizations integrate their content with the little garden, designing themed activities.

4.2 Community Children's Music Concert

The Community Children's Music Concert project, jointly initiated by the NICE commune and the Austrian Music Association, aims to explore innovative forms of music-themed community activities. Initially focused on children's music activities, it gradually evolved into two branches: one retained the original choir format but incorporated elements such as painting and dance, while the other focused on developing professional music skills.

Project Initiation. Two workshops were organized at the start of the project, with core members from both sides participating in the program's design. The association's team, leveraging their expertise in music education, provided relevant suggestions. In contrast, the NICE Commune members focused on systematic analysis to ensure the project's suitability and appeal to the community.

Planning and Preparation. After drafting the plan, the NICE Commune designed the project flow, content, materials, and props to enhance the participant experience. Since the activities were non-profit, parents were not just service recipients but also volunteered

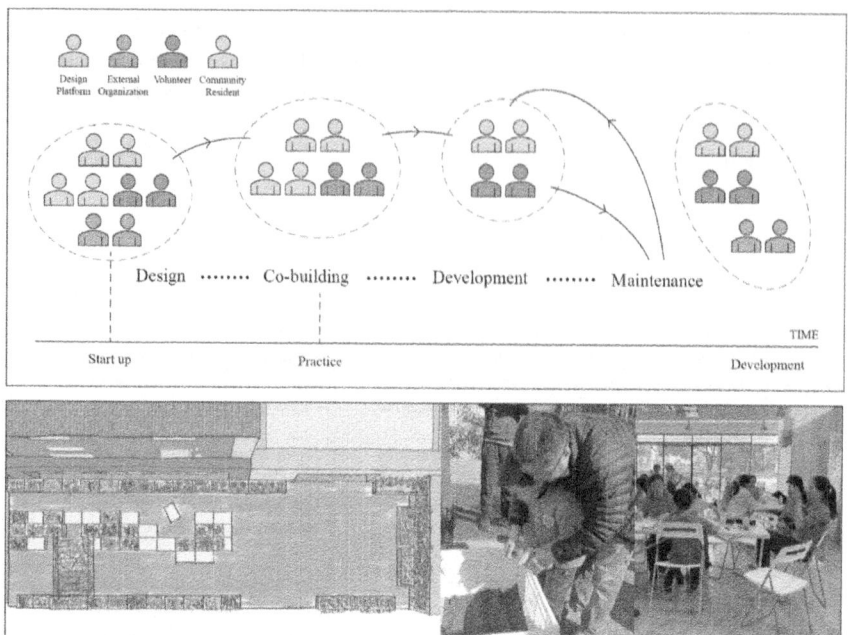

Fig. 1. Community Garden Co-Creation Project with Multi-Stakeholder Participation Content

to provide equipment and workforce. As the project progressed, some impracticalities and the hidden needs of various stakeholders became apparent. New three-way (NICE Commune, association, parents) co-creation workshops were deemed the best way to reflect and adjust during the process; with the help of co-creation tools, diverse needs from different perspectives emerged, fostering more empathetic understanding.

Activity Development. As the activities stabilized, considering the association's sustainable involvement and parents' educational aspirations for their children, two different development directions emerged: one branch retained the original choir format, iterating more new combinations by incorporating artistic elements like painting and dance. The other branch focused on cultivating children's professional knowledge through systematic music education to enhance their musical skills.

Reflection and Adjustment. Even after diverging into two activities, reflective summaries and agile adjustments were made to align with their unique community-oriented positioning.

Through these four stages of implementation, the Community Children's Music Concert project developed an effective participatory model for music-related activities in the community, whether for interest or educational purposes. It also revealed the differences in overall design and specification requirements due to the varied starting points of different types of activities (Fig. 2) (Table 2).

Table 2. Record of phases for Community Children's Music Concert Co-Creation

	Description	Construction	Observation
Phase 01	-Project seminar 1 -Project seminar 2	-NICE Commune core members -Austrian Music Association core members	In the scheme planning, designers take the lead, overseeing and coordinating the overall project.
Phase 02	-Community children's concert -Community children's choir	-NICE Commune core members -Austrian Music Association core members -Community parents	Designers are responsible for designing the activity content, materials, and props; They also propose enhancements to the activities and invite parents to participate in co-creation workshops.
Phase 03	-Community children's concert and painting -Community children's choir	-NICE Commune members (Volunteers) -Austrian Music Association members -Community parents (Volunteers)	Once the activity format is established, designers gradually delegate responsibilities to external organizations and parent volunteers to share the workload.
Phase 04	-Community children's concert and painting -Community children's choir	-NICE Commune core members -Austrian Music Association core members -Community parents	Designers regularly organize retrospectives on the activity process and content, providing feedback for iteration.

5 Process Results and Discussion

5.1 Design Inspiring Creative Thinking at the Project Initiation Stage

In the early stages of the project, the degree of design intervention was high, with significant effort and support invested to inject fresh content into the community by introducing external organizations. Within the community, design played the role of facilitator and motivator, using various visual expressions and innovative tools to guide residents in breaking traditional thinking patterns and igniting their enthusiasm for participation. For external participants, their usual goals when providing support are project success and community development. However, actual results indicate that the relationship between external organizations and the community is not just a one-way transfer of resources and technical support but a two-way learning process. Moreover, design thinking acted as a catalyst for change within external organizations, helping them improve and upgrade project content, subtly influencing the work patterns of organizational members, and fostering a culture of innovation within the broader business framework.

If viewing the community as a stable and somewhat closed environment, any attempt to introduce external elements may be disruptive, altering familiar lifestyles and community settings. Establishing emotional connections is the first step in successful community building. Transparent communication and information sharing are crucial for building

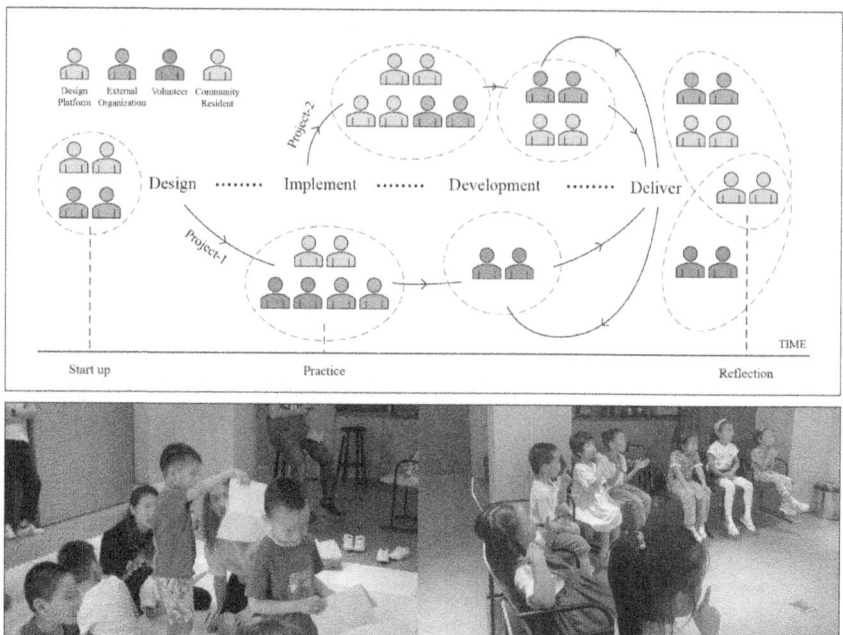

Fig. 2. Community Children's Music Concert Co-Creation Project with Multi-Stakeholder Participation Content

trust among the three parties, which is one reason for the high degree of design participation. Regularly hosting workshops and discussion meetings, the team maintained open communication with community members, ensuring all critical decisions and steps were publicly explained in detail, thus eliminating distrust due to information asymmetry. Through small successes, the team demonstrated their capability and commitment, making community members feel understood and supported, laying a solid foundation for the project's subsequent smooth progression.

5.2 Power Transfer During Project Development

As the project's content and frequency of activities stabilized, the initially solid tripartite collaboration gradually evolved. The NICE Commune team began transferring power to external teams and residents, forming a new mutual support structure that enabled them to drive the project's continuous progress autonomously. The process of transferring power and responsibility was gradual, allowing external teams and residents to accumulate the necessary skills and experience incrementally, taking on more management and operational tasks with the necessary guidance and support to alleviate the pressure and discomfort of sudden responsibilities. As participation deepened, participants developed a sense of belonging to the community, and collaboration further reinforced their sense of ownership. The gradually deepening integration of identity and responsibility helped enhance community autonomy and promote sustainable development.

Could excessive decentralization and democratization negatively impact sustainability? In community projects, increasing participation might achieve short-term continuity and stability, but overly dispersed power could lead to unclear responsibilities, ineffective governance structures, and weakened leadership. It could make decision-making processes lengthy and inefficient, increasing potential conflicts. Therefore, balancing the degree of decentralization is crucial for maintaining short-term and long-term sustainability.

5.3 Reflective Practice in Design

Finally, in regular review and iteration sessions, design is re-engaged as a diagnostic tool, breaking down complex processes into analyzable actions, carefully examining the outcomes of these actions, and making appropriate responses, forming a continuous improvement loop. This reflective practice promoted the professional growth of designers and played a vital role in the project's long-term success. Reflective practice cultivated systemic thinking, enabling designers to see broader impacts and interdependencies, thus formulating more comprehensive and sustainable design solutions. During the reflection process, not only did designers benefit personally, but the involvement of multiple stakeholders also ensured the comprehensiveness and practicality of the project improvement process. Unlike other research that typically focuses on outcomes, this approach emphasized learning and growth during the process and the professional development of different roles within the project.

6 Enhancing the Longevity of Community Participatory Design

Participatory design projects aim to ensure that users participate as full partners in the design process, emphasizing continuous interaction to optimize design solutions and engage in action throughout the design process [9]. In these projects, participatory design is not merely a tool for promoting community participation but a process that drives innovation and systemic change. One notable observation is that participatory design successfully breaks the boundaries of traditional design through cross-disciplinary collaboration and ongoing community involvement, creating a new form of social capital. This social capital is evident in the project's outcomes and the trust and cooperative relationships established among community members. Social capital can be defined as the resources formed through social networks, shared norms, and trust relationships, which help improve community cohesion and cooperative efficiency [10]. Putnam's theory of social capital posits that community social capital is enhanced through three key elements: networks, norms, and trust relationships. Social networks refer to the interconnectedness among community members; norms are the shared codes of conduct and values, and trust relationships indicate the degree of mutual trust among community members.

In this participatory design project, designers and community members build close social networks through continuous interaction and collaboration. It drives the success and sustainability of the projects and promotes overall community development and systemic change. These observations and analyses validate Putnam's social capital theory and demonstrate the significant potential of participatory design in enhancing community cohesion and cooperative efficiency. Another noteworthy observation is that in traditional participatory design models, designers often play the roles of leaders and decision-makers, while community members are typically passive participants. However, the NICE Community Garden project and the Community Children's Music Concert project illustrate how community members transform from passive participants to active builders and leaders. The application of Contingency Theory [11] in these cases reveals the profound impact of the dynamic adjustment of the designer's role and flexible leadership on project outcomes. Contingency Theory emphasizes that leadership and management strategies should be adjusted according to changing situations to improve organizational effectiveness. This flexible role transition, adopting different leadership styles and strategies at various stages to adapt to the evolving needs and environments of the projects, exemplifies the practical application and value of Contingency Theory and dynamic empowerment in participatory design.

In summary, promoting the longevity of community participatory design involves:

Building Social Capital. Continuous interaction and collaboration among designers and community members create robust social networks, shared norms, and trust relationships, enhancing community cohesion and cooperative efficiency.

Empowering Community Members. Transforming community members from passive participants to active builders and leaders increases their capabilities and confidence, improving project sustainability and success.

Flexible Leadership and Dynamic Adjustment. Applying Contingency Theory by adjusting leadership and management strategies to changing situations ensures the project's effectiveness and adapts to evolving needs and environments.

These strategies collectively foster a sustainable and effective participatory design process, ultimately contributing to the community's overall growth and systemic improvement.

References

1. Scariot, C.A., Heemann, A., Padovani, S.: Understanding the collaborative-participatory design. Work **41**(Supplement 1), 2701–2705 (2012)
2. Sanoff, H.: Participatory design: a historical perspective. J. Arts Architect. Res. Stud. **2**(3), 12–21 (2021)
3. Munby, H.: Reflection-in-action and reflection-on-action. Curr. Issues Educ. **9**(1), 31–42 (1989)
4. Sanoff, H.: Multiple views of participatory design. Focus **8**(1), 7 (2011)
5. Alexander introduced the concept of 'pattern language' in his book A Pattern Language: Towns, Buildings, Construction (1977)
6. Sanders, E.B.N.: From user-centered to participatory design approaches. Design and the social sciences, pp. 18–25. CRC Press (2002)
7. Sanders, E.B.N., Stappers, P.J.: Co-creation and the new landscapes of design. Co-design **4**(1), 5–18 (2008)
8. Schon, D.: donald schon (schön): learning, reflection and change. **11** (2004). Accessed April 1983

9. Robertson, T., Simonsen, J.: Challenges and opportunities in contemporary participatory design. Des. Issues **28**(3), 3–9 (2012)
10. Putnam, R.: Social capital: measurement and consequences. Can. J. Policy Res. **2**(1), 41–51 (2001)
11. Donaldson, L.: The contingency theory of organizations. Sage (2001)

Let the Music Play: How Can One Test the Impact of Auditory Stimuli on User Experience (UX)?

Abhijai Miglani[✉] and Anushi Singh Thakur

Gurugram, India
miglaniabhijai@gmail.com, anushisinghthakur@gmail.com

Abstract. The research covers a novel approach around how one can test the impact of inclusion of auditory stimulus on user experience at commonly occurring touch points on digital platforms like notifying, splash screens and payment success indication. The study initiates with a review around what is user experience, the domain of sound design and existing potential sound design testing methods. Then building up a new agile method of testing impact of these sounds on UX and brand identity by combining Attrakdiff questionnaire with brand traits and specific sound characteristics. The results from the study helped in identifying crucial brand traits for designing auditory stimulus specific to the brand along with the effect of designed sounds on the existing UX and the preference of sounds for the concepts being tested.

Keywords: User Experience · Sound design · Brand identity · Auditory stimulus · Card sorting · Sound characteristics · Attrakdiff · Survey · Notification sound · MOGO (Splash screen sound) · Payment success indication

1 Introduction

1.1 User Experience (UX)

With respect to user experience, Don Norman is considered as the father of UX. The term 'user experience' was first coined by Norman, Miller, & Henderson (1995) in their research focusing on the human interface systems at Apple. They define user experience as the experience between a human being and a system, which also covers concepts such as usability. As per Norman, user experience entails satisfaction of core user needs while interacting with a human interface system with the user not feeling frustrated. ISO 9241-210 (DIS 2010) also defines user experience as "a person's perceptions and responses that result from the use or anticipated use of a product, system or service". Post introduction of the term UX by Norman, various other definitions and frameworks were introduced. Berni & Borgianni (2021) explains some of the other evolved definitions for user experience (UX).

Usability on the other hand as defined in (ISO/TS 20282-2:2013(en) Usability of consumer products and products for public use—Part 2: Summative test method) is the

M. Kurosu et al. (Eds.): HCII 2024, LNCS 15374, pp. 124–173, 2025.
https://doi.org/10.1007/978-3-031-76803-3_9

"extent to which a product can be used by specified users to achieve specified goals with effectiveness, efficiency, and satisfaction in a specified context of use". Effectiveness in the definition of usability is fundamental as it is about achieving the intended goals.

1.2 Auditory Displays and Sound Design

Wickens, Lee, Liu, & Gordon-Becker (2003) explains some of the heuristic principles for auditory displays design. Like visual displays involve usage of visual senses to interact with the system, auditory displays involve usage of auditory senses to interact with the interface. Auditory displays can involve usage of different auditory mediums. Bhattacharya, Das, Sahu, Borah, & Mondal (2021) proposes a classification of sound with different audible mediums like environmental sound, speech and music. Some of the important heuristics for auditory display design as mentioned by Wickens are: a) The alarm must be heard over background noise (alarm should be tailored to be atleast 15dB above the threshold of hearing above the noise level/30dB difference above the noise level in order to guarantee detection), b) alarm should not be above the danger level of hearing, c) alarm should not be overly startling or abrupt, d) should not disturb other tasks like communication and the main task for which the sound is being provided, d) sound could be informative signaling the nature of emergency and indicating appropriate action to take, e) must not be confusing with other sounds/should not impose on the human's restrictive limits of absolute judgement.

A survey by Winn & Hereford (1994) specifies the state of the art of sound usage in Human-Computer Interaction domain. The main important topics of that overview are: Earcons (symbolic and iconic), and sound in data sonification and in virtual reality environments. The literature study further mentions successes and problems of these interfaces, encouraging the reader to explore further. The paper concludes with some guidelines for the interface designer who uses sound, encouraging to improve the knowledge about how people interpret auditory messages.

1.3 Existing and Potential Sound Design Testing Methods

Moesgaard, Hulgaard, & Bødker (2020) explains some of the participatory design methods/collaborative practices in the field of sonic interaction design. Some of the methods explored in their research are – sound walking, sound sketching, think-aloud etc. Sound walking as explained by (Westerkamp) is "any excursion whose main purpose is listening the environment". Sound walking as used in the research by Moesgaard et al. is a) without a recorder and headphones and b) with a recorder and headphones. Their research is about exploring the sounds at Copenhagen metro station and ideation around the same. After the soundwalk, the participants in the research by Moesgaard et al., were debriefed and interviewed in order to describe and analyse how moving through the sonic context of the metro felt. Leading up to an unstructured interview, the researcher conducted a short think-aloud procedure, asking the participants to tell what immediately stood out as significant for them. Sound sketching on the other hand as explained by Ekman & Rinott (2010) is a type of vocal prototyping method wherein designers vocalize sounds in the form of interaction gestures.

Jeon (2014) also explains other participatory methods in the sound design domain like sound card sorting, sound-emotion mapping, constructing dimensions and positioning etc. Sound card sorting is an exercise wherein one can map different sound stimulus with its functions. In the research, Jeon et al. has made sound cards representing different sound stimulus which the research participants can map with index cards representing different functions. Figure 1 describes the sound card sorting exercise. Sound-emotion mapping is done by Jeon et al. in the form of a smart digital application. In this application, research participants are presented with a question and an emotion (Like for instance, which sound represents the emotional keyword better – happy). For the question, there are two emotions given which are essentially two sound stimuli. Figure 2 shows a snapshot of the application. Constructing dimensions and positioning method on the other hand has a likert scale (with emotions adjectives) on which a sound stimulus is rated for its appropriateness. Based on the analysis done for the rating results, one can create maps like in Fig. 3.

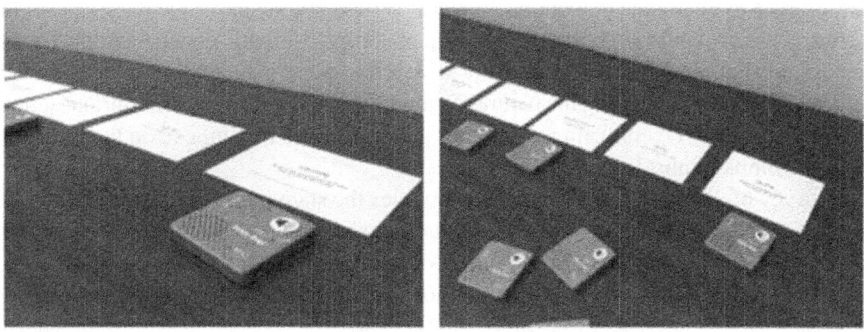

Fig. 1. Sound card sorting task. Participants are asked to make pairs between the index cards and the sound cards (Jeon 2014).

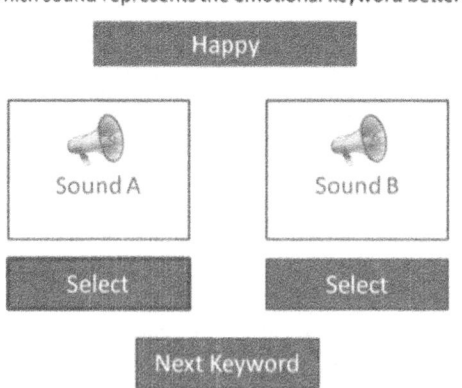

Fig. 2. Sound emotion mapping: participants compare the pairs (Jeon 2014)

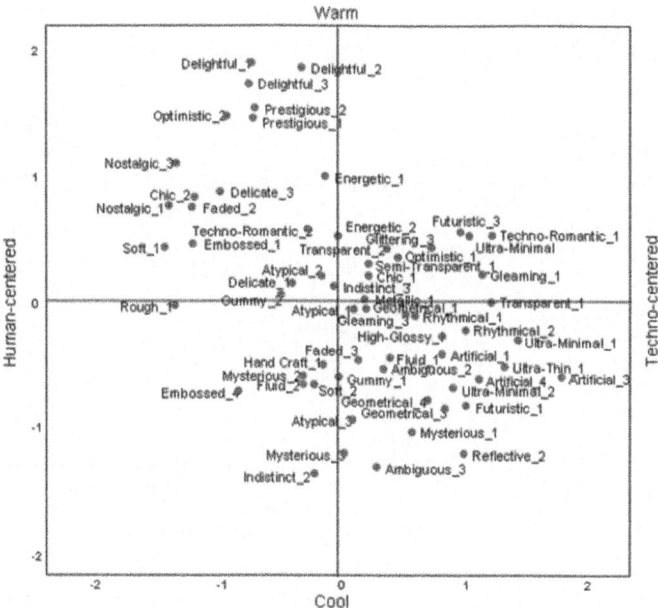

Fig. 3. Sound specific conceptual dimensions (Jeon 2014)

Furthermore, Hassenzahl, Burmester, & Koller (2003) presents Attrakdiff questionnaire for measuring hedonic and pragmatic attributes of user experience. Vieira, Providência, & Carva (2023) on the other hand has used a mini version of Attrakdiff questionnaire with 10 items for designing a smart garment. Attrakdiff questionnaire can be used to study how user experience varies with the introduction of auditory stimulus in a digital application.

Looka, a logo maker platform has derived 52 personality traits from Aaker (1997) dimensions of brand personality. These traits are further used in this research to get answers around the research questions related to brand recall. Figure 4 shows these personality traits.

Fig. 4. Brand personality traits as defined by Looka

2 Research Scope

The existing methods are either equipment heavy or time consuming in terms of taking user feedback, furthermore none of the existing methods aims at measuring impact of auditory stimulus on the existing UX and brand identity or identifying traits that are relevant to auditory stimulus.

The new method proposed is an effort to measure the mentioned points in a fast-paced environment to get quick feedback on sound designed for digital platforms.

3 Research Questions

The research questions were as follows:

- How does inclusion of different sound stimuli in different workflows of a digital application impact user experience?
- How are the proposed auditory concepts performing in terms of required characteristics, user expectations and brand recall?

4 Methodology

4.1 Tool for Data Collection

Since the study aimed at understanding larger sentiment and impact of auditory stimulus, quantitative approach was taken via surveys for data collection.

A survey was created (with referring to above mentioned questionnaires from Sect. 1.3) to get answers for the research questions and to distribute it to bigger audience – sample size considered was n = 180, with 60 participants in each of the 3 groups (between study design). The groups were different from each other with respect to the type of sound stimuli exposed to. Each group was further divided into 3 cohorts. The cohorts were different from each other with respect to whether they have subscribed to the digital application or not (application for which the different sound stimuli were made). Fair mix was also ensured across gender (18–60 years old), geography (Tier 1 and 2 PAN India cities), devices used to access the digital application and usage duration for the digital application.

The survey was created in a digital format and was filled by the participants in the presence of researchers. The researchers were present with the participants to address any questions, a participant may have. At a time, 2–3 participants (along with 2–3 researchers) were filling the survey in different rooms. Also, the survey was created in English and Hindi languages. For Hindi language, the Attrakdiff and Looka brand personality traits were also translated to Hindi. The same can be found out in the Appendix.

4.2 Instrument

There were 3 sections of the survey.

First Section. It was introductory section and was more like a screener to recruit the relevant audience cohorts and understand their demographics.

Second Section. Aimed at understanding the existing brand awareness by exposing the respondents to brand logo and taking inputs on their overall experience with the brand (Looka – as explained in Sect. 1) and UX of the platform being tested for (using Attrakdiff scale).

Based on the different auditory stimuli testing methods proposed in Sect. 1.3, it was decided to refer to Attrakdiff and Looka brand traits for answering the research questions. Attrakdiff questionnaire is a reliable and valid questionnaire to measure user experience and also the semantic differential adjectives used in the questionnaire resonated with the sound design domain, so a decision was taken to refer to Attrakdiff. Looka brand traits served as a ready to use list of brand traits covering the major brand archetypes in simpler words to take faster feedbacks.

Third Section. It focused on understanding the perception and recall of auditory stimulus to quantify the overall impact that sounds can bring to a platform and optimize the touchpoints for sound inclusion. Questions asked were: a) In what situations do you think sound is helpful to you (MCQ)?, b) Can you recall the applications on which you may have heard sounds (MCQ)?,

Then the participants were exposed to the auditory stimulus and the change in response was recorded for the same parameters as in section one with additional feedback on specific sound characteristics required for each touch point.

The respondents were also asked to arrange the different auditory stimulus in order of most to least resemblance to the brand and rate the concepts for their specific characteristics. For a particular group of auditory stimulus the following rating scale questions were asked:

- Group-1/MOGO sound: I would like to hear this sound every time I open the application - (5 point Likert)
- Group-2/Notification sound: The sound you selected is alerting – (5 point Likert)
- Group-2/Notification sound: I would like to have a distinct notification sound for the product – (5 point Likert)
- Group-2/Notification sound: I change my phone's notification settings - (5 point Likert)
- Group-3/Payment success sound: The sound I selected depicts completion/success - (5 point Likert)

A final question was asked around whether the respondents would like to hear the different auditory stimulus in the application itself and the reasons behind it to get some insights around why was a particular sound design appreciated or what made users not to opt for auditory stimulus.

5   Results and Discussion

5.1   Sample Size and Confidence Levels

For the given study, considering population as 10 crores (based on no. of application downloads on Playstore. Since this would also include repeated downloads and uninstallations it will balance the unaccounted Appstore downloads), sample size of 180 gives confidence level in between 80–85% with margin of error as 5% (Fig. 5).

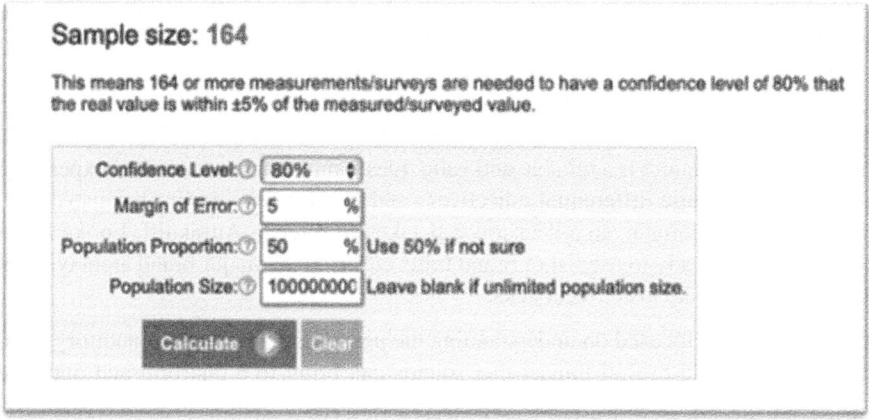

Fig. 5.   Sample size calculation from calculator.net

5.2   Existing Identity Awareness

177/180 participants were able to recall sonic branding from one brand or the other indicating that for majority of application/smart phone users sound does play an important role in creating recall for brands (Fig. 6).

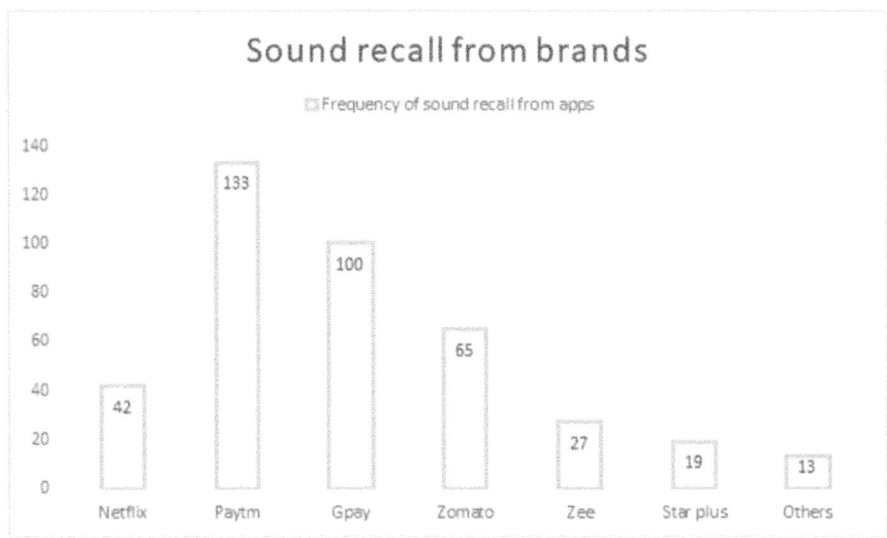

Fig. 6. Sound recall from different brands/ applications

Apart from given options users were able to recall sounds like mobile turning on, Ad alerts and sounds from applications like Candy saga, PhonePe, Voot, Jio etc.

5.3 Feedback on Sound

Agreement of Users on Wanting Sound Concepts Heard on Application. 139/180 Overall agreement of users on wanting concepts heard on the application. Majority of respondents who opted "No" were not the users of the application (Count - 23) (Fig. 7).

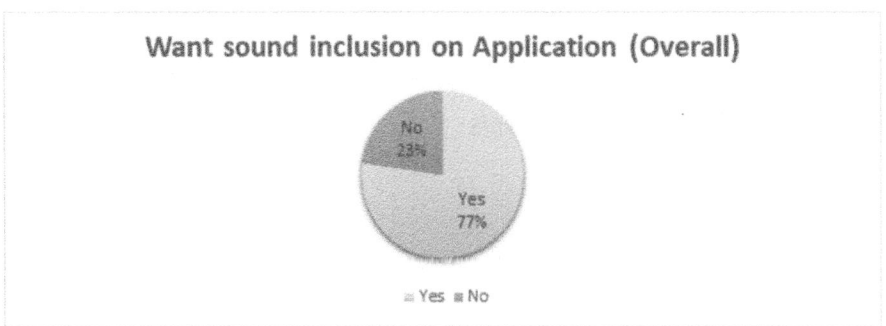

Fig. 7. Agreement of users on wanting concepts heard on application

Utility of Sound in Different Situations. Figure 8 shows the distribution of situations in which respondents found sound useful. Other situations they mentioned were – message alerts, refreshing their mood and giving cautionary indications.

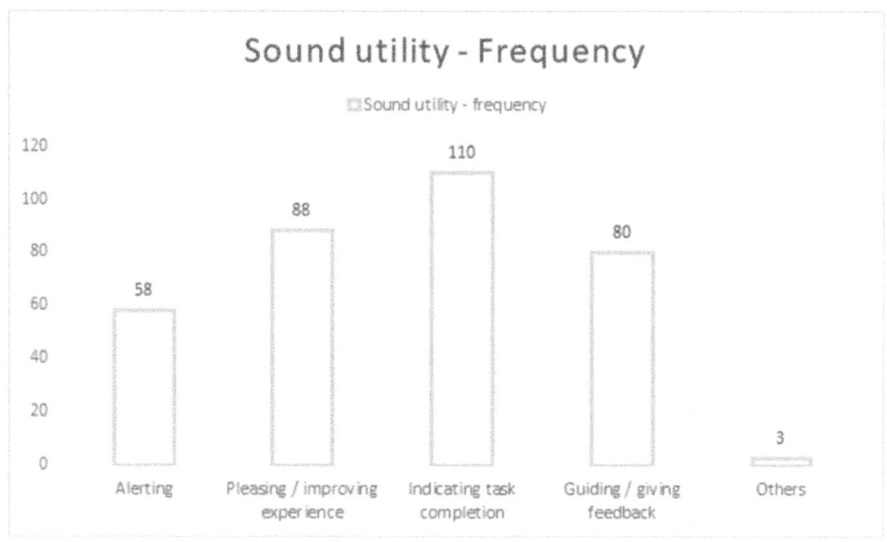

Fig. 8. Frequency of utility of sound in different situations

5.4 Feedback on Sound Concepts

Tests for normality and significance of preference order of different groups' sounds:

1. Mogo, notification as well as payment success all 3 sounds were not normally distributed as was concluded from Shapiro wilk test (p < 0.05) i.e. hence non parametric tests for inferential statistics were performed.
2. Friedman test was conducted for testing significance of ranking for specific groups (MOGO, notification and payment success). It was found that only for payment success, the ranking is significant.

    Details for the above-mentioned tests can be found out in Appendix.

5.5 Group-1/MOGO Sound Concepts

Fig. 9. Mean score of agreement on wanting to hear MOGO sound on opening the application

Figure 9 gives an overview of agreement on wanting to hear MOGO sound on opening the application. Respondents mentioned the following reasons for liking group-1 concepts:

- Newness: "If application is doing something new then it's really good as we always appreciate new things and the sound is very nice in listening"
- The sound was considered attractive, catching, innovative, alarming, pleasant, motivating, sophisticated, relaxing, unique, enjoyable, friendly, melodious and delightful by the respondents.

  "I liked the tones that I have just heard & and I would like to listen to them if it comes in the application."

  "I heard it & I feel it's amazing sound something special"

  " The music is full of positive vibes, It has a Dolby effect"

  "It is very melodious and clear sound; The sound has very relief kind of feeling which makes mind so relax and cool"

  " The sound has a motivating effect"

  "The sound is very sleek but sophisticated"

  " This sound is very attractive and soothing in hearing"

- It seems innovative and I will get the updates in a new way by this sound (5 people thought of it as way of getting updates), The sound is very alarming; As it has something new so I liked it; Every sound has something new in it so I like all the sounds that I heard
- Familiarity: "It seems familiar but still I like this sound, It seems some kind of very familiar sound"
- Point of difference: "This sound makes the application different from others.

  "The sound is quite nice and unique"

  " It's trying to increase enjoyment"

- Connection to brand:"it makes me feel connecting with the app; we can identify that its from the application brand considered in research"

  " it looks like advance technology so everyone can feel delightful"

Respondents mentioned the following reasons for NOT wanting MOGO on the application:

- Not using application: "I am not using this app so can't say anything"
- Unaffected: "It's not effecting me anymore,not so good not bad just"

  "I don't have any interest in sound ,I just love to watch the contents on the application; As I only watching"

- Old concept: "As I heard this sound it's feel like very old and have listened this type of tone many times; I am not feeling anything new in this sound"

" I don't like hearing the same tone again and again as it seems very common sound"

" I don't like it's notifications sound as it's not has anything new in it"

- Sharpness: "The sound is very sharp which is not pleasant to hear"

Group – 2/Notification Sound Concepts. Users showed satisfactory agreement on current notification concepts being alerting and wanting a distinct notification sound for the application. They also agreed that they willingly change their notification settings at times (Fig. 10, 11 and 12).

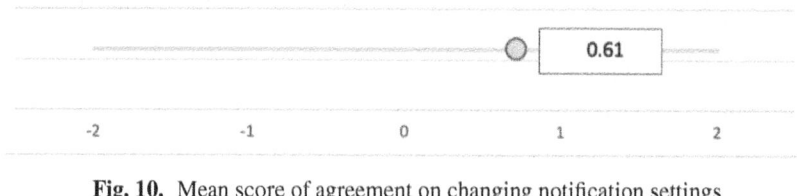

Fig. 10. Mean score of agreement on changing notification settings

Fig. 11. Mean score of agreement on wanting distinct notification for the application

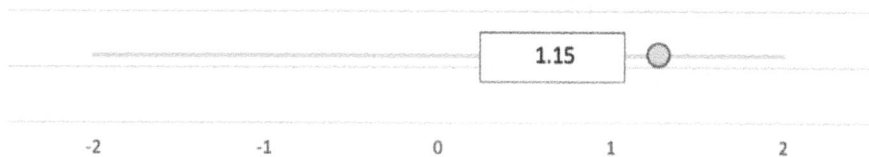

Fig. 12. Mean score of agreement on notification concepts being alerting

Respondents mentioned the following reasons for liking notifications concepts:

- They found the concepts clear, alerting (like a SMS), connecting, new, soothing, cool, familiar, refreshing, attractive and informing.

"It's very clear and I like this sound"

"The sound is good because its suits with the brand image"

"It's good in listening and helpful as an alert"

" It's like an alarm sound, but good in listening, It's like a SMS tone (many); It's good in listening and helpful as an alert"

"It's good thing if we will get anything new in the brand application and the sound is also very clear and soothing"

"The sound is very fresh and creative"

"This makes mind stress-free and has pleasant sound"

"because if we get notification sounds we will know that movie is there and we can click and see."

Respondents mentioned the following reasons for NOT wanting Notification concepts on the application:

- Old concept: "Not seems very new in hearing"; " I think I have heard this sound earlier before"
- Change:" I like the current sound of the application, as I have been using it for a long time and if it changes suddenly then it will not sound good to me."
- Unaffected: "Actually I don't have any such kind of comment to say as I have interest in only watching the contents in the application."
- Other: The sound seemed unrealistic and similar to sound of phone turning on

Group – 3/Payment Success Sound Concepts. Users agreed that payment success concepts did evoke some kind of feeling of completion or success on hearing (Fig. 13).

Fig. 13. Mean score of payment success concepts evoking feeling of completion/success

Respondents mentioned the following reasons for liking payment success concepts:

- Familiarity – "It's just like SMS tone which i heard many times,but nice"
- Classy – "It seems me old but classy"
- Unique – "It seems something unique"

"The sound is very attractive"

"I have heard some sounds in other apps also but it seems something new"

- Soft: "It is very light and soft kind of sound, I liked it"
- Short – "Sound clip is short and good in hearing"

Respondents mentioned the following reasons for NOT wanting Payment success concepts on the app:

- Alerting: "Music like some alert beep"
- Not special: "I am not feeling anything special while listening this sound"
- Very short: "It should change as its very short in listening"
- Old: "It's an old sound"
- Boring: "I am feeling bored after listening this sound"

5.6 Attrakdiff Results (UX Measurement)

Tests for Reliability and validity of AttrakDiff questionnaire in Hindi language (Note: reliability and validity for AttrakDiff English questionnaire wasn't performed separately as it has already been established):

- For all groups' sounds were not normally distributed as was concluded from Shapiro wilk test ($p < 0.05$) i.e., hence non parametric tests for inferential statistics were performed.
- Test for normality – Shapiro Wilk for pre and post exposure AttrakDiff has $p < 0.05$ which is why we used non parametric test - Wilcoxon
- Reliability for all 4 constructs is > 0.7 hence all 3 are significantly reliable.
- All items corelation are > 0.3 except for 2nd item (before sound exposure) but reliability didn't change the value much even after excluding the item.
- For item no. 9, 12, 15, 19, 21, 23, 27 Wilcoxon is insignificant before and after sound exposure, so effect of sound on these items is not significant.
- All items having r sum value > 0.31 (i.e. critical value of r) for pre & post exposure hence Attrakdiff is a valid measure for UX. Except for before exposure not being satisfied by 2nd item.

- All items value shifted to the little left side of scale post exposure indicating a little negative effect on the overall UX. Similar trend was observed when the scale was analysed for separate sound types, Cohort – Using the application more than a year and Tier 1 respondent.
- The items' value improved only in the case of tier 2 respondents majorly in constructs -Hedonic-identification usability and overall attractiveness (Fig. 14).

5.7 Perception on Brand Traits

Tests for reliability and validity of Brand traits questionnaire in English and Hindi languages:

Cronbach alpha value of brand traits for both before and after sound exposure came out to be < 0.7 and it was found that removal of none of the items would increase the Cronbach value to more than 0.7. Hence, brand traits questionnaire is not reliable.

Not all items have r sum value > 0.31 (i.e. critical value of r) for pre & post exposure (Hindi and English) hence brand trait questionnaire is not a valid measure for brand personality. However, it should be pointed out that for following items validity was established –

 i) Before exposure (English): 14,16,24,31,42 & 50
 ii) After exposure (English): 2,9,18,20,24,29,32,34,40,43 and 46
 iii) Before exposure (Hindi): 1,2,5,9,11,43 & 46
 iv) After exposure (Hindi): 3,8,9,32,34,40,42 & 46

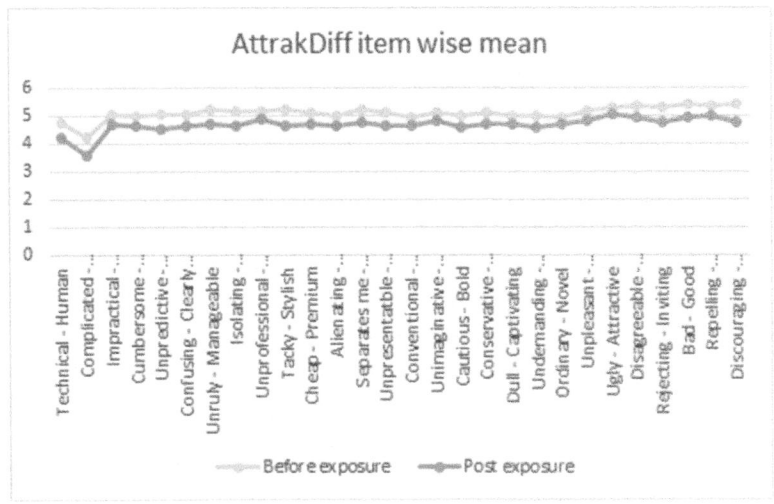

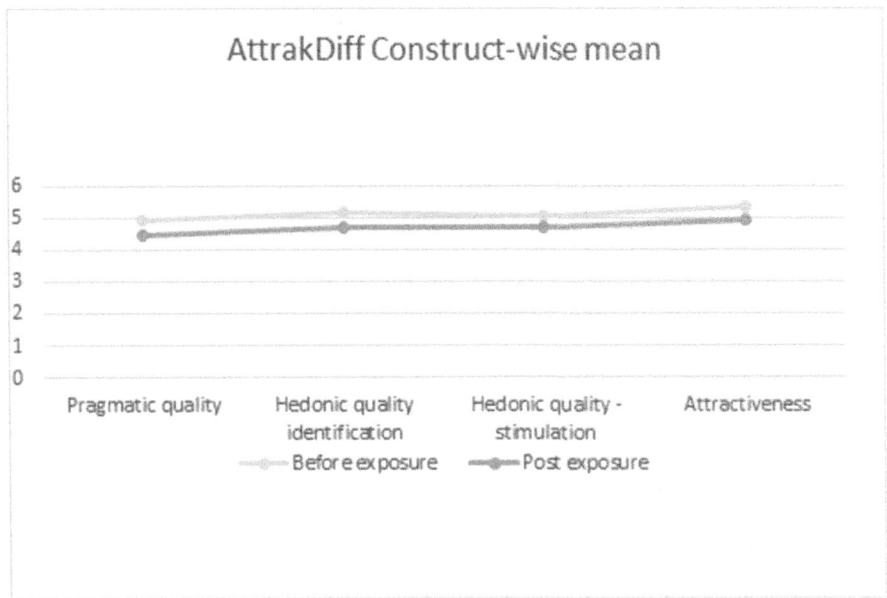

Fig. 14. Attrakdiff questionnaire results (before and after exposure of sound) – from top to bottom – 1. Attrakdiff item wise mean, 2. Attrakdiff construct wise mean, 3. Attrakdiff item wise mean for users who have used the application for more than a year, 4. Attrakdiff item wise mean for Mogo sound, 5. Attrakdiff item wise mean for Notification sound, 6. Attrakdiff item wise mean for Payment success sound, 7. Attrakdiff item wise mean for Tier – 1 city users

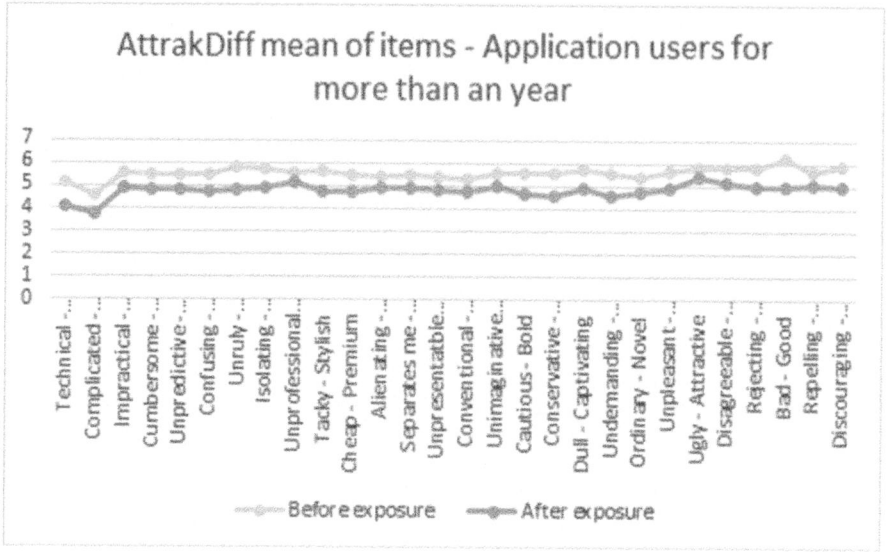

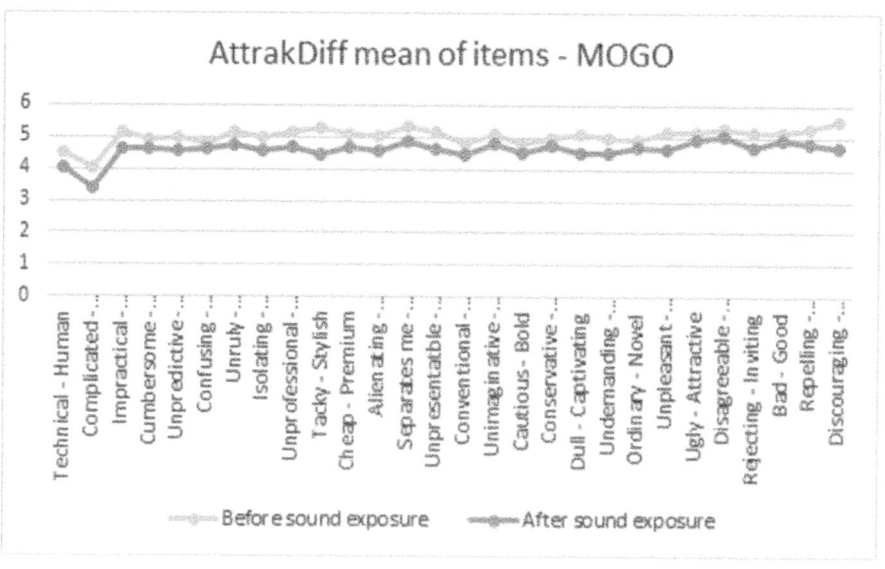

Fig. 14. (*continued*)

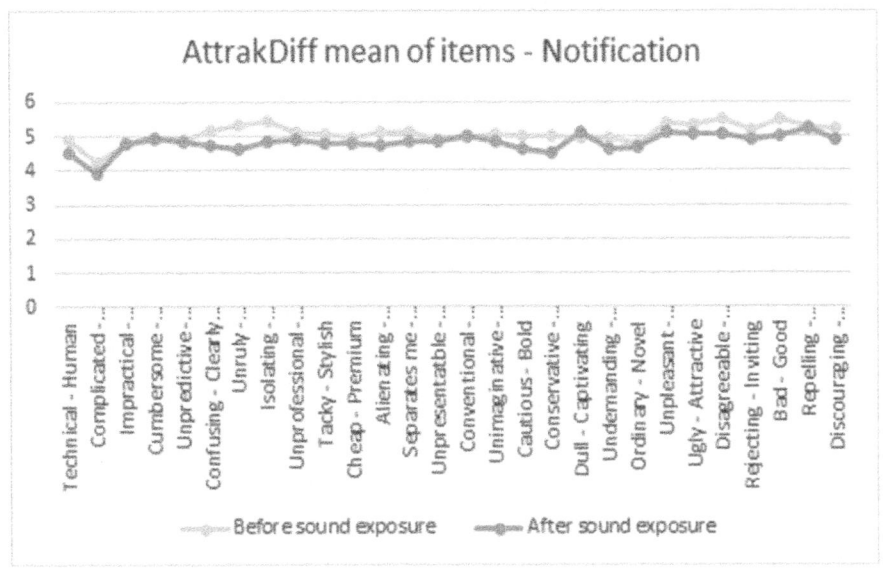

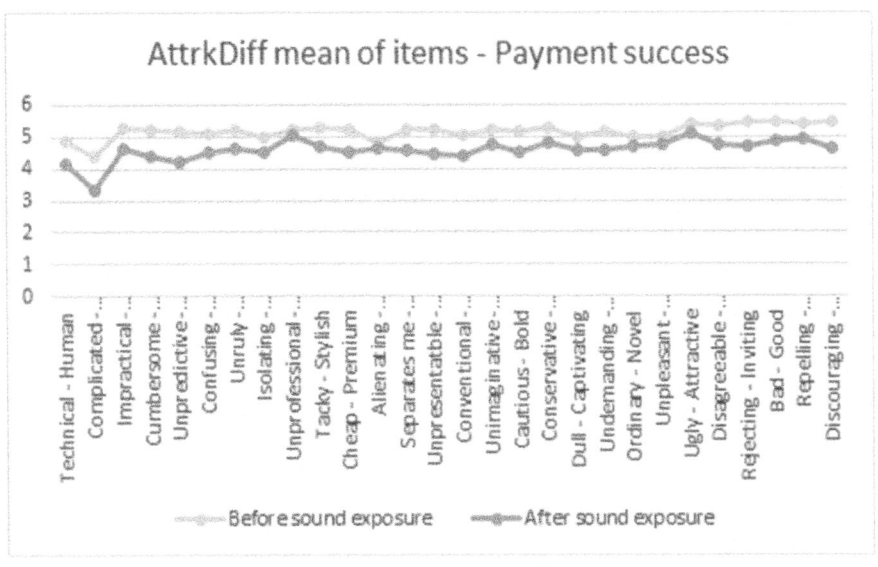

Fig. 14. (*continued*)

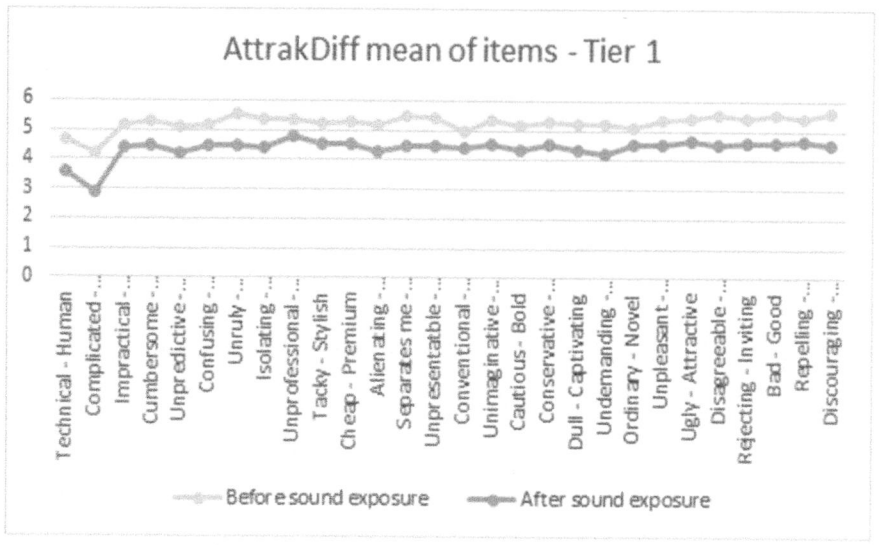

Fig. 14. (*continued*)

Out of 51 brand traits provided to choose from following were that traits that were most frequent. The left table in Fig. 15 mentions frequency of top 10 traits that define the application for respondents. The right table in Fig. 15 indicates top 10 traits that users selected their sound preference from. The traits that overlap in both the tables (highlighted in blue) are the ones that the application's sonic branding should be translating i.e. Classic, Cheerful, Friendly, Reliable, unique, familiar and flexible.

Before exposure traits		Sound prefrence based on	
Classic	72	Reliable	71
Cheerful	62	Classic	67
Friendly	59	Cheerful	66
Reliable	59	Flexible	66
Unique	58	Friendly	64
Familiar	56	Familiar	63
Flexibile	55	Creative	61
Playful	54	Unique	55
Cool	52	Fresh	54
Casual	52	Proffesional	53

Fig. 15. Count of top 10 traits for before exposure of sound (left) and basis for sound preference (right)

The following word clouds have the words as per their frequency (directly proposi-tional to their font size) to give gist of what were the prominent and not so prominent trait:

– Word cloud of the application brand traits (Fig. 16):

Fig. 16. Word cloud for the application brand traits

–   Word cloud for preferring sounds (Fig. 17):

Fig. 17.   Word cloud for preferring sounds

6   Conclusion

Majority of respondents had prominent brand recall through the sonic brandings and showed high willingness to have sounds included on the application specially for getting updates on content. Although users showed prominent willingness and likability towards having sound on the application and current concepts, it's positive effect on UX was only seen for cohort from tier 2 city. And no other significant correlations were found from demographic segregations like age group, subscription status, for specific sound type etc.

Respondents thought of sounds being most useful for indicating task completion and success followed by improving their experience. This can be used as basis for deciding where all sound can be included for the users.

It's recommended for sonic branding of the application to translate the traits - Classic, Cheerful, Friendly, Reliable, unique, familiar and flexible. However, please note that the reliability and validity of brand traits questionnaire was not established and these recommendations must be implemented with due care.

All the concepts gave satisfactory results for their relevant characteristics like Group 1 sounds were acceptable to be repetitive, notification concepts were alerting and accepted to be distinct for the application to get the updates as well as payment success concepts were providing the feeling of completion.

Some of the key and common characteristics that added to the likability of the concepts were – Innovative, familiarity, soothing, refreshing nature and melodious nature. Participants wanted the sounds to be unique and unheard from before.

7 Limitations and Future Research

The existing research targeted introduction of sound in different workflows in a digital application wherein the impact of sound exposure was studied. With the results, it was found out that inclusion of sound is promising. However, for some of the questionnaires like brand traits, reliability and validity was not established.

The fact that the survey was filled in the presence of a researcher, it could have lead to social desirability and acquiescence bias, which could have influence results. Also, as multiple researchers were moderating the study in different cities, differences in moderation of different researchers could have also influenced results.

In future, research might target identification of appropriate traits which are reliable, valid and suitable for studying brand personality. Also, similar survey can be conducting with a higher sample size to get significant results throughout all tests, which could also assure higher confidence levels. Given the scale and context of the research study, researchers are encouraged to utilise the research methodology described in the study, modify the same if needed (to minimise potential bias) and generalise the results for different geographies.

Appendix

Preference Order of Different Sounds

Test of Normality – MOGO/Group 1

	Kolmogorov-Smirnov[a]			Shapiro-Wilk		
	Statistic	df	Sig	Statistic	df	Sig.
VAR00001	.263	63	<.001	.789	63	<.001
VAR00002	.303	63	<.001	.751	63	<.001
VAR00003	.220	63	<.001	.800	63	<.001

Test of Normality – Notification/Group 2

	Kolmogorov-Smirnov[a]			Shapiro-Wilk		
	Statistic	df	Sig.	Statistic	df	Sig.
VAR00004	.299	59	<.001	.763	59	<.001
VAR00005	.269	59	<.001	.785	59	<.001
VAR00006	.223	59	<.001	.798	59	<.001

Test of Normality – Payment Success/Group 3

	Kolmogorov-Smirnov[a]			Shapiro-Wilk		
	Statistic	df	Sig.	Statistic	df	Sig.
VAR00007	.265	58	<.001	.784	58	<.001
VAR00008	.333	58	<.001	.739	58	<.001
VAR00009	.253	58	<.001	.794	58	<.001

Lilliefors Significance Correction

Test Statistics – MOGO/Group 1

N	63
Chi-Square	5.460
df	2
Asymp. Sig.	.065

Friedman Test

Test Statistics – Notification/Group 2

N	59
Chi-Square	5.831
df	2
Asymp. Sig.	.054

Friedman Test

Test Statistics – Payment Success/Group 3

N	58
Chi-Square	10.379
df	2
Asymp. Sig.	.006

Friedman Test

Attrakdiff Results (for Hindi Language)
Reliability Statistics Before Exposure of Stimuli

Cronbach's Alpha	N of Items
.932	28

Item Total Statistics Before Exposure of Stimuli

	Scale Mean if Item Deleted	Scale Variance if Item Deleted	Corrected Item-Total Correlation	Cronbach's Alpha if Item Deleted
VAR00001	133.7561	483.089	.257	.933
VAR00002	134.2195	492.376	.058	.937
VAR00003	133.4878	449.556	.715	.927
VAR00004	133.7073	469.012	.464	.931
VAR00005	133.3415	460.530	.569	.929
VAR00006	133.4634	463.155	.544	.929
VAR00007	133.5122	460.356	.555	.929
VAR00008	133.5122	455.406	.713	.927
VAR00009	133.3171	469.072	.466	.930
VAR00010	133.3171	454.372	.711	.927
VAR00011	133.3902	466.794	.568	.929
VAR00012	133.4878	471.256	.452	.931
VAR00013	133.5854	457.049	.738	.927
VAR00014	133.4390	463.952	.657	.928
VAR00015	133.7805	458.526	.623	.928
VAR00016	133.5122	465.906	.666	.928
VAR00017	133.4390	463.552	.581	.929
VAR00018	133.8537	456.678	.591	.929
VAR00019	133.6585	468.130	.593	.929
VAR00020	133.5366	477.055	.468	.930
VAR00021	133.6585	462.180	.621	.928
VAR00022	133.3902	464.744	.568	.929
VAR00023	133.0244	457.024	.679	.928
VAR00024	133.0488	463.598	.596	.929
VAR00025	133.3171	478.622	.396	.931
VAR00026	133.0244	466.924	.582	.929
VAR00027	133.2927	463.112	.591	.929
VAR00028	133.1220	465.760	.601	.929

Item Total Statistics Post Exposure of Stimuli

	Scale Mean if Item Deleted	Scale Variance if Item Deleted	Corrected Item-Total Correlation	Cronbach's Alpha if Item Deleted
VAR00001	123.7805	1134.476	.756	.975
VAR00002	124.6098	1160.394	.479	.977
VAR00003	123.4390	1121.302	.790	.975
VAR00004	123.9512	1145.948	.678	.976
VAR00005	124.0488	1136.048	.775	.975
VAR00006	123.8780	1137.260	.771	.975
VAR00007	123.9024	1140.190	.702	.976
VAR00008	123.7561	1134.439	.749	.975
VAR00009	123.7805	1136.826	.758	.975
VAR00010	123.9024	1132.290	.822	.975
VAR00011	123.9512	1135.748	.755	.975
VAR00012	123.6829	1128.672	.842	.975
VAR00013	123.8780	1138.160	.810	.975
VAR00014	123.8049	1128.411	.815	.975
VAR00015	123.7317	1136.051	.822	.975
VAR00016	123.4634	1132.555	.741	.975
VAR00017	124.0244	1131.624	.808	.975
VAR00018	123.7561	1139.839	.763	.975
VAR00019	123.8049	1129.261	.753	.975
VAR00020	123.7805	1144.126	.603	.976
VAR00021	123.6585	1139.430	.771	.975
VAR00022	123.3659	1122.988	.878	.975
VAR00023	123.4634	1124.705	.806	.975
VAR00024	123.3415	1116.880	.833	.975
VAR00025	123.6341	1137.988	.840	.975
VAR00026	123.2195	1123.026	.784	.975
VAR00027	123.2927	1124.012	.798	.975
VAR00028	123.6585	1139.130	.708	.976

Validity of Attrakdiff (Before Exposure)

Validity of Attrakdiff (Post Exposure)

Effect of Sound on UX

Tests of Normality (Pre Exposure Attrakdiff)

	Kolmogorov-Smirnov[a]			Shapiro-Wilk		
	Statistic	df	Sig.	Statistic	df	Sig.
VAR00001	.150	180	<.001	.913	180	<.001
VAR00002	.143	180	<.001	.923	180	<.001

(continued)

(continued)

	Kolmogorov-Smirnov[a]			Shapiro-Wilk		
	Statistic	df	Sig.	Statistic	df	Sig.
VAR00003	.146	180	<.001	.908	180	<.001
VAR00004	.140	180	<.001	.916	180	<.001
VAR00005	.169	180	<.001	.909	180	<.001
VAR00006	.164	180	<.001	.916	180	<.001
VAR00007	.171	180	<.001	.902	180	<.001
VAR00008	.159	180	<.001	.909	180	<.001
VAR00009	.162	180	<.001	.906	180	<.001
VAR00010	.192	180	<.001	.902	180	<.001
VAR00011	.158	180	<.001	.918	180	<.001
VAR00012	.174	180	<.001	.918	180	<.001
VAR00013	.183	180	<.001	.903	180	<.001
VAR00014	.157	180	<.001	.906	180	<.001
VAR00015	.172	180	<.001	.920	180	<.001
VAR00016	.198	180	<.001	.905	180	<.001
VAR00017	.185	180	<.001	.908	180	<.001
VAR00018	.195	180	<.001	.899	180	<.001
VAR00019	.151	180	<.001	.923	180	<.001
VAR00020	.168	180	<.001	.912	180	<.001
VAR00021	.161	180	<.001	.927	180	<.001
VAR00022	.180	180	<.001	.910	180	<.001
VAR00023	.197	180	<.001	.894	180	<.001
VAR00024	.181	180	<.001	.892	180	<.001
VAR00025	.176	180	<.001	.904	180	<.001
VAR00026	.198	180	<.001	.873	180	<.001
VAR00027	.186	180	<.001	.900	180	<.001
VAR00028	.196	180	<.001	.883	180	< .001

Tests of Normality (Post Exposure Attrakdiff)

	Kolmogorov-Smirnov[a]			Shapiro-Wilk		
	Statistic	df	Sig.	Statistic	Df	Sig.
VAR00001	.191	180	<.001	.905	180	<.001
VAR00002	.119	180	<.001	.936	180	<.001
VAR00003	.172	180	<.001	.924	180	<.001
VAR00004	.164	180	<.001	.922	180	<.001
VAR00005	.130	180	<.001	.928	180	<.001
VAR00006	.173	180	<.001	.926	180	<.001
VAR00007	.155	180	<.001	.912	180	<.001
VAR00008	.133	180	<.001	.932	180	<.001
VAR00009	.166	180	<.001	.921	180	<.001

(continued)

(*continued*)

	Kolmogorov-Smirnov[a]			Shapiro-Wilk		
	Statistic	df	Sig.	Statistic	Df	Sig.
VAR00010	.137	180	<.001	.918	180	<.001
VAR00011	.142	180	<.001	.924	180	<.001
VAR00012	.151	180	<.001	.919	180	<.001
VAR00013	.178	180	<.001	.920	180	<.001
VAR00014	.160	180	<.001	.918	180	<.001
VAR00015	.153	180	<.001	.913	180	<.001
VAR00016	.172	180	<.001	.904	180	<.001
VAR00017	.184	180	<.001	.912	180	<.001
VAR00018	.178	180	<.001	.905	180	<.001
VAR00019	.158	180	<.001	.916	180	<.001
VAR00020	.168	180	<.001	.907	180	<.001
VAR00021	.153	180	<.001	.928	180	<.001
VAR00022	.165	180	<.001	.897	180	<.001
VAR00023	.208	180	<.001	.879	180	<.001
VAR00024	.169	180	<.001	.874	180	<.001
VAR00025	.170	180	<.001	.917	180	<.001
VAR00026	.167	180	<.001	.883	180	<.001
VAR00027	.185	180	<.001	.888	180	<.001
VAR00028	.194	180	<.001	.896	180	<.001

a. Lilliefors Significance Correction

Wilcoxon Test Results (Pre-Post Exposure Attrakdiff)

Tests for Reliability and Validity of Brand Traits Questionnaire in English

Reliability Statistics Before Exposure

Cronbach's Alpha	Cronbach's Alpha Based on Standardized Items	N of Items
.602	.599	51

Reliability Statistics After Exposure

Cronbach's Alpha	Cronbach's Alpha Based on Standardized Items	N of Items
.569	.555	51

Item-Total Statistics (Before Exposure)

	Scale Mean if Item Deleted	Scale Variance if Item Deleted	Corrected Item-Total Correlation	Squared Multiple Correlation	Cronbach's Alpha if Item Deleted
VAR00001	10.4667	19.189	.139	.	.597
VAR00002	10.4111	19.104	.133	.	.597
VAR00003	10.3611	18.947	.156	.	.595
VAR00004	10.3722	19.743	−.059	.	.612
VAR00005	10.3000	19.664	−.043	.	.612
VAR00006	10.2444	18.610	.209	.	.590
VAR00007	10.1889	18.791	.156	.	.595
VAR00008	10.3833	19.835	−.084	.	.613
VAR00009	10.4000	19.560	−.005	.	.607
VAR00010	10.3056	19.130	.092	.	.600
VAR00011	10.3000	19.474	.004	.	.608
VAR00012	10.3556	18.644	.238	.	.588
VAR00013	10.4222	19.508	.015	.	.605
VAR00014	10.4333	19.644	-.025	.	.608
VAR00015	10.4278	18.391	.370	.	.580
VAR00016	10.4278	18.816	.233	.	.590
VAR00017	10.5222	18.910	.332	.	.588
VAR00018	10.4222	18.882	.208	.	.591

(*continued*)

(*continued*)

	Scale Mean if Item Deleted	Scale Variance if Item Deleted	Corrected Item-Total Correlation	Squared Multiple Correlation	Cronbach's Alpha if Item Deleted
VAR00019	10.4389	18.929	.205	.	.592
VAR00020	10.3056	18.806	.175	.	.593
VAR00021	10.2778	18.626	.213	.	.590
VAR00022	10.2833	19.567	-.021	.	.610
VAR00023	10.3556	19.035	.130	.	.597
VAR00024	10.2944	18.756	.185	.	.592
VAR00025	10.2611	18.172	.325	.	.579
VAR00026	10.2889	19.067	.104	.	.599
VAR00027	10.3833	19.310	.062	.	.602
VAR00028	10.4444	19.835	−.084	.	.611
VAR00029	10.4000	19.850	−.088	.	.613
VAR00030	10.3722	18.749	.217	.	.590
VAR00031	10.4611	19.434	.051	.	.602
VAR00032	10.4778	18.832	.280	.	.588
VAR00033	10.4389	18.683	.286	.	.586
VAR00034	10.5778	19.854	−.181	.	.606
VAR00035	10.4444	19.019	.180	.	.594
VAR00036	10.4278	19.062	.155	.	.595
VAR00037	10.2889	18.788	.175	.	.593
VAR00038	10.3667	18.949	.158	.	.595
VAR00039	10.3278	19.071	.112	.	.599
VAR00040	10.4000	19.694	−.044	.	.610
VAR00041	10.2667	19.012	.114	.	.599
VAR00042	10.2611	18.038	.359	.	.576
VAR00043	10.3278	19.015	.127	.	.597
VAR00044	10.3500	18.821	.187	.	.592
VAR00045	10.3722	18.525	.281	.	.585
VAR00046	10.4056	19.606	−.018	.	.608
VAR00047	10.4667	19.267	.111	.	.598
VAR00048	10.3556	18.130	.384	.	.576
VAR00049	10.5222	19.581	.024	.	.603
VAR00050	10.5278	19.223	.197	.	.595
VAR00051	10.5278	19.033	.289	.	.590

Item-Total Statistics (Post Exposure)

	Scale Mean if Item Deleted	Scale Variance if Item Deleted	Corrected Item-Total Correlation	Squared Multiple Correlation	Cronbach's Alpha if Item Deleted
VAR00001	10.5056	17.056	.347	.	.548
VAR00002	10.4722	17.725	.070	.	.568
VAR00003	10.3833	17.053	.236	.	.553
VAR00004	10.3778	17.856	.005	.	.574
VAR00005	10.3444	17.322	.145	.	.562
VAR00006	10.2500	17.071	.189	.	.557
VAR00007	10.2444	17.348	.118	.	.564
VAR00008	10.3944	17.950	−.018	.	.576
VAR00009	10.3833	18.003	−.034	.	.578
VAR00010	10.3667	17.004	.242	.	.552
VAR00011	10.3944	17.570	.090	.	.567
VAR00012	10.2778	17.688	.037	.	.573
VAR00013	10.4667	17.960	−.010	.	.574
VAR00014	10.4667	18.038	−.035	.	.576
VAR00015	10.4056	17.226	.196	.	.557
VAR00016	10.5500	17.701	.140	.	.563
VAR00017	10.5833	17.608	.277	.	.559
VAR00018	10.4222	17.486	.125	.	.563
VAR00019	10.3389	16.706	.314	.	.545
VAR00020	10.3667	17.127	.207	.	.556
VAR00021	10.2667	16.744	.277	.	.547
VAR00022	10.2500	17.675	.037	.	.573
VAR00023	10.4000	17.917	−.008	.	.575
VAR00024	10.3167	17.458	.102	.	.566
VAR00025	10.2611	16.764	.271	.	.548
VAR00026	10.3611	17.997	−.035	.	.578
VAR00027	10.4278	17.956	−.015	.	.575
VAR00028	10.4722	18.016	−.027	.	.575
VAR00029	10.4389	18.304	−.119	.	.583
VAR00030	10.4167	16.814	.329	.	.545
VAR00031	10.4667	17.815	.038	.	.570
VAR00032	10.5333	17.781	.086	.	.566

(*continued*)

(*continued*)

	Scale Mean if Item Deleted	Scale Variance if Item Deleted	Corrected Item-Total Correlation	Squared Multiple Correlation	Cronbach's Alpha if Item Deleted
VAR00033	10.5222	17.312	.271	.	.555
VAR00034	10.6111	18.138	−.134	.	.571
VAR00035	10.5000	17.168	.295	.	.552
VAR00036	10.4444	17.678	.074	.	.568
VAR00037	10.3556	17.135	.200	.	.556
VAR00038	10.4611	17.479	.147	.	.562
VAR00039	10.3222	17.404	.117	.	.564
VAR00040	10.3889	17.870	.003	.	.574
VAR00041	10.3111	17.154	.181	.	.558
VAR00042	10.2222	16.397	.358	.	.538
VAR00043	10.3611	17.584	.077	.	.568
VAR00044	10.3722	17.475	.110	.	.565
VAR00045	10.3889	16.988	.258	.	.551
VAR00046	10.4222	18.044	−.042	.	.578
VAR00047	10.4722	17.480	.154	.	.561
VAR00048	10.3778	16.951	.263	.	.551
VAR00049	10.5389	17.781	.091	.	.566
VAR00050	10.5778	17.921	.061	.	.568
VAR00051	10.5778	18.178	−.095	.	.574

Reliability Statistics (Before Exposure, Hindi)

Cronbach's Alpha	Cronbach's Alpha Based on Standardized Items	N of Items
.514	.539	50

Item-Total Statistics (Before Exposure, Hindi)

	Scale Mean if Item Deleted	Scale Variance if Item Deleted	Corrected Item-Total Correlation	Squared Multiple Correlation	Cronbach's Alpha if Item Deleted
VAR00001	10.4878	15.306	.358	.	.487

(*continued*)

(*continued*)

	Scale Mean if Item Deleted	Scale Variance if Item Deleted	Corrected Item-Total Correlation	Squared Multiple Correlation	Cronbach's Alpha if Item Deleted
VAR00002	10.3415	16.480	−.093	.	.531
VAR00003	10.3902	16.144	.007	.	.519
VAR00004	10.3171	16.872	−.196	.	.543
VAR00005	10.3171	16.172	−.011	.	.522
VAR00006	10.1951	15.661	.110	.	.508
VAR00007	10.2195	15.976	.032	.	.518
VAR00008	10.3415	16.680	−.147	.	.537
VAR00009	10.3902	15.994	.052	.	.514
VAR00010	10.3902	16.644	−.139	.	.534
VAR00011	10.3415	16.230	−.024	.	.523
VAR00012	10.3171	16.022	.030	.	.518
VAR00013	10.4390	15.602	.198	.	.500
VAR00014	10.4390	15.902	.098	.	.510
VAR00015	10.4878	15.356	.338	.	.489
VAR00016	10.4878	15.606	.240	.	.498
VAR00017	10.5610	16.152	.082	.	.511
VAR00018	10.4390	16.452	−.082	.	.527
VAR00019	10.3902	15.094	.330	.	.484
VAR00020	10.3171	16.672	−.144	.	.537
VAR00021	10.3171	15.822	.085	.	.511
VAR00022	10.3659	15.538	.180	.	.500
VAR00023	10.3902	15.744	.128	.	.506
VAR00024	10.2927	15.262	.234	.	.493
VAR00025	10.2439	14.889	.323	.	.481
VAR00026	10.2439	15.989	.030	.	.518
VAR00027	10.4146	16.649	−.142	.	.533
VAR00028	10.5122	16.606	−.144	.	.528
VAR00029	10.5366	16.305	−.014	.	.517
VAR00030	10.3659	15.588	.165	.	.502
VAR00031	10.5122	16.156	.040	.	.514
VAR00032	10.5610	15.852	.256	.	.502
VAR00033	10.5122	15.606	.273	.	.496
VAR00035	10.4390	15.852	.114	.	.508

(*continued*)

(*continued*)

	Scale Mean if Item Deleted	Scale Variance if Item Deleted	Corrected Item-Total Correlation	Squared Multiple Correlation	Cronbach's Alpha if Item Deleted
VAR00036	10.4878	16.006	.086	.	.511
VAR00037	10.3415	15.230	.261	.	.491
VAR00038	10.3902	16.444	−.081	.	.528
VAR00039	10.3415	14.980	.335	.	.482
VAR00040	10.4146	15.549	.200	.	.499
VAR00041	10.3415	16.430	−.079	.	.529
VAR00042	10.2439	14.189	.522	.	.454
VAR00043	10.4390	15.252	.318	.	.488
VAR00044	10.2927	15.062	.290	.	.486
VAR00045	10.4390	15.702	.164	.	.503
VAR00046	10.4146	16.349	−.051	.	.525
VAR00047	10.5122	16.056	.082	.	.511
VAR00048	10.3171	14.872	.355	.	.479
VAR00049	10.5122	16.006	.103	.	.509
VAR00050	10.5366	16.105	.080	.	.511
VAR00051	10.5366	15.505	.371	.	.491

Reliability Statistics (After Exposure, Hindi)

Cronbach's Alpha	Cronbach's Alpha Based on Standardized Items	N of Items
.547	.569	49

Item-Total Statistics (After Exposure, Hindi)

	Scale Mean if Item Deleted	Scale Variance if Item Deleted	Corrected Item-Total Correlation	Squared Multiple Correlation	Cronbach's Alpha if Item Deleted
VAR00001	10.9487	16.892	.233	.	.532
VAR00002	11.0000	17.263	.144	.	.540
VAR00003	10.8462	17.239	.079	.	.546
VAR00004	10.8462	17.449	.022	.	.551

(*continued*)

(continued)

	Scale Mean if Item Deleted	Scale Variance if Item Deleted	Corrected Item-Total Correlation	Squared Multiple Correlation	Cronbach's Alpha if Item Deleted
VAR00005	10.7692	17.287	.053	.	.549
VAR00006	10.8205	16.941	.154	.	.538
VAR00007	10.7436	16.827	.166	.	.536
VAR00008	10.8718	17.378	.047	.	.549
VAR00009	10.8974	17.779	−.064	.	.558
VAR00010	10.8718	16.957	.167	.	.537
VAR00011	10.8718	17.378	.047	.	.549
VAR00012	10.7436	18.617	−.269	.	.583
VAR00013	10.7949	17.273	.060	.	.548
VAR00014	10.9487	16.734	.287	.	.527
VAR00015	10.9231	16.915	.206	.	.534
VAR00016	11.0000	17.158	.186	.	.537
VAR00017	11.0769	17.757	−.042	.	.550
VAR00018	10.8718	17.641	−.027	.	.556
VAR00019	10.6923	17.534	−.014	.	.557
VAR00020	10.7949	17.325	.047	.	.549
VAR00021	10.6667	16.754	.175	.	.535
VAR00022	10.6154	16.769	.169	.	.536
VAR00023	10.8462	17.186	.094	.	.544
VAR00024	10.7436	17.038	.113	.	.542
VAR00025	10.7692	16.709	.202	.	.532
VAR00026	10.9487	18.260	−.214	.	.569
VAR00027	10.8718	17.641	−.027	.	.556
VAR00028	11.0000	17.368	.103	.	.543
VAR00029	10.9487	17.418	.057	.	.547
VAR00030	10.9744	16.447	.424	.	.518
VAR00031	11.0000	16.895	.292	.	.530
VAR00032	11.0000	16.842	.313	.	.528
VAR00033	11.0256	16.973	.306	.	.531
VAR00035	10.9487	17.155	.144	.	.540
VAR00036	10.8974	17.410	.043	.	.549
VAR00037	10.7949	17.062	.115	.	.542
VAR00038	10.9231	16.494	.342	.	.521

(continued)

(continued)

	Scale Mean if Item Deleted	Scale Variance if Item Deleted	Corrected Item-Total Correlation	Squared Multiple Correlation	Cronbach's Alpha if Item Deleted
VAR00039	10.9231	16.599	.308	.	.525
VAR00040	10.8718	17.009	.152	.	.538
VAR00041	10.7436	17.143	.086	.	.545
VAR00042	10.6923	15.955	.382	.	.511
VAR00043	10.7949	16.957	.143	.	.539
VAR00044	10.9744	17.762	−.053	.	.555
VAR00045	10.8205	16.414	.299	.	.522
VAR00046	10.8974	17.884	−.094	.	.561
VAR00047	11.0256	17.447	.092	.	.544
VAR00048	10.8205	16.783	.197	.	.533
VAR00049	11.0000	16.842	.313	.	.528
VAR00051	11.0513	17.787	−.059	.	.552

Validity for English Brand Traits (Before Exposure)

Validity for English Brand Traits (After Exposure)

Validity for Hindi Brand Traits (Before Exposure)

Validity for Hindi Brand Traits (After Exposure)

Hindi Language Questionnaires

Brand Traits

Pillar 1	पिलर 1
Accessible	आसानी से इस्तेमाल करने वाला
Approachable	पहुंच वाला
Bold	साहसी
Calm	स्थिर
Casual	सामान्य
Cheerful	मनोरंजक
Classic	श्रेष्ठ
Conservative	पुराने तरीके वाला
Contemporary	आधुनिक समय वाला
Convenient	सुविधाजनक
Cool	कूल
Creative	रचनात्मक
Custom	रीति रिवाज वाला
Cutting edge	अत्याधुनिक तकनीकि वाला
Delightful	आनंदमय
Easy	आसान
Efficient	योग्य
Pillar 2	पिलर 2
Elegant	बेहतरीन
Energetic	उर्जा से भरा हुआ
Exclusive	खास
Familiar	परिचित/जान पहचान वाला
Flexible	लचीला
Formal	औपचारिक
Fresh	तरोताजा रखने वाला

Friendly	दोस्ताना
Fun	मजेदार
Func-tional	काम करने वाला
Human	इंसान
Infor-mal	अनऔपचारिक
Innova-tive	नयी सोच वाला
Inviting	आमंत्रित करने वाला
Mature	पूरी तरह से विकसित
Modern	आधुनिक
No sense	किसी मतलब वाला नही
Pillar 3	पिलर 3
Per-sonal	व्यक्तिगत
Plain	सादा
Playful	चंचल
Pol-ished	अच्छी तरह से तैयार किया गया
Profes-sional	पेशेवर
Quirky	विचित्र
Unique	अलग
Reliable	भरोसेमंद
Secure	सुरक्षित
Serious	गंभीर
Sincere	ईमानदार
Sleek	आकर्षक
Sophisti-cated	जटिल
Trust-worthy	विश्वसनीय
Uncon-ven-tional	अपरंपरागत
Versa-tile	अनेक गुणों वाला
Warm	हार्दिक

Attrakdiff

Please rate Application on the following scales as per your opinion:	कृपया अपनी राय के अनुसार इन स्केल पर Application को रेटिंग दें:
Is Application technical or human?	क्या Application तकनीकी है या इंसान है?
Extremely human	बेहद इंसान
Extremely technical	बेहद तकनीकी
Is Application simple or complicated?	क्या Application आसान है या कठिन है?
Extremely complicated	बेहद कठिन है
Extremely simple	बेहद आसान है
Is Application impractical or practical?	क्या Application अव्यावहारिक है या व्यावहारिक है?
Extremely practical	बेहद व्यावहारिक
Extremely impractical	बेहद अव्यावहारिक
Is Application cumbersome or straightforward?	क्या Application कठिन है या एकदम सीधा समझ में आने वाला है
Extremely straightforward	बेहद एकदम सीधा समझ में आने वाला
Extremely cumbersome	बेहद कठिन है

Is Application unpredictable or predictable?	क्या Application का पूरी तरह से अनुमान नहीं लगाया जा सकता है या पूरी तरह से अनुमान लगाया जा सकता है
Extremely predictable	पूरी तरह से अनुमान लगाया जा सकता है
Extremely unpredictable	पूरी तरह से अनुमान नहीं लगाया जा सकता है
Is Application confusing or clearly structured?	क्या Application भ्रमित करने वाला है या साफ तौर से बना बनाया है?
Extremely clearly structured	बेहद साफ तौर से बना बनाया
Extremely confusing	बेहद भ्रमित करने वाला
Is Application unruly or manageable?	क्या Application को पूरी तरह से चलाया जा सकता है या पूरी तरह से नही चलाया जा सकता है?
Extremely manageable	पूरी तरह से चलाया जा सकता है
Extremely unruly	पूरी तरह से नही चलाया जा सकता

Please rate Application on the following scales as per your opinion:	कृपया अपनी राय के अनुसार इन स्केल पर Application को रेटिंग दें:
Is Application isolating or connective?	क्या Application अलग कर देने वाला या जोड़ने वाला है?
Extremely connective	पूरी तरह से जोड़ने वाला
Extremely isolating	पूरी तरह से अलग करने वाला
Is Application unprofessional or professional?	क्या Application गैर-पेशेवर या पेशेवर है?
Extremely professional	बेहद पेशेवर
Extremely unprofessional	बेहद गैर-पेशेवर
Is Application tacky or stylish?	क्या Application बेढंगा या स्टाइलिश है?
Extremely stylish	बेहद स्टाइलिश
Extremely tacky	बेहद बेढंगा
Is Application cheap or premium?	क्या Application सस्ता या प्रीमियम है ?
Extremely premium	बेहद प्रीमियम
Extremely cheap	बेहद सस्ता

Is Application alienating or integrating?	क्या Application अलग-थलग करने वाला है या एक करने वाला है?
Extremely integrating	बेहद एक करने वाला
Extremely alienating	बेहद अलग-थलग करने वाला
Does Application separates you or brings you closer?	क्या Application आपको दूर करने वाला है या करीब लाने वाला है?
Brings me closest	मुझे सबसे करीब लाने वाला है
Separates me the most	मुझे सबसे दूर करने वाला है
Is Application unpresentable or presentable?	क्या Application अप्रस्तुत या प्रस्तुत करने योग्य है?
Extremely presentable	बेहद प्रस्तुत करने योग्य
Extremely unpresentable	बेहद अप्रस्तुत
Please rate Application on the following scales as per your opinion:	कृपया अपनी राय के अनुसार इन स्केल पर Application को रेटिंग दें:
Is Application conventional or inventive?	क्या Application परंपरागत या आविष्कारशील है?

Extremely inventive	बेहद आविष्कारशील
Extremely conventional	बेहद परंपरागत
Is Application unimaginative or creative?	क्या Application अकल्पनीय या रचनात्मक है?
Extremely creative	बेहद रचनात्मक
Extremely unimaginative	बेहद अकल्पनीय
Is Application cautious or bold?	क्या Application सतर्क या साहसी है?
Extremely bold	बेहद साहसी
Extremely cautious	बेहद सतर्क
Is Application conservative or innovative?	क्या Application पुरानी सोच वाला या नयी सोच वाला है?
Extremely innovative	बेहद नयी सोच वाला
Extremely conservative	बेहद पुरानी सोच वाला
Is Application dull or captivating?	क्या Application सुस्त करने वाला या लुभावने वाला है?
Extremely captivating	बेहद लुभावने वाला
Extremely dull	बेहद सुस्त करने वाला
Is Application	क्या Application कम

undemanding or challenging?	उम्मीद करने वाला या चुनौती वाला है?
Extremely challenging	बेहद चुनौती वाला
Extremely undemanding	बेहद कम उम्मीद करने वाला
Is Application ordinary or novel?	क्या Application साधारण है या नया है?
Extremely novel	बेहद नया
Extremely ordinary	बेहद साधारण
Please rate Application on the following scales as per your opinion:	कृपया अपनी राय के अनुसार इन स्केल पर Application को रेटिंग दें:
Is Application unpleasant or pleasant?	क्या Application अप्रिय या सुखद है ?
Extremely pleasant	बेहद सुखद
Extremely unpleasant	बेहद अप्रिय
Is Application ugly or attractive?	क्या Application खराब या आकर्षक है?
Extremely attractive	बेहद आकर्षक
Extremely ugly	बेहद खराब
Is Application disagreeable or likeable?	क्या Application न पसंद करने या पसंद करने योग्य है?
Extremely likeable	बेहद पसंद करने योग्य

Extremely disagreeable	बेहद न पसंद करने योग्य
Is Application rejecting or inviting?	क्या Application अस्वीकार करने वाला है या आमंत्रित करने वाला है?
Extremely inviting	बेहद आमंत्रित करने वाला
Extremely rejecting	बेहद अस्वीकार करने वाला
Is Application bad or good?	क्या Application खराब है या अच्छा है?
Best	अच्छा
Worst	खराब
Is Application repelling or appealing?	क्या Application बेकार है या आकर्षक है?
Extremely appealing	बेहद आकर्षक
Extremely repelling	बेहद बेकार
Is Application discouraging or motivating?	क्या Application हतोत्साहित करने वाला है या प्रेरित करने वाला है?
Extremely motivating	बेहद प्रेरित करने वाला
Extremely discouraging	बेहद हतोत्साहित करने वाला

References

Jeon, M.: How can lay people participate in sound design?: Introduction to sound mapping tools and methods. In: International Conference on Auditory Displays (2014)

Hassenzahl, M., Burmester, M., Koller, F.: AttrakDiff: Ein Fragebogen zur Messung wahrgenommener hedonischer und pragmatischer Qualität. Mensch & Computer (2003)

Vieira, D., Providência, B., Carva, H.: Design of a smart garment for fencing: measuring attractiveness using the AttrakDiff Mini method. Human-Intelligent Systems Integration (2023)

Aaker, J.L.: Dimensions of brand personality. J. Mark. Res. (1997)

Bhattacharya, S., Das, N., Sahu, S., Borah, S., Mondal, A.: Deep classification of sound: a concise review. In: Proceeding of First Doctoral Symposium on Natural Computing Research, pp. 33–43 (2021)

Norman, D., Miller, J., Henderson, A.: What you see, some of what's in the future, and how we go about doing it: HI at Apple Computer. In: CHI 1995: Conference Companion on Human Factors in Computing Systems (1995)

DIS, I.: 9241–210: 2010. Ergonomics of human system interaction-Part 210: human-centred design for interactive systems (formerly known as 13407). International Standardization Organization (ISO) (2010)

Berni, A., Borgianni, A.: From the definition of user experience to a framework to classify its applications in design. In: Proceedings of the Design Society (2021)

ISO/TS 20282-2:2013(en) Usability of consumer products and products for public use — Part 2: Summative test method. (n.d.)

Wickens, C., Lee, J. D., Liu, Y., Gordon-Becker, S.: Introduction to Human Factors Engineering (2003)

Winn, W., Hereford, J.: Non-speech sound in human-computer interaction: a review and design guidelines. Educ. Comput. Res. (1994)

Moesgaard, F., Hulgaard, L., Bødker, M.: Involving users in sound design. HCI International (2020)

Westerkamp, H.: Soundwalking. Sound Heritage (n.d.)

Ekman, I., Rinott, M.: Using vocal sketching for designing sonic interactions. Designing Interactive Systems (2010)

Lexical Event Models for Multimodal Dialogues

James Pustejovsky$^{(\boxtimes)}$ⓘ and Yifan Zhuⓘ

Brandeis University, Waltham, MA 02453, USA
`jamesp@brandeis.edu`

Abstract. In order to understand multimodal interactions between humans or humans and machine, it is minimally necessary to identify the content of the agents' communicative acts in the dialogue. This can involve either overt linguistic expressions (speech or writing), content-bearing gesture, or the integration of both. But this content must be interpreted relative to a deeper understanding of an agent's Theory of Mind (one's mental state, desires, and intentions) in the context of the dialogue as it dynamically unfolds. This, in turn, can require identifying and tracking nonverbal behaviors, such as gaze, body posture, facial expressions, and actions, all of which contribute to understanding how expressions are contextualized in the dialogue, and interpreted relative to the epistemic attitudes of each agent. In this paper, we adopt Generative Lexicon's approach to event structure to provide a lexical semantics for ontic and epistemic actions as used in Bolander's interpretation of Dynamic Epistemic Logic, called *Lexical Event Modeling (LEM)*. This allows for the compositional construction of epistemic models of a dialogue state. We demonstrate how veridical and false belief scenarios are treated compositionally within this model.

Keywords: Theory of Mind · HCI · Epistemic Updating · Common ground tracking · multimodal dialogue · Generative Lexicon · Event Semantics

1 Introduction

With the introduction of large language models (LLMs) in the user experience for dialogue-based search and QA within HCI, much recent research has focused on aspects of Dialogue State Tracking (DST), the ability to identify and update the user's needs at each stage in the interaction, by taking into account the past dialogue moves and history. Such interactions are largely unimodal, characterized by linguistic queries and prompts from the human and linguistic responses by the system. Discourse policies for appropriateness or correctness of the system response can be arrived at by modeling such unimodal interactions, given the constrained nature of the context of the dialogue. Hence, most papers benchmarking the performance of dialogue models are often biased towards reflecting such interactions [9,19,26].

M. Kurosu et al. (Eds.): HCII 2024, LNCS 15374, pp. 174–192, 2025.
https://doi.org/10.1007/978-3-031-76803-3_10

When we move into the area of multimodal HCI or HRI dialogues, where information is conveyed through language, gesture, visual cues, and situated reference, interpretation becomes much more difficult [25]. Further, if we attempt to extend such interactions to model dialogues with multiple participants, we need to track not only the dialogue state, but also the *epistemic state* of each participant as well as the common ground of the entire group, as it develops during the dialogue [5]. This involves identifying the beliefs, desires, and intentions (Theory of Mind) for each actor in the interaction, as well as each actor's attitudes towards the other participants. These are constructed from not only the linguistic expressions uttered by each speaker, but from other communicative modalities, such as content-bearing gesture, as well as nonverbal behaviors, such as gaze, body posture, facial expressions, and actions, all of which contribute to understanding how expressions are contextualized in the dialogue, and interpreted relative to the epistemic attitudes of each agent.

In order to account for such representations, Dynamic Epistemic Logic has recently been implemented in the context of HCI and HRI to identify shared and divergent beliefs between participants [5,17]. For example, [5] demonstrates how epistemic updating and false beliefs can be modeled in an HRI task, illustrating the alignment of diverse modalities for determining belief states.

However, in multimodal dialogues, one of the major difficulties is determining how to compositionally construct epistemic models for the participants. There are three main dimensions of knowledge that need to be accounted for in such situations:

- **Language and gesture**: the different sources for the information that is announced or introduced into the context;
- **Gaze, posture, facial expressions**: nonverbal behaviors that indicate attention, co-attention, engagement, boredom, other emotional states;
- **Actions and objects in the world**: physical events that occur with the objects in the context.

The challenge for multimodal dialogue understanding is to determine how to compositionally construct epistemic models with these diverse sources of knowledge. More concretely, the question is how such representationally diverse sources are integrated, aligned, and harmonized into an operational form that fits within the mechanisms of Dynamic Epistemic Logic (DEL).

Given this challenge, in this paper, we study the creation of common ground in multimodal task-oriented interactions, in order to develop computational strategies and their models for representing and updating epistemic states. Our investigation involved studying the multimodal dialogue between a triad of co-situated students collaborating to solve a weights task for five blocks, using only a balance scale. The task is particularly suited for our purpose, because the participants naturally engage in the different modalities that are so crucial for understanding multimodal HCI: namely, speech, gesture, gaze, and of course joint actions. From the perspectives of both dialogue state modeling as well as common ground updating, there are several distinct action types and their effects that need to be identified and tracked:

(1) a. **Ontic actions**; interactions with and movements of the objects in the shared space; i.e., blocks and the balance scale;
b. **Epistemic actions**; changes to the epistemic state of one or more of the participants in the interaction.

We assume the architecture of the Common Ground Tracking model developed in [22,38,52], where an Evidence-based Dynamic Epistemic Logic is deployed to track common ground in a shared task. This involves two steps: applying recognition algorithms over each modality: speech [48], gesture [8], gaze detection [29], and action recognition [44]; aligning and interpreting the model results to determine common ground for the group [22].

In this paper, we extend this model by providing a compositional strategy for interpretation of each agent's epistemic state, given the current context. We present an extension of Bolander's model of DEL [5] adapted to multi-party dialogues, involving task-oriented interactions using multiple modalities. This approach, called *Lexical Event Modeling (LEM)*, enables the compositional construction of an epistemic model for a dialogue state as well as the updating to next state, given new information. The overall goal is to identify the epistemic content in situated dialogues, by interpreting the verbal and nonverbal behaviors of each agent, as well as referenced objects and situational relations in the context.

We proceed as follows. We examine the contribution of four distinct modalities (speech, gesture, action, and visual attention) to the information in a dialogue state and the associated update operations for determining epistemic content and common ground. In our model (as in the underlying corpus), each channel is encoded as an AMR-like representation, including: S-AMR for spoken language AMR [2]; GAMR for gesture [8]; Act-AMR for actions and events [44]; and the perception verb subset of PropBank from Act-AMR for attention. The predicative core for each AMR is based on the lexical resource, VerbNet-GL [47], which incorporates Generative Lexicon's dynamic event structure, distinguishing an event's *pre-state* and *post-state*, and the *program* mapping between them.

We distinguish verbal predicates as denoting either public or private events, and then provide an appropriate *epistemic framing* for the verb semantics, based on the role that belief, knowledge, doubt, or perception, plays relative to carrying out or performing this event. Two kinds of epistemic framing are identified: lexical and contextual. For example, an agent performing an action will believe (or know) that they are engaged in the act. Hence, for any verb containing an AGENT participant role, we presuppose an epistemic frame of belief towards that act. Similarly, in a dialogue, we contextualize a speech act as introducing an epistemic frame of belief (or the appropriate epistemic attitude) toward the proposition being uttered. A *lexical event model* will be identified as that component of the resulting Kripke structure, derived from an epistemic framing operation.

To illustrate how epistemic framing is interpreted from distinct modal descriptions, consider the dialogue state shown in Fig. 1, from one of the Weights Task Dataset videos [21]. In this scene, the participants in the image are denoted

Fig. 1. Example of a multimodal interaction

as p_1, p_2, and p_3 from left to right, respectively. Participant p_1 says of the scale, "It seems pretty balanced." Let us refer to this as b. At the same time, both p_2 and p_3 are visually attending to the situation which b refers to.

This scene shows information conveyed through two modalities (speech and vision), each of which has epistemic consequences. For example, the utterance introduces a public announcement of proposition b, which presupposes p_1's belief in b, and the audience's belief that p_1 believes b. Similarly, the visual perception of b for the other two participants presupposes that they each either believe or at least have evidence for b. We will demonstrate how this information is contributed compositionally from the lexical event models for each modality.

2   Related Work

This work draws on research on common ground and Theory of Mind, multimodal HCI, Dialogue State Tracking, and the role of gesture in multimodal interactions. Multimodal dialogue involves having a shared understanding of both utterance meaning (content) and the speaker's meaning in a specific context (intent), involves the ability to link these two in the act of situationally grounding meaning to the local context, what is typically referred to as "establishing the common ground" between speakers [1,10,15,42,46]. The concept of common ground refers to the set of shared beliefs among participants in a Human-Human interaction (HHI) [16,28,45], as well as HCI [23,31] and HRI interactions [13,24,41].

The role of nonverbal behavior in multimodal communication has recently taken on new interest within CL and the broader AI community. Gesture AMR (GAMR) [8] considers gestures that convey the same propositional content and intentionality as speech acts. Gesture may have meaning on its own, or it may enhance the meaning provided by the verbal modality [14]. Also critical to multimodal dialogue is human action, which in addition to communicating deictic and bridging information can also make lasting changes to the world, affecting the common ground [44]. Additionaly, gaze as a non-verbal behavior, also serve a important role in communicating intent [20,29].

Dynamic Epistemic Logic (DEL) has been used extensively to model the manner in which epistemic state among agents is updated in dialogue, with the introduction of dynamic operators to represent changes in knowledge and beliefs resulting from informational events [33,49]. Two notable variants of DEL, formulated by Pacuit [3,4,32] and Bolander [5,6], differ in their treatment of information updates and underlying semantics. While both methodologies aim to capture how agents modify their epistemic states upon acquiring new information, they employ distinct frameworks and principles to achieve this objective.

Theory of Mind has also been encoded within the DEL framework as developed by Bolander [5] to tackle the problem of false belief. This framework tackles the epistemic perspectives held by multiple participants concerning the ongoing actions within the interaction. This model formalizes an agent's erroneous belief concerning a dynamic environment, as well as the capacity of other agents to identify and deliberate upon this agent's inaccurate epistemic condition. However, this necessitates the incorporation of linguistic resources to account for the lexical semantics of events within a dynamic epistemic model, elucidating how agents perceive and assimilate information as events transpire throughout a discourse.

3   Experimental Domains

3.1   The Sally-Anne Narrative

The Sally-Anne narrative is a classic psychological tool used to investigate the understanding of false beliefs in children, particularly in the context of Theory of Mind development [51]. The story involves two characters, Sally and Anne. Sally has a basket, while Anne has a box. Sally first places a marble into her basket, then leaves the scene. While Sally is away, Anne moves the marble from the basket to her own box. Sally finally returns to the scene. From the Theory of Mind perspective, the question asked to the child is: "Where will Sally look for her marble?"

More formally, the Sally and Anne narrative encompasses a sequential series of five steps, as in 2, representing five distinct situations. The initial scenario involves Sally and Anne, where Sally possesses a basket and a marble, and both participants are aware of these objects. Additionally, Anne possesses a box, which is also observed by both individuals. Subsequently, in the second scenario, Sally proceeds to place the marble inside her basket, with both participants witnessing this action. The third situation involves Sally's departure, which is observed by Anne. Moving on to the fourth scenario, Anne proceeds to remove the marble from the basket and transfers it into the box. However, it is important to note that Sally does not perceive this action. Finally, in the fifth and final scenario, Sally returns, which is acknowledged by Anne's observation (Fig. 2).

3.2   The Weights Task Dataset

The Weights Task, explored in [21], entails collaborative problem-solving task among groups of three participants. Participants are provided with the weight

Fig. 2. Sally-Anne Experiment

of one block and are tasked with determining the weights of the remaining blocks and identifying the algebraic relationship between them (the Fibonacci Sequence). Given the task's context-dependent nature involving physical objects and reasoning about their properties, the communication can be annotated in several ways: speech with dense paraphrasing [48], gesture [8], action [44], non-verbal behaviors such as gaze [29] and body postures [40] as well as collaborative problem-solving (CPS) indicators following the framework of [43].

4   Dynamic Epistemic Logic

Dynamic Epistemic Logic (DEL) is an extension of classical epistemic logic that integrates dynamic operators to represent knowledge and belief changes resulting from information events. Two prominent variants of DEL, proposed by Pacuit and Bolander, diverge in their treatment of information updates and the underlying semantics. While both approaches strive to capture how agents modify their epistemic states upon receiving new information, they employ distinct structures and principles to achieve this objective.

Pacuit's approach to DEL introduces neighborhood models which employs a set of possible worlds (neighborhoods). In Pacuit's DEL framework, updates to an agent's epistemic state are captured through evidence models, which represent the information contained in an update and is used to modify the neighborhood models, resulting in an updated representation of the agent's epistemic state. The dynamic semantics of Pacuit's DEL are established by applying evidence models to neighborhood models, thereby transforming the neighborhoods to reflect the new information. This process involves mechanism to filter or adjust the neighborhoods based on the compatibility of the evidence with the agent's prior epistemic state. This model emphasizes the compatibility of new evidence and existing beliefs [3,4,32].

Bolander's approach to DEL differs from Pacuit's by predominantly employing traditional Kripke models that utilize possible worlds and accessibility relations to represent an agent's knowledge or beliefs. The update process in Bolander's DEL is performed by taking the product of the current epistemic model (Kripke model) with the action or event model, which results in a new Kripke model reflecting the updated epistemic state. The semantics of updates in Bolander's DEL is grounded in the transformation of Kripke models through the application of action or event models. This involves modifying the accessibility relations between possible worlds based on the information conveyed by the action or event. This model focuses on how events alter accessible worlds and relations [5,6].

Bolander's Evidence-based Dynamic Epistemic Logic (EB-DEL) in [5] provides a systematic framework for formalizing the understanding of Theory of Mind, elucidating how individuals interpret and attribute mental states to other agents. Within the DEL framework, states denote the epistemic updates occurring within agents, both within the actual world and within potential alternative realities accessible from the actual world. Additionally, an event model delineates the actions that trigger such epistemic change. The event model is defined as $\mathcal{E} = (E, Q, pre, post)$, which includes preconditions and postconditions to illustrate the event updates, where

- The domain, denoted as $\mathcal{E}$, is a finite non-empty set comprising events.
- The accessibility relation $\mathcal{Q}$ is a mapping from agents in $\mathcal{A}$ to subsets of event pairs in $E \times E$.
- Each event in E is associated with a precondition, denoted as *pre*, which can be any formula in the language $\mathcal{L}(P, \mathcal{A})$.
- Each event in E is assigned a postcondition, referred to as *post*. Postconditions are expressed as conjunctions of propositional literals, representing atomic propositions and their negations, including the constants $\top$ and $\bot$.

The above graph depicts an event in the context of the Sally-Anne experiment, which describes Anne's action of moving the marble from the basket to the box, shown in Fig. 3. The event is labeled as $\langle \top, \neg t \wedge x \rangle$, indicating that the precondition of the event is trivial, and the postcondition specifies that the marble is in the basket while not being in the box. Furthermore, the event is only accessible to Anne in the actual world (marked with ⊙), as indicated by an edge labeled with the name of the relevant accessibility agent, A.

5   Dynamic Event Structure

In this section, we explore how richer models of event semantics as developed
in lexical semantics can be adapted and integrated into DEL and the notion of
event model as discussed above. For this purpose, we adopt the view of event
structure as first developed within Generative Lexicon Theory [35,36] and in
terms of a dynamic event semantics, Dynamic Interval Temporal Logic (DITL)
[27,39].

Anne takes the marble out of the basket and puts it into the box.

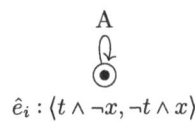

$$\hat{e}_i : \langle t \wedge \neg x, \neg t \wedge x \rangle$$

Fig. 3. Top: Anne's action of moving the marble from the basket to the box. Bottom:
Event model for this action.

On this view, activities and events are interpreted as programs, π, transi-
tioning between states or situations. A formula is interpreted as a propositional
expression, with assignment of a truth value in a specific state in the model. For
our purposes, a state is a set of propositions with assignments to variables at
a specific time index. Atomic programs are relations from states to states, and
hence interpreted over an input/output state-state pairing (cf. also [12,30]).

Following [39], we adopt the language of PDL to express an event structure
enriched to dynamically track object attributes modified in the course of the
event. All the events are represented as a sequence of states related by functions (programs) which go from state to state. The definitions of conventional
Aktionsarten can be given as follows [11,34,50]:

(2) a. **State:** φ – *happy, tall, closed, in a box.*
   b. **Process:** $\alpha; \alpha^*$ –*run, push, move.*
   c. **Achievement:** $? \neg \varphi; \alpha; ?\varphi$ – *dic, open, close*
   d. **Accomplishment:** $(? \neg \varphi; \alpha)^+; ?\varphi$ – *build, put, write.*

Specifically, consider the dynamic event structures below. The structure in (a)
below represents a **state**, e^i, at time i, with the propositional content, φ. The
event structure in (c) illustrates how program α takes the world from e^i with
content φ, to the adjacent state, e_2^{i+1}, where the propositional content has been
negated, $\neg \varphi$. This corresponds directly to **achievements**. From these two types,
the other two Vendlerian classes can be generated. **Processes** can be modeled

as an iteration of simple transitions, where two conditions hold: the transition is a change in the value of an identifiable attribute of the object; every iterated transition shares the same attribute being changed. This is illustrated in (b) below. Finally, **accomplishments** are built up by taking an underlying process event, $e{:}P$, denoting some change in an object's attribute, and synchronizing it with an achievement (simple transition): that is, $e{:}P$ is unfolding while ψ is true, until one last step of the program α makes it the case that $\neg\psi$ is now true.

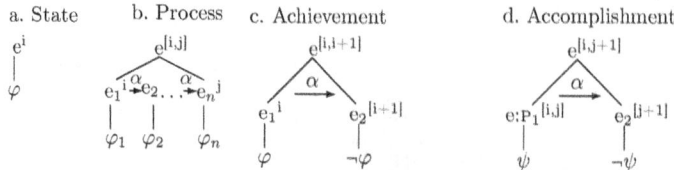

Of particular relevance to our present discussion, is GL's notion of opposition structure [36], and subsequent representations as pre-state and post-state conditions on event structures [18]. Simplified below, the transition from an initiating propositional content φ to its opposition $\neg\varphi$ is brought about by a program denoting the action inherent in the event.

Following the GL lexical representation for verbs presented in [7,37], we illustrate this with a simple transition predicate, such as *open*, (in "The door opened."), as shown below, where the CONST qualia role consists of *pre-state* and *post-state* components, encoding the opposition structure inherent in the change.

(3) λx
$$
\begin{bmatrix}
\textbf{open} \\
\text{ARGSTR} = \begin{bmatrix} \text{A1} = x ::\textbf{phys} \end{bmatrix} \\
\text{EVENTSTR} = \begin{bmatrix} \text{E1} = e_1:\textbf{state} \\ \text{E2} = e_2\textbf{state} \\ \text{P1} = p_1:\textbf{program} \end{bmatrix} \\
\text{QUALIA} = \begin{bmatrix} \text{CONST} = \begin{bmatrix} \text{PRE} = \neg open(e_1, x)) \\ \text{POST} = open(e_2, x) \end{bmatrix} \\ \text{FORMAL} = \textbf{simple\_transition} \\ \text{AGENTIVE} = nil \end{bmatrix}
\end{bmatrix}
$$

To illustrate the dynamic encoding of state and action information in a DES representation, consider the lexical semantics for the accomplishment verb *put*, shown below.

(4) $\lambda z \lambda y \lambda x$
$$
\begin{bmatrix}
\textbf{put} \\
\text{ARGSTR} = \begin{bmatrix} \text{A}_1 = \textbf{x:agent} \\ \text{A}_2 = \textbf{y:physobj} \\ \text{A}_3 = \textbf{z:location} \end{bmatrix} \\
\text{EVENTSTR} = \begin{bmatrix} \text{E1} = e_1:\textbf{state} \\ \text{E2} = e_2\textbf{state} \\ \text{P1} = p_1:\textbf{program} \end{bmatrix} \\
\text{QUALIA} = \begin{bmatrix} \text{CONST} = \begin{bmatrix} \text{PRE} = \neg at(e_1, y, z)) \\ \text{POST} = at(e_2, y, z) \end{bmatrix} \\ \text{FORMAL} = \textbf{accomp\_transition} \\ \text{AGENTIVE} = move(p_1, x, y) \end{bmatrix}
\end{bmatrix}
$$

In the next section, we show how the decompositional structure inherent in GL's event structure can be adapted to the event models as deployed in DEL's Kripke structures for agent epistemic modeling.

6   Lexical Event Models

In this section, we extend DEL's definition of event model to accommodate the event semantic information associated with specific predicates in the language. This is necessary if we are to compositionally create epistemic models for dialogue states, using data generated through automatic NLP and vision processing algorithms. This will involve two enhancements, described below:

- We retrieve the specific pre-state and post-state information for the verbal predicate associated with any action that has been recognized (annotated) within a dialogue state.
- We create an *epistemic framing* of an event or action, that can be lexically associated with a verbal predicate, encoded as part of a lexical resource.

A *lexical event model (LEM)* will be identified as that component of the resulting Kripke structure, derived from an epistemic framing operation.

Let's unpack each of these steps. The first step entails merely accessing the specific propositional content inherent in the oppposition structure for an action verb, as interpreted through the composition with its arguments. For example, consider the first agentive event in the Sally-Anne narrative, annotated as *Sally puts a marble in the basket*. Given the lexical semantics for the transition verb *put* shown in (4), the propositional content of *pre-state* and *post-state* after argument binding will be as follows (where m is marble and t is basket).

(5) a. *pre-state*: $\neg in(m, t)$
     b. *post-state*: $in(m, t)$

Now consider the introduction of the epistemic framing for an event. We wish to position an ontic action from the perspective of the participants who are present during the event. We first distinguish verbal predicates as denoting either *public* or *private* events. While attitudes and beliefs are private to an agent, most actions performed by an agent are potentially public or witnessed by others. In this sense, they are *self-announcing*, known at least to the agent performing them.

Given this distinction, we define the *epistemic framing* for an event as a modal subordination of the event from the perspective (accessibility relations) of any cognitive participant in the event, in particular the agent. That is, we can recover the epistemic attitude based on the role that belief, knowledge, doubt, or perception, plays relative to carrying out or performing a particular event.

For any public agentive event, $\hat{e}_i$, where $V(e_i, \text{AG}, \ldots)$, we introduce a default "audience" role, AU. This will be the "other agent(s)" in an epistemic embedding: $V(e_i, \text{AG}, \ldots, \text{AU})$. Hence, we now have the following enriched lexical semantics for a public agentive event, such as *put*.

(6) a. $\lambda z \lambda y \lambda x \lambda e[put(e, x{:}\textsc{ag}, y{:}\textsc{th}, z{:}\textsc{au})]$

We can now introduce the epistemic framing for a public agentive (PA) event as follows (where $\hat{e}$ denotes the propositional content that event e occurs):

(7) a. Agentive Awareness: $\forall e[PA(e) \rightarrow K_{ag}\hat{e}$
    b. Audience Witness: $\forall e[PA(e) \rightarrow B_{au}\hat{e}$

Similarly, in the context of a dialogue, we interpret a speech act as a public agentive event: hence it will fall under the application of epistemic framing, both for agent and audience. In particular, an agent performing a speech act, $V(e_{sa}, a, \varphi)$, will introduce an epistemic frame of belief (or the appropriate epistemic attitude) toward the proposition φ being uttered. For example, an agent a stating (a) will generate the epistemic frame shown in (b).

(8) a. The red block is the same weight as the blue block.
    b. B_a $r{=}b$.

Given this discussion, we now define the concept of *Lexical Event Modeling*. Adapting Bolander [5] we assume a lexical event model of $\mathcal{L}(P, \mathcal{A})$ is $\mathcal{E} = (E, Q, pre, post, in, out, ag, au)$, where

- The domain, denoted as $\mathcal{E}$, represents a finite non-empty set of events;
- The function $\mathcal{Q}\colon \mathcal{A} \rightarrow 2^{E \times E}$ assigns an "accessibility relation" $\mathcal{Q}(i)$ to each agent i in the set $\mathcal{A}$.
- The mapping $pre\colon E \rightarrow \mathcal{L}(P, \mathcal{A})$ associates a "precondition" with each event in E. The precondition can be formulated as any logical formula belonging to the language $\mathcal{L}(P, \mathcal{A})$.
- The mapping $post\colon E \rightarrow \mathcal{L}(P, \mathcal{A})$ assigns a "postcondition" to each event. Postconditions are expressed as conjunctions of propositional literals, specifically combinations of atomic propositions and their negations, which may include the logical constants $\top$ and $\bot$.
- $in\colon E \rightarrow \mathcal{L}(P, \mathcal{A})$ designates an "event input" for each event, indicating the input associated with the lexical event
- $out\colon E \rightarrow \mathcal{L}(P, \mathcal{A})$ assigns an "event output" to each event, representing the output produced by the lexical event.
- ag: for a public agentive event, denoted as e, for each $a \in \mathcal{A}$, a will possess the knowledge $K_a\hat{e}$.
- au: for a public agentive event e, for each $u \in \mathcal{A}$, u will hold the belief $B_u\hat{e}$.

As in [5], $\mathcal{Q}_i$ will be used to denote the relation $\mathcal{Q}(i)$. Within the context of the framework, when considering an element e belonging to the set E, the pair $(\mathcal{E}, e)$ is denoted as an "action" (or "pointed event model") of $\mathcal{L}(P, \mathcal{A})$. In this context, e is specifically referred to as the "actual lexical event". The two diagrams below illustrate the basic structures of a Lexical Event Model.

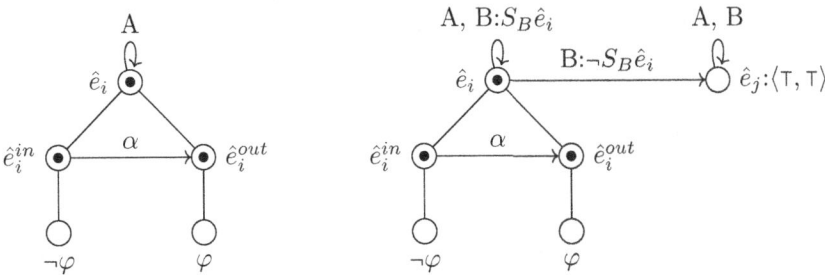

The graph on the left represents the lexical event model associated with an achievement verbal predicate, such as *close* or *die*, with opposition structure and transition program α. In this world, the audience sees the event e_i and the event is achieved.

The graph on the right is the same lexicon event mode with the same agent and audience. However, it introduces a conditional element: that is, if the audience does not see the event, then the agent and the audience will be in a world which is non-veridical, and in that world, event e_i has never been achieved.

Now let's see how lexical event models provide richer propositional content to a standard event model. Consider again the event depicted in Fig. 3. The action, *transfer* is implied by the disparity between the precondition and the postcondition, but no explicit content is provided. The propositional content of the pre- and post-states for the *transfer* act are derived from the lexical event semantics associated with the verb. To illustrate this, consider the diagram below, where the same event of Anne's action of transferring the marble from the basket to the box is viewed as a Lexical Event Model.

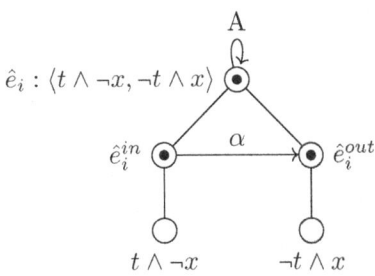

In this diagram, a lexical event has a pre-state and post-state designated, and a program α, carried out by an agent, A. The graph employs event input (designated as $\hat{e}_i^{in}$) and event output (referred to as $\hat{e}_i^{out}$) to denote the precondition and postcondition of an ontic alteration, where $t \wedge \neg x$ signifies "marble is in the basket and not in the box" and $\neg t \wedge x$ indicates "marble is not in the basket and in the box". Moreover, the manifestation of a transition is depicted by an edge labeled with the event α, which is *transfer* in this example. The relevant agent is identified by an edge labeled with their name, designated as A within this event.

Now consider the situated epistemic model, where we capture the visual attention or absence of attention by another agent, in this case Sally. We gloss this modal act below in (a) along with its modal form in (b).[1]

(9) a. Sally did not see the act of transfer.
    b. $\neg S_S \varphi$

We compose the epistemic framing associated with this and get the following compositional event model:

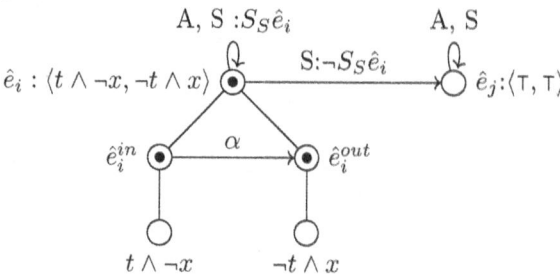

Hence, the epistemic consequences of the Lexical Event Modeling strategy introduced here can be summarized as follows (where the modal B_a represents belief of an agent a, DO is an action, and SA is a speech act):

(10) a. **Acting is Believing:** $DO_a\varphi \rightarrow B_a\varphi$ (you believe your own actions) As an agent participant in an event, you believe it has happened.
     b. **Saying is Believing:** $SA_a\varphi \rightarrow B_a\varphi$ (you believe what you say) As actor of a declarative speech act, you believe the proposition you express.
     c. **Seeing is Believing:** $S_a\varphi \rightarrow B_a\varphi$ (you believe what you see) As witness to a situation or event, you believe it to have occurred.

7   Constructing Epistemic Models from Annotations

In order to demonstrate the use and composition of lexical event models, we consider a case of the Weight Task with false belief as described by the following procedural steps, shown in Figs. 4, 5 and 6:

1. Both participants, p_1 and p_2, as well as p_3, possess knowledge regarding the weight of the red block, which is determined to be 10 g. p_1 places the green block on the left scale, while positioning the red and blue blocks on the opposite side of the scale. Throughout this process, p_1 and p_2 focus their attention on the scale and the blocks, whereas p_3 directs his attention towards the laptop.
2. Subsequently, p_2 asserts that the scale is balanced. Both p_1 and p_2 continue to observe the scale and the blocks, while p_3 maintains his attention on the laptop.

---

[1] We normalize the distinction between knowledge and belief so that we maintain a KD45 logic.

Fig. 4. Participants get information about the green block. (Color figure online)

Fig. 5. Participants get information about the blue block. (Color figure online)

Fig. 6. Participants get information about the purple block.

3. At this stage, p_1 points at the blocks and the scales, drawing $p_2's$ attention towards him. In response, p_2 places the blue block on the left scale, and positions the red block on the opposing side. Throughout this process, all participants (p_1, p_2, and p_3) direct their attention towards the scale and the blocks.
4. Following the arrangement, p_3 declares that the scale is balanced. Consequently, all participants (p_1, p_2, and p_3) continue to focus their attention on the scale and the blocks.
5. In the subsequent step, p_1 places the purple block on the left scale, while positioning the red and green blocks on the opposite side. Throughout this process, p_1, p_2, and p_3 concentrate their attention on the scale.
6. Finally, p_1 claims that the weight of the purple block is 30 g, while p_3 disputes this claim, stating that the purple block does not weigh 30 g.

In this example, p_3 holds a false belief regarding the purple block due to his lack of awareness of the actions performed by participant p_1 in the first step and the balanced state of the scale in the second step. In the first step, only participants p_1 and p_2 observe the actions performed by p_1. Consequently, the visual annotations for this scenario indicate that p_1 and p_2 see the action ($S_{p_1,p_2}\hat{e}_i$), while p_3 does not ($S_{p_3} \neg \hat{e}_i$), where $\hat{e}_i$ represents the action performed by p_1. The corresponding action annotations for this scenario can be represented as follows:

```
(p / put-01 :ARG0 (p / p1) :ARG1 (g / green block) :ARG2 (1 / left scale))
(p / put-01 :ARG0 (p / p1) :ARG1 (r / red block) :ARG2 (r1 / right scale))
(p / put-01 :ARG0 (p / p1) :ARG1 (b / blue block) :ARG2 (r / right scale))
```

In the second scenario, participant p_2 performs a speech act, indicating that the scale is balanced. Both p_1 and p_2 observe this balance, while p_3 does not. Therefore, the gaze annotations for this scenario indicate that p_1 and p_2 see the balanced scale ($S_{p_1,p_2}\hat{e}_j$), whereas p_3 does not ($\neg S_{p_3}\hat{e}_j$), where $\hat{e}_j$ represents the balanced state of the scale.

During the first step, all three participants are aware that the weight of the red block is 10 g. This knowledge is shared among them, leading to the belief:

$B_{p_1,p_2,p_3} red = 10g$. However, only participants p_1 and p_2 witness the actions performed by p_1. Based on the axiom "seeing is believing," we can infer that p_1 and p_2 believe in the occurrence of p_1's action ($B_{p_1,p_2} \hat{e}_i$), while p_3 holds the belief that it did not happen ($B_{p_3} \neg \hat{e}_i$). In the second step, drawing upon the axiom "you believe what you say" and the absence of objections from p_1, we can deduce that both p_1 and p_2 believe the scales to be balanced. Based on this perceived evidence, the participants conclude that the weight of the green block equals the combined weight of the red and blue blocks, expressed as $B_{p_1,p_2} green = red + blue$. However, p_3 lacks these beliefs and consequently does not hold the belief that $green = red + blue$. These two missing beliefs contribute to p_3's false belief in the sixth step.

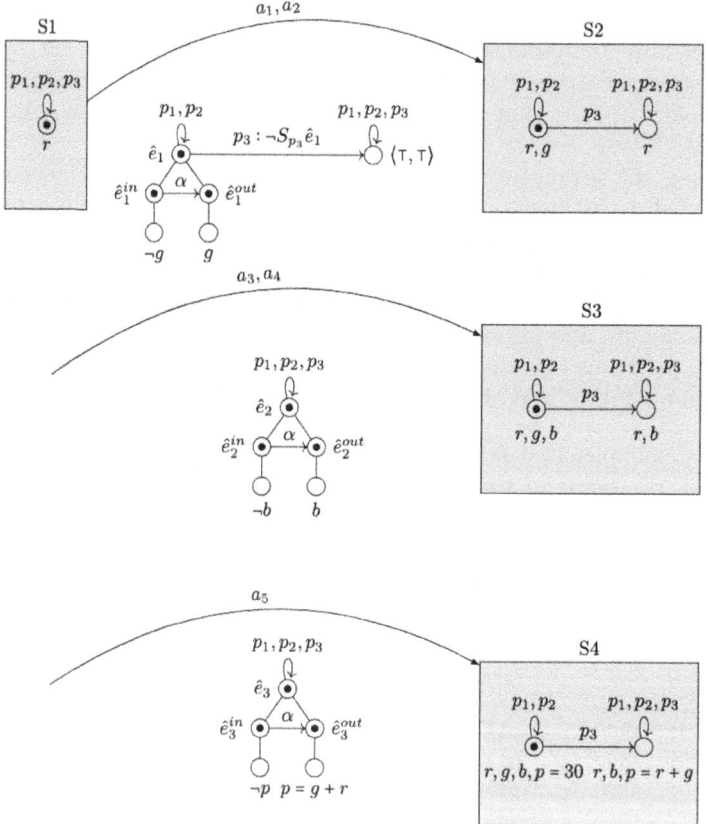

Fig. 7. The Weight Task Model

We employ Fig. 7 to illustrate the evidence-based epistemic updates of the exmaple. S_1 represents the participants' initial epistemic states wherein they all hold the belief that "red = 10 g". The actions performed by participant p_1

are represented by a_1, signifying the three put actions. The speech act from participant p_2 in the second step is represented by a_2. These actions are depicted as $\hat{e}_1$, with the output being that both p_1 and p_2 now believe that "green = red + blue" in S_2. As p_3 does not witness the put action and the balance of the scale, no changes occur for him, and consequently, he does not undergo any epistemic updates within the actual world S_2.

Moving on, a_3 and a_4 represent the third and fourth step, respectively. All three participants witness p_2 placing the blue and red blocks on opposite sides of the scale, observing that the scale is balanced. These actions are depicted as an event model $\hat{e}_2$. Based on this evidence, they all come to believe that the red block and the blue block possess equal weight. This update is reflected in S_3. It is worth noting that despite sharing the same knowledge regarding the blue block, S_3 still maintains two distinct epistemic worlds: only p_1 and p_2 possess comprehensive knowledge about the blocks in the actual world, while p_3 remains unaware of the green block due to their lack of previous epistemic updates.

The fifth step is represented by a_5. The action model illustrates that following the put action, observed by all participants, each individual revises their belief concerning the purple block. Specifically, they now believe that the weight of the purple block equals the combined weight of the red block and the green block. Drawing from this knowledge and the preceding epistemic updates regarding the green block, p_1 and p_2 further revise their beliefs concerning the weight of the purple block. However, since p_3 missed the belief updates regarding the green block, he is unable to perform the inference. Consequently, in S_4, p_3 lacks any knowledge updates regarding the actual weight of the purple block.

8   Conclusion and Future Work

In this paper, we examine the interpretation of multimodal dialogue and the contributions of ontic and epistemic events to the changes introduced in discourse. We introduce a technique for how lexical semantic information associated with verbal predicates can be integrated into epistemic event models as adopted in Dynamic Epistemic Logic, in order to faciliate a more compositional interpretation of epistemic state in dialogue modeling. To this end, we introduce the notion of Lexical Event Modeling (LEM), which encoded both the subeventual properties of events in a language, as well as the epistemic framing of agentive participants in these events. This is intended as the first step in the construction of a compositional procedure for computing an epistemic event model of a dialogue, by reading off the representations from multiple modalities in a discourse.

Acknowledgements. This work was supported in part by NSF grants DRL 2019805 and CNS 2033932 to Dr. Pustejovsky at Brandeis University. We would like to thank Nikhil Krishnaswamy, Ken Lai, Ricky Brutti, Chris Tam, and the reviewers for their comments and suggestions. The views expressed herein are ours alone.

References

1. Asher, N.: Common ground, corrections and coordination. J. Semantics **17**(4), 481–512 (1998)
2. Banarescu, L., et al.: Abstract meaning representation for sembanking. In: Proceedings of the 7th Linguistic Annotation Workshop and Interoperability with Discourse, pp. 178–186 (2013)
3. van Benthem, J., Fernández-Duque, D., Pacuit, E.: Evidence and plausibility in neighborhood structures. Ann. Pure Appl. Logic **165**(1), 106–133 (2014)
4. van Benthem, J., Pacuit, E.: Dynamic logics of evidence-based beliefs. Stud. Logica. **99**, 61–92 (2011)
5. Bolander, T.: Seeing is believing: Formalising false-belief tasks in dynamic epistemic logic. Jaakko Hintikka on knowledge and game-theoretical semantics, pp. 207–236 (2018)
6. Bolander, T., Andersen, M.B.: Epistemic planning for single-and multi-agent systems. J. Appl. Non-Classical Logics **21**(1), 9–34 (2011)
7. Brown, S.W., Bonn, J., Kazeminejad, G., Zaenen, A., Pustejovsky, J., Palmer, M.: Semantic representations for NLP using VerbNet and the generative lexicon. Front. Artif. Intell. **5**, 821697 (2022)
8. Brutti, R., Donatelli, L., Lai, K., Pustejovsky, J.: Abstract Meaning Representation for gesture. In: Proceedings of the Thirteenth Language Resources and Evaluation Conference, pp. 1576–1583. European Language Resources Association, Marseille, France (2022)
9. Budzianowski, P., et al.: MultiWOZ - a large-scale multi-domain Wizard-of-Oz dataset for task-oriented dialogue modelling. In: Proceedings of the 2018 Conference on Empirical Methods in Natural Language Processing, pp. 5016–5026. Association for Computational Linguistics, Brussels, Belgium (2018). https://doi. org/10.18653/v1/D18-1547, https://aclanthology.org/D18-1547
10. Clark, H.H., Brennan, S.E.: Grounding in communication. In: Resnick, L., B., L., John, M., Teasley, S., D (eds.) Perspectives on Socially Shared Cognition, pp. 13–1991. American Psychological Association (1991)
11. Dowty, D.R.: Word meaning and Montague grammar: The semantics of verbs and times in generative semantics and in Montague's PTQ, vol. 7. Springer (1979)
12. Fernando, T.: Situations in LTL as strings. Inf. Comput. **207**(10), 980–999 (2009)
13. Fischer, K.: How people talk with robots: designing dialog to reduce user uncertainty. AI Mag. **32**(4), 31–38 (2011)
14. Goldin-Meadow, S.: Hearing Gesture: How Our Hands Help Us Think, vol. 14 (2003). https://doi.org/10.2307/j.ctv1w9m9ds
15. Grice, H.P.: Logic and conversation. In: Speech acts, pp. 41–58. Brill (1975)
16. Hadley, L.V., Naylor, G., Hamilton, A.F.d.C.: A review of theories and methods in the science of face-to-face social interaction. Nat. Rev. Psychol. **1**(1), 42–54 (2022). https://doi.org/10.1038/s44159-021-00008-w, https://www.nature. com/articles/s44159-021-00008-w, number: 1 Publisher: Nature Publishing Group
17. Hansen, L.D., Bolander, T.: Implementing theory of mind on a robot using dynamic epistemic logic. In: Twenty-Ninth International Joint Conference on Artificial Intelligence, pp. 1615–1621. International Joint Conference on Artificial Intelligence Organization (2020)
18. Im, S., Pustejovsky, J.: Annotating lexically entailed subevents for textual inference tasks. In: Twenty-Third International Flairs Conference (2010)

19. Jacqmin, L., Barahona, L.M.R., Favre, B.: Äúdo you follow me?Äú: A survey of recent approaches in dialogue state tracking. In: Proceedings of the 23rd Annual Meeting of the Special Interest Group on Discourse and Dialogue, pp. 336–350 (2022)
20. Kendrick, K.H., Holler, J., Levinson, S.C.: Turn-taking in human face-to-face interaction is multimodal: gaze direction and manual gestures aid the coordination of turn transitions. Philos. Trans. R. Soc. B **378**(1875), 20210473 (2023)
21. Khebour, I., et al.: The weights task dataset: a multimodal dataset of collaboration in a situated task. J. Open Humanit. Data **10**(7), 1–7 (2024)
22. Khebour, I.K., et al.: Common ground tracking in multimodal dialogue. In: Proceedings of the 2024 Joint International Conference on Computational Linguistics, Language Resources and Evaluation (LREC-COLING 2024), pp. 3587–3602 (2024)
23. Krishnaswamy, N., Pustejovsky, J.: Generating a novel dataset of multimodal referring expressions. In: Proceedings of the 13th International Conference on Computational Semantics-Short Papers, pp. 44–51 (2019)
24. Kruijff, G.J.M., et al.: Situated dialogue processing for human-robot interaction. In: Cognitive systems, pp. 311–364. Springer (2010)
25. Li, K., Li, J., Guo, D., Yang, X., Wang, M.: Transformer-based visual grounding with cross-modality interaction. ACM Trans. Multimed. Comput. Commun. Appl. **19**(6), 1–19 (2023)
26. Liao, L., Long, L.H., Ma, Y., Lei, W., Chua, T.S.: Dialogue state tracking with incremental reasoning. Trans. Assoc. Comput. Linguist. **9**, 557–569 (2021)
27. Mani, I., Pustejovsky, J.: Interpreting Motion: Grounded Representations for Spatial Language. Oxford University Press (2012)
28. Markowska, M., Soubki, A., Mar, G., Mirroshandel, S.A., Rambow, O., Wasilewska, A.: Formal representation of common ground in dialogue
29. Miller, P.W.: Body language in the classroom. Tech. Connecting Educ. Careers **80**(8), 28–30 (2005)
30. Naumann, R.: Aspects of changes: a dynamic event semantics. J. Semant. **18**, 27–81 (2001)
31. Ohmer, X., Duda, M., Bruni, E.: Emergence of hierarchical reference systems in multi-agent communication. In: Proceedings of the 29th International Conference on Computational Linguistics, pp. 5689–5706 (2022)
32. Pacuit, E.: Neighborhood semantics for modal logic. Springer (2017)
33. Plaza, J.: Logics of public communications. Synthese **158**(2), 165–179 (2007)
34. Pustejovsky, J.: The syntax of event structure. Cognition **1**(41), 47–81 (1991)
35. Pustejovsky, J.: The Generative Lexicon. MIT Press, Cambridge, MA (1995)
36. Pustejovsky, J.: Events and the semantics of opposition. Events as grammatical objects, pp. 445–482 (2000)
37. Pustejovsky, J.: Dynamic event structure and habitat theory. In: Proceedings of the 6th International Conference on Generative Approaches to the Lexicon (GL2013), pp. 1–10. ACL (2013)
38. Pustejovsky, J., Krishnaswamy, N.: Embodied human computer interaction. KI-Künstliche Intelligenz **35**(3–4), 307–327 (2021)
39. Pustejovsky, J., Moszkowicz, J.: The qualitative spatial dynamics of motion. The Journal of Spatial Cognition and Computation (2011)
40. Radu, I., Tu, E., Schneider, B.: Relationships between body postures and collaborative learning states in an augmented reality study. In: Bittencourt, I.I., Cukurova, M., Muldner, K., Luckin, R., Millán, E. (eds.) AIED 2020. LNCS (LNAI), vol. 12164, pp. 257–262. Springer, Cham (2020). https://doi.org/10.1007/978-3-030-52240-7_47

41. Scheutz, M., Cantrell, R., Schermerhorn, P.: Toward humanlike task-based dialogue processing for human robot interaction. AI Mag. **32**(4), 77–84 (2011)
42. Stalnaker, R.: Common ground. Linguist. Philos. **25**(5-6), 701–721
43. Sun, C., Shute, V.J., Stewart, A., Yonehiro, J., Duran, N., D'Mello, S.: Towards a generalized competency model of collaborative problem solving. Comput. Educ. **143**, 103672 (2020)
44. Tam, C., Brutti, R., Lai, K., Pustejovsky, J.: Annotating situated actions in dialogue. In: Proceedings of the 4th International Workshop on Designing Meaning Representation (2023)
45. Traum, D.: A computational theory of grounding in natural language conversation. PhD thesis, University of Rochester (1994)
46. Traum, D.R., Larsson, S.: The information state approach to dialogue management. Current and new directions in discourse and dialogue, pp. 325–353 (2003)
47. Tu, J., et al.: GLAMR: augmenting AMR with GL-VerbNet event structure. In: Proceedings of the 2024 Joint International Conference on Computational Linguistics, Language Resources and Evaluation (LREC-COLING 2024), pp. 7746–7759 (2024)
48. Tu, J., Rim, K., Pustejovsky, J.: Competence-based question generation. In: Proceedings of the 29th International Conference on Computational Linguistics, pp. 1521–1533 (2022)
49. Van Ditmarsch, H., van Der Hoek, W., Kooi, B.: Dynamic epistemic logic, vol. 337. Springer Science (2007)
50. Vendler, Z.: Verbs and times. The philosophical review pp. 143–160 (1957)
51. Wimmer, H., Perner, J.: Beliefs about beliefs: representation and constraining function of wrong beliefs in young children's understanding of deception. Cognition **13**(1), 103–128 (1983)
52. Zhu, Y., et al.: Modeling theory of mind in multimodal HCI. In: International Conference on Human-Computer Interaction

Exploring the Dynamics of XR and AI Synergy in Architectural Design

Juan David Salazar Rodriguez$^{(\boxtimes)}$ ⓘ and Sam Conrad Joyce ⓘ

META Design Lab, Architecture and Sustainable Design Pillar,
Singapore University of Technology and Design, Singapore, Singapore
1008372@mymail.sutd.edu.sg, sam_joyce@sutd.edu.sg

Abstract. This study investigates the integration of Extended Reality (XR) and Artificial Intelligence (AI) in architectural design, examining their collective impact on design methodologies, stakeholder engagement, and project outcomes. Through a comprehensive review of existing literature, various applications of XR and AI across different stages of architectural design, including design exploration, building shape optimization, façade design, layout planning, floor plans, and energy performance, are identified and analyzed. The research proposes two key frameworks: the XR-AI Deployment Framework and the Vision Map for XR-AI integration. The XR-AI Deployment Framework offers a structured approach for effectively integrating XR and AI technologies into architectural projects, comprising preparation and planning, implementation process, and full-scale application phases. Meanwhile, the Vision Map provides a systematic methodology for understanding project objectives and requirements, guiding practitioners in gathering essential information to inform the deployment process. A practical case study illustrates the application of the XR-AI deployment framework, showcasing its adaptability and potential to revolutionize architectural design processes. This research highlights the transformative possibilities of XR and AI in architectural practice, while also addressing challenges such as technical complexity, data management, and ethical considerations. Ultimately, it emphasizes the need for ongoing research and educational advancements to ensure responsible and effective utilization of XR and AI technologies in architectural design.

Keywords: Extended Reality (XR) · Artificial Intelligence (AI) · Architectural design

1 Introduction

In recent years, the evolution of architectural design representation has seen a significant transformation from traditional 2D orthographic projection drawings, such as elevations, sections, and floor plans, to sophisticated digital 3D models or renderings [1]. These advancements have been facilitated by various software tools like Revit, AutoCAD, ArchiCAD and others, enhancing various aspects of the design process including improved communication, fluid development of design ideas, and early detection of potential deficiencies. However, these predominantly two-dimensional representations,

© The Author(s), under exclusive license to Springer Nature Switzerland AG 2025
M. Kurosu et al. (Eds.): HCII 2024, LNCS 15374, pp. 193–210, 2025.
https://doi.org/10.1007/978-3-031-76803-3_11

whether printed or displayed on screens, arguably have inherent limitations in intuitiveness due to their flat nature, which fails to convey the full depth and spatial characteristics of architectural designs.

The introduction of Extended Reality (XR) technologies, including Augmented Reality (AR), Virtual Reality (VR), and Mixed Reality (MR), marks a pivotal shift in architectural rendering and visualization [2]. XR technologies facilitate the creation of immersive environments where users can interact with both real and virtual elements, offering a more intuitive and engaging experience. The ability to merge holographic 3D models with the physical environment, as enabled by MR, enhances the user's understanding by providing spatially referenced information that supplements their knowledge of the design context [3]. This approach proves superior in the literature to traditional methods [4], offering solutions to previously cumbersome processes such as the generation of multiple physical models or the extensive use of paper in design reviews.

The integration of Artificial Intelligence (AI) with XR technologies is set to redefine architectural practices further [3, 5]. AI's analytical and predictive capabilities, when combined with XR's immersive and intuitive environments, arguably create a powerful toolset for architects. This synergy perhaps enables more efficient design reviews, accurate problem-solving in early project stages, and tailored design adaptations based on real-time data analysis [2]. The convergence of AI and XR in architectural design not only can streamline the design and construction process but also open up new avenues for creativity and innovation, thus the significance of the present paper.

Given these developments, this paper aims to explore the dynamics of XR and AI in architectural design comprehensively. This paper delves into the potential applications, benefits, and challenges of integrating these technologies into current architectural practices. By examining the impact of XR and AI on the architectural design process, we aim to provide insights into how these technologies can be harnessed to enhance design efficiency, client engagement, and overall project outcomes. This investigation seeks to contribute to the expanding body of knowledge on XR and AI in architecture, offering concrete results and recommendations for practitioners considering the adoption of these technologies.

Hence, the primary goal of this paper is to systematically explore the relationship between XR and AI within architectural design. We aim to:

- Identify how XR and AI individually and collectively influence design processes.
- Assess the current state of XR-AI integration across various architectural domains.
- Propose a framework for effectively implementing XR and AI technologies throughout the architectural design process.

2   Methodology

This literature review follows a systematic approach to explore the dynamics of Extended Reality (XR) and Artificial Intelligence (AI) within the field of architectural design. The methodology employed is aimed at ensuring a comprehensive and unbiased collection, analysis, and synthesis of relevant academic and industry literature. This systematic review was conducted in several stages (Fig. 1):

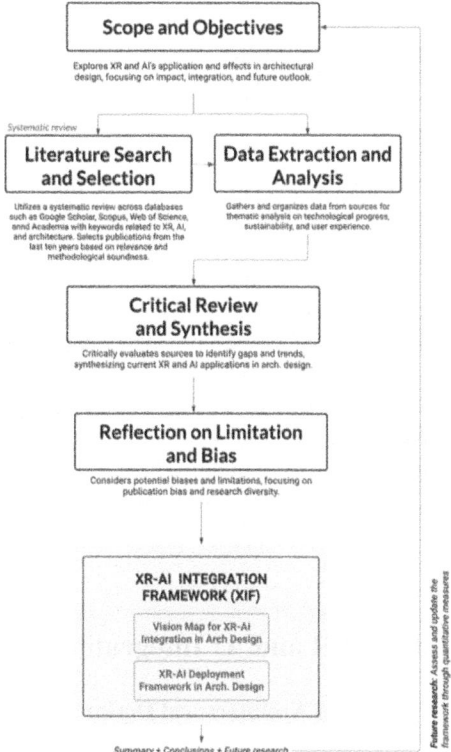

Fig. 1. Qualitative research methods and processes.

3 Background

3.1 Extended Reality (XR)

Extended Reality (XR), as defined by Fast-Berglind and Liang [3], encompasses both real and virtual environments, alongside human-machine interactions facilitated by computer technology and wearables. This fusion of realities enables the creation of immersive digital worlds with specific tools tailored to diverse objectives. The framework of XR, elucidated by Milgram and Colquhoun [6] through the Reality-Virtuality Continuum, delineates the spectrum of experiences. Augmented Reality (AR) enriches the real world with digital overlays, exemplified by technologies like "Google Glass" [7]. Conversely, Virtual Reality (VR) envelops users in entirely digital environments, typified by devices such as Facebook's Oculus Quest [7]. Mixed Reality (MR) occupies an intermediary position, blending virtual elements with real-world perceptions, epitomized by Microsoft HoloLens [8]. Apple's Vision Pro, released in 2024, promises a comprehensive XR experience across the continuum, revolutionizing user engagement.

Before the advent of Vision Pro, users had to select devices aligning with their specific XR goals. Despite Vision Pro's novelty, its contextual implications within XR's spectrum remain unexplored. Nevertheless, XR technology holds promise for enhancing design learning processes by mitigating communication ambiguities, thereby refining design rationale and review procedures [9].

3.2 Artificial Intelligence (AI)

AI, defined as machine intelligence by Diaz [10], encompasses various dimensions including structure, behavior, capabilities, function, and principles [11]. Stone et al. [12] describe AI as the pursuit of imbuing machines with foresight and appropriateness in their environments. Key capabilities include problem-solving, knowledge representation, reasoning, and learning.

The term "Artificial Intelligence" was coined in 1956 at Dartmouth College [13]. Early AI programs demonstrated remarkable feats like solving algebra word problems and learning language, but the complexity was underestimated, leading to inflated expectations and subsequent disillusionment. The 1970s witnessed the first AI winter characterized by diminished research interest and funding [14]. Despite setbacks, AI progressed under various names. The past decade marked the modern AI era, driven by advancements in computation, leading to subfields like Deep Learning, Machine Learning, Artificial General Intelligence, and Big Data.

4   The Current State of XR and AI Integration in Architecture

4.1   Current Trends in AI-Aided Architectural Design

The present paper has classified studies found in the literature by their application to different areas of conceptual design: design exploration, building shape, façade design, layout design, floor plans, and energy performance.

Design Explorations. The importance of exploratory design, particularly in the conceptual phase, is underscored, emphasizing the necessity for a clear understanding of the problem and the legitimacy of the solution before synthesis begins [15]. This iterative process in architectural design involves searching for both the design problem space and the constraints hindering a solution. Modern architecture relies on computer models to facilitate this exploration [16]. Parmee [16] proposes an integrated design concept that incorporates evolutionary computing at each stage of the design process, leveraging the designer's knowledge and intuition. Three stages—conceptual design, search, and detailed design—are identified, with emphasis on clarifying subsets of the system through design representation. Parmee [16] developed a system prioritizing designer interaction and knowledge during the conceptual phase, employing genetic algorithms for optimization and exploration. Their system aims to efficiently explore design variants while sustaining designer involvement.

Wen et al. [17] explore architectural form design using fractal algorithms for aesthetic purposes, emphasizing the need for further study into computational design techniques. Graham et al. [18] presented a system for user-driven selective breeding of architectural objects, aiming to aid designers in the conceptual phase. DeLanda [19] suggests that virtual evolution through genetic algorithms can expand the design space, offering surprise and impact, thus enhancing the design process. Research in design exploration seeks to expand the solution space, offering diverse models to assist designers rather than aiming for precise solutions. This interdisciplinary approach intersects AI and XR, potentially revolutionizing design conception and evolution.

Building Shape. In 2006, a methodology employing genetic algorithms (GAs) was introduced to optimize environmentally conscious building shapes, exemplified by a case study optimizing the floor shape of an office building [20]. Various methodologies, including H, L, T, U, and rectangular shapes, were explored to minimize energy use in residential buildings [21].

Caldas [22] introduced GENE-ARCH, a generative design system combining GAs and energy simulation for designing energy-efficient Islamic patio houses. Ekici et al. [23] proposed a self-adaptive multi-target differential evolution algorithm for shape optimization in high-rise buildings. Song et al. [24] suggested an Implicit Redundant Representation Genetic Algorithm (IRRG) for evolutionary architectural design, enhancing adaptability over time. Fang and Cho [25] utilized parametric design and GAs for energy performance optimization in small office buildings. Cubukcuoglu [26] presented robust, self-adaptive differential evolutionary algorithms for architectural design optimization.

Façade Design. Maria Skavara [27] investigated the potential of controlling cellular automaton behavior to develop adaptive, high-performance building façades for optimal lighting conditions. Implementing artificial neural networks and genetic algorithms, the approach trained the façade to adapt to structural characteristics, resulting in an adaptive and kinetic architectural entity. Gagne and Andersen [28] explored a genetic algorithm (GA) approach for performance-based exploration of façade designs. Combining micro-GA algorithms with user inputs and performance targets, the study generated numerous valid iterations while preserving the building's overall shape.

Chatzikonstantinou and Sariyildiz [29] proposed a decision-based support framework for design preferences, employing self-associated machine learning features derived through stochastic multi-objective optimization. The framework offers high-performance design solutions satisfying user-defined preferences. Agirbas [30] studied principles of cohesion, alignment, and separation from nature for architectural design and façade construction. Integrating user-defined morphodynamic perspectives and swarm intelligence-based automation, the study evaluated façade variations based on relative daylight capture.

Layout Design. In the domain of AI-assisted layout design, significant advancements have occurred, revolutionizing architectural practices. EvoArch, developed by Wong and Chan [31], utilizes a graph coding scheme to enhance the generation of architectural layout plans. Automated design techniques, employing real-coded genetic algorithms and differential evolution, have emerged for efficient space allocation in commercial building designs. Tools like EASE [32] optimize 3D space designs and facilitate the evaluation of multiple design alternatives. G-Shaper automates the design of modular residential housing, integrating personalization and production constraints through genetic algorithm strategies.

The architectural design landscape continues to evolve with the development of multilayered systems for layout and space processing optimization. Guo and Li [33] introduce systems for optimizing 3D layouts through simplified representations, reducing search spaces and streamlining design optimization processes. Furthermore, AI integration extends into conceptual design with graphically based automated learning systems. These systems utilize coded graphic neural networks for evaluating existing designs and generative adversarial networks (GANs) for creating novel designs. Despite advancements, human intervention is still required to evaluate AI-generated designs. In the context of XR-AI integration, immersive and interactive visualizations are highlighted as beneficial for enhancing spatial understanding and design decision-making. Such integration can aid in evaluating and optimizing architectural layouts, contributing to the advancement of architectural practices [34].

Floorplans. The evolution of AI-aided design in floor plan creation has progressed significantly over the years. In 1995, Gero and Schnier [35] introduced a pioneering approach utilizing genetic algorithms to centralize designs resembling a given example case, fostering creativity in design. Rosenman and Gero [36] further advanced this by focusing on viable research areas to navigate large design spaces. Rafiq et al. [37] developed a computational method optimizing multi-criteria conceptual design, aiming to reduce costs and enhance space flexibility while adhering to architectural criteria.

In 2001, GBRID, a decision-support system for conceptualizing commercial office buildings, was created, followed by the exploration of the BGRID system in 2003, showcasing the applicability of evolutionary computing in commercial office building design [38]. In 2013, a hybrid evolutionary technique was introduced for multi-level floor plan design, treating stairways and elevators as fixed points to generate coherent plans dynamically. Integration of AI with contemporary web-based tools and BIM software, such as Revit, represents a significant advancement. These tools enhance efficiency and precision in floor plan creation, offering functionalities from basic layout planning to comprehensive building information modeling. They facilitate efficient updates and coordination across project stages, reflecting a shift towards more integrated and collaborative architectural design processes.

Energy-Efficient Buildings. The growing concern over the environmental impact of buildings, especially regarding high energy consumption, has spurred significant research into AI applications aimed at enhancing efficiency, reducing costs, and mitigating ecological effects. Ghada and Negm [39] provide a comprehensive review of AI-based strategies in green architecture, highlighting genetic algorithms (GA), fuzzy logic (FL), and the Analytical Hierarchy Process (AHP) as pivotal techniques shaping the landscape. The Empire State Building's renovation serves as a transformative example of integrating AI with direct digital control systems, setting a new standard for intelligent building design and operational efficiency. These advancements not only enhance energy efficiency but also enable predictive maintenance, thus reducing operational costs and improving safety.

Research by Tsanas and Xifara [40] and others demonstrates the precision of machine learning in understanding and predicting energy dynamics within buildings. Robinson et al. [41] and Roy et al. [42] advocate for a balanced approach in selecting appropriate AI models based on specific building characteristics and data availability. Deng et al. [43] evaluate the application of machine learning to commercial energy use, suggesting careful algorithm selection to optimize performance. Innovations like Project

Dasher's integrated sensor networks and Li's intelligent data analysis method for electricity consumption prediction broaden the scope of AI applications in building management. Energy dashboards and advanced simulation software further enhance insights into energy consumption patterns, enabling better decision-making for energy savings.

4.2 Integration of XR and AI

Existing literature on XR and AI often delineates the contours of these technologies separately, rarely delving into their combined impact and potential, especially within architectural realms. For instance, Lampropoulos et al. [44] dissects the roles of deep learning, semantic web, and knowledge graphs in augmenting AR experiences, emphasizing enhancements in object detection, image processing, and computer vision. Yet, while AI's role in refining AR inputs like gestures or speech is acknowledged, the discussion remains generalized, lacking specificity in applicable techniques. Furthermore, reviews, such as those by Norouzi et al. [45], explore the domain-specific utilization of Intelligent Virtual Agents (IVAs) within AR, noting their emergent roles in assistive, therapeutic, and collaborative contexts. These reviews spotlight the critical need for IVAs to better understand their physical surroundings. However, such literature often focuses on isolated application domains—like education, professional training, or healthcare—without fully intersecting the broader vistas of XR and AI research [46].

Contrastingly, a handful of studies endeavor to bridge this divide. Luck and Aylett [47] introduce "intelligent virtual environments" discussing autonomy as a central theme, while Ribeiro de Oliveira et al. [48] evaluate VR and AI's problem-solving capabilities in sectors beyond architecture, like industry and healthcare, underlining issues like data scarcity and computational demands. Reiners et al. [49] further dissect the combined applications of XR and AI across diverse fields including medical training and autonomous vehicle simulation, yet these reviews primarily spotlight sector-specific applications without addressing fundamental research questions or the overarching synthesis of XR and AI technologies.

We found five topic clusters on XR and AI research. Most of the reviewed papers address topics related to using AI to create XR worlds [50], using AI to understand users [51], and using AI to support interaction [52]. The fourth topic cluster revolves around interacting with Vas [53], focusing on user perceptions such as emotions or trust but rarely presenting an implementation of agents. Lastly, there is minimal work on using XR for AI, which includes techniques to enhance understandability by visualizing AI models in VR or addressing the problem of limited training data in XR [46]. In the realm of architectural design, the integration of Extended Reality (XR) applications has initiated a paradigm shift, transforming traditional methodologies and introducing innovative affordances that significantly impact the design process. These transformations are not merely technological but also conceptual, affecting how architects and designers perceive and interact with their creations. This discussion section delves into the implications of these changes, focusing on the impact of AI and XR on architectural design, future directions, and the ethical and practical considerations associated with these advancements.

The integration of AI with XR enables a deeper understanding of design environments, facilitating simulation and validation of architectural solutions against real-world variables. Architects can utilize the Concept-Knowledge-Environment (CKE) theory to achieve a balance between creativity and practicality, ensuring innovative yet grounded designs. The Vision Map provides a strategic blueprint for systematic integration, emphasizing collaboration among stakeholders and the need for cross-disciplinary teams, regulatory frameworks, and educational initiatives. However, ethical and practical considerations arise, including privacy, data security, and the digital divide. Future directions in architectural practice must address these concerns by developing guidelines and standards for responsible and equitable use of AI and XR technologies. The Vision Map serves as a foundational context for discussions, highlighting the transformative impact of these technologies and offering a strategic approach to navigating challenges and opportunities (Fig. 2).

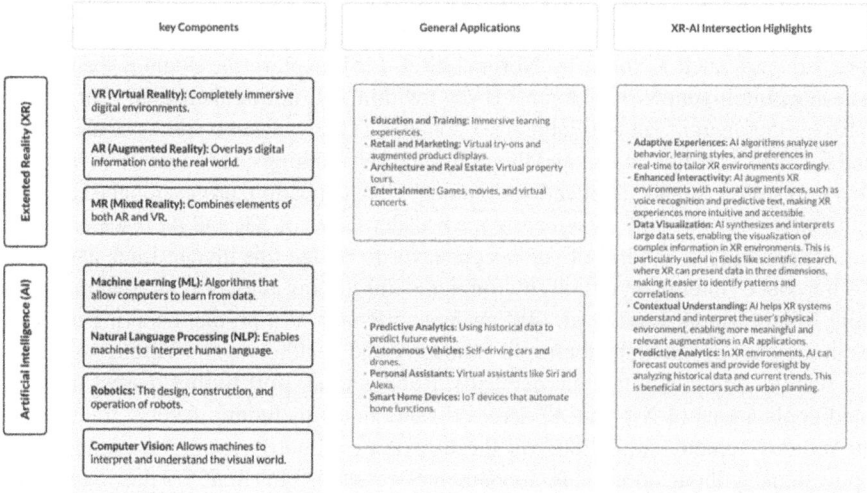

Fig. 2. Key components, applications, and intersection highlights of XR and AI Technologies.

5 Developing a Framework for XR-AI Integration

The integration of Extended Reality (XR) and Artificial Intelligence (AI) in architectural design represents a significant paradigm shift, enabling innovative, efficient, and highly interactive design processes. This integration is encapsulated within two comprehensive frameworks: the XR-AI Deployment Framework and the Mechanisms, Plans, and Procedures to inform Policy, also referred to as the Vision Map for XR-AI integration in architectural design.

5.1 XR-AI Deployment Framework

The XR-AI Deployment Framework outlines a structured approach for integrating XR and AI technologies into architectural projects. This framework is divided into three key phases:

Preparation and Planning. This initial phase focuses on understanding the project's specific requirements and establishing a solid foundation for XR and AI integration. Key activities include:

Assessment and Goal Setting. Identifying design challenges and objectives that XR and AI can address, such as enhancing visualization or streamlining collaboration.

Technology Selection. Choosing suitable XR and AI tools that align with the project's needs, whether it's virtual reality for immersive experiences or AI for data-driven design insights.

Skill Development and Training. Ensuring the project team is equipped with the necessary skills to effectively utilize selected technologies.

The deliverable from this phase, the "XR-AI Blueprint," serves as a comprehensive guide outlining the strategic approach for incorporating XR and AI into the architectural design process.

Implementation Process. The second phase involves the practical application of the XR-AI Blueprint. Key steps include:

Implementation Planning. Developing detailed plans for how XR and AI will be utilized throughout the design and construction phases.

Pilot Testing. Conducting initial tests to evaluate the integration's effectiveness and identify areas for improvement.

Feedback and Iteration. Refining the approach based on stakeholder feedback, ensuring the integration meets the project's goals and user needs.

This phase yields the "Pilot Integration Feedback," a document summarizing the outcomes of the pilot tests and recommendations for enhancing the XR-AI integration.

Full-Scale Application. The final phase involves scaling the refined integration approach to larger projects, continuously adapting to technological advancements and project feedback (Fig. 3).

In the "Assessment & Goal Setting" stage of the XR-AI deployment framework, a critical step involves engaging in a detailed inquiry to gather comprehensive information that will inform the entire deployment process. This inquiry should be adaptive, with the flexibility to cater to the specific demands and peculiarities of each project. The purpose of this step is two-fold: to ensure the resulting XR-AI tool is fully aligned with the client's vision and practical requirements, and to anticipate the needs of the end-users, thereby enhancing the efficacy and user experience of the design solution.

The following series of structured questions are designed to serve as a guide for practitioners to extract the depth of information required. These questions are categorized into distinct themes, each targeting crucial aspects of the design process: Contextual, Technical, Aesthetic and Design, Sustainable and Environmental and Stakeholder, Inquiries. Thus, this framework of inquiry encourages a holistic approach to understanding and defining the goals for the XR-AI tool, ensuring a tailored fit for the unique context of each architectural project (Table 1).

In order to ensure that the deployment of XR-AI tools in architectural design is not only innovative but also effective, it is crucial to establish a set of Key Performance

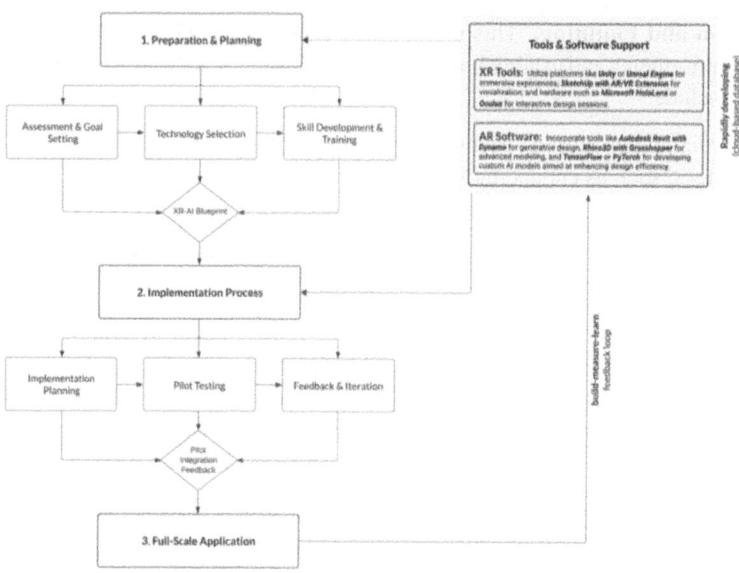

Fig. 3. Key components, applications, and intersection highlights of XR and AI Technologies.

Table 1. Key Questions for XR-AI Tool Development

Theme	Subtheme	Question
Contextual	Project scope	What is the desired scale and complexity of the project?
	End-User Profile	Who are the primary users, and what are their demographics?
	User Experience Goals	What are the key experiences that the XR-AI tool should deliver?
	Spatial Requirements	Are there specific spatial considerations or constraints?
Technical	Functional Requirements	What specific tasks should the XR-AI tool enable?
	Integration Needs	How should the XR-AI tool integrate with existing workflows or systems?
	Performance Metrics	What performance indicators will define success for the XR-AI tool?
Aesthetic and Design	Design Aesthetics	What are the aesthetic preferences or requirements?

(continued)

Table 1. (*continued*)

Theme	Subtheme	Question
	Interactivity Level	How interactive should the virtual environment be?
	Realism	How important is photorealism or accurate simulation of materials and lighting?
Sustainable and Environmental	Sustainability Goals	How should the XR-AI tool aid in achieving sustainability objectives?
	Environmental Impact Assessment	Are there environmental impacts that need to be visualized or mitigated through the design process?
Stakeholder	Stakeholder Input	What input is needed from various stakeholders (e.g., developer, community members, regulatory bodies)?
	Collaboration Methods	What collaborative features are necessary for stakeholder engagement?

Indicators (KPIs). These KPIs act as quantifiable metrics that facilitate the objective evaluation of tool performance against predefined targets, enabling the identification of successes and areas for improvement within the design process. The KPIs are integral to the 'Measure' phase of the build-measure-learn feedback loop and should be closely monitored to guide strategic decisions and iterative enhancements. Presented below is a comprehensive set of KPIs, each serving as a critical metric for evaluating various dimensions of XR-AI deployment (Table 2):

Table 2. Proposed KPIs to assess XR-AI tools.

Area	KPI	Description
Efficiency	Design Cycle Time	Measures the average duration from conceptualization to the final design, reflecting process efficiency
	Iteration Speed	Tracks the time required for modifications in design iterations, signifying agility in the design process
	Learning Curve	Assesses the time it takes for new users to reach proficiency with the XR-AI tools, indicating ease of adoption

(*continued*)

Table 2. (*continued*)

Area	KPI	Description
Cost-Related	Return on Investment (ROI)	Quantifies financial gains relative to the cost of XR-AI tool investment over a specific period
	Cost Savings	Evaluates the reduction in costs related to design inaccuracies, material wastage, and man-hours
	Budget Adherence	The proportion of projects completed within the allocated budget post XR-AI tool implementation
Quality	Error Rate Reduction	The decrease in frequency of design errors, indicating improved design accuracy
	Design Accuracy	The precision of measurements and representations when employing XR-AI tools
	User Satisfaction Score	Aggregate scores from user surveys assessing satisfaction with the design process and the final product
User Experience	Adoption Rate	The percentage of the team effectively integrating XR-AI tools into their standard workflow
	User Proficiency	Improvement in task completion efficiency as users become adept with the XR-AI tools
	Net Promoter Score (NPS):	The likelihood of users recommending the XR-AI tools to peers, a testament to user satisfaction
Sustainability	Material Efficiency	What input is needed from various stakeholders (e.g., developer, community members, regulatory bodies)?
	Energy Modeling Accuracy	What collaborative features are necessary for stakeholder engagement?
	Sustainable Design Features	The count of eco-friendly design elements incorporated per project, including impacts on Total Energy Use Intensity (TEUI)

These KPIs should be carefully selected to align with the specific goals of each project and the overarching objectives of the architectural team. The selection and implementation of KPIs necessitate a methodical approach, with careful consideration given to the specific context of the deployment, the intended outcomes, and the ability to accurately measure and interpret the data. Regular review and refinement of these KPIs are recommended to accommodate technological advancements and evolving project demands, ensuring that the design team remains at the forefront of industry best practices in XR-AI deployment.

5.2   Practical Application of the XR-AI Deployment Framework

To demonstrate the practical application of the proposed XR-AI deployment framework in architectural design, we present a case study where machine learning (ML) and extended reality (XR) technologies converge to create an adaptive interior design experience. The example project involves designing an interactive virtual environment for a client's new office space. The aim is to utilize ML algorithms to analyze user behavior and preferences, which then inform the dynamic adaptation of the interior design within an AR/VR setup. This approach enables real-time customization of the virtual space, enhancing user engagement and satisfaction. The application of the XR-AI Deployment Framework includes the following steps:

Preparation and Planning
Assessment & Goal Setting. The design team conducts interviews and surveys with the client to understand their vision and functional needs for the office space. They define goals for space optimization, user comfort, and aesthetic appeal.

Technology Selection. Based on the client's needs, a VR platform compatible with machine learning algorithms is selected for the project.

Skill Development & Training. Designers and stakeholders receive training on using the selected VR tools and providing feedback within the virtual environment.

Implementation Process
Implementation Planning. A schedule is created for the development and integration of the ML model with the VR platform.

Pilot Testing. A prototype VR environment is developed. A small user group interacts with the space, while the ML model records and analyzes their behavior and design preferences.

Feedback & Iteration. Feedback from the pilot test is used to refine the ML algorithms and update the virtual environment accordingly.

Full-Scale Application. The refined VR environment is deployed to a larger group of users. The ML model continues to learn and adapt the design in real-time based on user interactions.

Evaluating Deployment Through KPIs
Efficiency KPIs. The reduction in design cycle time is noted compared to traditional methods.

User Experience KPIs. User proficiency with the VR tool and satisfaction scores are collected and analyzed.

Innovation KPIs. The number of unique design adaptations suggested by the ML algorithm is recorded.

Build-Measure-Learn Feedback Loop
Build. The XR-AI environment is built with adaptive learning capabilities.

Measure. User interactions and preferences are measured and analyzed by the ML system.

Learn. Insights from the data are used to iteratively enhance the virtual environment and user experience.

This example illustrates the application of the proposed XR-AI deployment framework in a real-world scenario. It highlights the framework's adaptability and the value of integrating KPIs to measure the success of the deployment. Through iterative feedback and a data-driven approach, the project showcases the potential of XR-AI to revolutionize the architectural design process, providing a personalized and immersive experience that aligns with users' preferences.

5.3 Vision Map for XR-AI Integration in Architectural Design

The Vision Map for XR-AI integration in architectural design offers a long-term perspective, outlining the roles and responsibilities of various stakeholders from 2024 to 2050. It is structured around key stakeholder groups: Non-government organizations, Governments and Regulatory Bodies, Industry Professionals, Technology Developers, and Communities and End-users. Each stakeholder group is tasked with specific actions aligned with innovation, education, engagement, adoption, and advocacy, marked by milestones set for 2026, 2030, 2035, 2040, and 2050. This strategic vision ensures a collaborative, cross-sector approach to realizing the full potential of XR and AI in architectural design, emphasizing continuous learning, technological advancement, and policy development (Fig. 4).

Fig. 4. Vision map highlighting the holistic responsibilities of various stakeholders.

6 Conclusions

This review examines the integration of Extended Reality (XR) and Artificial Intelligence (AI) in architectural design, highlighting their significant impacts on methodologies, stakeholder involvement, and project outcomes. By blending theoretical insights with real-world applications, the review demonstrates how XR and AI are reshaping visualization, simulation, and optimization in architecture, leading to advances in innovation and operational efficiency. The formulation of an XR-AI integration framework offers architects actionable steps to leverage these technologies effectively.

As XR and AI technologies evolve, they promise to further revolutionize architectural design, providing advanced tools for crafting sustainable, efficient environments centered around user experience. This fusion of technologies is expected to empower architects to tackle complex design challenges with heightened creativity and accuracy, contributing to sustainable development objectives and responsive design processes.

However, the rapid pace of technological innovation necessitates ongoing research to assess the long-term effects of XR and AI integration on project quality and success. Future explorations should address ethical, privacy, and security concerns while developing enhanced XR-AI frameworks adaptable to technological advancements. Continuous scholarly inquiry is crucial to keep the architectural community at the forefront of technological progress, ensuring practitioners can employ XR and AI to create innovative, human-centric, and ecologically sustainable environments.

6.1 Future Applications and Implications

Incorporating Extended Reality (XR) and Artificial Intelligence (AI) into architectural practices presents a range of challenges and opportunities:

Technical and Adoption Challenges. Integrating XR and AI with traditional systems involves complex hardware and software requirements, extensive data management, and workflow adaptations. Professionals need enhanced capabilities, comprehensive training, and change management strategies to facilitate smooth integration. Addressing privacy concerns requires stringent security protocols and ethical standards compliance.

Innovative Opportunities and Educational Advancements. The integration offers opportunities like automated design-to-fabrication processes, real-time environmental impact simulations, and adaptive environments. AI and XR synergy can enhance sustainability, efficiency, and educational practices in architecture. Institutions should revise curricula to include XR and AI technologies, preparing future architects for a digitally enhanced design landscape and promoting lifelong learning among current practitioners.

Addressing these dimensions will ensure that the field of architecture navigates the complexities of XR and AI integration while capitalizing on the opportunities they offer, guiding the discipline toward a future characterized by sustainable, efficient, and user-focused design solutions.

Disclosure of Interests. The authors have no competing interests to declare that are relevant to the content of this article.

References

1. Zheng, X., Zheng, S., Kong, Y., et al.: Recent advances in surface defect inspection of industrial products using deep learning techniques. Int. J. Adv. Manufact. Technol. **113**(1), 35–58 (2021)
2. Carrasco, D.O.M., Po-Han Chen, P.H.: Application of mixed reality for improving architectural design comprehension effectiveness. Autom. Constr. **126**, 1–16 (2021). https://doi.org/10.1016/j.autcon.2021.103677
3. Fast-Berglund, Å., Liang, D.G.: Testing and validating extended reality (xR) technologies in manufacturing. Proc. Manuf. **25**, 31–38 (2018)
4. Dustin, P.S., Wang, X.: Mixed reality-based visualization interfaces. J. Constr. Eng. Manag. **12**(1301), 1301–1309 (2015). https://doi.org/10.1061/(ASCE)0733-9364(2005)131:
5. Castro-Pena, L.M., et al.: Artificial intelligence applied to conceptual design. A review of its use in architecture. Autom. Constr. **124**, 103550 (2021). https://doi.org/10.1016/j.autcon.2021.103550
6. Milgram, P., Colquhoun Jr., H.: A taxonomy of real and virtual world display integration. In: Mixed Reality: Merging Real and Virtual Worlds. Springer-Verlag Berlin Heidelberg, pp. 5–30 (1999)
7. Meta Technologies. Oculus. Retrieved March 06, 2024, from Meta: https://www.meta.com/ca/quest/products/quest-2/ (2023)
8. Bray, B.: What is Mixed Reality? Retrieved March 05, 2024, from Microsoft: https://learn.microsoft.com/en-us/windows/mixed-reality/discover/mixed-reality (2023)
9. Sampaio, A.Z., Martins, O.P.: The application of virtual reality technology in the construction of a bridge: the cantilever and incremental launching methods. Autom. Constr. **37**, 58–67 (2014). https://doi.org/10.1016/j.autcon.2013.10.015
10. Diaz, M.: What is AI? Everything to know about artificial intelligence. Retrieved March 04, 2024, from ZDNET: https://www.zdnet.com/article/what-is-ai-heres-everything-you-need-to-know-about-artificial-intelligence/, April 21 (2023)
11. Wang, P.: What do you mean by "AI"? In: Artificial General Intelligence 2008 Proceedings First AGI Conference, Amsterdam, The Netherlands: The Netherlands, IOS Press, pp. 362–373 (2008)
12. Stone, P., et al.: Artificial intelligence and life in 2030: one-hundred-year study on artificial intelligence. Stanford: Stanford University, Retrieved from https://ai100.stanford.edu/ (2016)
13. McCarthy, J., et al.: A proposal for the Dartmouth summer research project on artificial intelligence. ma Ética Para Quantos?, pp. 81–87 (2012)
14. Crevier, D.: AI: The Tumultuous History of the Search for Artificial Intelligence. Basic Books Inc, New York, NY, USA (1993)
15. Maher, L.M., Poon, J.: Modeling design exploration as co-evolution. Microcomputational Civ. Eng. **11**(3), 193–207 (1996)
16. Parmee, I. C.: Diverse evolutionary search for preliminary whole system design. In: Proceedings of the 4th International Conference on AI in Civil and Structural Engineering, Cvetkovic and Parmee (1999)
17. Wen, W., Hong, L., Xueqiang, M.: Application of fractals in architectural shape design. In: IEEE 2nd Symposium on Web Society, pp. 185–190 (2010)
18. Graham, I.J., Case, K., Wood, R.L.: Genetic algorithms in computer-aided design. J. Mater. Process. Technol. **117**(1–2), 216–222 (2011)
19. DeLanda, M.: Deleuze and the use of the genetic algorithm in architecture. Architectural Des. **71**(7), 9–12 (2012)
20. Lin, E.-S.H., Gerber, J.D.: Designing-in performance: a framework for evolutionary energy performance feedback in early-stage design. Autom. Constr. **38**, 59–73 (2014). https://doi.org/10.1016/j.autcon.2013.10.007

21. Tagaki, H.: Interactive evolutionary computation: fusion of the capabilities of EC optimization and human evaluation. IEEE **89**(9), 1275–1296 (2001). (Coates et al., 1996)
22. Caldas, L.: GENE_ARCH: an evolution-based generative design system for sustainable architecture. In: Intelligent Computing in Engineering and Architecture. EG-ICE 2006, I.F.C. Smith (Ed.), pp. 4200. Springer, Berlin, Heidelberg (2006). https://doi.org/10.1007/11888598_12
23. Ekici, B., et al.: A multiobjective self-adaptive differential evolution algorithm for conceptual high-rise building design. In: IEEE Congress on Evolutionary Computation (CEC), pp. 2272–2279 (2016)
24. Song, H., Ghaboussi, J., Kwon, H.T.: Architectural design of apartment buildings using the implicit redundant representation genetic algorithm. Autom. Constr. **72**, 166–173 (2016)
25. Fang, Y., Cho, S.: Design optimization of building geometry and fenestration for daylighting and energy performance. Sol. Energy **191**, 7–18 (2019)
26. Cubukcuoglu, C., et al.: OPTIMUS: self-adaptive differential evolution with ensemble of mutation strategies for grasshopper algorithmic modeling. Algorithms **12**(7), 141 (2019)
27. Skavara, M.M.E.: Learning Emergence: Adaptive Cellular Automata Façade Trained by Artificial Neural Networks. PhD Thesis, UCL, London (2009)
28. Gagne, J.M., Andersen, M.: Multi-objective genetic façade optimization for daylighting design using an algorithm. SimBuild **4**(1), 110–117 (2010)
29. Chatzikonstantinou, I., Sariyildiz, S.: Addressing design preferences via auto-associative connectionist models: application in sustainable architectural Façade design. Autom. Constr. **83**, 108–120 (2017). https://doi.org/10.1016/j.autcon.2017.08.007
30. Agirbas, A.: Façade form-finding with swarm intelligence. Autom. Constr. **99**, 140–151 (2019)
31. Wong, S.S., Chan, K.C.: EvoArch: an evolutionary algorithm for architectural layout design. Comput. Aided Des. **41**(9), 649–667 (2009)
32. Dino, I.G.: An evolutionary approach for 3D architectural space layout design exploration. Autom. Constr. **69**, 131–150 (2016)
33. Guo, Z., Li, B.: Evolutionary approach for spatial architecture layout design Evolutionary approach for spatial architecture layout design. Front. Architectural Res. **6**(1), 53–62 (2017)
34. As, I., Pal, S., Basu, P.: Artificial intelligence in architecture: generating conceptual design via deep learning. Int. J. Architectural Comput. **16**(4), 306–327 (2018). https://doi.org/10.1177/1478077118800982
35. Gero, J.S., Schnier, T.: Evolving representations of design cases and their use in creative design. In: Preprints Computational Models of Creative Design, Key Center of Design Computing, University of Sydney, Sydney (1995)
36. Rosenman, M.A., Gero, J.S.: Evolving designs by generating useful complex gene structures. In: Evolutionary Design by Computers, P. Bentley (Ed.), London (1999)
37. Rafiq, M.Y., Bugmann, G., Easterbrook, D.J.: Building concept generation using genetic algorithms integrated with neural networks. In: 6th Workshop of the European Group of the Structural Engineering Applications of Artificial Intelligence, pp. 165–174 (1999)
38. Sisk, G.M., Miles, J.C., Moore, C.J.: Designer centered development of GA-based DSS for conceptual design of buildings. J. Comput. Civ. Eng. **17**(3), 159–166 (2003)
39. Ghada, G.E., Negm, A.: AI technologies in green architecture field: statistical comparative analysis. Procedia Eng. **181**, 480–488 (2017). https://doi.org/10.1016/j.proeng.2017.02.419
40. Tsanas, A., Xifara, A.: Accurate quantitative estimation of energy performance of residential buildings using statistical machine learning tools. Energy Build. **49**, 560–567 (2012)
41. Robinson, C., et al.: Machine learning approaches for estimating commercial building energy consumption. Appl. Energy **208**, 889–904 (2017)
42. Roy, S., Balas, V.E.: Estimating heating load in buildings using multivariate adaptive regression splines, extreme learning machine, a hybrid model of MARS and ELM. Renew. Sustain. Energy Rev. **82**, 4256–4268 (2018)

43. Deng, H., Fannon, D., Eckelman, M.J.: Predictive modeling for US commercial building energy use: a comparison of existing statistical and machine learning algorithms using CBECS microdata. Energy Build. **163**, 34–43 (2018)

44. Lampropoulos, G., Keramopoulos, E., Diamantaras, K.: Enhancing the functionality of augmented reality using deep learning, semantic web and knowledge graphs: a review. Vis. Inform. **4**(1), 32–42 (2020). https://doi.org/10.1016/j.visinf.2020.01.001

45. Norouzi, N., et al.: A systematic literature review of embodied augmented reality agents in head-mounted display environments. In: ICATEGVE 2020 - International Conference on Artificial Reality and Telexistence and Eurographics Symposium on Virtual Environments (2020). https://doi.org/10.2312/egve.20201264

46. Hirzle, T., et al.: When XR and AI meet - a scoping review on extended reality and artificial intelligence. In: CHI '23: Proceedings of the 2023 CHI Conference on Human Factors in Computing Systems, pp. 1–45 (2023). https://doi.org/10.1145/3544548.3581072

47. Luck, M., Aylett, R.: Applying artificial intelligence to virtual reality: intelligent virtual environments. Appl. Artif. Intell. **14**(1), 3–32 (2000). https://doi.org/10.1080/088395100117142

48. de Oliveira, R., et al.: Systematic review of virtual reality solutions employing artificial intelligence methods. In: Symposium on Virtual and Augmented Reality (SVR'21), Association for Computing Machinery, New York, pp. 42–55 (2021). https://doi.org/10.1145/3488162.3488209

49. Reiners, D., et al.: The combination of artificial intelligence and extended reality: a systematic review. Front. Virtual Reality **2**, 721933 (2021)

50. Felbrich, B., et al.: Self-organizing maps for intuitive gesture-based geometric modeling in augmented reality. In: IEEE International Conference on Artificial Intelligence and Virtual Reality (AIVR), New York, pp. 61–67 (2018)

51. Chirra, V., Uyyala, S., Kolli, V.: Virtual facial expression recognition using deep CNN with ensemble learning. J. Ambient Intell. Humanized Comput. **12**, 10581–10599 (2021)

52. Buck, L., Park, S., Bodenheimer, B.: Determining peripersonal space boundaries and their plasticity in relation to object and agent characteristics in an immersive virtual environment. In: IEEE Conference on Virtual Reality and 3D User Interfaces (VR), New York, vol. 1, pp. 332–342 (2020)

53. Balasubramanian, S., Soundararajan, R.: Prediction of discomfort due to egomotion in immersive videos for virtual reality. In: IEEE International Symposium on Mixed and Augmented Reality (ISMAR), New York, vol. 1, pp. 169–177 (2019)

A Template Course for Teaching
the Development of Interactive Systems
to Students of Human-Computer
Interaction

Toni Schumacher⬤, Maged Mortaga⬤, and André Calero Valdez⁽⊠⁾⬤

Institute of Multimedia and Interactive Systeme, University of Lübeck, Ratzeburger
Allee 160, 23562 Lübeck, Germany
{t.schumacher,maged.mortaga,andre.calerovaldez}@uni-luebeck.de

Abstract. Human-Computer Interaction (HCI) is an essential skill for
the future. However, previous observations have revealed a discrepancy
between the programming training provided to HCI students and the
skillset required in the HCI field. This article describes the development and implementation of a course tailored for 3rd-semester bachelor
students of HCI to provide them with practical skills in programming
interactive systems. The course, named *Interactive Systems*, spans two
semesters and includes a combination of lectures and programming exercises, designed to meet the specific needs of HCI students. This module
aims to bridge the gap between general computer science programming
courses and the specialized requirements of HCI students. We present
the concept, realization, and evaluation of this module.

Keywords: Human-computer interaction · Education · Educational
Resources · Computer Science Didactics

1 Introduction

Human-computer interaction (HCI) is an interdisciplinary field that blends principles from computer science, design, psychology, and cognitive science to understand and improve the interaction between humans and computers. As technology continues to advance, the role of HCI professionals has become increasingly
critical in creating user-centered designs that enhance user experience and accessibility. Despite the growing importance of HCI, many university programs do
not provide specialized training that addresses the unique requirements of HCI
students. Instead, these students are often directed to traditional computer science courses, which may not fully cater to their educational needs.

A significant challenge for HCI students is the difficulty in focusing on the
core competencies of HCI, especially when it comes to implementation-related
tasks. Traditional computer science courses often emphasize theoretical concepts

M. Kurosu et al. (Eds.): HCII 2024, LNCS 15374, pp. 211–229, 2025.
https://doi.org/10.1007/978-3-031-76803-3_12

and programming skills without sufficiently covering HCI's practical, design-oriented aspects. This gap highlights the need to promote knowledge of implementation techniques through interactive, individualized approaches that include practical exercises and reflective activities.

To address these challenges, HCI education should incorporate more hands-on projects that simulate real-world scenarios, allowing students to apply their knowledge in practical settings. Collaborative projects can also be beneficial, as they mimic the multidisciplinary nature of professional HCI work, requiring students to integrate insights from psychology, design, and computer science.

Contribution. This article describes our efforts in developing a course for students of human-computer interaction to help them gain practical skills in programming interactive systems. The course, named *Interactive Systems* and held at the University of Lübeck, spans two semesters and includes lectures and exercises, requiring students to participate over a full academic year. Although the content of each semester is relatively independent, they are evaluated as a single joint module.

2   Motivation

The primary motivation for developing a specialized course for HCI students stems from the recognition that the skills and knowledge required in HCI significantly differ from those emphasized in conventional computer science curricula. Several key factors presented underscore the necessity of a tailored educational approach for HCI students.

2.1   Interdisciplinary Nature of HCI

HCI is inherently interdisciplinary, requiring knowledge from multiple domains, including cognitive psychology, ergonomics, design principles, and social sciences, in addition to technical skills in programming and software development. Traditional computer science courses predominantly focus on algorithmic thinking, data structures, and systems programming, which, while essential, do not cover the breadth of topics needed for a comprehensive HCI education. HCI students need to understand how to design and evaluate user interfaces, conduct usability testing, and apply human-centered design principles—all of which are not typically covered in depth in standard computer science programs.

2.2   Focus on User-Centered Design

Unlike students of traditional computer science who often focus on system performance and efficiency, HCI students prioritize user experience and usability. This user-centered approach requires different skills and methods, such as user research, prototyping, and iterative design processes. Standard programming courses may not address these aspects, leaving HCI students without the necessary tools to design effective and intuitive interactive systems. A specialized course can bridge this gap by integrating user-centered design practices with technical instruction.

2.3 Emerging Technologies and Frameworks

The landscape of interactive systems is rapidly evolving, with new technologies and frameworks continuously emerging. HCI students must stay ahead of the latest developments in web technologies, mobile applications, virtual and augmented reality, and ubiquitous computing. Traditional computer science curricula may not be agile enough to incorporate these rapidly changing technologies into their coursework. A dedicated HCI course can provide timely and relevant instruction on the latest tools and frameworks, ensuring that students are well-prepared for the current job market.

2.4 Focus on Web Development

Web development is integral to HCI education, providing a versatile foundation for creating user interfaces and experiences. Mastering web development equips students with essential skills for designing interactive and responsive interfaces and extends their capabilities beyond web applications. Modern frameworks like React Native and Electron allow HCI professionals to use web development principles to build native mobile apps and desktop applications, broadening their technical expertise and application scope.

2.5 Practical and Applied Learning

HCI education benefits greatly from a hands-on, applied learning approach. Students must engage in practical projects that allow them to apply theoretical knowledge to real-world problems. Standard computer science courses often emphasize theoretical concepts and abstract problem-solving, which, while valuable, do not always translate to the practical skills needed for HCI. A specialized course can focus on project-based learning, where students develop interactive systems, conduct usability studies, and iterate on their designs based on user feedback.

2.6 Collaboration and Teamwork

HCI projects often involve interdisciplinary teams, requiring strong collaboration and communication skills. Students must learn to work effectively with designers, psychologists, and other stakeholders. Traditional computer science courses may not emphasize these soft skills to the same extent. By incorporating collaborative projects and team-based assignments, a dedicated HCI course can better prepare students for the collaborative nature of the field.

2.7 Requirements

Given these considerations, it is clear that HCI students require a distinct educational path that addresses their unique needs and prepares them for the challenges of designing user-centered interactive systems. The *Interactive Systems* module is designed to fill this gap, providing HCI students with a comprehensive and practical learning experience that combines technical skills with a strong emphasis on user experience and usability. This tailored approach not only enhances the educational outcomes for HCI students but also ensures that they are well-equipped to contribute to the advancement of human-computer interaction in various professional contexts.

3 Didactic Approach

To help students attain advanced theoretical and practical competencies in the development of interactive systems, we chose didactic approaches that facilitate learning of both theoretical groundwork and practical skills in software development.

As a core guiding principle, we apply constructivist paradigms [9] that align with self-determination theory [4]. We try to pick the best fitting approach to the individual learning pieces and a wide range of teaching tools, ranging from classic lectures (passive learning) to methods such as problem-based learning [1,11] that have been shown to be effective for teaching applicable knowledge [5].

HCI education benefits greatly from a hands-on, applied learning approach. Students must engage in practical projects that allow them to apply theoretical knowledge to real-world problems. Kolb's experiential learning theory [7] states that knowledge is created through experience and reflection. By incorporating hands-on projects and real-world applications, our course allows students to engage deeply with select frameworks and ensures that they will be capable of creating an interactive system themselves after the course.

3.1 Individualized Learning and Motivation

One of the common challenges we encounter is the varying levels of prior education in software engineering and programming among students. Therefore, it is crucial to address these differences by providing individualized materials and helping students identify which skills and theories they have mastered and which ones they still need to work on.

To facilitate learning, we use a combination of didactic approaches. Our foundation is based on self-determination theory [4], which posits that task satisfaction is rooted in three innate psychological needs: autonomy, competence, and relatedness. We design our teaching methods around these principles. We encourage *autonomy* by allowing students to choose lessons and tasks they are comfortable with. We gradually increase the difficulty of problems to build *competence* over time. Finally, we let students select their challenges to foster a sense of *relatedness* in our approach.

3.2   Lectures and Flipped Classroom

We achieve this by employing a variety of methods that are uniquely combined for our system. Specifically, lectures focused on theory are conducted in person, facilitating peer discussions and reflections on different perspectives during the lecture. This approach is particularly effective when the content requires reflection to deepen understanding, even if it is not inherently difficult.

For practical learning, such as programming skills, we utilize flipped classrooms [2]. A flipped classroom means that the static instructional material usually received by the students in a passive learning environment is pre-recorded as learning videos that are available on a learning platform. Students have the flexibility to access these videos at their convenience, whether at home, during their commute, or any other preferred location, and engage in exercises alongside the video content. An overview of the recorded course content from the winter semester of 2023 and the summer semester of 2024 can be found in Fig. 1. In this model, students can learn at their own pace, allowing them to adjust the videos' speed to match their skill levels. This flexibility also enables students to revisit material they might have missed or found challenging. To deepen the skills introduced in learning videos, exercises are given to the students as learning sessions that require them to apply the skills learned. Moreover, for these sessions, we provide exercise office hours, where the instructors are present in the lecture room and assist students when problems occur while conducting the exercises.

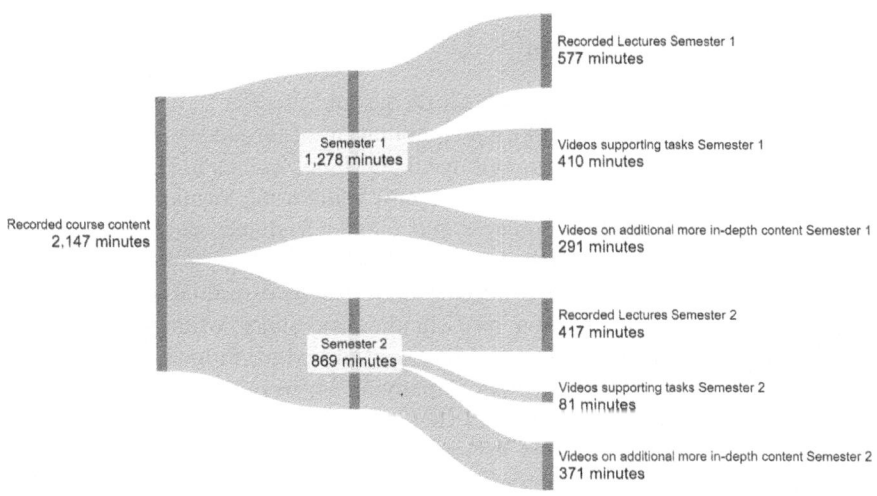

Fig. 1. Division of the recorded course content for each semester into recorded lectures, videos supporting the practical exercises and videos on additional more in-depth content. Information in total minutes of videos

3.3 Cooperative and Problem-Based Learning

Exercises must be handed in as groups, allowing more complex tasks and facilitating peer-to-peer cooperative learning. Cooperative learning [10] promotes direct communication within groups and fosters teamwork, thus improving communication skills, conflict resolution, and leadership skills [6].

These types of approaches address the required knowledge of the course. We consider them the baseline knowledge and skills. Beyond this baseline lays additional expert knowledge and skills necessary to give students a sense of competence. However, these skills quickly branch into separate sub-skills, which are hard to delineate from one another and rapidly evolve with technological progress. The possible "tree of knowledge" is obviously larger than a single student can learn in one year. Moreover, students may be more or less interested in different parts of this tree. Here, we provide autonomy to the students to pick a "mastery branch". Students pick a specific technology that they apply to a problem they have selected themselves.

For this project part of the course, we apply problem-based learning [1] as the core method for teaching. In self-selected groups, students take a required and maybe an additional optional project to apply their knowledge. These projects are small real-world scenarios that students choose themselves. Here, they can deepen their preferred knowledge branch and learn to apply it to a problem that is important to them. This fosters a sense of autonomy, competence, and relatedness. The required project is necessary to successfully complete the course, while the optional project can attain additional credit for the final exam.

3.4 Exams and Assessment

The module aims to teach students both theory and practice in developing interactive systems. Our course employs a combination of formative and summative assessments to provide a continuous feedback loop, enhancing student learning and performance. According to Black and Wiliam [3], formative assessment practices, including low-stakes quizzes and regular feedback, play a crucial role in raising educational standards.

Critical theoretical concepts introduced in lectures are evaluated interactively using an audience response system (e.g., in our case, Slido), while practical skills are assessed asynchronously through exercises tailored for flipped-classroom sessions. An example question with accompanying answers presented to the students is illustrated in Fig. 2. Students then select the correct answers, followed by the presentation of the correct responses. In cases where there is a significant discrepancy in students' selection of incorrect answers, the topic is revisited and discussed with the students.

Still, developing interactive systems is a holistic skill set that requires knowledge and competencies in a wide range of frameworks (e.g., backend technologies, frontend technologies, DevOps, version control, etc.); therefore, we assess this holistic skill set using projects, as stated above. The project results can be used as bonus credit in the summative final assessment in the form of a written exam and provide flexibility and internal differentiation. Students can—to a certain extent—pick their preferred way of attaining credit, providing an additional layer of autonomy.

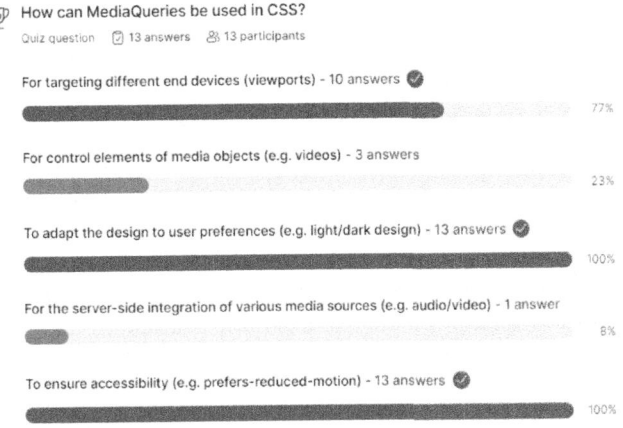

Fig. 2. Assessment of a sample question from a quiz. Following the students' selection of possible answers, the assessment is displayed. Correct responses are indicated in green, whereas incorrect ones remain gray. Both the question and answers were translated into English. (Color figure online)

3.5 Continuous Feedback and Improvement

To ensure that our approach aligns with the curriculum and students' interests and prerequisites, we elicit continuous feedback using different methods (e.g., short surveys at the end of lectures and formal university evaluation). The module has undergone three large overhauls and continuously improved from both the learner's and teachers' perspectives. In this article, we provide detailed feedback on the quality of those improvements.

4 Course Structure

The *Interactive Systems* module is structured over two semesters, with the first semester focusing on foundational skills and the second semester advancing to more complex technologies and applications.

4.1 Semester 1: Foundations of Web Development

The first semester aims to equip students with basic web development skills using HTML, CSS, and TypeScript. The course content is presented in the following sections.

Introduction to Guided Development. Students begin with an introduction to development tools, specifically open source tools such as Visual Studio Code[1] and git[2]. They learn git by solving gamified tasks from learngitbranching.js.org[3]. Students acquire skills in using git and GitLab[4] for project collaboration, resolving conflicts, merging branches, and writing README documents in Markdown. Additionally, students learn the benefits of using a code formatter, such as Prettier[5]. Furthermore, they gain an understanding of the basics of web page rendering by browsers and deepen their knowledge of web development tools, such as the browser's built-in developer tools.

HTML Basics. The second lecture addresses the fundamentals of HTML, including tags, nesting, and typical HTML data structures. Students also learn to use multimedia elements, such as `picture`, `audio`, and `video`. Additionally, they gain an understanding of the semantic meaning and appropriate usage of HTML elements. Students are then tasked with designing their own websites and sharing them in the GitLab repository.

Cascading Style Sheets (CSS) Basics. Students then learn the fundamentals of CSS, including key concepts such as cascading, inheritance, and specificity. Additionally, they gain an understanding of selectors, nesting, and advanced techniques such as animations, transitions, and transformations. Students apply their knowledge to solve gamified tasks, such as those found on flukeout.github.io[6]. Subsequently, they apply their skills to enhance the websites they previously developed.

CSS Layout. The fourth lecture concentrates on CSS layout mechanisms, specifically grid and flex layouts, media queries, float and position layout, to create responsive and accessible designs. The lecture emphasizes HCI aspects, such as developing accessible websites with media queries using principles of universal design and inclusive design, for instance, `prefers-reduced-motion` or `prefers-contrast`. Students apply their knowledge to solve gamified tasks,

---

[1] Visual Studio Code. (Microsoft). Integrated Development Environment for Code Editing. Retrieved from https://code.visualstudio.com/.

[2] git. (Software Freedom Conservancy). Distributed Version Control System. Retrieved from https://git-scm.com/.

[3] learngitbranching.js.org. (Peter Cottle). Repository visualizer and sandbox with educational tutorials and challenges. Retrieved from https://learngitbranching.js.org/.

[4] GitLab. (GitLab, Inc.). DevOps Platform. Retrieved from https://gitlab.com/.

[5] Prettier. (James Long and Prettier contributors). Code formatter. Retrieved from https://prettier.io/.

[6] flukeout.github.io. (Luke Pacholski). Learn CSS Layout. Retrieved from https://flukeout.github.io/.

such as Flexbox Froggy[7] to learn flexbox layout or Grid Garden[8] to learn grid layout, before applying their skills to enhance the websites they are developing.

DevOps Fundamentals. Students are introduced to basic client-server infrastructure, setting up a web development environment using pnpm[9] as package manager and Vite[10] as dev server and bundler, also applying pre- and post-processors for CSS and using tsc to transpile typescript.

CSS Frameworks. Students learn about CSS frameworks such as Tailwind CSS[11], daisyUI[12], OpenProps[13], UnoCSS[14], and Bootstrap[15]. They also explore Font Awesome[16] and Tabler Icons[17] for standardized iconography.

TypeScript Basics. The seventh lecture introduces TypeScript, emphasizing its benefits as a statically typed language. Students learn about the advantages of static code analysis using ESLint[18]. Additionally, they are taught about the DOM and Node API, events, and global functions. More advanced TypeScript topics, such as syntactic sugar and array functions, are also covered. Furthermore, students apply these concepts to their website projects.

Asynchronicity. In the eighth and ninth lectures, advanced asynchronicity techniques using TypeScript are covered. Students gain an understanding of

---

[7] Flexbox Froggy. (Codepip). An interactive game for learning CSS flexbox layout. Retrieved from https://flexboxfroggy.com/.

[8] Grid Garden. (Codepip). An interactive game for learning CSS grid layout. Retrieved from https://cssgridgarden.com/.

[9] pnpm. (contributors of pnpm). Fast, disk space efficient package manager. Retrieved from https://pnpm.io/.

[10] Vite. (Evan You & Vite Contributors). Fast and lean build tool for modern web projects. Retrieved from https://vitejs.dev/.

[11] Tailwind CSS (Tailwind Labs). Utility-First CSS Framework for Rapid UI Development. Retrieved from https://tailwindcss.com/.

[12] daisyUI. (Pouya Saadeghi). Component library for Tailwind CSS. Retrieved from https://daisyui.com/.

[13] OpenProps. (Adam Argyle). CSS library with custom properties to help accelerate adaptive and consistent design. Retrieved from https://open-props.style/.

[14] UnoCSS. (Anthony Fu). Instant on-demand atomic CSS engine.. Retrieved from https://unocss.dev/.

[15] Bootstrap. (The Bootstrap Authors). HTML, CSS, and JS library for developing responsive, mobile first projects on the web. Retrieved from https://getbootstrap.com/.

[16] Font Awesome. (Fonticons, Inc). Icon and font library. Retrieved from https://fontawesome.com/.

[17] Tabler Icons. (Paweł Kuna). Icon library. Retrieved from https://tabler.io/icons.

[18] ESLint. (OpenJS Foundation and ESLint contributors). Static code analysis tool for identifying problematic patterns found in web code. Retrieved from https://eslint.org/.

asynchronous function calls and promises. They also learn about syntactic sugar for promises using `async` and `await`. Additionally, students are introduced to the architectural software paradigm of Representational State Transfer (REST) and how to use REST APIs with the Fetch API. Students then apply these concepts to their website projects.

Client-Server Architecture. The final lecture of the first semester instructs students on setting up a Node.js server using the Express[19] framework, including a database with json-server[20], and developing an API in their client-server architecture for their website. Additionally, students are introduced to server-side implementation architectures, such as Server-Side Rendering (SSR), Client-Side Rendering (CSR), and Static Site Generation (SSG), as well as client-side implementations, including Single Page Applications (SPA) and Multi-Page Applications (MPA).

Optional Project. At the end of the first semester, students undertake a comprehensive software project that incorporates all the tools and concepts learned throughout the course. This optional project, which offers the opportunity to earn bonus points for the exam, involves pitching their own project ideas, receiving feedback, and presenting their final work. The project is designed to deepen the students' understanding of the concepts covered and includes implementing a website in form of a client-server architecture. Additionally, it emphasizes Human-Computer Interaction aspects by requiring the creation of a responsive website, adaptable for use on both smartphones up to desktop screens. Students are also instructed to implement accessible websites using the concepts they have learned. Examples of student work can be found in Sect. 5.

4.2   Semester 2: Advanced Web, Mobile and Desktop Development

In the second semester, students build on their foundational web development knowledge and transition to more advanced web, mobile and desktop technologies.

React Framework and Mobile Applications. The semester begins with an introduction to the React[21] framework for developing websites and mobile applications. Students learn React basics using TSX, virtual DOM, and reconciliation. They also explore React DevTools and integrate React into their deployment procedures using GitLab for continuous integration and continuous

---

[19] Express. (OpenJS Foundation). Fast, unopinionated, minimalist web framework for Node.js. Retrieved from https://expressjs.com/.

[20] json-server. (typicode). JSON-based REST-API mocking server. Retrieved from https://github.com/typicode/json-server.

[21] React. (Meta Platforms, Inc. and affiliates). JavaScript library for building component-based user interfaces. Retrieved from https://reactjs.org/.

deployment (CI/CD). Students are then tasked with designing their own websites using React and sharing them in the GitLab repository.

React Advanced Concepts. Students delve deeper into React by learning about props, event handlers, conditional rendering, states, the component life-cycle with hooks like (`useState` and `useEffect`). They also study routing using React Router and state management using Context-API. Furthermore, students apply these concepts to their website projects.

React Styling and Frameworks. The third week covers React styling and the use of CSS frameworks such as daisyUI, Mantine[22], and shadcn/ui[23] to create advanced and modern user interfaces. Additionally, students learn the benefits of using Component Workshops when implementing websites with component-based frameworks. The students are then tasked to apply styling to their React projects.

Web Applications and Progressive Web Apps (PWAs). Students learn about web applications and PWAs, including progressive enhancement, service worker and the Push Render Pre-cache Lazy-Load (PRPL) pattern. They discuss the benefits and downsides of PWAs compared to traditional web applications.

Native and Hybrid Mobile Applications. In the fifth week, students are introduced to native mobile app development for iOS and Android. They deepen their understanding of the software stacks for both iOS and Android, learning about the primary differences between the two operating systems and the apps developed for them. Additionally, students explore hybrid app development using frameworks such as React Native[24]. The course also covers the benefits and drawbacks of native app development and hybrid app development in comparison to web and progressive web development.

Desktop Applications. In the sixth week, students delve into desktop application development for operating systems such as Windows, macOS, and Linux. They discuss the differences between desktop applications and mobile applications. Furthermore, students are introduced to desktop app development frameworks, such as Electron[25].

---

[22] Mantine. (Vitaly Rtishchev). React component library. Retrieved from https://mantine.dev/.

[23] shadcn/ui. (shadcn). Component library. Retrieved from https://ui.shadcn.com/.

[24] React Native. (Meta Platforms, Inc.). JavaScript and React library for building native mobile apps. Retrieved from https://reactnative.dev/.

[25] Electron. (OpenJS Foundation and Electron contributors). Library for building cross-platform desktop apps with web standards like Vite and React. Retrieved from https://www.electronjs.org/.

Game Programming, Game Engines and Game Rendering. In the seventh, eighth, and ninth weeks, students are introduced to game engines, game programming, and rendering in games. They begin by exploring the fundamentals and concepts of game engines, with an introduction to game engines such as Unity[26]. Additionally, students learn about game programming, covering topics such as game genres and game production efforts. They delve into game concepts and the development of serious games, highlighting their significance in human-computer interaction and interactive systems. Finally, students study rendering in games, focusing on the rendering pipeline, particularly the 3D rendering pipeline as described by Malaka et al. [8], including concepts such as tessellation, culling, lighting, shading, clipping, and viewport mapping.

Specialized Frameworks. During the final eight weeks of the semester, students choose to specialize in React Native, Electron, or Unity for their programming project. Working in groups of up to three, they may develop a desktop application using Electron, a hybrid application using React Native, or delve into game programming using Unity. Fundamentals of using these frameworks is provided through prepared video content. Additionally, students can utilize help desk appointments to address their questions. The concept of individualized learning is presented in Sect. 3.

Optional Project. At the end of the second semester, students have the opportunity to participate in an additional project before pitching and presenting their final projects, which utilize the specialized frameworks Electron, React Native, or Unity. This optional project, which offers the opportunity to earn bonus points for the exam, involves evaluating the usability of the implemented applications to enhance their understanding of human-computer interaction.

5   Student Results

Following the acquisition of the foundations of web development, students were given the opportunity to pitch their own ideas for a web application, which they would then implement using the technologies learned during the course. This hands-on project allowed students to apply their knowledge in a real-world context, receive feedback, and, for students with prior experience, explore advanced technologies.

The project was optional in the first semester of the course, yet it received a positive response. Among the 61 total students, 28 opted to participate in the optional project. Participation in the project using specialized frameworks was made mandatory for the second semester. However, as of the time of writing, the student projects for the second semester are still ongoing and thus cannot be summarized.

---

[26] Unity. (Unity Technologies). Cross-platform game engine. Retrieved from https://unity.com/.

This chapter highlights the creativity and technical skills demonstrated by the students through a summary of selected projects from the first semester.

5.1 TankAlarm

The first highlighted project is called *TankAlarm*. It is a responsive website tailored for smartphones that is designed to notify users when a predetermined price threshold for a selected type of gasoline is reached at nearby gas stations. It achieves this by using the Tankerkönig API[27]. Users receive push notifications upon reaching the predetermined price threshold.

5.2 NoteSync

The next project showcased app is *NoteSync*, a learning app that allows students to take notes collaboratively and enhances group-based learning. The idea is to create groups with fellow students and to collect and share a collective knowledge base. The website also allows users to ask questions about certain posts within a group, facilitating peer-to-peer learning and support. The website operates in real-time, using WebSockets, allowing students to see updates and additions as they happen. The messages also support Markdown as well as KaTeX[28] to format the posts or questions (Fig. 3).

5.3 Flea

The final highlighted project is *Flea*. It is a website designed to help users search and discover flea markets. Additionally, users can create their own flea markets as well. The website offers easily accessible filters to help users find specific types of markets that align with their interests. It also features a map interface that allows users to view the location of different flea markets in their vicinity, providing a visual and intuitive way to explore flea markets (Fig. 4).

The students' projects demonstrate remarkable creativity, technical skills, and practical application. From *TankAlarm*, which uses modern web technologies to provide real-time price notifications to *NoteSync*, an innovative learning and knowledge base app facilitating collaborative note-taking, and *Flea*, a community-driven platform to create and discover flea markets, each student project showed their ability to address real-world problems with sophisticated solutions. These projects highlight not only the technical proficiency gained through the course but also the students' ability to understand and meet user needs. The diverse range of applications underscores the broad applicability of the skills learned and the students' readiness to tackle various challenges in the field of HCI. This chapter showcases some of their impressive outcomes, setting a high standard for future students and illustrating the course's effectiveness in preparing them.

---

[27] Tankerkönig API. (Tankerkönig). Real-time petrol API. Retrieved from https://creativecommons.tankerkoenig.de/.

[28] KaTeX. (Khan Academy and other contributors). Math typesetting library. Retrieved from https://katex.org/.

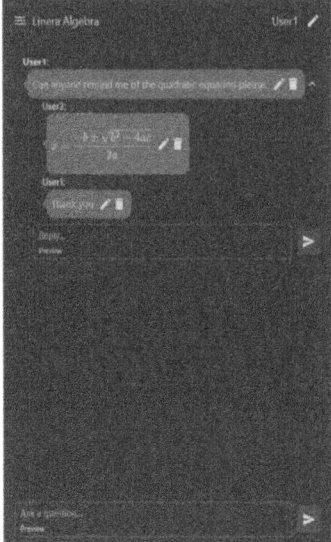 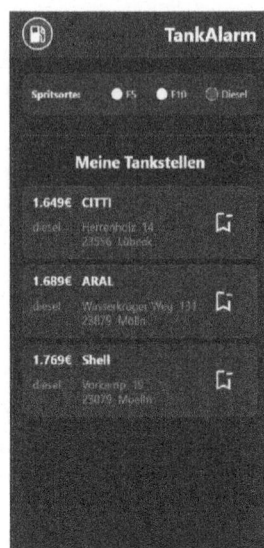

Fig. 3. Screenshot of the *NoteSync* (left) and *TankAlarm* (right) website interface

Fig. 4. Screenshot of the *Flea* website interface

6   Evaluation

To demonstrate how we ensure the success and continuous improvement of our
course, we showcase the results of a mid-semester evaluation. This section, shows
how we evaluate the *Interactive Systems* course based on data collected through
an online survey during the course.

Courses of Study of participants

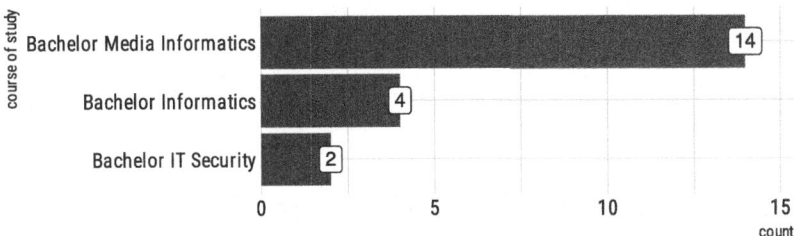

Fig. 5. Courses of study of participants

Did you take part in the optional project?

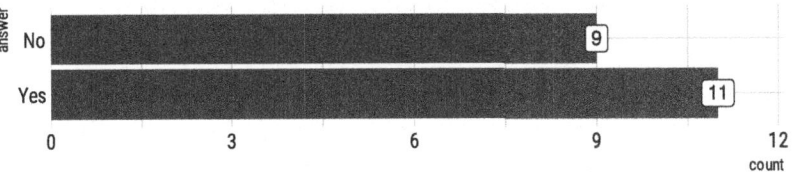

Fig. 6. Participation in optional projects

6.1 Sample

We collected our evaluation data through an online survey administered during the summer semester. Participation in the survey was voluntary. A total of twenty students ($n = 20$) participated, including fourteen from the Media Informatics program, four from the Computer Science program, and two from the IT Security program (see Fig. 5). Among these participants, eleven students engaged in the optional project offered during the course (see Fig. 6).

6.2 Method

We designed the survey to gather both quantitative and qualitative feedback from students about their experiences with the course. The survey included questions about their perceptions of learning success, specific elements of the course they found beneficial, and aspects they felt could be improved. We measured quantitative responses on a six-point anchored Likert scale (translated from the German school grades: 1 = very good, 2 = good, 3 = satisfying, 4 = sufficient, 5 = poor, 6 = unsatisfactory), while open-ended questions provided qualitative insights. Our survey focused on the following areas:

- Participation in the optional project and its perceived learning success.
- Evaluation of course components, including help desk sessions, quizzes, online lectures and recordings, and group work.
- Unique aspects of the course that distinguished it from other courses.

6.3   Results

Out of the 20 students, 11 participated in the optional project. Of these, 6 students reported that their learning success from the optional project was very high with absolute certainty, while 5 students indicated their learning success as mostly high (see Fig. 7).

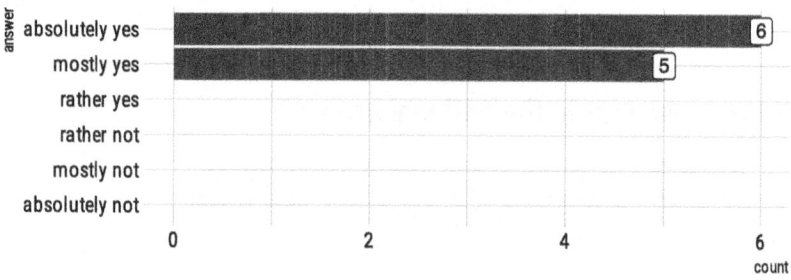

High learning success in the optional project

Count of participants who took part in optional project

Fig. 7. Students reporting high learning success in the optional project

The qualitative survey highlighted several positive aspects of the course (see Fig. 8:

- **HelpDesk Sessions**: Students appreciated the help desk sessions, noting that they provided valuable support and allowed for detailed questions to be addressed.
- **Quizzes**: The quizzes were well-received as they helped reinforce learning and provided a self-assessment tool for students.
- **Online Lectures and Recordings**: Students highly valued the availability of online lectures and recordings, which offered flexibility and the opportunity to review the material at their own pace.
- **Group Work**: Group projects and collaborative tasks were seen as beneficial, fostering teamwork and allowing students to apply their knowledge in practical settings.

Students particularly appreciated the following unique aspects of the course that stood out in comparison to other courses in their course of study (see Fig. 9):

- **Relatable Practical Content**: The course content was highly relevant and applicable to real-world scenarios, making it more engaging and useful for students.
- **Good Fit of Lectures**: The alignment of lectures with course objectives and practical exercises was noted as a strength, enhancing the overall learning experience.

What was good about the course and should be retained?

Most frequent mentions

Size determined by frequency of mentions

Fig. 8. Students reporting on what they liked most about the course

What distinguishes the InterSys course in your opinion compared to other courses?

Most frequent mentions

Size determined by frequency of mentions

Fig. 9. Students reporting on how the course stood our compared to other courses

The quantitative evaluation shows generally positive feedback for the course improvements (see Fig. 10), with the majority of aspects receiving high ratings (1 or 2). The most highly rated improvements were the enhancement of recordings with video jump marks and the restructuring of exercise sessions as a help desk format, both receiving overwhelmingly positive feedback. The listing of learning objectives in the Moodle course and the redesign of the Moodle course overview had more mixed reviews but were still generally well-received. The definition of learning objectives in the slide sets, labeling of asynchronous learning units, and reduction of exercise group sizes were also favorably rated, indicating that students appreciated these changes.

6.4   Conclusion

Our evaluation of the *Interactive Systems* course indicates a high level of student satisfaction, particularly with the practical, hands-on aspects of the course and the support provided through help desk sessions. The optional project was

Quantitative evaluation of the course improvements

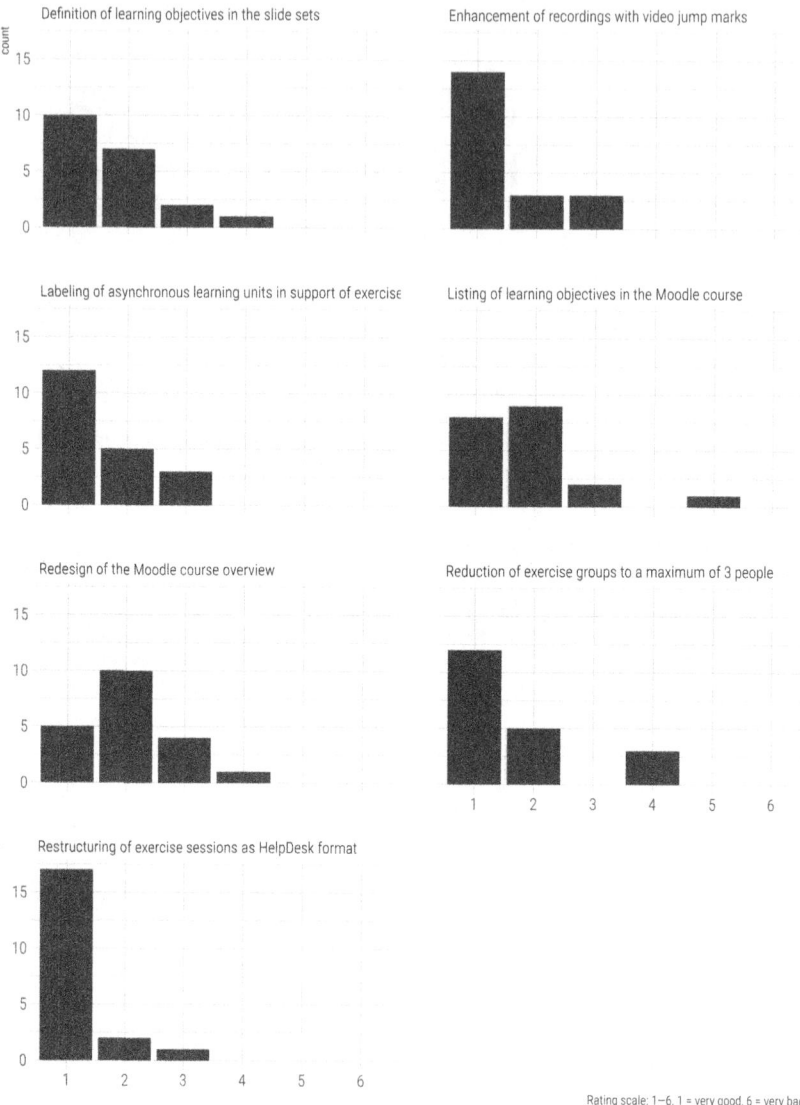

Fig. 10. Students reporting on how the course changes were perceived

a significant contributor to perceived learning success. The combination of theoretical and practical components, along with flexible learning options such as online lectures and recordings, contributed to a positive learning experience.

7   Conclusion and Future Work

The *Interactive Systems* module is designed to provide HCI students with a comprehensive and practical learning experience in programming interactive systems. By combining foundational skills with advanced technologies, the course ensures that students are well-equipped to meet the specific challenges of their field. The module also emphasizes flexibility, allowing students to learn at their own pace and focus on areas of personal interest.

At present, the course materials are only available in German. We intend to translate these materials into English to make them accessible to a broader audience. Furthermore, all course materials are developed with the objective of being transformed into open educational resources, thereby benefiting a wider academic community. Our future plans include creating a massive open online course (MOOC) featuring lecture content, individual gamified exercises, reflection tasks, and self-assessments for learners. The MOOC is intended to be a free learning resource available to everyone.

Acknowledgements. We would like to thank the students for their continuous feedback on how to improve this course. Translation of German qualitative data to English was done semi-automatically using ChatGPT 4o after checking for privacy issues. No privacy sensitive data was transmitted to OpenAI. A translation check was done manually by the authors.

References

1. Barrows, H.S., Tamblyn, R.M., et al.: Problem-Based Learning: An Approach to Medical Education, vol. 1. Springer Publishing Company (1980)
2. Bergmann, J., Sams, A.: Flip your classroom: reach every student in every class every day. Int. Soc. Technol. Educ. (2012)
3. Black, P., Wiliam, D.: Inside The Black Box: Raising Standards Through Classroom Assessment. Granada Learning (1998)
4. Deci, E.L., Ryan, R.M.: Self-determination theory. Handb. Theor. Soc. Psychol. **1**(20), 416–436 (2012)
5. Hmelo-Silver, C.E.: Problem-based learning: what and how do students learn? Educ. Psychol. Rev. **16**, 235–266 (2004)
6. Johnson, D.W., Johnson, R.T., Smith, K.A.: Cooperative learning returns to college what evidence is there that it works? Change: mag. high. learn. **30**(4), 26–35 (1998)
7. Kolb, D.: Experiential Learning: Experience as the Source of Learning and Development. Prentice Hall, Englewood Cliffs, NJ (1984)
8. Malaka, R., Butz, A., Hussmann, H.: Medieninformatik Eine Einführung. Pearson Deutschland (2009). https://elibrary.pearson.de/book/99.150005/9783863266523
9. Piaget, J.: Piaget's theory. In: Inhelder, B., Chipman, H.H., Zwingmann, C. (eds.) Piaget and His School: A Reader in Developmental Psychology, pp. 11–23. Springer Berlin Heidelberg, Berlin, Heidelberg (1976). https://doi.org/10.1007/978-3-642-46323-5_2
10. Slavin, R.E.: Research on cooperative learning and achievement: what we know, what we need to know. Contemp. Educ. Psychol. **21**(1), 43–69 (1996)
11. Wood, D.F.: Problem based learning. BMJ **326**(7384), 328–330 (2003)

Humans as Cultural Gatekeepers: A Reverse Turing Test Approach

Nanta Sooraksa[1], Chattraporn Noviram[1], and Pitikhate Sooraksa[2]([envelope])

[1] School of Human Resource Development, National Institute of Development Administration,
148 Seri Thai Rd., Bangkapi, Bangkok 10240, Thailand
`nanta.soo@nida.ac.th`
[2] School of Engineering, King Monkut's Institute of Technology, Ladkrabang1 Chalongrung 1,
Ladkrabang, Bangkok 10240, Thailand
`pitikhate.so@kmitl.ac.th`

Abstract. In this paper, we explore the role-play of humans as cultural gatekeepers via a reverse Turing approach where machines or agents are evaluated on their ability to understand human culture. The study is organized in four steps: Step 1, we first conduct a survey of CQ and overseas work adjustment aimed to provide a supporting contribution to the analysis of CQ and work adjustment to which Person-Environment Fit (PEF) theory has been applied. We collect the data at this step. Step 2, as humans, we analyze the results and perform statistical analysis to prepare the body of knowledge for benchmarking with the agents in the next step. Finally, in Step 3, humans evaluate an agent's understanding of cultural nuances by designing and administering tests that assess its ability to navigate the same given complex scenarios as humans did in Step 1. The results will be compared, analyzed, and discussed by humans. In the last step, Step 4, we reverse the direction of the test in Step 3 by using agents as the panel examiners. The results revealed a partial understanding of the CQ of the agents, and the reversed Turing test was incomplete.

Keywords: CQ · Cultural Intelligence · Human-machine Cultural Interaction · Cultural Intelligence · Reverse Turing Test

1 Introduction

Rapid evolution of AI in recent years makes AI smarter [1–3]. Hence these questions become more pressing. Even generative AI are performed quite impressive in many aspects but it seems to be the direction of cultural intelligent (CQ) may not yet be well-evaluated for assessing available agents. In fact, CQ is a key aspect of human interaction, including the ability to understand different perspectives, navigate social situation, and effectively communicate across cultures [4]. Nevertheless, evaluating AI's CQ remains a challenge. A This paper is an attempt to answer the question that: Can machines understand the cultural nuances making us human? Reversely, can human pass the CQ test if the agents serve as a panel evaluator?

The paper is organized into four sections: Sect. 1 is the Introduction. Section 2 provides concepts and critical benefits of CQ and Person-Environmental Fit (PEF) theory. Section 3 presents a study on the perceptions of expatriate teachers in international schools in Thailand regarding cultural intelligence (CQ) and their work adjustment. Results of the prior study in human subjects and statistical analysis are reported to prepare the body of knowledge for benchmarking with the agents in the next step. Section 4 illustrates Turing test results of an agent's understanding of cultural nuances by designing and administering tests that assess its ability to navigate the same given complex scenarios as humans from the previous section, as well as provides a reverse Turing test by using agents as the panel examiners. The last section, Sect. 5, yields concluding remarks.

2 Cultural Quotient and Personal-Environmental Fit

2.1 Cultural Quotient

Concepts. Cultural Intelligence, a 21st-century concept, determines the extent of workers' success in foreign cultures but also provides an answer to why dealing with issues that arise from cross-cultural problems can cause failure or success [4]. It is also a valuable personal resource that enables employees to interact and cooperate effectively with people from different cultures. Employees with high cultural intelligence could better adapt to cross-cultural working conditions and develop more positive emotions at work [6]. Earley and Aung [7] developed the concept of CQ based on Sterngerg's theory, which was constructed in 1986. They defined CQ as an individual's competence to successfully work with people from different national cultures at home or abroad. It is also described as a process in which an individual perceives, understands, and functions effectively in various cultural contexts. This overall capability or competence comprises four inter-related capabilities: CQ Strategy or Meta-Cognitive CQ, CQ Knowledge or Cognitive CQ, CQ Drive or Motivational CQ, and Behavioral CQ for Behavioral CQ [8–10]. Only two levels of headings should be numbered. Lower-level headings remain unnumbered; they are formatted as run-in headings.

Thomas and Inkson [11] emphasized and divided aspects of CQ into 3 main components knowledge, mindfulness, and behavior:

1. *Knowledge* is defined as an individual's knowledge of cultural differences. It is basic knowledge and understanding about appropriate behaviors in different cultural situations. This knowledge supports an individual's analysis of similarities and differences. However, knowledge will lead to an individual's behaviors only if it is urged by cognitive and motivational influences.
2. *Mindfulness* refers to the process of an individual's influencing knowledge into action. An individual who has high mindfulness is aware of sensations, perceptions, emotions, internal personal processes, as well as external stimuli. It also helps individuals evaluate situations from various perspectives based on their internal personal processes and external stimuli [12]. Regarding cross-cultural interaction, mindfulness is separated into 3 dimensions: mindful attention, mindful monitoring, and mindful regulation. Mindfulness attention is about being open-minded and applying all

senses to understand the contexts of situations. Mindfulness monitoring relates to an individual's awareness of understanding a problem through the lens of others. Mindfulness regulation involves appropriate behaviors and responses of an individual by developing new mental maps from different cultures [11]. Logan [13] mentioned that mindfulness helps an individual think wisely through cognitive processes before they lead to behaviors.

3. *Behavior* is an individual's ability to demonstrate appropriate actions in new cultural contexts. It could be separated into 2 main behaviors: an individual who appropriately behaves in different cultural contexts and has been accepted, and an individual who estimates situations of that cultural context first to ensure that their behaviors will be accepted and appropriate [14].

Key Benefits. The key benefits occur when an individual holds a high level of CQ and has the ability to effectively perform in cross-cultural situations, e.g., working with colleagues from different countries and working in international organizations [15]. When individuals and teams hold a high level of CQ, they will experience benefits in 3 aspects of outcomes: Psychological Outcomes, e.g., effective intercultural adjustment and greater interpersonal trust. Behavioral Outcomes, e.g., improved decision-making, higher confidence in sharing ideas, and creative collaboration among the teams. Performance Outcomes e.g. effective intercultural negotiations, increased work performance [16, 17]. Apart from individual and team aspects, the organization will also indirectly benefit from the high level of CQ like increased profitability and cost savings due to the adoption of more innovative methods, more expansion into international markets, better services that is tailored to specific needs of different group of customers, more effective HR practices on attracting talents to the organization in the context of diversity and global workforce [8, 9].

In the context of different or unfamiliar cultures, an individual with high CQ shows better emotional and psychological adjustment. They can live and work less stress and burnout, showing higher productivity and perseverance when encountering tough situations. An individual with high CQ can adjust themselves easily to uncertain and complex intercultural contexts [18–20].

It improved Cultural Judgment and Decision-Making. Individuals with high CQ can better understand and evaluate situations with multiple perspectives, leading to high-quality decision-making within intercultural contexts. CQ helps both individuals and teams to find the practical solutions that come from different perspectives [8, 10].

Greater Effectiveness in Intercultural Negotiations. Working in an international organization, negotiation is important, especially when it relates to agreements or contracts with clients or suppliers; in the school environment, it could refer to the talks between colleagues, teams, and parents. Individuals or teams with high CQ shows more patient and better ability to persist and collaborate across cultures to negotiate and develop 'win-win' agreements. These results come from their ability to better understand and incorporate diverse perspectives into negotiation process [21, 22].

Higher Levels of Trust, Idea-sharing, Information-Sharing and Creative Collaboration.
CQ enhances creativity and innovation for individuals and organization, individual and teams with high CQ are more capable of trusting each other which lead to higher levels of informational-sharing and idea-sharing. It causes the team members to engage and become more collaboration which can come up with innovative solutions. Furthermore, CQ creates higher psychological safety to the team due to positive level of CQ with higher trust [9, 23].

Increased Work Performance. Individuals with high CQ perform better in different cultural contexts compared to individuals with low CQ. Relevant studies stated the positive impacts of CQ and work adjustment, for example, high CQ positively impacts in terms of work performance, adaptive performance, and global leadership effectiveness [24, 25].

2.2 Personal-Environmental Fit

According to [26], the fit is the degree to which individual and organizational attributes are compatible. It relates to skills, abilities, goals, and values that fit the organization's culture and demands of an individual, including the fit of community and environment as well. There are many arguments for the measurement of work adjustment. However, one such attempt to measure adjustment has been through the person-environment fit theory (PE), which is generally defined as an individual's ability to fit into a work environment [26]. Dawis [27] also mentioned it is "one of the more venerable lines of psychological theorizing". Person-environment (PE) or organizational fit was first proposed by Parson (1909) to make professional choices by matching an individual's attributes such as personality, knowledge, past experiences, and environmental characteristics like norms and organizational structure. The interaction of an individual and the environment could also be measured as a statistical interaction [26]. It has also been defined as an "elusive criterion of fit" due to the multidimensions of people and environment. The PE consists of internal factors like personality, values, attitudes, skills, emotions, and goals. The external factors related to job requirements, expected behavior, organizational cultures, and collegiality [23].

The PE consists of 2 main types 1) supplementary fit and 2) complementary fit. Supplementary refers to similar characteristics of an individual to other individuals in the same environment. Complementary relates to the need of an individual which is offset by the environment or vice versa which could be separated into 2 fits: need-supplies fit Is the needs of an individual has been fulfilled by the environment. Or demands-abilities fit is the capabilities of an individual to fulfill the demands of the environment. Relevant research has stated that a positive relationship between the leader and follower will be achieved when both are alike and there is a supplementary fit in personality. However, the follower possibly requires autonomy and delegation to perform their tasks which an empowering leader would be needed [28]. This theory allows individuals to understand more on others' behaviors and easier apply their interpersonal interactions [29].

To be more specific, the summary of the aforementioned can be depicted as a conceptual model in Fig. 1 and will be used in Sect. 3.

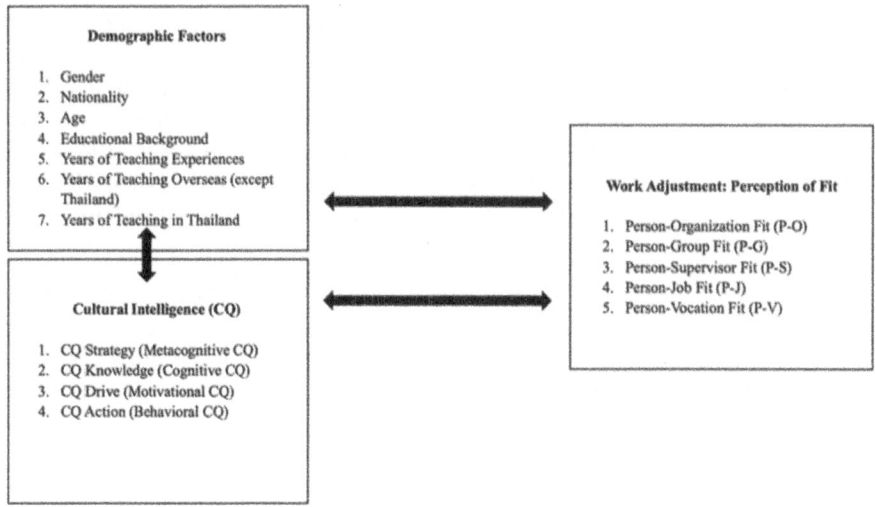

Fig. 1. A conceptual model of CQ and Work Adjustment [30]

3 CQ and Work Adjustment: Human Responses

3.1 Methodology

As discussed in Sect. 2, cultural intelligence (CQ) influences expatriate teachers' cross-cultural adjustment (CCQ) and work adjustment, resulting in their successful adjustment. Teachers who can adjust to the new culture and workplace may have high job satisfaction and intention to renew their employment contracts. Therefore, the researcher constructed a conceptual model, as shown in Fig. 1.

For the human response part, the research was conducted to study cultural intelligence (CQ) (independent variable), including demographic factors (control variables), and work adjustment (dependent variable) among expatriate teachers in international schools in Thailand. This study used a quantitative data collection method, in which the data was collected by the researcher through online questionnaires. This method allows many expatriate teachers to express their opinions about CQ and work adjustment.

Consent forms were sent to each international school's headmaster and the Human Resource Department to ask for approval before conducting the research. The invitation, consent form, and questionnaires will be sent to the potential participants, giving the details of this research and how the questionnaires are related, along with an option for the participants not involved in this research. From the time the invitation is sent out, the participants will have two weeks to complete the questionnaires, with a reminder email after one week.

Target Population and Samplings. This research represents the number of expatriate teachers working in international schools. The number of samplings is referred to by Krejcie and Morgan [31], 260 participants in the research samplings out of 800 teachers from 10 international schools as the target populations. The participants are male and female regardless of nationality, including those who experienced teaching overseas in other international schools and those who have worked here in Thailand as their first international teaching experience.

The Sampling Technique. This research utilizes convenience sampling to obtain the participants. Based on the 260 participants from 10 international schools located in Thailand, the online questionnaires were sent to the expatriate teachers in international schools through Google Forms regardless of their nationalities, age groups, educational backgrounds, and overseas and local teaching experiences to explore their perceptions and avoid bias.

Research Instrument. The research instrument is conducted as online questionnaires sent to participants' emails. The questionnaire is adapted from the Cultural Intelligence Scale (CQS) [7, 10]. And Person-Environment fit which the questionnaires of Person-Organization Fir (P-O), Person-Group Fit (P-G), Person-Supervisor Fit (P-S), Person-Job Fit (P-J) were developed by Vahidi et al. [32] and the Person-Vocation Fit (P-V) was modified and generated by Kennedy [33].

It consists of 3 different parts of the questionnaires: 1) Demographic Questions, 2) the Cultural Intelligence Scale, and 3) Work Adjustment: Perceptions of Fit, which has detail as follows:

1. *Demographic Questions.* Demographic questions have been constructed from items 1 to 7 regarding gender, nationality, age, education, years of teaching experience, years of teaching overseas (except Thailand), years of teaching in Thailand.
2. *The Cultural Intelligence Scale.* The scale has been constructed to measure the factors of CQ from items 8 to 27, measuring Metacognitive CQ, Cognitive CQ, Motivational CQ, and Behavioral CQ. The meta-cognitive CQ includes 4 questions from questions number 8 to 11 to assess the ability of teachers to understand cultural preferences. The cognitive CQ consists of 6 questions from questions 12 to 17 to determine teachers' knowledge related to economic, legal, and social systems. The motivational CQ includes 5 questions from questions number 18 to 22 related to teachers' motivation to adapt to different cultures and environments. The behavioral CQ consists of 5 questions from questions number 23 to 27 to assess the ability of teachers to interact with individuals from different cultures.

Work Adjustment: Perceptions of Fit. PEF have been constructed to measure self-reported teacher's work adjustment items 28 to 49 measuring factors of person-environment fit theory are Person-Organization Fit (P-O) from questions number 28 to 31, Person-Group Fit (P-G) from questions number 32 to 26, Person-Supervisor Fit (P-S) from questions number 37 to 40, Person-Job Fit (P-J) from questions number 41 to 44, and Person-Vocation Fit (P-V) from questions number 45 to 49.

The rating scale used in this research is based on Likert Scale (the 5-point scale) are shown in Table 1.

Reliability Test. The questionnaires have been adapted, which could be separated into 3 main categories: 1) Cultural Intelligence Scale (CQS) developed by Earley and Aung [7] and verified by Van Dyne et al. [10]. The Cronbach's alpha for each CQ factor were .84, .90, .89, and .86, respectively. 2) Person-Environment Fit questionnaires were developed by Vahidi et al. [31] which the reliability values of each fit factor are Person-Organization

Table 1. Table captions should be placed above the tables.

Scale	Meaning
1	Strongly disagree
2	Disagree
3	Neutral
4	Agree
5	Strongly agree

Fit (P-O), Person-Group Fit (P-G), Person-Supervisor Fit (P-S), and Person-Job Fit (P-J) were 0.70. Lastly, the questionnaires related to Person-Vocation Fit (P-V) individually, modified and generated by Kennedy [32], consisted of a reliability test scale of .82.

Data Analysis. In this section, the quantitative part, IBM SPSPP Statistics Software, was employed to analyze the factors between cultural intelligence (CQ) and work adjustment of the expatriate teachers by using descriptive statistics. The demographic part has been used frequency and percentile to see the majority of respondents. Mean and Standard Deviation (S.D.) have been used to see the overall Cultural Intelligence (CQ) and Person-Environment Fit factors. The Pearson's Correlation Coefficient has been used to analyze the relationship between Cultural Intelligence (CQ) and Person-Environment Fit factors.

3.2 Descriptive Statistics

Tables 2–8 show the model's inputs corresponding to Fig. 1. The number of respondents classified by gender is shown in Table 2. The majority of respondents were female (50.4%), followed by male (49.2%), and prefer not to say (0.4%), respectively.

The number of respondents classified by nationality group is shown in Table 3.

The sample group consisted of 260 expatriate teachers, divided into 4 nationalities, including American, Australian or New Zealand, British or other Europeans, and Chinese or other Asians with equal proportions of 25%.

The number of respondents classified by age group is shown in Table 4. The majority of respondents were 30 – 39 years old (56.2%), followed by 20 – 29 years old (18.8%), 40 – 49 years old (15.0%), and 50 years old or older (10.0%), respectively.

The number of respondents classified by educational background is shown in Table 5. The majority of respondents had a bachelor's degree (59.6%), followed by a master's degree (39.2%) and a doctoral degree (1.2%), respectively. The number of respondents classified by years of teaching experience is shown in Table 6. The majority of respondents had 6–10 years of teaching experience (37.3%), followed by 11–15 years (28.5%), 16 years or above (26.2%), and 1–5 years (8.1%), respectively.

Table 7 shows the number of respondents classified by years of teaching overseas (except Thailand). The majority of respondents had 1–5 years of teaching overseas (35.4%), followed by 6–10 years (31.2%), 11–15 years (19.2%), less than 1 year (8.5%), and 16 years or more (5.8%), respectively. The number of respondents classified by years

Table 2. Frequency and percentage of respondents classified by gender (n = 260)

Gender	Frequency	Percentage
Male	128	49.2
Female	131	50.4
Other	0	0
Prefer not to say	1	0.4
Total	260	100

Table 3. Frequency and percentage of respondents classified by Nationality Group (Geographic Region of Nationality) (n = 260)

Nationality Group (Geographic Region of Nationality)	Frequency	Percentage
American	65	25.0
Australian or New Zealand	65	25.0
British or other Europeans	65	25.0
Chinese or other Asians	65	25.0
Total	260	100

Table 4. Frequency and percentage of respondents classified by age group (n = 260)

Age Group	Frequency	Percentage
20 – 29 years old	49	18.8
30 – 39 years old	146	56.2
40 – 49 years old	39	15.0
50 years old or older	26	10.0
Total	260	100

of teaching in Thailand is shown in Table 8. The majority of respondents had 1–5 years of teaching in Thailand (56.9%), followed by 6–10 years (21.5%), less than 1 year (11.2%), 11–15 years (6.9%), and 16 years or more (3.5%), respectively.

Due to limitation of pages, correlation coefficient between CQ and other factors are not shown in all cases, but shows only in Table 9 as an example. From Table 9, the results indicated the overall Cultural Intelligence and Person-Vocation Fit (P-V) had moderate statistically significant positive correlations ($r = 0.543$). The Cultural Intelligence factors of Meta-Cognitive CQ, Cognitive CQ, Motivational CQ, Behavioral CQ had moderate statistically significant positive correlation with Person-Vocation Fit (P-V) at $r = 0.514$, 0.489, 0.441, and 0.464, respectively.

Table 5. Frequency and percentage of respondents classified by education background (n = 260)

Education background	Frequency	Percentage
Lower than a bachelor's degree	0	0
Bachelor's degree	155	59.6
Master's degree	102	39.2
Doctoral Degree	3	1.2
Total	260	100

Table 6. Frequency and percentage of respondents classified by years of teaching experience (n = 260)

Years of teaching experience	Frequency	Percentage
Less than 1 year	0	0
1–5 years	21	8.1
6–10 years	97	37.3
11–15 years	74	28.5
16 years or above	68	26.2
Total	260	100

Table 7. Frequency and percentage of respondents classified by years of teaching overseas (except Thailand) (n = 260)

Years of teaching overseas (except Thailand)	Frequency	Percentage
Less than 1 year	22	8.5
1–5 years	92	35.4
6–10 years	81	31.2
11–15 years	50	19.2
16 years or more	15	5.8
Total	260	100

3.3 Summary of Findings

Based on the results, the majority of respondents were female, male, and prefer not to say, respectively. In term of nationality group, the researcher tried to acquire respondents on each nationality group equally, therefore, the nationality groups have been divided into 4 main categories are American, Australian or New Zealand, British or other Europeans, Chinese or other Asians with the number of respondents 65 people on each group to avoid bias. The age group results found that most respondents are expatriate teachers

Table 8. Frequency and percentage of respondents classified by years of teaching in Thailand (n = 260)

Years of teaching in Thailand	Frequency	Percentage
Less than 1 year	29	11.2
1–5 years	148	56.9
6–10 years	56	21.5
11–15 years	18	6.9
16 years or more	9	3.5
Total	260	100

Table 9. Correlation Coefficient between Cultural Intelligence factors and Person-Vocation Fit (P-V) factor

Cultural Intelligence	Person-Vocation Fit (P-V)		
	Pearson's correlation (r)	p	Correlation Level
Meta-Cognitive CQ	0.514	0.000**	moderate correlation
Cognitive CQ	0.489	0.000**	moderate correlation
Motivational CQ	0.441	0.000**	moderate correlation
Behavioral CQ	0.464	0.000**	moderate correlation
Overall	0.543	0.000**	moderate correlation

** $p < 0.01$ (significant at the 0.01 level)

who are 30 – 39 years old, 20 – 29 years old, 40 – 49 years old, and 50 years old or older, respectively. Regarding education background, the results showed that the majority of respondents graduated with a bachelor's degree, master's degree, and doctoral degree, respectively – no respondent graduated lower than a bachelor's degree. Years of teaching experience have also been explored; the results presented that the majority of respondents have 6 – 10 years of teaching experience, 11 – 15 years of teaching experience, 16 years of teaching experience or above, and 1 – 5 years of teaching experience, respectively – there was no respondent has teaching experience less than 1 year. For the years of teaching overseas (except Thailand), most respondents have been overseas for 1 – 5 years, 6 – 10 years, 11 – 15 years, less than 1 year, and 16 years or more, respectively. In a particular aspect, years of teaching in Thailand, the results presented that most respondents have 1 – 5 years of teaching in Thailand, 6 – 10 years, less than 1 year, 11 – 15 years, and 16 years or more, respectively.

The results appear that there was a positive correlation between the cultural intelligence (CQ) and overall work adjustment of expatriate teachers in international schools in Thailand regardless of their genders, nationalities, education backgrounds, years of teaching experiences, years of teaching overseas (except Thailand), and years of teaching in Thailand. This result confirmed that the essential characteristics of expatriate teachers to adjust well to a new cultural context related to the high level of their CQ. In particular, the overall level of correlation of these variables is a high correlation, which is in line with the study of Guomundsdottir [18], which mentioned that expatriate teachers with a high level of CQ would be able to understand the new culture and adjust themselves to a new environment which they are involved.

Based on the descriptive statistics of each factor of cultural intelligence (CQ), expatriate teachers in international schools in Thailand hold the highest level of motivational CQ, which relates to the level of interest and dedication of expatriate teachers to experience Thai culture and interact with Thai people. Meta-Cognitive CQ is the second level, which is about the ability of expatriate teachers to be aware and understand different cultures, especially in Thailand, including their abilities to adjust and adequately interact with Thai people successfully. Not too different level, Behavioral CQ, is considered the third level of the expatriate teachers' CQ, which this study defined as the capability of expatriate teachers to appropriately use their verbal or non-verbal behaviors in dealing with Thai culture and Thai people, including their ability of adjust themselves to the norms, values, different nationalities, ethics, and organizational cultures of international schools located in Thailand. The last factor, Cognitive CQ, was interpreted as a neutral level of expatriate teachers' CQ, which is the ability of expatriate teachers to understand similarities and differences between Thai cultures and their home countries. It also relates to their ability to assess and respond appropriately to the Thai economic and legal systems, norms, social interactions, religious beliefs, and aesthetic values.

Regarding the factor of person-environment fit, which is challenging to the expatriate teachers in their work adjustment, the results appear that the expatriate teachers have a positive relationship with the person-environment fit, which the overall interpretation of descriptive statistics has been shown to agree. This means that the expatriate teachers in international schools in Thailand can adjust themselves to their surrounding work environments, such as organization, group, supervisor, job, and vocation at a high level overall. In particular, the interpretation of Person-Group Fit (P-G), Person-Supervisor Fit (P-S), Person-Job Fit (P-J), and Person-Vocation Fit (P-V) were strongly agree. There was only a person-organization fit, which was interpreted as an agreement. In this context, it seems like the school's culture and environment are challenging factors for expatriate teachers to adjust to, compared to other factors.

Being more specific on the correlation of each CQ to the Person-Organization Fit, the results show that the level of cognitive CQ is highly related to the person-organization fit. At the same time, other CQs like meta-cognitive CQ, motivational CQ, and behavioral CQ were moderately correlated. This means that the more a teacher can understand the similarities and differences between Thai cultures and their home country, the more they can adjust to the school's culture here in Thailand. However, all CQ factors were moderately correlated to the Person-Group Fit, so the CQs are related to the ability of teachers to get along well with their colleagues from various nationalities but at a medium level.

4   Results: Computer Interaction

4.1   A Turing Test

This section presents how humans evaluate agents' understanding of cultural nuances by designing and administering tests that assess their ability to navigate the same given complex scenarios as humans did in Sect. 3. In this test, like in [34], we selected three of the well-known generative agents: Microsoft's Copilot, ChatGPT from OpenAI, and Google Gemini. There are several more besides, but the selection was based on the free AI model rather than the paid-for versions. The same questionnaires were given to perform the test for those three AI models. Utilizing the framework in Fig. 1, the control and independent variables are defined as follows

Control Variables (Demographic Factors). CV1: Gender CV2: Nationality CV3: AgeCV4: Educational Background
   CV5: Years of Teaching Experience
   CV6: Years of Teaching Overseas (except Thailand)
   CV7: Years of Teaching in Thailand

Independent Variables. IV1: The CQ Strategy (Meta-Cognitive CQ) refers to the ability of expatriate teachers to be aware of and understand different cultures, especially in Thailand, including their ability to adjust and adequately interact with Thai people successfully. The questionnaires consist of four questions related to meta-cognitive CQ (MC), as stated on questions 8 to 11.

   IV2: **CQ Knowledge (Cognitive CQ)** is defined as the ability of expatriate teachers to understand similarities and differences between Thai cultures and their home countries. It also relates to their ability to assess and respond appropriately to the Thai economic and legal systems, norms, social interactions, religious beliefs, and aesthetic values. The questionnaires consist of 6 questions related to cognitive CQ (COG), as stated on questions 12 to 17.

   IV3: **CQ Drive (Motivational CQ)** is described as the level of interest and dedication of expatriate teachers to experiencing Thai culture and interacting with Thai people. The questionnaires consist of 5 questions related to motivational CQ (MOT), which is stated on questions 18 to 22.

   IV4: **CQ Action (Behavioral CQ)** is the capability of expatriate teachers to appropriately use their verbal or non-verbal behaviors in dealing with Thai culture and Thai people, including their ability to adjust themselves to the norms, values, different nationalities, ethics, and organizational cultures of international schools located in Thailand. The questionnaires consist of 5 questions related to behavioral CQ (BEH), as stated on the questionnaire's questions number 23 to 27.

   Before presenting the results of the Turing tests, we investigate the human case shown in Tables 10 and 11. From this point, tables show descriptive analysis for mean, standard deviation (S.D.), and interpretation of each question with the measurement scale as follows.

Range of Mean	Interpretation
4.21 – 5.00	Strongly agree
3.41 – 4.20	Agree
2.61 – 3.40	Neutral
1.81 – 2.60	Disagree
1.00 – 1.80	Strongly disagree

Table 10. Mean, S.D., and interpretation of Cultural Intelligence (Human)

Statements	Mean ($\bar{x}$)	Standard Deviation (S.D.)	Interpretation
Meta-Cognitive CQ	4.17	0.626	Agree
Cognitive CQ	3.18	0.826	Neutral
Motivational CQ	4.48	0.501	Strongly agree
Behavioral CQ	3.99	0.694	Agree
Overall	3.91	0.592	Agree

From Table 10, the results indicated that overall Cultural Intelligence is at an agree level (mean = 3.91, S.D. = 0.592). The highest mean is Motivational CQ (mean = 4.48, S.D. = 0.501), followed by Meta-Cognitive CQ (mean = 4.17, S.D. = 0.626), Behavioral CQ (mean = 3.99, S.D. = 0.694), and Cognitive CQ (mean = 3.18, S.D. = 0.826), respectively.

The results of the human case in Table 11 are now used to compare with those of the agents in Table 12. From Tables 11, 12, and 13, for example, the results indicated that the overall Meta-Cognitive CQ of those agents is at an agreeable level with mean = 4, S.D. = 0.816 (mean = 4.17, S.D. = 0.626 for the human case).

The highest mean in the case of humans is MC1, "I am conscious of the cultural knowledge I use when interacting with people from different cultural backgrounds." (mean = 4.22, S.D. = 0.647), followed by MC2, "I adjust my cultural knowledge as I interact with people from a culture that is unfamiliar to me." (mean = 4.20, S.D. = 0.640), MC3, "I am conscious of the cultural knowledge I apply to cross-cultural interactions." (mean = 4.20, S.D. = 0.640), and MC4, "I check the accuracy of my cultural knowledge as I interact with people from different cultures." (mean = 4.05, S.D. = 0.739), respectively.

The agents have not agreed upon this. The highest mean in the case of agents is MC4, "I check the accuracy of my cultural knowledge as I interact with people from different cultures." (mean = 4.33, S.D. = 0.943), followed by MC1, "I am conscious of the cultural knowledge I use when interacting with people from different cultural backgrounds." (mean = 4., S.D. = 0.816), MC3, "I am conscious of the cultural knowledge I apply to cross-cultural interactions." (mean = 4, S.D. = 0.816), and MC2, "I adjust my cultural knowledge as I interact with people from a culture that is unfamiliar to me." (mean = 3.67, S.D. = 0.943), respectively.

Table 11. Mean, S.D., and interpretation of Meta-Cognitive CQ (Human)

Statements	Mean ($\bar{x}$)	Standard Deviation (S.D.)	Interpretation
MC1: I am conscious of the cultural knowledge I use when interacting with people from different cultural backgrounds	4.22	0.647	Strongly agree
MC2: I adjust my cultural knowledge as I interact with people from a unfamiliar culture	4.20	0.640	Agree
MC3: I am conscious of the cultural knowledge I apply to cross-cultural interactions	4.20	0.640	Agree
MC4: I check the accuracy of my cultural knowledge as I interact with people from different cultures	4.05	0.739	Agree
Overall	4.17	0.626	Agree

Table 12. Interpretation of Meta-Cognitive CQ (Agents)

Statements	Copilot	ChatGPT	Gemini
MC1: I am conscious of the cultural knowledge I use when interacting with people from different cultural backgrounds	5	4	3
MC2: I adjust my cultural knowledge as I interact with people from a unfamiliar culture	5	3	3
MC3: I am conscious of the cultural knowledge I apply to cross-cultural interactions	5	4	3
MC4: I check the accuracy of my cultural knowledge as I interact with people from different cultures	5	5	3
Overall	5	4	3

For IV2-IV4, which are cognitive, motivational, and behavioral CQ, the results were not significantly different in most items, except those of COG1 and COG2. For COG1, "I know the legal and economic systems of other cultures," the average rate was Neutral (mean = 2.67, S.D. = 1.247). For COG2, "I know the rules (e.g., vocabulary, grammar) of other languages," the average rate was Neutral (mean = 3, S.D. = 1.414).

4.2 A Reverse Turing Test

In this test, as definition page 3 of [35], "we quantify humans' ability to simulate computer programs, however; rather than computer programs' ability to simulate humans.

Table 13. Mean, S.D., and interpretation of Meta-Cognitive CQ (Agents)

Statements	Mean ($\bar{x}$)	Standard Deviation (S.D.)	Interpretation
MC1: I am conscious of the cultural knowledge I use when interacting with people from different cultural backgrounds	4	0.816	Agree
MC2: I adjust my cultural knowledge as I interact with people from a unfamiliar culture	3.67	0.943	Agree
MC3: I am conscious of the cultural knowledge I apply to cross-cultural interactions	4	0.816	Agree
MC4: I check the accuracy of my cultural knowledge as I interact with people from different cultures	4.33	0.943	Agree
Overall	4	0.879	Agree

Specifically, we quantify humans' ability to predict the output of machine learning models given previously unseen examples." However, we have not fully adopted the entire protocol and framework suggested in [35] for this research, but we adopted the idea of using prediction by the human ability to predict the outputs of machine models based on the frameworks given in Fig. 1. The dependent variables for prediction were as follows.

Dependent Variables. DV1: **Person-Organization Fit (P-O)** refers to the level of fit of expatriate teachers' personal and organizational characteristics. In this case, it means the international schools where they currently work in Thailand. The questionnaires consist of 4 questions related to Person-Organization Fit (P-O), which has been stated in the questionnaire's questions number 28 to 31.

DV2: **Person-Group Fit (P-G)** is the ability of expatriate teachers to get along well with their colleagues from various nationalities, mainly related to demographics, goals, personalities, and skills. The questionnaires consist of 5 questions related to Person-Group Fit (P-G), as stated in questions 32 to 36.

DV3: **Person-Supervisor Fit (P-S)** means the ability of expatriate teachers to get along well with their supervisor in the international schools where they presently work. The questionnaires consist of 4 questions related to Person-Supervisor Fit (P-S), which are stated in the questionnaire's questions number 37 to 40.

DV4: **Person-Job Fit (P-J)** is the relationship between expatriate teachers and their job attributes like demands and workload, job security, promotion opportunities, role ambiguity, supervisor support, and autonomy of their job at their current school. The questionnaires consist of 4 questions related to Person-Job Fit (P-J), which are stated in the questionnaire's questions number 41 to 44.

DV5: **Person-Vocation Fit (P-V)** is defined as the fit of expatriate teachers and their professional outcomes, like satisfaction and performance at the current school. The questionnaires consist of 5 questions related to Person-Vocation Fit (P-V), which are stated in the questionnaire's questions number 45 to 49.

Based on various responses from agents obtained from Sect. 4.1, we carefully served as "cultural gatekeepers" to predict outputs from the agent models in this research's given scenarios. Upon reviewing the responses of the given scenarios in the previous subsection, we found that copilot gave a trend to maximize the rating, which was strongly agreed, followed by Gemini trended to neutralize the rate, and ChatGPT3.5 trended to guess the answer based on its assumption. For a giving situation involving human feelings or lacking the complete given information, Gemini would not give a rate but rather provide hints for possible rating based on condition. An example of results for P-O1 by agents, "My organization meets my primary requirement.", is shown in Fig. 2. In Fig. 2, the response from Gemini is not given because of no rating, only for the hints.

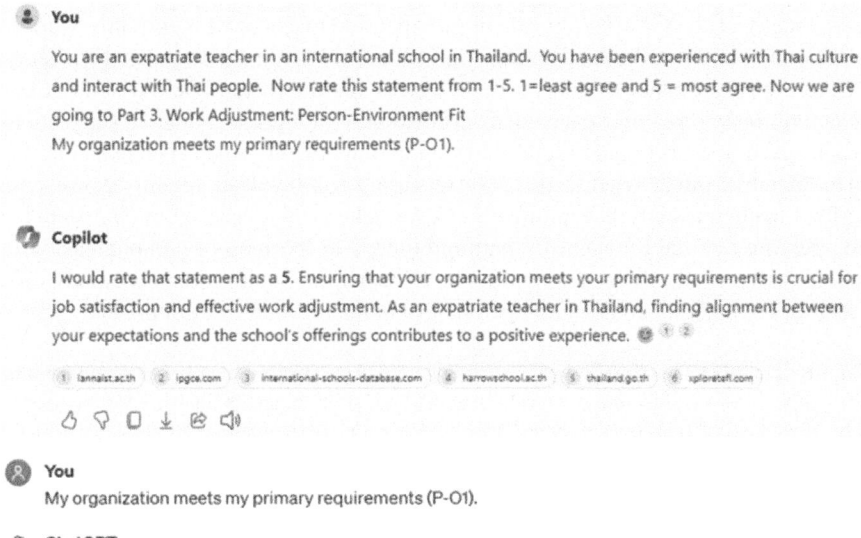

Fig. 2. An example of responses on P-O1 item by the agents

With "cognitive bias" including in the interpretation of the agents' responses and information from the human cases that a low correlation of meta-cognitive CQ has been shown in the result of Person-Supervisor Fit, it might be forward predicted that Copilot, ChatGPT and Gemini would give the highest rate 5, 4 and no rate (only a hint) as in the past observation by us. Our forward prediction results would be no surprise due to our inherent cognitive biases. Besides, we have previously known that other CQ factors were moderately correlated to the Person-Supervisor Fit. This could be explained by the fact that the ability of expatriate teachers to be aware and understand different cultures, including their abilities to adjust and appropriately interact with Thai people, is rarely related to their supervisor fit. This is because international schools typically hire native-speaker headmasters and teachers who come from the country where they brought the curriculum to teach here in Thailand.

5   Conclusion

We presented the role of humans as cultural gatekeepers via a reverse Turing test. The term of a reverse Turing test herein quantified humans' ability to simulate computer programs to predict the output of machine learning models given scenarios. The scenarios in our study were the investigation of the statistical correlation between Cultural Intelligence (CQ) and Work Adjustment of expatriate teachers who currently work in international schools in Thailand through the concept of Person-Environment Fit Theory.

Even the performance of generative AI agents and the forward perdition ability by human intuitions were impressive; in the evaluation of rating and providing suggestions on each given scenario, there were many limitations of this study. For example, the human cognitive model used in this reverse Turing test involved cognitive biases not described mathematically but intuitively. Nevertheless, this paper attempts to predict AI outputs in a cultural context by putting humans in the loop of comprehension of autonomous agents. Further investigation of this emerging topic would benefit not only the field of engineering and technology but also human resource development.

Acknowledgments. This paper is financially supported in part by the School of Human Resource Development, National Institute of Development Administration, and is financially supported in part by the School of Engineering, King Mongkut's Institute of Technology Ladkrabang.

Disclosure of Interests. The first and the second authors researched the parts involving human aspects, which were financially supported by the School of HRD, NIDA. The third author helped design and analyze the part involving generative AI or agents, which is financially supported by the School of Engineering, KMITL.

References

1. Semeraro, F., Griffiths, A., Cangelosi, A.: Human-robot collaboration and machine learning: a systematic review of recent research. Robot. Comput. Integr. Manufact. **79**(4), 102432 (2023)
2. Yadollahi, E., et al.: Explainability for human-robot collaboration. In: HRI '24: Companion of the 2024 ACM/IEEE International Conference on Human-Robot Interaction, pp. 1364–1366 (2024)
3. Lappromrattana, T., Sooraksa, P.: Quick prototyping of companion bots for elderly people. Sens. Mater. **35**, 1487–1495 (2023)
4. Garamvölgyi, J., Rudnák, I.: Exploring the relationship between cultural intelligence (CQ) and management competencies (MC). Sustainability **15**(7), 5734 (2023)

5. Kristof-Brown, A.L., Guay, R.P.: Person-environment fit. In: Zedeck, S. (ed.) American psychological association handbook of industrial and organizational psychology 3, pp. 3–50. American Psychological Association, Washington DC (2011)
6. He, G., An, R., Zhang, F.: Cultural intelligence and work-family conflict: a moderated mediation model based on conservation of resources theory. Int. J. Environ. Res. Public Health **16**(13), 2406 (2019)
7. Earley, P.C., Ang, S.: Cultural Intelligence—Individual Interactions Across Cultures. Stanford University Press, Stanford (2003)
8. Ang, S., Rockstuhl, T., Tan, M.L.: Cultural intelligence and competencies. Int. Encycl. Soc. Behav. Sci **2**, 433–439 (2015)
9. Livermore, D.: Leading with Cultural Intelligence: The Real Secret to Success, 2nd edn. AMACOM, New York (2015)
10. Van Dyne, L., Ang, S., Ng, K.Y., Rockstuhl, T., Tan, M.L.: Sub-dimensions of the four-factor model of cultural intelligence: Expanding the conceptualization and measurement of cultural intelligence. Soc. Personality Psychol. Compass **6**, 295–313 (2012)
11. Thomas, D.C., Inkson, K.: Cultural Intelligence: People Skills for Global Business. Berrett-Koehler, San Francisco (2004)
12. Gardner, H.: "Multiple intelligences" as a catalyst. English Journal, pp. 16–18 (1995)
13. Logan, R.: Flow and solitary ordeals. In: M. Csikszentmihalyi & I. Csikszentmihalyi (Eds.), Optimal experience. Cambridge University Press, Cambridge, MA (1989)
14. Thomas, D.C.: Domain and development of cultural intelligence the importance of mindfulness. Group Org. Manag. **31**(1), 78–99 (2006)
15. Fang, F., Schei, V., Selart, M.: Hype or hope? A new look at the research on cultural intelligence. Int. J. Intercultural Relat. **66**, 148–171 (2018)
16. Gelfand, M.J., Imai, L., Fehr, R.: Thinking Intelligently about Cultural Intelligence: The Road Ahead. In: Handbook of Cultural intelligence: Theory, Measurement and Applications, Ang, S. and L. Van Dyne (Eds.), Routledge, New York, pp. 375–387 (2015)
17. Leung, K., Ang, S., Tan, M.L.: Intercultural competence. Annual Rev. Organiz. Psychol. Organizat. Behav. **1**, 489–519 (2014)
18. Guomundsdottir, S.: Nordic expatriates in the US: the relationship between cultural intelligence and adjustment. Int. J. Intercultural Relat **47**, 175–186 (2015)
19. Lin, Y.C., Chen, A.S.Y., Song, Y.C.: Does your intelligence help to survive in a foreign jungle? The effects of cultural intelligence and emotional intelligence on cross-cultural adjustment. Int. J. Intercultural Relat **36**, 541–552 (2012)
20. Malek, M.A., Budhwar, P.: Cultural intelligence as a predictor of expatriate adjustment and performance in Malaysia. J. World Bus. **48**, 222–231 (2013)
21. Imai, L., Gelfand, M.J.: The culturally intelligent negotiator: the impact of cultural intelligence (CQ) on negotiation sequences and outcomes. Organiz. Behav. Human Dec. Processes **112**, 83–98 (2010)
22. Groves, K.S., Feyerherm, A., Gu, M.: Examining cultural intelligence and cross-cultural negotiation effectiveness. J. Manage. Educ **39**, 209–243 (2015)
23. Jansen, K.J., Kristof-Brown, A.: Toward a multidimensional theory of person- environment fit. J. Manag. **18**, 193–212 (2006)
24. Groves, K.S., Feyerherm, A.E.: Leader cultural intelligence in context: testing the moderating effects of team cultural diversity on leader and team performance. Group Organiz. Manage **36**, 535–566 (2011)
25. Presbitero, A.: Cultural intelligence (CQ) in virtual, cross-cultural interactions: generalizability of measure and links to personality dimensions and task performance. Int. J. Intercultural Relat **50**, 29–38 (2016)

26. Kristof-Brown, A.L., Zimmerman, R.D., Johnson, E.C.: Consequences of Individuals' fit at work: A meta-analysis of person-job, person-job, person-organization, person-group, and person supervisor fit. Pers. Psychol. **58**(2), 281–342 (2005)
27. Dawis, R.V.: Person–environment fit and job satisfaction. In: Cranny, C.J., Smith, P.C., Stone EF (Eds.), Job satisfaction: How people feel about their jobs and how it affects their performance. Lexington Books, New York (1992)
28. Sales, A., Mansur, J., Roth, S.: Fit for functional differentiation: new directions for personnel management and organizational change bridging the fit theory and social systems theory. Organ. Change Manag. **36**(2), 273–289 (2023)
29. Edwards, J.R., Cooper, C.L.: The person-environment fit approach to stress: recurring problems and some suggested solutions. J. Organ. Behav. **11**, 293–307 (1990)
30. Dawis, R.V., Lofquist, L.H.: A Psychological Theory of Work Adjustment. University of Minnesota Press, Minneapolis (1984)
31. Krejcie, R.V., Morgan, D.W.: Determining sample size for research activities. Educ. Psychol. Measur. **30**(3), 607–610 (1970)
32. Vahidi, N., Roslan, S., Abdullah, M.C., Omar, Z.: Relationship between need supply major fit and demand ability major fit with academic achievement. J. Educ. Hum. Dev. **5**(2), 196–206 (2016)
33. Kennedy, M.: An Integrative investigation of person-vocation of person-vocation fit, person-organization fit, and person-job fit perceptions. Doctoral dissertation. University of North Texas (2005)
34. Popular Science Homepage. http://www.popsci.com/technology/copilot-vs-chatgpt-vs-gemini. Accessed 19 May 2024
35. Gonzalez, A.V., Søgaard, A.: The reverse Turing test for evaluating interpretability methods on unknown tasks, NeurIPS 2020 Workshop on Human and Model in the Loop Evaluation and Training Strategies, ONLINE (2020)

Design and Responsible Research Innovation in the University-Industry Collaboration: An Ethnographic Study of Nice2035 Project-Based Community

Jing Wang[1]([✉]), Yunyun Weng[2], Mohammad Shidujaman[3], and Ying Jiang[1]

[1] College of Design and Innovation, Tongji University, Shanghai, China
wangjing7733@tongji.edu.cn, my.jiang@connect.polyu.hk
[2] Hangzhou College of Childhood Teachers' Education Zhejiang Normal University, Zhejiang, China
wengyunyun77@zjnu.edu.cn
[3] Department of Computer Science and Engineering, Independent University, Dhaka, Bangladesh
Shantothusets@iub.edu.bd

Abstract. Background: Responsible innovation is an assessing process before a new product/service put into commercial application. However, the designers' commitment and responsibility to the public means that designers cannot ignore or downplay the institutional framework. The significance of responsible innovation being discussed again is that the role of designers as cultural intermediaries in the opening innovation process remains to be clarified. **The objective** of this study is to explore designers 'new role in achieving sustainable community that economic prosperity, cultural regeneration, and vitality. **Participants and setting:** A total of 12 Chinese respondents with different work experience background (Government, research institutions, private enterprises) responded to a qualitative survey and interview research about design and responsible innovation. **Method:** This article using an ethnographic case study to investigate the writing practices of academic, and qualitative data that collected from participatory observation and interviews with experienced experts were analyzed using reflexive subject analysis and content analysis. **Result:** Findings from the case study support a model of sustainable community comprised of three overarching components: 1)Design Harvest Global Innovation and entrepreneurship Platform ;2)Artistic participation;3)Cultivating care economy. Thematic analyses also revealed that Socio-economic cooperation model is considered to be the way out of the depressed economic environment. **Conclusion:** The quality of community health care cannot be improved only through top-down health care systems, but must rely on socioeconomic and community upstream interventions. The public responsibility of designers convening citizen leaders to strengthen collective collaboration and reconnecting isolated people building stronger socioeconomic and cultural relationships, thus provide healthcare to the marginal community. Our results are consistent with previous surveys from China and the United States, highlighting the international relevance of these topics.

© The Author(s), under exclusive license to Springer Nature Switzerland AG 2025
M. Kurosu et al. (Eds.): HCII 2024, LNCS 15374, pp. 249–273, 2025.
https://doi.org/10.1007/978-3-031-76803-3_14

Keywords: Design for sustainability · Responsible research innovation · Collaborative design

1 Introduction

Increasingly, the designer is forced to re-examine her own role, especially in reflecting on what is a Sustainable society? and how to do some social design working together to tackle unsustainable crises? The famous Brundtland Report coined one of the most frequently cited definitions of sustainable development in 1987 as 'development team that meets the needs of the present without compromising the ability of future generations to meet their own needs'. Studies have shown that our theoretical understanding of the concept has evolved from a view that perceived sustainability as a static goal to a dynamic and moving target responding to our ever increasingly understanding of interdependencies between social and ecological systems.

Transition Management (TM) is a long-term policy design method that originated in the Netherlands and developed long-term vision methods to create path for change [1]. Social transformation is a systematic innovation which require the cooperation of socio-technical infrastructure and social culture [2], changing habits of current practice [3]. The general approach to transformation management is nurturing rather than controlling, creating space for learning and experimentation with relevant 'front-runner' stakeholder groups.

In this paper, the author presents a specific project —NICE2035 which implemented in a project-based community in Shanghai China, based on the concept of community resilience, and promotes more caring and inclusive sustainable communities development. **NICE2035** comes from The Shanghai Urban Master Plan (2017–2035) [4] that highlights the expansion from regional scope to the vision of open global interconnection and regional coordinated development. NICE2035 community-supported social innovation practice adopts a 'committee'-style flat management method, where entrepreneurs, capital, enterprises, and the government jointly manage platform resources [5]. The solution of social problems requires the participation of multiple stakeholders. The Social Solidarity Economy (SSE) consists of bottom-up grassroots actions such as cooperatives, mutual aid societies, associations, foundations and social enterprises, and the specific forms are very diverse.

1.1 Research Question

The purpose of this article is to promote sustainable communities that economic prosperity, cultural regeneration, social progress, and cultural vitality. However, Designers should be fully aware that the responsibility in revitalizing local economy is shared by shanghai public sector. Since public institutions (Governmental entities, Statutory bodies, Regulatory authority, Ministries department) and private institutions (Commercial companies, Non-governmental and Non-profit organizations) often involved in design research as funding agencies, participants, donors, sponsors and play an important role that designers cannot ignoring and downplaying the institutional framework [6]; Furthermore, designers should facilitate and encourage people to form a diverse team of professionals and institutions, so that both sides in the partnership can benefit from the development and implementation of projects.

This raised the following research questions [RQs]:

[RQ1] Is innovation socially responsible? What are socially responsible (people-centered) innovation?

[RQ2] What are the characteristics and components of a sustainable community? What are the interactions between the components of the NICE2035 project community?

[RQ3] How design strategies are used in NICE2035 project-based innovation ecosystem?

The specific study objectives were:

1. Open innovation process, through collaboration, co-design and design thinking integrates or combines economics, environment and science in order to transform science and industry, harmonize different specifications and establish multi-level shared spaces and activity venues to support and meet the needs of society.
2. Nice 2035 project-based community as a green infrastructure powered by renewable energy and improves the quality of air, soil and water, in which the residents are able to maintain their own sustainable lifestyles and benefit from the whole ecosystem which promote more cohesive community enterprise.

2   Theoretical Background

2.1   University-Industry Collaboration

As far back as Aristotle, in 335 B.C.E., one of the first examples of higher education institutions (HEIs) was the Lyceum, which focused on training the elite members of the community [7]. Now, in the 21st century, universities have become key actors in cultural and economic growth, as well as fostering competitiveness in the global arena. On the one side, over the past few decades, in addition to teaching and research, Universities have been increasingly pursuing a third mission namely activities that can "contribute to the social, economic and cultural development of the regions whereby they (the Universities) located, by transferring knowledge and technologies to industry and society" [8].On the other side, universities are also evolving more and more into institutions engaged with industry and society. 'The third mission' promotes the active engagement of universities in Knowledge commercialization activities, which are an important source of innovation and an engine of economic development for regions. University professors argue that the third mission cannot be achieved in isolation, and universities must collaborate with external organizations, particularly in industry, government and civil society.

Universities as custodians of scientific enquiry and new knowledge are at the forefront of exploring new design and engineering approaches. There has been a dramatic increase and recent acceleration over the past two decades in the number of university-industry collaborations. These collaborations include joint research projects, joint research centers, contract research and academic consulting. And yet, despite the value of university-industry collaboration, there is limited theoretical and practical advice on how to successfully manage interactions, and what the key elements for success are. There is limited understanding on how design methods support university-industry collaborations to produce both research and commercial outcomes.

In today's rapidly changing international environment, what are the key role of design at the level of strategic cooperation framework between universities and industry? Perhaps we can get some inspiration from the Danish Denmark's National Medicines Agency which has taken full advantage of healthcare system reform to reconfigure relationship with their clients, hospitals, drug manufacturers and Danish international health organization to expand their influence and create economic benefits.

Social capital in the partnership impacts collaborative and innovative outcomes, and identified success factors include positive interrelationships between individuals, open communication, trust and understanding during different phases of the project.

2.2 Codesign

A codesign approach supports sharing a 'third space', a conceptual space, where participants knowledge is combined to create new insights and plans for action. In university-industry collaboration this third space is separate from expectations and constraints of the university campus, head office or factory floor, becoming a neutral space for collaboration and participation. Irrespective of where design activities take place, the 'third space' is for articulating, clarifying, informing, challenging assumptions, learning reciprocally, and creating new ideas which emerge through negotiation, co-creation and conversations across and through existing differences, supporting plurality in design.

2.3 Design-Driven Innovation and Designers' Public Responsibility

Human-centered design is the core of knowledge economy era. The Made in China 2025 design policy initiated by the Chinese central government proposed to replace traditional design with innovation design and clarified the emerging role of design-driven innovation [9]. The innovative design includes four characteristics, namely green, low-carbon, networked and intelligent. The project leader of the Made in China 2025 research team pointed out that innovation design includes four characteristics: green and low carbon, networking and intelligence, openness and integration, and co-creation and sharing together. The joint project leader stated that innovation design consists of five key characteristics: arts, culture, technology, business and user-centeredness [9].

The current society's challenges is interconnected and systemic which is characterized by intractable and persistence [10]. Administration are trying to address complex policy issues through social innovation and co-creation, although it is still an emerging field of practice with various interpretations and institutional constraints [11]. Socio-economic cooperation model is considered to be the way out of the depressed economic environment. The relationship between design and local economy is mainly reflected in the following aspects: 1) The effectiveness of design on the local economy lies in the fact that it retains the ownership of local actors, stewardship of shared values, and retain the control of local finances; 2) dealing with the unsatisfied physical and social needs of the place and emphasizes the moral values of solidarity and reciprocity. Assisted by visualization techniques [12], designers think systematically and create visual prototypes [12], so as to assist social groups make achievement in complex social learning processes. Meanwhile, in order to generate sustainable actions [13] and reestablish urban relationships [14], designers continuously evaluate biological, social, and cultural diversity and promote urban regeneration [15]. Various studies explore co-creation methodologies, particularly the connection between co-creation and social innovation when experimenting with new forms of citizen participation in policy-making and public management processes.

3   Research Methodology

3.1   Ethnographic Study: NICE2035 Project-Based Community

'Design' does not have a universally agreed upon definition among design scholars and practitioners. In general, the design is characterized by being future-oriented and incorporating change as a functional pattern. Some design scholars describe 'design' as the act of improving or maintaining the relationship between people and their environment, that is, the livability of the world. Participatory observation is a critical research methodology in anthropology and sociology in which researchers actively participate in the environment under study to gain an intimate familiarity with the research object. The purpose of ethnographic research is to better understand the mechanism of design value creation in the co-creation process between designers and industry participants. The author therefore focused on a specific case – The NICE2035 project-based community – whilst combining participatory observations and semi-structured interviews. At the same time, the author observes the design practices and the scientific and cultural activities that occur around the Siping community in Shanghai that occur at the intersection area of communities and University. The author jointly participated in workshops, seminars, and workshops with the innovation and entrepreneurship actors and through structured and semi-structured interviews, documented the creation mechanism of design value.

The purpose of anthropology is to study local life and to comparatively understand culture, society, and humanity. In design research, ethnographic observation and conversation analysis help capture and record 'naturally occurring conversations and interactions'. Documentation of this process reveals how sequences of social action are accomplished, understand how design can be a useful tool [16] (Fig. 1).

Establish an Ongoing Dialogue with Stakeholders. Social innovation often uses the metaphor of "bees" and "pollen", which means "Bees" (small mobile organizations) pollinate "trees" (large, stable, entrenched organizations such as governments, large corporations, or non-governmental organizations). In the NICE2035 project community, the bee refers to bottom-up grassroots action and agents of social entrepreneurs. Trees refer to the public sector, government agencies, such as the central government in WIEE and WDCC. The paradigm of design-driven innovation refers to sub-elements of processes used to develop human interaction, social processes, product development, and practices that invent and reshape organizations and their services. University, as a potential incubator and disseminator of ideas [17], while community participation promotes the development of social learning and interpersonal relations, and the mutual benefit between them plays a powerful role in promoting social synergy. The embodiment of multi-stakeholder diversity in the NICE2035 community, as Vezzoli advocated, is a "broad social learning process" towards sustainability [17]. Social learning is the process of acquiring knowledge within a social group as well as learning from others,

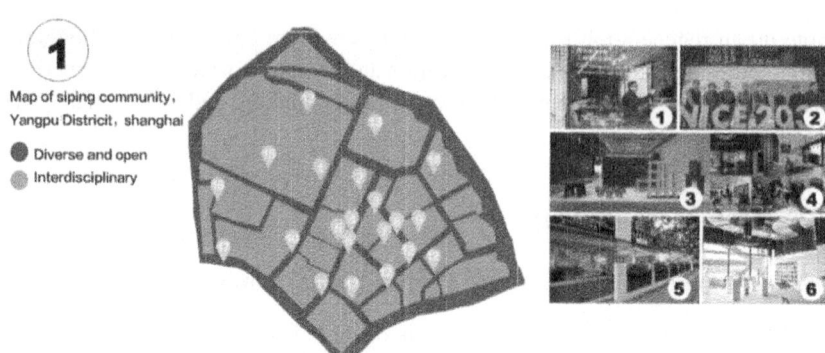

#	Projects	Space/Service	Role of DH Platform	Design Thinking
1	80 meter pocket park	Prototype lab		Sustainable behavior
2	Guidance system of Good Neighbor center			Green design
3	Skillful Auntie project			Emotionally durable design
4	Community kitchen project	Prototype lab	Endorser	
5	Coffee ground regeneration project	Artist		Ecological Design
6	Starbucks green workshop	Prototype lab		Product service system design
7	Creative citizenship project	Prototype lab	Endorser	
8	Telephone Art museum	Artist		
9	'Garage' swap parties	NICE Commune	Endorser	Cradle to Cradle Design
10	Community Garden project	Prototype lab		
11	'12 lines of poetry' floor fluorescent lighting project	Artist		Emotional design
12	Aldo Cibic Cabin project		Partner	
13	'Photosynthesis' community garden solar terms	Citizen		Sustainable behavior
14	Ren Ren market of Yangpu Binjiang		Prompter	
15	Sustainable lifestyle exhibition of Neini Department store	Citizen	Prompter	Sustainable behavior

Fig. 1. NICE2035 project-based community (Image source: Adapted by the Author)

which includes a series of knowledge exchange seminars, workshops, capacity building workshops, and discussions on community engagement. [17].

All regional design projects are shaped to the specifics of the region and its institutional setting. They are unique and have different aims and outcomes. As a co-creator and observer, the author, from the participation of daily life to the collection of second-hand data, provides an observation perspective for the transformation design in a sustainable society. The project for sustainable communities is initiated by the various prototype labs of the School of Design and innovation of Tongji University, examples include the TEL Art Gallery, the coffee grounds experiment, and the tailoring shop that conveys the design concept of regeneration, zero waste and sustainable circulation (Fig. 2).

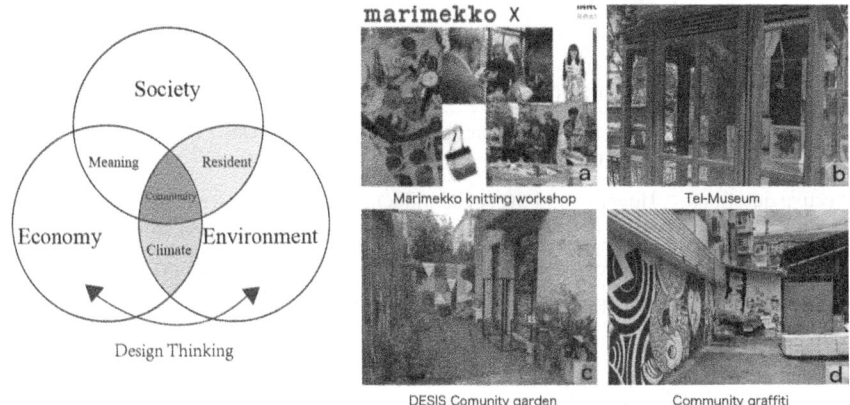

Fig. 2. NICE2035 project-based community: Interact with the community and build commons (Image source: Adapted by the Author)

3.2 Interview Guideline

The author developed an interview guide based on Pavie's responsible innovation theory (see Table 1 for main interview topics and sample questions). In the field of innovation management, Pavie proposed the concept of 'innovation-care', emphasizing how caring for the community and others are prerequisites for innovation and responsible business conduct [18]. Tronto's care ethics framework clarifies how to care for others in the innovation process and the interdependence determines the individual's access to power and resources, including social responsibility, empathy, competence, and responsiveness [19]. The method of semi-structured interview aims to identify the underlying Mechanisms that describe 'how' particular Outcomes are created by a design programme or intervention. For universities and Industry, an 'Outcome' was when the awareness of social responsibility in some way inspired by the design of intervention strategies.

Table 1. Interview Questionnaire (Table source: Drawn by the author)

Interview outline	List of Questions
Basic questions	How many years have you been in the industry?
	What specific areas of work are you engaged in? What are the specific responsibilities of your job?
	What do you think of corporate social responsibility?
	How do you understand a better society and economy?
In-depth questions	How do you think companies should enhance their ability to adapt to environmental changes? Do you think local government needs to give more support to the community?
	In order to enhance the cohesion of community enterprises, how you help promote the establishment of collaborative relationships between enterprises?
	What role do you think designers play in today's sustainable society Transformation?
Reflective questions	How to build the social influence of collaborative communities? What does community mean in corporate alliance action?
	Where does your driving force (Trigggor) come from?
	Why built a community?

3.3 Recruitment Interviews

The purpose of this study was to examine innovators' perceptions of what is and is not responsible innovation. The authors conducted an extensive online search of both for-profit and non-profit organizations to identify potential respondents. The author sent interview invitations via email and forwarded invitation emails through alumni associations, rehabilitation associations, disease book clubs, and business incubators to screen innovation partners who share a common interest in responsible innovation. Finally, the author received responses from 12 respondents. There were 8 males and 4 females, with an average age of 35.6 years. In 2021, 4 non-private industry workers agreed to be interviewed (1 male and 3 females, aged between 27 and 42 years old). In 2023, we included 2 more non-private sector workers who expressed willingness to be interviewed (2 males, aged 32 years). Four private sector workers were invited and agreed to be interviewed in 2023 and 2024 (3 men and 1 woman aged between 32 and 44 years old). In addition, the authors interviewed two local government officials to provide information that allowed us to gain insight into municipalities' perspectives on responsible innovation. Some interviews were conducted in person, however some, due to COVID-19 restrictions, were conducted online. Each interview took approximately one hour and was audio-recorded and transcribed. Participants provided written consent prior to interviews.

Interviewee come from diverse backgrounds: senior government executives, innovative researchers, civil servants, and grassroots entrepreneurs. The civil service employees were middle level management who were involved in the planning and strategy development of various agencies. Innovation researchers and CBO civil servants are active members, advocating for their causes at the local and national levels. 4 people work in the partner private sector, 2 people work in university laboratories or medical research centers, 3 people work in government departments (of which 2 people are in provincial offices and 1 person is in national level offices), 3 people are civil servants working in CBO Community Organization. The table below contains statistical details such as gender, age, current position. In addition, the authors also asked whether there are other factors unrelated to the project, such as previous work experience, that affect their understanding of responsible innovation (Table 2).

Table 2. Demographic details of the 12 Interviewees (Table source: Drawn by the author)

Interviewee	Sex	Age	Current position	Previous work experience
01	Male	47	Provincial Office Staff	National government organization
02	Male	32	NGO/Civil service	National government organization
03	Female	27	CBO/Community-based organizations	Private company
04	Female	27	Research/Consulting center(RCC)	National government organization
05	Female	42	Provincial Office Staff	National government organization, Municipal organization
06	Male	41	National government Office staff	Engineering Company
07	Male	32	Research/Consulting center(RCC)	National government organization
08	Male	37	Private Enterprise	Engineering Company
09	Male	32	Civil service	National government organization
10	Female	44	Private Enterprise	National government organization
11	Male	35	Private Enterprise	Engineering Company
12	Male	32	Private Enterprise	Private Enterprise

3.4 Analyzing Procedure

For the collected data, we employed thematic analysis [20] where all data collected were involved in a process of identifying themes throughout coding, categorizing and concepting towards aggregated themes. Different techniques were undertaken at each stage of the inquiry to establish credibility [20]. The analysis proceeded in three steps:

Step 1: First order categories was accomplished by re-listening to all recordings, reading ethnographic notes, and writing summaries of interview excerpts. During the first-level coding process, both interviewees reviewed their interviews and the first-order codes were discussed with both participants in the form of an initial member check. Transcripts were initially coded using NVivo 12 software, using the coding software to regroup notes in iterations and broader patterns to emerge through cycle coding;

Step 2: Second order concepts and the emerging themes were put through peer-debriefing, where an informed, but not directly involved peer, provided honest feedback on the lines of enquiry to maintain objectivity [21].

Step 3: The higher-level themes (aggregate Themes) were then put through 'formal checking'. The researchers organized a session to present preliminary interpretations of the study. Attendees were asked to provide feedback, and reflect on their own experiences to strengthen and advance the research.

In conducting an ethnographic study of data, The three-step analysis process helps summarize "key features of large body of data" [20], rather than focusing on a smaller number of interviewees in great detail. The researchers aimed to demonstrate patterns in the data and identify alignments in respondents' descriptions of their work practices. The comments did not challenge the findings, but rather the audience saw their working methods reflected in the findings (Table 3).

Table 3. Summary of coding process (Table source: Drawn by the author)

First order Categories	Second order Concepts	Aggregate Themes
Open innovation process…	Inclusive society	Design Harvest Global Innovation and entrepreneurship Platform
Creativity space… Public cultural resources…	Creative space	
Repair culture…	local administrative leadership	
Citizen empowerment…	Civic Infrastructure	
Citizenship education…		
Public image and added value of cooperation…		
Appreciative inquiry…	Public health	Artistic participation
Incentive mechanism	Resilience city	
Cross-department and cross-industry innovation collaboration… Cultural corridor…	Horizontal collective intelligence	

(*continued*)

Table 3. (*continued*)

First order Categories	Second order Concepts	Aggregate Themes
Create opportunities for knowledge exchange…	Emerging design culture	
Integrate capital…		
Transformation of science and industry…	Mixed benefit structure	Cultivating care economy
Scalability Expand insurance coverage	Technical experts	
Diversified financial support…	For-profit and non-profit Network	
Bottom-up legal, policy and communication systems…	Neighborhood economy	
Cultivating new partnerships… Revitalize local communities…	Regional Cooperative Alliance	

4 Case Study: Ethnographic Observation of the NICE2035 Design-Driven Innovation Ecosystem

4.1 Looking at the Future from History

When considering the history of a region, the temporal perspective of regional design can range from decades to centuries and centuries. Decades as a time dimension for thinking from a future perspective. This long-term future perspective can zoom in from the future to current month, or the current year, making current or future year reasoning tangible. The Sustainable Lifestyle Prototype becomes a city's way of exploring and experimenting with uncertainty, creates a space for discussion and reflection between all those involved in the experience, allowing them to speak freely about their aspirations and challenges, social vision, and many other issues of everyday life.

NICE2035 refers to the co-creation process of creating a better life for 2035. NICE means Neighborhood, Innovation, Creativity, and Entrepreneurship. It means the three innovative communities of innovation, entrepreneurship, and creation for 2035. The author uses the time node of project establishment as the main basis and simply divides it into four stages:

The First Stage: Early Creative Spaces and Civic Infrastructure

Since 2007, Design Harvest Innovation and Entrepreneurship Platform proposed an 'acupuncture' design strategy, through a series of small, interrelated design intervention projects, activated the exchange and interaction of urban and rural resources (talent, capital, knowledge, services) and stimulated rural potential and promote systemic change. Since then, the basic strategic framework founded by Design Harvest Platform has been derived a series of sub-projects, such as Open Your Space 72 Pilot in Siping (2015), Future Living Prototype blocks (2018), NICE communes and Future need laboratory (2018), WDCC Shanghai Design City (2020). These interconnected experimental pilots evolved into community networks, driven by numerous participants, ultimately formed a project cluster effect.

Design Harvest 2007, as a hub node composed of numerous prototype projects, is not only a platform for innovation and entrepreneurship, but also a collaborative design innovation network. For example, neighborhood gardens, vertical farming, micro experimental farms, and a series of educational and cultural spaces for composting, heating, rainwater collection, solar power generation, aquaponics, and experimental equipment for phytoremediation. These green lifestyles experiments managed by local residents, with regular serving as public facilities to accommodate collective action. The project is a successful example of citizen ecology, visualizing how Green Square residents connect to and shape the urban environment of shanghai. Creative spaces become strongholds for communities, fostering community cohesion and increasing civic engagement. Design knowledge used by designers and non-designers (individuals, communities, institutions, companies) in co-design processes [22], while creating high-quality job opportunities of economy. For example, design researchers and community residents jointly organize weaving workshops and create community gardens. Community residents voluntarily organize daily maintenance of the community garden, visits, receptions and exchanges and other daily affairs (Fig. 3).

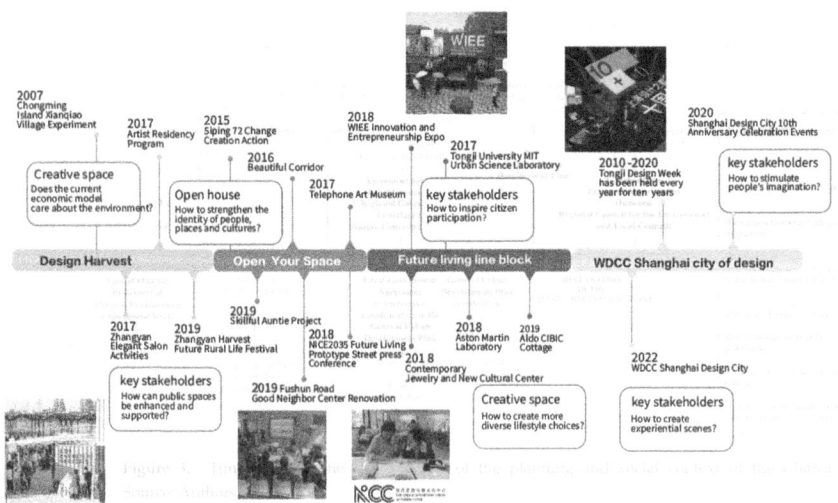

Fig. 3. The Time line of the NICE2035 project-based community (Picture source: Author drawing)

The Second Stage: Open Innovation Process

Started in 2015, Open Your Space (OYS) is a community service project that jointly organized by Siping Office of Yangpu District and Tongji University School of Design and Innovation. The open innovation process integrates the economy, environment and science through collaborative design to achieve the transformation of scientific research into daily applications. For example, the OYS design team invited OOP Street Culture and Creative Studio to paint graffiti on the wall of Siping Road Subway Exit 2. Various themes, colors, and patterns are blended together to bring fresh sensory stimulation to the community. Design serves the community, invited residents, businesses, and schools to participate in community creation, created a university city and a city university. The civic infrastructure that brings together the increasingly diverse society, heal old wounds and build a culture of repair. Creative spaces such as cultural corridors, artists, affordable housing as well as shared studios and workspaces and creative enterprises are scattered throughout the corners of Siping neighborhoods, especially backward and barren blocks. Creative Spaces can become a stronghold for communities, promoting community cohesion and participation, and creating employment (creative economy). From the stage of mass entrepreneurship 1.0 to 2.0, with the participation of mature entrepreneurial teams, the initial financial burden has been shifted from local governments to a basic framework sponsored by folk culture and art funds and corporate sponsorship. At the same time, the curatorial team of university teachers transformed some redundant spaces that had been abandoned for many years into exhibition spaces and artist work camps, or hotels and restaurants. These restored spaces have become a stop for artists and visitors, created economic value which has largely alleviated the financial expenditures on local government.

The Third Stage: Specialized Development and Strategic Resource Accumulation
In 2017, Future Living Prototyping Street has built 20 Prototype labs and introduced mature entrepreneurs join in and create Future Living demonstration site. In August 2017, witnessed by the president of Tongji University, Tongji University college of Design and Innovation and the MIT Media Laboratory formally signed a cooperation agreement, and join hand build the City Science Lab &Shanghai City Science Laboratory. The laboratory is dedicated to conducting the innovation and transformation of research policy based on the specific needs of Shanghai. In November 2018, The NEEDS Lab organized a design thinking exhibition at Gaobei 16, Shenzhen. Through academic lectures, exhibitions, workshop, visits, The NEEDS Lab injected the Tongji Spirit into the Shenzhen urban prosperity. Design-driven Industry innovation is promoted by three key events, the 10th anniversary of Shanghai Design City, WIEE innovation and Entrepreneurship Expo, and WDCC World Design Capital. In particular, the Shanghai Design Capital Conference serves as a mechanism for coordinating multi-party collaborations, paving the way for possible collaborations, and building highly responsive social networks.

The Fourth Stage: Expanding the Innovation Network
As the organization's reputation has grown, it attracted more donors, members, and even job seekers, so has the added value of the partnership. Strategic investments not only gain access to the human resources of more people, it also had a greater impact. For example, The increase number of membership of NICE Commune was due to the hiring of a member expert consultant (NICE Commune President— Lu zhou zhou), and increased staff responsible for law, policy and communications, specifically focused on improving the efficiency and public image of the organization. As a result, NICE Commune is no

longer dependent on subsidies from public funding schemes, has a spontaneous business model, and generates considerable benefits in terms of membership and funding (as well as reflected in the project's experts in quality, averageness and effectiveness).The various strategic divisions are working together on litigation communications and policy advocacy to bring more attention to the work of the alliance, and each of these divisions has formed a strong development and management team to ensure the sustainability and effectiveness of the project.

4.2   Characteristics of Nearby Institutions: Openness and Specificity

Mainstream economics views humans as isolated, selfish rational beings. However, orthodox economists prefer to regard people as social beings, who will show the characteristics of altruistic behavior and be more willing to assume corresponding social responsibilities. The social Innovation network formed by the 'social people' provides a favorable medium for the a new/future credit relationship in which collaboration-network replace hierarchical structures. However, there is little reflection on this 'unstructuredness', and found in other studies as well, is that in these hypothetical descriptions of use, the designer talk with very little definition about future users – e.g., they remain genderless, ageless, bodiless, etcetera.

As the survey suggested, the Siping community' economic situation is very pessimistic. Many commercial storefronts sit empty, housed are abandoned, and poor community conditions exacerbate health disparities. The Alliance for Community Health Equity and Development recognizes that real improvement in healthy environments cannot be achieved through the traditional national health system and that community well-being must rely on upstream interventions, bringing together diverse investment streams to advance community health.

Specificity. As regional design projects are shaped to the specifics of the region and its institutional setting, as was emphasized in the interviews. They are unique and have different aims and outcomes. Regional designing was for example said to be used to develop policy guidelines, to open up new regional vistas, to influence the political agenda, to coordinate developments of various stakeholders, to improve and develop relationships, and to design and structure the forthcoming stages of a spatial. Specificity relates to how the 'affordance' building-in-design facilitates particular uses [23]. 'Specificity' refers to that it can be used comfortably only for specific functions in a specific way by a limited group of people. By detailing the design for use, designers inevitably but also possibly deliberately afford or constrain certain social outcomes. The findings show that the designers are concerned with specificity at different levels – meaning imagining the role of their designs in people's behavior, social roles, and cultural meaning. Scenario-thinking is important in developing specificity. For example, Medical emergency aircraft of Chinese aviation system, as one of the derivatives of AIG21 (Business aircraft, official aircraft, helitanker), Whose usage scenarios include aviation medical emergency, aviation emergency transportation, medical assistance, emergency rescue. The special medical aircraft Medical emergency aircraft meet the needs of commercial flights along the Belt and Road Initiative surrounding China, and integrating more detailed rescue intensive care system, improve the domestic aviation medical rescue network (Patient monitoring experiment, portable diagnosis table, etc.) promoted rapid change of COMAC.

> *'The ECHO Project (Community Healthcare Extension) is a remote innovation mentoring program that brings together healthcare providers and domain experts to create virtual communities of learners through the use of video conferencing technology, short lecture presentations, and case-based or context-based learning' (07-RCC), 'Standard mechanisms for public services, such as regulations governing fund allocation and government contracts are not conducive to effective collaboration...these mechanisms hinder the efforts of synergy across organization and sectors...managers who deliver public services are more accustomed to working in specific environment with clear boundaries than work in new and challenging way with people come from different environment.' (09 – Civil service), 'Integrate capital implement a non-extractive investment method, the investor of the integrated capital think about if I don't support, what kind of risk will the community face...help those who are not belong to mainstream banks' (10-Private Enterprise) 'potentially therapeutic gardens are under lock and key and the windows can hardly be opened' (03—CBO), 'Signs reinforced accepted norms that the hospital, the patient's position in clinic load, made patients feel confused, processed and stressed...' (04-RCC)*

Openness. Create conditions for change, such as trusted spaces, relationships, local administrative leadership, and political environment in which change can be made. Whether top-down or bottom-up, the process of building environment for change must be ongoing. First, most industry conferences are problem-driven, the knowledge exchange conference provides capacity building, technical assistance, consulting, and industry seminars to create learning opportunities for investors. Training sessions ensure broad participation from industry representatives by expanding discussion topics: Second, organizations across sectors and industries come together, whether to adapt existing technologies to new products, or facilitate cross-sector investments in portfolios, drive collaboration through co-sponsored events, grants or investments, and provide inspiration for how different teams solve similar challenges. Finally, there are important relationships and interactions between behavioral social context and structural factors that need to be considered before developing sound solutions. Cooperation among participants promotes horizontal collective intelligence, in which everyone is considered for their true value. This spirit of cooperation encourages true equality between peoples and allows for better dissemination of information. Horizontal collective intelligence better adapted to complex and unstable environments. In contrast, pyramidal collective intelligence come from agricultural and patriarchal societies can only works in stable environments and has no adaptability.

4.3   Toward Sector-Level Change

In the context of university/industry interdependence, a consensus on adaptability has led to a shift in university and industry relations towards collaboration, while the anchoring approach relies on social mission of institution. Since Shanghai joined the United Nations

Creative Cities Network in 2010, the creative and design industries have flourished. In the new development stage, the design creative industry acts as a global innovation link, strengthening international cooperation and exchange in the city network, and promoting the transformation of potential innovation achievements into regional economic benefits (Fig. 4).

Fig. 4. International Industry-Academia-Research Cooperation Conference (Image Source: https://mp.weixin.qq.com/)

At the 2022 International Industry-University-Research Cooperation Conference, experts participating in the forum said that in the era of digital economy, better innovative cooperation models between universities and industries can effectively promote the high-quality development of education and the innovative transformation of enterprises. In the areas of research, education, welfare and urban development, It is a jointly entanglement process with various institutions such as municipalities (either as host or recipient), universities (involving researchers), research councils and private companies (providing funding and setting policy).

> *'Interdependence is a widespread motivating factor for cooperation. But for all stakeholders, working together to address the impacts of climate change requires a comprehensive and consistent analysis.' (Previous director of The Shang Hai Foundation's Environment Program). Qin Changwei, Secretary-General of the Chinese National Commission for UNESCO, delivered a speech'(...)Whether these clusters are related to processes, products or Service-related, both create potential new opportunities for competitive advantage, entrepreneurship helps transform potential innovation momentum into regional economic gains, When this activity gains momentum, diverse but specialized industrial clusters form. (Qin Changwei, Designer and technologist, 2022).The Mayor of Yangpu district Shanghai stressed that 'the city's resilient planning requires efficient coordination*

with universities as they are the most resourceful think tank of regional economic development. '(Xue Kan, Mayor of Yangpu District, 2022)

The Vision Report in which the symbolic resources, such copyright symbols, government logos and other visual assets were invented to support the establishment of a shared vision. Design tools play an important role in reinforcing official narratives and the positive impact of local government through rhetorical and visual techniques, and influencing public perceptions of the process. For example, the IEID (International forum on innovation and Emerging Industries Development (see Fig. 5 held in Shanghai in September 2020 was co-sponsored by the Chinese Academy of Engineering, the Shanghai Municipal People's Government, the Shanghai Ministry of Industry and Information Technology, and the Tongji University served as the organizer. Scholars, innovative entrepreneurs, government innovation management officials and other insightful people conducted open exchanges on disruptive innovation and the development of emerging industries, and provided innovative services such as achievement display and project docking. The conference size was about 1,800 people. The official website is: http:// ieid.cn. The resourcefulness positions resilience in a more positive way and links it to community empowerment and community governance.

Fig. 5. IEID International Conference on Emerging Industries (Image Source: https://mp.weixin. qq.com/s/axSDgkB43K9goS-PT-2wcg)

4.4 New Patient-Centered Design

Lab curation, as a generative process of emerging knowledge, highlights aspects of organization change, which relying on multiple dialogues to foster trusting and open relationships that bring different knowledge-making practices together. At the 2023 WDCC World Design Capital Expo, Emerging Industry pavilion was composed of fashion Hall, design achievements Hall, urban exhibition area and design carnival, where exhibitors from all over the world to show the design achievements and explore infinite possibilities of design. Interdisciplinary curatorial activity, leaving the comfort zone of 'everyday' control and confront the unknown of 'the unknown' by connecting a wide diversity of skills, cultures and perspectives (architects, designers, artists, playwrights and musicians). The Lab curation break down established notions at the level of methodological, interpretive and representative curatorial inquiry through the analysis of intercultural action, transport and appropriation. For example, the Design Capital Industry Pavilion at WDCC 2023, Showcasing the entrepreneurial partners of the health care alliance, bringing together civic leaders, health care providers and community sector executive leaders, to developed a joint investment strategy with the unified goal of maximizing the knowledge resources and actions of each organizations to improve the health of community residents. Rethinking Health is a computer modeling tool (Figure a) loaded with large amounts of data about residents' health, enabling communities to come up with innovative ideas for redesigning health care systems and providing a basis for evaluating investment decisions; CHEER lab is a R&D center for child-friendly medical experience composed of designers, engineers, artists, educators, administrators and researchers which is also an interdisciplinary joint research laboratory that focuses on improving medical experience, alleviating children's fear of medical treatment, soothing pain, and enhancing understanding (Figure b); SURGICAL AR Single-orifice endoscopic surgical robot, the hook section of the serpentine surgical arm is more flexible and can reach complex areas to achieve bends in any direction. The endoscopic robot operated by both arms can minimize the invasive damage caused by surgery, thus play a certain role in protecting the surrounding tissue of the patient's operative area (Figure c); MAD GPT Pfizer Medical Innovation center (Oncology center and patient lab) is combination of traditional non-profit and for-profit platforms which is a peer-to-peer element production network consisted of console, network Center and radiation Clinic, each interface is part symbiotic system of the platform (Figure d); MINDREY Air rescue has a complete life support system, which can complete the medical transfer of critically injured patients in the shortest possible time. Medical rescue aircraft is extremely important in the race against time rescue process, provides more efficient rescue measures for patients in cardiac arrest and gives them the best chance of survival (Figure e) (Fig. 6);

'Mainstream healthcare companies are not optimistic about telemedicine and are reluctant to provide medical resources to people in marginal areas, because such medical services or physician training are not profitable (10-Private Enterprise)'. 'ECHO telemedicine model provides professional care for patients who lack medical resources, and the patients trust local clinicians to provide culturally appropriate care in their native language...' (04-RCC). 'Three different organizational elements are integrated into ECHO's institutional design, and we call this new model a for-profit and non-profit peer-to-peer element production network. ECHO-clinics are often symbiotic with universities, medical centers, or other large organizations, where Mission control center, network hubs and spoke clinics together form the platform.' (04-RCC)

The steering committee of the Community Health Improvement Partnership is composed of 15 core members from medical hospitals, insurance companies, local public health agencies, Shanghai Centers for Disease Control and Prevention, and community health centers and health behavior providers. 'Job creation program had attracted large

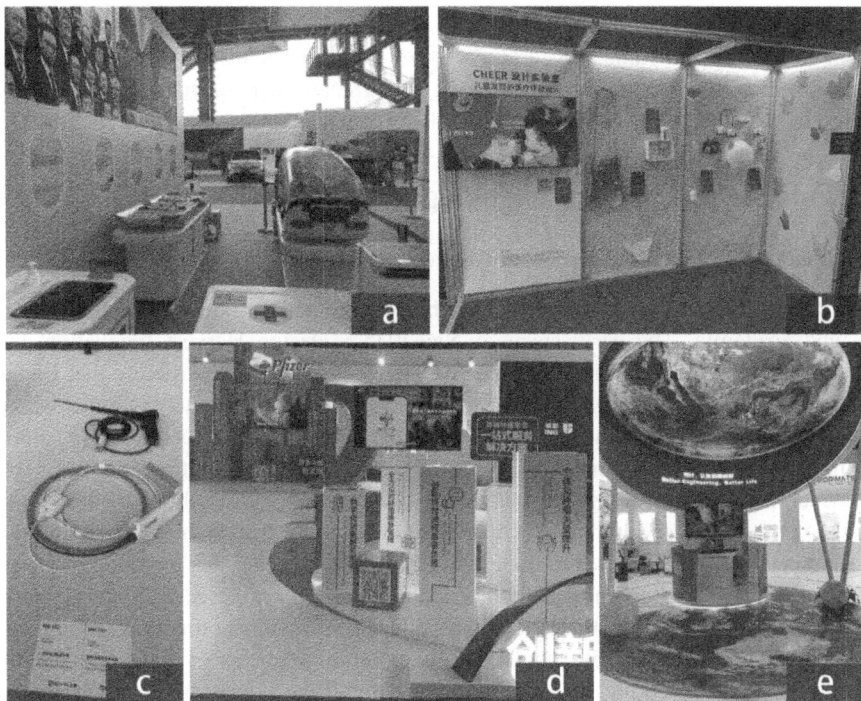

Fig. 6. AI+ Drug development: Medical robots as a digital solution (Picture source: taken by the author)

amounts of private capital' (03-CBO); 'The NHS involves clarifying the value of a variety of alternatives, from routine checkups, surgery, to community interventions, trying to capture the value that individuals derive from their health instead of getting sick… it is a framework for thinking about 'value':1) Strategic agenda for cooperation; 2) Potential health outcomes' (06-National government Office staff). 'A welfare corporation is an innovative form of organization, integrating broader objectives into its organizational governance purposes and legal statements… It also reflects the relationship between government, private capital, community and philanthropy' (01-Provincial Office Staff). At last, the author believe that the challenges facing the innovation projects and programs are to address structural problems in the economy, knowledge production and political power which are largely beyond the reach of researchers, without strategies to address structural change, these innovations will stagnant forever.

The authors argue that health has been recast as a permanent state of insecurity that relies on constant vigilance, assessment, and intervention. Further analysis of the health equity literature reaffirms how this metaphor has been explicitly used to redefine inequalities in health resources and to make recommendations working on underlying social and structural causes of policies making. Disease prevention means mobilizing skills, practices, and materials so that public health, clinical care, and water and sanitation systems can work together effectively. The partners in the collaborative network come from different sectors (direct and indirect participants) and act as facilitators, mentors to support health service. In this process, responsibilities are shared and a consensus is reached on the shared value of a certain region—Emerging industry of shanghai. All in all, adapting to changing needs of the times means greater interdependence and ensuring vulnerable citizens have access to appropriate, effective health care.

5 Understanding Design Thinking as a Change Strategy

5.1 Design Harvest Platform as an Anchor Institution for Cooperation

NICE2035 project-based community had direct influence on both professional practice and academia. The early stage of Nice2035 - Design Harvest Innovation and Entrepreneurship Platform, an early creative space and civic infrastructure that brings together the country's increasingly diverse society and advances a culture of repair which provided rich resources for the organizational ecosystem. Tongji universities have helped to build collective capacity in partnership with surrounding communities since the 2016. Advocates have proposed a transformative role of design through a culture of community engagement. A shared value model could engender a more sustainable, long-term relationship between design and community. Scholars and advocates have used the concept of "anchor institution" to capture the notion that large, place-based institutions could make a positive contribution to the health, wealth and well-being of their local communities. While universities have received the most attention as anchors, patient care facility have also been analyzed for their anchor role. Hospitals have increasingly committed to addressing social determinants of health rather than a simple medical model of disease. Hospitals can play a proactive role in improving health equity by measuring progress against community benefits indicators that span economic development, community building, education, and a healthy environment. University and industry anchors have the potential for an elevated collective impact through partnerships in which education, healthcare, faith-based institutions and even some corporations play complementary roles within an "anchor collaborative" (Fig. 7).

When designing at the infrastructure level, designers offer their expertise as a service to support community interaction. Designers not only provide coordination for the co-creation process, but also provide a multi-level structure for social action and public participation. In particular, new technologies have become a peer-to-peer social structure when coordinating collaboration, which means that the process of value creation is changing. Social capital is mainly reflected in the identity of designers as cultural operators. Designers, by designing products, communication, interaction, services, and spaces [25], create collaborative environments, such as multidisciplinary collaboration [26], cultivate entrepreneurs as cultural operators [27], and design social and cultural transformation framework [28]. Innovation means that social capital develops on a regional scale. Social entrepreneurship involves, on the one hand, collaboration with a wide variety of different groups of people and organizations; on the other hand, it involves the promotion and development of new networks of such diverse interests in pursuit of specific social goals. In the NICE2035 project community, the infrastructure building process includes project-based learning [29], distributed studio network [30], localizing, networking and distributing [31] configuration of social relations [32], knowledge transfer [33], and ultimately, the expansion of the innovation network [34]. Co-design as a solution to complex

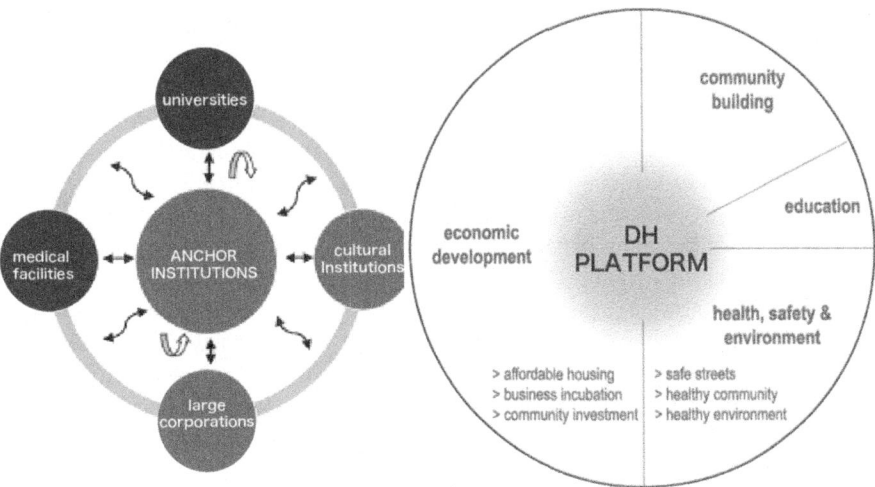

Fig. 7. Anchor institution for Collaboration (Image source: Adapted from Hannah M. Teicher [24])

social problems introduces users (in the case of NICE2035's project community residents) as experiential experts and as part of the design process. **Grassroots culture** is a resilient culture that is the opposite of authoritarian/authoritarian culture. Grassroots culture does not deliberately emphasize the superiority of professional designers, nor does it ignore the creative problem-solving abilities of ordinary people, lying on the boundary between professionals and non-professionals. The broad vision of grassroots communities is mainly reflected in the organic combination of cultural inheritance, cultural innovation and cultural tolerance, and gaining endogenous power from cultural roots. The neighborhood lanes of NICE2035 use immersive cultural and artistic methods, such as art installations and art exhibitions, to enhance the humanistic atmosphere of the community and provide public services.

5.2 Cultivating Regional and Solidarity Economy

Michael Porter's cluster theory research shows that it will take 10 years for a cluster to establish and develop in depth on a regional scale [35]. Cultivating production factors for innovation and entrepreneurship is a key factor in becoming a regional economy. Regional innovation does not necessarily occur within university or government laboratories influenced by regional economic dynamics. Increasingly, regional leaders are trying to connect the dots so that regional industries can take advantage of these new potential commercialization ideas [36]. At the 10th anniversary celebration of Shanghai Design City in 2020, Chen Mingbo, Shanghai Municipal Secretary-General delivered a speech affirming that design is the engine that drives innovation and empowers urban development. Creative design industry serves as an important node linking the global design innovation network. Industrial cluster network is a governance process involving multiple actors, including various enterprises, local governments, industry associations, universities and scientific research institutions, financial institutions and intermediaries.

National regulatory agencies and local financial services jointly promote regional socio-economic development. For example, the Shanghai Municipal Commission of Economy and Information Technology commissioned an alliance of 20 universities to jointly lead the construction of new think tanks, demonstrating new organizational forms through cooperative governance forms where investors and credit recipients share ownership, identify new ways of knowing, including knowledge of regulation, economics, governance, and local networks and resources. University-industry cooperation introduces the public sector as intervening departments (Shanghai Economic and Information Commission, Shanghai Municipal People's Government, Siping Community Service Department), and multi-knowledge institutions as cultural intermediaries whose work involves consecration and the transfer of symbolic capital and Establish new relationships with scientific knowledge through the activities of knowledge brokers. Cultural intermediaries serve as professional groups, promote intangible assets such as honor, prestige and reputation owned by subjects and explain the interactive forms of industrial innovation activities (Fig. 8).

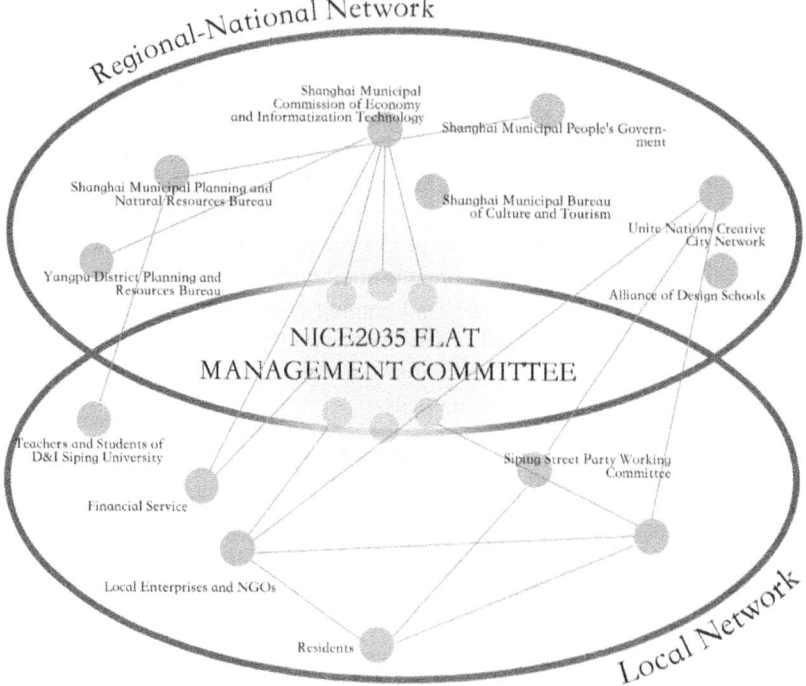

Fig. 8. Bottom-up local network and top-down regional-National Network (Image source: Adapted by the author)

6 Concluding and Remarks

The study into the principles of regional economy designing illustrates the involvement of design professionals and position of designers in vision development and strategy making. The author expect that this strategic kind of designing is here to stay and will grow in importance as one of the domains that design professionals engage with, and it adds new dimensions to the 'art' and culture of designing.

Public Fiduciary duty of Designers. Do designers often ignore voices that are misunderstood or deemed untrustworthy? Structural racism in healthcare refers to the totality of ways that social structures produce inequities in access to effective care, with financial (财政/金融), geographic, social, and political factors contributing [37]. The economic development of marginalized communities faces many challenges, and vulnerable citizens have inherent disadvantages in infrastructure such as bridges, roads, and emergency rescue system. The designer's new role is that of a facilitator supporting cohesive and professional teams, opening public information office to help connect scientific researchers and the public,thus break the stagnation situation of local economy. The NICE2035's public health care system creates new pathways for underserved patients to specialist care which increase the inclusion of vulnerable groups in the development of public sector services. Patients trust local clinicians who provided culturally appropriate care in their native language, alleviated the financial and psychological stress on patients. At last, it is important to note that although philanthropy plays an important role in public financing, philanthropy cannot replace public responsibility. As we all know, Philanthropy is often small and decentralized. Its advantages are independence and experimentation, but it cannot be regarded as a substitute for public funds.

Return to Human-Center and Interconnected Urban Life. The fact that society is isolated and separated from each other makes us realize that the socio-economic and cultural connections of urban residents are very weak. The author explored people's feelings of otherness and distant and disinterested, as well as their sense of safety and seclusion. A new generation of urban recycling infrastructure offers a more compelling vision, from economic equity to environmental health, that considers reconnecting isolated people and building stronger socioeconomic and cultural relationships. Design Harvest is the global alliance for health equity and community wealth building partnership led by the Institute of Public Health and the Reinvestment Fund, which recognizes that the real health improvements cannot rely on the traditional national health care systems, but must proactively involve socioeconomic and community-based upstream interventions. The Partnership alliance brings together community members with different professional backgrounds to provide technical assistance and pool sources of investment to promote community health and well-being.

References

1. Loorbach, D.: Transition management for sustainable development: a prescriptive, complexity-based governance framework. Governance **23**, 161–183 (2009)
2. Geels, F.: Co-evolution of technology and society: the transition in water supply and personal hygiene in the Netherlands (1850–1930)—a case study in multi-level perspective. Technol. Soc. **27**(3), 363–397 (2005)
3. van de Kerkhof, M., Wieczorek, A.: Learning and stakeholder participation in transition processes towards sustainability: Methodological considerations. Technol. Forecast. Soc. Change **72**(6), 733–747 (2005)
4. Planning, S.U.: Land Resource Administration Bureau (2018) Shanghai Master Plan (2017–2035) (2018)
5. Lou, Y.: NICE 2035: A Design-driven, community-supported Social Innovation Experiment (2018)
6. Huybrechts, L., Benesch, H., Geib, J.: Institutioning: participatory design, co-design and the public realm. CoDesign **13**(3), 148–159 (2017)
7. Enrico, B.: Profilo di Aristotele. Edizioni Studium Srl (2018)
8. Compagnucci, L., Spigarelli, F.: The third mission of the university: a systematic literature review on potentials and constraints. Technol. Forecast. Soc. Chang. **161**, 120284 (2020)
9. Liu, S.X., Liu, H., Zhang, Y.: The new role of design in innovation: a policy perspective from China. Des. J. **21**(1), 37–58 (2018)
10. Rittel, H.W.J., Webber, M.M.: Dilemmas in a general theory of planning. Policy. Sci. **4**(2), 155–169 (1973)
11. Hansson, K., Forlano, L., Choi, J.H等.: Provocation, conflict, and appropriation: the role of the designer in making publics. Des. Issues **34**(4), 3–7 (2018)
12. Hillgren, P.-A., Seravalli, A., Emilson, A.: Prototyping and infrastructuring in design for social innovation. CoDesign **7**, 169–183 (2011)
13. Sarmento, F., Moura, M.: Material Resignification in the Amazon. A way to construct sustainability scenarios. Des. J. **20**(sup1), S1852–S1868 (2017)
14. Di Prete, B., Mazzarello, M.: Towards a new "urban sensitivity". The role of design as support to social innovation. Des. J. **20**(sup1), S3589–S3600 (2017)
15. Bagaini, A., Balmas, Z., Koryakina, A等.: Multidisciplinary approach for a new vision of urban requalification. Multi-scale strategies of social innovation, economic improvement and environmental sustainability practices. Des. J. **20**(sup1), S4778–S4780 (2017)
16. Luck, R.: 'Doing designing': on the practical analysis of design in practice. Des. Stud. **33**(6), 521–529 (2012)
17. Manzini, E., Vezzoli, C.: A strategic design approach to develop sustainable product service systems: examples taken from the 'environmentally friendly innovation' Italian prize. J. Cleaner Prod. **11**(8), 851–857 (2003)
18. Pavie, X.: The importance of responsible innovation and the necessity of 'innovation-care.' Philos. Manag. **13**, 21–42 (2014)
19. Tronto, J.C.: Moral boundaries: A political argument for an ethic of care. Psychology Press (1993)
20. Braun, V., Clarke, V.: Using thematic analysis in psychology. Qual. Res. Psychol. **3**(2), 77–101 (2006)
21. Lincoln, Y.S., Guba, E.G.: Naturalistic inquiry. Sage (1985)
22. Manzini, E.: New design knowledge. Des. Stud. **30**(1), 4–12 (2009)
23. Stam, L., Verbeek, P.-P., Heylighen, A.: Between specificity and openness: how architects deal with design-use complexities. Des. Stud. **66**, 54–81 (2020)

24. Teicher, H.M.: Anchor institutions as adaptation allies: promises and pitfalls of joint urban/military adaptation planning in U.S. cities. Geoforum **142**, 103754 (2023)
25. Marcel de Arruda Torresa, P.: Design for socio-technical innovation: a proposed model to design the change. Des. J. **20**(sup1), S3035–S3046 (2017)
26. Bayrak, A.T.: Jamming as a design approach. Power of jamming for creative iteration. Des. J. **20**(sup1), S3945–S3953 (2017)
27. Pérez, D., Hands, D., McKeever, E.: Design for society: analysis of the adoption of design practices by early-stage social entrepreneurs. Des. J. **20**(sup1), S3020–S3034 (2017)
28. Kimbell, L.: Rethinking design thinking: Part I. Des. Cult. **3**(3), 285–306 (2011)
29. Easterday, M., Gerber, E., Rees Lewis, D.: Social innovation networks: a new approach to social design education and impact. Des. Issues **34**, 64–76 (2018)
30. Smirnov, N., Easterday, M., Gerber, E.: Infrastructuring distributed studio networks: a case study and design principles. J. Learn. Sci. **27**(4), 580–631 (2017)
31. Morelli, N.: Active, local, connected: strategic and methodological insights in three cases. Des. Issues **27**(2), 90–110 (2011)
32. Carvalho, L., Goodyear, P.: The architecture of productive learning networks. Routledge (2014)
33. Nimkulrat, N., Groth, C., Tomico, O等.: Knowing together – experiential knowledge and collaboration. CoDesign **16**(4), 267–273 (2020)
34. Nunes, V.G.A.: Designing more responsible behaviours through design education: reflections on a Brazilian pilot experience in social innovation for sustainability. Des. J. **20**(sup1), S1014–S1025 (2017)
35. Porter, M.E.: Clusters and the new economics of competition. Harvard Bus. Rev. **76**(6), 77–90 (1998)
36. Henton, D., Melville, J., Walesh, K.: The rise of the new civic revolutionaries: answering the call to stewardship in our times. Nat. Civ. Rev. **93**(1), 43–50 (2004)
37. Hailu, E.M., Maddali, S.R., Snowden, J.M等.: Structural racism and adverse maternal health outcomes: a systematic review. Health Place **78**, 102923 (2022)

Design Support Tool Based on the Analysis of Differences Between Japanese and Chinese E-commerce Sites

Xiaojiao Zou and Tomonari Kamba(✉)

Information Networking for Innovation and Design, Toyo University, 1-7-11 Akabanedai, Kita-ku, Tokyo 115-8650, Japan
kamba@iniad.org

Abstract. We quantitatively investigate and compare the design characteristics of Japanese and Chinese e-commerce (EC) sites and develop a design tool that reflects these characteristics for cross-border EC sites. When Japanese and Chinese EC companies build websites targeting users in their respective countries, matching the design to the customs and preferences of the other country may lead to the natural acceptance of the site and facilitate business expansion. The effectiveness of the tool was confirmed by evaluating its usability and the acceptability of the site design by users in the other country, with five people from each country creating the site and 11 people from each country evaluating it. In addition, we attempt to automatically interconvert product images by considering the characteristics of each country using CycleGAN, a type of generative AI. Cross-border EC is expected to expand further, and tools such as those described in this study have the potential to contribute to its development.

Keywords: Web design · Cultural difference · electronic commerce

1 Introduction

With the rapid growth of e-commerce (EC), cross-border sales across countries have become important for companies. Therefore, it is imperative for companies to not only translate their websites linguistically but also design websites that match the culture and tastes of each country or region so that they can be accepted by consumers in each country or region.

This study aims to develop a development support tool that is effective for companies in one country to provide EC sites to users in other countries, particularly for transactions between Japan and China. The scale of cross-border EC between Japan and China continues to grow rapidly, with Japan to China transactions accounting for 2,138.2 billion yen (9.7% growth) and China to Japan transactions for 36.5 billion yen (7.6% growth) in FY2021 [1]. In the following section, we describe the results of a quantitative analysis of Japanese and Chinese EC site designs, followed by a description of the design support tool created to reflect these results and the basic evaluation results.

M. Kurosu et al. (Eds.): HCII 2024, LNCS 15374, pp. 274–285, 2025.
https://doi.org/10.1007/978-3-031-76803-3_15

2   Related Research

2.1   Factors Affecting Web Site User Experience

Nielsen stated that a successful website design must consider the needs, abilities, and characteristics of different user groups, as well as the frequency of website use and experience with the Internet [2]. Coursaris et al. reported that the color of a website influences user experience and those cold colors exert a positive impact on usability by creating a clean and fresh impression, whereas warm colors enhance user enjoyment and increase willingness to purchase [3]. For example, when the number of pictures is the same, short descriptions increase user enjoyment, whereas long texts increase stress [4].

2.2   User Interface Design for EC Sites

Aslam et al. confirmed that the user interface (UI) of a consumer website affects user satisfaction [5]. Econsultancy reported that a poor UI of an EC site decreases the annual revenue by 24% [6]. Parboteeah et al. showed that the UI of EC sites affects users' purchasing behavior [7] and Lee et al. studied the relationship between various factors associated with online shopping quality, customer satisfaction, and willingness to buy and showed that the UI of the site affects total service quality and customer satisfaction [8]. Park et al. studied the relationship between various characteristics of Korean online bookstores and found that UI quality was significantly related to satisfaction and purchasing behavior [9].

These results indicate that in addition to the quality and selection of products sold on an EC site, UI is an important element that influences the purchasing behavior of customers.

2.3   UI Adaptation to Local Culture

In a study on cross-cultural UI design, Zhu demonstrated the need to adapt UI design to the local culture [10]. Singh et al. compared a standard website with a culturally adapted and customized website and found that the latter had better information acquisition and navigation usability [11]. Both studies demonstrated the effectiveness of customizing UIs to their respective local cultures.

3   Comparison of UIs Between Japanese and Chinese EC Sites

3.1   Survey Target

The survey targeted top-page designs for smartphones by selecting ten popular EC sites from Japan and China. The increasing use of smartphones for EC is the primary reason for targeting these sites. This trend is expected to continue growing in the years to come. The target sites, all representative EC sites in each country, are presented below. Examples of the site screens are shown in Fig. 1.

- Japan: Rakuten, ZOZOTOWN, UNIQLO, GU, Yahoo Shopping, Matsumoto Kiyoshi, BIC Camera, Nitori, SHOPLIST, and BOOKOFF
- China: Taobao, Jing Dong, PinDuoDuo, Dang Dang, Zhen Kuaile, Jing Xi, Suning, Xiaonu, Yanxuan and HUAWEI

(a) Japanese sites

(b) Chinese sites

Fig. 1. EC sites surveyed

3.2 Color Scheme

The ratio of warm to cold colors on the entire page was also investigated. Colors were detected using the image processing library OpenCV, which was converted into the HSV color space. Warm colors had a range of 60° hues, with red as the median, and cold colors had a range of 60° hues, with blue as the median. The color ratios were calculated as follows:

- Japan: white (58.5%), warm (6.7%), cold (3.1%)
- China: white (63.4%), warm (12.6%), cold (1.9%)

China has approximately twice as many warm colors as Japan and approximately 60% of the cold colors in Japan. At first glance, Fig. 1 gives the impression that the Japanese sites are subdued, whereas the Chinese sites are more flamboyant.

3.3   Layout, Columns, and Scrolling

In general, the layout of Japanese sites varies from site to site; however, the items displayed are similar. Of the ten Japanese sites, search bars appear on ten sites, banners on nine sites, and recommended products on eight sites. Although the layout of Chinese sites is almost uniform as shown in Fig. 2, the content tends to vary from site to site.

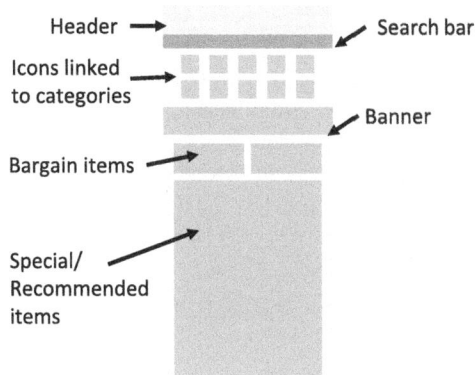

Fig. 2. Typical layout of Chinese sites

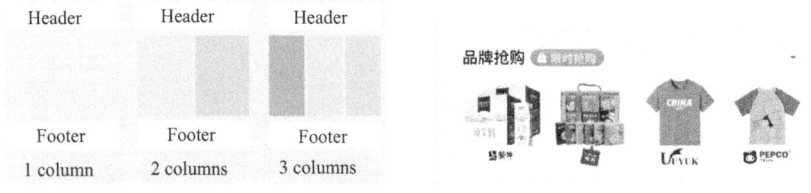

(a) Difference of columns   (b) Four elements in one columns

Fig. 3. Columns

In terms of column configuration, 80% of Japanese EC sites use three columns and 30% use two columns (some use both). By contrast, Chinese EC sites often use a composite combination of layouts with different numbers of columns throughout the page. In addition, they often arrange the four elements in one column without clearly separating them (Fig. 3b). Differences in scrolling were also observed. Sixty percent of the Japanese EC sites allow both horizontal and vertical scrolling. Chinese sites allow only vertical but infinite scrolling.

3.4   Images of the Products for Sale

For a screen width of 750 pixels, the average size of each area was 347×346 pixels in two columns and 220×220 pixels in three columns, whereas the image size for the four elements in a single column was 142×141 pixels. For Japanese EC sites, the average image size was 249×256 pixels in two columns and 209×209 pixels in three columns.

Regarding the characteristics of the images, Chinese product images generally display many words superimposed on the photo, whereas Japanese images simply display only the product and a white background.

4 Design Support Tool

4.1 Screen Layout

Figure 4 shows the screen layout of the system. By selecting a tab for Japan or China on the left (1), the design templates and components are displayed. In this area, when the designer selects the template or component to use, it appears in the editing area (2) at the center of the screen, where images can be embedded and the text can be modified. The upper-right button (3) is used to preview the design.

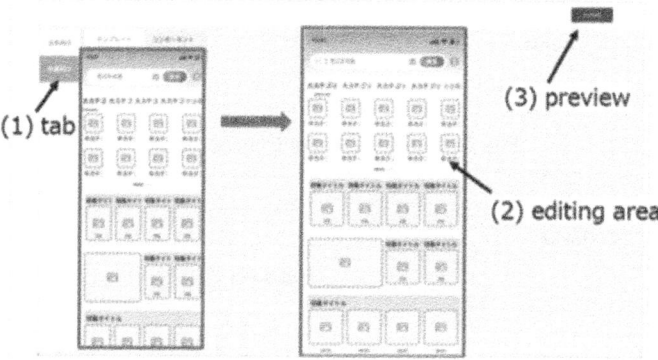

Fig. 4. Screen layout

4.2 Templates

Examples of these templates are shown in Fig. 5. Each template reflects the findings described in Sect. 3 as follows:

- Template for Chinese sites of Japanese EC: The color scheme uses many warm colors, and a complex combination of one, two, and three columns is used with reference to the layout of the Chinese sites. The header section has buttons for the "Contact," "Scan," and "Photo" functions found on Chinese sites, and the page is infinitely scrollable.
- Template for Japanese sites for Chinese EC: Cold colors are extensively used, providing an overall subdued atmosphere. The layout is designed based on elements commonly found on Japanese sites and adopts a three-column design common in Japan. The header feature buttons are the three most frequently used functions: "Cart," "Menu," and "Notices."

(a) A template for Chinese websites provided by Japanese EC

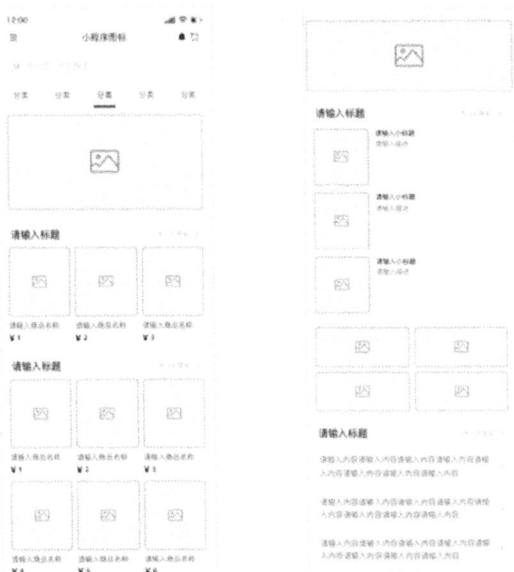

(b) A template for Japanese sites by Chinese EC (The right figure is located below the left one)

Fig. 5. Templates

4.3 Components

Although it is possible to create a site using the template as-is, a variety of components are available for further customization. These components include navigation and banners, which are common to both China and Japan. Some components are unique to one country, such as the "countdown" for Chinese sites and the "special features" for Japanese sites, and even the common components differ in design. Examples of content display components in China and Japan are shown in Fig. 6.

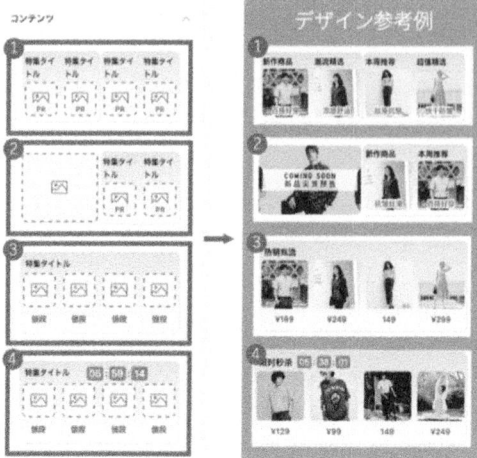

(a) Components for Chinese sites by Japanese EC

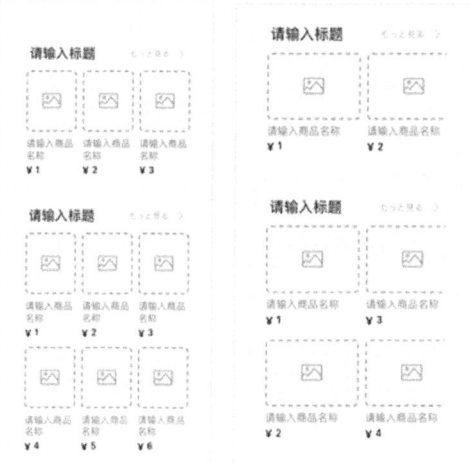

(b) Components for Japanese sites by Chinese EC

Fig. 6. Components for content display

5 Evaluation and Discussion

5.1 Tool Usability

This study involved ten participants: five Japanese and five Chinese individuals in their 20s and 30s. All participants possessed basic PC skills and could use typical office tools; however, they were not designers. They were asked to design an EC site for their partner country using our tool and image data, with reference to the original EC sites of their own country. UNIQLO and JINGDONG were used as reference sites for the Japanese and Chinese EC sites, respectively. When creating the site, we asked users to write texts in their own language; after completion, the texts were automatically translated into the language of their partner country. Each participant took approximately 50 min to complete their task, and after completion, a questionnaire regarding the usability of the tool was distributed, which generally received a high evaluation as shown in Fig. 7.

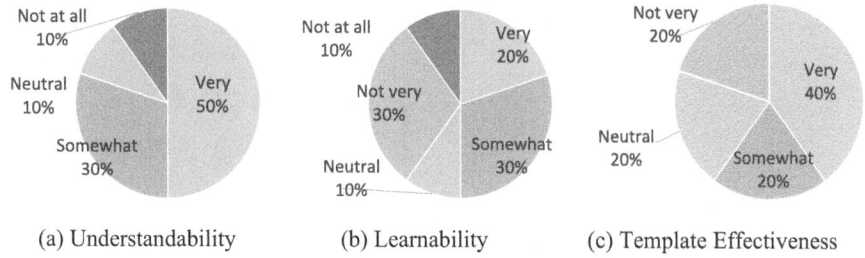

(a) Understandability   (b) Learnability   (c) Template Effectiveness

Fig. 7. Usability of the tool (n = 10)

Based on the experimental results, five designs were created for the Chinese site design of Japanese EC and the Japanese site design of the Chinese EC. The designs were validated based on the results.

Figure 8 shows the created designs. In both (a) and (b), the isolated leftmost image is directly translated from the original image. This was compared with five other designs displayed on the right side, which were created using our tool.

Chinese sites by Japanese EC. Eleven Chinese evaluators (four males and seven females) aged between 20 and 39 years participated in the study. Each evaluator was presented with six designs, including one image from the UNIQLO website translated into Chinese and five images of the design for Chinese users created using our tool (Fig. 8(a)). The results of the questionnaire are shown in Fig. 9. The results show that the designs created by our tool are familiar and well-liked by the Chinese subjects.

Japanese Sites by Chinese EC. Eleven Japanese evaluators (seven males and four females) in their 20s–50s participated in this study. Each evaluator was presented with six designs, including one image of the JINGDONG website translated into Japanese and five images of the designs created for Japanese users using our tool (Fig. 8(b)). The questionnaire results are shown in Fig. 10. Again, they show that the Japan sites created using our tool are highly rated.

5.2 Trial of Product Images Conversion

Finally, we conducted an experiment in which product images from Japan and China were mutually transformed using CycleGAN [12], a type of generative artificial intelligence (1,000 training images from each country and 200 epochs of learning). There are differences in the characteristics of the product images between the Japanese and Chinese sites, as described in Sect. 3. In China, it is common to have a background with

(a) Chinese sites by Japanese EC

(b) Japanese sites by Chinese EC

Fig. 8. Created designs (the left-most is a direct translation from the original site)

text on top of the product, whereas in Japan, only the product image is displayed and the background is often white. Although it will be impossible to automatically generate everything, it is helpful for the site creator to view the atmosphere of the images that are desirable for the counterpart country.

As shown in Fig. 11, images reflecting the characteristics of each country are sometimes generated. Figure 11 depicts a relatively successful case; however, there are cases in which part of the product image is lost or nothing changes because of the conversion. In the future, our intention is to evaluate this feature alongside other methods, such as image generation from text.

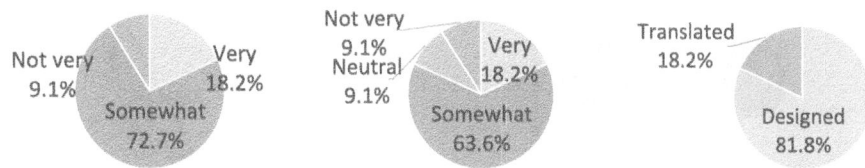

(a) Importance of Chinese style   (b) Similarity to familiar image   (c) Familiar design

(d) Preferred design   (e) Browsing convenience

Fig. 9. Evaluation of the China sites by Japanese EC

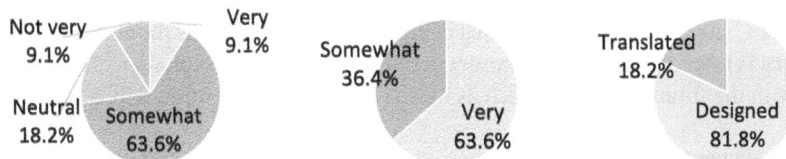

(a) Importance of Japanese style   (b) Similarity to familiar design   (c) Familiar design

(d) Preferred design   (e) Browsing convenience

Fig. 10. Evaluation of the Japan sites by Chinese EC

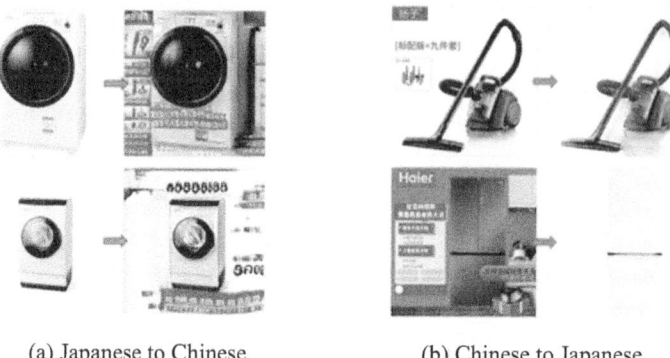

(a) Japanese to Chinese   (b) Chinese to Japanese

Fig. 11. Conversion of images by CycleGAN

6 Conclusion

In addition to quantitatively clarifying the design differences between Japanese and Chinese EC sites, we demonstrated that designing a site that reflects the characteristics of a country is favorably accepted by users in other countries. Cross-border EC is expected to grow in the future, and tools such as those presented in this study will be needed.

Acknowledgments. This study was supported by Toyo University Top Priority Research Program.

References

1. Ministry of Economy. Trade and Industry in Japan, FY2021 Market Research Report on Electronic Commerce. August 2023 (in Japanese), https://www.meti.go.jp/press/2022/08/202 20812005/20220812005-h.pdf. Accessed 28 Apr 2024
2. Nielsen, J.: Top 10 Mistakes in Web Design, Jan. 1, 2011., N N/g Nielsen Norman Group, https://www.nngroup.com/articles/top-10-mistakes-web-design/. Accessed 28 Apr 2024
3. Coursaris, C.K., van Osch, W.: A cognitive-affective model of perceived user satisfaction (CAMPUS): the complementary effects and interdependence of usability and aesthetics in IS design. Inf. Manag. **53**(2), 252–264 (2016)
4. Bufquin, D., et al.: Effects of hotel website photographs and length of textual descriptions on viewers' emotions and behavioral intentions. Int. J. Hospitality Manag. **87**, 102378 (2020)
5. Aslam, W., Hussain, A., Farhat, K., Arif, I.: Underlying factors influencing consumers' trust and loyalty in E-commerce. Bus. Perspect. Res. **8**(2), 186–204 (2020)
6. Reducing online customer struggle. Econsultancy's customer experience survey, August 2011. http://docs.media.bitpipe.com/io_10x/io_101973/item_460831/tealeaf-report_Econsu ltancy-Customer-Struggle-B.pdf. Accessed 28 Apr 2024
7. Parboteeah, D.V., Valacich, J.S., Wells, J.D.: The influence of website characteristics on a consumer's urge to buy impulsively. Inf. Syst. Res. **20**(1), 60–78 (2008)
8. Lee, G.G., Lin, H.F.: Customer perceptions of e-service quality in online shopping. Int. J. Retail Distrib. Manag. **33**(2), 161–176 (2005)

9. Park, C.H., Kim, Y.G.: Identifying key factors affecting consumer purchase behavior in an online shopping context. Int. J. Retail Distrib. Manag. **31**, 16–29 (2003)

10. Zhu, C.: Re-examining cross-cultural user interface design indicators: an empirical study. University of Twente student theses (2015)

11. Singh, N., et al.: A cross-cultural analysis of German Chinese and Indian consumers' perception of web site adaptation. J. Consum. Behav. **5**(1), 56–68 (2006)

12. CycleGAN. https://junyanz.github.io/CycleGAN/. Accessed 28 Apr 2024

Multimodal Interaction

Evaluation of Interactive Slider Design Utilizing Haptic Feedback

Yui Atarashi[✉] and Buntarou Shizuki

University of Tsukuba, 1-1-1 Tennodai, Tsukuba, Ibaraki 305-8573, Japan
{atarashi,shizuki}@iplab.cs.tsukuba.ac.jp

Abstract. A slider is a user interface component that allows users to select a value by moving a handle along a straight track. We propose a three-slider design utilizing haptic feedback. We conducted an experiment involving 12 people using the proposed sliders and collected data on task completion time, mental workload, and the participants' self-reported preferences. The results showed that the participants preferred the slider with haptic feedback to the normal slider without haptic feedback, with a lower workload, although it did not affect the operation time. In particular, we found that a slider that provides haptic feedback when the direction of the slider manipulation changes requires the least mental workload and is the most preferred.

Keywords: mobile interaction · mobile input · user interface design · value input · usability · workload

1 Introduction

A slider is a user interface (UI) component that allows users to select a value by moving a handle (a.k.a., knob or bar) along a straight track. It is commonly used to let users adjust volumes, modify the brightness and contrast of images, change settings within applications, and perform other tasks that involve manipulating a range of continuous values. Due to its intuitive operability, a slider is widely used across many applications.

Recently, applications that can be used on slate devices have become widespread, leading to sliders on mobile devices being used for adjustments requiring precision. For example, fine color adjustments in graphic design or photo editing, detailed volume or pitch adjustments in music production or audio editing, subtle adjustments to brightness or color in video editing, and specifying doses of medication in medical devices may all require accurate adjustments. When fine adjustments or precise value settings are necessary, it can often be difficult to slide to the exact position needed. This difficulty can be attributed to the limited operational area of sliders on small screens, such as those on smartphones. When using a finger to operate a slider, it is challenging to make fine adjustments in a narrow range, making it difficult for users to select the precise value they want. Additionally, when sliders cover a wide range of values (e.g.,

M. Kurosu et al. (Eds.): HCII 2024, LNCS 15374, pp. 289–298, 2025.
https://doi.org/10.1007/978-3-031-76803-3_16

from 0 to 100), slight slide movements can cause large value changes, making fine-tuning difficult. Given these issues, sliders displayed on mobile devices, especially in situations requiring precise input values, suffer from low usability and increased workloads.

Our goal is to improve the usability of sliders and reduce workload by utilizing haptic feedback. Haptic feedback is a form of haptic or kinesthetic communication that takes advantage of the sense of touch by applying forces, vibrations, or motions to the user. It conveys information or enhances interaction with digital devices and interfaces. By simulating the sensations of touch and movement, haptic feedback can provide users with a more immersive, efficient, and enjoyable experience [6]. Previous research has shown that using haptic feedback [3,5,8,9,13] can improve usability.

Various design guidelines have been published for slider design [1,2,11], but none mention slider design combined with haptic feedback. Although there are already published applications that use sliders combined with haptic feedback, the UI components of these haptic-focused sliders have not been studied, and the optimal design for the user remains unclear.

As an approach to the goal, we propose three slider designs utilizing haptic feedback. We then examined the performance of the three designs using the speed of operation, mental workload, and self-reported preferences as evaluation indicators in an experiment involving 12 participants.

2 Related Work

This research is based on haptic feedback, specifically usability improvement by utilizing haptic feedback in GUI operations. In this section, we describe research that has explored haptic feedback.

Haptic feedback has been used in various devices such as slate devices and pens [10,13] to improve the performance of operations. Previous studies have shown that adding haptic feedback to GUI elements improves usability [4,5,12]. For example, a study by Dennerlein et al. [4] demonstrated that providing a tactile channel in a steering task GUI using force feedback for mice resulted in an improvement of over 50% in movement time. Oakley et al. [12] added two haptic effects to the scrollbar, an indentation and a gravity well, allowing users to scroll without taking their eyes off the scrollable text. They found that when haptic feedback was enabled, participants made significantly fewer errors and perceived their workload as significantly lighter. However, the haptic feedback did not improve the task completion time. Fukumoto and Sugimura [5] used voice coil actuators attached to the body of a handheld computer to transmit haptic feedback to the user's hand holding the device. They compared haptic and audio feedback with touch-screen buttons and found that performance using haptic feedback was 5% faster in quiet environments and 15% faster in noisy environments compared to audio feedback. In another study [9] on the impact of haptic feedback on the usability of GUI elements (buttons, progress bars, and scrollbars) on touchscreens, the experimental results showed that adding haptic feedback to the progress bar and scrollbar tasks significantly improved task completion times. In addition to touchscreens, these studies used external haptic vibration devices to utilize haptic feedback.

Mobile device performance has improved in recent years. In the iPhone, a vibration device called "Taptic Engine" has been available in iPhones since the iPhone 6 s was released in 2015. The range of expressive haptic designs for mobile devices alone has been expanding. In this research, we do not use an external vibration device but rather a built-in haptic vibration device. We also focus on a slider, a UI component used for input.

3 Slider Design

We observed three individuals' slider operations and then obtained the following three types of slider designs with haptic feedback.

3.1 A Slider that Provides Haptic Feedback for Every Single Unit

This design provides haptic feedback with every single step change in the slider's value. It represents the most straightforward design and is commonly used in applications that incorporate haptic feedback into sliders.

3.2 A Slider that Provides Haptic Feedback When the Speed of Manipulation Decreases

This design provides haptic feedback when the manipulation speed decreases, specifically when the speed of a single unit action is longer than 0.5 s. Users initially move the slider quickly, slowing down as they approach the desired value. The time required to perceive feedback provided in single units increases when the speed of operation is slower than when it is faster. Therefore, we hypothesize that slow manipulation makes users perceive haptic feedback more readily. Namely, as the speed of manipulation decreases, haptic feedback becomes more perceptible. Considering these, the design utilizes the speed of the slider's manipulation as a trigger for activating haptic feedback (see Fig. 1).

3.3 A Slider that Provides Haptic Feedback When the Direction of the Slider Manipulation Changes

This design provides haptic feedback only after the direction of the slider's movement changes. Users typically accelerate the slider beyond the target value and then reverse direction to fine-tune it to the desired value. Additionally, providing haptic feedback at every step could overwhelm and potentially stress the user due to the increased perceptual load. The value at the point of direction change is often close to the desired input value. Therefore, offering haptic feedback only around the vicinity of the intended value would help eliminate unnecessary feedback (see Fig. 2). Note that using the change in direction as a trigger negates

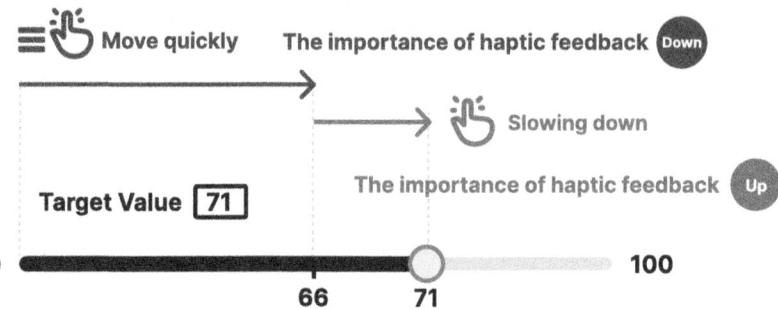

Fig. 1. A slider that provides haptic feedback when the slider manipulation speed decreases.

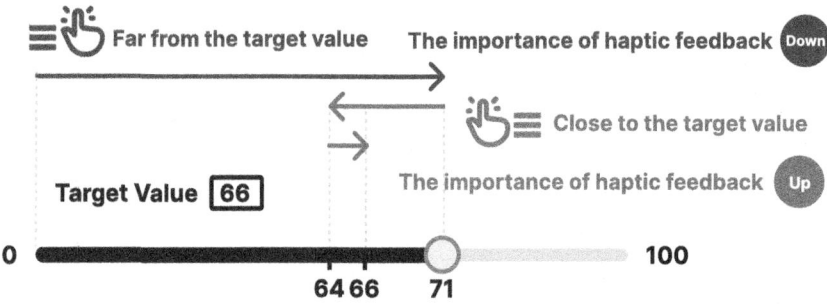

Fig. 2. A slider that provides haptic feedback when the slider manipulation direction changes.

the need for the system to determine the target value the user aims to input. Additionally note that reducing vibration also helps prevent battery consumption. Based on these considerations, we propose a slider design that employs the change in the slider's movement direction as the trigger for activating haptic feedback.

4   Evaluation

4.1   Participants and Apparatus

We recruited 12 participants (2 females and 10 males) from the local university as volunteers. All were right-handed. We used an iPhone 13, which includes a component that creates vibrations and haptic feedback. The development language is Swift, and the haptic implementation was done using Core Haptics, a framework that enables haptic feedback. We used haptic feedback, which is a transient vibration with a 1.0 intensity.

4.2   Design and Procedure

Participants were tasked with operating sliders under four conditions to input specified target values. Condition 1 (Without Haptic) featured a standard slider without haptic feedback. Condition 2 (Haptic by Unit) featured a slider that returns haptic feedback with every single unit adjustment. Condition 3 (Haptic by Speed) featured a slider that provides haptic feedback when the speed of the slider manipulation decreases. Condition 4 (Haptic by Direction) featured a slider that provides haptic feedback when the direction of the slider manipulation changes. The sliders allowed for inputting an integer ranging from 0 to 100, with the handle starting at the left position of 0. The current value was displayed at the top center, with the target value shown below it.

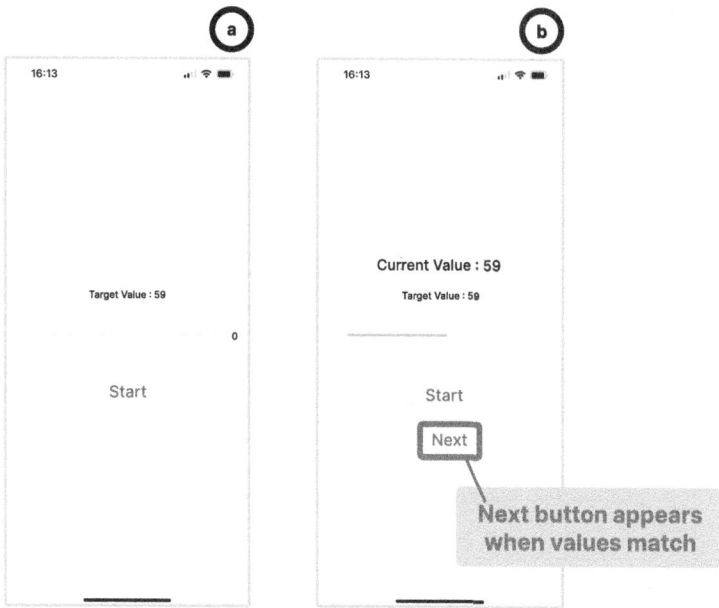

Fig. 3. Screens of the task used for evaluation. The screen before the slider manipulation, with the target value displayed (a). The screen when the slider is operated and the current value matches the target value (b).

The procedure for executing a single trial was as follows. Initially, participants are required to verify the displayed target value (see Fig. 3a). Subsequently, they press the start button. Next, they operate the slider to align the current value with the target value. Upon completion, they click the newly appeared NEXT button to transition to the subsequent trial (see Fig. 3b). This procedure was designed to assess the participant's ability to accurately and efficiently achieve the specified target value, providing insight into the usability and effectiveness of the proposed slider designs.

A session consisted of ten repetitions of this trial. Initially, participants practiced with a standard slider without haptic feedback for one session. Subsequently, two sessions of tasks were performed for each of the four sliders. In total, including one practice session, nine sessions are performed. The order of sliders was determined based on the Latin square method, setting unbiased sequences for 12 conditions. The presented target values were 10 fixed random numbers (76, 19, 45, 58, 65, 73, 10, 43, 96, and 30) with the same sequence in each session. A one-minute break was provided between each session, with a ten-minute break after the first five sessions. In the second half, participants were asked to fill out the NASA Task Load Index (NASA-TLX) [7] questionnaire and self-reported questionnaires after each session. In the self-reported questionnaire, participants were asked to rate their preference for the slider on a seven-point scale and to compare it without haptic feedback sliders. Each session took approximately one minute on average, with the total estimated time for the experiment being around 45 min. In total, we collected data from 960 trials from 12 participants (20 trials x 4 sliders x 12 participants).

5   Result

5.1   Task Completion Time

Figure 4 shows the task completion times of four sliders. The average time for each slider was as follows: Condition 1 had an average time of 3.41 s (SD = 0.99 s), Condition 2 had an average time of 3.38 s (SD = 1.09), Condition 3 had an average time of 3.52 s (SD = 0.96), and Condition 4 had an average time

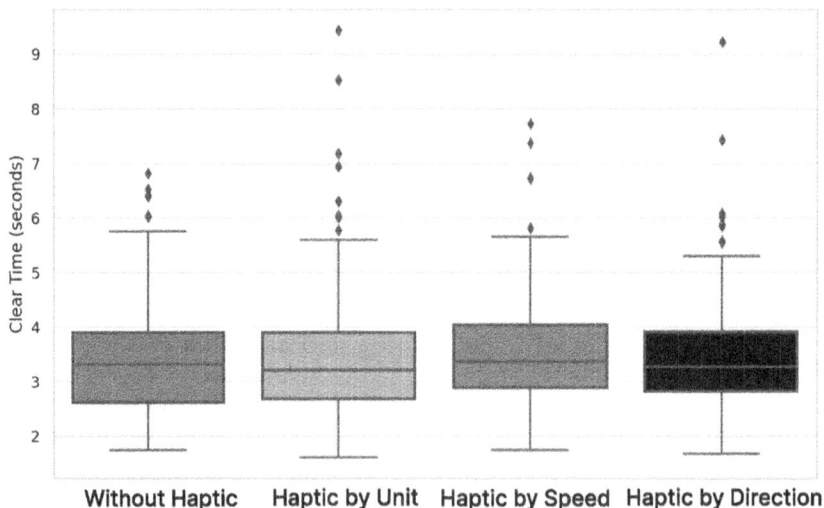

Fig. 4. Task completion times across four conditions.

of 3.44 s (SD = 0.94). After the Shapiro-Wilk test showed that the data did not follow a normal distribution, we used the Kruskal-Wallis test to check for differences in task completion times across four conditions. This test produced a statistic of 5.65 and a p-value of 0.13. These results suggest that there are no significant differences in the completion times among the four conditions (p ¿ 0.05). Furthermore, after conducting the Kruskal-Wallis test to examine for significant differences among the four conditions for each target value, it was found that there are no significant differences in task completion times for any of the target values. Therefore, it was concluded that using haptic feedback on sliders does not affect the time it takes to complete tasks.

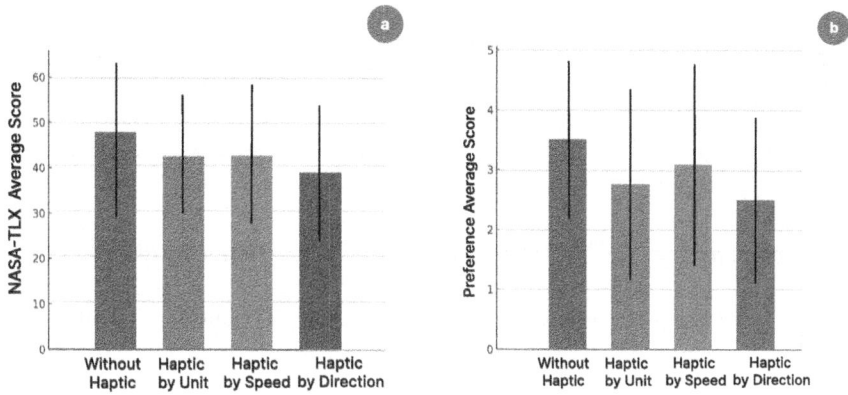

Fig. 5. The average NASA Task Load Index scores across the four conditions (a). The average preferences on a 7-point scale (1: like – 7: dislike) (b).

5.2 NASA-TLX

Participant's mental workload was evaluated using the NASA Task Load Index (NASA-TLX) [7] questionnaire. NASA-TLX assesses subjective workload across six dimensions: mental demand, physical demand, temporal demand, effort, performance, and frustration, using a scale from 0 to 100. A higher score indicates a higher perceived workload. The average scores and standard deviations for each condition are presented in Fig. 5a. Condition 1 had an average score of 46.03 (SD = 17.00), Condition 2 had an average score of 42.47 (SD = 12.98), Condition 3 had an average score of 42.67 (SD = 15.25), and Condition 4 had an average score of 39.00 (SD = 14.92). All data followed a normal distribution. We conducted a paired t-test to investigate significant differences between pairs under each condition. A significant difference is determined when the p-value is greater than 0.05. For Condition 1, significant differences were observed between Condition 2 (p-value = 0.039), Condition 3 (p-value = 0.043), and Condition 4 (p-value = 0.0011). On the other hand, there was no significant difference between Condition 2 and Condition 3 (p-value = 0.952). There were significant differences between

Condition 2 and Condition 4 (p-value = 0.032) and Condition 3 and Condition 4 (p-value = 0.048). Therefore, sliders without haptic feedback tended to have a slightly higher workload compared to sliders with haptic feedback. Furthermore, there was almost no difference in workload between the slider that provides haptic feedback for every single unit and the slider that provides haptic feedback when the speed of manipulation decreases. The sliders that provide haptic feedback when the direction of the slider manipulation changes were associated with the lowest workload.

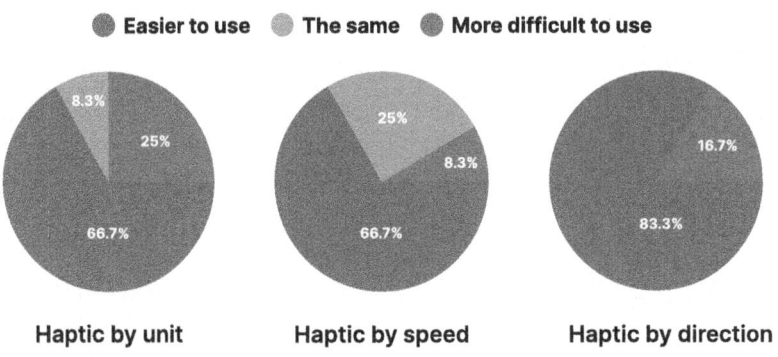

Fig. 6. Comparison with proposed sliders and the slider without haptic feedback.

5.3   Self-reported Preferences

Participants rated their preferences for sliders on a seven-point scale (1: like – 7: dislike). The results are shown in Fig. 5b. Condition 4 (M=2.5) was the most preferred, followed by Condition 2 (M=2.8), Condition 3 (M=3.1), and then Condition 1 (M=3.5). We performed the Wilcoxon rank-sum test and found significant differences between Condition 1 and Condition 2 (p-value = 0.021), Condition 1 and Condition 3 (p-value = 0.046), and Condition 1 and Condition 4 (p-value = 0.0057). Furthermore, significant differences were observed between Condition 2 and Condition 3 (p-value = 0.046), between Condition 2 and Condition 4 (p-value = 0.039), and between Condition 3 and Condition 4 (p-value = 0.0082). This indicates that sliders with haptic feedback were preferred sliders without haptic feedback. Moreover, sliders that provide haptic feedback when the direction of the slider operation changes (Condition 4) were the most favored among participants. The sliders that provide haptic feedback for every single unit (Condition 2) were slightly more preferred than those that provide haptic feedback when the manipulation speed decreases (Condition 3). Additionally, participants evaluated the usability in Conditions 2, 3, and 4 compared to a standard slider without haptic feedback in terms of being easier to use, the same, or more difficult to use. The results, shown in Fig. 6, revealed that 66.7% of participants in Condition 2 and 3 and 83.3% in Condition 4, found these sliders easier to use compared to the standard slider without any haptic feedback.

6 Discussion

The results presented above results revealed that haptic feedback does not affect the time taken to operate a slider. Furthermore, evaluations of workload using the NASA-TLX and preferences through self-reporting indicated that sliders equipped with haptic feedback tended to have lower workloads and be more preferred by users than sliders without haptic feedback. This implies that sliders with haptic feedback can reduce the user's workload without impacting the task completion time.

In addition, it was found that the slider that provides haptic feedback when the direction of the slider operation changes (Condition 3) resulted in the lowest workload and was the most preferred, while it is possible to lower the energy consumption of mobile devices related to haptic feedback compared to providing it with every single unit.

7 Limitations and Future Work

In the system used for the experiments, the current value was displayed on the slider, which inevitably introduced some visual influence during manipulation. To accurately assess the effects of haptic feedback without the influence of vision, it is necessary to adjust the position and size of the current value display in the design of the experimental system. Additionally, while the slider handle was placed at the left end of the bar, some sliders initially had the handle in the center. In such cases, the speed of manipulation and the range of manipulation differed, necessitating new experiments. Furthermore, while this study focused on the design of sliders, it is also conceivable to utilize haptic feedback in other design components, such as progress bars or accordions.

In addition, this experiment targeted healthy individuals in their 20 s, but using haptic feedback on sliders could significantly improve accessibility for the elderly and visually impaired. To investigate this effect, future experiments will include elderly and visually impaired individuals as participants.

8 Conclusion

Our goal is to improve the usability of sliders and reduce their workload. In this research, we proposed three types of interactive slider designs utilizing haptic feedback. Through experiments involving 12 participants, we found that sliders equipped with haptic feedback did not affect the manipulation time compared to traditional sliders without haptic feedback but did reduce the workload. It was also found that sliders with haptic feedback tended to be preferred by users. In particular, we found that a slider that provides haptic feedback when the direction of the slider manipulation changes has the lowest workload and is the most preferred.

References

1. Adobe: Slider adobe spectrum (2023). https://spectrum.adobe.com/page/slider/. Accessed 20 May 2024
2. Apple: Sliders human interface guidelines design (2023). https://developer.apple.com/design/human-interface-guidelines/sliders. Accessed 20 May 2024
3. Brewster, S., Chohan, F., Brown, L.: Tactile feedback for mobile interactions. In: Proceedings of the SIGCHI Conference on Human Factors in Computing Systems, pp. 159–162. CHI '07, Association for Computing Machinery, New York, NY, USA (2007). https://doi.org/10.1145/1240624.1240649
4. Dennerlein, J.T., Martin, D.B., Hasser, C.: Force-feedback improves performance for steering and combined steering-targeting tasks, pp. 423–429. In: CHI '00, Association for Computing Machinery, New York, NY, USA (2000). https://doi.org/10.1145/332040.332469
5. Fukumoto, M., Sugimura, T.: Active click: tactile feedback for touch panels. In: CHI '01 Extended Abstracts on Human Factors in Computing Systems, pp. 121–122. CHI EA '01, Association for Computing Machinery, New York, NY, USA (2001). https://doi.org/10.1145/634067.634141
6. Harrison, C., Hudson, S.E.: Providing dynamically changeable physical buttons on a visual display, pp. 299–308. In: CHI '09, Association for Computing Machinery, New York, NY, USA (2009). https://doi.org/10.1145/1518701.1518749
7. Hart, S.G., Staveland, L.E.: Development of NASA-TLX (task load index): results of empirical and theoretical research. In: Hancock, P.A., Meshkati, N. (eds.) Human Mental Workload, Advances in Psychology, vol. 52, pp. 139–183. North-Holland (1988). https://doi.org/10.1016/S0166-4115(08)62386-9
8. Koskinen, E., Kaaresoja, T., Laitinen, P.: Feel-good touch: finding the most pleasant tactile feedback for a mobile touch screen button. In: Proceedings of the 10th International Conference on Multimodal Interfaces, pp. 297–304. ICMI '08, Association for Computing Machinery, New York, NY, USA (2008). https://doi.org/10.1145/1452392.1452453
9. Leung, R., MacLean, K., Bertelsen, M.B., Saubhasik, M.: Evaluation of haptically augmented touchscreen GUI elements under cognitive load. In: Proceedings of the 9th International Conference on Multimodal Interfaces, pp. 374–381. ICMI '07, Association for Computing Machinery, New York, NY, USA (2007). https://doi.org/10.1145/1322192.1322258
10. Lüthi, G., Fender, A.R., Holz, C.: Deltapen: A device with integrated high-precision translation and rotation sensing on passive surfaces. In: Proceedings of the 35th Annual ACM Symposium on User Interface Software and Technology, pp. 1–12. UIST '22, Association for Computing Machinery, New York, NY, USA (2022). https://doi.org/10.1145/3526113.3545655
11. Microsoft: Slider fluent 2 design system microsoft design (2023). https://fluent2.microsoft.design/components/web/react/slider/usage/. Accessed 20 May 2024
12. Oakley, I., McGee, M.R., Brewster, S., Gray, P.: Putting the feel in 'look and feel'. In: Proceedings of the SIGCHI Conference on Human Factors in Computing Systems, pp. 415–422. CHI '00, Association for Computing Machinery, New York, NY, USA (2000). https://doi.org/10.1145/332040.332467
13. Poupyrev, I., Okabe, M., Maruyama, S.: Haptic feedback for pen computing: Directions and strategies, pp. 1309–1312. Association for Computing Machinery, New York, NY, USA (2004). https://doi.org/10.1145/985921.986051

Design of a Multimodal Robot-Based Conversational Interface: A Case Study with FURHAT

Rita Francese[✉], Madalina G. Ciobanu, Emilio Clemente, and Genoveffa Tortora

Computer Science Department, University of Salerno, Fisciano, Italy
{francese,mciobanu,tortora}@unisa.it, e.clemente3@studenti.unisa.it

Abstract. In this paper, we propose a system, named SO-Robot, which adopts a multimodal interface to support student orientation by providing information concerning the university's formative offer. A Furhat Robot acts as a secretary. We adopt NLP-based technology for the dialogues and query the university website database to obtain the needed information. The multimodal interface of the system enables the user to converse with the Furhat while additional content is shown on the board. In particular, we describe the adopted NLP process and the multimodal interface. Future work will be devoted to assessing user engagement and the system's usability.

Keywords: Multimodal Conversational Interface · Robotics · Artificial Intelligence · Human Robot Interaction · Natural Language Processing

1 Introduction

Nowadays, conversational interfaces and social robots [9] are relevant players in enhancing human-computer interaction. As technology advances, the need for seamless communication between users and automated systems becomes increasingly critical. Multimodal conversational interfaces - which combine verbal and nonverbal communication- have emerged as a promising solution to bridge this gap [8].

In face-to-face interactions, participants exchange a rich repertoire of communicative behaviors. Verbal information, gestures, facial expressions, and gaze all contribute to the intricate conversation process. Understanding the combination and co-occurrence of these modalities is essential for effective communication. To enhance human-robot communication researchers experimented with Natural Language Processing (NLP) techniques and Machine/Deep Learning models to develop effective chatbots [6]. Another relevant aspect to consider is the design of a multimodal conversational interface which requires careful selection of the interaction modalities that have to align user needs, task requirements, and contextual factors. The definition of the integration modalities of multiple inter- action channels is crucial, ensuring coherent and consistent feedback for users [7,8].

When designing multimodal conversational interfaces, the specific type of chatbot plays a significant role. Chatbots may have diverse applications, in this paper, we are interested in the development of an effective service chatbot [13], named SO-Robot (Student Orentation Robot), useful for students' support and efficiently addressing student inquiries.

SO-robot proposes a multimodal interface by equipping the Furhat robot with Artificial Intelligence features for detecting the user's intent and providing the appropriate answer, and with a digital board where contents related to the dialogue topic are shown. In this paper, we describe the SO-robot system and its multimodal interface.

The paper is organized as follows: Sect. 2 introduces the background concern- ing the Furhat robot and related work; Sect. 3 presents the proposed approach; finally, Sect. 4 concludes the paper with final remarks and future work.

2   Background

In this section, we introduce the main concept related to the Furhat robot and discuss the state-of-the-art work concerning multimodal robot-based interface.

2.1   The Furhat Robot

Social robots integrate the progress made in robotics, speech technology, and understanding of human behavior over the past century. This combination dis- tinguishes social robots from chatbots and avatars, which may simulate social interaction but lack physical embodiment, and from manufacturing robots, which are typically physical but lack social capabilities. Furhat [2,3] is an advanced social robot designed with a focus on human interaction. He can listen, answer questions, and express primary emotions: joy, sadness, anger, fear, disgust, and surprise, as shown in Fig. 2. It is the first robot with a back-projected face and, for this reason, it is also difficult to photograph.

The Furhat Robotics operating system for social robotics is named FurhatOS[1]. It includes subsystems essential for the technical operation of the robot. These components manage different functionalities, such as facial ani- mation, motion control, sensory perception, audio processing, visual processing, input/output handling, integration with cloud services, and operation and main- tenance tasks. Developed with Java and C++, Furhat subsystems communicate seamlessly through a structured event system facilitated by a messaging bus, ensuring efficient coordination and fulfilling soft real-time requirements.

---

[1] https://furhatrobotics.com/docs/Furhat-Robotics-Technical-Product-Overview. pdf.

Fuhrat can turn its head in a human-moving-like, which creates a natural head movement, up, down, and to the sides. On the robot's forehead, there is a 135° field-of-view camera. It also exposes two microphones and one speaker. The last version of Furhat has many face masks that vary from robot-like to woman and man-like to child-like or blank. Together with the projected faces, one can change the physical mask by choosing one of the different versions. Also for the voice, it is possible to choose between the available versions. To create interaction with Furhat, it is possible to use the Kotlin programming language or a visual programming environment based on Google Blockly[2]. It is not necessary to have the availability of the physical robot for development because its software enables us to program and test the results on a Virtual Furhat, an emulator of the robot. Shown in Fig. 1. All the Furhat developers may access the Furhat community, which is a global collection of developers. Furhat SDK (Software Development Kit) includes all the developer tools needed to create skills for the Furhat platform.

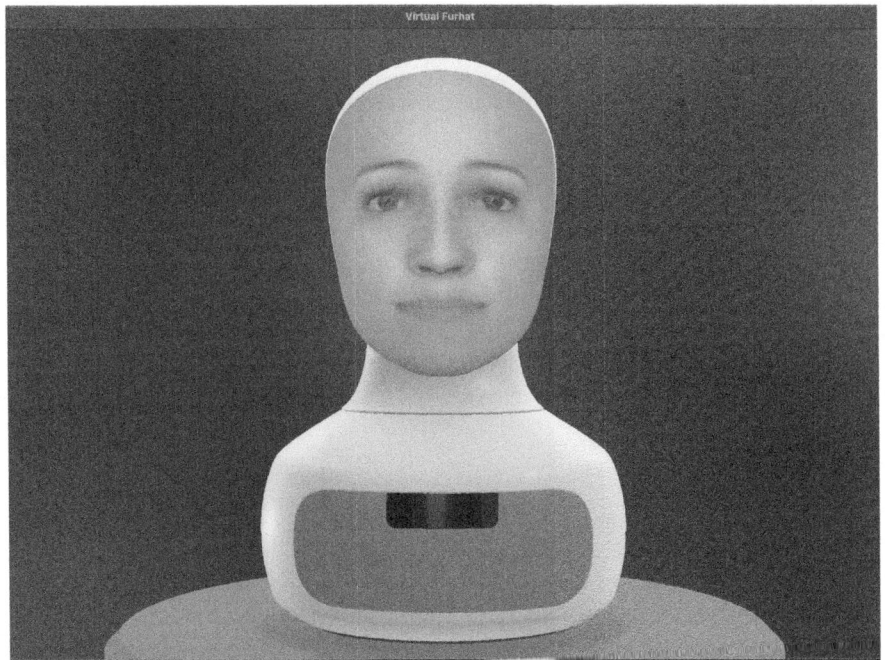

Fig. 1. Furhat Desktop Launcher displays the Furhat virtual simulator.

A Furhat skill is the foundational component for building applications running on the Furhat robot. These skills empower the robot to engage in intricate and dynamic interactions and may be classified as follows.

---

[2] https://developers.google.com/blockly.

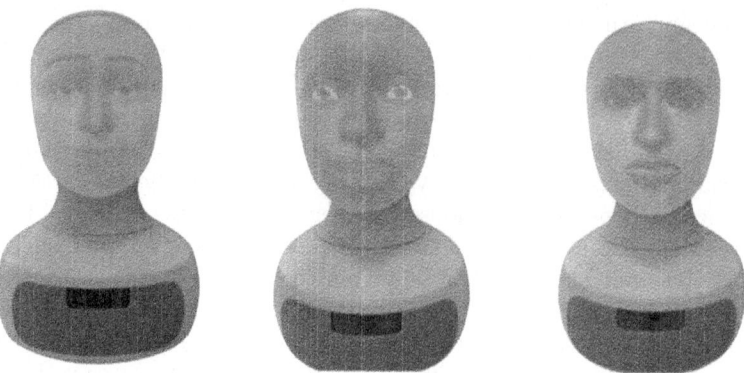

Fig. 2. Furhat: big smile, fear, anger

– *Flow or Dialog Flow.* A Furhat skill consists of a flow (also referred to as a dialog flow) that includes states with event handlers. These states define various interaction stages within the skill. It is like a script guiding the conversation between the robot and the user.
– *Intents and Entities.* Skills involve natural language understanding. Intents represent the user's intentions (e.g., asking a question, or making a request), while entities are specific information extracted from the user's input (e.g., identifying a date or location in a sentence).
– *Skill Files.* From a coding perspective, a Furhat skill comprises several files. The primary ones reside in the src folder[3]. These files define the robot's behavior, logic, and responses during interactions.
– *Skill Templates.* When creating a new skill, developers have at disposal various templates, such as skills for conducting a quiz or handling specific social scenarios.

2.2 Related Work

Since the realization of the first modern industrial robot in 1961, pioneered by George Devol for General Motors assembly lines, the field of robotics has undergone a remarkable evolution. The integration of robots into our daily lives is experiencing a remarkable surge. While initially conceived as mechanical arms, the concept of robots has since evolved significantly, now encompassing increasingly human-like features and capabilities, marking a profound shift in our relationship with technology [12].

Human-computer interaction has become challenging in recent decades. To enrich this communication in 1999 J. Casell [5] proposed the REA architecture,

---

[3] https://www.src/main/kotlin/furhatos/app/gettingstarted.

an embodied conversational agent capable of both multimodal input understanding and output generation in a limited application domain. Rea supports both social and task-oriented dialogue.

Gradually, the need was felt to make robots more similar to humans. Not only with human features but also with the voice and facial shapes that give the idea of having feelings. In short, empathetic robots are ready to become our "friends" who can help us in the professional field and our private lives. Thus, we are witnessing the evolution of robots from mechanical entities to social robots - machines designed not only to perform tasks but also to engage humans in social interactions. This transition signifies a pivotal moment in the evolution of robotics, where the aims are to encompass emotional intelligence, social cognition, and the ability to foster meaningful connections with humans.

Research is constantly evolving in human-robot interaction. Al Moubayed et al. [1] developed Furhat to support non-verbally and dynamically rich audio-visual synthesis and to study human-robot spoken interactions together with the IrisTK dialogue platform, both developed and utilized in multimodal multiparty embodied spoken dialogue systems.

Subsequently, robots, especially social ones, have been further enhanced by the integration of artificial intelligence (AI). This union has enhanced human-robot interaction, endowing machines with improved cognitive capabilities and the ability to perceive and respond to human emotions. Harnessing the power of artificial intelligence, social robots have moved beyond their mechanical origins to become more than passive tools, evolving into interactive companions capable of understanding, empathizing, and adapting to human needs and preferences. This marriage between robotics and artificial intelligence has not only broadened the horizons of technological innovation but has also opened up new possibilities for integrating intelligent machines in various sectors, including healthcare, education, entertainment, and personal care. We are witnessing a new era of human-robot collaboration. To obtain excellent results from human-computer interaction, studying a multimodal approach is of fundamental importance [11].

An example of a multimodal interface applied to a chatbot and board has been discussed and evaluated in [4] in an impmersive virtual reality collaborative work setting. Here, an embodied avatar-chatbot has been equipped with an interactive board for accomplishing a specific task: setting up a meeting in a virtual room. An empirical valuation has been conducted to assess the approach against the pre-existing menu-based interface.

3   The Proposed Approach

SO-Robot is a system aiming to support the orientation of students when approaching a university campus. In particular, it proposes a robot-secretary based on the Furhat robot, named Gianna, which provides information on the courses, the teachers' curriculum and activities, and the university's educational offer customized to the University of Salerno. To make the conversation more effective we adopted a multimodal interface, by enhancing the user-robot communication with visual content. In particular, we equipped Gianna with a screen displaying information related to Gianna's answers. Figure 3 shows Gianna while it provides the main information concerningo Professor Rita Francese, including her role, department, and teaching activities.

Fig. 3. The Multimodal Robot-based Conversational Interface.

The dialog process, depicted in Fig. 4, is the following:

1. the user asks for some information from the robot;
2. the robot converts the user's speech into text and generates an event for sending it to the web server;
3. the web server hosts the NLP functionalities and identifies the keywords of the user sentence. Then it takes the information from the database;
4. the web server provides the answers for Furhat and generates the web page for the browser;
5. the robot provides the vocal answer while the user browser displays the related content on the screen.

3.1   The SO-Robot Architecture

To effectively integrate the conversational robot Furhat, the architecture of the SO-Robot system consists of three subsystems: the Furhat robot, a server, and a web app, as shown in the Deployment Diagram in Fig. 4.

The server RESTful APIs, implemented in Python, constitute the core of the architecture, facilitating communication between the system's backend and the virtual assistant. This ensures smooth and scalable handling of user requests. Additionally, to provide an intuitive and accessible graphical user interface, a

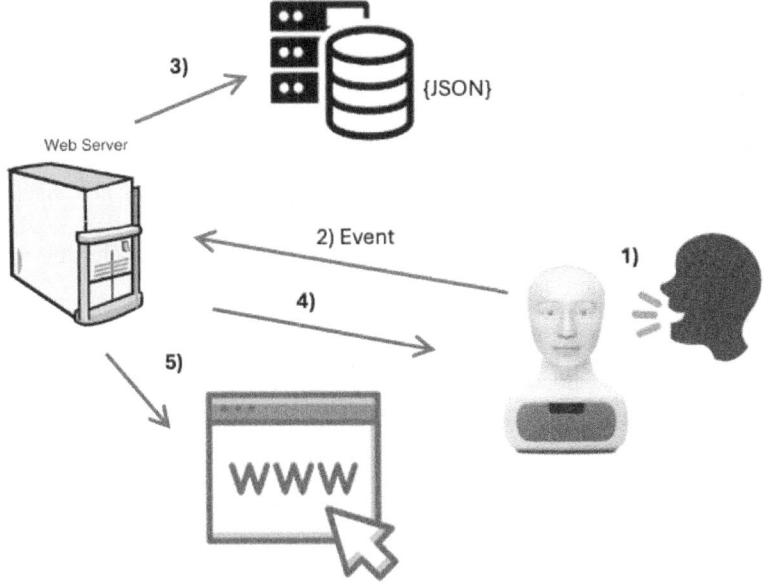

Fig. 4. The dialog process.

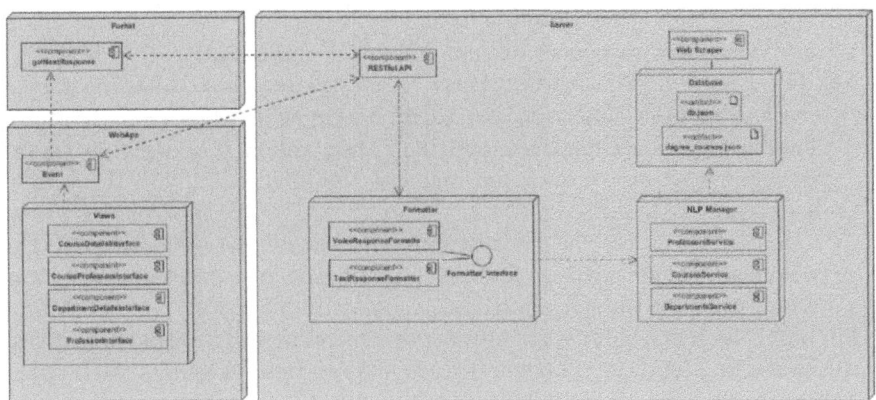

Fig. 5. The Deployment Diagram of SO-Robot.

web app was developed using Webpack, a powerful bundler for JavaScript applications in the Node.js environment. This choice optimized and organized the code of the web application, ensuring fast loading times and a seamless user experience across different devices.

In particular, the following components are shown in Fig. 4:

- **Web server**
  - *NLP Manager.* It manages NLP data-related services, including ProfessorsService, CoursesService and DepartmentsService. These services are essential for information management and retrieval specifications relating to teachers, courses, and departments. With the help of advanced NLP (Natural Language Processing) libraries such as SpaCy it is possible to efficiently direct the user's request towards the most relevant answer, optimizing the interaction process.
  - *Web Scraper.* It is responsible for data collection, and scraping information from predefined websites. This data is then sent to the database to be archived and made accessible. As part of the project, this scraper was developed to collect complex data from the official website of the University of Salerno. It was possible to collect detailed information on 1,278 teachers, including essential data such as office hours and relative locations, email and telephone contacts, information on teaching courses, timetables, course description sheets, images, and URLs of the teachers' pages. Data is organized in a CSV file structured as a relational database, facilitating data query and analysis using IDs and foreign keys.
  - *Formatter.* The Formatter takes care of converting the data into formats usable for the end user. In particular, it manages classes TextResponseFormatter and VoiceResponseFormatter, extending the Formatter Interface, to format responses textual and vocal, respectively.
  - *API RESTful.* The beating heart of the system, hosted on the server, receives requests and processes them, acting as a mediator between the database, the user interface, and the Furhat robot. It is essential for the dynamic flow' of the data and manages the interaction with the various services.
  - *Database.* It stores the information collected by the Web Scraper. The database includes several files, such as db.json and degree courses.json, which organize the data into structures easily retrievable by the API.
- **Furhat.** The social robot that interacts with the user. Through the getNextResponse function, the robot receives vocal questions, transmits them to the API, and communicates the response received to the user. This process occurs via asynchronous events, ensuring a natural and fluid conversation.
- **Web App:** The Web App acts as a visual interface of the system, showing information through a series of Views, such as CourseDetailsInterface, CourseProfessorsInterface, DepartmentDetailsInterface, and ProfessorsInterface. Each View is designed to respond to various events and user requests. When Furhat detects the voice input, via a specific event, the question is sent to the Web App, which processes the request and displays the information relevant to the user. This allows for smooth interaction vocal and visual, providing immediate feedback and making the experience more engaging and interactive.

3.2   Design of the Multimodal Interface

The SO-Robot system provides two types of information to the user:

- Feedback, includeing the results of operations performed by the system.
- Support information, guiding users on what they can or should do in subsequent interactions.

Combining spoken instructions with visual cues can enhance understanding and engagement. The challenge when designing this kind of interface is how to enhance the human-robot interaction by distributing the information between the robot and the board. We followed the guidelines proposed by [7]: we divided the information provided by the two interaction modalities in such a way that when designing the robot conversation, it's possible to omit information conveyed through other means, resulting in shorter and more efficient messages.

As suggested by the Furhat development team, to get effective communication with the robots it is better to give priority to Face-to-Face interaction, which is the main advantage offered by Furhat. We decided to show on the display additional content better supporting the information provided vocally by the robot, such as the teacher's picture or the map to reach her office and the list of the courses of a degree program. The spoken information provided by Furhat is integrated with the one displayed on the screen. Furhat provides the support information. We avoid using a touch screen[4] because the user may be distracted by this interaction modality and avoid interacting with the robot.

3.3   NLP Model Development

To design the interaction with the robot, we first identified the kind of chatbot interaction (user-driven dialogue) [10]; in this kind of dialogue, the user drives the conversation. Then, we specified the support the robot should provide, such as describing how to reach the teacher's room and the feedback it has to produce. Successively, we developed the NLP model for understanding the user's needs by defining the intents the robot should process. We also accurately designed the interface from a graphical and a communication point of view, by highlighting how the different communication approaches should combine the two elements (robot and board) to avoid overloading or confusing the user.

We create a dataset for model training by analyzing the human-robot dialogues that may be conducted in the domain of university formative courses and activities. In particular, we asked 30 students to ask for information from one of the researchers simulating the system behavior. An example of one of these dialogues is reported in Table 1.

---

[4] https://furhatrobotics.com/blog/should-social-robots-have-touch-screens/.

Table 1. The student orientation domain. A transcript of the dialog with the SO-Robot system concerning the teacher's activities.

Gianna	Hello. My name is Gianna. I'm the secretary. I can help you by providing information on the University of Salerno and its programs. What are you interested in?
Student	Who is Rita Francese?
Gianna	Rita Francese is an associate professor at the Computer Science Department.
Student	When can I find Rita Francese?
Gianna	Her office hours are Monday at 10.30 a.m. and Wednesday at 11.30 a.m.
Student	What courses does Rita Francese teach?
Gianna	She teaches web programming and enterprise mobile application development.

The NLP component uses SpaCy[5], an open-source software library for advanced NLP written in Python and Cython. SpaCy provides support for:

- Part-of-Speech Tagging (POS). It enables us to analyze text and identify parts of speech (such as nouns, verbs, adjectives, etc.) to each word.
- Named Entity Recognition (NER): useful to recognize entities such as names of people, organizations, locations, and dates.
- Dependency Parsing. To analyze the grammatical structure of sentences and represent it as a parse tree.
- Word Vectors. It provides pre-trained word vectors that capture semantic meanings of words.
- Customization and Extension. SpaCy can be customized with components and attributes to implement a specific NLP feature.
- Large Language Models (LLMs). The spacy-llm package integrates Large Language Models (LLMs) into spaCy, allowing fast prototyping and robust outputs for various NLP tasks without requiring training data. In our case, SpaCy is loaded with the model *it_core_news_lg*, a large model for the Italian language.

Listing 1.1. Question category identification.

```
question_categories = {
    "teaching": ["which professors teach", "who teaches", ...],
    "course_offer": ["course details", "course objectives", ...],
    "department_field": ["teachers belonging to", ...],
    "department_course_offer": ["professors' offerings", ...],
    "teacher_questions": ["office hours", ...],
    "all_information": ["what do you know about", ...],
    "contact": ["how to contact", ...],
    "courses_taught": ["courses taught by", ...],
    "general_info": ["who is", ...],
    "help": ["what can you do", "help", ...]
}
```

---

[5] https://spacy.io/.

```
for category, phrases in question_categories.items():
    for phrase in phrases:
        if any(phrase.lower() in question for question in phrases):
            ...
```

We adopted the feature offered by SpaCy for implementing the following functions useful to address the user intents:

– *extract_department_or_field*. This function extracts the name of the department or field of study from the question by looking for specific keywords and identifying the relevant part of the sentence.
– *find_department_by_department_name*. This function compares the user query with department names, using lemmatization to normalize the keywords in both the query and the department names. A lemma representation of the query and department keywords is created, ignoring stop words and punctuation. The best match is then found by comparing the expanded keywords from the query with the departments.
– *extract_course_name*. It extracts the course name from the user's question by cleaning the question and creating a SpaCy document. It uses keywords to identify the starting point for extracting the course name and converts any Arabic numbers in the course name to Roman numerals, lemmatization helps identify the keywords that indicate the beginning of the course name. Once the keywords are identified, the function extracts and lemmatizes the subsequent words to obtain the full course name.
– *extract_prof_name*. This function extracts the professor's name from the question by looking for proper nouns and concatenating tokens identified as proper nouns until it encounters a token that is not a proper noun. The sentence analysis via SpaCy helps identify the proper nouns (PROPN) that make up the professor's name, improving the accuracy of name extraction.

The detected keywords are used to classify user questions into different categories and to trigger the appropriate functions to respond to these questions. This process primarily occurs in the *answer_a_question* function as follows.

Identification of the question category. The *answer_a_question* function contains a dictionary called *answer_category* that maps key phrases to specific question categories. For example, the categories include teaching, courses, department_area, reception_times, contacts, courses_taught, general_information, and help.

Matching key phrases. The function compares the user's question with the key phrases in each category. If one of the key phrases is present in the question, the function identifies the corresponding category.

Activation of appropriate functions:

– Teacher categories (e.g., *reception_time*, *all_information*). If the question concerns a specific teacher, identified by the *extract_prof_name function*, the *find_teacher* function is used to find the teacher's detailed data. Then, *manage_response_category_on_professors* is called to generate the appropriate response based on the category.

- Specific categories (e.g., course, degree_program). If the question matches a specific category, the *manage_category_answer* function is called with the question, data (professors or departments), response format, and the identified category. The *manage_category_answer* function adopts the appropriate formatter to generate the answer.
- Help. If the question asks for help or information on how to use the chatbot, the *how_to_use_this_chatbot* function is called to explain the chatbot's functionalities.

The example in Table 2 shows how the student questions are analyzed and assigned to specific categories. In particular, the keywords in the user questions determine which function to call and how to format the response, enabling the chatbot to understand and answer a wide range of questions.

Table 2. An example of the application of NLP analysis procedure.

Student	Which professors teach Programming I?
Category identification	The phrase "teach" matches the "teaching" category.
Information retrieval	The data related to the teachers teaching Programming 1 are retrieved in the database.
Function activation	*gestisci_categoria_risposta* is called with the question, teachers' data, response format, and the course category.
Response generation	The formatter function (e.g., *VoiceResponseFormatter* or *TextResponseFormatter*) specific to the course category is used to format and return the list of teachers who teach the specified course and generates the content for both the Furhat and the screen.

4   Conclusion

In this paper, we proposed a multimodal interaction approach by equipping a Fuhrat robot with a display. The assistant facilitates access to information for university students and staff. It helps the students search the educational options offered by the University of Salerno and make informed decisions about their academic and professional future. The project aims to break down informational barriers, promoting an inclusive and accessible university experience for everybody.

In the future, we plan to perform a wide evaluation to assess the human-robot dialogues, the usability of the system, and user engagement.

Acknowlegment. This project has been financially supported by the European Union NEXTGenerationEU project and by the Italian Ministry of the University and Research MUR, a Research Projects of Significant National Interest (PRIN) 2022 PNRR, project n. D53D23017290001 entitled "Supporting schizophrenia PatiEnts Care wiTh aRtificiAl intelligence (SPECTRA)".

References

1. Al Moubayed, S., et al.: Human-robot collaborative tutoring using multiparty multimodal spoken dialogue. In: ACM/IEEE International Conference on Human-Robot Interaction, pp. 112–113 (2014). https://doi.org/10.1145/2559636.2563681
2. Al Moubayed, S., Beskow, J., Skantze, G., Granström, B.: Furhat: A back-projected human-like robot head for multiparty human-machine interaction (2012). https://doi.org/10.1007/978-3-642-34584-5_9
3. Al Moubayed, S., Skantze, G., Beskow, J.: The furhat back-projected humanoid head-lip reading, gaze and multi-party interaction. Int. J. Humanoid Robot. **10**, 1350005 (2013). https://doi.org/10.1142/S0219843613500059
4. Barra, P., et al.: A task-oriented multimodal conversational interface for a CSCW immersive virtual environment. In: Proceedings of the The 22nd European Conference on Computer-Supported Cooperative Work - to appear (2024)
5. Cassell, J., et al.: Embodiment in conversational interfaces: Rea. pp. 520–527 (1999). https://doi.org/10.1145/302979.303150
6. Clavel, C., Labeau, M., Cassell, J.: Socio-conversational systems: three challenges at the crossroads of fields. Front. Robot. AI **9**, 937825 (2022)
7. Crovari, P., Pidó, S., Garzotto, F., Ceri, S.: Show, don't tell. Reflections on the design of multi-modal conversational interfaces. In: Følstad, A., et al. (eds.) CONVERSATIONS 2020. LNCS, vol. 12604, pp. 64–77. Springer, Cham (2021). https://doi.org/10.1007/978-3-030-68288-0_5
8. Francese, R., Guercio, A., Rossano, V., Bhati, D.: A multimodal conversational interface to support the creation of customized social stories for people with ASD. In: Bottoni, P., Panizzi, E. (eds.) AVI 2022: International Conference on Advanced Visual Interfaces, Frascati, Rome, Italy, June 6 - 10, 2022, pp. 19:1–19:5. ACM (2022). https://doi.org/10.1145/3531073.3531118
9. Hegel, F., Muhl, C., Wrede, B., Hielscher-Fastabend, M., Sagerer, G.: Understanding social robots. In: Proceedings of the 2nd International Conferences on Advances in Computer-Human Interactions, ACHI 2009, pp. 169–174 (02 2009).https://doi.org/10.1109/ACHI.2009.51
10. Mohamad Suhaili, S., Salim, N., Jambli, M.N.: Service chatbots: a systematic review. Expert Syst. Appl. **184**, 115461 (2021). https://doi.org/10.1016/j.eswa.2021.115461
11. Safavi, F., et al.: Emerging frontiers in human-robot interaction. J. Intell. Robot. Syst. **110**, 45 (2024). https://doi.org/10.1007/s10846-024-02074-7
12. Sheridan, T.: Human-robot interaction: status and challenges. Hum. Factors **58**, 525–532 (2016). https://doi.org/10.1177/0018720816644364
13. Suhaili, S.M., Salim, N., Jambli, M.N.: Service chatbots: a systematic review. Expert Syst. Appl. **184**, 115461 (2021)

Effect of Olfactory Presentation Timing on Memory Retention: Relationship to Default Mode Network Activity

Takuto Fukushima[1] and Takehiko Yamaguchi[2(✉)]

[1] Tokyo Institute of Technology, Ookayama 2-12-1, Meguro-City, Japan
[2] Suwa University of Science, Chino-Shi, Toyohira 5000-1, Japan
tk-ymgch@rs.sus.ac.jp

Abstract. Various effects of olfactory stimulus presentation on the retention of memory have been reported. However, no previous studies have determined the best method of olfactory presentation for improving memory retention. Therefore, this study compares olfactory pulse presentation, which induces olfactory adaptation with olfactory pulse presentation and reduces adaptation. In addition, the temporal pattern of the pulse presentation is focused on memory consolidation. This olfactory presentation during default mode network (DMN) activity. DMN is observed when information is organized in the brain. No differences were found between in the results of the memory test between continuous presentation and DMN presentation after a video was viewed. However, when the test was repeated one week later, the results showed there was a difference between the pre- and post-weekly results of the continuous presentation. However, no difference was observed between the pre- and post-weekly results of the DMN presentation. This suggests that memory retention was maintained over time after the DMN presentation. However, the temporal pattern of DMN activity may have been altered by the olfactory presentation, which suggests the need for further investigation into the temporal pattern of olfactory presentation.

Keywords: Olfactory Presentation · Memory Retention · Default Mode Network

1 Introduction

1.1 Relation Between Olfaction and Memory

There is a close relationship between olfaction and memory, and it has been shown that stimuli perceived by the sense of smell activate the hippocampus [1]. In addition, various studies have shown that olfactory presentation improves memory consolidation. As an example, a study on memory performance in an environment in which coffee aroma was presented continuously over a long period of time compared with an environment without aroma showed that performance increased was better when the coffee aroma was present [2]. However, this research presents the problem of olfactory adaptation, in which olfactory sensitivity gradually decreases with prolonged and sustained stimulus presentation. Therefore, it is essential to prevent olfactory adaptation when measuring memory retention.

M. Kurosu et al. (Eds.): HCII 2024, LNCS 15374, pp. 312–324, 2025.
https://doi.org/10.1007/978-3-031-76803-3_18

1.2 Olfactory Presentation to Reduce Olfactory Adaptation

One method of olfactory stimulus presentation that reduces olfactory adaptation is pulsed olfactory presentation, where the odorant is presented at intervals. This method has been shown to reduce olfactory adaptation [3]. Therefore, in the case of long-lasting stimulus presentations, the use of a pulsed presentation may result in less olfactory adaptation than the use of a continuous presentation of olfactory stimuli. In the present study, we focus on the difference in memory retention between pulsed and continuous stimuli presentations.

The temporal pattern of olfactory pulse presentation is critical to olfactory presentation. In conventional pulse presentation, the temporal pattern of an olfactory stimulus presentation is indexed to respiration. However, this type of presentation focuses on the perception of aroma and not on the memory retention effects of olfaction. Therefore, to investigate the effects of olfaction on memory, it is necessary to select a new and different temporal pattern of olfactory presentation.

1.3 Temporal Pattern of Olfactory Stimulus Presentation

The selection of the temporal pattern of olfactory stimulus presentation should consider the effect of temporal patterns on memory. In a previous study [3] on the reduction of olfactory adaptation, the temporal pattern of inhalation was used as the temporal pattern of olfactory stimulus presentation. However, another study [4] observed brain activity during breathing using functional magnetic resonance imaging (fMRI) and reported that the temporal pattern of inhalation reduced activity in the brain regions that control concentration and attention, which resulted in reduced cognitive function. For this reason, the use of the breathing temporal pattern may have the effect of decreasing memory, as it has in previous studies. Therefore, we propose another temporal pattern of olfactory stimulus presentation that increases brain activity during memory as a temporal pattern for improving memory retention.

1.4 Olfactory Stimulus Presentation in Elevated Brain Activity During Memory

fMRI measurements that observe brain activity interfere with a subject's consciousness. fMRI is a large device that is used to generate a high magnetic field for the observation of changes in cerebral blood flow. Therefore, the increase in brain activity observed by fMRI has the inherent problem of interference with memory. For this reason, it is important to observe brain activity without using fMRI measurements.

To observe brain activity without fMRI, physiological indices can be used. Among the physiologic indices, blinking may be used for observing brain activity in memory consolidation. It is said that the organization of information in memory consolidation is largely related to the activity of the default mode network (DMN), which is a neural network in the brain. It has been shown that blinking is induced during DMN activity [5]. Therefore, olfactory stimulus presentation during eye blinking in DMN activity can have a significant effect on memory by providing olfactory stimulus presentation at the temporal pattern of the increase in brain activity during memory.

1.5 Blinking by DMN

A study that observed blinking during DMN activity [5] reported that the blinking could be identified synchronously between and within subjects. By using this property, it is possible to distinguish the blinking during DMN activity from blinks related to other factors such as eye fatigue and dryness.

The visual stimulus used in the study in which blink synchrony was observed was a narrative video of Mr. Bean, which is a British comedy act. Therefore, we propose using a similar video in this study to confirm the synchrony of blinking.

1.6 Purpose of the Study

The purpose of this study is to clarify whether the effect of olfaction on memory retention is affected by the method of olfactory stimulus presentation. Specifically, we carried out continuous olfactory stimulus presentation and pulsed olfactory stimulus presentation (DMN presentation) using eye blinking during DMN activity as an indicator. We hypothesized that DMN presentation would be more effective in improving memory retention because it reduces the olfactory adaptation induced by continuous presentation. Therefore, the detailed purpose of this study is to investigate methods for improving memory retention that involve the temporal pattern of olfactory stimulus presentation.

2 Methods

2.1 Proposed Methods

In various previous studies, memory retention was measured using a test In the present study, a test is also used. However, because the information to be memorized by the subjects in this study uses images like those in the previous study [5], it is difficult to compare them in terms of working memory, as was done in the previous study [2]. Therefore, the experimental method we use to measure memory retention in this study is important. As mentioned earlier, it is necessary to distinguish between blinks during DMN activity and blinks for reasons such as dryness. For this purpose, the temporal pattern during DMN activity must be observed prior to the actual presentation of the olfactory stimulus. Therefore, in a Preliminary Experiment, we measured the blinking during DMN activity when subjects were viewing images to be stored in memory.

The Preliminary Experiment for distinguishing blink factors was intended to define the synchronized blinking temporal pattern during the viewing of the images used in this study. It was stated in a previous study [5] that the blinking during DMN activity is synchronized across subjects. Because it is not clear whether the method of olfactory stimulus presentation during DMN activity reduces olfactory adaptation, it is necessary to confirm olfactory perception during DMN presentation in another experiment.

In the experiment to confirm the intensity of olfactory perception during DMN presentation, we checked whether olfactory adaptation was induced by comparing the intensity of olfactory perception before and after DMN presentation. The experiment in which olfactory adaptation was confirmed by DMN presentation was designated as Preliminary

Experiment 2, and the experiment in which the temporal pattern of DMN activity was designated as Preliminary Experiment 1.

The main experiment measured memory retention and was conducted after the Preliminary Experiments 1 and 2 were conducted. As it was difficult to use the methods from the previous study [2] in the present experiment, we referred to study [6], which measured video memory.

2.2   Experimental Environment

All the experiments in this study were conducted in the environment shown in Figs. 1 and 2.

The olfactory stimulus presentation device used in this study, Aroma Shooter 3, can be controlled on Unity. Thus, any fragrance could be injected at any given time. However, if the Aroma Shooter 3 were placed in front of the eyes, it could block the subject's view and affect their vision. Similarly, the same problem could occur if a blink measurement device were used. For this reason, we used virtual reality (VR) technology for blink measurement and for the presentation of video in the experiment. The VR device used in this study was the VIVE Pro Eye developed by HTC. In addition, Liberty Air 2 Pro noise-canceling earphones were used as earplugs to remove auditory influence. Because a previous study [2] reported that coffee aroma improves memory retention, we also presented a coffee aroma was as the olfactory stimulus in this study. To prevent different olfactory perception, the position of the nose was fixed using a chin rest, as shown in Fig. 1.

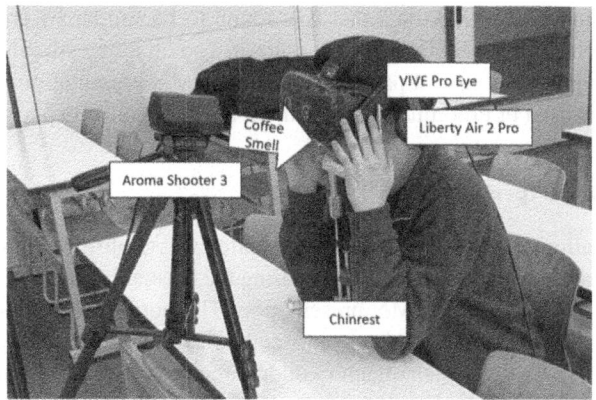

Fig. 1. Real environment

The visual stimulus presented using the VIVE Pro Eye was a virtual environment, as shown in Fig. 2. The virtual environment contained a desk and a chair, as in the real environment. The video to be memorized was presented on a monitor on the desk. To present the aroma of coffee as the olfactory stimulus, a mug with coffee poured into it was added in the virtual space to prevent the user from feeling uncomfortable with the aroma. The video to be memorized was a 10-min video of Mr. Bean.

Fig. 2. Virtual environment

2.3 Preliminary Experiment 1

In this experiment, the temporal pattern of the DMN activity in the video to be remembered was observed. The synchronized blinks that occurred during the DMN activity were measured using the VIVE Pro Eye shown in Fig. 1. The peak blink time was calculated from the data obtained. Next, to confirm whether the blink peak data at the peak time were synchronized, the peak blink data were analyzed by cross-correlational analysis.

The peak time of the blink data that was found to be similar by cross-correlation analysis was defined as the DMN temporal pattern. The olfactory stimulus presentation according to this DMN temporal pattern was called DMN presentation, and this DMN presentation was used in Preliminary Experiment 2 and the main experiment.

2.4 Preliminary Experiment 2

Olfactory adaptation in the defined DMN presentation was confirmed in this experiment. Olfactory adaptation was confirmed by comparing the normal intensity of olfaction with the intensity of olfaction after DMN presentation. The normal olfactory intensity was the perceived intensity of an odor after its presentation. To measure olfactory sensitivity, we measured the intensity of each olfactory odor perceived on a 6-point subjective rating scale of 0 to 5, as shown in Table 1 of the study [7], which measured olfactory sensitivity. The higher the perceived olfactory intensity, the higher the numerical value; if the DMN presentation causes olfactory adaptation, we would expect the rated value of olfactory intensity to be lower than the normal olfactory intensity.

2.5 Main Experiment

In this experiment, we compare the effects of different methods of olfactory stimulus presentation on memory consolidation. The measures of olfactory stimulus presentation

Table 1. Questionnaire on olfactory intensity

Questions
0: Odorless
1: Barely perceptible
2: Strong enough to detect what it smells like
3: Easily detectable
4: Strong
5: Intense

are continuous presentation and DMN presentation. A previous study [2] showed that the aroma of coffee improves memory retention. Therefore, in this experiment, we did not conduct baseline measurements with no olfactory stimulus presentation.

In this experiment, each olfactory stimulus presentation is made during the viewing of the video. This is followed by a test related to the video. For the test, a scene from the Mr. Bean video and a scene from a Mr. Bean video that was not included in the presentation were presented. The participants were asked to answer "Yes" if they remembered watching the scene and "No" if they did not remember watching the scene. This confirmation test was conducted again one week later to check the effect on long-term memory as well as on short-term memory.

It has been said that olfactory perception changes with the impression of a smell [8]. For this reason, the data to be obtained from this experiment in addition to the measurement of memory using the confirmation test were used to confirm the content of the video and impressions by smells by administering a questionnaire, which is shown in Table 2. The questionnaire was designed so that participants were asked to answer "Yes" or "No" to Q1–1, 1–7, 1–8, and 2–1, and to give a higher number, from 1 to 7, in answer to the other questions if they felt strongly about them. In addition, as in the Preliminary Experiment 1, blink data during the olfactory stimulus presentation were also obtained. From this data, we compared the differences in the temporal pattern of DMN activity between the different methods of olfactory stimulus presentation.

The results of the confirmation test immediately after the olfactory stimulus presentation are based on a previous study [2], and we hypothesize that no difference in memory performance will be observed due to the olfactory stimulus presentation method. However, as the DMN presentation approaches the time of DMN activity, it is possible that memory could be stored for a longer period. Therefore, we hypothesize that a difference will be observed in the confirmation test performance after one week.

Table 2. Questionnaire on video content and olfactory stimulus presentation

1.About the video content	2.About olfactory presentation
1. Viewing the video made feel sick	1. Olfactory presentation made feel sick
2. Impression of the video	2. Impression of the scent
3. Preference for the video	3. Preference for the scent
4. Enjoyment of the video	4. Unnaturalness of the scent
5. Degree of concentration on the video	5. Disturbance of consciousness by olfactory presentation
6. Sleepiness while viewing the video	
7. Degree of disturbance to viewing the video	
8. Experience of watching the video	

3   Results and Discussion

3.1   Preliminary Experiment 1

Figure 3 shows the time series of the blink rates. There are five subjects in this experiment. The incidence at any given point in time is calculated at 20% intervals. In Fig. 3, the peaks in blink incidence are at 15, 23, 27, 141, 362, 368, 469, and 523 s.

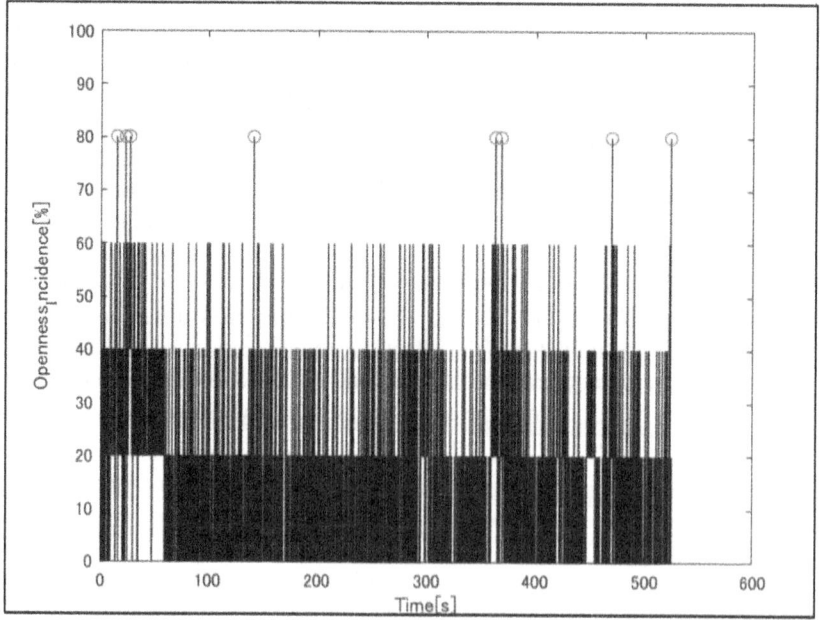

Fig. 3. Blink incidence

However, the temporal pattern revealed in the above figure is the temporal pattern of the moment when most blinks occur. Therefore, it is not known whether it is the beginning or the end of the blink in each subject. For this reason, the peak blink is not a synchronized blink. To examine the synchronization of blinks, the similarity in the data before and after the peak blink must be analyzed by cross-correlation.

Figure 4 shows the results of cross-correlation analysis on the blink data at 141 s. As can be seen from the figure, significant correlations were obtained with very small lags for all subjects except one. The one subject who did not synchronize had never used the VR equipment used in the experiment. From this result, we concluded that the reason for the lack of synchronization was that the subject was not concentrating on the images and felt anxious.

Figure 4 shows the blink data at the 141 s time point, but the same analysis was conducted for a different location at the peak, and the same significant correlation was obtained with a small lag. Thus, all the blink data at peak incidence were similar. Considering this, we defined the peak incidence as the blink synchronized by the DMN, and we defined the temporal pattern of this peak as the DMN temporal pattern. All DMN presentations in future experiments refer to olfactory stimulus presentations at this peak temporal pattern.

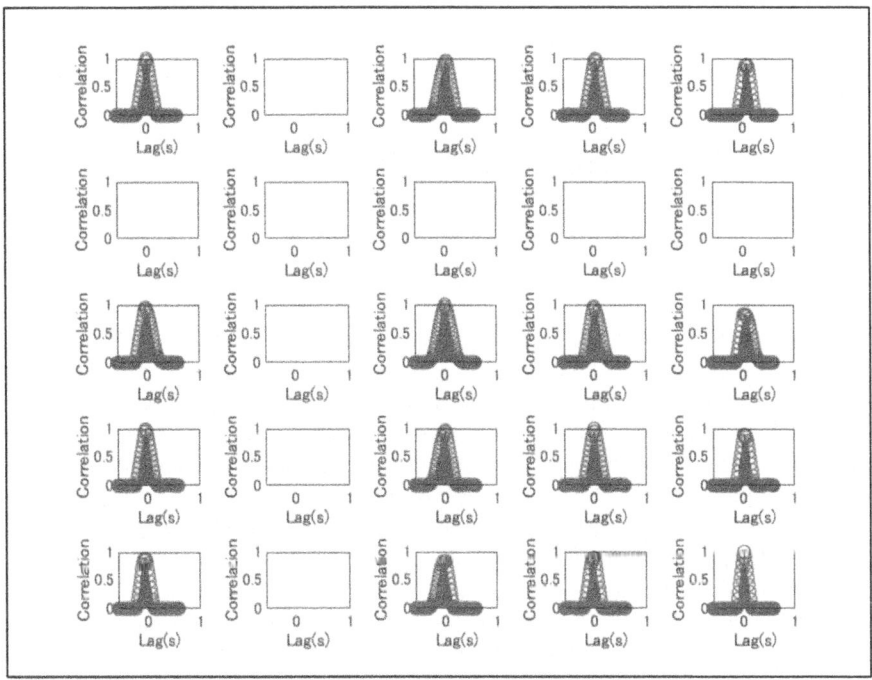

Fig. 4. Cross-correlation analysis results

3.2 Preliminary Experiment 2

The olfactory sensitivity intensity of the defined DMN presentation before [pre] and after [post] presentation was obtained and is shown in Fig. 5. A comparison of the olfactory sensitivity intensity before and after presentation by the U-test revealed a significant increase with $p < 0.05$. The result of no decrease in olfactory sensitivity would suggest that DMN presentation is unlikely to induce olfactory adaptation. Therefore, it is possible that DMN presentation may induce different cognitive functions than does a continuous presentation that would induce olfactory adaptation.

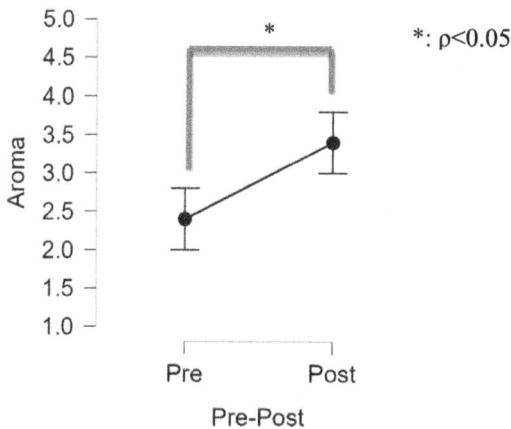

Fig. 5. Olfactory sensitivity plot

3.3 Main Experiment

Questionnaire Results. Table 3 presents a comparison of the results of the question-naires in this experiment. It compares the questionnaire results for the continuous and the DMN presentations of stimuli using the Mann–Whitney U-test. The results for Q1–1 and 2–1 did not show that all subjects felt worse. However, some subjects felt disturbed by the environmental noise from Q1–7 during viewing, and some subjects who knew the video content from Q1–8 were excluded from this experiment.

Table 3 shows that there were no significant differences between the questionnaires. Therefore, there was no difference in the subjective evaluation of the perception of visual and olfactory stimuli according to the olfactory stimulus presentation method. From this result, it can be assumed that there was no difference in the sensory reception of the stimuli between the different olfactory stimulus presentation methods.

Results of Confirmation Test. In the analysis of the test performance, four groups were analyzed: pre-, post-, continuous-, and DMN presentation. As in a previous study [6], the test performance was calculated as the Corrected Recognition Score (CRS), which is the proportion of correct responses (hit rate) minus the proportion of incorrect responses (miss rate).

Table 3. U-test results

Question	W	ρ	R-B Correlation	SE R-B Correlation
1–1	No subject was offended by the video presentation			
1–2	33.000	0.268	0.347	0.309
1–3	17.000	0.355	− 0.306	0.309
1–4	14.000	0.176	− 0.429	0.309
1–5	29.000	0.582	0.184	0.309
1–6	23.000	0.895	− 0.061	0.309
1–7	One subject was disturbed (and was excluded from the group of subjects)			
1–8	One subject (had experienced watching the video (and was excluded from the group of subjects			
2–1	No subjects were sickened by the presentation of the olfactory stimulus			
2–2	18.000	0.430	− 0.265	0.309
2–3	23.000	0.897	− 0.061	0.309
2–4	19.000	0.515	− 0.224	0.309
2–5	17.500	0.290	− 0.286	0.309

As equal variance and normality were observed in the CRS for each subject group, an analysis of variance was performed. Figure 6 shows the results of the two-way ANOVA for the four groups. There was no effect of olfactory stimulus presentation on the short-term memory performance in the immediate post-memory period. However, one week later, different results were obtained that depended on the method of olfactory stimulus presentation. For the continuous presentation, there was a significant difference between the pre and post results. This was because the subjects' memories were lost over time. This result suggests that the subjects in the continuous presentation did not exhibit long-term memory. However, the DMN presentation showed there was no significant difference between pre and post. This suggests that the content may have been retained even one week after the memory. This suggests that the DMN presentation may increase memory retention and enable longer retention than does the continuous presentation. A significant difference ($\rho < 0.05$) was also observed for the interaction between the two factors. This result suggests that an effect of olfactory stimulus presentation on memory retention may appear over time.

The results of a previous study [9] might have been related to the factors that led to these results. The previous study [9] observed brain activity during sustained olfactory stimulus presentations, such as the continuous presentation in this experiment. The results [9] revealed that the brain's cognitive processing speed decreased during continuous presentation. In addition, the longer the olfactory stimulus presentation time, the greater the activation in the regions of the brain that control emotion, whereas activation in the regions that control memory were not augmented. These results suggest that the

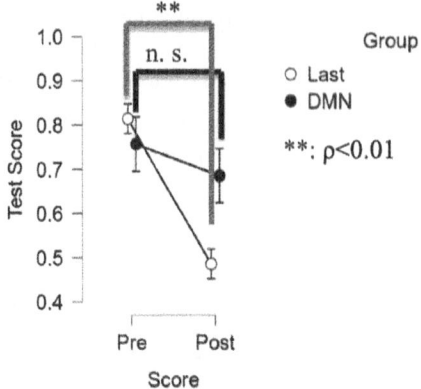

Fig. 6. CRS mean plot

memory regions in the brain were activated more during DMN presentation than during continuous presentation, and that this may have resulted in a difference in memory retention.

Blink Data. As in Preliminary Experiment 1, we analyzed the blink data in this experiment to calculate the temporal pattern of DMN activity. Figure 7 presents a plot of the incidence of blinks during continuous presentation, and Fig. 8 plots the incidence during DMN presentation.

It is clear from the figures that the peak temporal patterns of the incidence are different. This suggests that the temporal pattern of DMN activity may vary depending on the olfactory stimulus presentation method. The peak temporal patterns in Fig. 7 and Fig. 8 are different from the peak incidence temporal pattern in Preliminary Experiment 1, which suggests that the DMN activity temporal pattern may also change with or without olfactory stimulus presentation. In this experiment, olfactory stimulus presentation according to the temporal pattern of DMN activity defined in Preliminary Experiment 1 was used to improve memory retention. However, if olfactory stimulus presentation changes the temporal pattern of DMN activity, the improvement in memory retention by DMN presentation may not be due to DMN activity. Therefore, the improvement in memory retention revealed by the two-way ANOVA suggests that the method of olfactory stimulus presentation, which was pulse presentation, might have affected memory retention, rather than the temporal pattern of olfactory stimulus presentation being important.

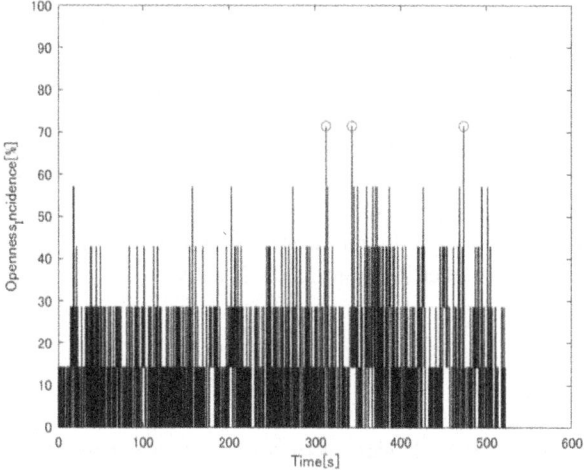

Fig. 7. Blink incidence [continuous presentation]

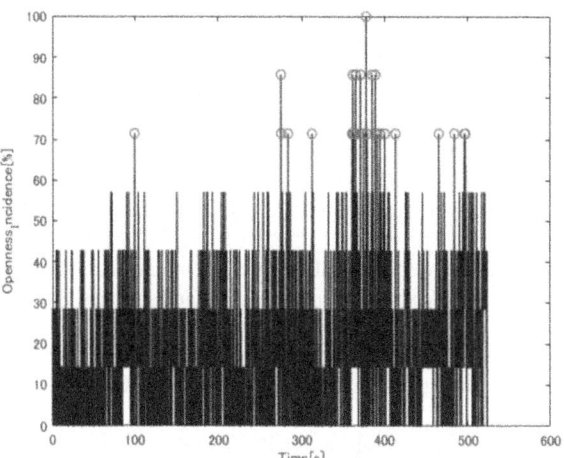

Fig. 8. Blink incidence [DMN presentation]

4 Conclusion

In this study, we found that the effect on long-term memory varied depending on the method of olfactory stimulus presentation. One of the methods of olfactory stimulus presentation focused on the DMN, which is active during memory consolidation. We compared the degree of memory consolidation between the DMN presentation during DMN activity and the conventional continuous presentation. The results suggest that visual images may be retained for as long as one week after DMN presentation. However, continuous presentation showed a lack of memory content, in line with the Ebbinghaus forgetting curve. This indicates that different olfactory stimulus presentation methods have different effects on memory.

As a result of other, it was not possible to clarify the relationship between DMN and memory. The DMN presentation used in this experiment was a method of olfactory stimulus presentation during DMN activity. However, the results did not indicate that DMN activity affected memory, because the temporal pattern of DMN activity was altered by olfactory stimulus presentation. For these reasons, further investigation into the factors that enhance memory retention is needed, such as comparing pulse presentations that use temporal patterns other than during DMN activity.

References

1. Igarashi, K.M., Lu, L., Colgin, L.L., Moser, M.-B., Moser, E.I.: Coordination of entorhinal-hippocampal ensemble activity during associative learning. Nature **510**(7503), 143–147 (2014)
2. Hawiset, T.: Effect of one-time coffee fragrance inhalation on working memory, mood, and salivary cortisol level in healthy young volunteers: a randomized placebo-controlled trial. Integr. Med. Res. **8**(4), 273–278 (2019)
3. Kadowaki, A., Sato, J., Bannai, Y., Okada, K.-I.: presentation technique of scent to avoid olfactory adaptation. In: 17th International Conference on Artificial Reality and Telexistence (ICAT 2007), pp. 97–104 (2007)
4. Nakamura, N.H., Fukunaga, M., Yamamoto, T., Sadato, N., Oku, Y.: Respiration-timing-dependent changes in activation of neural substrates during cognitive processes. Cereb. Cortex Commun. **3**(4), tgac038 (2022)
5. Nakano, T., Yamamoto, Y., Kitajo, K., Takahashi, T., Kitazawa, S.: Synchronization of spontaneous eyeblinks while viewing video stories. Proc. R. Soc. B: Biol. Sci. **276**(1673), 3635–3644 (2009)
6. Yoshioka, K., Iwanaga, M.: Memory facilitation effect in interaction between video clips and music, bulletin of the graduate school of integrated arts and sciences. Stud. Hum. Sci. **2**, 35–45 (2007)
7. Saito, S., Ayabe-Kanamura, S., Kobayakawa, T.: Relation of time intensity curves with perceptual characteristics during odor exposure. J. Jpn. Assoc. Odor Environ. **39**(6), 399–407 (2008)
8. Sakai, N., Kobayakawa, T., Saito, S.: Effect of description of odor on perception and adaptation of the odor. J. Jpn. Assoc. Odor Environ. **35**(1), 22–25 (2004)
9. Tang, B.-B., et al.: The effect of odor exposure time on olfactory cognitive processing: an ERP study. J. Integr. Neurosci. **18**(1), 87–93 (2019)

A Stereohaptics Accessory for Spatial Computing Platforms

Ali Israr[1,3]([✉]), Asad Tirmizi[1], Bo Zhu[2], Dehao Zhao[2], Erting Cheng[2], and Zachary Schwemler[1]

[1] Pico Immersive US Inc., Bellevue, WA 98004, USA
ali.israr@bytedance.com
[2] Pico Immersive China, Beijing, China
[3] ViiVai Inc, Seattle, USA

Abstract. We present a stereohaptic accessory mounted on the back of a head mounted display (HMD) to enable spatial haptic interactions in spatial computing applications. The accessory consists of two broadband haptic actuators placed symmetric to the sagittal plane of the back of the head, and digitally connects to the HMD via the USB port. We provide design guidelines to achieve engineering performance and human-factor requirements, and build a prototype module. We utilize Android's audio support to independently control dual haptic channels. To accommodate haptic content design, we utilize audio based authoring tools and custom algorithms to auto generate haptic content directly from the audio media. We use these development tools to build haptic experience for watching videos, bare hand interactions, and mitigating cybersickness. Our evaluation shows that the accessory increases immersion, engagement, user efficiency and reduces VR sickness in dynamic spatial environments.

Keywords: Stereohaptics · Cybersickness · Bare Hand Interactions · Head Haptic feedback · Haptic Videos

1 Introduction

In the era of spatial computing, technologies are poised to render multisensory information around the user (or users) while logging their activities, status and intents. Many spatial computing platforms, such as Meta Quest 3 and Apple Vision Pro, completely or partially overlay the real world with audio-visual content and associate it to head, hand and body movements to increase user throughput between real and digital worlds. These platforms deploy high resolution, low latency and wide field-of-view of sensory feedback with seamless tracking, thereby making interactions natural, intuitive, enjoyable, comfortable and efficient. Almost all platforms accommodate high-definition stereoscopic visual feeds with two speakers to render multisensory spatial experience for their users. In this paper, we design and test a dual channel stereohaptic accessory mounted on the back of the head to render broadband directional vibration feedback (see

M. Kurosu et al. (Eds.): HCII 2024, LNCS 15374, pp. 325–340, 2025.
https://doi.org/10.1007/978-3-031-76803-3_19

Fig. 1). This way, users not only see and hear but also feel the spatial haptic feedback corresponding to activities and audio-visual feeds, and enhances the sensory experience while playing games, watching videos, navigating places, and social interactions, etc.

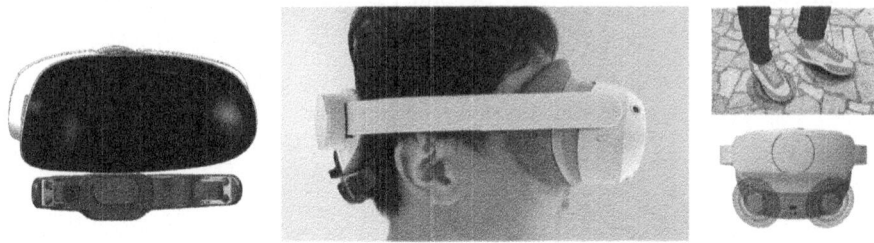

Fig. 1. A stereohaptic accessory attached on the back of a VR device. Foot steps are mapped to the two haptic units on the back of the head.

While hand controllers are commonly used for user inputs, modern spatial computing devices use camera systems, inertial measurement units (IMUs), and computer vision (CV) inspired multimodal machine learning techniques to track user head, hand and body movements, thereby removing the need of controllers during typical manual interactions [1]. These bare hand interactions combined with gaze input reduce user effort during manual tasks, while increasing the task efficiency using adaptive AI-based interaction models [2]. However, lack of haptic feedback to close the action confirmation loop during selection and manipulation tasks overloads audio-visual pathways, creating uncertainty and confusion in users and consequently increases errors and reduces efficiency in spatial tasks [3]. In preliminary studies, we evaluated haptic feedback presented on the back of the head during manual input for 'selection' and 'manipulation' tasks and observed that users quickly learnt the referred feedback when actions were performed on the hands and feedback was provided on the back of the head. We also compared the efficiency of 'text input' with gaze-pinch input and showed that selection with haptic feedback yielded lower errors and faster typing speed.

Another challenge with spatial computing platforms is the "virtual dizziness" (or cybersickness) induced due to sensory mismatch between the dynamic visual content and body movements sensed in the inner ear (vestibular system) [4]. Low resolution, high latency and weight of head mounted displays amplify cybersickness and increase discomfort in users, resulting in low retention rates and customers satisfaction [5]. Mitigation techniques include modifying the field-of-view to limit peripheral vision, playing pleasant music and odors [6,7], electric nerve stimulations (ENS) applied on the neck, legs and ears [8,9], and head vibrations [10,11]. We hypothesize that transcutaneous stimulation of the occipital bone on the back of the head will alleviate cybersickness in dynamic virtual scenes. We utilize the dual-channel haptic accessory as a mitigation scheme while users navigate through VR spaces by walking, running, climbing, and zip lining, and evaluated the influence of haptic feedback.

The organization of the paper is as follows. In Sect. 2, we describe the design of the haptic accessory and guidelines to build a prototype module. We evaluate the design with structural tests to meet engineering criteria and with subjective user tests to rate the quality of vibrations and human factor metrics. In Sect. 3, we describe a software development kit (SDK) to integrate the haptic accessory into spatial computing applications, and describe a haptic content development pipeline to author haptic content from scratch or from audio-visual feeds. In Sect. 4, we describe interactive scenarios to illustrate use cases of the dual-channel haptic accessory, and report a series of preliminary user studies to verify the value added by the haptic accessory in spatial computation applications. Particularly, we show that synchronized haptic feedback on the back of the head i) increases user engagement and immersion while playing video games and watching videos, ii) closes the action-confirmation loop and improves user efficiency in bare hand and gaze input scenarios, and iii) alleviates cybersickness evaluated by a standard simulator sickness questionnaire (SSQ). Finally, the paper concludes with Sect. 5.

2 Device Design and Prototype Build

We performed both structural and industrial design exercises to converge on a set of device-design guidelines that accounted for many practical and engineering constraints. We built a set of intermediate prototypes, and evaluated them using subjective and objective measures to converge on acceptable solutions. Finally, we built the prototype and verified design decisions. These exercises and guidelines are described in this section.

Key design criteria for the haptic accessory device was to enable seamless hand-free haptic feedback while ensuring natural, intuitive and comfortable user experience. The design should also justify the cost, size, weight and power requirements, in addition to reducing structural noise, improving perceivability, and user acceptability. This section describes the design pipeline for a viable haptic prototype.

2.1 Location of Haptic Stimulation

Several parameters were considered to determine the location of haptic stimulation for spatial computing applications. These included device form factor, device donning and doffing, anatomical and perceptual characteristics, user mobility, interaction models, and user acceptance. First, we evaluated wristbands, palm-rings and rings which were worn on the arm close to hand interactions. These wearable solutions can be used as an independent standalone accessory but adds constraints for data communication and electric power. Spatial computing platforms mainly consist of a head-mounted display that provides compute, power and sensors for user tracking. Therefore, we selected the head as a source of vibration and designed a detachable accessory for a typical head mounted display.

Several head locations were evaluated to account for anatomical variations, user perception, structural noise and sensor interference. Figure 2 shows early prototypes to conduct preliminary tests, and Fig. 3 shows comparative analysis of five head locations by 5 participants. We avoided direct stimulation to the upper skull because one, the sensitivity of vibration at the skull is low, and two, it's direct anatomical association with the neocortex.

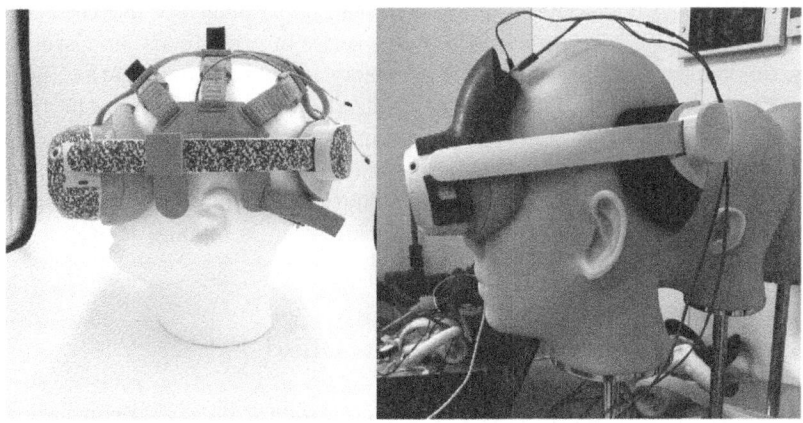

Fig. 2. Early prototypes used to evaluate structure resonance and location and number of channels.

	Front	Temple	Side	Back	Back Bottom	Specification
HMD Shaking and vibrations	High	High	Mid	Mid	Mid	No or low no shaking of the front HMD
Audio Interference	Low	High	High	Mid	Low	No or low noise interference
Comfortable	Mid	Low	Mid	Mid	High	High comfort
Vibration Sensitivity	High	High	High	Low	Mid	High sensitivity to intensity and frequency
Vibration Pleasantness	Low	Mid	Mid	Mid	High	Highly pleasant

Fig. 3. Comparison of vibrations at different head locations. The table shows mode of the user responses (N=5).

Vibrations at the front of the head created structural resonance that resulted in shaking of the headset, particularly the optical system and embedded IMU.

Vibrations on the temporal bones were audible and interfered with the audio content. Vibrations on the back were less sensitive to localization, and vibrations on the lower back of the head (i.e., subcutaneous vibrations to the occipital bone) were recognizable, pleasant and interfered less with components in the front of the HMD. Therefore, we selected the back of the head for haptic stimulation.

2.2 Number and Placement of Haptic Actuators

We evaluated 1, 2, 3, 4 or 6 vibration channels systemically placed around the head. A single haptic channel provided pleasant feedback, had less structural issues but completely eliminated the spatial aspect of haptics. Three and above channels rendered high-resolution 360 and 3D haptic locations and movements around the head, but they also increased weight, power, structural resonance, computational and component costs. A good compromise was to use two haptic channels that provided a dual-channel solution for left-and-right spatial feedback. In addition, dual-channel haptics are synonym to stereo-audio channels available as a standard in almost all HMDs and operating systems, and are shown to render localized and moving sensory illusions [12].

We determined rendering parameters of illusory locations and movements between the two channels and synchronized them with audio-visual feeds to create spatial feedback on the head. We conducted a preliminary study to determine the separation between two haptic actuators on the back of the head. Three inter-stimulus-distance (ISD) were tested on three participants. The location of haptic actuators on the back of the head are shown in Fig. 4(a). Participants had difficulty in locating the direction of tactile illusion when the channels were 3 in. apart, while 7 in. separation was too wide to elicit continuous illusory motion without gaps. ISD of 5 in. yielded acceptable location detection and feeling of continuous motion.

2.3 Type of Haptic Stimulation

We tested two broadband voice coil motors (VCM) to evaluate the sensitivity and pleasantness of vibrations on the head. These VCMs were Tectonic Audio Labs' TEAX25C05-8 (tectonicaudiolabs.com) and ThorEngine's M05 (thorinnovation.com). Mono-frequency vibrations below 30 Hz were imperceptible at the back of the head even at full intensity due to small device movement (up to a 3 mm), low tactile sensitivity and cushioning due to the hair [13]. Vibrations above 250 Hz were audible and felt synthetic. Therefore, we tested intermediate frequencies between 30–250 Hz at various intensity levels to evaluate the sensitivity and hedonic features of vibrations on the back of the head.

Generally vibrations in the 15–30 dBSL (dB sensation level, 0 dBSL is the detection threshold level) were easily detected, localized and differentiable, and was determined to be a useful intensity range for haptic feedback. Vibrations above 40 dBSL generated structural noise and felt uncomfortable. Low frequency vibrations were generally pleasant but felt weak. Most pleasant ratings were given

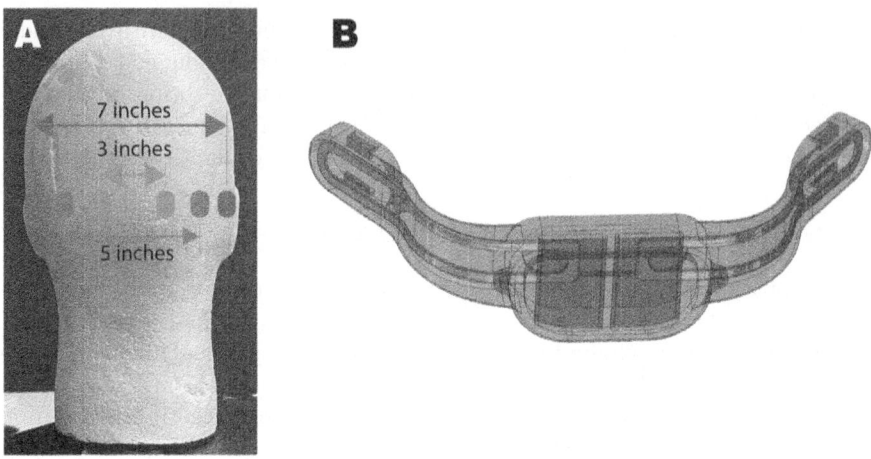

Fig. 4. (a) Inter-stimulus-distance tested on the back of the head to determine acceptable separation. (b) Structural design of the accessory with an inner core.

to vibrations between 80–120 Hz in the intensity range. Therefore, we used 80–120 Hz vibrations as a base driving signal for creating the haptic content.

Low frequency pressure-indentations and skin-stretch haptic feedback were considered early in the design phases but not prototyped. This would require designing a complex structure, using bigger and heavier motors, and consuming higher power [14,15]. Electric stimulation was also investigated but determined complex due to electrode design, skin contact, safety and subjective variability. We will resume these investigations in our future research.

2.4 Structural Design

The structural design of the haptic accessory is to ensure 1) vibrations are localized at the point of stimulation under contact loading, 2) the fidelity of vibrations are preserved instead of fading in the structure, and 3) structural resonance due to vibrations are reduced to accepted levels.

Rigid structures, such as plastic, dampened vibrations at the source and transmitted them to the whole structure resulting in increased resonance and low haptic saliency. Structures made of entire soft materials (such as rubber or elastomers) increased vibration fidelity but did not maintain consistent contact conditions and structural rigidity. Therefore, a hybrid approach was taken where the core of the accessory was made from a thin high strength resin and the outer layer was injected molded with 40A black pourable urethane rubber (Smooth-On KX Flex 40). Haptic actuators were attached to the extreme ends of the structure using 3M VHB (4991) adhesive tape and enclosed in a silicone housing for consistent conformable contact with the head. Figure 4(b) shows the main structure of the accessory with the rigid inner core connecting the central housing to the actuators.

Finite element analysis and detailed structural evaluation are beyond the scope of the work presented here. We conducted a preliminary structural analysis and compared the performance between rigid and hybrid designs. The accessory was attached to the HMD and mounted on a dummy head. A reference test signal

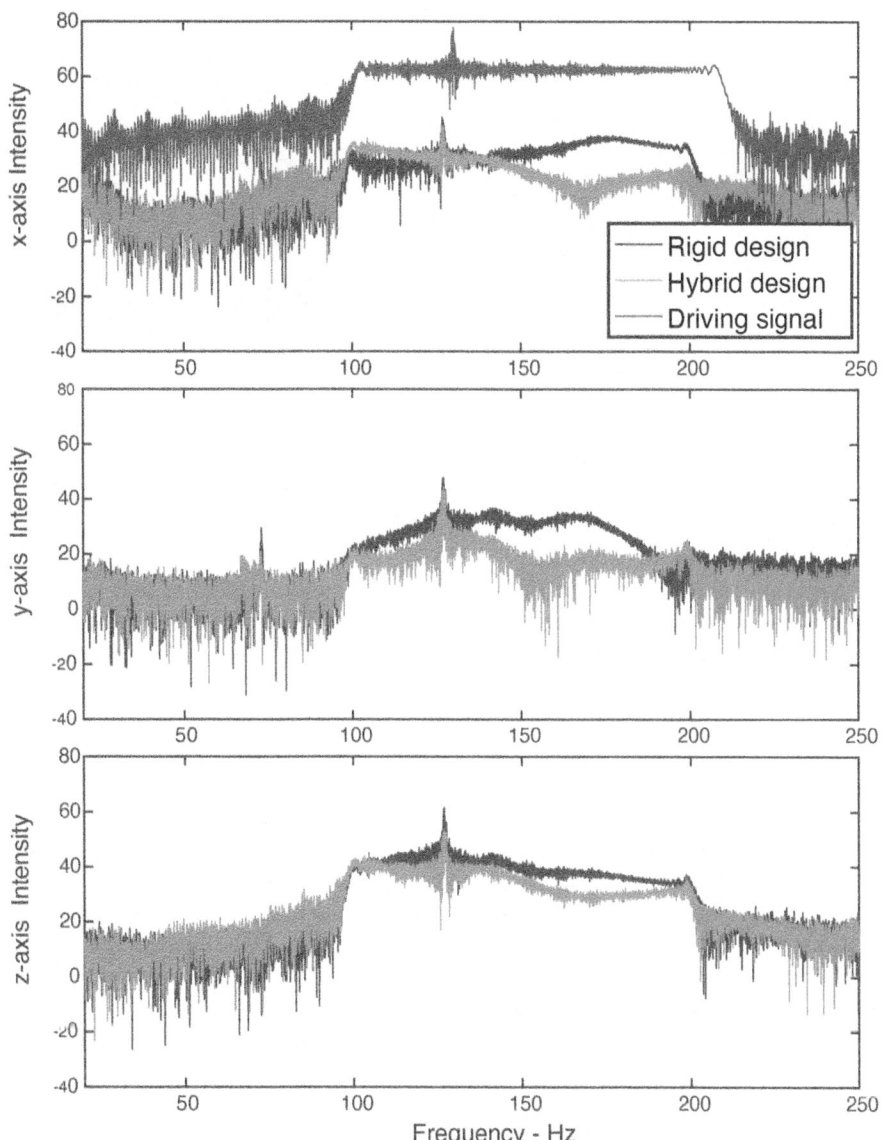

Fig. 5. Frequency response (FFT) of the rigit and hybrid structural along x-axis (top), y-axis (center) and z-axis (bottom). Overall the hydrid design (green curve) reduces the vibration intensity compared with the rigid design (blue curve). (Color figure online)

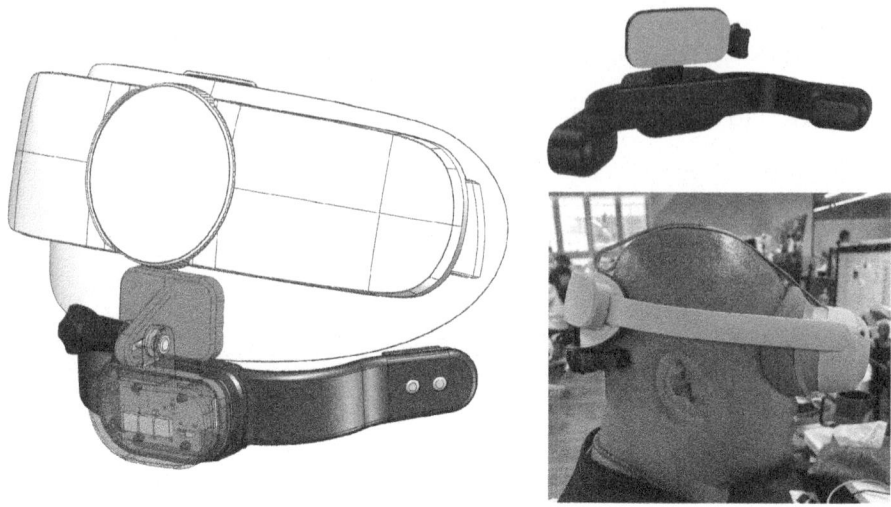

Fig. 6. Final design of the accessory to stimulate the lower back head.

composed of broadband haptic effects was played through the two channels, and the three-axes acceleration was measured using a built-in IMU sensor placed in the front of the headset. The frequency responses of the reference signal (red) and acceleration data is shown in Fig. 5.

In all three axes, the structural resonance collected on the front of the headset was reduced in the hybrid design, compared to the rigid design, specifically above 150 Hz. The overall intensity of vibration was below the threshold for head tracking algorithm and did not produce uncomfortable shaking experience with the hybrid design.

2.5   Wearability and Outlook

Several design choices were accommodated in order to ensure user comfort, long term wearability, easy usability, and sleek and modern outlook. The final design of the accessory is shown in Fig. 6. The accessory was made symmetric to counter mass distribution on the head during head movements. The flexural arm structure ensured comfortable and consistent contact pressure while users sat down or moved around while wearing the headset. A knob and a quick-release connection scheme allowed removal of the accessory from the headset, and a slot on the back allowed quick adjustment to conform the accessory around various head shapes and sizes. A PCB was placed in the back central panel with a UBC-C connector and an LED to light up the device during operation. The overall design did not interfere with donning and doffing the head mounted device. The total weight of the accessory (including connectors, PCB and actuators) was 63 g. This weight did not bother users because i) it was distributed along the shape of the head and ii) it countered the weight of the display system of the HMD.

3   SW Framework and Content Generation Tools

In order for the developers to quickly integrate the accessory in their applications, we utilized the audio architecture to playback haptic signals. We also report development tools and algorithms for quick development of haptic content and render them with audio-visual feeds.

3.1   SW Framework and SDK

Two common operating systems in the spatial computing device market, i.e. iOS and Android, support multiple audio channels. Default Android playback is tested for multichannel support to eight channels. In order to reduce new software development and increase user adaptability, we utilized two audio channels for haptics playback, similar to stereo-audio channels [12]. Once the accessory is attached to the USB-C port of the HMD, the software detects a haptic accessory, and uses haptics channels independent from the speaker output. This way, users can playback haptics experience without interfering with the audio throughput.

We updated these features in the SDK provided by Pico Immersive [16], and used the "buffered haptics" framework to support .WAV files to pass through the haptic accessory attached to the Pico 4 XR device [17]. In addition, when the haptic accessory was connected to the PC (both Windows, MacOS), then the accessory appeared as a new audio device and users directly output haptic signal through the audio device. This provided flexibility to operate the accessory using audio tools without developing a new processing, real-time and communication architecture. In the current implementation, haptic signals were generated and stored ahead of time. Future work will integrate real-time haptic content generation and parametric haptic rendering engine. The next subsection describes a development pipeline and tools to generate haptic content for the scenarios discussed in Sect. 4. All interactions scenarios are made with the Unity game engine (https://unity.com/).

3.2   Haptic Content Design

A set of tools were realized to create haptic content. These include audio-based editor tools to generate and save haptic signals, and an algorithm to auto-generate haptic media directly from the audio content. The editor tool allowed video, audio and haptics to overlay in the same timeline, adjust and play them simultaneously to the content creator's satisfaction, and save them for deployment in applications. Figure 7(a) shows a screenshot of CapCut [18], an AI driven video and audio creative platform, with video, audio and haptic tracks shown in the timeline. Haptic tracks can be modified using audio filters and exported as .WAV file.

In addition to the editor tools, we accommodated audio-to-haptic algorithms to generate haptic content from directly translating the audio content. This reduces creators' time and effort, as well as applies audio-based Large Language Models (LLMs) and AI algorithms for generating haptic content. The algorithm

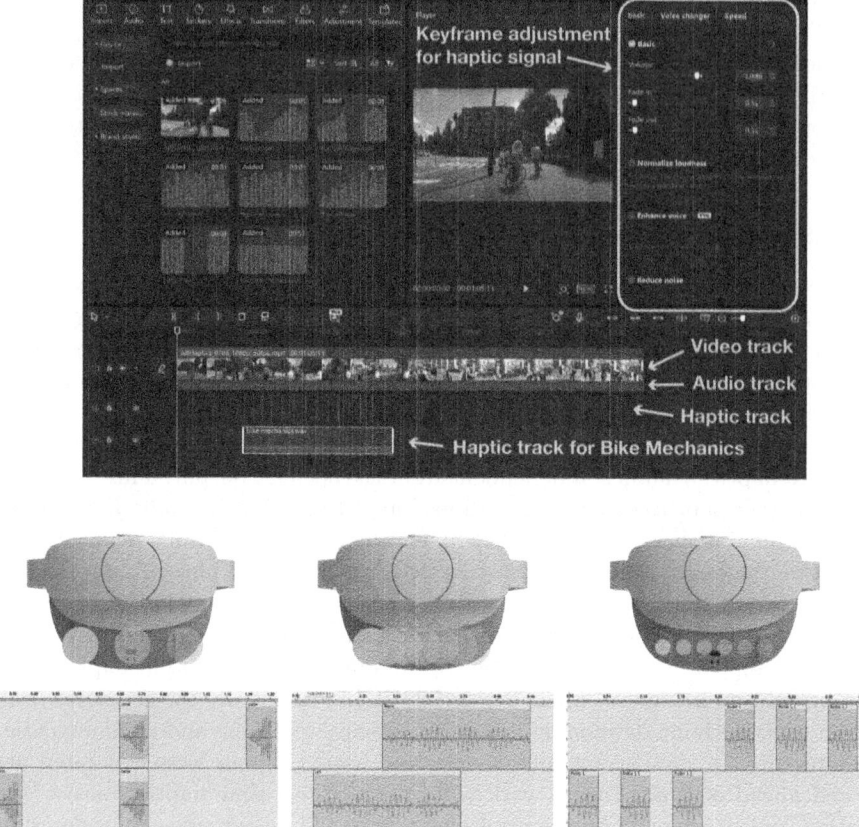

Fig. 7. (Top) Typical editor tool for audio-video content is utilized for haptic content creation and tuning. (Bottom) Three sensory illusions created on the back of the head by modulating the amplitude, duration and time offset between the two actuators

removed vocals from the audio signal, preserved spatial features, and compressed the broadband audio signal to narrow band haptic signal. Details of the algorithm and its applications with LLMs will be discussed in detail in another publication. The algorithm was used to process audio signals from movies, music, and games to generate haptic content.

Finally, we developed psychophysical models to elicit sensory illusions between the two actuators, as described in [12]. These models are accounted for the actuators in the accessory and optimized for the back of the head. Figure 7(b) shows signal parameters to elicit three common sensory illusions. Three participants evaluated these illusions and affirmed the sensation of location, motion and saltation illusions. These models were used to create spatial haptic patterns, and saved as .WAV files.

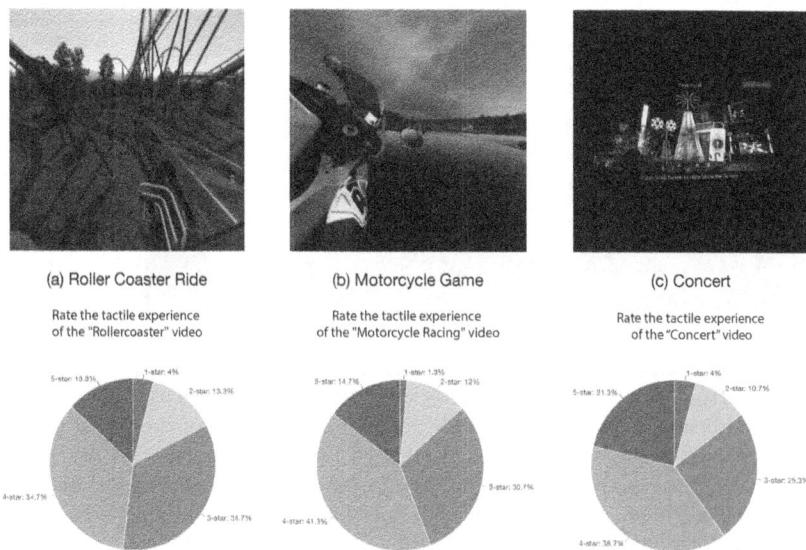

Fig. 8. 3D videos are enhanced by coherent haptic feedback to enjoy (a) a roller coaster ride, (b) a motorcycle game, and (c) an enhanced experience, and subjective ratings by n=75 participants

4   Interaction Scenarios

In this section, we evaluated haptic feedback presented on the back of the head during interactions within spatial computing scenarios. The purpose of haptic feedback is to i) increase immersion during playing games, watching 3D videos, and listening to music, ii) increase user efficiency during hand-free interactions, and iii) alleviate VR dizziness.

4.1   Enhancing 3D Videos

Three video experiences were realized to be viewed in VR (Fig. 8). Video 1 was a clip of a 1-minute long roller coaster ride, where spatial haptic feedback associated with speed and head movements was rendered with the accessory. The speed of the roller coaster was mapped to the intensity of haptic signal and turns were mapped to the location of haptics on the head, i.e., left tuning roller coaster activated the left haptic channel and right turning activated the right channel. Straight movements activated both channels. Therefore, left-to-right turns are felt as haptic movements also moving from the left side of the head to the right side. Rumbles from the tracks were detected from the audio of the clip, and mapped to the source haptic outputs.

Video 2 was a footage taken from a motorcycle game, and stereohaptic feedback associated with engine rumble, gear shifts, body tilts and road textures were rendered. The location of vibrations moved on the head based on player

Fig. 9. The application showing three interaction scenarios with bare hands. (a) Confirmation of button clicks reduced the errors for button presses, (b) Dragging a folder felt different and heavier than dragging a file, and (c) the location of the vibration moved with the location along a 1D slider. (d) UI used for the typing task. A user gazes to highlight the "Backspace" key and pinches to select it. (e) Text input comparisons with a gaze-controller (black), gaze-pinch coordination (light grey), and gaze-pinch coordination with haptic feedback (dark grey) (Color figure online)

tilt, i.e., the right tilt triggered right vibrations and the left tilt triggered left vibrations. Similarly, vibrations morphed from smooth to textured as the player slid from the center of the road to side pavement. Video 3 was an enhanced concert experience of "We will rock you" by Queen, enhanced by LED light patterns and haptic feedback. All haptic effects were built using the audio-to-haptic algorithm and modified using the editor tool describe in the last section.

The videos were demonstrated to 75 participants, who rated each video on a 1-star to 5-star rating scale. Average rating scores were 3.4-star, 3.6-star and 3.6-star for the roller coaster, motorcycle and concert experience, respectively (see Fig. 8). When asked if haptic feedback reduced dizziness in the virtual experience, 51 of the 75 participants (68%) responded affirmatively. Some participants mentioned that they were very sensitive to motion sickness in VR but these experiences did not induce discomfort.

4.2 Hand-Free and Hand-Gaze Interactions

One main feature of the spatial computing platform is to enable hand free interactions, allowing users to have natural, effortless and error free experience during manual spatial tasks. Hand and body tracking are accomplished by sensors and cameras mounted on the HMD and use sophisticated machine learning algorithms to recognize user gestures. However these algorithms are not perfect and are prone to errors, and therefore demand higher visual attention and yield low efficiency. We utilized haptic feedback on the back of the head to close the action confirmation loop, and hypothesize that timely haptic feedback on the back of the head is intuitive and improves user efficiency.

We evaluated the efficacy of the stereohaptic accessory in two applications, one with hand-free interaction and the other using hand-gaze interactions. In the first application, we tested three UI widgets, namely, button clicks, select and drag files, and a 1D horizontal slider (see Fig. 9). The HMD tracked user hands and their actions, and provided feedback on the back of the head. The user felt feedback to confirm their actions associated with pressing buttons clicks, snapping on files and dragging friction forces associated with the size of the files and user motion, and spatial haptic feedback associated with the location of the slider. As the user moved the slider from extreme left to extreme right then the haptic feedback on the back of the head gradually moved from the left side of the head to the right side.

We tested the application with five participants and collected their feedback. The evaluation indicated that the feedback was quickly learnt by participants, who felt spatial feedback associated with different file types and slider locations, therefore allowing users eyes-away interactions while performing spatial tasks. Users were more confident about their action and encountered lesser errors in the presence of haptic feedback. A detailed user study will evaluate the efficacy and quantitative improvements in the presence of haptics feedback.

In the second application, we evaluated the efficiency of haptic feedback during text input using gaze. The gaze input was estimated by the eye tracking feature of the Pico 4 device. Five users participated in a preliminary study, where users gazed over a keyboard to move the cursor at the location of gaze, and then pressed the key using a pinch by any of their hands. Each participant entered six 4 word sentences in two test conditions, with and without haptic feedback. The order of the test conditions and sentences were randomly selected for each participants. Participant could press "Backspace" to correct any errors they made or pressed the "Enter" key to finish a trial.

Figure 9 shows the screenshot of the application. Before the study started, users calibrated their eye tracking using the build-in application. A small training session was completed before the test session, for the users to get familiar with the task. On average, participants took 23.25 s per sentence entry without haptic feedback, compared to 21.23 s when haptic feedback was used to confirm the text entry. Participants reported to prefer haptic feedback (4-star rating) compared to no haptic feedback (2-star) conditions.

4.3   Haptic Feedback to Alleviate Cybersickness

A study was conducted to evaluate if haptic feedback reduced cybersickness (or motion sickness) while a user performed activities in a VR environment. A custom application was made in Unity for the participants to complete four activity phases. Phase 1 was walking through a maze on the grass, phase 2 was climbing rocky stairs, phase 3 was climbing a wall, and phase 4 was going down a hill using a zip-line.

During virtual walking, gait pattern and pace were mapped to spatial haptic feedback and synced with audio, therefore, feedback on the left and right were adjusted for walking and running. Feedback for phase 2 was same as phase 1, except haptic feedback was crispier to imitate rocky texture of the stairs. Feedback for climbing a wall moved from the hand controllers to the head, giving

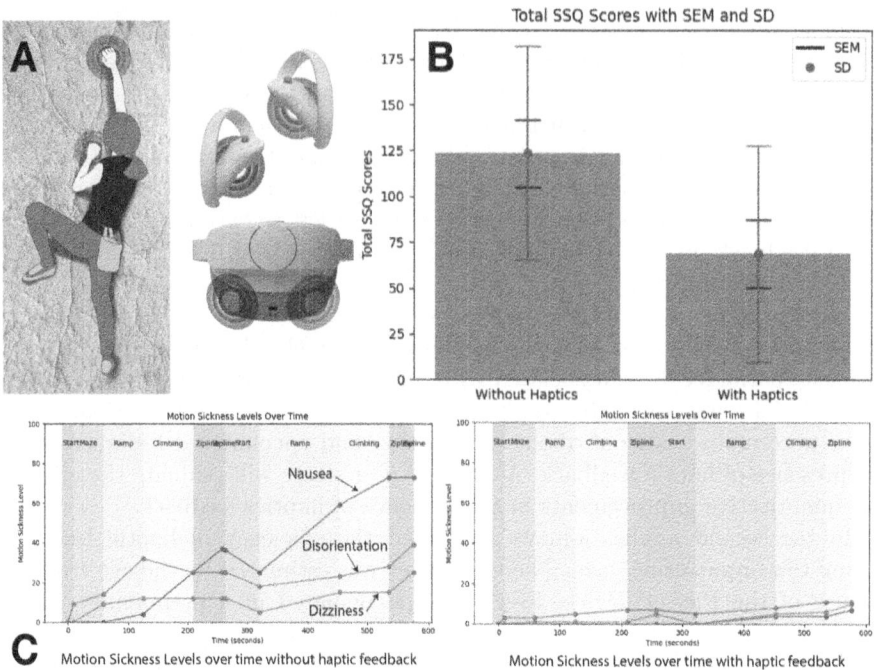

Fig. 10. A. Haptic feedback associated with climbing. B. Overall SSQ scores in the VR activities without haptic feedback and with haptic feedback. C. SSQ scores over time without haptic feedback and with haptic feedback.

them the sense of progression, and feedback for zip-lining was a continuous feedback with changing location and intensity associated with body tilting and user speed. Figure 10 shows haptic feedback associated with activities.

After each phase, participants completed a simulator sickness questionnaire (SSQ) [22]. SSQ scores are a measure of how much cybersickness was caused. A result above 100 is generally considered high. Scores approaching 200 mean the subject was in active pain. Ten participants first completed the activities with no feedback to measure the baseline SSQ scores, and two days later they completed the activities again with haptic feedback. SSQ scores after completing all phases were compared for haptics and no haptic conditions. Eight out of ten participants had significant reduction of cybersickness due to haptic feedback. One participant had no influence (net change of 3 points) and another participant had a negative influence (SSQ scores with haptic feedback were higher). Overall, the average SSQ score was 123.5 with no haptic feedback compared to 68.8 with haptic feedback. This is a 34.6% reduction (p¡0.05) of SSQ score with haptic feedback.

5   Concluding Remarks

The paper presents an a dual channel haptic accessory that can be attached to a typical spatial computing head mounted device. The design of the accessory ensured user comfort, while wearing for long duration or during donning and doffing, and rendering broadband haptic feedback on the back of the head. We evaluated the location, type, and number of stimulation points while reducing structural resonance and maintaining haptic saliency. In order to make the accessory adopted by developers, we utilized the audio framework to create, fine tune and playback haptics, and provided algorithms to quickly generate dynamic and spatial haptic experiences. Finally we evaluated the accessory in three application scenarios.

Users enjoyed haptic experience while watching movies, playing games and listening to music, making the experience immersive with synchronized multi sensory feedback. Haptic feedback on the back of the head during bare hand interactions showed quick adaptation of the feedback for manual tasks and indicated eye free interactions during spatial tasks. Finally, synchronized feedback on the back of the head associated with user movements alleviated motion sickness (cybersickness), provided an alternative mitigating scheme for high sensitive individual.

Acknowledgments. We like to thank Danny Saetern, Yufei Lu, Guanqun Zhang, Alice Liu, Shuo Liu, Yuzhou Gong, Yangfei Xu, Ming Li, FeiFei Ding, Jiabin Zhao, Wei Chen for hardware, software, HCI and Unity support, and flushed out many ideas and implementations. We also like to thank Bytedance Inc. for supporting this work.

References

1. Nguyen, R., Gouin-Vallerand, C., Amiri, M.: Hand interaction designs in mixed and augmented reality head mounted display: a scoping review and classification. Front. Virtual Reality **4**, 1171230 (2023)
2. Sendhilnathan, N., Zhang, T., Lafreniere, B., Grossman, T., Jonker, T.R.: Detecting input recognition errors and user errors using gaze dynamics in virtual reality. In: Proceedings of the 35th Annual ACM Symposium on User Interface Software and Technology, Article no. 38, pp. 1–19. ACM, New York USA (2022)
3. Gupta, A., Sendhilnathan, N., Hartcher-O'Brien, J., Pezent, E., Benko, H., Jonker, T.R.: Investigating eyes-away mid-air typing in virtual reality using squeeze haptics-based postural reinforcement. In: Proceedings of the 2023 CHI Conference on Human Factors in Computing Systems, Article no. 230, pp. 1–11. ACM, New York USA (2023)
4. Chang, E., Kim, H.T., Yoo, B.: Virtual reality sickness: a review of causes and measurements. Int. J. Hum. Comput. Interact. **36**(17), 1658–1682 (2020)
5. Thompson, S.: Motion Sickness in VR: Why it happens and how to minimise it (2023). https://virtualspeech.com/blog/motion-sickness-vr. Accessed 30 Apr 2024
6. Keshavarz, B., Hecht, H.: Pleasant music as a countermeasure against visually induced motion sickness. Appl. Ergon. **45**(3), 521–527 (2014)

7. Keshavarz, B., Stelzmann, D., Paillard, A., Hecht, H.: Visually induced motion sickness can be alleviated by pleasant odors. Exp. Brain Res. **233**(5), 1353–1364 (2015)
8. Molefi, E., McLoughlin, Ia., Palaniappan, R.: On the potential of transauricular electrical stimulation to reduce visually induced motion sickness. Sci. Rep. **13**, 3272 (2023)
9. Chu, H., Li, M.-H., Juan, S.-H., Chiou, W.-Y.: Effects of transcutaneous electrical nerve stimulation on motion sickness induced by rotary chair: a crossover study. J. Altern. Complement. Med. **18**(5), 494–500 (2012)
10. Peng, Y.-H., et al.: WalkingVibe: reducing virtual reality sickness and improving realism while walking in VR using unobtrusive head-mounted vibrotactile feedback. In: Proceedings of the 2020 CHI Conference on Human Factors in Computing Systems, pp. 1–12. ACM, New York USA (2020)
11. Tirmizi, A., Culbertson, H.: Haptics for Mitigation of Cyber-Sickness in XR environments. In: Workshop in IEEE World Haptics Conference (2023)
12. Israr, A., Zhao, S., Schwemler, Z., Fritz, A.: Stereohaptics toolkit for dynamic tactile experiences. In: Stephanidis, C. (ed.) HCII 2019. LNCS, vol. 11786, pp. 217–232. Springer, Cham (2019). https://doi.org/10.1007/978-3-030-30033-3_17
13. Israr, A., Choi, S., Tan, H. Z.: Mechanical impedance of the hand holding a spherical tool at threshold and suprathreshold stimulation levels. In: Proceedings of Second Joint EuroHaptics Conference and Symposium on Haptic Interfaces for Virtual Environment and Teleoperator Systems (WHC'07), pp. 56–60. IEEE (2007)
14. Berning, M., Braun, F., Riedel, T., Beigl, M.: ProximityHat: a head-worn system for subtle sensory augmentation with tactile stimulation. In Proceedings of the 2015 ACM International Symposium on Wearable Computers, pp. 31–38. ACM, New York USA (2020)
15. Preechayasomboon, P., Israr, A., Samad, M.: Chasm: a screw based expressive compact haptic actuator. Proceedings of the 2020 CHI Conference on Human Factors in Computing Systems, pp. 1–13. ACM, New York USA (2020)
16. Pico Unity Integration SDK. https://www.picoxr.com/global. Accessed 30 Apr 2024
17. Haptic Feedback for Pico Unity SDK. https://developer-global.pico-interactive.com/document/unity/haptic-feedback/. Accessed 30 Apr 2024
18. CapCut, Free all-in-one video editor for everyone to create anything anywhere. https://www.capcut.com/. Accessed 30 Apr 2024
19. de Jesus Oliveira, V.A., Brayda, L., Nedel, L., Maciel, A.: Designing a vibrotactile head-mounted display for spatial awareness in 3D spaces. IEEE Trans. Visual Comput. Graphics **23**(4), 1409–1417 (2017)
20. Kaul, O. B., Rohs, M.: Wearable head-mounted 3D tactile display application scenarios. In: Proceedings of the 18th International Conference on Human-Computer Interaction with Mobile Devices and Services Adjunct, pp. 1163–1167. ACM, New York USA (2016)
21. Kerdegari, H., Kim, Y., Prescott, T.: Tactile language for a head-mounted sensory augmentation device. In: Wilson, S. P.. Verschure, P., Mura, A., Prescott, T. J. (eds.) Biomimetic and Biohybrid Systems, pp. 359–365. Springer International Publishing (2015)
22. Kennedy, R.S., Lane, N.E., Berbaum, K.S., Lilienthal, M.G.: Simulator sickness questionnaire: an enhanced method for quantifying simulator sickness. Int. J. Aviat. Psychol. **3**(3), 203–220 (1993)

EEGMobile: Enhancing Speed and Accuracy in EEG-Based Gaze Prediction with Advanced Mobile Architectures

Teng Liang[1]([⊠]) [iD] and Andrews Damoah[2] [iD]

[1] Palo Alto High School, Palo Alto, USA
`t140355@pausd.us`
[2] University of Maryland, College Park, USA
`adamoah@terpmail.umd.edu`

Abstract. Electroencephalography (EEG) analysis is an important domain in the realm of Brain-Computer Interface (BCI) research. To ensure BCI devices are capable of providing practical applications in the real world, brain signal processing techniques must be fast, accurate, and resource-conscious to deliver low-latency neural analytics. This study presents a model that leverages a pre-trained MobileViT alongside Knowledge Distillation (KD) for EEG regression tasks. Our results showcase that this model performs at a level comparable to the previous State-of-the-Art (SOTA) on the EEGEyeNet Absolute Position Task, achieving a Root Mean Squared Error (RMSE) of 53.6, a 3% reduction in accuracy, while being 33% faster and 60% smaller. Our research presents a cost-effective model applicable to resource-constrained devices and contributes to expanding future research on lightweight, mobile-friendly models for EEG regression.

Keywords: Electroencephalography · Deep Learning · Brain-Computer Interfaces · Mobile Networks · Knowledge Distillation · Gaze Prediction · Human Computer Interaction

1 Introduction

Electroencephalography (EEG) signal analysis is a pivotal research subject contributing to the advancement of Brain-Computer Interfaces (BCI). Furthermore, the application of Machine Learning (ML) and Deep Learning (DL) algorithms has become a key component for EEG analysis, which has only grown steadily across the years (Qu et al. 2020b; Sun and Mou 2023). The EEGEyeNet dataset has become the centerpiece in this field fusing advanced EEG data compilation with cutting-edge ML and DL techniques (Dou et al. 2022; Farago et al. 2022; Murungi et al. 2023a; Rolff et al. 2022; Wolf et al. 2022). Its popularity is underscored by its large collection of high-quality EEG and eye-tracking (ET) recordings alongside baseline ML and DL models to benchmark accuracy on a variety of ET tasks. The advent of EEGEyeNet has spurred further research into applications of new DL algorithms for EEG-ET tasks Yang and Modesitt (2023); Modesitt et al. (2024); Dou et al. (2022); Rolff et al. (2022). While much of this research is focused on improving predictive accuracy, for these methods to be practical in real-world scenarios, there is a need to develop more computationally efficient models.

As such, this study explores the efficacy of integrating a pre-trained MobileViT network into the existing EEG-based transformer model (EEGViT-TCNet) alongside incorporating knowledge distillation during training with a fine-tuned EEGViT-TCNet teacher model for EEG-based gaze estimation. This unique approach allows our model, dubbed EEGMobile, to leverage the MobileViT's effective design to increase computational efficiency. The use of knowledge distillation also enhances task performance, allowing our model to exhibit accuracy comparable to the current SOTA.

This research provides an extensive evaluation of EEGMobile and contrasts it with previous models focused on the same task, in terms of speed, size, and accuracy. We aim to highlight the strengths of the individual components that comprise our model and illustrate how these components unite to form a cost-effective model for EEG regression. Our research has the potential to expand the efficiency and scalability of practical applications of DL models for EEG analysis across a plethora of domains. Our code is publically available at: https://github.com/t0nyliang/EEGMobile.

1.1 Research Question

– Is a MobileViT-based model viable for faster, SOTA-comparable accuracy on the EEGEyeNet dataset?

Table 1. Abbreviation Table

Abbreviation	Definition
EEG	Electroencephalography
ET	Eye-Tracking
HCI	Human-Computer Interaction
BCI	Brain-Computer Interfaces
AI	Artificial Intelligence
ML	Machine Learning
DL	Deep Learning
ViT	Vision Transformer
CNN	Convolutional Neural Network
TCN	Temporal Convolutional Network
KD	Knowledge Distillation
SOTA	State Of The Art
RMSE	Root Mean Squared Error

By answering this question, we hope to contribute to research into the development of more memory-conscious models designed for resource-constrained devices, such as mobile phones. Our research contributions highlight the potential for expanding the accessibility of EEG-based eye-tracking technology to a wider audience, further interpolating neuroscience and Human-Computer Interaction (HCI) for medical applications (Table 1).

2   Related Work

Table 2. Root Mean Squared Error (RMSE) of EEGEyeNet Random guessing and baseline DL models, EEGViT, and EEGViT-TCN (Kastrati et al. 2021; Yang and Modesitt 2023)

Model	Absolute Position RMSE (mm)
Naive Guessing	123.3 ± 0.0
CNN	70.4 ± 1.1
PyramidalCNN	73.9 ± 1.9
EEGNet	81.3 ± 1.0
InceptionTime	70.7 ± 0.8
Xception	78.7 ± 1.6
ViT-Base	58.1 ± 0.6
ViT-Base	61.5 ± 0.6
ViT-Base (Pre-trained)	58.1 ± 0.6
EEGViT	61.7 ± 0.6
EEGViT (Pre-trained)	55.4 ± 0.2
EEGViT-TCN	51.8 ± 0.2

2.1   EEG and Deep Learning

EEG and deep learning research have been in close proximity for decades, with advancements in both fields contributing to strides in our understanding of the brain (Craik et al. 2019; Murungi et al. 2023b; Qu et al. 2020a; Roy et al. 2019; Yi and Qu 2022). Deep learning algorithms have been extremely popular in the context of EEG analysis, as their ability to extrapolate and generalize input information makes them perfect for decoding the complexities and noise within EEG signals into interpretable outputs. The research presented in the EEGEyeNet study encapsulates this main point, presenting a large-scale EEG and eye-tracking dataset, designed specifically for ML and DL research Kastrati et al. (2021). The study also presents a robust baseline for comparing the performance of new models on gaze estimation tasks. Due to its high-quality and accessible dataset, EEGEyeNet has been used by numerous studies experimenting with various DL techniques and architectures to improve performance. Their results, shown in Table 2, specifically highlight Convolutional Neural Networks (CNNs) as having a profound ability to interpret complex EEG data accurately, achieving a Root Mean Squared Error (RMSE) value of 70.4. The contributions of combined EEG and deep learning heavily deepen our understanding of the brain and thus influence several related fields. EEG-based Artificial Intelligence (AI) systems can allow for the automated detection and monitoring of various neurological states and conditions, advancing fields such as neuroscience and BCI. In the case of EEGEyeNet, behavioral and neurological information can be deduced from eye tracking, further highlighting the importance of enhancing the capabilities of deep learning algorithms for EEG regression Cao (2020).

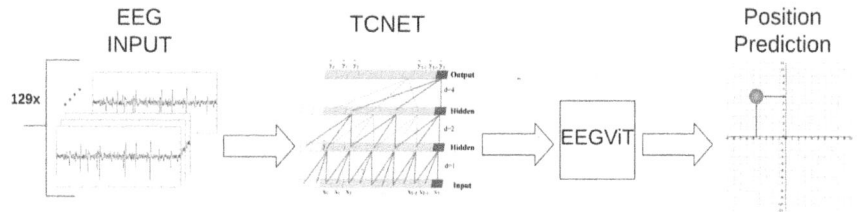

Fig. 1. EEGViT-TCNet Model Diagram (Modesitt et al. 2024).

2.2 Vision Transformers for EEG Regression

Vision Transformers are well regarded as being extremely adept at performing a wide variety of image tasks when pre-trained on large datasets Dosovitskiy et al.(2021). This is a result of the self-attention mechanism, which captures information across sequences of pixel patches, allowing the model to build a more robust representation of the entire image. While ViTs have been nominally utilized in image analysis, recent research has unmasked the applicability of ViTs for EEG analysis. The study presenting the EEGViT model highlighted how transformers' strong global and sequential data processing performs better at regression on time-series EEG data Yang and Modesitt (2023). Furthermore, the addition of prior feature extraction layers, such as a Temporal Convolutional Network (TCN) block shown in Fig. 1, as discussed in EEGViT-TCNet, further extracts temporal features within sequences of EEG signals (Ingolfsson et al. 2020).

The strength of pre-trained ViTs for EEG regression lies in their ability to interpret sequence data as a whole and apply image-related priors to the EEG space. Moreover, evidence seems to suggest that decreased local connectivity may lead to more subject and noise invariance, broadening the variety of signal patterns that can be processed. Overall, ViTs prove to be an exceptional tool in the field of EEG signal analysis, overcoming the many limitations of other DL algorithms specific to EEG (Table 2) Yang and Modesitt (2023).

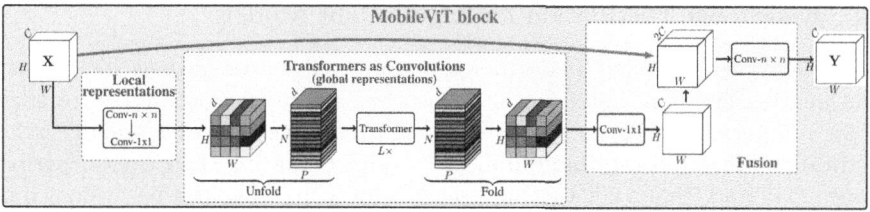

Fig. 2. Model diagram for the MobileViT block, primary innovation of the MobileViT, fusing both Convolution and Transformer layers for local and global processing (Mehta and Rastegari 2022a).

2.3 Lightweight and Mobile Networks

The use of lightweight models is the standard for vision tasks on mobile or resource-constrained devices. Typically, these models are adapted from CNNs, which, due to their spatial inductive bias, yield better performance than ViTs at lower parameter sizes. Lightweight CNNs can also be more effortlessly adapted for downstream tasks and are generally easier to optimize than ViTs, which require extensive data augmentation and regularization Xiao et al.(2021). However, to learn global representations, ViTs need to be integrated in some manner. MobileViT introduces a hybrid, lightweight model that treats transformers as convolutions Mehta and Rastegari(2022a). They achieve this by modifying standard convolution operations to encode global features via a transformer, seen in Fig. 2, permitting both local and global processing, resulting in better accuracy than other lightweight networks. Further optimizations were made to MobileViT, which was subsequently named MobileViTV2. This primarily involved altering the self-attention mechanism from using the multi-headed standard to a separable approach. Using this method, rather than attention scores being computed with respect to each patch, they are computed with respect to a single latent token, reducing the time complexity from quadratic to linear with respect to the number of patches. Additionally, the removal of the skip connection within the MobileViT block provided a minor improvement to the model's task performance.

The advancements of lightweight networks have implications directly related to building more deployable AI systems. Faster and more accurate models improve vision-related tasks on mobile devices, such as image recognition and augmented reality functionality. This extends outward from solely mobile phones and can apply to other resource-constrained devices, such as drones and wearable technology. When it comes to EEG analysis, both CNNs and Transformers are proven to be powerful tools for enhancing performance, and the adaptation of mobile networks can make strides in the practical application of DL in EEG signal processing Kastrati et al. (2021); Yang and Modesitt (2023); Modesitt et al. (2024).

2.4   Knowledge Distillation for Lightweight Models

While lightweight models perform reasonably well across various image task benchmarks, they still fall short in terms of accuracy when compared to their larger counterparts. Due to the necessity of a resource-conscious design, architectural modifications are more difficult to make, limiting their overall performance Gao and Zhou (2023). One proven way to improve the performance of lightweight models is through model compression, with knowledge distillation being one well-known technique to achieve this. The main methodology behind this procedure is to have a larger, more complex network (teacher) with a smaller, simpler model (student) and train the student model using a "distillation loss" calculated from the combined losses of the student and teacher models Hinton et al. (2015). This causes the student model to mimic the teacher model's behavior, effectively "compressing" the teacher into a smaller network. This is especially good for lightweight networks, as they are able to enjoy enhanced predictive accuracy alongside their computational efficiency.

Knowledge distillation is an incredibly popular and useful technique in designing deployable DL models for resource-constrained devices, as this training procedure can result in better accuracy without affecting the model's size or speed Cui et al. (2024). This makes it an attractive method to aid in developing enhanced lightweight networks for EEG analysis. These networks, with higher accuracy and efficiency, are particularly relevant for applications in medical contexts, where speed and accuracy are vital.

3   Methods

In our study, we concentrated on the Absolute Position task within the EEGEyeNet dataset, opting for the MobileViT architecture due to its proven superior performance relative to other similarly sized models. We incorporated a meticulously fine-tuned EEGViT-TCNet as the teacher model in our knowledge distillation process, aimed at enhancing the MobileViT student model's accuracy. The accuracy of our proposed model was rigorously evaluated using the Root Mean Squared Error (RMSE) on the test set, in addition to measuring the computational speed during inference, and the model's parameter count.

3.1   Dataset

This study employed the EEGEyeNet dataset for the training and validation of our model (Fuhl et al. 2023; Mishra et al. 2023; Modesitt et al. 2023; Wang and Wang 2022; Xiang and Abdelmonsef 2022). This dataset encompasses EEG and ET recordings from 356 adults, 190 of whom were female and 166 were male, ranging in age from 18 to 80 years old. Researchers obtained written consent from all participants prior to data collection and compensated participants monetarily. The EEG data was recorded on the EEG Geodesic Hydrocel system with 128 channels and a 500 Hz sampling rate. The impedance of each electrode was analyzed between recording sessions and kept at a maximum of 40 KOhm. Eye positions were concurrently recorded with an EyeLink 1000 Plus at the same sampling rate. The eye tracking was calibrated using a 9-point grid before each recording and validated to ensure an average error of less than 1° for the measurement of all points. Participants were seated 68 cm from a 24-inch monitor with a resolution of 800×600 pixels, with their heads stabilized in a chin rest position.

To address artifacts present in the EEG recordings as a result of environmental and psychological noise, the necessary preprocessing steps were taken. This process involved the detection and correction of bad electrodes, along with running a 40 Hz high-pass filter and a 0.5 Hz low-pass filter on the data. The EEG data was then synchronized alongside the eye-tracking data to ensure time-locked analyses at the onset of relevant events with errors not exceeding 2 ms.

In the Large Grid Paradigm, participants were asked to focus on a sequence of 25 dots located in different positions on the screen. Dots were each presented for roughly 1.5 to 1.8 s, and their positions were selected to ensure maximal coverage of the screen area. This procedure was separated into five experimental blocks, each displaying a series of 27 dots, with the center dot appearing three times in a pseudo-randomized order to reduce the predictability of subsequent dots. This entire experiment was then repeated six times.

The Absolute Position benchmark data was performed using the Large Grid Paradigm. This task involves determining the subject's gaze position as an XY coordinate pair. Each sample of one second describes a single fixation from a participant. The benchmark contains 21464 samples from 27 participants. This task was specifically important for our research as it provided a diverse array of gaze positions combined with a high sample count, allowing for a more comprehensive analysis of EEG-ET patterns, integral to determining the XY coordinate positions (Kastrati et al., 2021).

3.2   Model Architecture

The architecture of our model can be seen in Fig. 3. Our model design is adapted from the EEGViT-TCNet architecture and includes three main components that construct the entire network architecture.

Temporal Convolutional Network Block: The TCN block is initialized with a 129-dimension input layer, specifically attuned to the number of EEG channels with an extra dimension for encoding grounding information. Three additional layers with channel sizes 64, 128, and 256 are utilized to build a comprehensive representation of the temporal dependencies within the recorded EEG signals. A uniform kernel of size 3 coupled with ReLU activation is applied to all layers with a dropout rate of 0.75 to counteract overfitting. Finally, causality and weight normalization are applied to improve stability Bai et al. (2018).

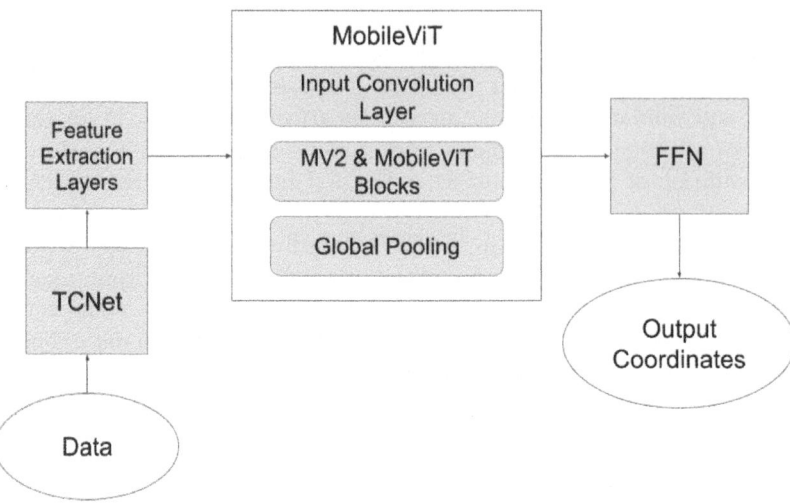

Fig. 3. EEGMobile Model Flow Chart: MV2 refers to MobileNetV2 and FFN refers to Feed Forward Network.

Feature Extraction Layers: This block consists of two convolutional layers designed to initiate feature extraction on the data output by TCN in preparation to be fed to the MobileViT layer. The first layer consists of a convolutional kernel of size (1, 36) scaling the input up to 256 channels, initiating spatial feature extraction from the input data. The second layer consists of a kernel of size (256, 1), further scaling the data to 768 channels and compressing spatial information in preparation for the transformer component Yang and Modesitt (2023).

MobileViT Network: This final block consists of a pre-trained MobileViTV2 network configured from the Hugging Face "apple/mobilevitv2-1.0-imagenet1k-256" model. The model is initialized with an input dimensionality of 768, perfectly aligning with the previous feature extraction component, along with a kernel size of (3, 3) for the internal convolutional layers and a patch size of (1, 1) for the internal transformers. Lastly, a classifier head is comprised of a classifier layer followed by a dropout of 0.1, finally connecting to a linear layer that outputs the final XY coordinate gaze prediction Mehta and Rastegari (2022a; 2022b); Yang and Modesitt (2023).

3.3 Training and Evaluation

Data from the Absolute Position tasks was split 70% for training, 15% for validation, and 15% for testing. To maintain data integrity, we ensured data points with eye positions outside of the 800-by-600 pixel range were excluded. Our model was then trained for a total of 15 epochs, with each training iteration consisting of 64 sample batches Kastrati et al. (2021). Our model utilized the Adam optimizer with a learning rate of 1e–3 and weight decay of 0.3, and a learning rate scheduler with a step size of 6 was utilized to prevent overfitting. Additionally, we employed knowledge distillation using a fine-tuned EEGViT-TCN teacher model to train our EEGMobile student model, due to its superior performance over other models on the Absolute Position Task. The loss was calculated as a function of a lambda-controlled, weighted sum between the Mean Square Error (MSE) between the student predictions and observed values, the "true loss", and the Kullback-Leibler divergence loss of the soft targets of both models, the "distillation loss". We set the temperature parameter, controlling the strength of the distillation, to 20 and lambda to 0.9, giving a higher weight to the distillation loss. Hinton et al. (2015).

Model accuracy was evaluated as the Euclidean distance between the model's predictions and observed values in millimeters, represented as the RMSE Kastrati et al. (2021). We also evaluated the model's speed through an inference test, where the model was set to run inferencing across the entire Absolute Position task dataset ten times, after which the runtime in minutes was computed. Finally, we report parameter counts for the compared models to examine their relative sizes. All training and testing were conducted on the same machine using a single P5000 GPU.

4   Results

Results from our exhaustive evaluation illustrate EEGMobile's ability to deliver SOTA-comparable accuracy at a faster inferencing speed and smaller size, outperforming the other transformer-based models.

Table 3. RMSE indicates validation error in millimeters. Runtime measures the time to complete inferencing on the entire dataset 10 times. Parameter count is measured in millions. All values represent the mean and standard deviation of 5 runs. All tests were run on the same hardware.

Model	RMSE (mm)	Runtime (mins)	Parameter Count
CNN Kastrati et al. (2021)	70.4 ± 1.1	2.1 ± 0.2	0.6 M
EEGViT Yang and Modesitt (2023)	55.4 ± 0.2	78.8 ± 0.2	86.0 M
EEGViT-TCN Modesitt et al. (2024)	51.8 ± 0.2	12.1 ± 1.6	137.2 M
EEGMobile (Ours)	**53.6 ± 0.6**	**8.1 ± 0.9**	**55.9 M**

Table 3 shows that our EEGMobile architecture attains an impressively low RMSE of 53.6 mm. This eclipses all EEGEyeNet baseline models, the lowest of which is the CNN with an RMSE of 70.4 (Kastrati et al. 2021). Likewise, our model outperforms the highest-performing EEGViT model with an RMSE of 55.4 (Yang and Modesitt, 2023). EEGMobile also attains a similar accuracy to

EEGViT-TCNet, just 3% shy of its 51.8 RMSE (Modesitt et al., 2024). This notable performance accuracy underscores the robustness of EEGMobile and its ability to capture and generalize key information within the training data.

In addition to evaluating the accuracy, we also assessed EEGMobile's computational efficiency through an inference speed test and analyzed the model's relative size. Compared to the other EEG-based ViT architectures, our model boasts a 33% increase in inferencing speed when compared to EEGViT-TCNet and is over 9.7× faster than the original EEGViT with a runtime of about 8.1 min, compared to 78.8 and 12.1 min for EEGViT and EEGViT-TCNet, respectively. However, EEGMobile is still slower than the baseline CNN model by about 3.9×. Furthermore, we find that while EEGMobile has a smaller size compared to the other ViT architectures, with 55.9 million parameters, followed by EEGViT with 86 million and EEGViT-TCN with 137.2 million, It is still much larger than the CNN model with only 609 thousand parameters. These sizes indicate that while EEGMobile is still about 91.7× larger than the CNN, it is also about 35% smaller than EEGViT and 60% smaller than EEGViT-TCN. This noteworthy improvement to both speed and size highlights EEGMobile's efficiency over the other transformer-based models and is especially paramount for applications involving real-time predictions on memory-restricted devices.

5   Discussion

Our meticulous performance evaluation legitimizes EEGMobile as a robust model capable of executing EEG-ET tasks efficiently when compared to other transformer-based models, reinforcing the viability of combining lightweight networks with distillation techniques to develop cost-effective models. Our RMSE results suggest that EEGMobile is capable of providing predictive capabilities comparable to the other transformer models on EEG gaze estimation tasks and can gain a robust interpretation of the EEG data despite its small size. Similarly, without the use of KD, EEGMobile has a much higher RMSE of about 76.8. This alludes to the idea that KD aids in guiding the model to learn better representations, enhancing its accuracy. This is further highlighted by the high temperature and lambda parameters, which greatly increased the strength and effect of distillation. We also note that EEGMobile's memory and time efficiency are still very much below those of CNN. However, when examining the components of all three ViT-based models, a significant amount of the total parameter counts stem from the feature extraction layers, which contain over 50 million parameters. As such, there is a strong possibility that integrating feature extraction methods with significantly fewer parameters may further close the size gap between EEGMobile and CNN in terms of speed and size. Our analysis of EEGMobile's size, speed, and task performance illustrates its potential as an efficient model for practical EEG signal analysis, especially on weaker devices, across various domains.

This improved efficiency is material to real-time EEG and eye-tracking applications, where speed and accuracy are important EL Menshawy et al. (2015).

Our findings are also particularly relevant to the HCI community, such as in the integration of EEG recording devices into virtual reality and augmented reality technologies to improve interactivity Xiang and Abdelmonsef (2022); Rolff et al. (2022); Xu et al. (2023). Additionally, due to the model's low parameter count, there are also memory efficiency benefits when it is utilized by resource-constrained BCI devices, allowing the model to be run on-device, making medical diagnostic tools more accessible to the average person Jebelli et al. (2019).

Due to time constraints, our experiment only tested the MobileViT and MobileViTV2 architectures, ultimately selecting the V2 in our final results. However, a MobileViTV3, which makes a number of improvements to further enhance the model's performance, has also been developed Wadekar and Chaurasia(2022). Not only does utilizing this pre-trained model have the potential to improve our results, but it would also be more representative of the capabilities of MobileViT on the Absolute Position Task. Similarly, testing our model on other EEG datasets would allow us to better evaluate its robustness for EEG analysis as a whole.

In future studies, exploring alternative model architectures could enhance both accuracy and computational efficiency (An et al. 2023a,b; Chen et al. 2021; Chen at al. 2024; Li et al. 2024; Lu et al. 2023a,b, 2024). Similarly, experimenting with alternative distillation techniques, such as feature distillation, may also lead to better performance (Gui et al. 2024; Tan et al. 2023a,b; Tang et al. 2023; Wang et al. 2023; Yunoki et al. 2023; Zhao et al. 2024, 2022b). Furthermore, due to the distillation paradigm, in theory, there is no constraint on what teacher model is used (Jiang et al. 2023; Ma 2022; Ma et al. 2024; Zhang et al. 2022, 2023; Zhao et al. 2022a) Consequently, there is potential for research into developing a large, high-performance model that can then be used as a teacher to train a smaller model for more practical use using the same training procedure as for EEGMobile. One notable concern regarding the current methodology is the independent training of both the teacher and student model, as required by knowledge distillation. This process can be quite inefficient, especially when working with a very large and slow teacher model. As such, research parallelizing this training process may increase the scalability of these types of models.

6   Conclusion

This study highlights the efficacy of lightweight models for EEG-ET tasks. By integrating the MobileViT architecture into a Hybrid Transformer model and utilizing knowledge distillation techniques, we present a model with enhanced speed and size with a minimal cost to accuracy compared to the SOTA. Our findings further validate the potential of lightweight networks on EEG regression tasks, but further expand the accessibility of DL-based EEG analysis tools for real-world applications, especially on resource-constrained devices, with the potential to advance the unification of neuroscience and HCI.

References

An, S., Bhat, G., Gumussoy, S., Ogras, U.: Transfer learning for human activity recognition using representational analysis of neural networks. ACM Trans. Comput. Healthc. **4**(1), 1–21 (2023)

An, S., Tuncel, Y., Basaklar, T., Ogras, U.Y.: A survey of embedded machine learning for smart and sustainable healthcare applications. In:Embedded Machine Learning for Cyber-Physical, IoT, and Edge Computing: Use Cases and Emerging Challenges, pp. 127–150. Springer, Heidelberg (2023b)

Bai, S., Kolter, J.Z., Koltun, V.: An empirical evaluation of generic convolutional and recurrent networks for sequence modeling. arXiv preprint arXiv:1803.01271 (2018)

Cao, Z.: A review of artificial intelligence for eeg-based braincomputer interfaces and applications. Brain Sci. Adv. **6**(3), 162–170 (2020). https://doi.org/10.26599/BSA. 2020.9050017

Chen, P., Ding, H., Araki, J., Huang, R.: Explicitly capturing relations between entity mentions via graph neural networks for domain-specific named entity recognition. In: Proceedings of the 59th Annual Meeting of the Association for Computational Linguistics and the 11th International Joint Conference on Natural Language Processing, vol. 2: Short Papers, pp. 735–742 (2021)

Chen, P., et al.: Hytrel: hypergraph-enhanced tabular data representation learning. In: Advances in Neural Information Processing Systems, vol. 36 (2024)

Craik, A., He, Y., Contreras-Vidal, J.L.: Deep learning for electroencephalogram (EEG) classification tasks: a review. J. Neural Eng. **16**(3), 031001 (2019)

Cui, Y., et al.: Lightweight neural network with knowledge distillation for csi feedback (2024)

Dosovitskiy, A., et al.: An image is worth 16×16 words: transformers for image recognition at scale (2021)

Dou, G., Zhou, Z., Qu, X.: Time majority voting, a pc-based eeg classifier for non-expert users. In: International Conference on Human-Computer Interaction, pp. 415–428. Springer, Heidelberg (2022)

EL Menshawy, M., Benharref, A., Serhani, M.: An automatic mobile-health based approach for eeg epileptic seizures detection. Expert Syst. Appl. **42**(20), 7157–7174 (2015). ISSN 0957-4174. https://doi.org/10.1016/j.eswa.2015.04.068. https://www. sciencedirect.com/science/article/pii/S0957417415003103

Farago, E., Law, A.J., Hajra, S.G., Chan, A.D.C.: Blink and saccade detection from forehead eeg. In: 2022 IEEE International Instrumentation and Measurement Technology Conference (I2MTC), pp. 1–6. IEEE (2022)

Fuhl, W., et al.: One step closer to eeg based eye tracking. In: Proceedings of the 2023 Symposium on Eye Tracking Research and Applications, pp. 1–7 (2023)

Gao, D., Zhou, D.: A very lightweight and efficient image super-resolution network. Expert Syst. Appl. **213**, 118898 (2023). ISSN 0957-4174. https://doi.org/ 10.1016/j.eswa.2022.118898. https://www.sciencedirect.com/science/article/pii/ S0957417422019169

Gui, S., Song, S., Qin, R., Tang, Y.: Remote sensing object detection in the deep learning era-a review. Remote Sens. **16**(2), 327 (2024)

Hinton, G., Vinyals, O., Dean, J.: Distilling the knowledge in a neural network (2015)

Ingolfsson, T.M., Hersche, M., Wang, X., Kobayashi, N., Cavigelli, L., Benini, L.: Eegtcnet: an accurate temporal convolutional network for embedded motor-imagery brain-machine interfaces. In: 2020 IEEE International Conference on Systems, Man, and Cybernetics (SMC), pp. 2958–2965 (2020). https://doi.org/10.1109/SMC42975. 2020.9283028

Jebelli, H., Khalili, M.M., Lee, S.H.: Mobile EEG-based workers' stress recognition by applying deep neural network. In: Mutis, I., Hartmann, T. (eds.) Advances in Informatics and Computing in Civil and Construction Engineering, pp. 173–180. Springer, Cham (2019). https://doi.org/10.1007/978-3-030-00220-6_21 ISBN 978-3-030-00220-6

Jiang, C., Hui, B., Liu, B., Yan, D.: Successfully applying lottery ticket hypothesis to diffusion model. arXiv preprint arXiv:2310.18823 (2023)

Kastrati, A., et al.: Eegeyenet: a simultaneous electroencephalography and eye-tracking dataset and benchmark for eye movement prediction (2021)

Li, H., et al.: Spherehead: stable 3d full-head synthesis with spherical tri-plane representation. arXiv preprint arXiv:2404.05680 (2024)

Lu, Y., Sato, K., Wang, J.: Deep learning based multi-label image classification of protest activities. arXiv preprint arXiv:2301.04212 (2023a)

Lu, Y., et al.: Machine learning for synthetic data generation: a review. arXiv preprint arXiv:2302.04062 (2023b)

Yingzhou, L., Chen, T., Hao, N., Van Rechem, C., Chen, J., Tianfan, F.: Uncertainty quantification and interpretability for clinical trial approval prediction. Health Data Sci. 4, 0126 (2024)

Ma, X.: Traffic performance evaluation using statistical and machine learning methods. PhD thesis, The University of Arizona (2022)

Ma, X., Karimpour, A., Wu, Y.J.: Data-driven transfer learning framework for estimating on-ramp and off-ramp traffic flows. J. Intell. Transport. Syst. 1–14 (2024)

Mehta, S., Rastegari, M.: Mobilevit: light-weight, general-purpose, and mobile-friendly vision transformer (2022a)

Mehta, S., Rastegari, M.: Separable self-attention for mobile vision transformers (2022b)

Mishra, A.R., et al.: Signeeg v1. 0: Multimodal electroencephalography and signature database for biometric systems. bioRxiv, pp. 2023–09 (2023)

Modesitt, E., Yang, R., Liu, Q.: Two heads are better than one: a bio-inspired method for improving classification on eeg-et data. In: International Conference on Human-Computer Interaction, pp. 382–390. Springer, Heidelberg (2023)

Modesitt, E., Yin, H., Wang, W.H., Lu, B.: Fusing pretrained vits with tcnet for enhanced eeg regression (2024)

Murungi, N.K., Pham, M.V., Dai, X., Qu, X.: Trends in machine learning and electroencephalogram (eeg): a review for undergraduate researchers. In: International Conference on Human-Computer Interaction, pp. 426–443. Springer, Heidelberg (2023a)

Murungi, N.K., Pham, M.V., Dai, X.C., Qu, X.: Empowering computer science students in electroencephalography (eeg) analysis: a review of machine learning algorithms for eeg datasets. In: Proceedings of the 29th ACM SIGKDD Conference on Knowledge Discovery and Data Mining, pp. 1728–1739 (2023b)

Qu, X., Liu, P., Li, Z., Hickey, T.: Multi-class time continuity voting for EEG classification. In: Frasson, C., Bamidis, P., Vlamos, P. (eds.) BFAL 2020. LNCS (LNAI), vol. 12462, pp. 24–33. Springer, Cham (2020). https://doi.org/10.1007/978-3-030-60735-7_3

Qu, X., Mei, Q., Liu, P., Hickey, T.: Using EEG to distinguish between writing and typing for the same cognitive task. In: Frasson, C., Bamidis, P., Vlamos, P. (eds.) BFAL 2020. LNCS (LNAI), vol. 12462, pp. 66–74. Springer, Cham (2020). https://doi.org/10.1007/978-3-030-60735-7_7

Rolff, T., Harms, H.M., Steinicke, F., Frintrop, S.: Gazetransformer: gaze forecasting for virtual reality using transformer networks. In: DAGM German Conference on Pattern Recognition, pp. 577–593. Springer, Heidelberg (2022)

Roy, Y., et al.: Deep learning-based electroencephalography analysis: a systematic review. J. Neural Eng. **16**(5), 051001 (2019)

Sun, C., Mou, C.: Survey on the research direction of eeg-based signal processing. Front. Neurosci. (2023). ISSN 1662-453X. https://doi.org/10.3389/fnins.2023.1203059

Tan, J., et al.: Audio-induced medial prefrontal cortical dynamics enhances coadaptive learning in brain-machine interfaces. J. Neural Eng. **20**(5), 056035 (2023)

Tan, J., Zhang, X., Wu, S., Wang, Y.: State-space model based inverse reinforcement learning for reward function estimation in brain-machine interfaces. In: 2023 45th Annual International Conference of the IEEE Engineering in Medicine & Biology Society (EMBC), pp. 1–4. IEEE (2023b)

Tang, Y., Song, S., Gui, S., Chao, W., Cheng, C., Qin, R.: Active and low-cost hyper-spectral imaging for the spectral analysis of a low-light environment. Sensors **23**(3), 1437 (2023)

Wadekar, S.N., Chaurasia, A.: Mobilevitv3: mobile-friendly vision transformer with simple and effective fusion of local, global and input features (2022)

Wang, J., Chang, R., Zhao, Z., Pahwa, R.S.: Robust detection, segmentation, and metrology of high bandwidth memory 3d scans using an improved semi-supervised deep learning approach. Sensors **23**(12), 5470 (2023)

Wang, X., Wang, Z.: Cnn with self-attention in eeg classification. In: International Conference on Human-Computer Interaction, pp. 512–526. Springer, Heidelberg (2022)

Wolf, L., et al.: A deep learning approach for the segmentation of electroencephalography data in eye tracking applications. arXiv preprint arXiv:2206.08672 (2022)

Xiang, B., Abdelmonsef, A.: Vector-based data improves left-right eye-tracking classifier performance after a covariate distributional shift. In: International Conference on Human-Computer Interaction, pp. 617–632. Springer, Heidelberg (2022)

Xiao, T., Singh, M., Mintun, E., Darrell, T., Dollár, P., Girshick, R.: Early convolutions help transformers see better (2021)

Xu, X., Yang, L., Yan, Y., Li, C.: Cmfs-net: common mode features suppression network for gaze estimation. In: Proceedings of the 2023 Workshop on Advanced Multimedia Computing for Smart Manufacturing and Engineering, AMC-SME 2023, pp. 25–29. Association for Computing Machinery, New York (2023). ISBN 9798400702730. https://doi.org/10.1145/3606042.3616449

Yang, R., Modesitt, E.: Vit2eeg: leveraging hybrid pretrained vision transformers for eeg data (2023)

Yi, L., Qu, X.: Attention-based cnn capturing eeg recording's average voltage and local change. In: Artificial Intelligence in HCI: 3rd International Conference, AI-HCI 2022, Held as Part of the 24th HCI International Conference, HCII 2022, Virtual Event, 26 June–1 July 2022, Proceedings, pp. 448–459. Springer, Heidelberg (2022)

Yunoki, I., Berreby, G., D'Andrea, N., Lu, Y., Qu, X.: Exploring ai music generation: a review of deep learning algorithms and datasets for undergraduate researchers. In: International Conference on Human-Computer Interaction, pp. 102–116. Springer, Heidelberg (2023)

Zhang, Z., Tian, R., Sherony, R., Domeyer, J., Ding, Z.: Attention-based interrelation modeling for explainable automated driving. IEEE Trans. Intell. Veh. **8**(2), 1564–1573 (2022)

Zhang, Z., Tian, R., Ding, Z.: Trep: transformer-based evidential prediction for pedestrian intention with uncertainty. In: Proceedings of the AAAI Conference on Artificial Intelligence, vol. 37, pp. 3534–3542 (2023)

Zhao, H., Du, H., Yang, S., Yao, F.: Rec-rn: user representations learning over the knowledge graph for recommendation systems. In: 2022 4th International Conference on Machine Learning, Big Data and Business Intelligence (MLBDBI), pp. 228–233. IEEE (2022a)

Zhao, S., et al.: Deep learning based cetsa feature prediction cross multiple cell lines with latent space representation. Sci. Rep. **14**(1), 1878 (2024)

Zhao, Z., Zhou, F., Xu, K., Zeng, Z., Guan, C., Zhou, S.K.: LE-UDA: label-efficient unsupervised domain adaptation for medical image segmentation. IEEE Trans. Med. Imaging **42**(3), 633–646 (2022)

Foam Magnetic Tactile Sensors
for Spatial Computing Input

Wade Marquette[1,2]([✉]), Ali Israr[1], and Mohammed Al-Rubaiai[1]

[1] Pico Immersive, ByteDance Inc, Bellevue, WA 98004, USA
[2] Mechanical Engineering, University of Washington, Seattle, WA 98105, USA
wm25@uw.edu

Abstract. This work explores the development and implementation of a silicone foam soft sensor used in input devices for spatial computing, targeting low-effort, comfortable, compact, and discreet interfaces for interacting within three-dimensional environments. The soft sensor is composed of thin foam encapsulating a small magnet, and the deformation of the foam is monitored by a Hall effect sensor. Sensor characterizations quantified the sub-millimeter spatial sensing capabilities achieving a spatial resolution of 0.56 mm. Moreover, the sensor was scaled to three input devices, namely, a soft three-dimensional (3D) joystick for spatial control, a soft grip controller for multipoint grip input, and a force myography (FMG) wristband for hand gesture recognition. We evaluated the application of the sensor in a user study of the soft FMG wristband, where displacement of the wrist tendons were measured while users performed five typical hand gestures. Machine learning models were fit to quantify the accuracy of gesture recognition using the wristband. Our findings demonstrate the potential of the sensor used in input devices to enhance user interaction within spatial computing environments.

Keywords: Spatial computing · Soft sensing · Input devices · Virtual reality · Force myography · Wearable technology · Gesture recognition

1 Introduction

As spatial computing continues to rapidly evolve, the development of new input devices for interacting with spatial environments becomes essential for navigation and manipulation within three-dimensional spaces. For these input devices to gain widespread acceptance, it's beneficial if they are low-effort, compact, and robust to both environment and user variability. Furthermore, for interactions to be integrated into everyday use, it's important that they are comfortable and socially acceptable; hence, the spatial computing input devices should remain subtle and discreet. This work focuses on creating input devices using soft sensors designed for spatial computing interfaces.

Creating spatial computing input devices from soft sensors enables low-effort and comfortable wearable interfaces for users. Traditional soft tactile sensors

© The Author(s), under exclusive license to Springer Nature Switzerland AG 2025
M. Kurosu et al. (Eds.): HCII 2024, LNCS 15374, pp. 356–371, 2025.
https://doi.org/10.1007/978-3-031-76803-3_21

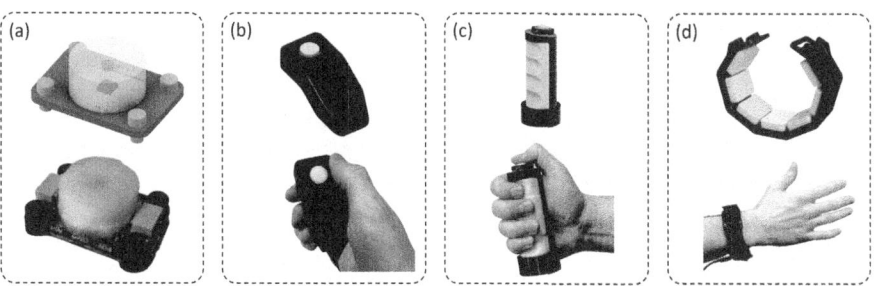

Fig. 1. (a) Foam magnetic tactile sensor applied to (b) the soft three-dimensional joystick for 3D spatial control, (c) the soft grip controller, SensiGrip, and (d) the FMG wristband for gesture recognition.

such as those based on resistance, capacitance, piezoelectric, optics, and magnetics have been examined extensively, with each having its strengths and limitations [2]. In this work, we utilize soft magnetic tactile sensors as they enable compact input devices by measuring a high degree of spatial information from a single interaction point.

In magnetic soft tactile sensing, a magnet or magnetic film is embedded in a soft material near a Hall effect sensor which measures the magnetic flux density as the soft material is deformed and the magnet is displaced. By utilizing a three-dimensional Hall effect sensor to measure three-axis magnetic field readings, high spatial information can be captured from a single sensor [9]. The measurement from the Hall effect sensor is then used to identify tactile information of the interaction such as contact point localization or interaction force.

Soft magnetic tactile sensors have been calibrated as force sensors [6,10–12,16,17,22] and have been arranged in arrays for robotic skins [14,20,21,23]. Recent developments explored the spatial super-resolution, where spatial sensing resolution beyond the Hall effect element spacing is achieved through machine learning techniques [8,9,14,23].

The main contribution of this work is two-fold. First, we fabricate a soft magnetic tactile sensor with the material selection of a silicone foam elastomer which creates a soft interface compared to similar magnetic tactile sensors while being classified as a non-irritant (Fig. 1(a)). Second, we integrate the foam magnetic tactile sensor into three spatial computing input devices (Fig. 1(b-d)). We characterized the spatial sensing of the foam magnetic tactile sensor before using it to create a soft three-dimensional (3D) joystick for spatial cursor control, a soft grip controller, SensiGrip, enabling full finger input, and a force myography (FMG) wristband for gesture recognition. We performed a user study on the FMG wristband to quantify the performance of the sensor in an input device form factor.

2   Sensor Design

Soft magnetic tactile sensors are designed to either embed rigid magnets within an elastomer body or to distribute magnetic particles throughout an elastomer film. The former provides benefits in designing a general purpose input device which enables multiple interaction modes. With the same sensor interface, three-dimensional rigid magnet measurements can distinguish motion generated from surface pressure, shear forces, and magnet rotation with understanding of the magnetic field [22], whereas thin magnetic films may only detect surface pressure unless complex magnetization procedures are performed [23]. Therefore, we adopt a sensor architecture of a rigid magnet embedded within an elastomer body.

The foam magnetic tactile sensor design integrated a single three-dimensional Hall effect sensor and cylindrical magnet embedded within a 15 mm diameter cylindrical silicone foam body, as shown in Fig. 2a. The elastomer body of the sensor consisted of Soma Foama^{TM} 15 silicone foam from Smooth-On Inc. with a density of 15 lb/ft^3. This elastomer was observed to benefit from characteristics associated with both silicone rubbers and polyurethane foams used in similar sensors [8]. The silicone foam body demonstrated a nonporous outer surface finish typical of silicone rubbers, protecting a soft, porous inner foam body commonly associated with polyurethane foams. The sensing element consisted of a TLV493D Hall effect sensor, with a range of +/- 130 mT and an RMS error of 0.1 mT, integrated into a printed circuit board. Embedded within the foam was an N52 cylindrical permanent magnet with a magnetization strength of 1450 mT, thickness of 1 mm, and diameter of 2.5 mm.

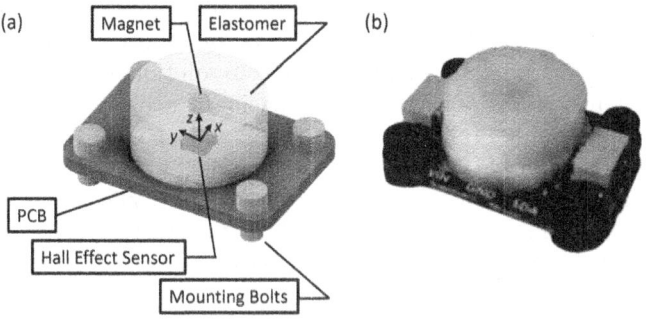

Fig. 2. Sensor (a) diagram of components with Hall effect sensing element axes and (b) photo.

The bottom surface of the magnet was embedded 4 mm above the sensitive element in the Hall effect sensor, aligning the cylindrical magnet's axis to the z-axis of the Hall effect sensor. The magnet's top surface was embedded 1 mm below the planar surface of the foam. The total height of the sensor was 8 mm.

Using the Magpylib simulation tool [15], we performed simulations verifying that the sensitive element of the Hall effect sensor would not saturate during maximum compression.

3   Sensor Fabrication

We designed two stages of two-part molds for casting the silicone foam from a two-part resin onto the printed circuit board containing the Hall effect sensor. Compared with silicone rubbers found in sensors with similar fabrication processes [17], the silicone foam fabrication process is simplified as it does not require degassing in a vacuum chamber. However, the foam expands to four times its original volume once mixed, and may compromise surface finish if the expansion traps air bubbles against the walls of the mold. Therefore, the molds were completely filled with the mixed, unexpanded resin, and excess expanded material pushed through escape holes which were experimentally determined to resist the flow of the liquid resin mixture prior to expansion. The first stage mold was designed to cast the bottom of the cylindrical foam body with a recess for the magnet to be placed. The walls of the mold were lined with 3 mm diameter circular holes at a 6 mm spacing shown in Fig. 3(a). The second stage mold enabled application of a thin layer of foam over the cast foam cylinder, embedding the magnet. A 1 mm thick slot in the mold wall allowed excess material to escape.

Carrying out the fabrication procedure, each mold was sprayed with mold release, lightly brushed, and left undisturbed to dry for 5 min. The sensor was then fabricated following the two-stage casting process. In the first stage, the printed circuit board and sensor were bolted to the base mold. The two part Soma Foama^{TM} 15 components were mixed rapidly in the instructed ratio of 2A:1B for 30 s. The mixture was poured to fill the mold, and the two-part mold was bolted together, allowing excess material from the foam expansion to escape from the holes in the mold sides. The mixture was left to cure for 1 h before removing the sensor from the first stage, resulting in a cylinder with a cylindrical recess left for embedding the magnet. A magnet was placed in the recess left from the first stage mold with it's north pole facing up. In the second stage, the procedure from the first stage was repeated to add a cylindrical layer of 1 mm, embedding the magnet in the foam body. Finally, excess foam was carefully cut from the foam body using a razor blade. A diagram of the fabrication process is visualized in Fig. 3.

4   Sensor Characterization

Soft magnetic tactile sensors demonstrate a high degree of sensing with the ability to distinguish various spatial interactions from a single magnetic sensing element. The sensor effectively manages both simple interactions, such as measuring uniform compression, and complex interactions, such as contact point localization. We carried out two characterizations of the foam magnetic tactile sensor, demonstrating its sub-millimeter spatial sensing properties.

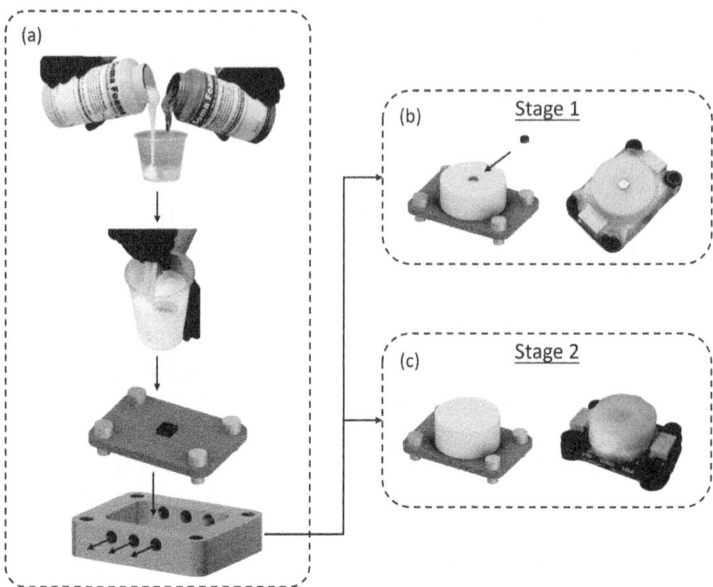

Fig. 3. Diagram of sensor fabrication process (a) depicting the material mixing and pouring onto the Hall effect sensor element in the mold which is performed in two stages, (b) the result after the Stage 1 casting where a magnet was embedded in the recess and (c) the finished sensor after Stage 2 casting.

4.1   Test Setup

To characterize the tactile displacement sensing capabilities of the sensor, the sensor was bolted with four fasteners to a three-axis motorized CNC machine via a 3D printed mounting bracket. The mounting bracket geometry included a lip to align with the edge of the CNC bed, aligning the axes of the Hall effect sensor. The three-axis magnetic flux densities, denoted as B_x, B_y, and B_z, were streamed via a micro controller and returned the sensor readings to a computer for data storage and processing through serial communication. The CNC testbed with the sensor and mounting bracket are shown in Fig. 4.

To characterize the spatial properties of the sensor, two probes for two characterization experiments were installed on the CNC testbed. First, to quantify the sensor's uniform compression resolution, a 15 mm diameter cylindrical tipped probe was installed to compress the entire foam body uniformly along the z-axis. To properly align the probe with the sensor, the probe was manually aligned with the cylindrical profile of the sensor's surface before zeroing the machine. Next, the spatial resolution of the sensor was tested similarly to previous works by probing the sensor radially at a specified depth with a probe [8,14,23]. This work utilized a 3D printed 5 mm diameter cylindrical probe for the spatial resolution tests. To properly align the probe with the sensor, a homing indent matching the cylindrical probe's profile was created in the mounting bracket at a known

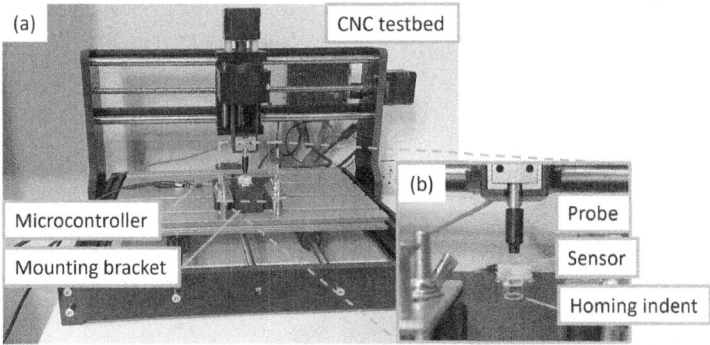

Fig. 4. (a) CNC testbed with the microcontroller and (b) probe above sensor installed in mounting bracket with homing indent used in probe alignment.

distance from the sensor's top and center. The probe was manually aligned to this indent before zeroing the machine.

4.2   Uniform Compression Resolution

Characterizing the uniform compression of the sensor quantifies performance for simple interactions where displacement is limited to the sensor's z-axis. Input devices equipped with soft buttons can incorporate this modality to either continuously measure the compression or detect a discrete press using a threshold. In wearable applications, both wear status and device tightness can be quantified in this way.

Uniform compression characterization was carried out by probing the sensor with the 15 mm diameter cylindrical probe in intervals of 0.1 mm between depths of 0 and 3 mm. The probe is fully retracted from the sensor between each measurement. This probing sequence was repeated a total of 10 times. The data collected relating the compression depth, z, to the z-axis magnetic flux density, B_z, is shown in Fig. 5(a).

Given the quadratic nature of estimating the z-axis displacement from the measured magnetic field within in the compression range, we applied a quadratic regression model. The model fit the displacement, zz, from the zz-axis magnetic flux density, B_z, with $R^2 = 0.994$. To further evaluate the model, 200 uniformly distributed random compression depths were generated and probed between depths of 0 and 3 mm. The model was applied to predict each compression depth from the sensor measurement. The error obtained from randomly selected test points shows an average estimation error of 0.06 mm with a maximum estimation error of 0.21 mm.

4.3   Spatial Resolution

Measuring spatial resolution of the sensor, although more complex than measuring uniform compression resolution, quantifies the sensor's capabilities for several

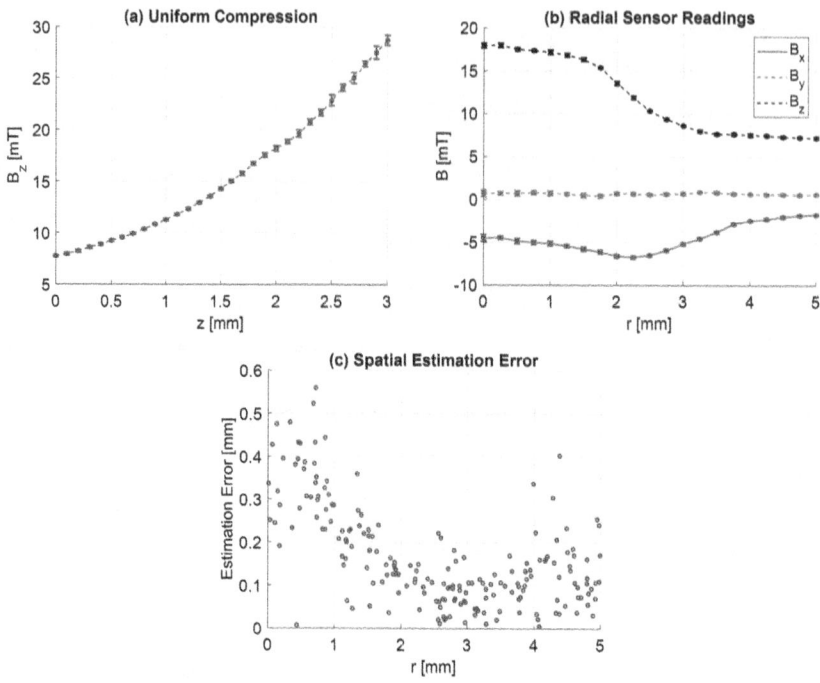

Fig. 5. (a) Sensor measurements, B_z, collected from uniform compression characterization over varying depths, z. (b) Sensor measurements, B_x, B_y, and B_z, collected from radial probing along at the x-axis at varying radii, r. (c) Estimation error in probe location along at the x-axis at varying radii, r.

additional applications. The sensor's ability to detect various spatial interactions enables applications of input devices such as soft smart surfaces and touchpads. In wearable applications, the sensor can comfortably be arranged directly in contact with the skin, measuring forces and displacement.

Due to the symmetry of the cylindrical magnet, the radial magnetic flux density, B_r, is equivalent in every radial direction from the magnet center. Therefore, experiments quantifying the sensor's spatial resolution were conducted along a single radial axis only. Assuming a model can be fit relating (B_r, B_z) to r, the (x, y) interaction coordinates can be localized at any point of contact along the surface from measurements of B_x, B_y, and B_z through computation [22]. In this work, the measurements were taken radially along the x-axis, but the results are representative over the whole sensor surface.

The sensor was probed along the x-axis in increments of 0.25 mm from the sensor center to a distance of 5 mm. The cylindrical probe with a diameter of 5 mm probed at a depth of 2 mm for this study. This probing sequence was repeated a total of 10 times. Figure 5(b) shows the three-axis magnetic flux density measurements taken radially from the sensor's center.

Figure 5(b) demonstrates that the curves correlating B_r and B_z to r do not align with any conventional surface functions for mapping the measurements to the probing radius. This complex functional relationship is a result of the probe and magnet geometry. However, a regression model is still required for analyzing the spatial resolution of the sensor. Therefore, the non-parametric surface fitting technique of locally-weighted surface smoothing (LOWESS) is applied to the regression problem [4]. LOWESS is fit with the Curve Fitting Toolbox in MATLAB with a span of 0.3 using the collected radial data [19].

The spatial resolution of the two sensors was quantified from experimental data through the metric of localization error. 200 uniformly sampled radial values between 0 and 5 mm were selected for probing the sensor at a depth of 2 mm. The measurements of B_r and B_z were interpolated using the fit LOWESS surface to obtain the estimated probing radius to compare with the actual randomly selected probing radius. The absolute localization error is plotted in Fig. 5(c). The error obtained from randomly selected test points shows an average estimation error of 0.17 mm with a maximum estimation error of 0.56 mm.

5   User Interface Concepts and Prototypes

5.1   Soft 3D Joystick

We incorporated the developed sensor into the soft 3D joystick. This input device provides a thumb-controlled interface, offering a compact solution for three-dimensional cursor control within spatial environments (Fig. 6). It can measure changes in the magnetic field as a user applies a combination of one-dimensional normal force and two-dimensional shear forces with their thumb, enabling three-dimensional input. This form factor bypasses the need for conventional reaching and pointing interactions commonly used in spatial computing applications, resulting in a compact and discreet spatial computing input device.

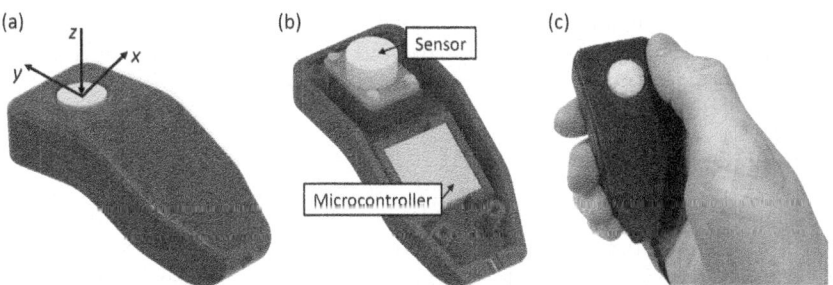

Fig. 6. (a) Soft 3D joystick model with labeled control axes, (b) diagram of the main soft 3D joystick components and packaging, and (c) photo of soft 3D joystick held by a user.

The soft 3D joystick design encased the sensor in a 3D printed housing with a microcontroller. The microcontroller returned three-axis magnetic field readings from the Hall effect sensor via serial communication at 75 Hz for use in spatial control.

Five participants signed consent forms and participated in a preliminary user study approved by the organization's ethical committee, using the soft 3D joystick to control a three-dimensional cursor in a virtual reality environment. Each participant was tasked with moving the cubic cursor within a $1.5\,\text{m}^3$ workspace, located $0.25\,\text{m}$ in front of the participant's head, into a cubic target 100 times. Once selected by the cursor, the target respawned in a random location within the workspace at a uniformly distributed random size between 0.1 and $0.5\,\text{m}$. The study was designed similarly to previous work modelling virtual reality reaching tasks using Fitts' law [3].

Relative to the participant's view, the cursor moved horizontally and vertically from the x- and y-axis magnetic field measurements, respectively, when the user placed their thumb at the joystick's center and slid it across the two-dimensional surface. Mirroring the operation of a conventional thumb joystick, this movement specified cursor velocity, specifiying speed by multiplying the change in sensor measurements by a factor of 0.1. Cursor depth was controlled as the user pushed into the soft 3D joystick. As this motion is unidirectional, changes in the z-axis measurements between two thresholds of 4 mT and 25 mT were linearly mapped to a cursor depth position between $0\,\text{m}$ and $1.5\,\text{m}$ into the workspace. Once the cursor and target overlapped, participants pressed a button held in their non-dominant hand.

All participants successfully performed the task and completed a subjective questionnaire, asking participants to rank on a seven point scale (1: Strongly Disagree to 7: Strongly Agree) statements about the soft 3D joystick. When prompted "The soft 3D joystick was easy to use," participants responded with a mean and standard deviation of 4±1. When prompted "Using the soft 3D joystick was tiring," participants responded with a mean and standard deviation of 2.6±1.3. The responses are encouraging as participants felt neutral of the device's ease of use, despite being first time users. Furthermore, the soft interface appears low effort, as participants did not find the repeated task tiring. Future work will further analyze both qualitative and quantitative aspects of this study, aiming to fit the soft 3D joystick with a Fitts' law model.

5.2 SensiGrip

We incorporated four of the developed sensors into a finger grip form factor, stacked within a single foam body to create SensiGrip, a soft grip controller (Fig. 7). Each finger grip embedded a foam magnetic tactile sensor for measuring continuous grip force or discrete finger presses, creating a highly capable full-finger and low-effort input device. SensiGrip's top integrates an additional sensor, functional as a button or soft 3D joystick input. The sensors were measured using an I^2C multiplexer and microcontroller in the base of the device, and the measurements were transferred via serial communication at 35 Hz for use. SensiGrip has applications in immersive virtual reality gaming experiences and general-purpose full-finger interactions.

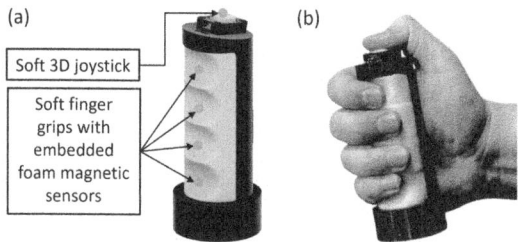

Fig. 7. (a) Diagram showing the soft grip controller, SensiGrip, sensor placement and (b) photo of SensiGrip held by a user.

5.3   FMG Wristband

In wrist-worn FMG, tendon forces and displacements from an array of sensors located on the wrist are measured and used for gesture recognition. Several FMG wristbands have been developed using a variety of sensors [1,5,13,18,24]. We introduce the implementation of the foam magnetic tactile sensor for wrist-worn FMG, creating a soft and discreet wearable input device for gesture recognition. The FMG wristband, featuring an array of seven foam magnetic tactile sensors (Fig. 8), can detect hand and wrist gestures by analyzing changes in magnetic fields from wrist movements measured over the sensor pads' surfaces. Changes in magnetic field measurements are classified as gestures using machine learning techniques. In applications of spatial computing, this approach enables gesture recognition in the presence of visual occlusion from cameras. The gestures may control discrete actions such as selecting buttons or continuous actions such as navigating a cursor across a virtual screen by measuring continuous wrist motion.

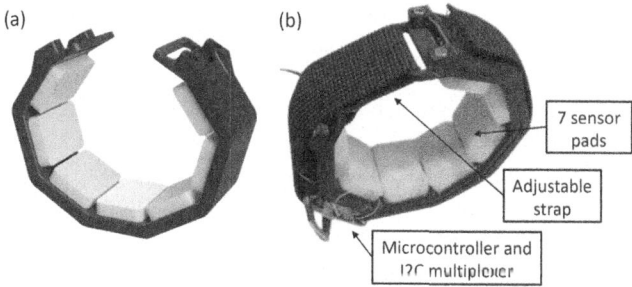

Fig. 8. (a) The FMG wristband model and (b) a photo of the FMG wristband labeled with main components and features.

To adapt to the wristband application, we cast the foam over the entirety of the printed circuit board, creating a uniform surface to avoid any hard contact with the skin. Furthermore, the foam was cast in a thinner mold with a total pad height of 4 mm to match expected wrist tendon displacements. This reduction in pad thickness moved the magnets closer to the sensing element, increasing the sensitivity. Aside from varied dimensions, the fabrication process remained unchanged.

An adjustable Velcro strap was used to tighten the wristband for different users. While the wristband consisted of rigid printed circuit boards and a plastic 3D printed case, the wristband structure was thin enough to adapt to variation in wrist sizes. The sensors were measured using an I^2C multiplexer and microcontroller located on the wristband strap. The sensor measurements were transferred via serial communication at 35 Hz for gesture recognition use in spatial computing applications.

6   User Study: FMG Wristband Gesture Recognition

We conducted a small-scale user study, approved by the organization's ethical committee, where the FMG wristband was trained using a feedforward neural network for classification to detect a mixture of wrist and hand gestures which act as control inputs for spatial environments. The study addressed challenges in the wrist-worn FMG field, demonstrating robustness against re-donning and user variation.

6.1   Methods

Three participants with mean and standard deviation wrist circumferences of 16.8 ± 0.8 cm, long wrist diameters of 54.0 ± 1.7 mm, and short wrist diameters of 39.7 ± 1.2 mm signed consent forms and performed the user study. Participants were instructed to position the wristband such that the center sensor pad aligned with the underside center of their right wrist, ensuring that the edge of the wristband rested on the forearm just behind the ulnar styloid. This placement was intuitive to explain to the participants and kept the wristband far enough from the bending location to avoid hindering user motion while simultaneously avoiding large measurement disturbances caused by small wrist bend angles.

A combination of five wrist and hand gestures were selected for gesture recognition. The gestures consisted of hand open, wrist left, wrist right, wrist down, and fist. Participants made the gestures in a pose with the hand held in front of the participant with the elbow bent at a $90°$ angle. The pose and gestures are shown in Fig. 9.

Before data collection, the participants practiced making each gesture in the pose to become familiar with the task. Before each set of gestures was collected, the wristband was calibrated by zeroing the sensor measurements in the hand open gesture. The change in magnetic field from the zeroed pose was used for training the gesture classification machine learning model.

Each gesture set was collected five times, redonning and recalibrating the wristband before recording each set. This approach ensured that the trained

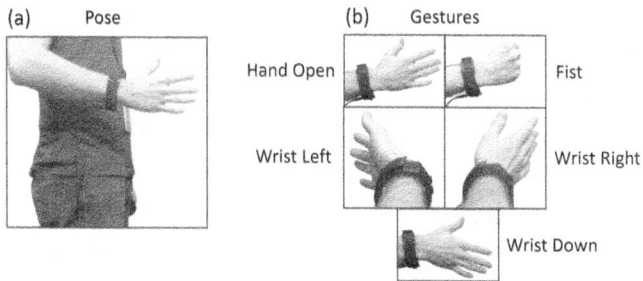

Fig. 9. (a) Pose and (b) wrist and hand gestures used in the FMG wristband study.

gesture recognition models remained robust against variation introduced during redonning the band. The participants were instructed to make each gesture loosely for 5 s without strain such that they would be comfortable holding the gesture for long periods of time. This ensured that the recorded data resulted in recognizing comfortable gestures, enabling the input device to be used for long durations without fatigue. During each 5 s gesture, each user generated 175 data points. To ensure variability in the gesture data throughout the 5 s, the participants were asked to slowly and continuously move their hand within a 15 cm diameter circle and bend their wrist within 10° in either direction from their default pose.

The data was used to train a gesture recognition machine learning model. A feedforward neural network was selected, consisting of 21 inputs from the magnetic field readings of the seven sensors, passed through a 60 node hidden layer using a rectified linear activation function. A softmax output was used to output a probability of the estimated gesture which could be useful in tuning precision and recall for input device applications. The model architecture was designed to be compact enough for potential integration on a microcontroller.

6.2   Results

Similar to previous works [5, 13, 24], k-fold cross validation was used to quantify the gesture recognition performance. 5-fold cross validation was applied in this study, holding out a unique wristband donning from each user at each fold. The models were then trained using a cross entropy loss function with the Adam optimizer and a batch size of 8.

To demonstrate the performance of the redonned band in a personalized model, 5-fold cross validation was applied to a single user, and the corresponding confusion matrix is shown in Fig. 10(a). This result shows all gestures were classified with an accuracy of 97% or greater in this personalized model. The effect of increasing the number of users is demonstrated in Fig. 10(b), where the 5-fold cross validation was performed on a combined dataset from all the participants, reporting a gesture recognition accuracy above 82% across all gestures.

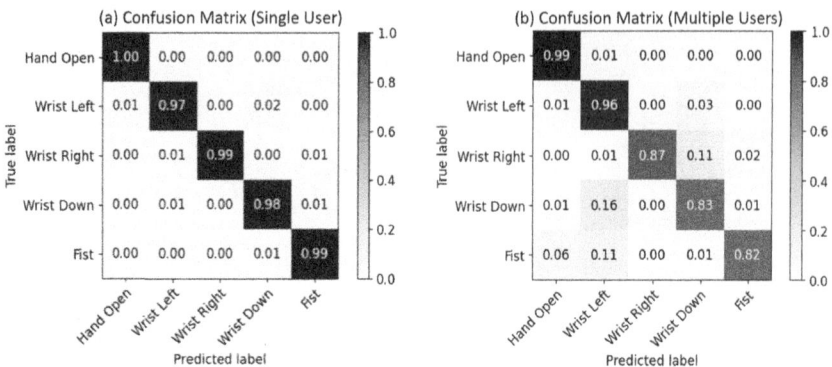

Fig. 10. Gesture recognition 5-fold cross validation confusion matrices with re-donning at folds for (a) a single participant and (b) combined dataset of all participants.

7   Discussion

7.1   Sensor Performance

We observed sub-millimeter resolution of the soft sensor under various modes of spatial interaction, enabling several human computer interface applications. Both the sensor uniform compression and spatial resolution characterizations demonstrated spatial estimation accuracy similar to state-of-the-art soft magnet tactile sensors [23]. These characterizations applied directly to the FMG wristband application as spatial patterns pressed into the sensor surfaces from wrist tendon displacement. The plot of the spatial measurements and estimation in Fig. 5(b)(c) demonstrates the relationship between magnetic field measurement sensitivity with respect to radial distance and estimation error for the chosen sensor architecture. Future sensor designs can optimize the magnet placement with respect to the sensing element to maximize sensitivity for specific applications to reduce estimation errors.

7.2   FMG Wristband Performance

The small-scale FMG wristband user study shows promising results for the foam magnetic tactile sensor's use in future spatial computing input devices. All reported results in the FMG wristband user study consider redonning the band, which has resulted in significantly decreased accuracy in previous studies. For example, WristFlex demonstrated a decrease in accuracy from 80% to 67.5% once considering wristband replacement in finger gesture recognition [5]. The results of the personalized model consisting of a single user reported gesture recognition accuracy above 97% across all five gestures. Considering this personalized model, similar gesture recognition accuracy is achieved compared to studies using the same gestures without redonning [18]. We infer that robustness against redonning is attributed to the spatial sensing capabilities of the sensing elements compared with other sensing modes.

Upon increasing the dataset to include all participants, gesture recognition accuracy across all gestures decreased which is expected based on prior work [1]. MyoSpring, a customizable 3D printed flexible magnetic wristband, emphasized importance in physical wristband customization for higher gesture recognition accuracy [13]. This work further demonstrates benefits of personalized learning models. We anticipate the future use of one-shot or few-shot learning to calibrate gestures for individual users, allowing for fast algorithmic customization [7].

8   Conclusion

This paper presents the development of foam magnetic tactile sensors and their integration into various input devices providing low-effort, compact, and discreet spatial computing interfaces. The developed sensor was applied to the soft 3D joystick, soft grip controller, and FMG wristband input devices, each with unique form factors. Through spatial resolution characterizations and an FMG wristband user study, the high resolution sensor demonstrated robustness when applied in an input device application. Future work seeks to further optimize the sensor designs through finite element modeling and to perform extended sensor characterizations capturing shear responses used in the soft 3D joystick. Each input device prototypes' use case within spatial environments can be further defined based on their strengths and limitations explored through additional user studies. Overall, this work contributes to the development of spatial computing interfaces, paving the way for improved interactions in virtual and augmented reality environments through three-dimensional soft sensing technology.

References

1. Barioul, R., Gharbi, S.F., Abbasi, M.B., Fasih, A., Ben-Jmeaa-Derbel, H., Kanoun, O.: Wrist force myography (FMG) exploitation for finger signs distinguishing. In: 2019 5th International Conference on Nanotechnology for Instrumentation and Measurement (NanofIM), pp. 1–6 (2019). https://doi.org/10.1109/NanofIM49467.2019.9233484
2. Chi, C., Sun, X., Xue, N., Li, T., Liu, C.: Recent progress in technologies for tactile sensors. Sensors 18(4), 948 (2018). https://doi.org/10.3390/s18040948
3. Clark, L.D., Bhagat, A.B., Riggs, S.L.: Extending Fitts' law in three-dimensional virtual environments with current low-cost virtual reality technology. Int. J. Hum. Comput. Stud. 139, 102413 (2020). https://doi.org/10.1016/j.ijhcs.2020.102413
4. Cleveland, W.S.: Robust locally weighted regression and smoothing scatterplots. J. Am. Stat. Assoc. 74(368), 829–836 (1979)
5. Dementyev, A., Paradiso, J.A.: WristFlex: low-power gesture input with wrist-worn pressure sensors. In: Proceedings of the 27th Annual ACM Symposium on User Interface Software and Technology, pp. 161–166. UIST '14, Association for Computing Machinery, New York, NY, USA (2014). https://doi.org/10.1145/2642918.2647396
6. Dwivedi, A., Ramakrishnan, A., Reddy, A., Patel, K., Ozel, S., Onal, C.D.: Design, modeling, and validation of a soft magnetic 3-D force sensor. IEEE Sens. J. 18(9), 3852–3863 (2018). https://doi.org/10.1109/JSEN.2018.2814839

7. Ganesha, H., Gupta, R., Gupta, S.H., Rajan, S.: Few-shot transfer learning for wearable IMU-based human activity recognition. Neural Comput. Appl. **36**(18), 1–13 (2024)
8. Hellebrekers, T., Chang, N., Chin, K., Ford, M.J., Kroemer, O., Majidi, C.: Soft magnetic tactile skin for continuous force and location estimation using neural networks. IEEE Robot. Autom. Lett. **5**(3), 3892–3898 (2020)
9. Hu, H., et al.: Wireless flexible magnetic tactile sensor with super-resolution in large-areas. ACS Nano **16**(11), 19271–19280 (2022). https://doi.org/10.1021/acsnano.2c08664
10. Jamone, L., Natale, L., Metta, G., Sandini, G.: Highly sensitive soft tactile sensors for an anthropomorphic robotic hand. IEEE Sens. J. **15**(8), 4226–4233 (2015). https://doi.org/10.1109/JSEN.2015.2417759
11. Jones, D., et al.: Design and evaluation of magnetic hall effect tactile sensors for use in sensorized splints. Sensors **20**(4), 1123 (2020). https://doi.org/10.3390/s20041123
12. Ledermann, C., Wirges, S., Oertel, D., Mende, M., Woern, H.: Tactile sensor on a magnetic basis using novel 3D hall sensor - first prototypes and results. In: 2013 IEEE 17th International Conference on Intelligent Engineering Systems (INES), pp. 55–60 (2013). https://doi.org/10.1109/INES.2013.6632782
13. Lin, S.S.r., Gamage, N.M., Herath, K., Withana, A.: MyoSpring: 3D printing mechanomyographic sensors for subtle finger gesture recognition. In: Sixteenth International Conference on Tangible, Embedded, and Embodied Interaction, pp. 1–13 (2022)
14. Mohammadi, A., Xu, Y., Tan, Y., Choong, P., Oetomo, D.: Magnetic-based soft tactile sensors with deformable continuous force transfer medium for resolving contact locations in robotic grasping and manipulation. Sensors **19**(22), 4925 (2019). https://doi.org/10.3390/s19224925, https://www.mdpi.com/1424-8220/19/22/4925
15. Ortner, M., Bandeira, L.G.C.: Magpylib: a free python package for magnetic field computation. SoftwareX **11**, 100466 (2020)
16. Paulino, T., et al.: Low-cost 3-axis soft tactile sensors for the human-friendly robot vizzy. In: 2017 IEEE International Conference on Robotics and Automation (ICRA), pp. 966–971 (2017). https://doi.org/10.1109/ICRA.2017.7989118
17. Rehan, M., Saleem, M.M., Tiwana, M.I., Shakoor, R.I., Cheung, R.: A soft multi-axis high force range magnetic tactile sensor for force feedback in robotic surgical systems. Sensors **22**(9), 3500 (2022).https://doi.org/10.3390/s22093500, https://www.mdpi.com/1424-8220/22/9/3500
18. Shull, P.B., Jiang, S., Zhu, Y., Zhu, X.: Hand gesture recognition and finger angle estimation via wrist-worn modified barometric pressure sensing. IEEE Trans. Neural Syst. Rehabil. Eng. **27**(4), 724–732 (2019)
19. The MathWorks, I.: Curve Fitting Toolbox. Natick, Massachusetts, United State (2020). https://www.mathworks.com/products/curvefitting.html
20. Tomo, T.P., et al.: Covering a robot fingertip with uSkin: a soft electronic skin with distributed 3-axis force sensitive elements for robot hands. IEEE Robot. Autom. Lett. **3**(1), 124–131 (2018). https://doi.org/10.1109/LRA.2017.2734965
21. Tomo, T.P., et al.: Design and characterization of a three-axis hall effect-based soft skin sensor. Sensors **16**(4), 491 (2016). https://doi.org/10.3390/s16040491, https://www.mdpi.com/1424-8220/16/4/491
22. Wang, H., et al.: Design methodology for magnetic field-based soft tri-axis tactile sensors. Sensors **16**(9), 1356 (2016)

23. Yan, Y., et al.: Soft magnetic skin for super-resolution tactile sensing with force self-decoupling. Sci. Robot. **6**(51), eabc8801 (2021). https://doi.org/10.1126/scirobotics.abc8801, https://www.science.org/doi/abs/10.1126/scirobotics.abc8801

24. Zhang, Y., Liu, B., Liu, Z.: Recognizing hand gestures with pressure-sensor-based motion sensing. IEEE Trans. Biomed. Circuits Syst. **13**(6), 1425–1436 (2019). https://doi.org/10.1109/TBCAS.2019.2940030

Decoding Elbow Movement Intentions from EMG Signals for Exosuit/Exoskeleton Control

Siddharth Rajesh Patil and Deep Seth$^{(\boxtimes)}$

Department of Mechanical and Aerospace Engineering, Ecole Centrale School of
Engineering, Mahindra University, Hyderabad, India, Survey No. 62/1A,
Bahadurpally, Hyderabad, India
{se23pmee002,deep.seth}@mahindrauniversity.edu.in

Abstract. This research investigates the potential of electromyography
(EMG) signals to understand a user's intention for upper-limb rehabilitation. We focused on classifying elbow flexion and extension movements
using EMG data collected from healthy participants. By analyzing EMG
signals alongside elbow joint angle, torque, and velocity, we identified a
time delay between when a user intends to move and when the movement actually begins. The study also highlighted the influence of individual differences in how EMG signals manifest, emphasizing the need
for robust classification techniques that can account for this variability.
These findings provide a valuable foundation for developing EMG-based
control systems for exoskeletons used in rehabilitation. Future work will
explore more advanced classification algorithms, incorporate a normalization technique to account for variations in muscle strength across
users, and expand the study to include individuals with neurological
conditions. This broader investigation will be crucial for developing control systems that can be applied in real-world rehabilitation settings for
a wider range of patients.

Keywords: Electromyography (EMG) · intent detection ·
rehabilitation · Muscle modelling · EMG based actuation

1 Introduction

Electromyography (EMG) is a technique for measuring the electrical activity of
muscles. When muscles contract to move our limbs, they generate tiny electrical
signals. By recording these signals, EMG provides valuable information about
how our muscles work and how we control our movements.

The strength of these EMG signals can vary a lot from person to person
[1,2]. This can be due to differences in muscle makeup or how the nervous system activates the muscles. This variation is especially noticeable in people with
conditions like stroke or paralysis [3,4], who may have difficulty generating strong
EMG signals.

M. Kurosu et al. (Eds.): HCII 2024, LNCS 15374, pp. 372–386, 2025.
https://doi.org/10.1007/978-3-031-76803-3_22

EMG is used in a variety of applications. Doctors use it to diagnose movement disorders [5], nerve problems [6], and muscle conditions [7]. Therapists use it to help patients recover from injuries or learn new movement patterns. Beyond medicine, EMG is also being used in exciting new technologies. Engineers are using EMG signals to create robots and computer interfaces that can mimic human movement [7–10]. Prosthetic limbs are being developed that patients can control using their own muscle signals [11]. Exoskeletons, wearable suits that can help people move, are also being designed to use EMG for more natural control [12,13].

This paper describes a new approach for developing a closed-loop control system for rehabilitation. A closed-loop system means it constantly adjusts based on what's happening. In this case, the system will use EMG signals to understand what a patient wants to do. Unlike some existing rehabilitation techniques that use pre-programmed movements, this system focuses on the patient's own intentions. The goal is for the patient to be in control, with the exoskeleton acting as a helper rather than taking over completely.

By analyzing the EMG signals, the system can figure out what the patient is trying to do. It can tell which muscles the patient is trying to use, how hard they're trying, and what kind of movement they want to make. This information is then used to create a model that can understand the patient's intentions. This model is used by the closed-loop control system to adjust the exoskeleton in real-time to best assist the patient's movements. Additionally, by monitoring the EMG signals over time, the system can track the patient's progress and adjust the level of assistance provided by the exoskeleton as they get stronger.

With the growing need for better rehabilitation options, technologies like intent detection and gesture recognition are becoming increasingly important. This research focuses on helping people with conditions like stroke, paralysis, or limb loss by developing innovative rehabilitation strategies based on EMG signals. Specifically, we propose a novel approach for a closed-loop control system in upper-limb exoskeletons that decodes user intent for basic elbow movements in real-time. This approach aims to overcome limitations of pre-programmed rehabilitation techniques by allowing patients to control the exoskeleton with their own muscle signals, promoting a more natural and user-centric rehabilitation experience.

2   Literature Review

The early stages of research on EMG and hand gesture recognition models started from 1970s [14], these were the initial stages of research in the field of human intent recognition, which mapped a relationship between the muscle activity and hand motions [15]. In this era basic signal processing techniques were implemented on the EMG signals for analysis and basic feature extraction. The classification algorithms for human hand recognition were very basic and used thresholding techniques and simple statistical methods [1].

After the machine learning was introduced in 1990s, their were advancements in computational capabilities which lead to a significant development in the area of research for EMG. At this time more sophisticated algorithms like ANN(Artificial Neural Network), KNN (K-Nearest Neighbour) [16], (SVM) Support Vector Machine [17] and (HMM) Hidden Markov Models [18] were developed for classification and recognition of hand gestures.

Later in 2010s the research started shifting towards mechanical systems to perform in Real-time and recognize more complex gestures with high degree of freedom. This period integrated the advanced signal processing techniques with machine learning algorithm, including deep-learning models like (CNN) convolutional Neural Networks and (RNN)Recurrent Neural Networks [19]. Also, the use of wearable EMG devices emerged from this era.

With time many advancements have been made in the signal processing techniques of EMG. The need for signal processing of EMG is an important part, while developing a control based on EMG, as the signal has a lot of noise embedded within itself. The cause for noise detected while recording EMG are sources like: Inherent noise present in the Electrode, Movement Artifacts, Electromagnetic Noises, Cross-Talks, Internal Noises, Electrocardiography (ECG) Artifacts. These noises present in the EMG signal carries frequency components which ranges to a thousand Hz. The need to cancel out these noises from EMG are worked upon to avoid unwanted signals that may cause hindrance in the output necessary for our application. And so, to remove these noises from the EMG several signal processing techniques are used like: Amplification, Filtering, Rectification and Envelope. Amplification the EMG signal [20] is done to amplify or enhance the intensity of the EMG signal received, because the intensity of EMG signal varies from person to person, some people are able to generate high intensity EMG, some people generate less intensity EMG, for example patients. The next step is implementation of different filtering techniques, i.e. using digital filters like band-pass filters, High-pass filters, Low-pass filters and Notch filters etc. to remove the unwanted high or low frequencies present in the EMG signal. Later, full-wave rectification of EMG is done and the negative values of data are converted into positive and plotted [21]. The next step is creating an envelope of the rectified data for easy visualization and draw conclusions out of it.

The next step for gesture recognition after signal processing is Feature extraction. The feature extraction of the EMG signal is very important aspect necessary for classification of the motion that is to be derived from the recorded EMG. Some features like: Integrated EMG, Mean Absolute value (MAV), Simple Square Integral (SSI), Variance of EMG, Root Mean Square (RMS), Waveform Length and many more feature are extracted. Further different classification techniques are implemented on these extracted features for gesture recognition [2, 22].

One of the most widely used techniques for classification of EMG data is SVM (support vector machine) [23], Neural Networks [24] and LDA (Linear

Discriminant Analysis), the accuracy of the above discussed techniques depends on which extracted feature has been used for classifying the motion [25]. In recent researches Deep Learning and Double-deep Q-networks are being used for gesture recognition based on EMG signals [26]. [27]. Also, the use of Reinforcement learning offers a wide area for research and scope of future development in the area of gesture recognition using EMG [28].

While significant progress has been made in EMG-based gesture recognition, challenges remain in achieving robust real-time control, especially for applications like upper-limb rehabilitation exoskeletons. These challenges include accounting for user variability, noise reduction in EMG signals, and efficient classification algorithms for real-time implementation. Our research aims to address some of these limitations by focusing on a specific application (upper-limb rehabilitation) and prioritizing real-time control of basic elbow movements.

Deep learning and reinforcement learning offer promising advancements for future EMG research. While this research utilizes traditional classification techniques, future work could explore the integration of deep learning models for improved accuracy and recognition of more complex movements. Additionally, reinforcement learning techniques could be investigated to enhance the adaptability of the closed-loop control system based on user feedback and progress.

3   Objective

The primary objective of this research is to assess the feasibility of using EMG signals to decode user intent for controlling elbow flexion and extension movements in upper-limb rehabilitation applications. The specific objectives are mentioned below:

- Analyze EMG signals to identify features that differentiate between elbow flexion and extension movements.
- Investigate the relationship between EMG signal characteristics, user intent, and actual elbow movement.
- Evaluate the time delay between the detection of EMG activity and the initiation of movement.
- Explore the limitations and challenges associated with using EMG signals for user intent decoding in a rehabilitation setting.

4   Methodology: Decoding User Intent Through EMG Signals

This section outlines the methodology employed to investigate the feasibility of using EMG signals to decode user intent for upper-limb rehabilitation applications. Here, we focus on classifying elbow flexion and extension movements using EMG data collected from healthy subjects.

4.1 Data Collection

Four healthy subjects participated in the study and their anthropometric data is shown in Table 1. An established protocol was implemented for data collection, though we opted against MVC (Maximum Voluntary Contraction) normalization at this stage. MVC normalization, a common practice in EMG analysis, involves recording the maximum EMG signal produced by a muscle during a maximal voluntary contraction. This step accounts for baseline differences in muscle strength between subjects. Future work will incorporate MVC normalization [7, 9, 29].

Table 1. Anthropometric data of 4 subjects who were part of the conducted experiment.

Subject	Age	Weight	Height	UpperArm(cm)	Forearm(cm)
Subject 1	24	80.2	183.5	31.5	28
Subject 2	20	69.8	180.1	30	29.5
Subject 3	26	62.2	172.8	28.5	27
Subject 4	27	66	181	29.5	26.5

The experiment focused on recording EMG activity from muscles involved in elbow flexion and extension movements. Subjects performed repetitive elbow flexion and extension exercises in an isotonic dynamometer within a vertical plane. The range of motion (ROM) considered was 70°, encompassing −20° (extension) and 50° (flexion) [30], as shown in Fig. 1.

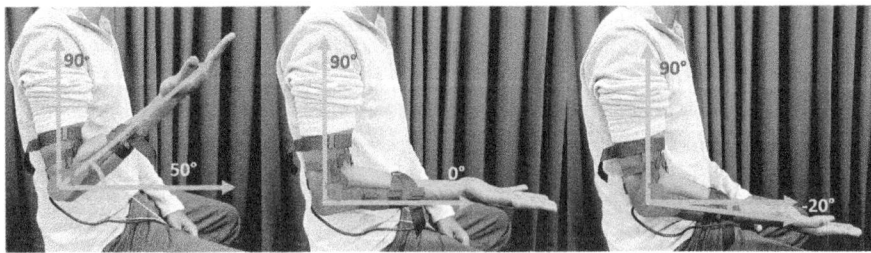

Fig. 1. The above figure shows the ROM for elbow joint taken into consideration for our experiment.

The protocol involved one-minute intervals of continuous elbow flexion and extension movements. Twenty cycles of flexion and extension were recorded per minute, followed by rest periods. This exercise continued until subjects reached exhaustion. To restrict unwanted backward motion, support was provided behind the upper arm during the exercises.

4.2   Rationale for Non-normalization

While MVC normalization is a common practice, we did not perform this study for two reasons. The initial study focused on establishing the feasibility of user-intent decoding using EMG signals for basic elbow movement. Additionally, individuals with stroke/paralysis can be the target population for future rehabilitation application. They may not be able to perform MVC due to their condition. Therefore, we opted for a data collection protocol that would be applicable in a real-world rehabilitation setting.

4.3   Data Recording

The data we have recorded is for the Flexion and Extension movement of Elbow joint in vertical plane. The data collected includes:

- EMG signals from relevant muscles (Biceps for elbow flexion and, Triceps for elbow extension)
- Elbow joint angle
- Torque exerted during movement
- Velocity of elbow movement

4.4   Data Processing

The data processing steps typically involves:

- Filtering the EMG signals to remove noise
- Signal rectification to convert negative voltages to positive
- Feature extraction to identify relevant characteristics of the EMG signal for classification

We have been using MATLAB for processing of raw EMG data from muscles. Signal processing of the raw EMG data includes FFT of the data initially, followed by 4th order Butterworth bandpass filter at high-pass cut-off frequency of 30 Hz and lowpass cut-off frequency of 300 Hz, next the filtered data is fully rectified and RMS enveloping is done and plotted against the rectified signal. The data after RMS enveloping is very useful for easy understanding and visualization of the peaks, analysing the changes in the movements and how the muscles act while performing a certain gesture or movement. As we are interested in developing a control system for an Exo-suit which is suitable for rehabilitation of stroke/paralyzed patients. We are trying to develop an Exo-suit whose actuation mechanism is dependent on the human intent (i.e. EMG data from muscles).

Let, $P_{F_{n-1}}$ and P_{F_n} be the EMG values at different times for a sample time window of 10ms(milliseconds) for 20 cycles.

$$\triangle P_{F_n} = P_{F_n} - P_{F_{n-1}} \tag{1}$$

Then, let Eq. 1, be the difference between the amplitude of EMG for flexion at different time.

Similarly,

$$\triangle P_{E_n} = P_{E_n} - P_{E_{n-1}} \tag{2}$$

let Eq. 2, be the difference between the amplitude of EMG for extension at different time.

Next, we check the conditions for flexion/extention EMG detected

- Initially, we check the condition, if $P_{F_n} > P_{E_n}$. If the condition satisfies, we check for more condition,
  - first, if $\triangle P_{F_n} < \triangle P_{F_{n-1}}$ for the duration of sample time, no motion is detected.
  - Next, if $\triangle P_{F_n} \geq \triangle P_{F_{n-1}}$ for the duration of sample time, which implies that the plot for flexion EMG is incrementing consistently.
  - Then, the initial value P_{F_0} of the sample time window at which plot increments consistently is considered as threshold value, i.e. $P_{F_0} = P_{F_{Threshold}}$, this is represented by 'Red' lines in Figs. 3, 4, 5, 6 in results and discussion section. And all the upcoming values are $P_{F_n} \geq P_{F_{Threshold}}$, this implies that the EMG for flexion is detected.
- Next, if the above condition doesn't satisfy, the next condition is $\triangle P_{F_n} > \triangle P_{F_{n-1}}$, further
  - if $\triangle P_{F_n} > \triangle P_{F_{n-1}}$, for the duration of sample time, no motion is detected.
  - Next, if $\triangle P_{F_n} \leq \triangle P_{F_{n-1}}$, for the duration of sample time, which implies that the plot for flexion EMG is decrementing consistently.
  - Then, the initial value P_{F_0} of the sample time at which plot decrements consistently is considered as threshold value, i.e. $P_{F_0} = P_{F_{Threshold}}$, which is represented by 'Black' lines in Figs. 3, 4, 5, 6 in results and discussion section. And all the upcoming values are $P_{F_n} \leq P_{F_{Threshold}}$, this implies that the EMG for Extension is detected.
- For marking the points at which actual motion starts can be easily done by setting a threshold value for the flexion/extension motion in 'Position' plot in Figs. 3, 4, 5, 6 represented by 'Green' lines.

Future studies will incorporate MVC normalization and expand the subject pool to include individuals with neurological conditions. The research will also explore more sophisticated classification algorithms for improved accuracy in decoding user intent from EMG signals.

5   Results and Discussion

With the analysis of data collected from 4 healthy subjects, we can assess the feasibility of using EMG signals for decoding user intent in upper-limb rehabilitation application. As discussed before we are focusing on classifying elbow

Extracted Data of Subject 1

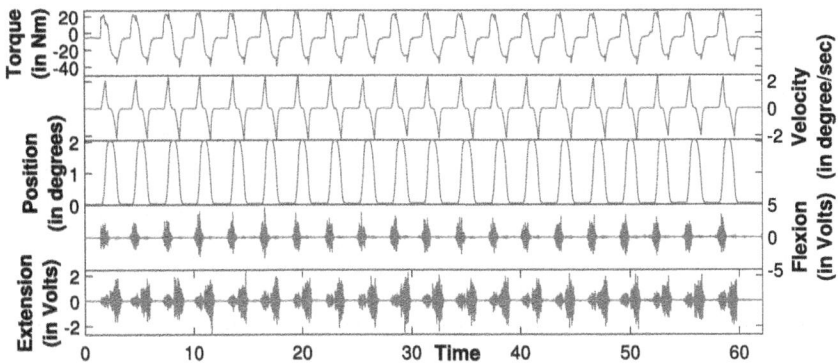

Fig. 2. Data plot of 20 cycles for subject 1

flexion and extension movements. As we can see, Fig. 2 represents 20 cycles of data for Elbow Flexion and Extension movements for studying and classifying Elbow joint movements.

Here, we analyzed and understand that how muscles generate impulses in the form of EMG signal, and how useful information can be extracted from the signal. In Table 2 we have extracted some features from the data presented in Fig. 2. To make our study convenient we have taken into consideration a sample of 5 cycles from the original data comprising of 20 cycles and make conclusions out of it. In Figs. 3, 4, 5 and 6, we can observe how the Torque, velocity of hand movement and changes in position of hand varies with EMG(i.e. muscle intent) during Flexion and Extension movements. Here the 'Red' and 'Black' lines are used to represent the time instance at which the detection of EMG for flexion/extension starts and the 'Green' line depicts the time instance at which the actual flexion/extension motion starts.

The 'Red' and 'Black' lines in the Figs. 3, 4, 5, and 6, are marked in the graph by checking the conditions of the recorded flexion/extension EMG to be increasing continuously with time for a sample window of 10ms(milliseconds), and making the initial value of the sample window as threshold and marking it as the point on which we can say flexion/extension EMG is detected. And the 'Green' lines are marked with respect to the point at which we can observe the actual motion of the elbow joint to be increasing consistently for flexion, and decreasing consistently for extension, in the 'Position' data plot. The above conditions are applicable to the data extracted for all the 4 subjects.

In the Figs. 3, 4, 5 and 6, we have plotted a graph for 4 subjects using MATLAB, which shows changes in the Position, Velocity and Torque of Elbow joint, During Flexion and Extension movement. We were able to make a lot of observations from the graph.

Table 2. Features Extracted from EMG data of 4 subjects

Sr. no.	Features Extracted	Subject 1	Subject 2	Subject 3	Subject 4
1	RMS of rectified flexion data	0.514922	0.499113	0.620227	1.340792
2	RMS of rectified extension data	0.253098	0.229577	0.081108	0.251690
3	Mean of rectified flexion data	0.135680	0.153222	0.179067	0.240317
4	Mean of rectified extension data	0.134157	0.100527	0.088944	0.148166
5	Median of rectified flexion data	0.022033	0.040966	0.032577	0.037466
6	Median of rectified extension data	0.033009	0.018273	0.030340	0.057468
7	Variance of rectified flexion data	0.091326	0.087153	0.125792	0.236675
8	Variance of rectified extension data	0.050432	0.037427	0.017370	0.050052
9	Standard Deviation of rectified flexion data	0.295217	0.458357	0.354671	0.486493
10	Standard Deviation of rectified extension data	0.193460	0.242659	0.131794	0.223723
11	Maximum Value of rectified flexion data	4.221870	6.409619	4.434485	6.788736
12	Maximum Value of rectified extension data	4.164597	2.728131	1.495233	3.117257
13	Minimum Value of rectified flexion data	0.00	0.00	0.00	0.00
14	Minimum Value of rectified extension data	0.00	0.00	0.00	0.00
15	Mean of envelope flexion data	0.169342	0.187888	0.215229	0.294093
16	Mean of envelope extension data	0.167474	0.124315	0.108711	0.178954

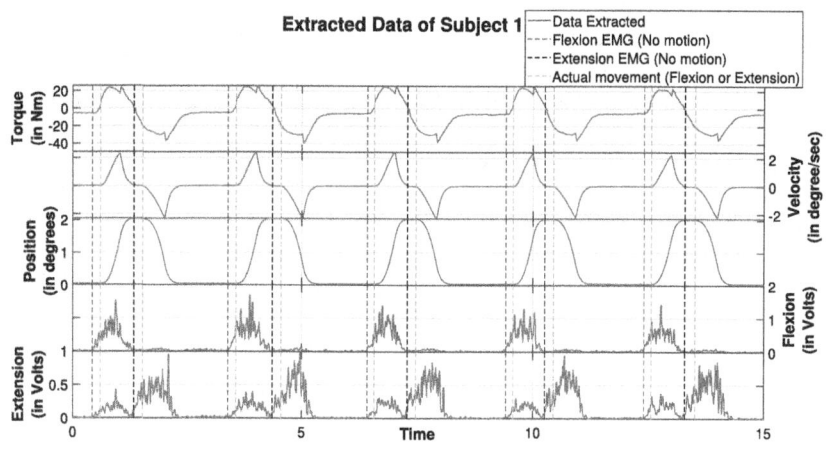

Fig. 3. Data Plot of Subject 1

When analyzing a single flexion and extension cycle of the elbow, we observed some electrical activity (EMG) from the triceps muscle (responsible for extension) even during flexion. However, the triceps EMG signal was always weaker than the bicep EMG signal (responsible for flexion). Similarly, there was minimal bicep activity during elbow extension, with the triceps EMG signal being consistently stronger.

Additionally, the graphs shown in Figs. 3, 4, 5 and 6, revealed a time difference between the initial detection of EMG activity (represented by the red and black

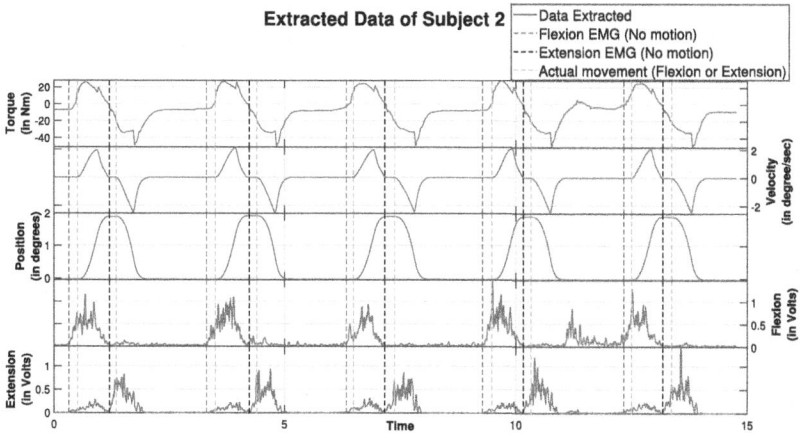

Fig. 4. Data Plot of Subject 2

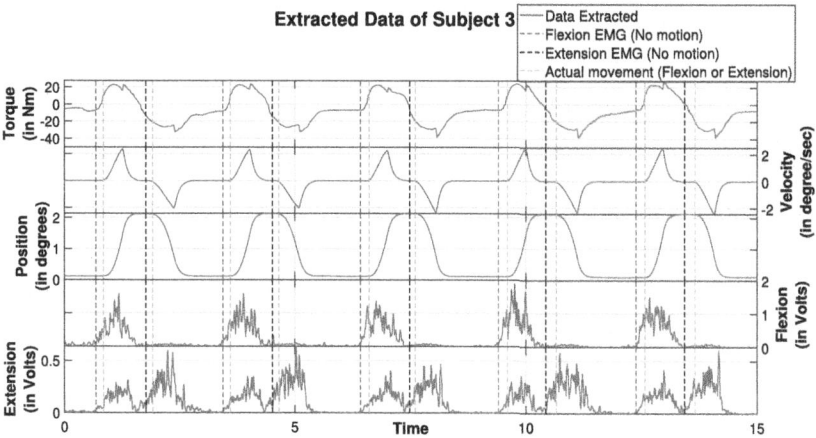

Fig. 5. Data Plot of Subject 3

lines) and the actual start of movement (represented by the green line). This indicates a delay between the brain sending signals to the muscles (EMG) and the muscles generating enough force to initiate movement. This delay is followed by changes in the elbow's position, speed (velocity), and torque.

As you can see in Table 3, The analysis revealed several key observations regarding the relationship between EMG signals, user intent, and elbow movement:

Time Delay Between Intent and Movement: A consistent time delay was observed between the detection of EMG signal (indicating user intent) and the actual initiation of elbow flexion/extension movement. This delay varied between

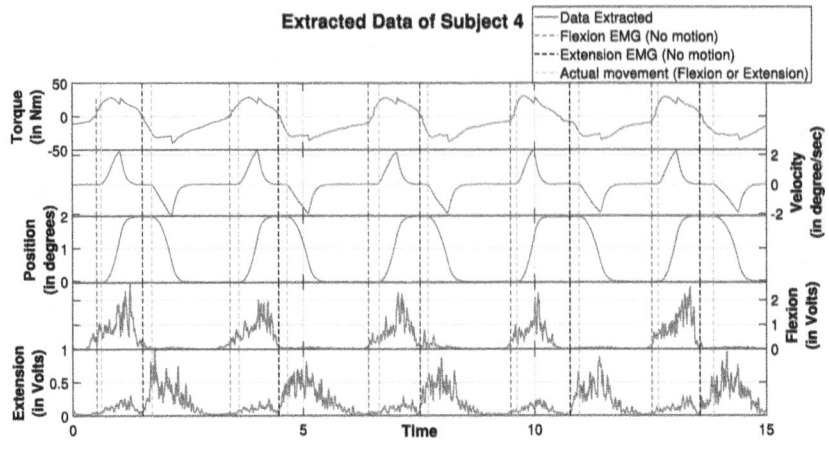

Fig. 6. Data Plot of Subject 4

Table 3. The table above presents the Time difference and average time difference between the EMG getting detected and Actual motion being started for flexion and extension movements of elbow joint

Subjects	No. of Cycles	EMG Detected		Actual Moment		Difference		Average	
		Flexion	Extension	Flexion	Extension	Flexion	Extension	Flexion	Extension
Subject 1	1	0.429	1.345	0.6055	1.5345	0.1765	0.1895	**0.1628**	**0.1946**
	2	3.415	4.3625	3.589	4.548	0.174	0.1855		
	3	6.4265	7.2785	6.574	7.465	0.1475	0.1865		
	4	9.4045	10.2555	9.564	10.445	0.1595	0.1895		
	5	12.398	13.2795	12.5545	13.5015	0.1565	0.222		
Subject 2	1	0.32	1.2075	0.507	1.3555	0.187	0.148	**0.1791**	**0.1766**
	2	3.313	4.2335	3.5015	4.3985	0.1885	0.165		
	3	6.335	7.1625	6.485	7.376	0.15	0.2135		
	4	9.283	10.1615	9.4835	10.33	0.2005	0.1685		
	5	12.3215	13.1665	12.491	13.3545	0.1695	0.188		
Subject 3	1	0.6805	1.769	0.846	1.918	0.1655	0.149	**0.1802**	**0.1773**
	2	3.445	4.5075	3.602	4.6545	0.157	0.147		
	3	6.4155	7.464	6.606	7.6005	0.1905	0.1365		
	4	9.403	10.427	9.598	10.6575	0.195	0.2305		
	5	12.3695	13.4245	12.5625	13.648	0.193	0.2235		
Subject 4	1	0.5145	1.526	0.615	1.727	0.1005	0.201	**0.158**	**0.2081**
	2	3.4335	4.4775	3.6245	4.662	0.191	0.1845		
	3	6.4125	7.5165	6.642	7.6875	0.2295	0.171		
	4	9.476	10.7555	9.6075	10.9535	0.1315	0.198		
	5	12.523	13.558	12.6605	13.844	0.1375	0.286		

subjects, with an average ranging from 162.8 ms to 194.6 ms for subject 1. This highlights the need to account for this delay when designing control algorithms for exoskeletons.

EMG Signal Variations: The amplitude of the EMG signal differed between the initiation of intent and the actual movement for both flexion and extension. While the difference wasn't significant for consecutive cycles within a subject, it varied considerably between subjects. This suggests that relying solely on EMG amplitude for intent classification might be challenging.

Torque and Velocity: The torque required to initiate movement began increasing before the actual elbow motion. For flexion, a notable increase in torque occurred upon movement initiation. Conversely, for extension, torque increased steadily in the opposite direction. The maximum angular velocity for elbow motion was around 2.2 degrees/second for all subjects.

Limitations of Range of Motion: EMG signals continued even after the elbow reached its flexion/extension limits. This necessitates incorporating range-of-motion constraints into control systems to prevent overexertion or injury.

Developing effective control for our exosuit hinges on synchronizing actuator activation and deactivation with user intent, while accounting for anatomical limitations. Ideally, upon detecting actual elbow flexion/extension, the actuator would initiate movement transmission to the exosuit/exoskeleton with minimal delay. However, delaying actuation until actual movement is detected based solely on EMG introduces a further latency, potentially compromising user intent capture and hindering real-time control.

The human upper limb possesses 7 degrees-of-freedom (DOF), with each joint having a specific range of motion (ROM). During elbow flexion/extension, EMG signal generation precedes actual movement. While this allows for recording, analysis, and subsequent actuation based on EMG. Even after reaching its flexion/extension limit, the elbow continues to generate EMG, despite the absence of further movement. To address this, actuator operation needs to be limited based on the defined ROM, ensuring deactivation upon reaching the elbow's anatomical limits even if EMG persists.

We have extracted out the data for Flexion-Extension movements. Initially we find the mean of amplitude of EMG (in volts), when Flexion and Extension starts which can be visualised in the plots by 'RED' (for Flexion) and 'BLACK' (for Extension) dotted lines (Please see Figs. 3, 4, 5 and 6). The 'Red' and 'Black' lines actually shows that the Flexion/Extension movements has been initiated but the actual movement of the hand has not started yet. The actual movement starts with some delay, after the Flexion/Extension movement is detected. This actual movement in the graph can be visualized by the 'GREEN' lines, also it is easy to verify when the actual movement starts with the plot of change in Positions (in degrees), we can also observe changes in Torque (in N-m) and Velocity (in degrees/second) of the hand with changes in position of the arm.

5.1 Implications for Controls Based on Suggested Method

The above findings provide valuable insight for developing EMG based control system. Here, we discuss some key-points and future considerations.

Addressing Time Delay: The observed delay between EMG detection and movement initiation underscores the importance of incorporating this factor into control algorithms. Strategies can be explored to minimize the perceived delay and improve responsiveness.

EMG Signal Classification: The variability of EMG signal amplitude across subjects emphasizes the need for robust classification techniques. Future work will investigate machine learning algorithms and feature extraction methods to enhance classification accuracy.

Importance of MVC Normalization: While not implemented in this study, including MVC normalization in future data collection will account for baseline muscle strength variations between subjects.

Fatigue Analysis: Expanding the study to include fatigue analysis is crucial. The impact of muscle fatigue on EMG signal characteristics needs to be investigated to ensure reliable control during extended use.

Control System Design: Building upon these findings, the next steps involve designing and evaluating control algorithms for an exoskeleton based on real-time EMG data and incorporating range-of-motion constraints.

6   Conclusion

This study successfully investigated the feasibility of using EMG signals for user intent recognition in upper-limb rehabilitation. Analyzing EMG data during elbow flexion and extension tasks identified a time delay between user intent detection and actual movement. Furthermore, the study underscored the impact of user variability on EMG signal characteristics. These findings highlight the importance of incorporating time delay compensation and robust classification techniques when designing EMG-based control systems for exoskeletons. Future research will focus on refining classification algorithms using machine learning, incorporating muscle force normalization for enhanced user independence, and exploring the influence of muscle fatigue on EMG signals. Expanding the subject pool to include individuals with neurological conditions will be crucial for developing generalizable control strategies applicable to real-world rehabilitation settings.

Acknowledgement. We would like to thank IHFC, New Delhi (Grant no.: GP/2021/RR/017) for funding the Project. We acknowledge all the subjects who participated in research help us to collect the data. Also, we would like to thank Mahindra University, Hyderabad, India to support the research and provide related infrastructure.

References

1. Reaz, M.B.I., Hussain, M.S., Mohd-Yasin, F.: Techniques of EMG signal analysis: detection, processing, classification and applications. Biol. Proced. Online **8**(1), 11–35 (2006)
2. Chowdhury, R., Reaz, M., Ali, M., Bakar, A., Chellappan, K., Chang, T.: Surface electromyography signal processing and classification techniques. Sensors **13**(9), 12431–12466 (2013)
3. Yang, H., Wan, J., Jin, Y., Xixia, Yu., Fang, Y.: EEG- and EMG-driven poststroke rehabilitation: a review. IEEE Sens. J. **22**(24), 23649–23660 (2022)
4. Cesqui, B., Tropea, P., Micera, S., Krebs, H.: EMG-based pattern recognition approach in post stroke robot-aided rehabilitation: a feasibility study. J. Neuroeng. Rehabil. **10**(1), 75 (2013)
5. Kai-Hsiang Stanley Chen and Robert Chen: Principles of electrophysiological assessments for movement disorders. J. Mov. Disord. **13**(1), 27–38 (2020)
6. Sadikoglu, F., Kavalcioglu, C., Dagman, B.: Electromyogram (EMG) signal detection, classification of EMG signals and diagnosis of neuropathy muscle disease. Procedia Comput. Sci. **120**, 422–429 (2017)
7. Seth, D., Chablat, D., Bennis, F., Sakka, S., Jubeau, M., Nordez, A.: Validation of a new dynamic muscle fatigue model and DMET analysis. Int. J. Virtual Reality **16**(1), 22–32 (2016)
8. Meattini, R., Benatti, S., Scarcia, U., De Gregorio, D., Benini, L., Melchiorri, C.: An sEMG-based human-robot interface for robotic hands using machine learning and synergies. IEEE Trans. Compon. Packag. Manufact. Technol. **8**(7), 1149–1158 (2018)
9. Seth, D., Chablat, D., Bennis, F., Sakka, S., Jubeau, M., Nordez, A.: New dynamic muscle fatigue model to limit musculo-skeletal disorder. In: Proceedings of the 2016 Virtual Reality International Conference, VRIC '16. ACM (2016)
10. Chen, M., Liu, H.: Robot arm control method using forearm EMG signals. MATEC Web Conf. **309**, 04007 (2020)
11. Fleming, A., Stafford, N., Huang, S., Hu, X., Ferris, D.P., Huang, H.: Myoelectric control of robotic lower limb prostheses: a review of electromyography interfaces, control paradigms, challenges and future directions. J. Neural Eng. **18**(4), 041004 (2021)
12. Lotti, N., et al.: Adaptive model-based myoelectric control for a soft wearable arm exosuit: a new generation of wearable robot control. IEEE Robot. Autom. Mag. **27**(1), 43–53 (2020)
13. Seth, D., Vardhan Varma, V.K.H., Anirudh, P., Kalyan, P.: Preliminary design of soft Exo-suit for arm rehabilitation. In: Duffy, V.G. (ed.) HCII 2019. LNCS, vol. 11582, pp. 284–294. Springer, Cham (2019). https://doi.org/10.1007/978-3-030-?????-2_22
14. Hallett, M., Shahani, B.T., Young, R.R.: EMG analysis of stereotyped voluntary movements in man. J. Neurol. Neurosurg. Psychiatry **38**(12), 1154–1162 (1975)
15. Viitasalo, J.H.T., Komi, P.V.: Signal characteristics of EMG during fatigue. Eur. J. Appl. Physiol. Occup. Physiol. **37**(2), 111–121 (1977)
16. Pattichis, C.S., Schizas, C.N., Middleton, L.T.: Neural network models in EMG diagnosis. IEEE Trans. Biomed. Eng. **42**(5), 486–496 (1995)
17. Fatma Güler, N., Koçer, S.: Classification of EMG signals using PCA and fit. J. Med. Syst. **29**(3), 241–250 (2005)

18. Bengacemi, H., Gharbi, A.H., Ravier, P., Abed-Meraim, K., Buttelli, O.: Surface EMG signal segmentation based on hmm modelling: application on Parkinson's disease. ENP Eng. Sci. J. **1**(1), 63–74 (2021)
19. Zheng, M., Crouch, M.S., Eggleston, M.S.: Surface electromyography as a natural human-machine interface: a review. IEEE Sens. J. **22**(10), 9198–9214 (2022)
20. Phinyomark, A., Campbell, E., Scheme, E.: Surface electromyography (EMG) signal processing, classification, and practical considerations. In: Naik, G. (ed.) Biomedical Signal Processing. SB, pp. 3–29. Springer, Singapore (2020). https://doi.org/10.1007/978-981-13-9097-5_1
21. Martinek, R., et al.: Advanced bioelectrical signal processing methods: past, present, and future approach-part III: other Biosignals. Sensors **21**(18), 6064 (2021)
22. Phinyomark, A., Khushaba, R.N., Scheme, E.: Feature extraction and selection for myoelectric control based on wearable EMG sensors. Sensors **18**(5), 1615 (2018)
23. Paul, Y., Goyal, V., Jaswal, R.A.: Comparative analysis between SVM & KNN classifier for EMG signal classification on elementary time domain features. In: 2017 4th International Conference on Signal Processing, Computing and Control (ISPCC). IEEE (2017)
24. Lee, K.H., Min, J.Y., Byun, S.: Electromyogram-based classification of hand and finger gestures using artificial neural networks. Sensors **22**(1), 225 (2021)
25. Seyidbayli, C., Salhi, F., Akdogan, E.: Comparison of machine learning algorithms for EMG signal classification. Periodicals Eng. Nat. Sci. **8**(2), 1165–1176 (2020)
26. Caraguay, Á.L.V., Vásconez, J.P., López, L.I.B., Benalcázar, M.E.: Recognition of hand gestures based on EMG signals with deep and double-deep q-networks. Sensors **23**(8), 3905 (2023)
27. Li, W., Shi, P., Yu, H.: Gesture recognition using surface electromyography and deep learning for prostheses hand: state-of-the-art, challenges, and future. Front. Neurosci. **15**, 621885 (2021)
28. Vásconez, J.P., Barona López, L.I., Caraguay, Á.L.V., Benalcázar, M.E.: A comparison of EMG-based hand gesture recognition systems based on supervised and reinforcement learning. Eng. Appl. Artif. Intell. **123**, 106327 (2023)
29. Seth, D., Chablat, D., Sakka, S., Bennis, F.: Experimental validation of a new dynamic muscle fatigue model. In: Duffy, V.G.G. (ed.) DHM 2016. LNCS, vol. 9745, pp. 54–65. Springer, Cham (2016). https://doi.org/10.1007/978-3-319-40247-5_6
30. Zwerus, E.L., Willigenburg, N.W., Scholtes, V.A., Somford, M.P., Eygendaal, D., van den Bekerom, M.P.J.: Normative values and affecting factors for the elbow range of motion. Shoulder Elbow **11**(3), 215–224 (2017)

On-Skin Interaction System and Smart Wearable Research Based on Innovative Gesture Input

Chen Wang[✉]

School of Industrial Design, China Academy of Art, Hangzhou, China
wangchen6171@sina.com

Abstract. The rapid development of technology has greatly contributed to the innovation and popularization of smart wearables, which has not only made significant breakthroughs in functionality, design aesthetics, and user experience but also pushed forward the advancement of related technologies. However, existing research has found that one of the main limitations of current smart wearable devices lies in the limited nature of the interaction interface - especially the limitations of the screen size and the singularity of the input function. Skin is a permanent, portable, and flexible natural interaction interface that can be used as a novel interaction carrier. In this study, an innovative on-skin input and output system is proposed based on the exploration of skin properties and improved sensing techniques. It is designed to use human skin as a virtual interaction medium, allowing users to issue various operation commands by executing different interaction gestures on the arm skin to realize different functional applications; in addition, feedback information is provided intuitively and dynamically by projecting a virtual interface on the skin on both sides of the arm and the back of the hand as the visual output of a dual-screen display. The main contribution of this study lies in its exploration of future interfaces, especially the potential of using skin as an interface to realize physical and virtual interactions. This not only provides a theoretical basis for understanding new dimensions of human-computer interaction but also opens up an under-explored interaction space, bringing new design ideas and possibilities to the smart application market.

Keywords: On-Skin Interaction · Future Interface · Innovative Gesture Input · Smart Wearable · On-Skin Display

1 Introduction

In the current technological era, smart wearable devices and other digital accessories are evolving, driving innovation in human-computer interaction interfaces. However, these devices generally face a significant problem - the limitation of the size of the interaction space. This limitation not only narrows the interaction area but also tends to obscure part of the screen with the user's fingers during use, further reducing the efficiency and comfort of the interaction. Moreover, current input functions are relatively basic, usually limited to limited key operations or basic gesture recognition. In the face of this challenge, researchers and developers are actively exploring new technologies and approaches to break through the existing constraints. Voice interaction, mixed reality, and even more cutting-edge brain-computer interaction are all considered potential solutions. But in fact, there is one seemingly overlooked member of the future user interface team that has a distinct advantage over the rest. That is on-skin interaction.

Human skin, as the largest organ in the human body, has the advantage of being readily available without the need to worry about portability. From a physiological point of view, the sensory ability of the skin provides humans with precise proprioception, allowing us to interact with the body precisely without the limitation of the eyes, a characteristic that makes skin-based interaction provide a more natural and intuitive user experience. Utilizing skin as an interaction platform not only expands the variety of interaction gestures but also enables fine-grained physical and virtual interactions through innovative touch technologies. In addition, although differences in skin color and skin texture may have some impact on the effectiveness of skin as a display vehicle, existing studies have shown that the resolution, frame rate, and overall quality can be achieved at a relatively satisfactory level.

This study aims to explore the unique properties of skin as a novel interaction carrier. Through an in-depth study of the skin's sensory mechanism and interaction potential, the author developed a series of innovative skin-based interaction gestures and combined them with advanced touch technology to construct a new skin interface interaction system. This system not only breaks the limitation of interaction space size but also brings a more natural and smooth interaction experience for users. Through this study, the author expects to take a key step in realizing a richer, more flexible, and seamless interaction experience, thus promoting the further development of smart wearable devices and their applications.

2   Literature Review

2.1   The Evolution and Limitations of Smart Wear

The concept of smart wearables dates back as far as the 1970s when research focused on wearable computing devices that could support simple computing and data processing tasks. Most of the early devices were bulky and limited in functionality, but they laid the foundation for the development of smart wearable technology. It wasn't until the beginning of the 21st century, with the rapid development of high-precision sensors, low-power processors, wireless communications, biometrics, and other technologies, that the concept gained widespread application and development. Nowadays, smart wearables, as an emerging technology product, have shown great application potential in many fields such as healthcare, personal entertainment, sports, and industrial military. It possesses more complex and diversified application scenarios, providing users with real-time health monitoring, intelligent notification, GPS navigation, mobile payment and social interaction, etc., and becoming an indispensable part of people's daily lives [1].

Despite the significant advances in functionality and convenience, smart wearables still face many limitations and challenges. Today's smart wearables, especially smart-watches and other digital wearables, typically have small physical dimensions due to their design requirements. This results in devices with very limited input surfaces (e.g., touchscreens, buttons), making it difficult to perform complex gestures or precise inputs. When users interact on such small-sized interfaces, they often encounter problems such as finger occlusion and mis-touching, which limits the naturalness and smoothness of user interaction [2]. In addition, the small interaction area also increases the difficulty of designing the interaction interface, and designers need to create intuitive and easy-to-use user interfaces within the limited space. At the same time, the miniaturized output interface not only affects the richness and readability of the information display but also restricts the display effect of multimedia content. For applications that need to display complex data, navigate maps, or receive detailed notifications, a small screen significantly reduces the ease of use of information and the efficiency of user interaction.

To summarize, while smart wearables show great potential in several areas, their limitations cannot be ignored. These limitations mainly stem from the physical size of the device and the challenges of technical implementation. It carries two main functions: (1) input, receiving the human's operation intention, and (2) output, presenting the results. It is possible to move the interactive interface from the screen to other interactive media, enhance the functionality and experience of smart wearables by developing new input/output technologies, and explore new interaction methods.

2.2 Skin Characteristics and Interface Properties

Skin is the largest organ of the human body, and human skin is a physical interface between human beings and the environment. However, it is not just a layer of "skin" or a layer of "protective film" that wraps the body, but a "strategy and mind" that adapts life to the environment. The development of smart wearables is inseparable from the study of the interface, and skin and interface are both similar and different. Similarly, human beings perceive some information from the outside world through the skin, and interact with the body through being touched; while machines receive feedback information through the interface, and then interact with the outside world. The difference is that the skin belongs to humans and the interface belongs to machines. So, can human skin be used as some kind of interface to realize human-machine interaction?

First of all, skin is always on our body, always available, no need to think about "carrying" it. Secondly, physiologically, the skin can perfectly support human proprioception and tactile perception (Fig. 1). Proprioception refers to the individual's ability to perceive the location of body parts, the state of movement, and the characteristics of external objects, and is the basis for human interaction with the environment. It is capable of capturing a wide range of sensory information such as temperature, pressure, touch, pain, etc. through the abundant nerve endings distributed in the epidermis and dermis. This information is crucial for forming an awareness of one's body state and the external environment and is directly involved in the formation of proprioception. Tactile feedback is an integral part of proprioception. The skin's tactile perceptual capabilities, including sensitivity to light touch, pressure changes, and texture differences, provide the body with a precise and immediate feedback mechanism. Thus, the skin itself is likely to be a

390   C. Wang

new type of touch-sensitive interactive surface with several special user interface properties [3]: it has a very large input and output surface area, is easy to reach, and permits
direct, subtle, and discreet interaction. This applies to a wide range of mobile activities,
including walking, running, driving a car, or taking public transportation. Finally, in
exploring the potential of using skin as a visual output display vehicle, differences in
human skin tone and skin texture, such as color depth, glossiness, and texture coarseness
and orientation, can have an impact on the quality of the projected image. In particular,
during light penetration and reflection, different skin tones and textures scatter light in
different ways, affecting image clarity and color accuracy. However, existing studies
have shown that the display resolution, frame rate, and overall image quality of skin
as a carrier for output display can reach a satisfactory level by using advanced image
processing techniques and optical systems [4].

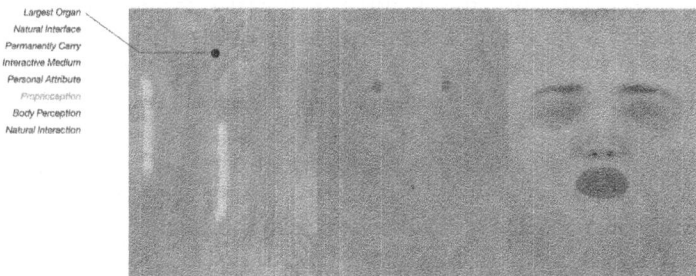

Fig. 1. Skin characteristics.

To sum up, the structural and functional properties of skin make it an ideal medium for
supporting human proprioception. The development of technologies that utilize skin for
human-computer interaction is not only feasible but also has significant potential through
an in-depth study of the correlation between skin properties and interface attributes.
Although the diversity of skin color and texture poses a challenge for achieving high-
quality skin displays, through current technological advances and future research directions, we can foresee the strong performance of skin as an interactive interface to provide
a more natural, intuitive, and efficient user experience.

2.3 Smart Wear Based on On-Skin Interaction

In the field of contemporary scientific research, smart wearable technologies based on
on-skin interaction are considered a cutting-edge and interdisciplinary research topic. Its
core objective is to deeply explore the potential application value of skin - as the largest
and directly connected natural surface of the human body - to drive technological innovation and development in the context of human-computer interaction. It has been shown
that in the context of skin interfaces, researchers have analyzed these most commonly
used wearability factors in the design of wearable devices based on both body aspects
(location, body movements, body characteristics) and device aspects (weight, attach-
ment method, accessibility, interaction, aesthetics, conductors, insulation, device care,

connection, communication, battery life), and have added novel skin interface-specific factors, opening up the possibility of creating novel on-skin interactions [5].

In addition, wearable research around skin covers a wide range of fields such as bio-skin, e-skin, and artificial skin (Fig. 2). These cases not only demonstrate the integration and innovation of interdisciplinary technologies but also provide substantial research basis and technical support for the future innovation of human-computer interaction. For example, OmniTouch and Multi-Touch Skin [6, 8], which explored and prototyped skin-based multi-touch input; SkinMarks [9], which demonstrated novel interaction techniques utilizing skin markers' unique touch, squeeze, and bend sensing with integrated visual outputs; SkinWire [10], PhysioSkin and SkinKit [11, 12], which investigate and design flexible electronic skins to transform wearable devices from their traditional box-like form to a fully self-contained, on-skin form; SkinPaper [13], which proposes woven paper as a wearable material for interacting with the skin, utilizing paper's versatility to lower the barriers to rapid prototyping of skin interfaces, providing a new user-friendly design strategy and potential for the creation of sustainable skin interfaces.

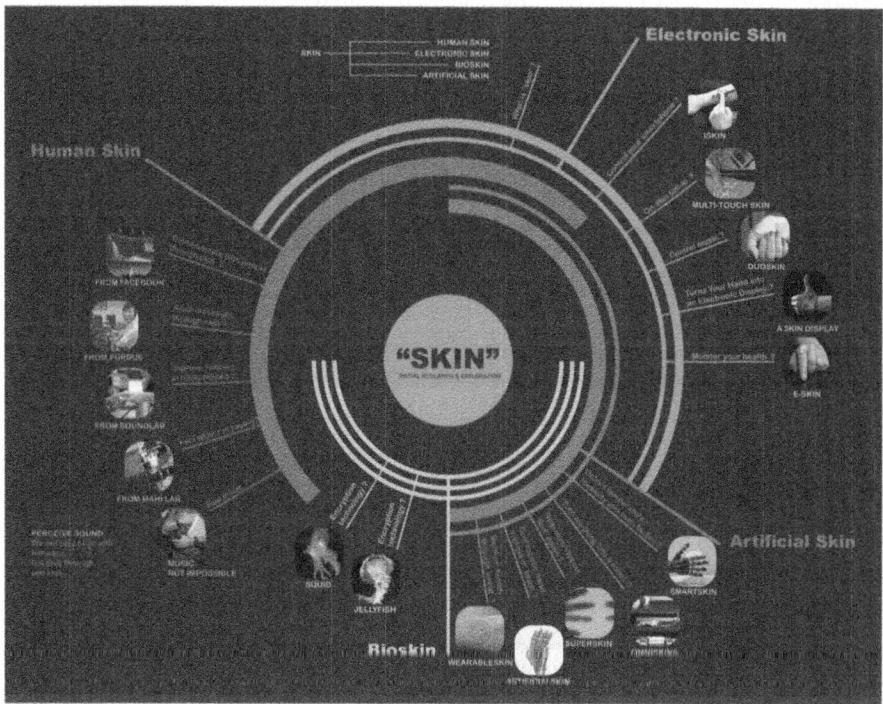

Fig. 2. Cases of skin interaction.

Researchers in the field of human-computer interaction have been exploring the possibility of using skin as an input and output surface. Currently, there are these tech-nological means for possible on-skin inputs: optical, acoustics, and radio frequency [2, 7, 8] (Fig. 3). (1) Among the optical means, infrared sensing is the most used one.

Infrared sensors are used to detect the deformation of the skin brought about by the user after the skin manipulation, thus recognizing the different manipulations; (2) Detecting the distance and position of a touch on the skin can be done not only optically, but also acoustically, like bats flying at night for localization. By using ultrasound sensors, simple user interactions on the arm can be detected. For example, pause, play, switch, etc. can be performed on the arm to control the device's player. Another way is to use inertial sensors and microphone devices to detect the bioacoustics propagation caused by vibrations interacting on the skin, and then use artificial intelligence algorithms to hypothesize the interaction events that occurred; (3) RF means can also be used to recognize inputs on the skin. Using the technique of electric field sensing, but requiring the wearing of a device, the skin is covered with an electric field at a certain distance around the device, which then recognizes the user's actions on the skin. Or using SFCS (Swept frequency capacitive sensing), which can turn almost any object into a device that is sensitive to human touch, which senses multiple frequencies emitted from body parts and then analyzes how the user interacts. As for skin output, effective solutions for visual information output are dominated by projection. Current skin projection displays are more likely to consist of projection devices that are well-placed in the environment. For example, performing a surgical procedure and providing visual aids to the surgeon through a targeted projection display. Another is Skinput [2], which is more in line with the human imagination of skin interaction, where the user's input is detected by the previously mentioned methods, and the output of the interface is controlled by a small video camera that is carried with the user.

Fig. 3. Technological analysis.

Based on the above research cases, it can be concluded that this research field is currently in a stage of rapid development, not only making important progress in theoretical research but also showing great potential in practical applications. Facing the future, research in this field will need to address the integration of more interdisciplinary technologies. Despite the challenges of technological realization, such as biocompatibility and durability of materials, miniaturization of integrated circuits, and how to ensure the comfort and stability of long-term wear, with the continuous progress in the fields of materials science, electrical engineering, biomedicine, and artificial intelligence, smart wearable devices based on skin interaction will provide a more natural, rich, and innovative solution for human-computer interaction, and also will human life and work will bring revolutionary changes.

3   Methodology

3.1   Research Objects and Methods

This study mainly adopts the experimental method and cooperates with the interview method, questionnaire method, observation method, and measurement method to carry out the investigation. The subjects of the study include users who have used smart wearable devices and users who love smart interactive products, aim to understand their attitudes and feedback on the input location, output location, input influence factors, output influence factors, input gestures, and output instruction of on-skin interaction. A total of 30 users aged between 15 and 65 years old participated in this study. The data collected from all the experiments will inform further case studies in this area.

3.2   Research Process and Experiments

The study was divided into six parts (Table 1). The first and second parts are the testing of input location and output location. The author proposed upper extremity input and output locations for the subjects to try (forearm, hand, fingers, etc.) because these are the most commonly used locations that are easy to reach and see, and they have also been shown to be highly socially acceptable. Also, the author proposed more non-traditional locations, such as the face, neck, and chest, to be explored as input locations. This phase of testing does not use any specific sensing technology, nor does it provide any form of inputs and outputs, and is intended to allow the author to examine the complete design space of inputs and outputs, independent of the constraints imposed by existing technology. Subjects were evaluated around the area of use, flexibility, ease of use, comfort, and preference for different input and output locations.

Table 1. Research steps.

No.	Experiment Method	Experiment Content	Target Users
1	Experiments, Questionnaires	Input Location Testing	users who
2	Experiments, Questionnaires	Output Location Testing	have used smart
3	Experiments, Observation	Input Influence Factor Testing	wear / users
4	Experiments, Observation	Output Influence Factor Testing	who love smart
5	Experiments, Measurement	Input Gesture Testing	interactive
6	Experiments, Measurement	Output Instruction Testing	products

The third and fourth parts are the tests of input and output influence factors. This part of the study used a combination of experimental and observational methods to do a series of tests on the effects of bone structure, skin texture, body hair, skin elasticity, and skin color on the on-skin interaction of the subject's skin, and an in-depth analysis of each of the influencing factors was conducted.

The fifth part is input gesture testing, which focuses on what the characteristics of skin-specific input modalities are and what gestures the user can perform on the skin.

Since existing sensor technologies can only capture some of the input modalities that may be present on the skin, the author asked the participants to perform gestural interactions directly on their bare skin without any technological aids or bodily instrumentation and to imagine that their skin would sense their inputs through something that has not yet been invented. Furthermore, to avoid the participants being distracted by a specific form or location of output, this testing phase chose not to provide output in any way that would ensure direct, natural haptic feedback.

The sixth part is the output instruction testing. The output instructions corresponding to each input gesture are tested for accuracy and validity by performing visual interactions based on the gesture form and skin deformation when the input gesture interacts with the skin.

4   Experimental Results and Analysis

4.1   Input Location Testing

The main question explored in the input location testing is where the preferred location for gesture input is. Not only did the author propose upper extremity locations (forearm, hand, fingers, etc.) that have been shown to have high social acceptance for testing, but more non-traditional locations (face, neck, chest, etc.) were also proposed for the experimental subjects to try out (Fig. 4). During the process, the test did not provide any form of technology to interfere with the exploration of input positions, and the experimental subjects evaluated and ranked the different input positions around 5 aspects (use area, flexibility, ease of use, comfort, and preference) for additional suggestions (Table 2).

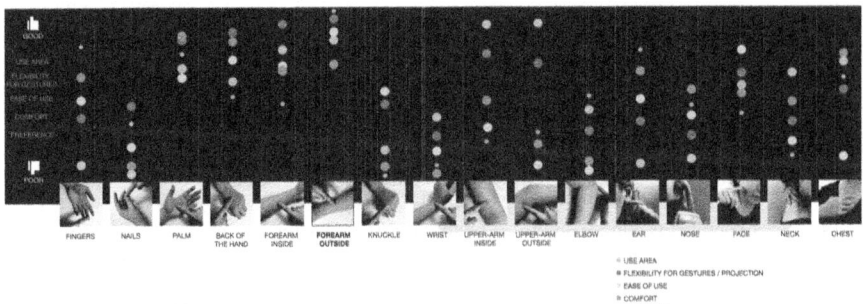

Fig. 4. Test contents and results of the input location.

Table 2. Satisfaction ranking of test contents in input location.

Experiment Content	Experiment Subject	Test Content	Top 3 for Satisfaction
		Use Area	Upper-arm outside= inside> Forearm outside
		Flexibility	Forearm outside>Forearm inside> Back of the hand
	30 Users	Ease of Use	Forearm outside> Face> Back of the hand
Input		Comfort	Palm> Back of the hand> Forearm out-side
Location		Preference	Forearm outside> Fingers> Ear

The results show that (1) the outside of the forearm is the preferred location for input and can be used for gesture input; (2) the inside of the forearm, the back of the hand, and the palm are also frequently used by users as input locations; (3) as input locations, the upper arm and the joint area are rarely used; and (4) for nontraditional locations, they do not fit the user's habit of use.

4.2   Output Location Testing

In the output location testing, the question focused on where the preferred location for visual output is. Again, the author presented upper extremity locations (forearm, hand, fingers, etc.) that have been shown to have high social acceptability for experimental subjects to explore (Fig. 5), but did not present more nontraditional locations as was done in the input location testing. In the process, the test used projection as the output medium, and experimental subjects evaluated and ranked (Table 3) around 5 aspects (use area, flexibility, ease of use, comfort, and preference) of the different output positions for additional possibilities.

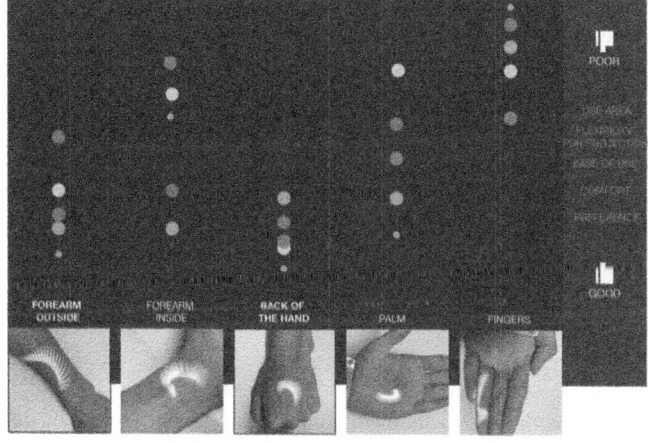

Fig. 5. Test contents and results of the output location.

Table 3. Satisfaction ranking of test contents in output location.

Experiment Content	Experiment Subject	Test Content	Top 3 for Satisfaction
		Use Area	Forearm outside=Forearm inside>Back of the hand
		Flexibility	Back of the hand>Forearm outside>Forearm inside
	30 Users	Ease of Use	Back of the hand>Forearm outside>Forearm inside
Output Location		Comfort	Back of the hand>Palm>Forearm outside
		Preference	Back of the hand> Forearm outside>Palm

The results of the analysis show that both the outside of the forearm and the back of the hand are better output locations. However, in the previous input position testing, it has been concluded that the outside of the forearm is the best position for gesture input. Also, in the initial research, it has been concluded that input and output cannot be performed in the same position. (This is because skin input patterns that produce strong distortions may interfere with the output effect, distorting the projected surface and affecting the user's experience. Similarly, users performing gesture inputs directly on the visual outputs would obscure the visual information.)

Therefore, it was further concluded that (1) the back of the hand is the preferred location for output and can be used for visual output; (2) the palm and the inside of the forearm can be used as output locations but cannot be used for long periods and the user will feel fatigued and uncomfortable; and (3) as an output location, the finger area is rarely used due to its lack of flatness.

4.3 Input Influence Factor Testing

In the input influence factor testing, the main research is about which factors of the skin will be affected by the gesture input, and to what extent. The author sampled the skin of different experimental subjects for the study and conducted an in-depth analysis of the bone structure, skin texture, body hair, skin elasticity, and skin color on their skin one by one (Table 4).

The main findings suggest that (1) variations in bone structure, skin texture, body hair, skin elasticity, and skin color on the skin provide many recognizable signs to the body; (2) skin texture and skin color do not affect input, but skin elasticity and body hair slightly affect the degree of gesture input; (3) the form of gesture input is largely influenced and limited by bone structure; and (4) these visual and spatial cues of the body can help to localize the body interface and guide input on the body.

4.4 Output Influence Factor Testing

In the output influence factor testing, the focus of the inquiry is on what factors of the skin affect the visual output and to what extent. The author sampled the skin of different experimental subjects and conducted an in-depth analysis of the bone structure, skin texture, body hair, skin elasticity, and skin color on the skin one by one (Table 5).

Table 4. Analysis of input influence factor.

Experiment Content	Experiment Subject	Test Content	Analysis Results
Input Influence Factor	30 Users	Bone Structure	Bone structure is made up of bones and joints in the body, resulting in curved surface geometries. Gesture input is affected and limited by it to some extent.
		Skin Texture	Skin texture, thickness and orientation of skin texture can be accurately touched and felt, but does not affect gesture input.
		Body Hair	Body hair generally has little effect on gesture input, but overly dense body hair may inconvenience input.
		Skin Elasticity	Skin elasticity varies with body location and depends on the amount of elastin in the dermis. These soft landmarks provide localized skin deformations that can slightly affect the degree of gesture input.
		Skin Color	Skin color depends on genetic, racial and external factors, among others, but does not affect gesture input.

Table 5. Analysis of output influence factor.

Experiment Content	Experiment Subject	Test Content	Analysis Results
Output Influence Factor	30 Users	Bone Structure	Bone structure is made up of bones and joints in the body, resulting in curved surface geometries. The hand visual output will be largely influenced and limited by it.
		Skin Texture	The texture, thickness and orientation of the skin texture scatters the projected light in different ways, but does not affect the clarity and accuracy of the visual output.
		Body Hair	Body hair generally has little effect on visual output, but overly dense body hair may have an effect on the clarity of the output.
		Skin Elasticity	Skin elasticity varies with body location and depends on the amount of elastin in the dermis. These soft landmarks provide localized skin deformation but do not affect the output at all.
		Skin Color	Skin pigmentation varies and therefore their visual properties are prominent. The darker the skin color, the more pronounced the effect on the output, especially on the accuracy of the colors.

The research results show that (1) skin elasticity does not affect the output at all; (2) skin texture and body hair slightly affect the clarity of the visual output, but are negligible; (3) skin color affects the color of the output content, and the darker the skin color, the more pronounced the effect is, but does not affect the accuracy of the output content; and (4) the form of the visual output is largely influenced by the bone structure of the influence and limitation. Flat skin areas will render the output content perfectly, while curved and uneven surfaces, like finger areas, will distort the projection badly.

4.5 Input Gesture Testing

In the input gesture testing, the main questions explored were what characterizes skin-specific input modalities and what gestures users can perform on their skin. The author asked experimental subjects to interact directly on their bare skin without any technological augmentation and to imagine that their skin would perceive their gestural input through something that had not yet been invented. During the test, some participants were performing gestures over the skin as if there was a virtual screen on their arm, with an input pattern similar to traditional touch gestures. Some participants performed gestures on the surface of the skin, which they explored more deeply and naturally compared to the former.

Characteristics of On-Skin Input Patterns. The analysis shows that on-skin input has a dual characterization. First, it is compatible with many existing smartphone gestures. Participants successfully transferred common multi-touch gestures from the touchscreen to on-skin input. This applies to typical commands common to smartphones, such as zooming in or out, swiping left or right, and moving content.

Input Gestures for Deep Interaction. Skin is fundamentally different from traditional touch surfaces. Due to its flexibility, skin can not only be touched, but also pulled, squeezed, and twisted, among other things. This increases the input space for skin-to-skin interactions and enables a much wider variety of forms of interaction, which is very promising. In addition, skin interactions have a strong personal emotional component. Such interactions allow for more personalized modes of interaction. These modalities are defined from the user's point of view, rather than being defined in a technology-centered way. Thus, the main findings suggest that (1) participants intuitively utilized the properties of the skin to obtain more expressive commands and be more expressive than traditional touch surfaces; (2) established multi-touch gestures can be transferred to skin input, so based on this, the author developed the first set of skin input gestures; (3) participants can effectively interact on the skin without visual output. Haptic cues can replace visual cues for precise localization on hypothetical interface elements.

User-Defined Input Gestures. Skin-specific interactions have great potential to enhance the user experience of on-skin input. During the experiments and research, the author has completed the first set of input gesture models (12 basic input gestures and instructions), as shown in Fig. 6. These gestures can be used as inspiration for on-skin gestures to encourage users to interact with electronic devices in a more personalized way.

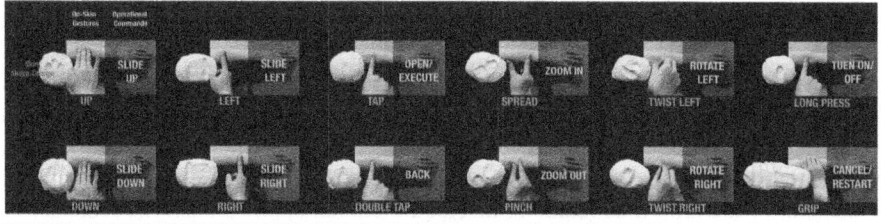

Fig. 6. 12 Basic Input Gestures and Instructions.

4.6   Output Instruction Testing

In the output instruction testing, the main purpose of the study is to use a complete set of forms to visualize the operation instructions of input gestures. Eventually, according to the gesture form and skin deformation when the input gesture interacts with the skin, the author designed the corresponding visual animation effect to show the accuracy and effectiveness of each input gesture visually and interestingly (Fig. 7). The 12 input gestures designed so far are only the basic gestures in the on-skin interaction system, which can fulfill the basic operation instructions. More input gestures can be custom-designed according to the user's needs and preferences to achieve personalized interaction. This part will be further explored and practiced in future research.

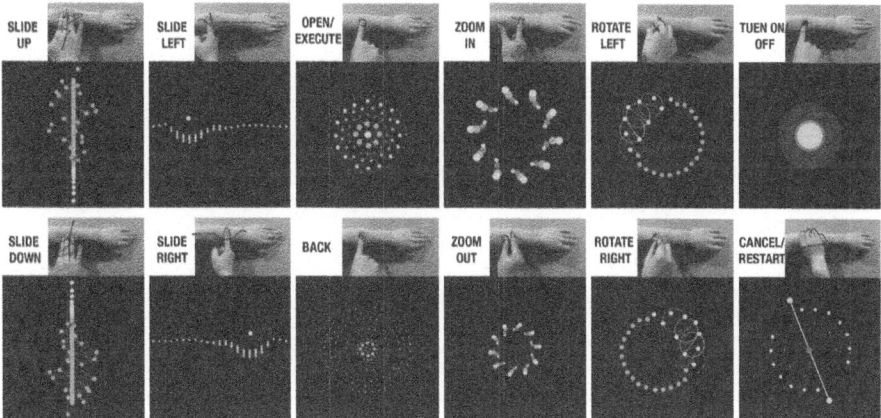

Fig. 7. Output display.

5   SKiNFINITY

5.1   Design Concept

This project is an exploratory design on on-skin interaction, aiming to explore a wide range of possibilities for future interfaces. After an in-depth study of the limitations of the current interaction interfaces faced by smart wearable devices, we realized that skin, as a permanently portable natural interaction interface, possesses great potential as a new type of interaction carrier. To this end, based on the exploration of skin properties and the improvement of sensing technology, the author has designed and realized an innovative on-skin input and output system: SKiNFINITY (Fig. 8). It uses human skin as a virtual interaction medium, allowing users to issue different operation instructions by executing various interaction gestures, such as sliding, pressing, pulling, and twisting, on the skin of the arm, thus realizing diverse functional applications. The feedback is presented intuitively and dynamically by projecting a virtual interface on the skin of the arm and the back of the hand as a visual output of the dual-screen display. In this way, SKiNFINITY realizes a kind of physical-virtual interaction with the skin as the interface, extends the boundary of the interaction interface, opens up a new and under-explored interaction mode, and brings new perspectives and inspirations to the smart application market.

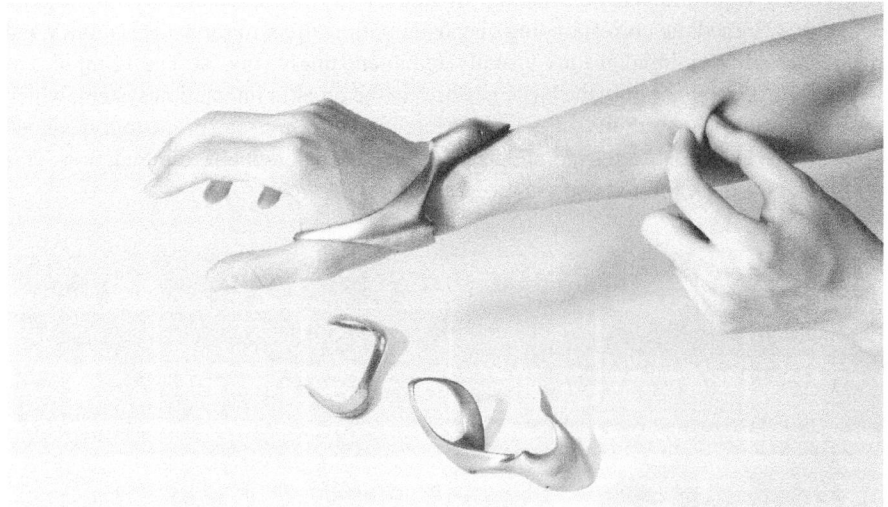

Fig. 8. SKiNFINITY.

Design Aesthetics. In this study, the author designed a simple and organic-shaped interaction device inspired by the natural form of bones and muscles within the human body to better suit the core theme of on-skin interaction. This design not only mimics the natural growth pattern of the body's internal structure but also demonstrates a unique fashion aesthetic through its smooth curves and elegant wrapping that fits snugly around the wrist. To further enhance the user experience, the author chose a flexible material as the main constituent element, which not only fits the ergonomic principle but also realizes the seamless integration between the hardware device and the human skin, thus providing the user with a more comfortable wearing experience. Through this design concept and choice of materials, the author aims to break through the limitations of traditional hardware devices that are cold and rigid and explore a more harmonious and symbiotic interaction with the human body. The design of the device not only reflects an in-depth understanding of and respect for the theme of skin interaction but also reflects a forward-thinking approach to future human-computer interaction. While realizing the technical functions, it also emphasizes the concern for user experience through its unique shape and materials, reflecting a design philosophy in the new era, i.e., the combination of technology and humanistic care (Fig. 9).

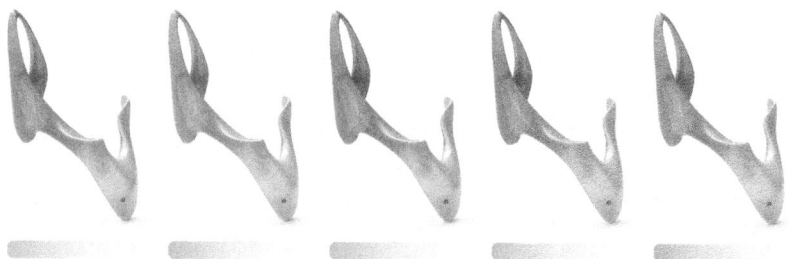

Fig. 9. Modeling design.

5.2 Technical Prototype

On-Skin Input Information Collection and Information Recognition. This project employs advanced micro-camera technology to capture information from specified skin regions and directly outputs the node positions of the hand via a convolutional neural network (CNN). Through in-depth deep learning research, the author has established an efficient gesture-skin interaction model, which consists of the following key steps: (1) designing a network that incorporates a before output of the node positions of the hand; (2) based on the predicted node positions, employing a refinement network for each node to carry out more precise position correction, a process that can be iteratively performed several times to further improve the accuracy of node localization.

In this study, the author compared four different network architectures: shallow network, deep network, multi-scale network, and deep network with prior. The comparison results show that the multi-scale network outperforms the deep network, which in turn outperforms the shallow network. This suggests that a multi-scale and deep network architecture is better able to handle high degree-of-freedom gesture actions in complex gesture recognition tasks. To reduce the learning difficulty of the network and to introduce prior knowledge, we introduce a bottleneck layer in the network, which uses a smaller number of neurons to force the network to learn representations in lower dimensional spaces. In addition, by performing the principal component analysis (PCA) on the training data, we match the number of neurons in the bottleneck layer with the PCA component, thus initializing the weights of the last layer of the network to the corresponding PCA component, a design that significantly improves the learning efficiency and output accuracy of the network.

The combination of camera sensing technology and deep learning used in this study shows significant advantages over traditional vibration recognition techniques. The stability of camera acquisition is not affected by light and signal frequency, ensuring higher recognition stability. In addition, with the help of a supercomputer in the cloud, faster recognition speeds are achieved compared to local recognition, resulting in a more miniaturized device with reduced costs. During the development of the gesture input and skin interaction model, the author collected and analyzed a large amount of data (Fig. 10), and achieved a continuous improvement in the accuracy and stability of gesture recognition by continuously optimizing the deep learning model.

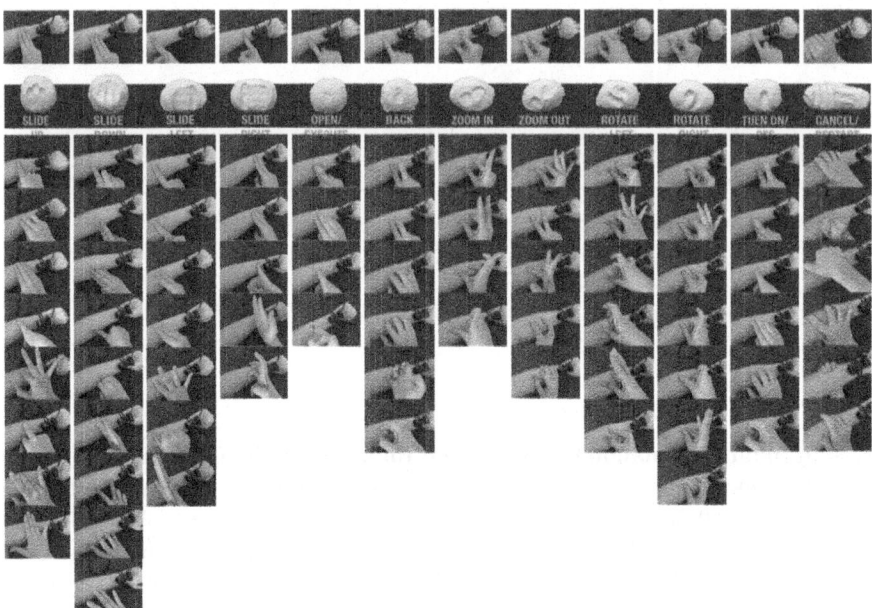

Fig. 10. On-skin input information collection.

On-Skin Output Information and Laser Display. In terms of on-skin output, we faced several challenges. Firstly, the shortest projection distances of the micro-projector modules available on the market today generally exceed 20 cm, which significantly exceeds our need for back-of-hand projection - a very short projection distance of less than 1.5 cm (Fig. 11). Second, solving this problem involves not only hardware improvements but more importantly, how to ensure that the projected image is effectively corrected for image distortion when projected from a low angle onto an irregular surface, ensuring that the display on the other hand meets the expected standard. Finally, considering the differences in where and how each user wears the device, designing an algorithm that can automatically correct the projection position becomes the key to realizing a personalized projection display.

After further research and exploration, the section finally adopted the ultra-short focus laser projection technology. The reflection layer of this projection module consists of multiple micro-raised structural units that are arranged in an upper semicircular pattern. From the center of the circle outward, the acute angle formed by the tangent of the receiving light surface of each micro-convex and the reflection layer gradually

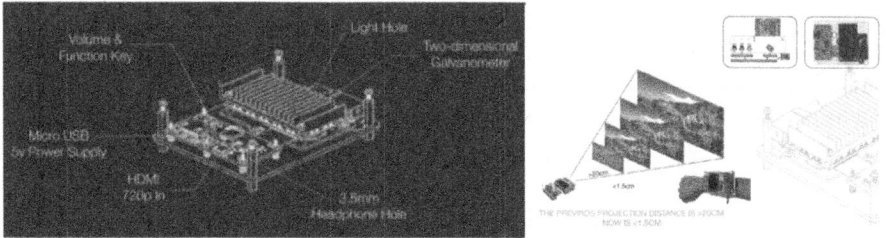

Fig. 11. Ultra-short focus laser projection module.

increases, so that the light emitted from the ultrashort-focus lens can be reflected out parallelly or subparallelly after hitting the reflection layer. By taking advantage of the constant property of its projection ratio, the author has realized that by simply adjusting the projection distance, changing only the pixel point density and the projected screen size, and combining it with a specially developed image correction algorithm, the author has successfully achieved accurate mapping of the surface skin even at ultrashort distances, avoiding any graphical distortion (Fig. 12).

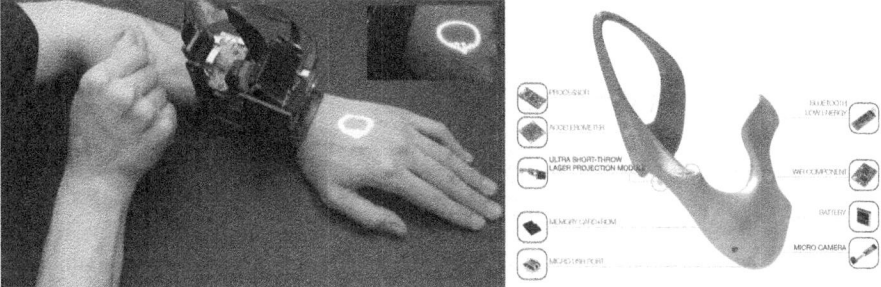

Fig. 12. Technical prototype and components.

5.3 Application Scenarios

With the development of society, people's pursuit of intelligent life is increasing, in the role of smart wearable devices is becoming more and more prominent. This study explores an innovative on-skin interaction system, which can realize the display and interaction of information directly on the user's skin, bringing a breakthrough in the field of wearable technology. Through this system, the author designed a series of rich application functions (mobile payment, GPS navigation, design tool, checking email, emergency call, remote control, etc.), as shown in Fig. 13. In addition, the system also supports remote control of daily electronic devices, such as cell phones, TVs, home projectors and smart home accessories. These features greatly increase user bonding and reuse frequency. It is worth noting that the application scenarios of the system are far from being limited to first aid, security, education, and sports. In the future, the author expects to develop more innovative applications and support users to make customized settings to further enhance the functionality and practicality of the skin interaction system. Through continuous technological innovation and application exploration, skin interaction technology will play an increasingly important role in the evolution of intelligent lifestyles.

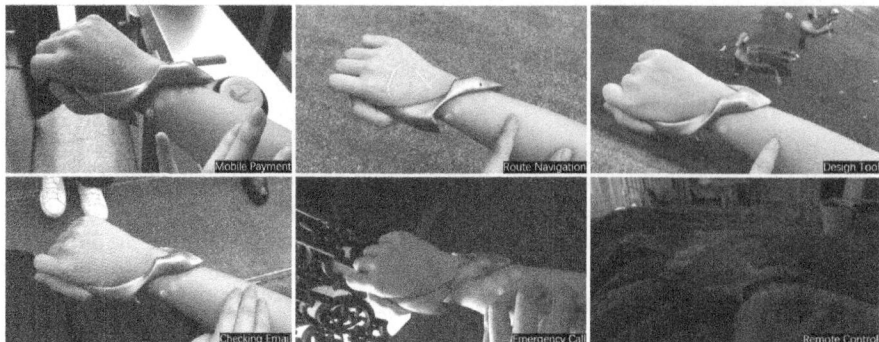

Fig. 13. Usage scenarios.

6 Conclusion and Prospect

In summary, this study adopted the experimental method as the main research method, and combined questionnaires, interviews, observations, and measurements with 30 users aged between 15 and 65 years old, who have experience in using smart wearable devices and are interested in smart interactive products, to explore, analyze and designing the skin interaction through a series of tests on the input location, output location, input and output influence factors, input gestures and output instructions The results of these studies provide a substantial real-world basis for subsequent design practices and reveal several key findings: (1) skin as an input interface provides a vast interaction space, and its accessibility and rapid responsiveness make it an ideal input surface for mobile devices, demonstrating great potential as an input medium; (2) skin is fundamentally different compared to traditional touch surfaces. Due to its elasticity, the skin supports a wider variety of input modalities, such as pulling, squeezing, and twisting, which enriches the interaction possibilities and introduces a more diverse range of gestures; (3) the complex physical properties of the skin and people's psychological connection with different body parts make the interaction on the skin strongly emotional, offering the possibility of more personalized interactions; (4) the skin serves as the output display carrier, its display resolution, frame rate, and overall image quality can reach a relatively satisfactory level; (5) due to proprioception and haptic feedback, all recognized gestures can be completed without relying on vision, demonstrating the input and output potential of skin as a virtual interface carrier.

This study shows that although existing smart wearable devices are favored for their portability and computing power, their small physical size limits the interaction space, which affects the usability and functionality of the devices. Therefore, exploring new interaction interfaces becomes crucial to enhance the user experience of small mobile systems. The author turns his attention to an often-overlooked input surface - the skin. The human body is a seductive input device, and skin is a permanently portable natural interaction interface. It perfectly supports an individual's proprioception, allowing us to interact with the body with precision without the limitations of our eyes. Few other external input systems can achieve this level of precision, as well as having input properties that are not limited by vision and such a large response area. Therefore, based on the exploration of skin properties and the improvement of sensing technology, the author designed an innovative on-skin input and output system: SKiNFINITY. It uses human skin as a virtual interaction medium, and it mainly contains two parts of functionality: gesture input and visual output. Based on the exploration of the complex physical properties of the skin, the author has designed a set of innovative input gestures, that allow users to issue commands by executing different interactive gestures (sliding, pressing, pulling, twisting, etc.) on the arm to realize different interactive functions; meanwhile, the virtual interface projected on the back of the hand and the skin of the arm serves as the visual output to receive feedback content and information. The innovative skin input mode and skin virtual interface form an innovative on-skin interaction system, which provides users with a brand-new interaction experience and opens up a new direction for the smart application market.

Despite the results of this study, there are still some limitations. In terms of social acceptability and ethics, the application of on-skin interaction needs to ensure that the technology is safe and not harmful to health. In addition, there is a need to consider people's acceptability from an ethical perspective and to ensure that personal privacy can be effectively protected against the misuse of sensitive body data. These challenges require a strong interdisciplinary discourse as well as a new set of methods and standards for human-computer engineering. However, the author believes that in the future, smart devices on the skin will no longer be black boxes and confusing. Instead, they will converge towards user-friendliness, scalability, and aesthetics of body adornment, creating a level of integration to the point of seeming to have disappeared, achieving a harmonious symbiosis with the human body. The future holds countless possibilities for the skin as an input and output carrier with myriad benefits.

References

1. Seng, K.P., Ang, L.M., Peter, E., Mmonyi, A.: Machine learning and AI technologies for smart wearables. Electronics **12**(7), 1509 (2023)
2. Harrison, C., Tan, D., Morris, D.: Skinput: appropriating the skin as an interactive canvas. Commun. ACM **54**(8), 111–118 (2011)
3. Nittala, A.S., Steimle, J.: Next steps in epidermal computing: opportunities and challenges for soft on-skin devices. In: Proceedings of the 2022 CHI Conference on Human Factors in Computing Systems, pp. 1–22 (2022)
4. Kao, C.H.L., Hung, M.W., Zhang, X., Huang, P.C., You, C.W.: Probing user perceptions of on-skin notification displays. Proc. ACM Hum. Comput. Interact. **4**(CSCW3), 1–20 (2021)
5. Liu, X., Vega, K., Maes, P., Paradiso, J.A.: Wearability factors for skin interfaces. In Proceedings of the 7th Augmented Human International Conference 2016, pp. 1–8 (2016)

6. Harrison, C., Benko, H., Wilson, A.D.: OmniTouch: wearable multitouch interaction everywhere. In: Proceedings of the 24th Annual ACM Symposium on User Interface Software and Technology, pp. 441–450 (2011)

7. Monisha, M., Preethi, R., Roshini, N.R., Priyadharshini, A.S.: Skinput the human body as touch screen. Int. J. Eng. Res. Technol. (IJERT) 7(11), 2278–0181 (2019)

8. Nittala, A.S., Withana, A., Pourjafarian, N., Steimle, J.: Multi-touch skin: a thin and flexible multi-touch sensor for on-skin input. In: Proceedings of the 2018 CHI Conference on Human Factors in Computing Systems, pp. 1–12 (2018)

9. Weigel, M., Nittala, A.S., Olwal, A., Steimle, J.: SkinMarks: enabling interactions on body landmarks using conformal skin electronics. In: proceedings of the 2017 CHI Conference on Human Factors in Computing Systems, pp. 3095–3105 (2017)

10. Kao, H.L.C., Bedri, A., Lyons, K.: SkinWire: fabricating a self-contained on-skin PCB for the hand. Proc. ACM Interact. Mob. Wearable Ubiquitous Technol. 2(3), 1–23 (2018)

11. Nittala, A.S., Khan, A., Kruttwig, K., Kraus, T., Steimle, J.: PhysioSkin: rapid fabrication of skin-conformal physiological interfaces. In: Proceedings of the 2020 CHI Conference on Human Factors in Computing Systems, pp. 1–10 (2020)

12. Ku, P.S., Molla, M.T.I., Huang, K., Kattappurath, P., Ranjan, K., Kao, H.L.C.: SkinKit: construction kit for on-skin interface prototyping. Proc. ACM Interact. Mob. Wearable Ubiquitous Technol. 5(4), 1–23 (2021)

13. Zhu, J., El Nesr, N., Rettenmaier, N., Kao, C.H.L.: SkinPaper: exploring Opportunities for woven paper as a wearable material for on-skin interactions. In Proceedings of the 2023 CHI Conference on Human Factors in Computing Systems, pp. 1–16 (2023)

Refining Human-Data Interaction: Advanced Techniques for EEGEyeNet Dataset Precision

Jade Wu[1] , Jingwen Dou[2] , and Sofia Utoft[3(✉)]

[1] Henry M. Gunn Senior High School, Palo Alto, USA
jw32946@pausd.us
[2] New York University, New York, USA
jd5668@nyu.edu
[3] Boston College, Chestnut Hill, USA
utoft@bc.edu

Abstract. The EEGEyeNet dataset merges EEG data with eye-tracking technology to advance cognitive research at the intersection of brain dynamics and eye movement. By developing machine learning models to predict eye movements from EEG data, we gain insights into perceptual, attentional, and cognitive processes. However, dataset outliers can compromise model integrity and accuracy. This paper explores the impact of outliers on the state-of-the-art model and highlights the benefits of outlier removal. By identifying and eliminating outliers, we improved the dataset to enhance model performance. Through the integration of advanced modeling techniques from EEGViT and EEGViT-TCNet, we set a new standard in eye-tracking precision, reducing the RMSE from 51.8 to 48.9. Despite removing only 15 outliers out of the 21,464 total data points, we reduced the RMSE by 2.9 mm. This study underscores the critical role of data refinement in advancing Brain-Computer Interfaces (BCI) and their applications.

Keywords: EEG · Gaze Prediction · Machine Learning · Vision Transformer · EEGEyeNet · Data Preprocessing

1 Introduction

The EEGEyeNet dataset has become a cornerstone in the realm of cognitive neuroscience and machine learning, facilitating the advancement of eye-tracking technologies through the integration of electroencephalography (EEG) data (Skoglund et al. (2022); Murungi et al. (2023a); Dou et al. (2022); Wolf et al. (2022); Murungi et al. (2023b); Rolff et al. (2022); Kastrati et al. (2023); Farago et al. (2022)). The fusion of these disciplines aims to enhance the precision of eye position prediction, a critical aspect in understanding visual attention and neurological behavior. However, the integrity of the EEGEyeNet dataset is

M. Kurosu et al. (Eds.): HCII 2024, LNCS 15374, pp. 407–419, 2025.
https://doi.org/10.1007/978-3-031-76803-3_24

compromised by the presence of data points exhibiting eye positions that surpass the physical boundaries of the experimental screen, leading to potential inaccuracies in subsequent analyses and model training.

This paper investigates the impact of such outliers on the performance of predictive models and explores the benefits of outlier pruning to maintain the dataset's integrity. Through meticulous data cleaning, we identified and removed these anomalous data points, aiming to refine the dataset for more accurate model training. By removing only a few outliers, the model's representation of EEG signals is drastically improved. Extending beyond simple outlier removal, our study incorporates advanced modeling techniques from the domains of the EEG Vision Transformer (EEGViT) and EEGViT-TCNet to establish a new benchmark in eye-tracking accuracy. Precise gaze estimation models have numerous applications across various fields such as behavioral science (Nakano and Ishii 2010), user experience (Rolff et al. (2022)), or assistive technology (Skoglund et al. (2022)). This demonstrates the significance of reliable models, which require accurate data.

1.1   Research Question

In addressing these objectives, our study aims to answer two key questions:

– How do outliers in the EEGEyeNet Dataset affect predictions of current state-of-the-art (SOTA) models and what do they reveal about the data?
– Can we develop a model with a specific data pruning technique to surpass the current SOTA model by reducing the Root Mean Squared Error (RMSE)?

By addressing these questions, we contribute to the ongoing discourse on EEG data preprocessing and model development, ultimately advancing eye-tracking technology and its applications. Our findings are particularly relevant

Table 1. Abbreviation Table

Abbreviation	Definition
AI	Artificial Intelligence
ML	Machine Learning
DL	Deep Learning
EEG	Electroencephalography
ET	Eye-Tracking
BCI	Brain-Computer Interfaces
HCI	Human-Computer Interaction
ViT	Vision Transformer
CNN	Convolutional Neural Network
TCNet	Temporal Convolutional Network
SOTA	State Of The Art
RMSE	Root Mean Squared Error

to the HCI community, as they provide a pathway to more accurate and responsive gaze-based interaction systems, enhancing the overall user experience and expanding the potential of assistive technologies. The full set of source code can be found at https://github.com/JadeW7/EEGViT-TCNet-pruned (Table 1).

2   Related Work

2.1   Deep Learning in EEG

The history of EEG signal processing has seen a notable evolution, especially with the advent of deep learning techniques. Traditional machine learning methods, although effective to a certain extent, often struggle to capture the intricate and high-dimensional nature of EEG data. However, the landscape changed with the introduction of deep learning models, notably convolutional neural networks (CNNs) and recurrent neural networks (RNNs), which brought about a paradigm shift in this field.

Moreover, the application of the Transformer architecture has transcended various domains within deep learning (Wang and Wang (2022); Fuhl et al. (2023); Xiang and Abdelmonsef (2022); Modesitt et al. (2023); Mishra et al. (2023)). The Vision Transformer (ViT) particularly stands out for its impact on both Computer Vision and EEG analysis (Yang and Modesitt 2023), showcasing its versatility and effectiveness in handling complex data structures such as EEG signals.

2.2   Vision Transformers

ViTs have generated significant impacts in numerous fields and are utilized for their excellent performance in many tasks, often surpassing the results of state-of-the-art Convolutional Neural Networks (CNNs) when trained on large datasets (Dosovitskiy et al. (2020)). Although initially designed for classifying images, ViTs are surprisingly accurate at analyzing EEG data due to their effectiveness with grid-like data. The key to their success lies in their self-attention mechanism, which plays a crucial role in capturing long-range dependencies. Unlike traditional CNNs, which rely on convolutional layers to process local receptive fields and gradually build up global context through multiple layers, ViTs can capture long-range dependencies in the data directly. This is achieved through self-attention, which allows the model to weigh the importance of each part of the input data relative to every other part, facilitating a more holistic understanding of the data's structure and relationships. This capability is crucial for tasks requiring a comprehensive understanding of spatial and temporal relationships within the data.

2.3   Temporal Convolutional Networks

Additionally, the Temporal Convolutional Network (TCNet) has become a favored option across different domains in deep learning, including EEG signal processing (Ingolfsson et al. 2020). Specialized architectures such as TCNet enhance the detection of subtle features that might be overlooked when using CNN models alone (Bai et al. 2018). TCNet enhances temporal feature detection through causal convolutions and dilations, allowing it to handle long-range dependencies and temporal correlations more effectively (Fig. 1).

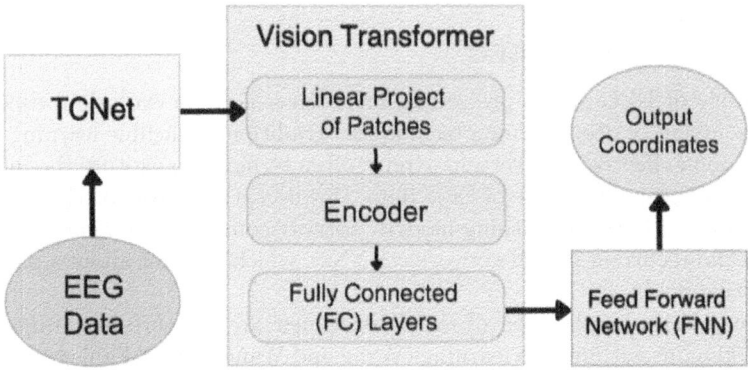

Fig. 1. The architecture of the EEGViT-TCNet. The model comprises three main components: TCNet, convolutional and batch normalization layers, and the Vision Transformer (ViT). TCNet processes EEG signals with three sequential layers, utilizing a kernel size of 3 and a dropout rate of 0.75. Convolutional layers bridge TCNet and ViT, extracting spatial features and compressing spatial information. The ViT component, adapted from "google/vit-base-patch16-224" model, includes patch embeddings projection and a classifier head for predicting gaze XY coordinates.

2.4 Fusing Pre-trained ViTs with TCNet

The integration of pre-trained Vision Transformers (ViTs) with Temporal Convolutional Networks (TCNet) represents a cutting-edge methodology in the realm of EEG regression (Modesitt et al. (2024)). This fusion combines the spatial feature extraction capabilities of ViTs with the temporal analysis strengths of TCNet, resulting in significantly improved model performance for EEG signal analysis. The EEGViT-TCNet model, composed of three primary components, is designed to process EEG data and predict gaze XY coordinates. The TCNet component, tailored to address the intricacies of EEG data, consists of three sequential layers with increasing channel dimensions (64, 128, 256) and a fixed kernel size of 3. Equipped to handle an input dimensionality of 129 channels, corresponding to the number of EEG channels plus one for grounding information, TCNet employs a dropout rate of 0.75 and weight normalization with ReLU activation to prevent overfitting and enhance stability and performance. The subsequent convolutional and batch normalization layers connect TCNet to ViT. These layers employ two convolutional layers, with the first layer initiating spatial feature extraction using 256 filters and a (1, 36) kernel size, followed by batch normalization and ReLU activation. The second layer increases the channel dimension to 768, aligning with ViT's input specifications, and compresses spatial information with a (256, 1) kernel size. The ViT component adapts EEG data using the "google/vit-base-patch16-224" model, projecting patch embeddings via a 1D convolutional layer to integrate output from preceding stages. Finally, the model concludes with a classifier head consisting of linear layers and a dropout layer (p=0.1), facilitating the prediction of gaze XY coordinates. This approach integrates TCNet's handling of EEG data complexities with spatial feature extraction and compression through convolutional layers, ultimately enabling accurate gaze prediction through the ViT component.

2.5   Outlier Detection in EEG Data

Previous studies have extensively explored outlier detection methodologies within EEG datasets. These methodologies encompass various approaches, including statistical methods, clustering techniques, and machine learning algorithms (Boukerche et al. (2020a), Boukerche et al. (2020b)). Outliers within EEG datasets pose a significant challenge, potentially distorting model accuracy and reliability. However, through rigorous outlier detection and removal processes, researchers have demonstrated substantial improvements in model performance and robustness. The integration of outlier detection mechanisms is essential for ensuring the integrity of EEG-based analyses and advancing the field's understanding of brain dynamics and cognitive processes.

3   Methods

3.1   The EEGEyeNet Dataset

Obtaining eye-tracking data involves intricate and costly procedures, demanding specialized equipment, skilled operators, and participant approval. The integration of such data with EEG recordings further complicates the data collection process. Consequently, studies exploring the interplay between brain activity and eye movements often encounter limitations due to the scarcity of suitable datasets. The introduction of the EEGEyeNet dataset (Kastrati et al. (2021)) alleviates this challenge by providing a comprehensive dataset incorporating both EEG and eye-tracking data. The EEGEyeNet dataset is a collection of electroencephalogram and eye-tracking data of 356 participants, 190 males, and 166 females, with ages ranging from 18 to 80, consisting of three benchmark tasks: Left-right, Angle/Amplitude, and Absolute position.

Collection Method/Details. EEG data was collected through the EEG Geodesic Hydrocel system, containing 128 channels and capturing at 500 Hz. Prior to recording, the impedance of each electrode was ensured at levels below 40 kOhm (kilo-ohms, a unit of electrical resistance). The eye position was also recorded with the ET EyeLink 1000 Plus, an infrared video system, also at the same sampling rate of 500 Hz. Participants then maintained a stable head position via a chin rest, placed 68 cm away from a 24-inch monitor.

Task Description. While there are three tasks for which data is collected, the pre-trained EEGViT-TCNet utilizes the large grid data, where participants are asked to fixate on a series of dots as shown in Fig. 2. 25 dots placed in all areas of the screen are displayed in a pseudo-randomized order for 1.5 to 1.8 s each. 27 dots per block were measured with a total of five random blocks repeated 6 times during the measurement, resulting in 810 stimuli for each participant.

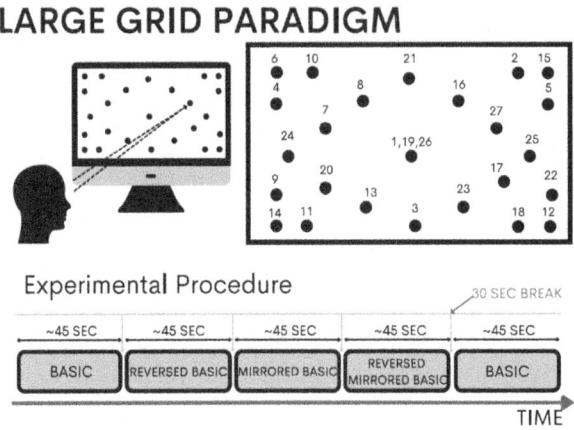

Fig. 2. Schematic diagram of the experimental setup and the placement of stimuli on the screen (Kastrati et al. 2021).

EEGEyeNet Initial Preprocessing. Because of the various external factors (temperature, air humidity, or outside noise), the EEG data collected from each participant could have resulted in more prominent signals of interest through reflexive eye movements, muscular noise, or heart signals. As such, the EEG data from the original EEGEyeNet dataset was preprocessed minimally or maximally with the toolbox from Pedroni et al. (2019). Maximal preprocessing addresses the aforementioned unwanted physiological signals by applying an independent component analysis in combination with Pion-Tonachini et al. (2019), a pre-trained classifier that allows for the removal of data that has a probability estimation of larger than 0.8 for reflecting external activity. Minimal preprocessing involves determining and filtering data with a 40 Hz high-pass filter and a 0.5 Hz low-pass filter. Given that the state-of-the-art model employs minimally preprocessed data, our focus was aligned with this approach to preserve consistency. The minimal preprocessing ensures the preservation of signal integrity and reduces the risk of information loss.

3.2 Data Preprocessing

We conducted a meticulous data-cleaning process of the minimally preprocessed data regarding the absolute position task on the large grid paradigm. We eliminated all data points with eye positions outside the experiment screen's dimensions of 800×600 pixels (Kastrati et al. 2021). As shown in Fig. 3, we found that these outliers make up 15 out of 21,464 total samples. As such, data points with coordinates outside of this dimension can reasonably be considered errors. This scrutiny of each data point's x and y coordinates ensured the retention of only valid, physically plausible samples for model training and testing.

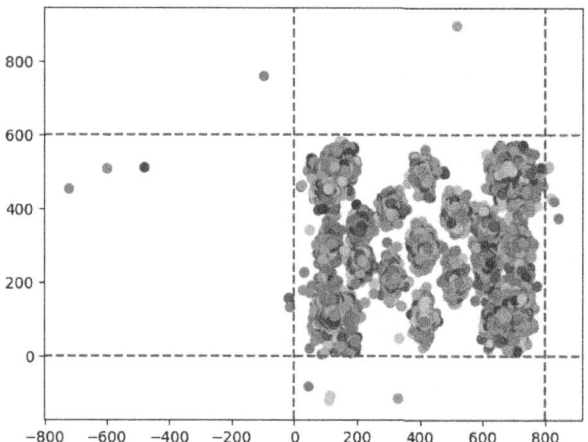

Fig. 3. Visualization of the EEGEyeNet Absolute Position data. 15 outliers lie outside of the designated (0–800, 0–600) range.

3.3 Application of Pruned Data

Building upon the foundations laid by EEGViT and EEGViT-TCNet, our research leverages the synergistic potential of Vision Transformers and Temporal Convolutional Networks. These technologies, known for their prowess in advanced machine learning regression tasks, were integrated into our model

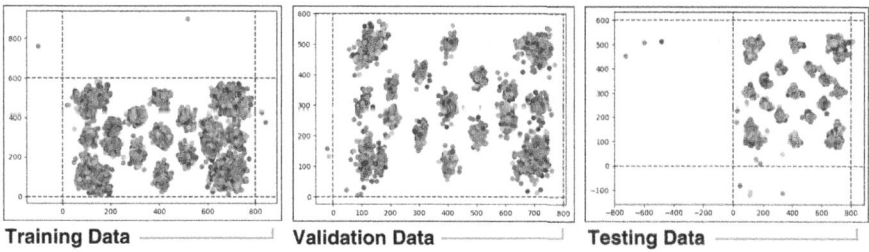

Fig. 4. Visualization of how the SOTA model splits the EEGEyeNet Absolute Position data into training, validation, and testing subsets. Several outliers lie outside the designated range of (0–800, 0–600).

architecture to refine EEG-signal analysis, enhancing the precision of eye-position predictions. We fed our cleaned data into the EEGViT-TCNet model to discern the effects of the outliers on the accuracy. Previously, the EEGViT and the EEGViT-TCNet split the data into the same subsets for training, testing, and validation, as shown in Fig. 4.

Figure 4 elucidates the distribution of the outliers across the training, testing, and validation sets. The EEGViT-TCNet was trained on a subset of the data with 5 outliers, validated on a subset of the data with 3 outliers, and tested on a subset of the data with 7 outliers. Thus, by eliminating these outliers, we have removed any potential adverse effect in all phases of the model development process.

4　Results

Subsequent retraining of the state-of-the-art model on this pruned dataset yielded significant improvements in predictive accuracy. This enhancement was

Table 2. Root Mean Squared Error (RMSE) loss in millimeters for different models on the Absolute Position Task. Lower RMSE values indicate better performance as they represent closer estimations to the actual values. The values represent the mean and standard deviation of 5 runs. All Transformers in the table are pre-trained.

Model	Absolute Position RMSE (mm)
Naive Guessing	123.3　0.0
KNN	119.7　0
RBF SVR	123　0
Linear Regression	118.3　0
Ridge Regression	118.2　0
Lasso Regression	118　0
Elastic Net	118.1　0
Random Forest	116.7　0.1
Gradient Boost	117　0.1
AdaBoost	119.4　0.1
XGBoost	118　0
CNN	70.4　1.1
PyramidalCNN	73.9　1.9
EEGNet	81.3　1.0
InceptionTime	70.7　0.8
Xception	78.7　1.6
ViT-Base	58.1　0.6
EEGViT	55.4　0.2
EEGViT-TCNet	51.8　0.2
EEGViT-TCNet (Pruned)	**48.9　0.2**

measured by the Root Mean Squared Error (RMSE), representing the Euclidean distance in millimeters between the predicted and actual gaze positions. Our findings in Table 2 revealed a marked enhancement in model performance, with RMSE values decreasing from 51.8 to 48.9. By removing only 15 data points, and only 5 in the training data, or stimuli, in the dataset, 0.07% of the total data, there was a reduction in RMSE of 2.9 mm on the SOTA model.

Our research establishes the pruned version of EEGViT-TCNet as the current benchmark, the most accurate model for the absolute position grid task of EEGEyeNet. In comparison to the baseline Naive Guessing model, which had an RMSE of 123.3, the pruned EEGViT-TCNet model's RMSE of 48.9 represents a substantial reduction, reinforcing the importance of data integrity and preprocessing in achieving high model performance.

5   Discussion

Our study not only highlights the critical importance of data integrity but also showcases the efficacy of combining advanced machine learning techniques, like those in EEGViT and EEGViT-TCNet, for precise gaze estimation applications. Demonstrated by notable enhancements in RMSE for the state-of-the-art model in EEGEyeNet, existing outliers pose a risk to both the overall accuracy and the integrity of the model, even throughout the training phase.

The distribution of outliers across the training, testing, and validation sets of the EEGViT-TCNet (Fig. 4) may partially elucidate the impact of anomalous points. The influence of these outliers on other models might differ from that on the state-of-the-art model, owing not only to differences in model architecture but also to the varying methods researchers used to split the EEGEyeNet dataset. Nonetheless, the reduction in RMSE observed when training the EEGViT-TCNet on the cleaned data highlights the potential for similar improvements in other models. Models previously developed for the absolute position task on the EEGEyeNet data might also experience comparable accuracy increases. Given that each model learns to predict absolute position uniquely, there is a possibility for an even greater reduction in RMSE with other models.

The continuous improvement in accuracy underscores the importance of building upon previous research, resulting in a total reduction of 74.4 RMSE from the baseline of Naive Guessing, which was 123.3 RMSE. However, all of the foundational research was conducted on data containing outliers. With the identification of these outliers and the availability of pruned data, future research can potentially achieve even greater error reduction.

Reporting anomalies in EEG data is valuable for researchers in intersecting fields (Murungi et al. 2023b; Qu et al. 2020a,b; Yi and Qu 2022). Understanding outliers can identify human errors, mislabeling, or unique phenomena, improving data accuracy and experimental protocols. These outliers might reveal unusual cognitive or perceptual events, rare neurological conditions, or specific responses to stimuli, providing deeper insights into brain functions. Investigating these anomalies can enhance cognitive and perceptual research by uncovering new neural patterns and improving human-computer interaction designs. It can challenge and refine existing theoretical models of brain function, leading to more robust frameworks. Additionally, identifying outliers can highlight new research directions. Overall, analyzing outliers in EEG data not only enhances data quality and model accuracy but also contributes to a more nuanced understanding of human-computer interactions.

The implications of our findings extend beyond cognitive research to practical applications in Human-Computer Interaction. Enhanced EEG and eye-tracking models can significantly improve adaptive user interfaces, making them more responsive and intuitive. This refinement can benefit assistive technologies, enabling better communication aids for individuals with disabilities. Additionally, the precision improvements can elevate virtual and augmented reality experiences, making interactions more seamless and immersive.

Future research avenues should explore additional data-cleaning techniques and their application to diverse EEG datasets for validation purposes. (An et al. (2023a; 2023b); Li et al. (2024); Chen et al. (2024, 2021); Lu et al. (2023b, 2024, 2023a)) As EEG classification and feature extraction architectures continue to evolve, our study emphasizes the importance of meticulous data preprocessing in enhancing model performance and reliability for real-world applications. In future studies, exploring alternative model architectures could lead to improved accuracy. (Zhao et al. (2024 2022b); Wang et al. (2023); Tang et al. (2023); Gui et al. (2024); Yunoki et al. (2023); Tan et al. (2023a,2023b); Zhang et al. (2022, 2023); Zhao et al. (2022a); Ma (2022); Ma et al. (2024); Jiang et al. (2023)).

Moving forward, it would be valuable to continue exploring data preprocessing techniques along with the integration of Transformers and CNN-like architectures to further enhance accuracy with EEG data. Such advancements will not only elevate the performance of predictive models but also expand the potential of HCI technologies, driving innovation in user-centric applications and setting new standards for BCI development.

6   Conclusion

Through rigorous data-cleaning procedures, we systematically eliminated outlier observations from the EEGEyeNet dataset, ensuring its integrity and reliability by removing data points lying outside the screen's dimensions. Our findings demonstrate a significant enhancement in predictive accuracy, highlighting the pivotal role of data integrity in machine learning applications. Despite the removal of only 0.07% of the data, we achieved a noteworthy 2.9mm decrease in RMSE. The observed reduction in RMSE for the EEGViT-TCNet model suggests potential improvements in other models when outliers are meticulously managed. This study establishes a benchmark for EEG-ET predictive models, emphasizing the significance of data quality in advancing Brain-Computer Interfaces, adaptive user interfaces, and assistive technologies.

References

An, S., Bhat, G., Gumussoy, S., Ogras, U.: Transfer learning for human activity recognition using representational analysis of neural networks. ACM Trans. Comput. Healthc. 4(1), 1–21 (2023)

An, S., Tuncel, Y., Basaklar, T., Ogras, U.Y.: A survey of embedded machine learning for smart and sustainable healthcare applications. In: Embedded Machine Learning for Cyber-Physical, IoT, and Edge Computing: Use Cases and Emerging Challenges, pp. 127–150. Springer, Heidelberg (2023b)

Bai, S., Kolter, J.Z., Koltun, V.: An empirical evaluation of generic convolutional and recurrent networks for sequence modeling. arXiv preprint arXiv:1803.01271 (2018)

Boukerche, A., Zheng, L., Alfandi, O.: Outlier detection: methods, models, and classification. ACM Comput. Surv. (CSUR) 53(3), 1–37 (2020)

Boukerche, A., Zheng, L., Alfandi, O.: Outlier detection: methods, models, and classification. ACM Comput. Surv. (CSUR) 53(3), 1–37 (2020). https://doi.org/10.1145/3381028. ISSN 0360-0300

Chen, P., Ding, H., Araki, J., Huang, R.: Explicitly capturing relations between entity mentions via graph neural networks for domain-specific named entity recognition. In: Proceedings of the 59th Annual Meeting of the Association for Computational Linguistics and the 11th International Joint Conference on Natural Language Processing, vol. 2: Short Papers, pp. 735–742 (2021)

Chen, P., et al.: Hytrel: hypergraph-enhanced tabular data representation learning. In: Advances in Neural Information Processing Systems, vol. 36 (2024)

Dosovitskiy, A., et al.: An image is worth 16x16 words: transformers for image recognition at scale. arXiv preprint arXiv:2010.11929 (2020)

Dou, G., Zhou, Z., Qu, X.: Time majority voting, a pc-based eeg classifier for non-expert users. In: International Conference on Human-Computer Interaction, pp. 415–428. Springer, Heidelberg (2022)

Farago, E., Law, A.J., Hajra, S.G., Chan, A.D.C.: Blink and saccade detection from forehead eeg. In: 2022 IEEE International Instrumentation and Measurement Technology Conference (I2MTC), pp. 1–6. IEEE (2022)

Fuhl, W., et al.: One step closer to eeg-based eye tracking. In: Proceedings of the 2023 Symposium on Eye Tracking Research and Applications, pp. 1–7 (2023)

Gui, S., Song, S., Qin, R., Tang, Y.: Remote sensing object detection in the deep learning era-a review. Remote Sens. 16(2), 327 (2024)

Ingolfsson, T.M., et al.: Eeg-tcnet: an accurate temporal convolutional network for embedded motor-imagery brain-machine interfaces. In: 2020 IEEE International Conference on Systems, Man, and Cybernetics (SMC). IEEE (2020)

Jiang, C., Hui, B., Liu, B., Yan, D.: Successfully applying lottery ticket hypothesis to diffusion model. arXiv preprint arXiv:2310.18823 (2023)

Kastrati, A., Płomecka, M.D., Küchler, J., Langer, N., Wattenhofer, R.: Electrode clustering and bandpass analysis of eeg data for gaze estimation. In: Annual Conference on Neural Information Processing Systems, pp. 50–65. PMLR (2023)

Kastrati, A., et al.: Eegeyenet: a simultaneous electroencephalography and eye-tracking dataset and benchmark for eye movement prediction. arXiv preprint arXiv:2111.05100 (2021)

Li, H., et al.: Spherehead: stable 3d full-head synthesis with spherical tri-plane representation. arXiv preprint arXiv:2404.05680 (2024)

Lu, Y., Sato, K., Wang, J.: Deep learning based multi-label image classification of protest activities. arXiv preprint arXiv:2301.04212 (2023a)

Lu, Y., Shen, M., Wang, H., Wang, X., van Rechem, C., Wei, W.: Machine learning for synthetic data generation: a review. arXiv preprint arXiv:2302.04062 (2023b)

Yingzhou, L., Chen, T., Hao, N., Van Rechem, C., Chen, J., Tianfan, F.: Uncertainty quantification and interpretability for clinical trial approval prediction. Health Data Sci. **4**, 0126 (2024)

Ma, X.: Traffic performance evaluation using statistical and machine learning methods. PhD thesis, The University of Arizona (2022)

Ma, X., Karimpour, A., Wu, Y.J.: Data-driven transfer learning framework for estimating on-ramp and off-ramp traffic flows. J. Intell. Transport. Syst. 1–14 (2024)

Mishra, A.R., et al.: Signeeg v1. 0: Multimodal electroencephalography and signature database for biometric systems. bioRxiv, pp. 2023–09 (2023)

Modesitt, E., Yang, R., Liu, Q.: Two heads are better than one: a bio-inspired method for improving classification on eeg-et data. In: International Conference on Human-Computer Interaction, pp. 382–390. Springer, Heidelberg (2023)

Modesitt, E., Huang Wang, H., Yin, H., Lu, B.: Fusing pretrained vits with tcnet for enhanced eeg regression (2024)

Murungi, N.K., Pham, M.V., Dai, X., Qu, X.: Trends in machine learning and electroencephalogram (eeg): a review for undergraduate researchers. In: International Conference on Human-Computer Interaction, pp. 426–443. Springer, Heidelberg (2023a)

Murungi, N.K., Pham, M.V., Dai, X.C., Qu, X.: Empowering computer science students in electroencephalography (eeg) analysis: A review of machine learning algorithms for eeg datasets. In: Proceedings of the 29th ACM SIGKDD Conference on Knowledge Discovery and Data Mining, pp. 1728–1739 (2023b)

Nakano, Y.I., Ishii, R.: Estimating user's engagement from eye-gaze behaviors in human-agent conversations. In: Proceedings of the 15th International Conference on Intelligent User Interfaces, IUI 2010, pp. 139-148. Association for Computing Machinery, New York (2010). ISBN 9781605585154. https://doi.org/10.1145/1719970.1719990

Pedroni, A., Bahreini, A., Langer, N.: Automagic: standardized preprocessing of big eeg data. Neuroimage **200**, pp. 460–473 (2019). https://doi.org/10.1016/j.neuroimage.2019.06.046

Pion-Tonachini, L., Kreutz-Delgado, K., Makeig, S.: Iclabel: an automated electroencephalographic independent component classifier, dataset, and website. Neuroimage **198**, 181–197 (2019)

Qu, X., Liu, P., Li, Z., Hickey, T.: Multi-class time continuity voting for EEG classification. In: Frasson, C., Bamidis, P., Vlamos, P. (eds.) BFAL 2020. LNCS (LNAI), vol. 12462, pp. 24–33. Springer, Cham (2020). https://doi.org/10.1007/978-3-030-60735-7_3

Qu, X., Mei, Q., Liu, P., Hickey, T.: Using EEG to distinguish between writing and typing for the same cognitive task. In: Frasson, C., Bamidis, P., Vlamos, P. (eds.) BFAL 2020. LNCS (LNAI), vol. 12462, pp. 66–74. Springer, Cham (2020). https://doi.org/10.1007/978-3-030-60735-7_7

Rolff, T., Harms, H.M., Steinicke, F., Frintrop, S.: Gazetransformer: gaze forecasting for virtual reality using transformer networks. In: DAGM German Conference on Pattern Recognition, pp. 577–593. Springer, Heidelberg (2022)

Skoglund, M.A., Andersen, M., Shiell, M.M., Keidser, G., Rank, M.L., Rotger-Griful, S.: Comparing in-ear eog for eye-movement estimation with eye-tracking: accuracy, calibration, and speech comprehension. Front. Neurosci. **16**, 873201 (2022)

Tan, J., Zhang, X., Shenghui, W., Song, Z., Chen, S., Huang, Y., Wang, Y.: Audio-induced medial prefrontal cortical dynamics enhances coadaptive learning in brain-machine interfaces. J. Neural Eng. **20**(5), 056035 (2023)

Tan, J., Zhang, X., Wu, S., Wang, Y.: State-space model based inverse reinforcement learning for reward function estimation in brain-machine interfaces. In: 2023 45th Annual International Conference of the IEEE Engineering in Medicine & Biology Society (EMBC), pp. 1–4. IEEE (2023b)

Tang, Y., Song, S., Gui, S., Chao, W., Cheng, C., Qin, R.: Active and low-cost hyperspectral imaging for the spectral analysis of a low-light environment. Sensors **23**(3), 1437 (2023)

Wang, J., Chang, R., Zhao, Z., Pahwa, R.S.: Robust detection, segmentation, and metrology of high bandwidth memory 3D scans using an improved semi-supervised deep learning approach. Sensors **23**(12), 5470 (2023)

Wang, X., Wang, Z.: Cnn with self-attention in eeg classification. In: International Conference on Human-Computer Interaction, pp. 512–526. Springer, Heidelberg (2022)

Wolf, L., et al.: A deep learning approach for the segmentation of electroencephalography data in eye tracking applications. arXiv preprint arXiv:2206.08672 (2022)

Xiang, B., Abdelmonsef, A.: Vector-based data improves left-right eye-tracking classifier performance after a covariate distributional shift. In: International Conference on Human-Computer Interaction, pp. 617–632. Springer (2022)

Yang, R., Modesitt, E.: Vit2eeg: leveraging hybrid pretrained vision transformers for eeg data. arXiv preprint arXiv:2308.00454 (2023)

Yi, L., Qu, X.: Attention-based cnn capturing eeg recording's average voltage and local change. In: Artificial Intelligence in HCI: 3rd International Conference, AI-HCI 2022, Held as Part of the 24th HCI International Conference, HCII 2022, Virtual Event, 26 June–1 July 2022, Proceedings, pp. 448–459. Springer, Heidelberg (2022)

Yunoki, I., Berreby, G., D'Andrea, N., Lu, Y., Qu, X.: Exploring ai music generation: a review of deep learning algorithms and datasets for undergraduate researchers. In: International Conference on Human-Computer Interaction, pp. 102–116. Springer, Heidelberg (2023)

Zhang, Z., Tian, R., Sherony, R., Domeyer, J., Ding, Z.: Attention-based interrelation modeling for explainable automated driving. IEEE Trans. Intell. Veh. **8**(2), 1564–1573 (2022)

Zhang, Z., Tian, R., Ding, Z.: Trep: transformer-based evidential prediction for pedestrian intention with uncertainty. In: Proceedings of the AAAI Conference on Artificial Intelligence, vol. 37, pp. 3534–3542 (2023)

Zhao, H., Du, H., Yang, S., Yao, F.: Rec-rn: user representations learning over the knowledge graph for recommendation systems. In: 2022 4th International Conference on Machine Learning, Big Data and Business Intelligence (MLBDBI), pp. 228–233. IEEE (2022a)

Zhao, S., et al.: Deep learning based cetsa feature prediction cross multiple cell lines with latent space representation. Sci. Rep. **14**(1), 1878 (2024)

Zhao, Z., et al.: Le-uda: label-efficient unsupervised domain adaptation for medical image segmentation. IEEE Trans. Med. Imaging **42**(3), 633 646 (2022b)

Author Index

A

Al-Rubaiai, Mohammed   356
Atarashi, Yui   289

C

Chen, Hao   52
Cheng, Erting   325
Chiou, Wen-Ko   52
Ciobanu, Madalina G.   299
Clemente, Emilio   299
Couto, Fábio   3
Curado Malta, Mariana   3

D

Damoah, Andrews   341
de Oliveira, Marcelo Henrique   23
Diniz de Souza, Adler   23
Dou, Jingwen   407

F

Francese, Rita   299
Fu, Zhiyong   83
Fukushima, Takuto   312

G

Gücük, Gian-Luca   63

H

Heuer, Marvin   42
Hsu, Szu-Erh   52
Huang, Liying   111

I

Israr, Ali   325, 356

J

Jiang, Ying   249
Joyce, Sam Conrad   193

K

Kamba, Tomonari   274

L

Leible, Stephan   63
Liang, Teng   341
Lin, Lin-mei   52
Liu, Chao   52
Liu, Yuqi   83

M

Ma, Yue   97
Marquette, Wade   356
Meng, Yichen   111
Miglani, Abhijai   124
Mortaga, Maged   211

N

Noviram, Chattraporn   230

P

Patil, Siddharth Rajesh   372
Pustejovsky, James   174

R

Rosa, Ferrucio de Franco   23

S

Salazar Rodriguez, Juan David   193
Schumacher, Toni   211
Schwemler, Zachary   325
Seth, Deep   372
Shen, Po-Chen   52
Shidujaman, Mohammad   249
Shizuki, Buntarou   289
Simic, Dejan   63
Sooraksa, Nanta   230
Sooraksa, Pitikhate   230

© The Editor(s) (if applicable) and The Author(s), under exclusive license
to Springer Nature Switzerland AG 2025
M. Kurosu et al. (Eds.): HCII 2024, LNCS 15374, pp. 421–422, 2025.
https://doi.org/10.1007/978-3-031-76803-3

T
Thakur, Anushi Singh   124
Tirmizi, Asad   325
Tortora, Genoveffa   299

U
Uba, Chikaodi   42
Utoft, Sofia   407

V
Valdez, André Calero   211
von Brackel-Schmidt, Constantin   63

W
Wang, Chen   387
Wang, Jing   249
Weng, Yunyun   249
Wu, Jade   407

Y
Yamaguchi, Takehiko   312

Z
Zhao, Dehao   325
Zhu, Bo   325
Zhu, Yifan   174
Zou, Xiaojiao   274

GPSR Compliance

The European Union's (EU) General Product Safety Regulation (GPSR) is a set of rules that requires consumer products to be safe and our obligations to ensure this.

If you have any concerns about our products, you can contact us on ProductSafety@springernature.com

In case Publisher is established outside the EU, the EU authorized representative is:

Springer Nature Customer Service Center GmbH
Europaplatz 3
69115 Heidelberg, Germany

The manufacturer's authorised representative in the EU is Springer
Nature Customer Service Centre GmbH, Europaplatz 3, 69115 Heidelberg,
Germany. If you have any concerns regarding our products, please
contact ProductSafety@springernature.com

Printed and bound by CPI Group (UK) Ltd, Croydon, CR0 4YY

06/05/2026

02103601-0003